FOR REFERENCE

Do Not Take From This Room

ENCYCLOPEDIA OF AMERICAN ENVIRONMENTAL HISTORY

VOLUME II

Edited by Kathleen A. Brosnan

Facts On File
An imprint of Infobase Publishing

Encyclopedia of American Environmental History

Copyright © 2011 Kathleen A. Brosnan

Facts On File, Inc.
An imprint of Infobase Publishing
132 West 31st Street
New York NY 10001

Library of Congress Cataloging-in-Publication Data

Encyclopedia of American environmental history / edited by Kathleen A. Brosnan.
p. cm.
Includes bibliographical references and index.
ISBN 978-0-8160-6793-0 (alk. paper)
1. United States—Environmental conditions—History—Encyclopedias.
2. Environmental policy—United States—History—Encyclopedias.
3. Environmentalism—United States—History—Encyclopedias.
I. Brosnan, Kathleen A., 1960–
GE150.E53 2010   333.720973—dc22
2010021963

Facts On File books are available at special discounts when purchased in bulk
quantities for businesses, associations, institutions, or sales promotions.
Please call our Special Sales Department in New York
at (212) 967-8800 or (800) 322-8755.

You can find Facts On File on the World Wide Web at http://www.factsonfile.com

Text design by Erika K. Arroyo
Composition by Mary Susan Ryan-Flynn
Maps by Dale Williams, Jeremy Eagle, and Sholto Ainslie
Cover printed by Sheridan Books, Ann Arbor, Mich.
Book printed and bound by Sheridan Books, Ann Arbor, Mich.
Date printed: November 2010
Printed in the United States of America

10 9 8 7 6 5 4 3 2 1

This book is printed on acid-free paper.

Contents

VOLUME I

Overview Maps

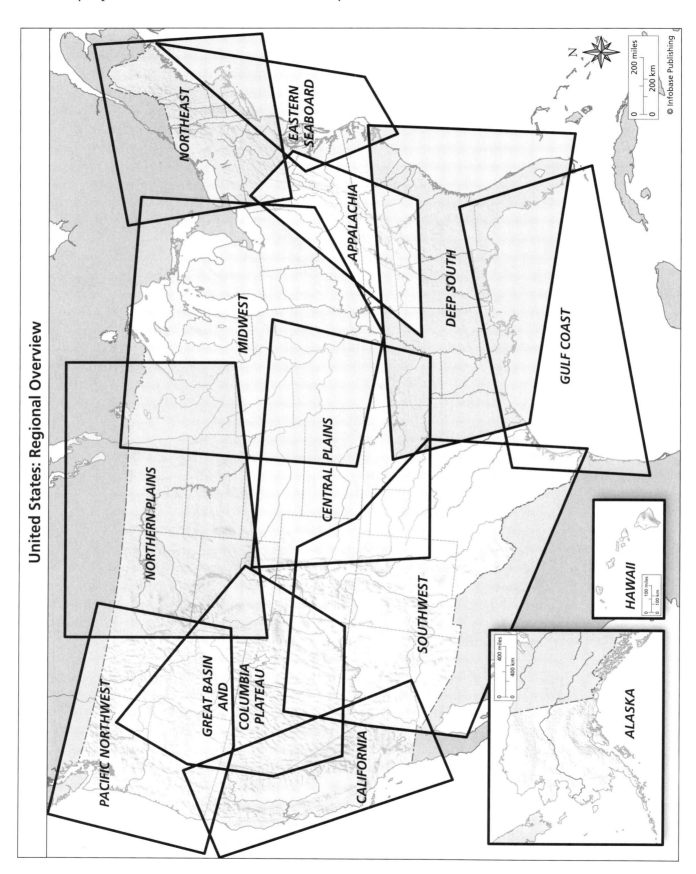

United States: Regional Overview

NORTHEAST

EASTERN SEABOARD

APPALACHIA

DEEP SOUTH

GULF COAST

MIDWEST

NORTHERN PLAINS

CENTRAL PLAINS

SOUTHWEST

PACIFIC NORTHWEST

GREAT BASIN AND COLUMBIA PLATEAU

CALIFORNIA

HAWAII

ALASKA

N

200 miles
200 km

100 miles
100 km

400 miles
400 km

© Infobase Publishing

United States

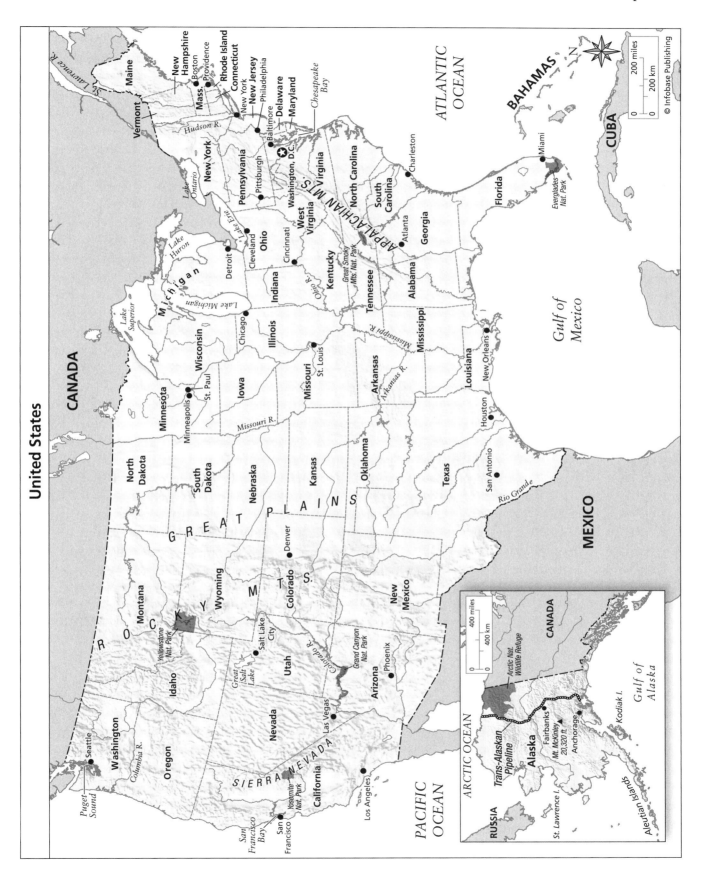

Entries D–H

dams, reservoirs, and artificial lakes

Dams hold a special place in environmental history because of the way that they are used to control water on the landscape and foster economic growth. In simplest terms, dams obstruct the flow of a stream or watercourse and thereby change the riparian environment. Some of these changes occur because water is backed up (or impounded) by the dam and the area upstream from the dam is inundated. Other changes occur when water flow is reduced or blocked by a dam and once-lush WETLANDS lying downstream disappear because their water supply is cut off. For spawning FISH, dams can present major obstacles affecting both upstream and downstream migration. And even when a flow of water downstream from a dam is maintained, the local aquatic environment can be altered because the temperature of water released from a reservoir is lower than the temperature of water in a naturally free-flowing stream—this change in water temperature may have major impacts on fish species. There is no single way that dams affect the environment, and their impact is tied to a multitude of local factors.

Dams do not bring about environmental change by accident: That is why they are built. Dams are *intended* to change the environment by making water available in locations and in quantities that differ from what natural conditions would provide.

ANTECEDENTS TO MODERN DAMS

Some of the earliest dams built in ancient Mesopotamia millennia ago were intended to divert water of the Tigris or Euphrates Rivers and into IRRIGATION canals; in turn, these canals allowed water to be dispersed over otherwise dry desert land and fostered the nourishment of crops. Irrigation represents a dramatic transformation of arid lands and, in a phrase that become popular in the 20th century, can "make the desert bloom." Since ancient times, dams have been built for myriad purposes including power (where water wheels drive mills), navigation (where dams inundate rocky stretches of rivers to facilitate boat and barge traffic), LOGGING (where dams store water for springtime release of floating logs), fish ponds (fostering early forms of aquaculture), mining (for both power and to help separate gold particles

from rock debris) and, at times, recreation (the Roman dams at Subiaco were built by Emperor Nero [37–68 C.E.] at his country villa in the Aniene Valley for no apparent utilitarian motive). In all these instances, dams altered natural river flow—and the riparian environment—to serve some human purpose or fulfill some desire.

LARGER DAMS FOR CITIES

In the 19th century, the size of dams began to increase in response to urban growth and the desire of cities in Europe and North America to deliver large quantities of water to urban consumers via large-scale aqueducts. These water supply systems extended into rural hinterlands as cities sought water relatively unpolluted from human settlement. From an engineering and public health perspective, the strategy proved sound, as water quality for densely populated urban areas improved dramatically with the implementation of new water supply systems, such as NEW YORK CITY's Croton Aqueduct, completed in Westchester County, north of the city, in 1842. In order to provide copious amounts of water for these systems, however, it was often necessary to build large storage reservoirs to capture spring snowmelt and storm runoff; only in this way could reliable water supplies be made available during seasons of low precipitation and periodic DROUGHTS. And with the creation of large reservoirs in once-remote valleys, the natural landscape began to change in dramatic ways.

The first major environmental controversy to arise over a major municipal water supply reservoir occurred in the 1870s, when the city of Manchester in western England proposed to transport water from Lake Thirlmere via a 100-mile-long aqueduct. Located in the romanticized "Lake District" of northwest England, Lake Thirlmere was to be transformed into a much larger artificial reservoir/lake by the construction of a 50-foot-high dam across the outlet stream. A cultural battle erupted as to whether the transformation of the lake into a reservoir—and the changes this would cause as water levels fluctuated in response not to natural conditions but to municipal demands—was in the best interests of British society. In the end, efforts to protect the natural lake came to naught, and in the 1890s, city officials trumpeted their success over "sentimentalism" in "conferring upon a large and crowded population the inestimable boon of a good supply of water." At Thirlmere, the environmental cost associated with large reservoirs entered the public arena, and the controversy presaged key issues that, in a global context, were to arise again in the 20th century. Similar controversies arose in the United States.

The most famous dam controversy in environmental history moved to the fore shortly after the turn of the 20th century, when SAN FRANCISCO, CALIFORNIA, proposed a municipal water supply reservoir high in the SIERRA NEVADA of California. From the perspective of city boosters, HETCH HETCHY VALLEY represented an ideal location for a reservoir—high in the mountains with water feeding in from an almost pristine, undeveloped watershed. To many preservationists in the newly founded SIERRA CLUB, including the famed naturalist and author JOHN MUIR, the city's proposal was an unmitigated travesty, an attempt to drown a wonderful valley in the northern reaches of YOSEMITE NATIONAL PARK simply to serve the short-sighted interests of San Francisco growth proponents. To other conservationists, including the U.S. president THEODORE ROOSEVELT and his colleague GIF-

FORD PINCHOT, use of Hetch Hetchy Valley for a municipally owned reservoir represented an instance where the utilitarian philosophy of providing for the "greatest good for the greatest number" held sway. To Roosevelt and Pinchot, the benefit of using Hetch Hetchy in order to furnish San Franciscans with a bountiful supply of pure water was so great that it trumped any desire to prevent the inundation of a valley that, in Muir's eyes, rivaled the grandeur of the main Yosemite Valley 15 miles to the south. Muir drew upon inspired, religiously toned rhetoric in castigating use of the valley to support urban commercial growth. As he famously phrased it: "These temple destroyers, devotees of ravaging commercialism, seem to have a perfect contempt for Nature, and, instead of lifting their eyes to the God of the mountains, lift them to the Almighty Dollar. Dam Hetch Hetchy! As well dam for water-tanks the people's cathedrals and churches, for no holier temple has ever been consecrated by the heart of man."

In the end, the fate of Hetch Hetchy was determined by the persuasiveness of a massive 400-plus-page report prepared for the city by the engineer John R. Freeman (1855–1932). Published in 1912, Freeman's report laid out practical arguments and justifications for why Hetch Hetchy was ideally suited as

Built in the 1930s and operated by the Bureau of Reclamation, the Grand Coulee Dam spans the Columbia River and is the nation's largest hydroelectric producer, while enabling irrigation of more than 600,000 acres of the Pacific Northwest.   *(Library of Congress)*

a water supply for San Francisco. Just as importantly, it also sought to demonstrate how development of an artificial lake in the valley could actually *enhance* scenic values and how the city's project could actually attract *more* people into the park to enjoy its pleasures. Freeman's attempt to portray the dam and reservoir as a means of *improving* nature enraged preservationists, but in order to counter his argument that only a few elite "nature lovers" were benefiting from visits to Hetch Hetchy, schemes were concocted to build a hotel in the valley and open it to upscale commercial tourism. Muir and his supporters were incapable of making much of an assault on the final component of Freeman's argument: hydroelectric power generation. As Freeman demonstrated, up to 200,000 horsepower could be developed by power plants below the reservoir, and this argument helped win final congressional approval of the city's project in 1913. At Hetch Hetchy, conservationist values extolling the public benefit of improved water supply and electric power clashed with preservationist desire to maintain rural and natural landscapes in order to serve a larger public good. It was not the last time that battles over "public interest" engaged preservationists opposing a dam.

THE NEW DEAL

While no other dam project in the early 20th century spurred opposition comparable to Hetch Hetchy, as more large dams were built, recognition of the environmental cost they incurred began to grow. For example, construction of the Winsor Dam/Quabbin Reservoir in western Massachusetts, in the 1930s, engendered much regional anger because of the local towns and settlements that it flooded; this anger was heightened because the reservoir was not for local use but was to quench the thirst of municipal users in the BOSTON, MASSACHUSETTS, area, almost 100 miles to the east. As with many of the dams built in the 1930s under the aegis of President FRANKLIN D. ROOSEVELT's NEW DEAL, planning for nonfederal Winsor Dam had begun in the 1920s.

However, unlike Winsor Dam, many other water development projects could not have gone forward without strong federal support and financing. Most prominently these included the dams of the TENNESSEE VALLEY AUTHORITY, U.S. BUREAU OF RECLAMATION projects such as Grand Coulee Dam in Washington State and Shasta Dam in northern California, and U.S. ARMY CORPS OF ENGINEERS projects such as the Tygart Valley flood control dam in West Virginia and the Bonneville hydroelectric power dam on the COLUMBIA RIVER east of Portland, Oregon. In addition, there were state-sponsored hydroelectric dams such as the Grand Dam in Oklahoma and the Santee Dam in South Carolina that received federal support through New Deal programs such as the Public Works Administration.

Heralded as "multipurpose" dams because they provided a multitude of benefits to society (for example, Hoover Dam was to provide water for both irrigation and municipal use as well as provide electric power and flood control protection for Southern California), New Deal era dams accrued environmental costs that did not attract much public attention; or at least such attention proved insufficient to force significant changes to engineering plans. When state and local officials in South Carolina lobbied Congress and President Roosevelt for federal support to build the Santee Dam, local opposition arose because of the many historic homes to be inundated and the wetlands and bird habitats to be destroyed. Such complaining fell on deaf ears as the project went through without significant modification. On the Pacific coast, major dams prompted public concern over impacts on spawning fish populations, which led to the design and construction of large-scale fish ladders at Bonneville Dam by the Corps of Engineers. But for large-scale storage dams such as Grand Coulee and Shasta, where building fish ladders was impractical, the Bureau of Reclamation made no attempt to mitigate the dams' effect on blocking upstream migration, and as a result, vast areas of the Upper Columbia and Sacramento River WATERSHEDS were eliminated as spawning grounds.

THE GO-GO YEARS AND ENVIRONMENTAL OPPOSITION TO DAMS

After the New Deal set the stage for the "Go-Go" years of dam building in the 1940s through the 1960s, most Americans perceived most dam projects as economically desirable, but environmental opposition did arise. For example, when Bureau of Reclamation plans for a major hydroelectric power dam across the Snake River on the Idaho-Oregon border were proposed after WORLD WAR II (1941–45), much opposition arose from proponents of private (not public) electric power development, but there was also concern raised about the impact to spawning fish. Even more important, when the Bureau of Reclamation proposed to build a large hydroelectric power dam across the Green River at Echo Park in eastern Utah, objections surfaced because of Echo Park's location within the boundaries of Dinosaur National Monument (a federal enclave administered by the NATIONAL PARK SERVICE). Sierra Club members and other antidam activists were able to thwart federal authorization of the Echo Park Dam in the mid-1950s, but they could not simultaneously block construction of the 704-foot-high GLEN CANYON DAM across the COLORADO RIVER near the Utah-Arizona border.

Designed to complement the HOOVER DAM lower down on the river, Glen Canyon Dam was intended to generate huge quantities of hydroelectric power and to facilitate expanded water use by the seven states lying within the Colorado River watershed. Soon after federal authorization of Glen Canyon Dam in 1956, the Sierra Club president DAVID R. BROWER undertook a major (and ultimately unsuccessful) public relations campaign to stop construction. In 1964, the Sierra Club published a major book *(The Place No One Knew)* highlighting the canyon landscape that would soon disappear under the rising waters of Lake Powell. With this, opposition to dam construction became a major part of the Sierra Club's mission, a focus that only intensified in the 1970s, as environmental groups began to see dams as symbols of a consumer-driven society that had lost appreciation of the natural world. Significantly, one of the most popular books within the environmental movement of the 1970s was EDWARD ABBEY's *The Monkey Wrench Gang* (1975), a celebration of the counterculture in which the four protagonists are energized by a (never-fulfilled) desire to blow up the Glen Canyon Dam with dynamite.

In the last quarter of the 20th century, dams attracted sustained attention from environmentalists, who wished to reduce their impact on the local ecologies and the natural landscape. For example, in the late 1970s, the proposed Tellico Dam in the Southeast United States was (temporarily) blocked over concern for the endangered "snail darter" fish, whose riparian habitat was threatened with inundation. In the Pacific Northwest, dwindling numbers of spawning SALMON spurred efforts both to remove existing dams as well as to find ways of mitigating the destructive effects of hydroelectric power dams through construction of improved fish ladders and other technologies. At Glen Canyon Dam, changes were made to the way in which water was released for electric power generation in hopes of restoring riparian conditions in downstream GRAND CANYON National Park. And local interest in removing small-scale dams, often dating back to the 19th century, swelled as communities sought to restore rivers and restore native fish and plant life.

INTERNATIONAL INFLUENCES

Internationally, large dams in developing nations such as India and China generated controversy because of the large numbers of people who would need to be relocated from reservoir areas and because of impacts on regional ecologies and endangered flora and fauna. U.S. government officials and engineering firms frequently consulted on these projects. In particular, the Three Gorges Dam on the Yangtze River in China has attracted opposition. Led by the U.S. Bureau of Reclamation's chief design engineer John L. Savage (1879–1967), head of the design effort for Hoover Dam, bureau engineers surveyed the area in 1944 and developed preliminary plans for a huge dam across the Yangtze. The bureau also helped train Chinese engineers in the United States prior to the communist victory in the Chinese civil war that ended in 1949. The Chinese government resurrected the Three Gorges project in the 1980s, and construction began in 1994 with technical support from American (as well as European) engineers.

Opposition to the dam arose in China, the United States, and elsewhere, because it displaced more than one million people and the 400-mile-long reservoir wrought other ecological changes. Conversely, proponents of the project pointed to the more than 22 million kilowatts of electric power capacity made possible by the dam and to how such power would help reduce China's reliance of COAL-fired, CO_2-emitting steam power plants. At Three Gorges, advocates of the dam won out, and the project is scheduled to be completed in the second decade of the 21st century.

CONCLUSION

Environmental interest in removing or blocking dams remains strong. In America, growing cities, burgeoning suburbs, and large tracts of irrigated agriculture continue to depend on the water stored and the power generated by dams. At the same time, public desire to protect natural landscapes and promote BIODIVERSITY remains strong, and interest in finding ways to remove dams and restore riparian ecologies does not appear to be abating. As the United States and other societies around the world struggle to find a balance between economic growth and natural resources protection, the construction and continued operation of dams will no doubt remain a contentious issue for decades.

See also BONNEVILLE POWER ADMINISTRATION; CENTRAL ARIZONA PROJECT; CENTRAL VALLEY PROJECT; CONSERVATION; ENDANGERED SPECIES ACT; ENERGY, HYDRAULIC; ENVIRONMENTALISM, MAINSTREAM; ENVIRONMENTALISM, RADICAL; LOS ANGELES, CALIFORNIA; MULHOLLAND, WILLIAM; PORTER, ELIOT; PRESERVATION; URBANIZATION.

Donald C. Jackson

Further Reading

Billington, David P., and Donald C. Jackson. *Big Dams of the New Deal Era: A Confluence of Water and Politics.* Norman: University of Oklahoma Press, 2006.

Brooks, Karl. *Public Power, Private Dams: The Hell's Canyon High Dam Controversy.* Seattle: University of Washington Press, 2006.

Goldsmith, Edward, and Nicholas Hildyard. *The Social and Environmental Effects of Large Dams.* San Francisco: Sierra Club Books, 1984.

Harvey, Mark. *A Symbol of Wilderness: Echo Park and the American Conservation Movement.* Seattle: University of Washington Press, 2000.

Jones, Holway R. *John Muir and the Sierra Club: The Battle for Yosemite.* San Francisco: Sierra Club Books, 1965.

McCully, Patrick. *Silence Rivers: The Ecology and Politics of Large Dams.* London: Zed Books, 1996.

Schnitter, Nicholas. *A History of Dams: The Useful Pyramids.* Brookfield, Vt.: Balkemas, 1994.

Darwin, Charles (1809–1882) *British biologist, naturalist, scientist*

Charles Darwin is perhaps the best known scientist who ever lived. He famously argued in his 1859 book *On the Origin of Species* that natural selection was the mechanism by which all life evolved. Natural selection is the competition among animals for finite resources that led certain species to survive and others to become extinct. The publication of Darwin's *On the Origins of Species* helped to develop the fields of ECOLOGY and population biology, and it revolutionized economics, psychology, political science, sociology, and a host of other intellectual disciplines, including environmental history.

Born in Shrewsbury, England, on February 12, 1809, Darwin grew up among a close-knit extended family of Unitarian physicians and textile producers. He was expected, as had his eminent grandfather, the physician and naturalist Erasmus Darwin (1731–1802), to attend medical school at Edinburgh University. Upon his arrival at Edinburgh, Darwin recoiled at the amputation of a child's arm and quit medical school. Darwin transferred to Christ College at the University of Cambridge with plans to become a clergyman. At Cambridge, Darwin developed an intense interest in the natural world under the tutelage of a prominent botanist, the Reverend John Henslow (1796–1861).

Upon graduation, Darwin convinced his father to pay for his voyage to Latin America onboard the HMS *Beagle* as the ship's resident naturalist. During the trip, he also visited New Zealand, Australia, and Cape Town in the Cape Colony (now part of South Africa). In Latin America, and throughout the Pacific, Darwin witnessed the dispersal of animal species, many of which were seemingly similar but yet strikingly different. This voyage provided him with the information to publish a variety of scientific papers and his first book, *The Voyage of the Beagle* (1839). Upon his return home to England in 1836, Darwin became a self-financed gentleman of science in London.

In 1837, Darwin first began thinking of EVOLUTION in terms of natural selection. Darwin's views were shaped by his direct interaction with new people, plants, and animals on his trip. His journey to Latin America was largely patterned after the German naturalist Alexander von Humboldt's (1769–1859) travels to the region during the late 18th and early 19th centuries. Humboldt and Darwin were just two of an increasing number of European explorers and botanists since the 17th century who tended to think of the world as an interconnected entity that could be understood through the application of reason and empirical induction. By viewing the forces of nature as materially driven, and by trying to draw connections between different animals across the world, Darwin observed that the differences of many animals and species could be understood through geographic terms. However, he did not know what caused these changes over time and space until he read Thomas Malthus's (1766–1834) *An Essay on the Principle of Population* (1798), in 1838, while in London. This book, which argued that population growth outpaced the expansion of resources, provided him the spark to believe that the mechanism for evolution was competition for finite resources.

Darwin continued to develop his evolutionary theory through conducting his own plant experiments, talking with

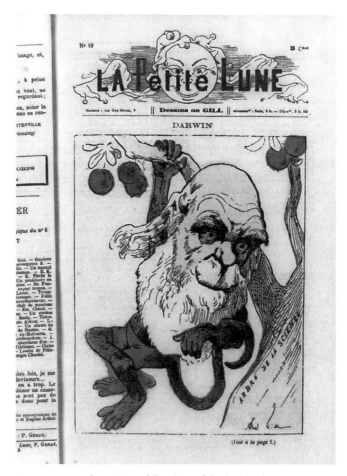

A response to the 1871 publication of the book *The Descent of Man,* this caricature on the cover of *La petite Lune* shows the book's author, English naturalist Charles Darwin, as a monkey hanging from a tree of science. *(Library of Congress)*

animal breeders, and continually corresponding with scientists throughout the United Kingdom and around the world. For more than 20 years—from 1838 to 1858—Darwin slowly and methodically crafted the theory of natural selection in his mind and in his private writings. On June 18, 1858, Darwin received a jolt that provided him the spark finally to write *On the Origin of Species* when he received a letter from Alfred Wallace (1823–1913), an explorer and private collector of animal and plant specimens who was working in the Malay Archipelago. In the letter, Wallace proposed his own theory of natural selection based upon his own observations traveling through Brazil and Southeast Asia. Interestingly, Wallace's reading of Malthus was also the spark that ignited his theory. On the advice of the British geologist Charles Lyell (1797–1875) and the British botanist Joseph Dalton Hooker (1814–79), Darwin decided to copublish his own ideas with Wallace's in the *Proceedings of the Linnaean Society*. This provided the impetus for Darwin quickly to write a "short" treatise of his idea. Darwin swiftly prepared his book, which had been 20 years in the making, for publication in London on November 22, 1859.

The reception of Darwin's *On the Origin of Species* was characterized by controversy. The book was widely discussed in the United Kingdom and, later, throughout the world. Many conservatives and official members of the Church of England rejected, mocked, and strongly criticized the book. It found a welcome reception among many who had already believed in EVOLUTION but did not know its mechanism. The book was read, but its influence remained limited throughout much of the 1860s until two acolytes of Darwin's, the German biologist Ernst Haeckel (1834–1919) and the English biologist Thomas Huxley (1825–95), later known as "Darwin's bulldog," promoted the book. With the help of Haeckel, Hooker, and Huxley—who debated people in public about the merits of Darwin's theory—the theory of evolution became a powerful idea in the late 19th century throughout the world.

Darwin continued to publish important works toward the end of his life. In 1871, Darwin put forward his theory of human evolution in *The Descent of Man, and Selection in Relation to Sex.* He published his last widely influential book, *The Expressions of the Emotions in Man and Animals,* the next year (1872); in it, he argued that psychology, culture, and biological evolution were intrinsically linked. These works provided the foundations for modern anthropology and evolutionary psychology, although they were never as influential and important as *On the Origin of Species.* On April 19, 1882, Charles Darwin died in his home in Downe at the age of 73.

Darwin's work helped to popularize evolution in the late 19th century, but it was not until the late 1930s that Darwin's concept of natural selection became the dominant method of explaining evolution after scientists had learned more about GENETICS. His theory of natural selection eventually became the leading explanation for evolution in the late 1930s, after scientists found that population genetics corresponded with Darwin's theory of natural selection. This synthesis of Darwinian natural selection and Mendelian genetics is called modern evolutionary synthesis. Modern evolutionary synthesis has influenced almost every single intellectual discipline, and it is likely one of the most influential concepts in the 20th and 21st centuries.

More than 200 years after his birth, Darwin and his theories remain controversial in the United States, although the scientific community and environmental historians have long accepted the basic principles of evolutionary theory. Other Americans have long clung to a biblical interpretation of the origin of life on Earth, believing that Darwin's theories undermine the role of God. The SCOPES TRIAL in Dayton, Tennessee, in 1925 remains the most famous episode in the American ideological debate over the teaching of evolutionary theory or various forms of creationism. In 1987, in *Edwards v. Aguillard* (482 U.S. 578), the Supreme Court ruled that a Louisiana law requiring educators to teach creation science along with evolu-

tion in public schools violated the First Amendment of the U.S. CONSTITUTION because it had no legitimate secular purpose and instead advanced a particular religion.

In the 1990s and early 21st century, its proponents attempted to reassert creationism in public schools in the guise of intelligent design. They claim intelligent design is a science, positing that life on Earth is a result of some intelligent cause rather than an undirected process such as natural selection. The U.S. National Academy of Sciences, the U.S. National Science Teachers Association, and the American Association for the Advancement of Science state that intelligent design is pseudoscience because it does not adhere to scientific methodology based on observable, empirical, or quantifiable evidence. The debate over evolution also represents the larger struggle between the scientific consensus and the fundamentalist skepticism about scientific authority that has pervaded American debates on the environment and public policy, reflected in some Americans' rejection of warnings about GLOBAL WARMING, for example.

See also BOTANY; ENLIGHTENMENT, THE; EXTINCTION; NATURAL HISTORY; ZOOLOGY.

Brett Bennett

Further Reading
Browne, Janet. *Charles Darwin.* Vol. 1, *Voyaging.* London: Jonathon Cape, 1995.
——. *Charles Darwin.* Vol. 2, *The Power of Place.* London: Jonathon Cape, 2002.
Desmond, Adrian, and James More. *Darwin.* London: Michael Joseph, 1991.
Worster, Donald. *Nature's Economy: A History of Ecological Ideas.* 2d ed. Cambridge: Cambridge University Press, 1994.

DDT

DDT is the abbreviation for *dichlorodiphenyltrichloroethane,* a synthetic insecticide belonging to the class of chlorinated hydrocarbons. DDT was first synthesized, in 1873, by Othmar Zeidler (1859–1911), a German graduate student. Dr. Paul Müller, a chemist at the Swiss corporation Geigy, discovered the insecticidal properties of DDT in 1924.

DDT is a powerful technology for PEST CONTROL because it is highly toxic to many INSECTS, especially flies and MOSQUITOES, but relatively harmless to mammals. The widespread use of DDT in the 1940s, 1950s, and 1960s represented the first time in human history that a chemical was used to kill insects without an immediate impact on humans.

In World War II, DDT was used extensively by the Allied forces to reduce mosquito populations in tropical areas and fight lice in urban areas. Some historians cite the use of DDT as being critical to the success of Allied forces in the Pacific theater against the Japanese, who did not employ DDT for

MALARIA control. Another success involved the use of DDT to control a typhus epidemic in Naples in 1944.

After the war, DDT became a regular part of American life. Farmers sprayed it on crops for all types of insects, and local governments sprayed DDT to control mosquitoes in residential and resort areas. The greater effectiveness of DDT than of other materials is demonstrated by the changes in pesticide production during the 1950s. Prior to the introduction of DDT, arsenic-based PESTICIDES were the primary chemical means of reducing insect damage to crops. In 1937, 100 million pounds of arsenic-containing insecticides was produced. By 1959, the production of this class of pesticides dropped to just 31 million pounds. Production of DDT increased from 38 million pounds in 1953 to 125 million pounds in 1959. The price of DDT also fell during this period, making it a more cost-effective choice.

The extensive use of DDT had an immediate downside. Insects are some of the most adaptable animals. There is great genetic diversity within a single insect species. When an environment changes, individual insects with a genetic advantage under the new conditions will survive more often than other individuals with a different set of genes. Their offspring will be better adapted to the new environment. This process of selection of the best-adapted individuals continues generation to generation. Because insects have a very short time span between generations, this process of adaptation can occur very quickly. The spraying of PESTICIDES drives this type of selection process, leading to populations of insects who have become resistant or immune to the effects of those pesticides. The first case of insects' becoming resistant to DDT was documented in Sweden in 1946. With the application of DDT and other insecticides against every pest on the farm, in the landscape, and in the home, many species of insects became resistant. By 1986, more than 477 species of insects had developed resistance to DDT or other insecticides.

The extensive use of DDT between 1940 and 1960 resulted in other environmental damage as well. RACHEL CARSON published the landmark book *Silent Spring* in 1962, sounding an alarm bell about the impacts of pesticides on the global environment. The importance of *Silent Spring* to American environmental history is hard to overstate. Carson discusses the impact of DDT on bird populations through a process called biomagnification.

DDT is not broken down completely when digested by any organism. Instead, it collects in the fatty tissue of that organism. DDT released into the environment ends up in water, where it is concentrated, albeit at very low concentrations, in zooplankton and other aquatic plants. These plants are eaten by fish that also fail to metabolize or excrete DDT, and the concentration in their bodies is even higher. This process of increasing concentration continues up the food chain to the highest-level predators in the system. In predatory birds, such as the peregrine falcon, osprey, and bald EAGLE, DDT has the effect of making the shells of eggs thinner and less rigid, leading to the death of the embryo before hatching. Other birds are affected as well.

Public outcry about the detrimental effects of DDT on birds and other possible environmental impacts led to the banning of DDT in the United States in 1972. Other industrialized nations also banned DDT. Nations where malaria is widespread have been less willing to ban it because of its success in controlling the disease. DDT is so successful at reducing deaths from malaria that the Swiss chemist Paul Müller was awarded the Nobel Prize in medicine in 1948 for "discovering" DDT.

Although DDT is widely considered in the United States to be the quintessential example of how damaging pesticides can be, it is still the most effective and least expensive means of preventing deaths from malaria in tropical countries. One of the most widely cited examples of both the successes and failures of DDT against malaria is Sri Lanka. In the mid-1940s, approximately three million cases of malaria were reported per year, killing 2 percent of the population annually. After spraying DDT, from 1948 to 1963, to control mosquito populations, the number of cases dropped to 7,300 annually with no reported deaths. In 1964, only 29 cases of malaria were reported; 1964 was also the year that spraying DDT for malaria control ended in Sri Lanka. It is now believed that mosquito populations in Sri Lanka have developed resistance to DDT. Cases and deaths from malaria in Sri Lanka began to rise again in the late 1960s. Early hopes that malaria had been eliminated were dashed.

Although agricultural use has declined globally, DDT continues to be employed in many nations, especially for disease control. The international debate over the balance between environmental damage and human health will continue into the foreseeable future. In place of DDT exists a wide range of insecticides, some based on or containing naturally occurring compounds. Many of these new compounds are designed to affect certain species of insects more than others. These pesticides are called "targeted," or "selective," insecticides. Pesticides are also designed to degrade in the environment so as not to result in biomagnifications or other long-term pollution. The widespread use of these materials, even if deemed less damaging than DDT, means the risks of insects' developing resistance to these compounds and unintended effects on other species remain.

See also BIODIVERSITY; DISEASES, HUMAN; EVOLUTION; GENETICS.

Craig Macmillan

Further Reading
Carson, Rachel. *Silent Spring*. New York: Houghton Mifflin, 1962.
Dunlap, Thomas R. *DDT: Scientists, Citizens, and Public Policy.* Princeton, N.J.: Princeton University Press, 1981.
Tren, Richard, and Roger Bate. *Malaria and the DDT Story.* London: Institute of Economic Affairs, 2001.

Winston, Mark L. *Nature Wars: People vs. Pests.* Cambridge, Mass.: Harvard University Press, 1997.

death   *See* DYING, DEATH, AND BODY DISPOSAL.

DeBow, J. D. B. (James Dunwoody Brownson DeBow) (1820–1867) *southern publisher, secessionist*

An American publisher and statistician, James Dunwoody Brownson (J. D. B.) DeBow founded a magazine, *DeBow's Review,* that advocated the extension of southern agriculture and slavery into new territories in the 1840s and 1850s and increasingly promoted the South's secession in the late 1850s. In critiquing the southern economic model, DeBow frequently focused on the region's abuse of natural resources.

DeBow was born on July 10, 1820, in CHARLESTON, SOUTH CAROLINA. His father, a once-prosperous merchant who moved from New Jersey to the South, died when J. D. B. was six, leaving the family impoverished. DeBow worked odd jobs, saving enough money to study at Charleston College. After graduation, he moved to NEW ORLEANS, LOUISIANA, where he became editor of the *Southern Quarterly Review.* In January 1846, DeBow founded the *Commercial Review of the South and South West,* later known as *DeBow's Review,* a journal that advocated greater investment in manufacturing in the South and the expansion of southern agriculture in an effort to end the South's economic dependence on the North. Among other issues, DeBow criticized southern COTTON farmers for their abuse of the land, believing they too frequently exhausted soil fertility, abandoned lands to EROSION, and moved on to new fields. In repeating this process, they failed to build the necessary infrastructure—roads, CANALS, RAILROADS—to facilitate transportation and enable manufacturing growth.

With his new journal, DeBow initially planned to deal with economic matters and avoid politics. However, it was not long before he penned openly political articles. For example, in an influential 1848 article, DeBow proposed that southern agricultural systems, including slavery, should expand into new territories acquired by the United States in 1848 at the end of the MEXICAN-AMERICAN WAR (1846–48). DeBow argued that without such expansion, demographic and economic trends would allow the northern states increasingly to dominate the country's economy and politics, a fact reflected by the more entrenched northern majority in the U.S. House of Representatives. DeBow and other southerners contended that the South needed to maintain its numbers in the U.S. Senate so as to balance political power between the nation's different sections. Senator Henry Clay (1777–1852) of Kentucky proposed a compromise with respect to California, part of the new territory. The California GOLD rush of 1849 prompted such an influx of people that California quickly had the population to achieve statehood. At the time, there were 15 slave states and 15 free states. Under the COMPROMISE OF 1850, California joined the Union as a free state, while CONGRESS tightened the Fugitive Slave Law, allowing slaves to be returned to their southern owners more easily. Although conscious of the South's economic problems for many years, DeBow grew to appreciate the South's demographic and political problems far more when he served as director of the U.S. Census from 1853 until 1857.

By 1857, however, DeBow had become closely associated with the "fire eaters," a term applied to extreme southern politicians who stated that they would prefer to "eat fire" than sit down with northerners. He increasingly saw secession as the means to southern economic independence, while repeatedly calling for planters to restructure their practices and reduce reliance on supplies from the North. He urged southern leaders to build more railways. Some improvements occurred in the late 1850s, contributing, in part, to the CONFEDERACY's ability to sustain the CIVIL WAR (1861–65)—which broke out in 1861—for four years despite its demographic and economic disadvantages. During the war, DeBow worked as the Confederacy's chief agent for the purchase and sale of cotton.

After the war, DeBow became the first president of the Tennessee and Pacific Railroad, but he did not see the railroad built. He died on February 27, 1867, in New Jersey. *DeBow's Review* continued to be published until 1880.

See also PLANTATIONS; SECTIONALISM; SOIL CONSERVATION; UNITED STATES—CALIFORNIA; UNITED STATES—DEEP SOUTH; UNITED STATES—GULF COAST; UNITED STATES—TIDEWATER.

Justin Corfield

Further Reading

McCardell, John. *The Idea of a Southern Nation.* New York: W. W. Norton, 1979.

Paskoff, Paul F., and Daniel J. Wilson, eds. *The Cause of the South: Selections from DeBow's Review, 1846–1867.* Baton Rouge: Louisiana State University Press, 1982.

Skipper, Ottis Clark. *J. D. B. DeBow: Magazinist of the Old South.* Athens: University of Georgia Press, 1958.

The South's Stagnant Economy
J. D. B. DeBow (1847)

J. D. B. DeBow, publisher of DeBow's Review, *an influential southern journal in the mid-19th century, feared the South's lack of manufacturing had condemned it to a colonial relationship with the North. A large part of the problem, he observed in this 1847 article in the* Commercial Review of the South and the West, *was attributable to abuses of the environment, particularly with the expansion of cotton into Mississippi, Louisiana, and Texas.*

If one unacquainted with the present condition of the southwest were told that the cotton-growing district alone had sold the crop for fifty millions of dollars per annum for the last twenty years, he would naturally conclude that this must be the richest community in the world. He might well imagine that the planters all dwell in palaces upon estates improved by every device of art, and that their most common utensils were made of the precious metals; that canals, turnpikes, railway, and every other improvement designed either for use or for ornament, abounded in every part of the lands, and that the want of money had never been felt or heard of in its limits. He would conclude that the most splendid edifices dedicated to the purposes of religion and learning were everywhere to be found, and that all the liberal arts had here found their reward and a home. But what would be his surprise when told that so far from dwelling in palaces, many of these planters dwell in habitations of the most primitive construction, and these so inartificially built as to be incapable of protecting the inmates from the winds and rains of heaven; that instead of any artistical improvement this rude dwelling was surrounded by cotton fields, or probably by fields exhausted, washed into gullies and abandoned; that instead of canals, the navigable streams remain unimproved, to the great detriment of transportation; that the common roads of the country were scarcely passable; that the edifices erected for the accommodation of learning and religion were frequently built of logs and covered with boards; and that the line arts were but little encouraged or cared for. Upon receiving this information he would imagine that this was surely the country of misers.—that they had been hoarding up all the money of the world, to the great detriment of the balance of mankind. But his surprise would be greatly increased when informed that instead of being misers and hoarders of money, these people were generally scarce of it, and many of them embarrassed and bankrupt. Upon what principle could a stranger to the country account for this condition of things? How could he account for the expenditure of the enormous sum of one *billion of dollars* in the short space of twenty years? Indeed, I think it would puzzle the most observing individual in the country to account for so strange a result.

It is true that much has been paid for public lands within this period of twenty years, but the price of two crops would more than cover that account. The purchase of slaves and private lands should not be taken into the account, because the money paid for these should have remained in the country, except that portion paid for the slaves purchased out of the cotton region, which

is inconsiderable when compared to the number brought into it by emigrants; and as to the natural increase of the slaves in the cotton region, that has no relation to the subject.

What, then, has become of the other nine hundred millions of dollars? Much of it has been paid to the neighboring States for provisions, mules, horses, and implements of husbandry; much has been paid for clothing and other articles of manufactures, all induced by the system of applying *all* or nearly all the labor of the country to the production of one staple only, and by neglecting the encouragement of manufactures. No mind can look back upon the history of this region for the last twenty years, and not feel convinced that the labor bestowed in cotton growing during that period has been a total loss to this part of the country. It is true that some of the neighboring States have been benefited to some extent, and it has served to swell the general commerce of the nation; the manufacturer of the raw material has given employment to foreign capital and to foreign labor, and has also served to swell the volume of foreign commerce. But the country of its production has gained nothing, and lost much;—it has lost much because it has not kept its relative position in the rapid march of improvement which marks the progress of other countries, and more than all, in the transportation of its *produce,* it has transported much of the productive and essential principles of the soil, which can never be returned, thereby sapping the very foundation of its wealth.

No country has ever acquired permanent wealth by exporting its unmanufactured products. And if any such case could be found in history the experience of the southwest would furnish satisfactory testimony that the exportation of the commodities produced here, tends rather to impoverish than to enrich the country. With the experience and the lights of the past before them it would seem to be madness to persevere in a course so detrimental to their interest.

Source: J. D. B. DeBow. "Domestic Manufactures in the South and West." In *The Commercial Review of the South and the West.* Vol. 3. New Orleans: Commercial Review, 1847, 200–201.

Debs, Eugene V. (1855–1926) *socialist, labor organizer, presidential candidate*

Eugene V. Debs was a labor leader and socialist who ran for president five times in the early 1900s. Although dedicated to the cause of working people, Debs was also a conservationist who argued that America's abundant natural resources belonged to all the people and should be protected by the federal government.

Eugene Victor Debs was born on November 5, 1855, in Terre Haute, Indiana, the eldest son of parents who had emigrated from Alsace. At the age of 14, he began to work, holding jobs in railroad shops of his hometown, in a grocery store, then as a locomotive fireman. In 1874, he gave up fireman duty to help organize a lodge of the Brotherhood of Locomotive Firemen. A national officer of the brotherhood and editor of its principal organ, the *Locomotive Firemen's Magazine,* Debs gave his first major speech in 1877 to the firemen's national convention. He also began a brief career in local and state Democratic politics, first serving as city clerk from 1880 to 1884, then briefly in the Indiana State Legislature from 1885 to 1887.

Frustrated by state politics—pressured to achieve DEMOCRATIC PARTY objectives and unable to realize meaningful gains for the working people he cared so much about—Debs turned to "industrial" organization. He spearheaded the founding of the American Railway Union (ARU), opening it to all railway workers. The ARU rapidly became the largest union in the nation and found significant successes in advocating better wages for workers through collective bargaining. In 1894, victorious in its first struggle against the Great Northern Railroad, the ARU was tested—and almost immediately destroyed—by its participation in the disastrous Pullman strikes in CHICAGO, ILLINOIS. The ARU's two major goals were to achieve higher wages and attain better working conditions for members and all railroad employees. In the midst of a severe economic depression in 1893, the Pullman Company cut workers' wages but refused to lower rents inside the company town of Pullman, where many workers lived. Pullman workers, many of them already ARU members, went on strike.

By then president of the ARU, Debs launched a boycott in which ARU members refused to operate or work on trains containing Pullman cars. Railroad attorneys secured an injunction barring union leaders from supporting the strike and ordering workers to cease their boycott. U.S. marshals and U.S. troops broke up the strike. Debs was arrested, indicted, and convicted of contempt for violating the injunction. He was sentenced to six months in jail. In writings later in life, he cited this period in jail as formative, the time when he fully converted to socialism. Thereafter and over the course of the ensuing 30 years, Debs became the figurehead for American socialism and what became the Socialist Party of America (SPA).

Never the intellectual leader of socialists in the United States, Debs was the movement's most prominent speaker and advocate. In 1897, he helped to form the Social Democratic Party, which merged with another group to become the Socialist Party in 1901. Debs's specific views deepened over time but were always centered on a radical critique of American CAPITALISM and an effort to overcome contemporary economic and social conditions by pushing a socialist agenda and revolution at the ballot box. He firmly believed that U.S. workers could and would adopt socialism. He focused his efforts on convincing working people to throw off the shackles of "party" and "class" and reorganize America to achieve equal distribution of wealth through the benefits of productive laborers rather than capitalists.

Often arguing for the equality of men and women, and against racial discrimination, Debs was more concerned with workingmen and industrial and craft organizations rather than with farmers, land, or the environment. Over the course of his long career, Debs maintained that America's natural resources were more than plentiful enough for all the citizens to share in harmony and comfort the "great banquet of Nature." CONSERVATION, while never a major part of Debs's socioeconomic views, held great appeal to him as part of his wider "producerist" efforts to get land out of private and corporate hands and into the protection of the federal government.

Debs was the Socialist candidate for president in 1900, 1904, 1908, 1912, and 1920. In 1912, he received almost 6 percent of the vote, just more than 900,000 votes, one of the largest proportions for a nonmainstream candidate in American history. An outspoken critic of the draft and of U.S. entry into WORLD WAR I (1914–18), Debs expressed those views forcefully in a speech in Canton, Ohio, in 1918. He was arrested, convicted, and sentenced to 10 years in prison for violating the Espionage Act. The imprisoned Debs ran for president again as the Socialist candidate in 1920 and secured an astonishing 919,801 votes, which amounted to 3.5 percent of the total vote. President Warren G. Harding (1865–1923) commuted Debs's sentence on Christmas 1921. In the last years of his life, Debs edited the Socialist weekly *American Appeal,* penned a book entitled *Walls and Bars,* wrote articles on prison conditions, and tried to prevent the Socialist Party from splintering. He died on October 20, 1926, in Elmhurst, Illinois.

See also ENVIRONMENTAL JUSTICE; JUDICIARY; LABOR, EXTRACTIVE INDUSTRIES; LABOR, MANUFACTURING; LABOR MOVEMENTS, RAILROADS.

Christopher McKnight Nichols

Further Reading

Constantine, J. Robert, ed. *Letters of Eugene Debs.* Urbana: University of Illinois Press, 1990.
Ginger, Ray. *The Bending Cross: A Biography of Eugene Victor Debs.* New Brunswick, N.J.: Rutgers University Press, 1949.
Kipnis, Ira. *The American Socialist Movement, 1897–1912.* Westport, Conn.: Greenwood Press, 1952.
Radosh, Ronald, ed. *Debs.* Englewood Cliffs, N.J.: Prentice Hall, 1971.

Salvatore, Nick. *Eugene V. Debs: Citizen and Socialist.* Urbana: University of Illinois Press, 1984.

Shannon, David. *The Socialist Party of America.* New York: Macmillan, 1955.

Weinstein, James. *The Decline of Socialism in America, 1912–1925.* New York: Monthly Review Press, 1967.

Writings and Speeches of Eugene V. Debs. New York: Hermitage Press, 1948.

Declaration of Independence (1776)

Adopted by the Continental Congress on July 4, 1776, the Declaration of Independence signaled America's official break with England and the onset of the AMERICAN REVOLUTION (1775–83), which had begun the preceding year. The Revolution, in turn, launched territorial and economic exploitation of the natural resources of the North American continent with the removal of restrictive British MERCANTILISM. Concepts of nature and reason from the 18th-century thinking of THE ENLIGHTENMENT infused the Declaration of Independence. It asserted that humans possessed certain natural rights, including a right to revolution.

The first such document of its kind, this declaration stated the justifications for an unprecedented formal political separation of the citizens of the thirteen North American colonies from the authority of the British Empire and their repudiation of allegiance to King George III (1738–1820). The declaration's primary author, THOMAS JEFFERSON, defined the colonists' position in terms of the discussion of rights that informed British political history and produced the evolution of individual political and property rights within a constitutional monarchy, the intellectual heritage of the Protestant Reformation, and the Enlightenment. The defiant colonists asserted their individual rights to property and to participation in the process by which that property could be taxed. They denied the monarch's ownership of natural resources that promised to become items of lucrative trade on the world market.

The format of the declaration mimicked a legal brief. The first of its four parts, the preamble, appealed to world public opinion for acknowledgment and affirmation of the justice of their unprecedented denial of British authority by asserting the rights of the governed according to divine and NATURAL LAW. The theory of natural law suggests that nature determines certain laws and rights that are valid everywhere and supersede the authority of a monarch or any government. The text of the preamble assumed patriarchal values inherent in the Protestant Reformation, which proved compatible with the rise of capitalism and interpreted the passage in Genesis to grant humans the right of domination over the planet and its resources. It also invoked a more recent secular assertion of the natural rights of men promoted by the Enlightenment. The second portion, the statement of philosophy of government, utilized the social contract theory of government to distinguish the rectitude and patriotism of the revolutionaries in their renunciation of their status as subjects of British monarchial authority. This innovative application of developing British constitutionalism suggested that consent of the governed was necessary to establish the legitimacy of a government.

The third and longest section of the declaration presented an extensive indictment of George III, listed the many actions of the British government, sanctioned by His Majesty, that constituted assault on the colonists' political and economic rights. It established George III as unfit to rule the colonists and validated their denial of British authority. In particular, it emphasized the British forbiddance of the colonials' free exploitation of the abundant natural resources in North America. In the concluding political manifesto, the colonists declared their intent to be free of British authority through diplomacy or by military resistance and claimed their status as a new member among the nations of the world, the United States of America.

Armed conflict between the colonists and the British military and naval forces prior to 1776 created the situation to which the declaration responded. After the FRENCH AND INDIAN WAR (1754–63), the British authority announced the Proclamation Line of 1763, which restricted colonists' western territorial expansion beyond the APPALACHIAN MOUNTAINS in deference to the profitable British FUR TRADE with Native Americans. Access to the resources of this WILDERNESS and the property rights to western lands were crucial to the acquisition of wealth in North America. To retire their enormous debt from the French and Indian War, the British sought to reorganize a newly expanded empire to assure that the economic contribution of the colonies exceeded the cost of their administration and defense. To strengthen enforcement of the Navigation Acts that defined British regulation of colonial trade, the British authorities reorganized their collection of the customs fees and increased the profits of the mercantilism that governed trade within the British Empire. The British established an increased postwar presence of the British military and added the Royal Navy to serve customs duty collection in North America and curb the lucrative smuggling by the colonists in evasion of the Navigation Acts.

The Declaration of Independence signaled the paradox of the anti-imperialist intent of the politically active citizens of the newly established nation by renouncing British imperialism. In asserting the rights of Americans to the natural resources of the North American continent, however, the declaration helped launch an ideology of expansionism that would transform the nation's environment by facilitating westward expansion and giving Americans license to exploit those resources with minimal regulation or restriction before the second half of the 20th century and with little concern for the Indians who occupied many of those lands.

See also ARTICLES OF CONFEDERATION; BOSTON TEA PARTY; ENGLISH EXPLORATION AND SETTLEMENT—CANADA AND NEW ENGLAND; ENGLISH EXPLORATION AND SETTLEMENT—THE MIDDLE COLONIES; ENGLISH EXPLORATION AND SETTLEMENT—THE SOUTH; IMPERIALISM; WASHINGTON, GEORGE.

Angela Marie Howard

Further Reading

Jennings, Francis. *The Invasion of America: Indians, Colonialism, and the Cant of Conquest.* New York: W. W. Norton, 1976.

Opie, John. *Nature's Nation: An Environmental History of the United States.* Fort Worth, Tex.: Harcourt Brace, 1998.

Petulla, Joseph M. *American Environmental History: The Exploitation and Conservatism of Natural Resources.* Boston: Boyd and Fraser, 1988.

The Declaration of Independence (1776)

Primarily authored by Thomas Jefferson, the Declaration of Independence set forth the reasons why the American colonists sought to break their political bonds with England. Adopted by the Continental Congress on July 4, 1776, the declaration identified "self-evident truths." Grounded in natural law, it asserted that nature is the source of law and human rights.

IN CONGRESS, July 4, 1776.

The unanimous Declaration of the thirteen united States of America,

When in the Course of human events, it becomes necessary for one people to dissolve the political bands which have connected them with another, and to assume among the powers of the earth, the separate and equal station to which the Laws of Nature and of Nature's God entitle them, a decent respect to the opinions of mankind requires that they should declare the causes which impel them to the separation.

We hold these truths to be self-evident, that all men are created equal, that they are endowed by their Creator with certain unalienable Rights, that among these are Life, Liberty and the pursuit of Happiness.—That to secure these rights, Governments are instituted among Men, deriving their just powers from the consent of the governed,—That whenever any Form of Government becomes destructive of these ends, it is the Right of the People to alter or to abolish it, and to institute new Government, laying its foundation on such

principles and organizing its powers in such form, as to them shall seem most likely to effect their Safety and Happiness. . . . The history of the present King of Great Britain is a history of repeated injuries and usurpations, all having in direct object the establishment of an absolute Tyranny over these States. To prove this, let Facts be submitted to a candid world.—He has refused his Assent to Laws, the most wholesome and necessary for the public good. . . .—He has refused to pass other Laws for the accommodation of large districts of people, unless those people would relinquish the right of Representation in the Legislature, a right inestimable to them and formidable to tyrants only. . . . He has endeavoured to prevent the population of these States; for that purpose obstructing the Laws for Naturalization of Foreigners; refusing to pass others to encourage their migrations hither, and raising the conditions of new Appropriations of Lands. . . .—He has combined with others to subject us to a jurisdiction foreign to our constitution, and unacknowledged by our laws; giving his Assent to their Acts of pretended Legislation: . . . For cutting off our Trade with all parts of the world. . . . He has abdicated Government here, by declaring us out of his Protection and waging War against us. He has plundered our seas, ravaged our Coasts, burnt our towns, and destroyed the lives of our people. . . . He has excited domestic insurrections amongst us, and has endeavoured to bring on the inhabitants of our frontiers, the merciless Indian Savages, whose known rule of warfare, is an undistinguished destruction of all ages, sexes and conditions. . . .

We, therefore, the Representatives of the United States of America, in General Congress, Assembled, appealing to the Supreme Judge of the world for the rectitude of our intentions, do, in the Name, and by Authority of the good People of these Colonies, solemnly publish and declare, That these United Colonies are, and of Right ought to be Free and Independent States; that they are Absolved from all Allegiance to the British Crown, and that all political connection between them and the State of Great Britain, is and ought to be totally dissolved; and that as Free and Independent States, they have full Power to levy War, conclude Peace, contract Alliances, establish Commerce, and to do all other Acts and Things which Independent States may of right do. And for the support of this Declaration, with a firm reliance on the protection of divine Providence, we mutually pledge to each other our Lives, our Fortunes and our sacred Honor.

❖

Source: The National Archives. Available online. URL: http://www.archives.gov/exhibits/charters/declaration.html. Accessed February 7, 2009.

Deep South *See* UNITED STATES—DEEP SOUTH.

deer

Deer have interacted with people in North America for at least the last 10,000 years, since the end of the last ICE AGE. The animals thrive in nearly every habitat on the continent, from western ponderosa forests to southern swamps and northeastern woodlands. Hoofed, ruminant animals with deciduous antlers in the male, deer belong to the family Cer-

vidae, and common North American species include mule deer and white-tailed deer. The roles deer play in human culture are varied; people have used them for food, clothing, tools, and symbols.

Before contact with Europeans, American Indians organized their deer hunting through kinship networks. Extended families had the right to hunt in a particular place, and they could extend this right to other families as they saw fit. They passed the place from one generation to the next, and in many Native cultures, deer-hunting grounds consequently became a source of tribal identity. The fall deer hunt also reinforced gender roles; after men hunted the animal, women prepared the meat for eating and the hides for wearing. Children helped their parents, and so tribes passed down the ritual of the hunt from generation to generation, just as they bequeathed the place of the hunt.

When Europeans began to settle in North America, they introduced new ways of managing deer with them. English colonists had known deer as the property of nobility, who ritually killed the largest deer—a stag or a hart—to demonstrate

Mule deer near Clear Lake, California. Humans have interacted with deer for millennia through hunting and skin trading. Management of deer populations in suburban, exurban, and rural areas is now a responsibility of many federal and state wildlife organizations. *(Tupper Ansel Blake, U.S. Fish and Wildlife Service)*

their control over England's forests. Peasants had often resented this enclosure of a once commonly held resource. In 1642, for example, English peasants protested by killing more than 600 deer belonging to an absentee landlord.

Many colonists considered deer hunting frivolous recreation, probably because it had been the pastime of idle nobles. But other colonists—especially those on the FRONTIER—hunted deer for subsistence, something they could not do in Europe. Their farms reshaped the North American landscape, often destroying Native hunting grounds or prohibiting American Indians from using them. Beyond the farms, Natives' relationships with deer changed as well. In the Mississippi Valley, Choctaw Indians used the horse to expand deer hunting and transport the hides to market. Between 1720 and 1780, French Louisiana exported three million deerskins. Intensive hunting pushed the Choctaw and other tribes into new hunting grounds, creating conflict or necessitating alliances with neighbors. The deerskin trade reordered Native political economy, one family's hunting ground at a time. In this way, transatlantic commerce took on a local character with deer in the North American backcountry.

The deerskin trade diminished as more and more Euro-Americans settled the continent in the 19th century. In the early 20th century, conservation agencies—the U.S. FOREST SERVICE, the NATIONAL PARK SERVICE, and state game commissions—began regulating deer hunting and, consequently, impeded local hunting for subsistence or barter. President THEODORE ROOSEVELT made the Kaibab Plateau in Arizona a national game preserve in 1906 and outlawed deer hunting there, much to the dismay of the Native Southern Paiute and Navajo. In Wyoming, the establishment of YELLOWSTONE National Park also made deer hunting illegal for local ranchers. The process of closing these local hunting commons mirrored the enclosure movement in England hundreds of years earlier and frequently produced similar unrest among locals, who resented outside control of deer.

The CONSERVATION movement protected deer largely because the animals represented natural abundance at a time when eastern herds were rapidly declining. Wildlife experts such as WILLIAM HORNADAY warned of possible species extinctions. In the *Saturday Evening Post* in 1922, the writer Emerson Hough called for the creation of a "President's Forest" that would maintain large herds and advertise America's natural abundance. Tourists visiting national parks in the American West found deer plentiful and associated them with nature unspoiled by industry. This "virgin" status also helped the national public think of deer as innocent—a point reiterated in the DISNEY film *Bambi* (1942).

When deer herds became overabundant—as on the Kaibab Plateau in the 1920s—the public came to terms with the need to cull herds, lest they die of starvation. In his famous *A Sand County Almanac* (1949), ALDO LEOPOLD argued for a more ecological approach to game management—one that

included not just deer but hunters and predators. Both deer hunters and supporters of wolf reintroductions have found this "land ethic" useful. Among suburban homeowners, deer hunting has earned support as herd overpopulations destroy gardens and make driving dangerous. Today, deer hunting is a multimillion-dollar industry. Many Americans, however, still see deer as innocent, and the animal is thus a point of tension in American culture.

See also ENGLISH EXPLORATION AND SETTLEMENT—CANADA AND NEW ENGLAND; FIRE; GRAND CANYON; HUNTING, COMMERCIAL; HUNTING, RECREATIONAL; HUNTING, SUBSISTENCE; INDIANS, DEEP SOUTH; INDIANS, GULF COAST; INDIANS, MIDWEST; INDIANS, NORTHEAST; SUBURBANIZATION; UNITED STATES—COLUMBIA PLATEAU AND GREAT BASIN; UNITED STATES—SOUTHWEST.

Neil Prendergast

Further Reading

Cronon, William. *Changes in the Land: Indians, Colonists, and the Ecology of New England.* New York: Hill & Wang, 1983.

Nelson, Richard. *Heart and Blood: Living with Deer in America.* New York: Random House, 1997.

Usner, Daniel. *Indians, Settlers, and Slaves in a Frontier Exchange Economy: The Lower Mississippi Valley before 1783.* Chapel Hill: University of North Carolina Press, 1992.

Warren, Louis. *The Hunter's Game: Poachers and Conservationists in Twentieth-Century America.* New Haven, Conn.: Yale University Press, 1997.

Defense, Department of

The United States Department of Defense (DOD) coordinates all agencies and functions of the federal government relating to the military and national security. It comprises the Department of the Army, the Department of the Air Force, and the Department of the Navy. It also includes DOD agencies such as the Pentagon Force Protection Agency (PFPA), the Defense Advanced Research Projects Agency (DARPA), the National Security Agency (NSA), and the Defense Intelligence Agency (DIA), among others. Given the size and depth of its global operations, the DOD is one of the world's largest consumers of fossil fuel and other environmental resources.

The modern DOD dates to September 18, 1947, when the National Security Act of 1947 unified the Department of War (founded in 1789), the Department of the Navy (founded in 1798), and the Department of the Air Force (also created on September 18, 1947) and consolidated them into a single department under one cabinet-level secretary. The modern DOD is a large organization, headquartered at the Pentagon in Arlington, Virginia, across the Potomac River from WASHINGTON, D.C. According to the Office of the Under Secretary of Defense (Comptroller), the DOD's annual budget reached approximately $786 billion in 2007.

NUCLEAR WEAPONS

Nuclear weapons testing and nuclear fallout emerged in the 1950s as the first significant environmental controversy affecting the DOD. In the immediate post–World War II (1941–45) period, the United States, France, Britain, and the Soviet Union all tested nuclear weapons in remote areas of the Pacific Ocean. However, despite the geographical isolation of these testing sites, many Pacific Islanders were adversely affected by the nuclear tests. For instance, the United States conducted 67 nuclear tests in the Pacific between 1946 and 1962. The most famous of these occurred in the Marshall Islands, specifically on Bikini Atoll. In 1946, approximately 167 islanders agreed to a temporary evacuation from their homeland, in order that the DOD could conduct nuclear tests. As late as 1954, however, bomb testing continued, with the most noteworthy American test occurring on March 1, 1954, when the United States dropped a hydrogen bomb code-named *Bravo* on the atoll. Controversies surrounding the environmental and cultural impacts of these tests, including potential genetic damage, dislocation and dispossession of Pacific communities, and radioactive fallout, influenced the U.S. decision to sign the Limited Test Ban Treaty with Britain and the Soviet Union in 1963. In 1969, the U.S. government prepared an eight-year plan for the resettlement of Bikini Atoll citizens to their homeland. Finally, as a result of a lawsuit filed by Bikini Atoll islanders and their descendants, the Nuclear Claims Tribunal awarded $560 million to the islanders as compensation for loss of property value, restoration costs, and suffering and hardship.

Nuclear testing and nuclear weapons storage remain significant environmental issues for the U.S. military. For instance, in the 1980s, political controversy arose—domestically and internationally—over President Ronald Reagan's proposed Strategic Defense Initiative (nicknamed Star Wars). In addition to concerns that implementation of a strategic defense initiative would undermine existing nonproliferation treaties with the Soviet Union, environmentalists argued that such a program would encourage a space-based nuclear power race among the United States, the Soviet Union, and China. In addition, critics of the Reagan proposal argued that the militarization of space increased the possibility of accidental atmospheric pollution.

THE MILITARY AND ENVIRONMENTAL LAWS

After the end of the cold war in the late 1980s, calculating the environmental consequences and costs of military base closures became a federal priority. According to the Congressional Research Service, the DOD decommissioned approximately 20 percent of its cold war domestic infrastructure in a series of base closings in 1988, 1991, 1993, and 1995. Section 120(h) of the Comprehensive Environmental Response, Compensation and Liability Act (CERCLA, also known as Superfund) of 1980 requires the DOD to clean up closed

Department of Defense Cleanup Sites

bases prior to releasing them for civilian use and economic development. DOD negotiates land-use plans with local communities. Land designated for industrial use is the least expensive to clean up, while land designated for residential development is the most expensive and must meet the highest regulatory standards.

The Sikes Act, originally signed in 1960 and amended several times since, authorized the DOD (as well as the Department of the Interior and the Department of Agriculture) to cooperate with state agencies in developing programs for the conservation and rehabilitation of fish and wildlife resources on its public lands. The Endangered Species Act of 1973 further strengthened federal protection for endangered species.

However, the sheer scale of the public land under DOD management makes balancing the needs of national security and military training with environmental protection an ongoing policy challenge. For example, the U.S. Air Force is trustee to more than eight million acres of natural habitat. According to the Air Force Center for Engineering and the Environment (AFCEE), this land includes 234,000 acres of wetlands, 200 miles of coastline, 570,000 acres of forested landscapes, and habitat for more 70 threatened and endangered species. The air force has used an integrated conservation management approach toward species conservation in order to balance the preservation of critical habitat with the requirements of military missions. In another example, the Marine Corps Base Camp Lejeune in North Carolina includes habitat for nine federally listed endangered species, including the American alligator, loggerhead sea

Military dump at Rat Harbor, Amchitka Island, Alaska, 1950. Ships introduced rats to the island, and the trash supplied sustenance to the invasive species.   *(Robert D. Jones, Jr., U.S. Fish and Wildlife Service)*

turtle, and American bald eagle. As a federal agency, the DOD must endeavor to protect endangered species from harm and harassment, manage listed species with a goal of species recovery, and consult the U.S. FISH AND WILDLIFE SERVICE and the National Marine Fisheries Service when its actions might compromise the management of listed species. In total, the DOD currently manages nearly 25 million acres of public land in the United States and ranks third among federal agencies in terms of listed species in its jurisdiction.

EXEMPTIONS TO ENVIRONMENTAL LAWS

The DOD often argues that strict adherence to environmental laws undermines its ability to provide high-level training for its troops and to protect America's national interests and security. In 2002, it submitted the Readiness and Range Preservation Initiative (RRPI) to CONGRESS, seeking exemption from several laws such as the CLEAN AIR ACT, the Solid Waste Disposal Act, and CERCLA. The RRPI ultimately sought to ensure that military readiness would be accorded equal status to economic and environmental factors in regulatory decisions. Congress did not pass the initiative in its entirety but did grant the military's request for an exemption from the MIGRATORY BIRD TREATY act. Under the exemption, the DOD would not be cited for unintentional takings of protected birds killed during routine training and operations. In 2003, Congress granted additional exemptions under the RRPI. It amended the definition of *harassment* contained in the Marine Mammal Protection Act in order to facilitate underwater sonar testing and training by the U.S. Navy. It also provided for national security exemptions under the act. Congress also authorized the military, with the prior approval of the Department of the Interior, to substitute Integrated Natural Resource Management Plans in place of critical habitat designations (thereby overriding the normal requirements of the Endangered Species Act).

Military exemptions from laws designed to protect endangered species are very controversial. For example, in its 2008 decision in *Winter, Secretary of the Navy v. National Resources Defense Council,* the U.S. Supreme Court, in a 5-4 decision, overruled the lower courts of California and lifted restrictions on the navy's use of midfrequency active (MFA) sonar. The navy argued that this decision was a victory for national security and emphasized that sonar training is a necessary part of its Anti–Submarine Warfare mission. According to the Navy Office of Information, the navy is a world leader in marine mammal research, with a large research program dedicated to the study of the care, diagnosis, and treatment of marine mammal diseases. However, for environmental groups such as the Natural Resources Defense Council, underwater sonar training constitutes a significant threat to the health and well-being of marine mammals such as whales and dolphins, as the interference with their natural communication systems can cause distress, disorientation, and even death.

In the first decade of the 21st century, the Department of Defense, which is among the nation's major polluters, if not the major polluter, resisted orders from the Environmental Protection Agency (EPA) to clean up Fort Meade in Maryland, Tyndall Air Force Base in Florida, and McGuire Air Force Base in New Jersey, where, the EPA claims, dumped chemicals threaten public health and the environment. Although some branches of the military have been more cooperative than others, tensions between the DOD and the EPA grew as the DOD refused to sign EPA-drafted orders to clean up these three bases and other Superfund sites. The DOD believes the provisions are unreasonable. The EPA has expressed concern that contaminants from military bases are leaching into aquifers and soils. DOD officials have argued that they need not comply with EPA orders because they are voluntarily cleaning up these three bases and other facilities. By 2009, the DOD had 129 sites on the Superfund list of 1,255 sites, the most of any entity, and more than 25,000 contaminated sites across the 50 states. No matter how this particular debate is resolved, cleanup of these facilities will cost billions.

CLIMATE CHANGE

Climate change is another major area in which the military often clashes with environmental groups. The latter criticize the military's large ecological footprint, pointing to the fact that the DOD consumes the largest share of oil of any government anywhere in the world. According to the U.S. Defense Energy Support Center, the U.S. military consumed 132.5 million barrels of oil in the 2007 fiscal year—a year that included significant military operations in Iraq and Afghanistan. From this perspective, the U.S. military is one of the largest greenhouse gas emitters on Earth. However, the U.S. military is also likely to be called upon to respond to humanitarian emergencies around the globe if the worst-case scenarios of climate change catastrophe occur. In 2007, the Army Environmental Policy Institute (AEPI) released the paper "Climate Change and Army Sustainability." It emphasizes the consensus reached by the Intergovernmental Panel on Climate Change (IPCC) about the significance of human-induced global warming. The report anticipates increased media scrutiny of the U.S. Armed Services and its energy consumption and points to the possibility of increased security conflicts arising in developing and vulnerable countries if desertification, extreme weather events, and water scarcity increase.

The AEPI report draws upon the work of the CNA Corporation, a not-for-profit research institute with a military advisory board that includes retired generals, admirals, vice admirals, and lieutenant generals from the army, navy, air force, and marine corps. In a highly influential 2007 report, the board concluded that climate change could become a significant security threat to America's domestic and international interests. It recommends that the United States increase its global cooperative efforts on climate mitigation initiatives and that the military pursue increased energy efficiency and sustainable fuel supplies. A hearing by the House Select Committee on Energy Independence and Global Warming in June 2008 to discuss "The National Intelligence Assessment on the National Security Implications of Global Climate Change to 2030," a report prepared by the National Intelligence Council in 2008, clarified the policy links of climate change, the military, and national security. Witnesses testified that although global warming cannot be directly linked to state failure, the impacts of significant global warming could nonetheless worsen existing social and environmental problems in vulnerable countries. The U.S. military, therefore, must plan for the possibility of future operations in which it will be called upon to intervene in environmental-humanitarian disasters, especially in the Pacific and in Africa.

SUSTAINABILITY

Today, the U.S. military also focuses increasingly on sustainability. The Green Procurement Program (GPP), for example, is an important tool by which the modern military reduces its ecological footprint. The Resource Conservation and Recovery Act (RCRA), signed by President Gerald Ford in 1976, regulates the disposal of solid waste and hazardous waste and authorizes federal agencies to implement green procurement policies when purchasing materials and supplies. Additional regulations for environmentally friendly procurement are found in Executive Order 13101 (Greening the Government through Waste Prevention, Recycling and Federal Acquisition), the 2002 Farm Bill, and Federal Acquisition Regulations. The six mandatory provisions of the GPP include purchasing products manufactured from recycled materials, biobased products (such as soy inks), energy-efficient lighting equipment, non-ozone-depleting substances, substitutes for chemicals prioritized as hazardous by the Environment Protection Agency, and alternative fueled vehicles (AFVs). Exemptions from the GPP can be sought on the grounds of cost (relative to that of a nonrecycled product), quality (does not meet technical requirements), or time (product is not available within a reasonable time frame).

A 2004 report, "Sustain the Mission—Secure the Future: The Army Strategy for the Environment," defined the triple bottom line of sustainability: mission, environment, and community. The strategy document outlines a shift in military thinking from a compliance-based environmental program (in which strict adherence to environmental regulations is the paramount goal) to a mission-oriented approach built upon not only compliance but also on the principles of sustainability. Prior to the 2004 report, the army's most recent environmental strategy was published in 1992. It focused on CONSERVATION, pollution prevention, and compliance. Seeking to build upon the knowledge gained in the intervening 12 years, the army's most recent strategy is a much more ambitious environmental blueprint for a military that must contend with a variety of nontraditional security issues—such as climate change—and with complex operations ranging from war to counterinsurgency to humanitarian operations.

See also ARMY CORPS OF ENGINEERS, U.S.; EAGLE ENERGY, RENEWABLE; FISH AND OTHER AQUATIC ORGANISMS; FUELS, FOSSIL; GREENHOUSE EFFECT; NONGOVERNMENTAL ORGANIZATIONS; OCEANS; OIL, DOMESTIC; OIL, IMPORTED; PUBLIC DOMAIN; TREATIES AND INTERNATIONAL LAW; UNITED STATES—HAWAII AND THE PACIFIC ISLANDS.

Amy Lynn Fletcher

Further Reading
Air Force Center for Engineering and the Environment. Available online. URL: http://www.afcee.af.mil. Accessed June 8, 2009.

Army Environmental Policy Institute. *July 07: Climate Change and Army Sustainability.* Edition 4.1. Arlington, Va.: Army Environmental Policy Institute, 2007.

Bearden, David M. *Exemptions from Environmental Law for the Department of Defense: Background and Issues for Congress.* Order Code RS22149. Washington, D.C.: Congressional Research Service, May 15, 2007.

———. *Military Base Closures: Roles and Costs of Environmental Cleanup.* Order Code RS22065. Washington, D.C.: Congressional Research Service, April 11, 2006.

CNA Corporation. *National Security and the Threat of Climate Change.* Alexandria, Va.: 2007.

Layton, Lindsey. "Pentagon Fights EPA on Pollution Cleanup." *Washington Post,* 30 June 2008, A01. Available online. URL: http://www.washingtonpost.com/wp-dyn/content/article/2008/06/29/AR2008062901977.html?sid=ST2008063001979. Accessed June 8, 2009.

Marine Corps Base, Camp Lejeune. "Threatened and Endangered Species." Available online. URL: http://www.lejeune.usmc.mil/EMD/TE/HOMETE.HTM. Accessed June 8, 2009.

Navy Office of Information. Available online. URL: http://chinfo.navy.mil. Accessed June 5, 2009.

Office of the Assistant Secretary of the Army for Installations and Environment. "Sustain the Mission—Secure the Future: The Army Strategy for the Environment." Washington, D.C.: 2004. Available online. URL: http://www.asaie.army.mil. Accessed June 5, 2009.

United States Defense Energy Support Center. Available online. URL: http://www.desc.dla.mil. Accessed June 5, 2009.

deforestation

Deforestation is the geological term that describes the clearing of trees. In much of the world and in parts of the United States in the 21st century, current and past clearings constitute an ecological crisis. Natural disasters have caused some episodes of deforestation, but the term usually refers to the destruction of FORESTS by humans. Many people believe that deforestation is a relatively recent global phenomenon occurring since WORLD WAR II (1941–45), but degradation of forests is as old as human history.

Humans began to use FIRE about 1.5 million years ago. Around 500,000 years ago, humans began to use fires for many purposes, including deforestation. Controlled burning of forests made hunting more predictable and more efficient because it allowed people to drive game into more accessible areas. Humans subsequently cleared forests so that they could plant crops. Humans obtained wood as fuel for heating and cooking and used fire to protect themselves from wild animals and to craft various tools. Fire was the major factor that changed the ancient hunting and gathering society into an agricultural one, until new sources of energy allowed the agricultural society to become an industrial society. With the invention of commercially viable steam engines in the 17th century, trees became an important fuel in producing power by steam until producers turned to COAL. Coal MINING, in turn, became a major contributor to deforestation. Surface mining removed the soil and rock overlying the coal. Knowledge of the Industrial Revolution spread from country to country, in part, through the art of printing. Paper, however, originated from trees and became a hidden contributor to deforestation. Industrialization also contributed to greater urbanization across the world over the past three centuries, and sprawling cities exacerbated forest loss.

When European colonizers arrived in North America in the 16th century, many of them assumed that they were encountering a pristine WILDERNESS. They were wrong. Across the continent, Native Americans ensured their subsistence by utilizing a variety of methods to manage their forests. They regularly employed fire to cut back or burn off vegetation, to facilitate foraging and hunting, and to clear fields for crops. Indigenous people altered forests by selectively cultivating those trees, shrubs, and plants they found useful, a practice that in turn affected the distribution of animal and plant species. Their impact on forests was greater than the European arrivals recognized.

Timber was one of the many resources that attracted European colonizers and settlers to North America. In the 16th century, denuded English forests, for example, were unable to meet the needs of society. Shipbuilders required wood to construct their vessels. Many commodities were stored or shipped in wooden barrels. Wood was the main fuel for the artisan crafts and burgeoning factories. Wood held together houses and supported mine shafts. By 1640, New England forests facilitated much of the trade in the Atlantic world, providing the wood for barrels and other containers that moved commodities. In the southern colonies, a 100-mile-wide swath of longleaf pine trees stretched 1,500 miles from Virginia to Texas. These trees, which are among the first to grow in recently burned or cleared forests, revealed the extent of Native Americans' manipulation of the forests. They also became an important source of pitch, tar, and other NAVAL STORES. Colonial cities placed a double burden on forests by usurping land and demanding wood for residences and other buildings.

Forests also presented an obstacle to colonial settlers who planned to farm. They initially confiscated land cleared by Indians, but with greater settlement, farmers began to

Three men in a devastated forest in the Cascade Mountains, near Seattle, Washington, 1906 *(Library of Congress)*

clear large sections of forests. In the northern colonies, they chopped down trees. Southern colonists more frequently used girdling—a system in which they removed the bark and cambium of the circumference of a tree in order to stop the flow of sap and kill the tree. Given the demands that TOBACCO placed on the soil and given the availability of land (assuming Indian claims were ignored), southerners began to shift agriculture by abandoning depleted fields, moving to new land, and burning forests to release nutrients and clear trees for crops. Well into the 19th century, land was a secondary resource in a southern society that based its wealth on slavery. As Americans populated much of the remaining continental United States, many continued to believe that AGRARIANISM offered the best future for the nation, while others saw nascent factories and extractive industries as the key to long-term economic success. With either vision, the demands of the American market economy contributed to extensive deforestation.

The loss of forests affected ECOSYSTEMS. It destroyed animal habitat and undermined BIODIVERSITY, although other species sometimes flourished in the new environments. Deforestation also contributed to CLIMATE CHANGE, allowing for greater weather extremes by removing tree roots and canopies that moderated the effects of cold and heat, respectively. Finally, this depletion affected rivers. Without tree roots to absorb water, more water flowed into streams. With the loss of tree roots, there was greater EROSION and soil sediment clogged rivers. Both of these factors contributed to greater flooding. In more arid areas, rapid runoff led to DROUGHTS.

As a U.S. diplomat in Europe, GEORGE PERKINS MARSH had observed the destruction of Mediterranean forests and believed that it contributed to the decline of nature and society. In his seminal book, *Man and Nature* (1864), Marsh explained how the loss of forests led to erosion and robbed soils of their nutrients. He feared that the trends he observed in Europe were being repeated in the United States. The popularity of his book suggested that other Americans were equally concerned about resource depletion. Marsh influenced the CONSERVATION movement that emerged at the end of the 19th century. Foresters, who had trained in FORESTRY at European schools, helped establish national forests and the Division of Forestry in 1891, which became the U.S. FOREST SERVICE in 1905.

Nonetheless, demands on American forests continued to grow as the U.S. economy became increasingly more industrialized, urbanized, and specialized. In the first half of the 20th century, new FOREST PRODUCTS emerged, such as pulp paper, packaging materials, and plywood. At the same time, traditional uses of trees in industry, construction, and energy continued. In some parts of the United States, particularly New England, Americans abandoned lands that were difficult to farm as COMMERCIAL AGRICULTURE shifted to new areas in the West. Many of these lands reverted to forest. The housing boom that followed World War II led to increased deforestation in other parts of the country, however. New building techniques in suburban track houses, such as balloon-frame construction, put new demands on American forests.

In recent decades, however, afforestation (the process of establishing a forest on land that was not forest before or has not been forest for an extend period) has led to an overall increase in the nation's forest cover. Today, the United States, as does much of northern Europe, has more forest cover than it did at the beginning of the 20th century. Between 1990 and 2000, for example, the United States regained an average of 1,400 square miles a year. These gains are attributable to reclaimed agricultural land, improved forestry practices in the national forests and on private lands, and increased plantings of seedlings by environmental activists, among other factors.

Deforestation, however, continues to be a problem in parts of the United States that currently are undergoing greater urbanization and around the globe, particularly in developing countries eager to close the economic gap. It repeatedly has led to erosion, drought, ACID RAIN, GLOBAL WARMING, and a loss of biodiversity. With an increasing global population, the demands for wood and cropland have grown commensurately. Many nations have undertaken afforestation or reforestation projects to reverse the effects of deforestation and to increase the available timber supplies.

See also FLOODS; FUEL, WOOD; HOUSING, PRIVATE; HOUSING, PUBLIC; LOGGING AND LUMBERING; MERCANTILISM; PRISTINE MYTH.

Subin Kim

Further Reading

Chew, Sing C. *World Ecological Degradation: Accumulation, Urbanization, and Deforestation, 3000 B.C.–2000 A.D.* New York: Oxford University Press, 2001.

Ehrhardt-Martinez, Karen. "Social Determinant of Deforestation in Developing Countries: A Cross-National Study." *Social Forces* 77, no. 2 (December 1988): 567–586.

Steinberg, Ted. *Down to Earth: Nature's Role in American History.* New York: Oxford University Press, 2002.

Williams, Michael. *Americans and Their Forests: A Historical Geography.* New York: Cambridge University Press, 1989.

———. *Deforesting the Earth: From Prehistory to Global Crisis.* Chicago: University of Chicago Press, 2003.

democracy

Democracy, in the sense of rule by the will of "the people" rather than a self-appointed elite, is an ancient idea. The first democracies developed at the village level in India, perhaps 4,000 years ago, and such systems of governance still exist. Democratic institutions at the village level have always been important because they often allocated environmental resources fairly and in a sustainable way. In the Indonesian island of Bali, *adat* (customary law), as administered democratically at village level, allocates water to rice growers on terraced slopes so that each grower, from top to bottom, receives adequate water. In such societies, democracy and environmental management are inseparable.

ORIGINS OF AMERICAN DEMOCRACY

Western ideas of democracy are derived from ancient Greek and Roman models that operate at the level of larger units—the town, city, and nation. Some of these communities practiced relatively "direct" democracy, as decisions were made by resolution of the citizenry. Such communities have their counterpart in the New England "town meeting." Most democracies, however, have been representative, operating via assemblies elected to represent the citizens.

Initially, the United States was a limited representative democracy with only property-owning white males having the vote. The franchise was expanded via the extension of the franchise to most free adult white males in the 1820s and 1830s, the abolition of slavery (1865) and extension of the ballot to black men in 1870, the extension of the vote to women in 1920, and the civil rights legislation of the 1960s that removed de facto barriers to voting for African Americans in many states. Throughout much of the nation's history, American democracy has not equally included Native Americans, who were deprived of their lands and faced systematic policies designed to destroy their cultures. Nonetheless, in comparison to other countries, the United States was a relatively democratic nation after the AMERICAN REVOLUTION (1775–83) and independence from Great Britain. Unlike European nations, it did not emerge from a tradition of hereditary authority.

American democracy found its philosophical basis, in part, in the writings of the British philosopher John Locke (1632–1704), whose ideas influenced the framers of the U.S. CONSTITUTION. In Locke's philosophy, the environment, in the form of land and natural resources, is valued purely as property, as a means to an end. Land that is not owned, Locke believed, should be available to anyone. According to Locke, land becomes one's legitimate and exclusive property if one "mixes his labour" with it, to make it productive. A person is therefore exclusively entitled to the fruits of his or her labor on that land. This radical idea challenged the idea of property rights as God-given, or hereditary, or derived from conquest.

DEMOCRACY AND AGRARIAN VIRTUE

What became the United States of America was an enormous area, colonized by a very small number of European people, to whom it seemed that limitless resources were available. In his inaugural address, in 1801, President THOMAS JEFFERSON referred to America as having "room enough for our descendants to the thousandth and thousandth generation." Jefferson's political views were closely connected to his ideas of land use. He believed that the best elements of American society were the small freehold landowners, who exemplified the virtues that he admired, such as independence, hard work, thrift, and commitment to family. People who both owned their land and directly worked it, he thought, were likely to be both committed republicans and suspicious of what today is called "big government." In contrast, he saw cities as cesspits of vice, disease, and corruption.

The French philosopher ALEXIS DE TOCQUEVILLE, who visited the United States in the 1830s, wrote *Democracy in America*. Produced in two volumes in 1835 and 1840, this book offered an insightful analysis of why republican representative democracy flourished in a relatively young United States. Among other factors, Tocqueville argued, nature had provided endless opportunities for the common American to obtain property through his own labor. With the extension of the franchise in the 1820s, however, political power gradually passed to the urban populations. The United States became more industrialized and more urban over the course of the 19th century, and by 1920, a majority of its citizens lived in urban areas. As cities grew, most voters had less and less contact with the land. Federal land policies remained essential to the American character in the 19th century, with many Americans believing that access to free or relatively inexpensive land provided the best means to economic opportunity. Nonetheless, with industrialization, fewer and fewer citizens worked the land. Today, there are few family farms left in the United States, though advocates of the small farm such as WENDELL BERRY and Marty Strange emphasize the value of farming as a way of life, committed to environmental sustainability and working with the land as a partner.

Even in Jefferson and Tocqueville's times, democratic political control of land was weak; early federal policies had favored large landowners. The 1841 Preemption Act (repealed 1891) and 1862 Homestead Act (not repealed until 1976) were designed to make it easier for would-be farmers to obtain publicly owned land at zero or very little cost. Even these acts were much abused, with claimants regularly acting as fronts for large corporations that cared little for SUSTAINABILITY.

THE POLITICAL PROCESS

While the people arguably possess all the power in a democracy, special interest groups have often influenced policy decisions, particularly in environmental matters. For example, there has been considerable destruction of wildlife in the 400 years since European colonization began, yet no president before THEODORE ROOSEVELT, in the early 20th century, expressed any concern about this loss. Roosevelt's actions were not attributable to democratic political pressure but rather to his personal convictions and the influence of JOHN MUIR, who took the president on a camping trip to YOSEMITE NATIONAL PARK. Although Yosemite had become a national park in 1890, the state of California continued to manage parts of it, including Yosemite Valley. Influenced by Muir and what he himself observed on the trip, Roosevelt subsequently persuaded Congress to transfer full control of a unified Yosemite National Park from state to federal government.

In 1892, Muir founded the SIERRA CLUB, which has been perhaps the most influential lobby group for environmental protection. However, he was unsuccessful in his attempts to prevent the flooding of the HETCH HETCHY VALLEY in Yosemite for a dam; after the 1906 SAN FRANCISCO, CALIFORNIA, earthquake, the DEPARTMENT OF THE INTERIOR was under intense pressure to allow the dam, which ensured water for the city and was authorized in the Raker Act of 1913.

The debate over Hetch Hetchy was perhaps the first example of a major environmental policy issue being determined primarily by lobbyists and special interest groups. It also raised issues about the extent to which control of resources should be determined by national or local interests and by experts or public opinion. This was a major aspect of environmental policy for much of the 20th century, notably the politically influenced allocation of resources to the management of organizations such as the U.S. ARMY CORPS OF ENGINEERS and the TENNESSEE VALLEY AUTHORITY. Another major influence on environmental policy is the political allocation of "pork barrel" projects designed to win votes by providing short-term economic boosts in targeted congressional districts.

More positively, environmental issues have become political issues with widespread democratic support since the 1960s with the rise of mass movements, symbolized by the first EARTH DAY in 1970, as well as community-based projects such as the Los Angeles Community Garden (which was, however, demolished in 2006). Public opinion forced politicians to pass laws that helped improve air and water quality in the 1960s and 1970s. Public opinion has prevented the construction of any new nuclear power facilities since the accident at the THREE MILE ISLAND nuclear facility in 1979. The Democratic Party candidate ALBERT GORE, JR. who made environmental issues a central part of his campaign, received the majority of the popular vote in the 2000 presidential election but lost in the electoral college.

On paper, the United States has very strong, widely supported environmental laws, protecting everything from ENDANGERED SPECIES to clean air and water. Indeed, a Pew report shows that most Americans support measures to move beyond current law and policy and tackle GLOBAL WARMING and improved energy efficiency. However, such attitudes are not always evidenced in voting behavior and often seem contradicted by Americans' personal energy consumption habits. Nonetheless, some scholars have argued that in pluralist regimes such as the United States, scientists, politicians, special interest groups, and ordinary citizens have grown more adept over time in handling the legacy of industrialization and URBANIZATION through the creation of regulations and agencies that work for present and future generations. Standing in contrast to totalitarian and authoritarian regimes, the United States offers more than one political party, universal suffrage, and an accessible legal system. These democratic mechanisms encourage public participation in decisions about resource management and environmental protection.

See also CRÈVECOEUR, J. HECTOR ST. JOHN DE; DECLARATION OF INDEPENDENCE; NATURAL LAW; FEDERAL LAW— AND POLICIES; YEOMAN.

Alastair Gunn

Further Reading

Josephson, Paul R. *Resources under Regimes: Technology, Environment and the State.* Cambridge, Mass.: Harvard University Press, 2006.
Pew Trusts. Voters Support Congressional Action on Comprehensive Energy and Global Warming Legislation. Available online. URL: http://www.pewtrusts.org/news_room_detail.aspx?id=52044. Accessed May 31, 2009.
Taliaferro, Charles. "Farms." In *Life Science Ethics,* edited by Gary L. Comstock. New York: Wiley-Blackwell, 2002.
Van Dyke, Fred, Michael J. Bigelow, Jo Ebihara, and Lauren Anderson. *Conservation Biology.* New York: Springer, 2008.
Wilentz, Sean. *The Rise of American Democracy: Jefferson to Lincoln.* New York: W. W. Norton, 2005.

Democratic Party

Of the two main political parties in the United States in the 21st century, the Democratic Party is better known for its ENVIRONMENTALISM than its REPUBLICAN PARTY counterpart. The Democrats generally believe that it is their responsibility to protect the natural resources of the United States and that there is a link between protection of the environment and a strong economy and healthy families. In addition, the Democratic Party argues that the federal government should take a leading role in the protection of the environment.

Some critics of the Democratic Party's environmentalism charge that some Democratic policies force people to choose between a healthy economy and a healthy environment. Democrats counter with the argument that numerous industries, including fishing, farming, and tourism, require a healthy environment. Those industries generate billions of dollars each year. Democrats also promote new technologies for creating and providing alternative energy sources, which create jobs. The Democratic Party also contends that creating a sensible energy policy is good for national security, as one of the goals is reducing dependence on foreign oil.

Historically, Democratic presidents and vice presidents often made the improvement of nature a priority, believing the federal government should be the primary agent of change. President FRANKLIN D. ROOSEVELT employed CONSERVATION as a central part of the NEW DEAL. He signed measures to provide IRRIGATION water to California's Central Valley, for example, through the construction of large multipurpose DAMS. He also prioritized rural electrification projects. Most notably, the TENNESSEE VALLEY AUTHORITY, a federally owned corporation founded in 1933, was designed to modernize the seven states touched by the Tennessee River watershed through dams that provided flood control and generated power. From 1933 to 1942, the Civilian Conservation Corps was a federal relief project that put more than three million men to work improving the nation's parks, constructing infrastructure, or planting three billion trees in decimated forests or as shelterbelts.

President LYNDON B. JOHNSON signed numerous environment-related measures into law as part of his GREAT SOCIETY program of the 1960s. His administration and the Democratic-controlled Congress enacted a number of laws that addressed the impact of American industry on the quality of human life and on wildlife, while maintaining a strong legacy of conservation. The Democratic Party had long outpaced Republicans in the number of national and STATE PARKS established and in the total acreage protected. During the Johnson presidency (1963–69), the federal government passed the Clear Air, Water Quality and Clean Water Restoration Acts (1965, 1966); the Solid Waste Disposal Act (1965); the Motor Vehicle Air Pollution Control Act (1965); the Endangered Species Preservation Act (1966); and more typical conservation measures such as the WILDERNESS ACT OF 1964 and the National Historic Preservation Act (1965).

Democrats were instrumental in the movements that brought about the ENVIRONMENTAL PROTECTION AGENCY, the CLEAN WATER ACT, and the CLEAN AIR ACT. An impetus of those movements was the publication in 1962 of RACHEL CARSON's *Silent Spring,* which illustrated the dangers of using PESTICIDES. By 1970, there was enough support in CONGRESS for the creation of the Environmental Protection Agency, tasked with repairing the damage already evident in the natural environment and establishing rules and regulations to prevent future damage. In 1972, Congress passed the Clean Water Act, which employs a variety of tools to reduce direct pollutant discharges into waterways sharply. It should be noted that many of these measures received support from Republicans in the 1970s as well. However, with the 1980 election of the Republican president RONALD REAGAN, most Republicans abandoned their support of environmental issues, arguing that such issues were matters for state governments and that environmental regulations created unnecessary restrictions on industry and commerce.

Most recently, the former Democratic vice president ALBERT GORE, JR., who served with President BILL CLINTON from 1993 to 2001, has made protecting the environment a worldwide issue. Upon leaving office, he focused on warning the world about the dangers of GLOBAL WARMING and pressed for strict regulation of greenhouse gases. He was awarded the Nobel Peace Prize in 2007 for his efforts.

See also AGRICULTURE, COMMERCIAL; CENTRAL VALLEY PROJECT; FISHING, COMMERCIAL; GREENHOUSE EFFECT; NATIONAL PARK SERVICE; OIL, IMPORTED; TRAVEL AND TOURISM.

James E. Seelye, Jr.

Further Reading

Carson, Rachel. *Silent Spring.* Greenwich, Conn.: Fawcett, 1962.

Dallek, Robert. *Flawed Giant: Lyndon Johnson and His Times, 1961–1973.* New York: Oxford University Press, 1999.

Gore, Albert, Jr. *An Inconvenient Truth: The Planetary Emergency of Global Warming and What We Can Do about It.* New York: Rodale Books, 2006.

Schlesinger, Arthur, Jr. *The Age of Roosevelt.* Vol. 2, *The Coming of the New Deal, 1933–1935.* Boston: Mariner Books, 2003.

Denver, Colorado

Denver, the capital of Colorado, finds its origins in the 1858 discovery of GOLD. Never as powerful as SAN FRANCISCO, CALIFORNIA, in the American West, Denver nonetheless dominated communities along the Front Range (or eastern face) of the ROCKY MOUNTAINS as it intersects with the Great Plains. The city influenced an urban network reaching westward to SALT LAKE CITY, UTAH, east to Omaha, NEBRASKA, north to Canada, and south to Mexico. Standing at an elevation of 5,277 feet, Denver earned the nickname of the "Mile High City," and from its beginning, it was a city of nature, tied to its mountains and plains. Growth and survival in the 19th century depended upon extracting, processing, shipping, and marketing the region's natural capital—metals, coal, timber, iron, livestock, grain, sugar beets, and even scenery and climate.

For centuries before gold was found, Native Americans traveled in the mountains' shadow, along the Platte and Arkansas Rivers flowing eastward. In 1858, two tribes, the Arapaho and the Cheyenne, occupied the area. The Arapaho had fled the GREAT LAKES in the 18th century under pressure from the Sioux and advancing Euro-Americans. Also escaping the Sioux, the Cheyenne became nomadic hunters dependent

Placer mining in Colorado, pictured here between 1890 and 1905, contributed to soil erosion and deforestation in the Rocky Mountains. *(Library of Congress)*

on BISON. They encountered the Arapaho in the Black Hills. Sharing similar traditions, the Southern Cheyenne and Arapaho moved southward along the Rockies and pushed out the Kiowa by 1815. Spain and later Mexico claimed title to this land but remained ineffective, if not invisible, forces.

The Indians hunted and lived along the Front Range and adjacent plains where Denver and its sister cities later appeared. An early American visitor, Major Stephen Long, foresaw little chance for occupation by his compatriots after his 1820 expedition. Long labeled the plains the "GREAT AMERICAN DESERT" and, misconstruing the complex production systems of the different Indians who lived there, concluded that the plains were uninhabitable by people dependent upon commercial agriculture.

Sparked by Mexican independence in 1821, a burgeoning FUR TRADE attracted American and European trappers and traders and doubled the region's human population. By 1830, bison hides replaced beaver pelts as the medium of exchange. Hides required processing, and Front Range trading posts appeared. Indian women provided labor. The bison economy proved short-lived, however, as markets declined by 1850. Both Indian hunting methods and other factors left herds in disarray. Indians selected cows, whose hides were easier to process, undermining bison reproduction. The introduction of cattle from Mexico introduced bovine diseases for which bison had no immunities. Envi-

ronmental pressures intensified when a two-decade drought forced cattle, horses, and bison to compete for limited water and grass.

An 1851 treaty with the United States guaranteed the Arapaho and Cheyenne land from the Continental Divide in the Rocky Mountains to western Kansas and Nebraska, where they already lived. Dependent on a shrinking bison population and floundering fur trade, the Arapaho and Cheyenne rarely received promised government reparations and faced near-starvation in the 1850s, although the region remained relatively peaceful. The Colorado GOLD rush at the end of the decade challenged this peace with larger numbers of people whose communities had no room for Indians. They found themselves isolated, denied access to hunting grounds, and destitute. Tensions rose between whites and Indians, and in 1864, in an event known as the Sand Creek Massacre, a Denver-based militia slaughtered 160 Indians supposedly living under army protection. Three more years of violence completely removed the Cheyenne and Arapaho from Colorado.

Gold had propelled the changes. In summer 1858, prospectors discovered gold at the base of the Rockies near the confluence of Cherry Creek and the South Platte River. News spread eastward. Most prospectors waited until spring to begin their trek, earning the sobriquet "fifty-niners."

Urban entrepreneurs had not waited. They anticipated that whatever market center emerged to control the mineral trade would become an important city. A decade earlier, San Francisco, for example, had dominated mining in the Sierra Nevada, which enhanced the nation's international role, expanded its credit, and created a trade surplus. Many towns aspired to this position of regional leadership, but Denver emerged as the preeminent city along the Front Range and in the Southwest. Its position was not preordained. Its physical location offered no advantages. Placers (water-based mineral deposits) in its immediate vicinity played out quickly. Other towns were closer to MINING districts and migration routes along the Platte River or the Santa Fe Trail. Americans historically built metropolises on major waterways. Denver stood at the confluence of the nonnavigable South Platte and Cherry Creek. They often became torrents in springtime, but their frequently dry beds provided inadequate water.

Established in autumn 1858, Denver enjoyed other advantages. Its entrepreneurs recognized that a central city offered greater, more consistent wealth than scattered gold camps. Diggings had shifted to the adjacent mountains, but Denver anchored the nascent economy when the fifty-niners arrived. In a form of "urban primogeniture" earned as the first city and as the locus of the first finds, prospectors associated Denver with their future fortunes. Unprepared and inexperienced, many moved west without necessary equipment. Denver merchants and tradesmen exploited their needs.

Denver boosters also offered experience from other western communities, with whom they maintained ties. They captured important systems of exchange and thus determined the movement of people, goods, information, and money within the region. Before RAILROADS reached the Southwest, Denverites grabbed cross-country and intraregional freight wagon lines, built warehouses, offered relatively steady employment, and set prices. Denver published the region's first newspaper and became the Western Union telegraph terminus in 1863. Given its primogeniture and booster connections, Denver attracted more and more capable bankers. By 1863, they successfully petitioned Congress for a branch mint and the region's first national bank. (The mint still functions today, as shown by the D found on all coins minted in Denver.) Already the territorial capital, Denver retained this status when Colorado became a state in 1876, reinforcing its importance to the region.

In its first 12 years from 1858 to 1870, Denver's permanent population only grew tenfold to 4,759, but hundreds of thousands traveled through its doors. When the transcontinental railroad decided to bypass Denver in 1867, threatening the city's future, its elites raised capital to guarantee that local railroads reached the main line by 1870 and thus secured Denver's primacy. By 1880, its population reached 35,629.

By dominating finances, communications, and transportation, Denverites controlled mining in the mountains. For example, Jerome Chaffee and David Moffat used the First National Bank of Denver to gain information about viable mines and to attract and manage distant investments as gold and silver mines spread across Colorado. When mines opened in other western states, Denverites often were among the most influential investors.

These Denverites also recognized that minerals alone ensured neither prosperity nor posterity. A competitive economy required diversification and viable agriculture. Moreover, 19th-century Americans believed that farm families provided social stability badly needed on the frontier. Working with local railroads, Denver boosters established land companies to recruit farmers. They proposed that the "Great American Desert" could be defeated through cooperative projects because the IRRIGATION required for success was too expensive and too backbreaking for individuals alone. Often organized in the East or Midwest, colonies purchased land from Denver-based railroads or companies. Occupying a former trading post and desolate military reservation, the Fort Collins Agricultural Colony settled north of Denver and built canals for settlers. Other colonies survived at Greeley and Loveland, but many failed, overwhelmed by irrigation costs and the difficulties of arid farming.

In addition to directing the mining and agricultural economies of mountains and plains, respectively, Denver dominated other Front Range cities and their hinterlands. Coalfields near Boulder, approximately 30 miles to the northwest, fed Denver's railroads and nascent factories. In the shadow of Pikes Peak, some 70 miles to the south, Colorado Springs was designed from its 1871 beginning as a resort town, packaging amorphous resources such as scenery, climate, and altitude. Boosters there and in Denver marketed nearby mountains to American and European elites as a pristine WILDERNESS and built resorts and sanatoria. Some travelers sought respite for respiratory ailments (most frequently TUBERCULOSIS) as emigrants wrote of gentle winters and dry air's healing qualities. The Denver-based Board of Immigration promoted the entire state as a "sanatorium" and reinforced the expression of an ancient belief that environment improved individual chemistry and health. Only wealthy consumptives, however, usually could afford the journey west.

Established during the gold rush, some 100 miles south of Denver, Pueblo struggled until the 1870s, when it emerged as a manufacturing center. Regionally based companies developed nearby COAL and iron resources. Denver and Pueblo became smelting centers, and their entrepreneurs built smelters in distant western communities, where they invested in mining and attendant industries. The

Colorado Fuel & Iron Company (CF&I) in Pueblo was the only STEEL-manufacturing plant west of the Mississippi River. Denver and Pueblo businessmen dominated its early management. By 1910, CF&I employed one out of 10 Coloradoans.

Denver entrepreneurs linked Front Range cities, the mountains, and the plains in one large regional economy. In turn, they linked them in environmental change. Regional actors believed underdeveloped resources were wasted. They assumed nature offered infinite rewards and possessed restorative powers, but their demands proved almost insatiable. One such resource was wood. Most buildings were wooden, and mineral-processing facilities burned wood or charred it for charcoal to fuel their enterprises. Wooden sluices, troughs, and flumes stretched across acres. Timbers supported miles of shafts running through underground lodes. Pollution from smelters and mills killed the remaining vegetation on denuded hills. Almost 85 percent of Colorado's FORESTS—once considered endless—disappeared by 1900. Effects reached across ECOSYSTEMS. Without protection from large trees, wind and sun reduced winter snowpack and interrupted the regular flow of water to agricultural areas. Heavily dependent on irrigation from mountain-based streams, farmers contributed to their own woes, as salinity and siltation, common problems with irrigation, decreased production.

Still tied to volatile mining and agricultural industries, Denver's regional economy stagnated between the two world wars. Colorado's overall population stalled, but a trend toward fewer, larger urban areas that began in the 19th century intensified in the 20th century, particularly during and after WORLD WAR II. Metropolitan Denver accounted for 34 percent of Colorado's population in 1940 and 56 percent by 1970. As do all metropolises, Denver left a large ECOLOGICAL FOOTPRINT—the land needed to provide the necessary resources and absorb community wastes. Denver, for example, depended on distant water sources. Starting in 1867, residents began building ditches into canyons along the Front Range to serve as aqueducts, some nearly 100 miles in length. In the 20th century, tunnels reached through the Rockies and across the Continental Divide to carry water from the COLORADO RIVER to Denver. In 1989, the ENVIRONMENTAL PROTECTION AGENCY thwarted ambitious Denver plans for one of the West's largest dam and water storage facilities, forcing the city and its residents to adopt more conservative measures for water usage, such as limitations on watering lawns, incorporation of xeric (low-moisture) landscaping, and enforcement of higher utility charges.

World War II had given Denver new life. The federal government pumped $400 million into the region. Denver's Rocky Mountain Arsenal, for example, occupied 17,000 acres, where 15,000 people produced chemical weapons, such as mustard gas, white phosphorus, and napalm. The army also leased facilities to private chemical companies to make PESTICIDES from 1946 to 1982.

Colorado's Front Range remained home to many scientific-research-military installations during the COLD WAR. From 1952 to 1988, the ATOMIC ENERGY COMMISSION (later the DEPARTMENT OF ENERGY) oversaw the Rocky Flats Plant, a nuclear weapons production facility on Denver's fringe, managed under private contract by the Dow Chemical Company and Rockwell International Corporation. The presence of the plant and so many other federal agencies led commentators to call Denver the nation's second capital. In 1988, the DEPARTMENT OF DEFENSE spent 8 percent of its research budget in the Denver-Boulder area. Regional manufacturing became more diversified after the war, but often in conjunction with the defense and aerospace industries. Older businesses, such as CF&I, closed.

Denver experienced pollution common to major cities, but military-industrial connections presented other, more serious problems. The Rocky Mountain Arsenal and Rocky Flats Plant became SUPERFUND sites. At the arsenal, the army and chemical companies had dumped liquid wastes in trenches and basins and contaminated groundwater. By 2006, approximately half of its cleanup projects were completed. At the same time, 330 wildlife species inhabited the now-unused land, and 5,000 acres was transferred to the U.S. FISH AND WILDLIFE SERVICE for the establishment of the Rocky Mountain Arsenal National Wildlife Refuge. At Rocky Flats, under government and private operation, radioactive wastes had leaked into groundwater, and plutonium contamination occurred throughout the facility. In 2006, the year after the cleanup was completed, a federal jury awarded adjacent landowners $350 million from Dow and Rockwell. In 2008, the district court judge tacked on 8 percent interest compounded annually from the time the suit was filed in 1990, raising the value of the award to more than $900 million. As of January 2010, the case remained on appeal.

Denver and its immediate suburbs constituted the 22nd largest metropolitan area in the United States by 2000 with a population of 2,330,000. With similarly booming economies, Fort Collins, Boulder, Colorado Springs, and Pueblo grew in both population and physical size in the second half of the 20th century and have almost merged with Denver and each other to form one unending megametropolis along Colorado's Front Range, with a population nearing 3,500,000. As do many places in the SUNBELT that boomed during and after World War II, the region lacks any meaningful public transportation systems. Thus, in the 21st century, Denver and its sister cities face particularly urgent environmental problems associated with an automobile-dependent population, such as air and noise pollution, an excess of greenhouse gases, and an increase in urban temperatures associated with the loss of green spaces to road construction.

See also CORPORATIONS, CHEMICAL; INDIANS, CENTRAL PLAINS; INDIANS, SOUTHWEST; MILITARY-INDUSTRIAL COMPLEX; NUCLEAR WEAPONS AND TESTING; ROCKY MOUNTAINS; UNITED STATES—SOUTHWEST.

Kathleen A. Brosnan

Further Reading

Abbott, Carl. *Colorado: A History of the Centennial State.* Boulder: Colorado Associated University Press, 1976.

Barth, Gunther. *Instant Cities: Urbanization and the Rise of San Francisco and Denver.* New York: Oxford University Press, 1965.

Brosnan, Kathleen A. *Uniting Mountain and Plain: Cities, Law, and Environmental Change along the Front Range.* Albuquerque: University of New Mexico Press, 2002.

Leonard, Stephen J., and Thomas J. Noel. *Denver: Mining Camp to Metropolis.* Niwot: University Press of Colorado, 1990.

"Region 8." U.S. Environmental Protection Agency. Available online. URL: http://www.epa.gov/region8. Accessed January 15, 2009.

West, Elliott. *The Contested Plains: Indians, Goldseekers, and the Rush to Colorado.* Lawrence: University Press of Kansas, 1998.

Detroit, Michigan

The city of Detroit, Michigan, began as a colonial FUR TRADE post but experienced its greatest growth in the 20th century as the manufacturing center for American AUTOMOBILES. As such, it helped remake the nation's landscape and would embody some of the worst environmental aspects of industrialization, such as AIR POLLUTION, URBAN SPRAWL, and environmental injustice.

EARLY SETTLEMENT

The settlement that came to be known as Detroit was founded in 1701 by some 100 French traders and soldiers. They hoped to expand their fur trade westward in North America and to prevent the English and the Iroquois from doing likewise. Their leader, Antoine Laumet de Lamothe Cadillac, chose the location because it was on the Detroit River. The city's name and the name of the river are based on a description of their geographic setting; *Détroit* is French for "strait." Flowing from Lake St. Clair to Lake Erie, the Detroit River was the crucial means of transporting furs from the area to eastern markets, as well as providing DRINKING WATER, water for crops, and a source of FOOD. Cadillac located the settlement at the river's narrowest point. With defense in mind, he selected a site with a high bank and good visibility up and down the river.

The early French settlement consisted of a fort, inside which the residents lived, and farm plots outside the fort. Called ribbon farms, the plots were long and narrow, extending from the Detroit River back as much as two or more miles. French Detroit remained a small town, its residents engaged primarily in the fur trade and farming. Cadillac persuaded Huron, Potawotami, Fox, Ottawa, and other groups of Native Americans to settle nearby to trade BEAVER and other pelts with the French. Thus, Detroit became an important outpost from which many furs were sent and eventually sold in Europe.

As a result of the FRENCH AND INDIAN WAR (1754–63), the defeated French relinquished their claim to Detroit to the British in 1760. The English proved more ruthless to their neighbors than had been the French. Relations between the town and neighboring tribes deteriorated, and conflicts increased. The English continued to use Detroit as a base of operations for the fur trade but also began to build ships in the city using oak from the surrounding FORESTS.

An event that proved significant to the geography of present-day Detroit was the June 1805 FIRE that nearly destroyed the town's entire infrastructure. Rather than rebuilding Detroit exactly as it had been, the town rebuilt by following, in part, a plan by Judge Augustus Woodward (1774–1827). Woodward's plan created wider streets than Cadillac had set up more than a century earlier, set aside open spaces for plazas, and built streets out from the plaza reminiscent of spokes on a wheel, rather than using the grid street system that existed in cities such as PHILADELPHIA, PENNSYLVANIA, and NEW YORK CITY. Although his plan was much more extensive than what was implemented, the part that was put into effect changed the layout of the town substantially and is still evident in the major streets that begin at Campus Martius in downtown Detroit and extend radially into the city and suburbs. Woodward's emphasis on more space between streets than in the early town also led to less dense settlement and, ultimately, to an extremely high rate of single-family homes instead of apartments. This layout and propensity for individual dwelling units have contributed to the difficulty of securing effective MASS TRANSIT for Detroiters in the 20th and 21st centuries.

URBAN GROWTH

Detroit was an important site of battle in the WAR OF 1812 (1812–15), which pitted Americans against the British and several Native American tribes that allied themselves with the British. As a result of the war, Native Americans in the Detroit area were forced to cede their land to the United States, thus providing more land for settlers around the city of Detroit. In the 1830s and 1840s, Detroit's population increased rapidly as a result of the invention of the steamboat, completion of the Erie Canal, the availability of nearby land that had previously belonged to Native Americans, and a positive publicity campaign by the Michigan territorial governor Lewis Cass to counteract previous reports of the area's swampy nature. Michigan became a state in 1837.

The steamboat greatly reduced the length of travel time by water, and when the Erie Canal was completed in 1825, Detroit became connected by rivers and lakes to eastern markets. Steamboats from Buffalo, New York, carried tens of thousands of people to Detroit in the two decades after the canal was built. Some did not stay in Detroit but instead landed in the city and traveled inland to settle in more remote areas. Records indicate that on many days there were several steamboats that discharged passengers in Detroit. On their return trip, the boats carried furs and other goods to sell.

At the same time that Detroit became more accessible by water, it was also made more accessible by train. Workers built RAILROADS to the north, west, and south, allowing both people and goods to travel to and from Detroit. The railroads greatly increased ease of obtaining and transporting natural resources in the city's hinterlands, resources that fueled the growth of industries in Detroit. In the second half of the 19th century, TOBACCO became one of the city's biggest industries, but there was a wide variety of industries. Although tobacco was not grown in the area, Detroit became a major site for the manufacture of cigars and chewing tobacco. Soon after the rise of tobacco companies, Detroit became a center for the production of other manufactured goods, with stoves, for example, becoming a major industry. Manufacturers in Detroit also produced furniture, bicycles, and carriage wheels.

RISE OF THE AUTOMOBILE INDUSTRY

In part because of the existing carriage and bicycle industry, Detroit became home to several early car manufacturers in the early 1900s. After HENRY FORD implemented the assembly line for mass production of the car he created, automobile manufacturing began to expand rapidly in the city, and the automobile became an increasingly common form of transportation both for wealthy Detroiters and for Americans in general. Detroit was nicknamed the "Motor City," and the three major automobile manufacturers, General Motors (GM), Ford, and Chrysler, became known as "the Big Three." Along with the growth of the auto industry, related manufacturers took a prominent place in the local economy. Closely linked to the health of the auto industry, Detroit's economy magnified national trends, experiencing both extreme prosperity (particularly during the 1920s and WORLD WAR II [1941–45]) and, during the 1930s, extreme depression.

Detroit's auto industries stopped civilian car production during World War II and contracted with the federal government to build war machinery, including tanks and planes. Although thousands emigrated from the southern United States, Detroit factories faced chronic labor shortages during the war. The mass migration of southern whites and African Americans strained the city's infrastructure and services, and the lack of housing, especially for African Americans, who

were relegated to already-overcrowded sections of the city, became an acute problem. Racial tensions erupted in June 1943 into RACE RIOTS begun on Belle Isle, one of the city parks. The riot spread across the city, and photographs that captured whites beating blacks with police acquiescence spread around the world.

POSTWAR PROSPERITY AND SUBURBANIZATION

During World War II, workers in Detroit's war industries accrued high wages but could not spend them on all of the items they wanted, since many—such as civilian automobiles—were not produced during the war. After the war, a car-centric culture swept across the nation, with Detroit at the forefront. As cars became more commonplace as transportation for even short trips, alternative forms of transportation such as trolleys became scarce. The decline of mass transit and dominance of individual cars created more AIR POLLUTION, and by the beginning of the 21st century, Detroit had the lowest air quality of any city in the country.

In the prosperous postwar era, the landscape of Detroit changed substantially, reflecting the increasing dominance of the automobile. Highways cut through the city and connected to suburbs, where existing communities expanded in population and new neighborhoods were quickly built. African-American and ethnic neighborhoods in Detroit were disproportionately likely to be chosen as sites for highway construction, and many communities were dislocated and divided up, including Detroit's two largest African-American neighborhoods, Paradise Valley and Black Bottom. In 1951, Detroit's largest retailer, Hudson's department store, built a shopping mall on the outskirts of the city. One of the first malls in the country, and the most profitable during its first decade, Northland Mall made it easy for suburban residents to do their shopping in the suburbs instead of traveling to downtown Detroit. At the same time that highways physically connected the city and suburbs, the area began to trace a trajectory in which city and suburbs became increasingly distinct in population, types of industry, and levels of prosperity. By 1960, the population of Detroit's suburbs was greater than the population of the city itself.

These demographic changes led to an extreme discrepancy between city and suburbs, with northern suburbs making neighboring Oakland County one of the wealthiest counties in the nation and Detroit continually beset by financial troubles and declining public services. In recent decades, issues related to ENVIRONMENTAL JUSTICE have been particularly pronounced in the city of Detroit, especially air and WATER POLLUTION from local industries. The city is home to the country's largest INCINERATION facility.

POPULATION AND JOB LOSS

Deindustrialization trends in the second half of the 20th century hit Detroit hard. A strong union town, Detroit suffered when manufacturers moved south or overseas in search of cheaper labor. As manufacturing jobs left the city, what service jobs moved into the area tended to establish themselves in suburbs. The racial composition of the city shifted to a majority African-American population as whites left to live in suburban communities en masse. Poverty, lack of jobs, and crime have plagued the city since the 1960s and 1970s and defined Detroit in the minds of many Americans. With the dispersion of jobs to suburbs, the area's lack of mass transit and extreme reliance on private automobiles for transportation became glaring problems for those without cars. The "Big Three" slowly lost their dominance to foreign automakers, and the fortunes of all three companies precipitously declined. As a result, GM, Ford, and Chrysler cut more jobs in the area. Detroit's dependence on the auto industry became all too apparent, with no major industries to fill the void. From a population of more than 1.8 million in 1950, the city's population had fallen below one million in 2000.

Since the 1980s, however, many Detroiters have undertaken revitalization efforts to improve communities within the city. There has been increased attention paid to the city's natural environment, with groups such as the Greening of Detroit planting trees and greenery throughout the city, the growing popularity of community gardens, and investment in developing a walkway and tourism along the riverfront in downtown.

Facing perhaps the worst urban blight in the United States and a long-stagnating local economy, residents of Detroit in the first decade of the 21st century have attempted to improve their city and reverse its image of industrial decline and devastation. Steeped in GRASSROOTS ENVIRONMENTALISM, activists have planted more than 800 community gardens on abandoned lots, established peace zones for public safety, and begun green retrofitting of empty houses. The long-term impact of these programs remains to be seen.

See also CANADA AND THE UNITED STATES; CANALS; FRENCH EXPLORATION AND SETTLEMENT—ACADIA AND CANADA; FRENCH EXPLORATION AND SETTLEMENT—ST. LOUIS AND THE MIDWEST; GREAT LAKES; HOUSING, PRIVATE; INDIANS, MIDWEST; INTERSTATE HIGHWAY SYSTEM; LABOR, MANUFACTURING; MERCANTILISM; RACISM AND DISCRIMINATION; RIVER TRANSPORTATION; SUBURBANIZATION; UNITED STATES—MIDWEST; URBANIZATION; URBAN RENEWAL.

Sarah Frohardt-Lane

Further Reading

Henrickson, Wilma Wood. *Detroit Perspectives: Crossroads and Turning Points.* Detroit: Wayne State University Press, 1991.

Parkins, Almon Ernest. *The Historical Geography of Detroit.* Lansing: Michigan Historical Commission, 1918.

Sugrue, Thomas J. *The Origins of the Urban Crisis: Race and Inequality in Postwar Detroit.* Princeton, N.J.: Princeton University Press, 1996.

Thompson, Heather. *Whose Detroit? Politics, Labor, and Race in a Modern American City.* Ithaca, N.Y.: Cornell University Press, 2001.

Woodford, Arthur M. *This Is Detroit: 1701–2001.* Detroit: Wayne State University Press, 2001.

Zunz, Olivier. *The Changing Face of Inequality: Urbanization, Industrial Development, and Immigrants in Detroit, 1880–1920.* Chicago: University of Chicago Press, 1982.

DeVoto, Bernard (1897–1955) *author, critic, historian of the American West*

Best known for his writing about the western FRONTIER, Bernard DeVoto spent a considerable portion of his life east of that mythical dividing line. He championed public lands and CONSERVATION and challenged triumphalist stories of American settlement by considering its environmental consequences. DeVoto viewed the West as a plundered province, stripped of its resources by eastern capital.

Born in Ogden, Utah, on January 11, 1897, DeVoto spent a year at the University of Utah before moving east to attend Harvard University in Cambridge, Massachusetts. After a short stint in the U.S. Army, DeVoto completed his Harvard degree and returned to Utah for a year to teach junior high school. Shortly thereafter, however, DeVoto became a professor of English at Northwestern University from 1922 to 1927 and began publishing. In 1927, DeVoto returned to Cambridge, Massachusetts, in order to make a living as a writer.

Although he served briefly as an instructor and lecturer at Harvard, DeVoto spent the rest of his life publishing fiction and essays (often under pseudonyms), serving as an editor for national publications such as the *Saturday Review of Literature,* making his regular Easy Chair contributions to *Harper's,* and producing edited collections such as *The Portable Mark Twain* (1946) and *The Journal of Lewis and Clark* (1953). He won the National Book Award for the latter collection, which remains an important edition of the early American explorers' journals to this day. DeVoto, however, is most distinguished for his work as a historian of the American West. In particular, his trilogy of westward expansion—*The Year of Decision: 1846* (1943), *Across the Wide Missouri* (1947), and *The Course of Empire* (1952)—serve as landmark texts. DeVoto received the Pulitzer Prize in history in 1948 for *Across the Wide Missouri.*

The familiar figures of the American frontier—early explorers and adventurers, settlers, pioneers, missionaries, American Indians, politicians, and artists—all play important roles in DeVoto's work on the West. An equally prominent consideration for his western histories, and the trilogy in particular, however, was the impact of expansion on the western environment. In exploring and inhabiting the lands west of the MISSOURI RIVER, Euro-Americans learned about endless miles of PRAIRIES, FORESTS, mountains, riparian and coastal landscapes, all of which found their way into DeVoto's writing. He chronicled the ecological implications of settlement, Indian removal, agriculture, trade, and expansion in general. DeVoto was both romantic and realistic in his portrayal of western environments. Playing to his romantic side, DeVoto opened *The Year of Decision: 1846* with a long passage from HENRY DAVID THOREAU's 1862 essay "Walking," from which he quoted: "It is hard for me to believe that I shall find fair landscapes or sufficient wildness and freedom beyond the eastern horizon . . . but I believe that the forest which I see in the western horizon stretches uninterruptedly toward the setting sun, and there are no towns nor cities in it of enough consequence to disturb me."

More often, however, DeVoto revealed in deceptively simple passages a keen awareness of just what environmental changes were wrought by the American settlement of the West. In writing about the Columbia Cascades encountered by the LEWIS AND CLARK EXPEDITION in *The Course of Empire,* for example, DeVoto noted that "there are no Cascades now; the water impounded by Bonneville Dam covers them. But this is the gorge which the Columbia cuts through the Cascade Mountains and before Bonneville there were the Upper and Lower Cascades." Americans drastically altered landscapes even in the short time since their first explorers arrived in the region. DeVoto died on November 13, 1955.

See also AGRICULTURE, COMMERCIAL; BONNEVILLE POWER ADMINISTRATION; COLUMBIA RIVER; DAMS, RESERVOIRS, AND ARTIFICIAL LAKES; INDIANS, CALIFORNIA; INDIANS, COLUMBIA PLATEAU AND GREAT BASIN; INDIANS, PACIFIC NORTHWEST; INDIANS, SOUTHWEST; MANIFEST DESTINY; UNITED STATES—CALIFORNIA; UNITED STATES—COLUMBIA PLATEAU AND GREAT BASIN; UNITED STATES—PACIFIC NORTHWEST; UNITED STATES—SOUTHWEST.

Matthew Low

Further Reading

DeVoto, Bernard. *Across the Wide Missouri.* Boston: Mariner Books, 1998.
——. *The Course of Empire.* Boston: Mariner Books, 1998.
——. *DeVoto's West: History, Conservation, and the Public Good.* Edited by Edward K. Muller. Athens, Ohio: Swallow Press, 2005.
——. *The Journals of Lewis and Clark.* Edited by Bernard DeVoto. Boston: Mariner Books, 1997.
——. *Mark Twain's America.* Lincoln, Nebr.: Bison Books, 1997.
——. *The Western Paradox: A Bernard DeVoto Conservation Reader.* Edited by Douglas Brinkley and Patricia Nelson Limerick. New Haven, Conn.: Yale University Press, 2001.
——. *The Year of Decision: 1846.* New York: St. Martin's Griffin, 2000.
Sawey, Orlan. *Bernard DeVoto.* New York: Twayne, 1969.
Stegner, Wallace. *The Uneasy Chair: A Biography of Bernard DeVoto.* Lincoln, Nebr.: Bison Books, 2001.
Thomas, John L. *A Country in the Mind.* New York: Routledge, 2002.

disasters

As of 2008, the U.S. DEPARTMENT OF HEALTH AND HUMAN SERVICES (HSS) defined natural disasters on its Web site as "naturally occurring events which can directly or indirectly cause severe threats to public health and/or well-being." The department expanded the definition by explaining that "because they are naturally occurring natural disasters pose an ever present threat which can only be dealt with through proper planning and preparedness." EARTHQUAKES, FIRE or wildfire, FLOODS, HURRICANES, landslides, thunderstorms, tsunamis, VOLCANOES, and extreme cold and heat constitute some of the phenomena that periodically threaten the United States. Yet, despite recommendations for preparedness, human responses to these unanticipated natural occurrences often have exacerbated the calamities, suggesting that they might be described more aptly as human disasters.

Most Americans traditionally viewed TORNADOES, floods, and earthquakes as exclusively natural phenomena and blamed nature for the subsequent destruction of life and property. This emphasis on natural factors, however, diminishes the centrality of social and economic forces in these phenomena. Natural calamities require human interaction, whether in the form of preparedness or response. Throughout history, however, the focus on disasters as unpredictable, freakish happenings has led decision makers to downplay the important human role, leaving unacknowledged the complicity of humans in the devastation wrought by natural disasters.

Human mishandling was evident in the SAN FRANCISCO, CALIFORNIA, earthquake in 1906. This major earthquake measured 7.9 to 8.3 on the Richter scale, which indicates the amount of seismic energy released as vibrations. It violently shook the city for 28 seconds on the morning of April 18, 1906. The quake ruptured gas mains and sparked fires throughout the city. An estimated 3,000 people died from the combined forces of the earthquake and fires. When the shaking stopped and the fires subsided, the recovering city gained much attention as the site of the "Big One." However, business leaders in San Francisco feared that a focus on the area's potential for unpredictable natural calamities would hamper the city's rapid commercial recovery. Moreover, many INSURANCE policies covered fires but not earthquake

Hurricane Katrina devastated New Orleans in August 2005, leaving 80 percent of the city flooded.   *(Alex Neauville/Shutterstock)*

damage. This fact influenced city leaders to blame the loss of property on the fires. Thus, largely through the influence of city leaders, the impact of the earthquake was recast; they blamed destruction of property and life on the fires rather than the earthquake.

The 1906 earthquake became a catalyst for some forms of earthquake preparedness, such as stronger building codes in the central business district and research on the causes of earthquakes. However, entrepreneurs' emphasis on the fires temporarily pushed aside the belief that San Francisco faced major threats from earthquakes and facilitated continued economic development. When another disastrous earthquake rocked the city on June 29, 1925, it surprised many San Franciscans. Moreover, despite an increased awareness of the region's earthquake potential, the city expanded into areas that proved dangerous. An earthquake on October 17, 1989, was particularly destructive in the city's Marina District. The district stood on filled land made up of sand, dirt, and much of the rubble from the 1906 earthquake. The quake liquefied this loose soil mixture, and stylish apartments pancaked as they crumpled to the ground.

Human complicity in the destruction caused by natural disasters continued throughout the late 20th century, as revealed, for example, by the events that transpired in Dade County, Florida, prior to Hurricane Andrew. The hurricane slammed into Southeast Florida on the morning of August 24, 1992, as a category 4 hurricane and then moved into Louisiana. During the 1980s, Dade County saw a rush in the demand for housing. Cheap and fast, rather than solid, became the building standard in this hurricane-prone region. Building inspectors aided in the sloppy production of houses by overlooking code violations; a state investigation after the hurricane revealed that some inspectors took bribes from contractors. In the decade preceding Hurricane Andrew, housing inspectors and construction companies favored economic gain while ignoring or minimizing the risk of potential hurricanes. Poorly built houses exacerbated the damage caused by the 1992 natural disaster. Andrew left Americans with an estimated $26.5 million in damages. Homeowners in Dade County felt particularly assaulted by Andrew and the contractors and home inspectors who had prioritized profits. Their feelings were warranted; houses built since 1980 in Dade County were 68 percent more likely to be uninhabitable after the hurricane than homes built before the housing boom.

In some ways, the federal government exacerbated natural disasters by providing disaster assistance. In the past, the federal role in disaster relief had been supplementary. That is, the federal government, under the Federal Emergency Management Agency (FEMA), covered 75 percent of the costs of disasters, with state and local governments providing the remainder. Recently, under the administrations of GEORGE H. W. BUSH, from 1989 to 1993, and BILL CLINTON from 1993 to 2001, the federal government provided 90 percent of disaster relief. Some critics contend that citizens gained a false sense of security, knowing that if homes are destroyed, they will receive government relief. Moreover, the National Flood Insurance Program (NFIP), established under the National Flood Insurance Act of 1968, provided federal flood insurance to more than 20,000 communities. Thus, in flood-prone regions that private insurance companies refused to cover, the federal government made flood protection available to homeowners, renters, and businesses.

On August 29, 2005, Hurricane Katrina made landfall in NEW ORLEANS, LOUISIANA, as a category 3 storm. Built on an alluvial floodplain, New Orleans relied on a system of levees commissioned under the U.S. ARMY CORPS OF ENGINEERS under the Flood Control Act of 1965 for protection. Once the levees were completed, local levee boards were expected to maintain the works. On August 29, however, the construction was only 60–90 percent complete. Fifty-three levees were breached during the storm, leaving 80 percent of the city flooded. More than 1,400 people died in New Orleans. Another 500 died (and some 700 were missing) in the hurricane and subsequent flooding across the larger Gulf Coast affected by Hurricane Katrina.

While many disasters, such as earthquakes and hurricanes, remain difficult to predict, the history of disasters illustrates that humans frequently made worse the destruction caused by nature by trading off economic gain for adequate preparedness. Furthermore, many Americans ignored the disastrous power of nature, choosing to build their communities in disaster-prone regions. Consequently, both nature and humans have been responsible for the destruction that has followed unexpected natural phenomena and severe weather disturbances.

See also ARCHITECTURE; DUST BOWL; UNITED STATES— CALIFORNIA; UNITED STATES—GULF COAST.

Natalie M. Schuster

Further Reading

Colten, Craig E. *An Unnatural Metropolis: Wresting New Orleans from Nature.* Baton Rouge: Louisiana State University Press, 2005.

Davis, Mike. *Ecology of Fear: Los Angeles and the Imagination of Disaster.* New York: Vintage Books, 1998.

Federal Emergency Management Agency. Available online. URL: http://www.fema.gov/. Accessed November 24, 2008.

Steinberg, Ted. *Acts of God: The Unnatural History of Natural Disaster.* 2d ed. Oxford: Oxford University Press, 2000.

U.S. Department of Health and Human Services. Available online. URL: http://www.hhs.gov/. Accessed November 24, 2008.

diseases, animal

Sometime around the dawn of agriculture in the Nile Valley thousands of years ago, a virus seems to have passed through enough camels to evolve in its genetic makeup in such a way that it could infect people. Actually, camels may have been an intermediary host between monkeys and humans. But as susceptible populations grew with farming, this virus had the chance to become more or less virulent. Probably, many viruses jumped species to their dead end, but this one became the single-greatest scourge of humanity: SMALLPOX. For most of history, it alone accounted for half the deaths of all children who died before age five. Fortunately, it is now gone—globally eradicated by vaccination with cowpox virus in 1980, representing medicine's only complete victory against an infectious disease. Ironically, another human virus, possibly of monkey origin, HIV (human immunodeficiency virus), appeared on the world stage precisely as smallpox exited.

PATHOGENS

Crowding is the circumstance in which pathogens evolve into diseases and become epidemics affecting humans or epizootics affecting other animals. Natural crowding of animals occurs when, for example, the climate favors a rising birth rate, or a predator population falls off. Artificial crowding, however, is the greater bane and, for animals, is a consequence of agriculture. Native Americans took domesticated DOGS with them from Asia and very possibly transited rabies as well—at least folktales of Natives of the Pacific coast suggest this.

Animal diseases, or the pathogens from which they evolve, were part of the COLUMBIAN EXCHANGE between the Eastern and Western Hemispheres in the 16th, 17th, and 18th centuries. Europeans transported rabies with them to the Atlantic coast of the Americas, though they may have encountered it there as well. In any case, rabies presented two forms: one "furious" and the other "dumb" (paralytic). As the two forms of variola virus cause major and minor smallpox, rabies strains evolved in relation to the animal populations they penetrated, afflicting wild and domesticated animals alike. The French chemist and microbiologist Louis Pasteur (1822–95), in developing an attenuated virus vaccine and using it for the first time on a nine-year-old boy in 1885, not only discovered a treatment for this relatively rare but terrifying zoonose (a disease that can be passed from other animals to humans) but also commenced the germ theory of disease in human and VETERINARY MEDICINE. In a sense, 1885 became a demarcation point, before which people conceived of any disease as an imbalance of vital fluids—the so-called humoral theory of disease. Bleeding, purging, novel medicines (such as a boiled-down extract of two newborn puppies in white wine with ginger, pepper, and sugar), and empirical therapies (e.g., inhaled urine) worked, supposedly, by rebalancing animal humors. Often, though, diseases were complete mysteries—in both cause and cure.

CATTLE FEVER AND HOG CHOLERA

During the early 19th century, two diseases—CATTLE fever and hog cholera—were particularly vexing. Cattle fever was a tick-borne (Boophilus), protozoan (Babesia bigemina) disease that first became notable in the hearth of southern cattle raising—the Piedmont of Georgia and South Carolina, and the Panhandle of Florida. It went by several names: in Georgia, cattlemen called it Spanish fever (implicating Florida); in South Carolina, they called it Georgia murrain; and in Virginia, they called it Carolina distemper. When drovers moved cattle west, babesiosis became Texas cattle fever, though the southeastern states, where the ticks were endemic, remained the disease's reservoir, afflicting both domesticated and wild animals. In the late 1880s, microbiology had progressed far enough for researchers—Cooper Curtice (1856–1939), Fred Kilbourne (1857–1936), and Theobald Smith (1859–1934), working for the U.S. DEPARTMENT OF AGRICULTURE's Bureau of Animal Industry—to identify the microparasite, establish the means of transmission, and begin developing control methods (insecticide dips). Cattle fever was finally eradicated from the United States in 1943.

The origin of hog cholera—a highly infectious viral disease—remains a mystery. It only arises in hogs but was unknown among European swine. Possibly, it was an immigrant pathogen that remained asymptomatic or mildly so until it became more virulent from passing through large swine populations that existed in the OHIO RIVER valley during the 1830s. At that time, CINCINNATI, OHIO, had so many meatpacking factories its nickname was "Porkopolis." Herds succumbed in droves; half or more of all the PIGS AND HOGS in Kentucky and Tennessee died of this disease during the 1840s. Penned-up breeding sows infected their shoats, which perished in heaps. The virus survived in processed meat and rendered fat, so that soap or axle grease became means for new outbreaks. Eventually, hog cholera followed the traffic patterns of ROADS AND TURNPIKES and RAILROADS across the country. The only significant control method was slaughter and burning the carcasses, and by those means hog cholera was eradicated from the United States in 1978.

GLANDERS

Long before the CIVIL WAR (1861–65), equine glanders was a feared disease. Indeed, the ancient Greek physician Hippocrates described it in ancient times, but rarely had it reached epizootic proportions in the United States because great herds of HORSES were relatively unseen until the huge Union and Confederate armies assembled them. Federal forces built expansive horse depots at ST. LOUIS, MISSOURI;

Greenville, Louisiana; Nashville, Tennessee; Harrisburg, Pennsylvania; Wilmington, Delaware; and the largest of all, for the Army of the Potomac, at Giesboro Point in the District of Columbia. Giesboro Depot was factorylike, with barracks, warehouses, and wharves; a horseshoeing shed where more than 100 blacksmiths worked; 32 stables providing 6,000 stalls; a veterinary hospital that could handle 2,650 head at one time; and several corrals, each capable of holding 1,000 horses. Its hay station handled 4,000 tons a month, and the combined operating expense of this post typically ran above $1 million a day. Glanders appeared almost as soon as the facilities opened, and over a course of about 16 months, only one morning report, on August 22, 1864, recorded no dead horses. More often, they died by the dozens; horses that appeared sick were shot and either burned, buried, or thrown into the Potomac River. In all, Giesboro handled 170,622 horses; 17,147 died on the post, 48,721 were sold as unfit, and the rest—some sick, some healthy—went to the war.

Confederate forces had similar depots, with the main one for the Army of Northern Virginia in the supply center at Lynchburg. During its time of operations, two Confederate army surgeons, John R. Page (1830–1901) and John J. Terrell (1829–1922), investigated the cause of so many horses dying. Page, who had studied medicine in Paris, France, where the pioneering comparative pathologist Pierre François Olive Rayer (1793–1867) had addressed pulmonary diseases in horses and humans, had probably learned about glanders symptoms then. In Lynchburg, Page and Terrell observed the full course of the disease—from an initial watery nasal discharge to final hemorrhaging through the nose and death. They performed necropsies on several horses and followed the infection from the nose to the lungs. And they inoculated several healthy horses with pathological materials to recreate the course of disease. They eventually published their findings as a Confederate Army Quartermaster pamphlet, which, ironically, was the first extensive clinical study of an animal disease in the United States. Except for not identifying the causative pathogen, a bacterium, *Pseudomonas mallei,* Page and Terrell's study was thorough and accurate. Perhaps as remarkable was the fact that they did not contract glanders themselves, as it is transmissible to humans. After the Civil War ended, glanders subsided along with the crowding, but it returned in the period of World War I, when it also became a secret biological weapon of German agents infecting American horses as they were shipped to the Allies in Europe.

TUBERCULOSIS AND BRUCELLOSIS

With western railroad construction and the Homestead Act of 1862, animal diseases spread across the prairies and plains—most notably TUBERCULOSIS and contagious abortion (brucellosis) among cattle. Both were transmissible to humans, though bovine tuberculosis, which can result in

the bone deformity of people called "humpback," was not the great scourge of human pulmonary tuberculosis. Several strains of the bacteria *Brucella* infect animals, including cattle, horses, sheep and goats, swine, dogs, and reindeer, and, occasionally, certain people, such as ovine slaughterhouse workers. *Brucella abortus* was highly contagious among cattle, and cattle were particularly vulnerable because of a high-level nutrient, erythritol, the pathogen needed and found in the placenta of calves. Cows could contract the disease from contaminated feed or water but more often from licking infected genitals or recently aborted fetuses. Bulls sexually transmitted the bacteria. Once the pathogen appeared in a herd, most of the pregnant cows aborted immediately and with subsequent pregnancies. Those that, somehow, continued having live births, gave little milk to their calves, and both cows and bulls could become sterile.

Contagious abortion probably existed in North America during colonial times but became a notable problem, in the 1840s, in New England, where cattlemen kept their stock relatively confined on small pastures. Cattle raising in the West often relied on the open range, where animals spread out. But that same land was where BISON roamed, millions upon millions. The conventional interpretation for the demise of the American bison is that they were hunted to near-EXTINCTION by the 1880s. There is ample evidence that, indeed, people moving west slaughtered herds for skins and sport, to protect railroads, and to drive away the Indians. But the hunting hypothesis, which fits so nicely with mythology of gun culture, hardly seems adequate for explaining how 50 to 100 million bison declined to a few hundred in so brief a window of time, when the herds also dropped in Canada and northern Mexico without intentional extermination. Further, heavily hunted species can respond to that pressure with increased fertility. Whether hunting was the chief factor, and contagious abortion a contributing one, or the other way around, the bisons' social instinct to herd was a natural crowding that figured in their demise. During the 1930s, the U.S. Department of Agriculture veterinary researchers developed a weakened culture of *B. abortus,* called "Strain 19," that they used to immunize calves, and over time brucellosis declined but never entirely disappeared. More commonly today, the disease is found among the 200,000 wild bison that remain on protected ranges and national park land—and the reason why western cattle ranchers are likely to shoot any bison that roam off their reservations.

FOOT AND MOUTH DISEASE

All diseases exhibit variability in their morbidity and mortality, partly because of biology of the pathogenic organism, and partly due to genomic individuality of hosts. Cattle plague, or rinderpest, from a highly contagious and extremely deadly virus, never entered the United States, though it ravaged all cloven-hoofed animals in Europe, Asia, and Africa. During the 1950s, the English veterinarian Walter Plowright (1923–) used a cell-cultured method for producing live, attenuated virus to produce an effective vaccine—which may eradicate cattle plague globally very soon (predicted for 2010). Foot and mouth disease (FMD) offers an interesting comparison. It, too, is viral and a highly contagious disease of all cloven-hoofed animals, but not highly fatal. Seven different strains of attenuated vaccine exist, though no one offers cross-protections against all seven serotypes, and none confers long-term immunity as Plowright's vaccine does. Consequently, massive slaughter of all susceptible species surrounding an outbreak area remains the main control method for FMD, as it has been since the 19th century.

The United States experienced eight serious FMD outbreaks, between 1870 and 1929. Most were small and brief, except for one in 1914, just as World War I began in Europe. American farmers anticipated a bonanza from selling live animals and meats abroad, but FMD reached the Chicago STOCKYARDS and from there quickly spread, infecting 3,500 herds across the country. Most countries to which the United States exported livestock restricted trade for fear of disease spread. By the time the United States entered the war in 1917, however, FMD was eliminated and animal exports resumed.

AFRICAN SWINE FEVER

There is another animal disease example, however, that has some of the pathological and economic features of both cattle plague and foot and mouth disease: African swine fever (ASF), as it affected Haiti in the early 1980s. Similar to both cattle plague and hog cholera, ASF is a highly contagious, usually fatal viral disease. It was not known outside Africa until 1957, when it appeared on the Iberian Peninsula and then spread with devastating effects to France and Italy, before migrating to Cuba and the Dominican Republic in the early 1970s. The Dominican Republic and Haiti share the island of Hispaniola, where CHRISTOPHER COLUMBUS introduced swine to the Western Hemisphere in 1493. The "Creole" pig was a descendant of its Spanish progenitors and lived much as the *pata negra* (black footed) Iberian swine did, roaming free until fattening season, when it was confined before butchering. Because ASF presented an enormous threat to U.S. hog farmers, the American government proposed a Creole pig eradication program to Haiti that offered compensation to farmers and replacement animals of "more productive" American types. Between 1980 and 1983, Haitian officials of the corrupt Duvalier government carried out the slaughter of an estimated 1.2 million Creole pigs but never passed along the compensation to the pigs' owners. Hog breeds from the United States fared poorly in tropical impoverishment. The Creole pig had been the main-

stay of Haiti's rural economy—providing food, a kind of savings account for financial emergencies, and a living currency. Its near-eradication, then, not only undermined farmers' income-producing capacity but contributed to environmental degradation—mainly DEFORESTATION and soil EROSION—as country people scrounged for survival.

Animal and human diseases have interfacing stories, but the main characteristic they share is that sickness or health influences all other aims and achievements. Over the course of human history, they have disrupted military actions and devastated domestic livestock, but epizootics also have prompted scientific advancements and new understandings of disease processes.

See also AIDS; BACTERIA; CANADA AND THE UNITED STATES; CONFEDERACY; ECOLOGICAL IMPERIALISM; HEALTH AND MEDICINE; MEXICO AND THE UNITED STATES; TICK FEVER; WEAPONS, BIOLOGICAL AND CHEMICAL.

G. Terry Sharrer

Further Reading
Bierer, Bert W. *A Short History of Veterinary Medicine in America.* East Lansing: Michigan State University Press, 1955.

Morse, Stephen S. *Emerging Viruses.* New York: Oxford University Press, 1993.

Sharrer, G. Terry. *A Kind of Fate: Agricultural Change in Virginia, 1861–1920.* Ames: Iowa State University Press, 2000.

Stalheim, O. H. V. *The Winning of Animal Health: 100 Years of Veterinary Medicine.* Ames: Iowa State University Press, 1994.

Wilkinson, Lise. *Animals and Disease: An Introduction to the History of Comparative Medicine.* Cambridge: Cambridge University Press, 1992.

Wiser, Vivian, Larry Mark, and H. Graham Purchase. *100 Years of Animal Health.* Beltsville, Md.: Associates of the National Agricultural Library, 1987.

diseases, human

Disease, broadly defined, can describe almost any condition that negatively affects human health. Infectious microbes cause some diseases; others result directly from a person's genes, lifestyle choices, or environment. In 2003, according to the U.S. National Center for Health Statistics, only one of the 10 leading causes of death in the United States—unintentional injuries—did not result from disease. Heart disease led the list, followed by cancer and cerebrovascular diseases. Although the particulars have changed from year to year, the 2003 list is reasonably representative of the previous three decades of U.S. mortality statistics. Diseases have dramatically affected the course of human history, leading societies to alter the shape of both their natural environment and the BUILT ENVIRONMENT dramatically.

Diseases fall loosely into two categories: infectious and noninfectious. Infectious diseases, such as INFLUENZA and SMALLPOX, can pass from one person to another. Noninfectious diseases, such as heart disease and lung cancer, do not normally pass from one person to another.

Some infectious diseases spread readily from person to person; these diseases can cause epidemics. An epidemic occurs when a disease spreads with unexpected speed through a population, sickening or killing large numbers of people. In 1793, for instance, a YELLOW FEVER epidemic killed almost 10 percent of the population of PHILADELPHIA, PENNSYLVANIA, forcing prominent citizens such as President GEORGE WASHINGTON and Treasury Secretary ALEXANDER HAMILTON to flee what was, at the time, the nation's capital.

Some diseases can only survive in particular areas or particular climates. The epidemic in Philadelphia partially resulted from weather conditions that favored the MOSQUITOES carrying the infection. The arrival of winter weather in the city, and the end of the mosquito season, halted the epidemic. Some diseases, however, spread more easily through human populations regardless of environmental conditions. Rather than remaining in one place, these epidemics can

MAJOR EUROPEAN DISEASE EPIDEMICS IN NORTH AMERICA AND CARIBBEAN, 1493–1802
(locations identified by contemporary names)

1493	Influenza reached Hispaniola, perhaps in livestock brought by Columbus. Indian traders may have carried disease to rest of Caribbean and possibly to Florida.
1507–19	Two smallpox epidemics killed perhaps 33–50 percent of indigenous population of Cuba, Haiti, and Puerto Rico. Indian traders carried disease to Mexico and killed many Mayans.
1520	Perhaps 3 million Arawak Indians in Caribbean died from European diseases by 1520.
1520	Smallpox reached the Aztec capital of Tenochtitlán.
1531–33	Measles epidemic swept through Sonora, Mexico, and into Arizona.
1539	Spanish explorer de Soto travels through southeastern United States. His men and their livestock brought diseases that killed some 75 percent of the Indians in the region.
1540	Spanish explorer Coronado and his livestock spread diseases through the American Southwest.
1559	Influenza epidemic swept through Caribbean.
1576	Typhoid fever killed thousands in Mexico.
1585	English settlers spread diseases to Indians around Roanoke Island.
1592–96	Measles moved through Seneca Indians of central New York.
1607	By this date, perhaps half of the Timucuan Indians had died from European diseases.
1613	Bubonic plague killed half the Indians who had converted to Christianity under missionaries in Florida.
1617–19	Fishing crews brought smallpox to Massachusetts, killing perhaps 90 percent of the Indian population and leaving few Indians present when the *Mayflower* arrives in 1620.
1630	Huron Indians in Ontario fell victim to smallpox epidemic.
1630–45	Smallpox killed many of the remaining New England Indians and spread westward to the Great Lakes, killing perhaps 10,000 Huron Indians.
1634	Dutch-introduced smallpox killed 95 percent of the Indians living along the Connecticut River.
1637	Scarlet fever spread from New England to the Great Lakes, killing thousands of Indians.
1638	European diseases had killed one-third of the Pueblo Indians in the Southwest.
1647	Influenza epidemic occurred in northeastern United States.
1649	New England Indians experienced another smallpox epidemic.
1658	Measles epidemic swept through New England.
1662	Smallpox epidemic killed more than 1,000 in New York.
1669	New England and the Great Lakes experienced another smallpox epidemic.
1674	Smallpox broke out among the Cherokee Indians in the Southeast.

spread across the entire world; epidemiologists (scientists who study the spread of disease) refer to these events as pandemics. In 1918, a particularly virulent strain of influenza caused a pandemic, sickening large numbers of people in almost every population center on Earth and killing between 50 and 100 million people worldwide.

Instead of (or in addition to) dividing diseases into infectious and noninfectious categories, scientists sometimes classify diseases based on the cause. Viral diseases, for instance, result from infections of the body by VIRUSES. AIDS (acquired immune deficiency syndrome), yellow fever,

influenza, and smallpox all result from viral infections. Other microorganisms, including BACTERIA, fungi, protozoa, amoeba, and animal parasites (such as the HOOKWORM), can also cause disease. *Genetic* diseases, by contrast, result from abnormal, harmful sequences in a person's deoxyribonucleic acid (DNA) rather than infections. Huntington's disease and sickle-cell anemia both fall into this category. *Occupational* diseases, such as black lung, result directly from hazards endemic to a particular workplace environment. These examples represent only a few of the causes of disease. Because many factors contribute to disease, the list of causes

1675	Influenza reappeared in the Northeast.
1687	Smallpox occurred again in New England.
1690	Malaria reached the southeastern United States and killed thousands of Indians.
1692	Another measles epidemic struck New England.
1713–15	Measles recurred in New England and the Great Lakes.
1715–21	Particularly virulent smallpox virus swept from Texas to New England.
1717–37	Malaria devastated the Miami Indians of the Midwest.
1729–33	Smallpox epidemic stretched from Texas to Hudson Bay.
1735–36	Diphtheria entered New England and killed hundreds, perhaps thousands of Indians.
1738	Smallpox epidemic took half of the Cherokee population in the Southeast.
1743	Russian fur traders spread new diseases to the Aleuts. The Aleut population declined nearly 90 percent by 1800.
1746	Typhoid fever moved along the St. Lawrence River in Canada, killing many MicMac Indians.
1750–52	Indians from Texas to the Great Lakes experienced another smallpox epidemic.
1753	Smallpox struck Cherokee Indians again.
1761	Influenza spread across North America.
1763	Smallpox outbreak undermined the loose Indian confederation around the Great Lakes during Pontiac's Rebellion.
1768–70	Measles killed thousands of Indians in the Southwest.
1770–79	Smallpox killed one-third of the Indians along the Pacific Coast.
1775–83	Smallpox reached from Mexico to Canada.
1777	Influenza killed Canadian Indians living in missions.
1780–99	Measles moved across Texas and Mexico.
1781	Deadly smallpox reached the Blackfeet Indians in Montana.
1782	Deadly smallpox reached Indians along the Columbia Plateau.
1785–87	Deadly smallpox reached indigenous people in the arctic areas of Canada and Alaska.
1788	Smallpox killed many Pueblo Indians in the Southwest.
1802	Two-thirds of the Omaha Indians in Nebraska died from smallpox epidemic.
1802	Pneumonia and diphtheria killed many California Indians.

Source: Timeline of European Disease Epidemics among American Indians. Available online. URL: http://www.kporterfield.com/aicttw/articles/disease.html. Accessed June 9, 2009; and John W. Verano and Douglas H. Ubelaker, eds. *Disease and Demography in the Americas.* Washington, D.C.: Smithsonian Institution Press, 1992.

is long and varied, and many causes overlap—heart disease, for instance, can result from a combination of genetic factors and a diet high in saturated fat.

Environmental factors influence diseases in many ways. Toxic substances are the most common direct environmental cause of disease. Cancer, for instance, can result directly from a patient's exposure to CARCINOGENS in the environment. Exposure to airborne asbestos, for instance, has been directly linked to various lung diseases, including lung cancer. Black lung, a widespread disease among COAL miners, arises when those workers inhale carbon particles (in this case, coal dust) that float in the air around them.

Environmental factors can also indirectly influence the spread of disease in human populations. Hot, humid environments, for instance, tend to support MOSQUITOES better than cold or arid climates. Many diseases, including MALARIA, yellow fever, West Nile virus, and several varieties of encephalitis, depend on mosquitoes to infect new victims. In the case of Philadelphia's yellow fever epidemic in 1793, hot weather did not *cause* the disease, but the environment *facilitated* the disease by sustaining the mosquito population. When the environment changed (with the arrival of cooler weather), the mosquitoes died, and the epidemic ended.

Many societies have at least partially understood the connections, both direct and indirect, between the environment and disease. As a result, disease has dramatically affected human interactions both with and within particular environments. In some cases, societies have done great damage to local environments in an effort to eradicate the diseases that flourish in these environments. In other cases, a particular understanding of the relationship between the environment and disease has led to dramatic alterations in the built environment of homes and cities.

One understanding of the relationship between disease and the environment, the "filth" or "miasma" theory of disease, influenced city construction in the 19th century. According to this theory, decaying organic matter (filth), such as GARBAGE or human waste, produced disease-causing chemicals. People believed that some chemicals hung in the air in the form of pestilential fogs—so-called MIASMAS—and infected anyone who passed through them; the presence of these miasmas supposedly explained the ability of a disease such as yellow fever to infect large numbers of people in a particular area. This miasma theory dramatically affected the built environment of 19th-century cities. It led cities, for instance, to construct large public sewer systems, designed to carry household wastes, with their clouds of miasma, away from people. The germ theory of disease, which posited microorganisms as the cause of many diseases, eventually supplanted the miasma theory.

As an example of the influence of disease on human interactions with the nonbuilt environment, it makes sense to turn back to the mosquito. In 1881, a Cuban doctor, Car-los Finlay (1833–1915), proposed that mosquitoes spread yellow fever through their bites, picking up the disease by biting an infected person and infecting healthy people with subsequent bites. A team of medical researchers from the U.S. Army, led by Walter Reed (1851–1902), confirmed Finlay's work, firmly establishing the environmental connection between mosquitoes and disease. This new understanding led to tremendous human interventions in the environment. In an effort to eliminate mosquito breeding grounds, some communities drained nearby WETLANDS. Many communities began (and continue) to use PESTICIDES, such as DDT (dichlorodiphenyltrichloroethane), to control mosquito populations. These interventions into environments and ECO-SYSTEMS dramatically reduced the incidence of diseases such as malaria and yellow fever, which disappeared from many parts of the world, including the United States, by the end of the 20th century. These interventions, however, also had harmful consequences for the environment, such as the loss of wetlands and the buildup of toxic substances in the food chain. The environment, in such instances, became a casualty in humanity's war against disease.

Diseases highlight the connections between humans and the environment. They represent one of the natural world's greatest threats to humanity, forcing people to reshape their built environment and leading us to intervene in the natural environment—often with unanticipated consequences. Despite their best efforts to control this part of our environment, humans remain at the mercy of some of Earth's tiniest inhabitants.

See also CARSON, RACHEL; CENTERS FOR DISEASE CONTROL AND PREVENTION AND NATIONAL INSTITUTES OF HEALTH; CHOLERA; HEALTH AND MEDICINE; LABOR, EXTRACTIVE INDUSTRIES; PANAMA CANAL; WASTE DISPOSAL AND MANAGEMENT; WORLD WAR I.

Jeffrey Womack

Further Reading

Grob, Gerald N. *The Deadly Truth: A History of Disease in America.* Cambridge, Mass.: Harvard University Press, 2002.

Oldstone, Michael B. A. *Viruses, Plagues, and History.* New York: Oxford University Press, 1998.

Tomes, Nancy. *The Gospel of Germs: Men, Women, and the Microbe in American Life.* Cambridge, Mass.: Harvard University Press, 1998.

Watts, Sheldon. *Disease and Medicine in World History.* New York: Routledge, 2003.

diseases, plant

All living things on Earth are subject to disease, including plants. Disease represents an abnormal or harmful condition that lasts long enough to disrupt or halt vital physiological

Introduced accidentally to the United States in the first decade of the 20th century, chestnut blight, also known as chestnut bark disease, is caused by a fungus that gains entry through wounds on a tree's bark. Once inside, it spreads and kills the cells that transport water and nutrients within the tree. Continued reinfections cause growth impairment and the death of twigs and branches; eventually the tree itself may die.   *(Kevin R. Williams/Shutterstock)*

processes. The term *plant disease* broadly describes malfunctions of plants caused by various environmental conditions such as pathogens, infectious diseases, and other physiological factors. In the United States, plant diseases ranging from Pierce's disease to CHESTNUT BLIGHT have altered American landscapes and disrupted commercial activity. As have other people, Americans have developed methods to attenuate and minimize the impact of plant disease and ensure the supply of healthy plants.

Throughout the Earth's history, plant disease was just one natural phenomenon that balanced the number of plants and animals in the ecological circulation. Fossil evidence reveals that plant diseases have existed for 250 million years. The Bible offers one of the earliest written records of plant disease, suggesting that mildew, pests, and bad weather occurred as a result of God's displeasure. Ancient Greek and Roman writers similarly observed that their gods expressed anger through epidemics such as plant rust. Although predecessors for the modern microscope existed since the late 16th century, it took several centuries for people to understand the mechanisms of plant disease. When the blight that affected POTATOES spread across Western Europe and North America in the 1830s, 1840s, and 1850s, undermining a major FOOD source and threatening millions of human lives, scientists began a more systematic study of the causes and potential cures of plant diseases. Heinrich Anton de Bary (1831–88), the German botanist and microbiologist, finally succeeded in identifying various fungi that debilitated plants, including, in 1861, the pathogen responsible for potato blight. He helped found modern plant pathology, or phytopathology.

Plant pathology developed as the United States experienced the growth of COMMERCIAL AGRICULTURE and the injection of new AGRICULTURAL TECHNOLOGY. American farmers in the 19th and 20th centuries increasingly planted crops in a MONOCULTURE system, which enhanced potential profits but also made crops more susceptible to diseases and epidemics. In Southern California, for example, *Xylella fastidiosa*, now known as Pierce's disease, destroyed tens of thousands of vineyards in the 1870s and 1880s, after the introduction of the glassy-winged sharpshooter, the vector for the disease, from the southeastern United States.

In the first two decades of the 20th century, stem rust epidemic destroyed WHEAT fields across the MIDWEST. In 1917, the U.S. DEPARTMENT OF AGRICULTURE launched an eradiprogram to remove barberry bushes near wheat fields and ensure the domestic food supply and food exports for the Allies during WORLD WAR I (1914–18). The parasitic fungus that causes rust used the barberry to move from crop to crop and remained dormant on the barberry between crops. The barberry served as a breeding ground for new pathogens. The eradication program reached most wheat-producing states by 1955. While this program substantially eradicated the bushes and reduced widespread epidemics, stem rust still occurred periodically, in the last half of the 20th century, because there are other sources for the fungus.

Plant diseases affected horticulture and domestic landscapes as well as agriculture. In the early 20th century, chestnut blight arrived in the United States with the importation of Asian chestnut trees. This fungal disease essentially destroyed the American chestnut tree, which possessed no natural immunity. The elm bark beetle, another native of Asia, carried a different fungus, known as DUTCH ELM DISEASE. Slowly spreading from New England, in the late 1920s, to Minnesota, in the 1970s, it devastated native elm trees across a broad swath of the country.

Consequently, Americans have economic reasons for securing healthy plants. In the United States, phytopathology has developed in partnerships of universities, agribusiness, and government agencies. An integrative science that draws on other specialties, phytopathology considers not only the causes of diseases and disorders but also their prevention and treatment. Phytopathology has a three-sided interface with (1) physical sciences and mathematics such as chemistry, physics, meteorology, and statistics to aid in measurements and observation; (2) biological sciences such as microbiology, virology, mycology, nematology, entomology, weed science, taxonomy, GENETICS, physiology, and ecology, to help understand the functioning and relations of diseases with plants and animals; and (3) agricultural technology and sciences such as horticulture, FORESTRY, soil science, land use, and CONSERVATION, to facilitate fulfillment of human needs.

Phytopathologists have discovered multiple causes for the more than 50,000 plant diseases and disorders on Earth. Infectious plant diseases require three conditions: a host plant, an adequate environment, and a pathogen. A pathogen is an organism, excluding insects, that cannot produce life-sustaining nutrients without a host. Plant pathogens include fungi oomycetes (funguslike organisms), BACTERIA, VIRUSES, nematodes (multicellular, wormlike creatures living in soil), and parasitic plants, all of which are invisible to the naked human eye. Other plant disorders result from noninfectious agents, such as improper nutrition; acidity or alkalinity of the soil; the lack, excess, or poor quality of water; the introduction of pests and other invasive species; and climatic or environmental shifts such as temperature changes or wildfires. Humans also contribute to plant disorders through contaminated soil, WATER POLLUTION, and the use of PESTICIDES, fungicides, and herbicides that also threaten the health of humans and other animals. Concerned about these human impacts, some consumers have turned to organically grown plants, risking exposure to diseased plants so as to be free from such chemical treatments.

Historically, people tried to control plant diseases or disorders through crop management techniques, such as terracing, fertilization, and grafting, or biological systems, such as crop rotation, and through quarantines. In the 20th century, farmers and scientists often combined variations of these traditional methods with modern innovations involving the use of synthetic compounds and genetic manipulations designed to increase resistance to disease. Since the 1970s, scientists have developed genetically modified organisms (GMOs) that add new genetic material to a genome.

GMOs potentially offer many advantages, such as creating more nutritious foods, generating new sources for vaccines, and increasing resistance to disease, but many consumers and environmentalists have resisted them. Among other things, they fear that such foods will lead to domination by a few large agribusinesses and more industrialized nations that control the technology, challenge the propriety of mixing genes from different species, and question whether the long-term health effects of such foods can be known. In any event, Americans will continue to struggle to control plant diseases that undermine domestic landscapes and agricultural production, even while humans often remain responsible for the conditions that spread those diseases.

See also PEST CONTROL; PLANT SUCCESSION; SPECIES, EXOTIC AND INVASIVE; SPECIES, INDIGENOUS; UNITED STATES—CENTRAL PLAINS; UNITED STATES—MIDWEST; UNITED STATES—NORTHERN PLAINS; WEEDS.

Subin Kim

Further Reading
Ainsworth, Geoffrey C. *Introduction to the History of Plant Pathology.* Cambridge: Cambridge University Press, 1981.
Horsfall, James G., and Ellis B. Cowling, eds. *Plant Disease: An Advanced Treatise.* Vol. 1. New York: Academic Press, 1977.
Ingram, David, and Noel Robertson. *Plant Disease: A Natural History.* London: HarperCollins, 1999.
Stakman, Elvin C., and J. George Harrar. *Principles of Plant Pathology.* New York: Ronald Press, 1957.

Disney

A word signifying a man, a corporation, a place, and a state of mind, *Disney*—in the form of Walter Elias Disney (1901–66), his films, his corporation, and his amusement parks—has shaped American environmental attitudes and landscapes for the better part of a century. Disney's influence ranges from his first 1920s cartoons featuring the adventures of an anthropomorphized mouse to Celebration, Florida, a "New Urbanist" residential community constructed in the 1990s adjacent to Disney World, one of several parks created during and after his lifetime. Disney's ability to combine small-town values and American optimism with mass entertainment and corporate growth made him one of the most successful media magnates of the 20th century. In a nation undergoing rapid URBANIZATION and technological change, and buffeted by global events, Disney's comforting view of nature, community, and life proved hugely popular.

Disney was born on December 5, 1901, in CHICAGO, ILLINOIS, a city where his father a decade earlier had helped construct the "White City" at the Columbian Exposition of 1893—a precursor to his son's future constructions. Though living in larger cities and spending much of his life in Southern California, the place Walt Disney remembered as his home was the small community of Marceline, Missouri, where he lived for part of his childhood. Marceline's downtown served as the model for "Main Street, U.S.A.," and the society of that small railroad and farming town remained a social and moral model Disney clung to and presented in his films and parks.

Disney's short cartoons and animated films contained a menagerie of anthropomorphized animals, from the ubiquitous Mickey Mouse to innumerable animal characters providing comic relief in films as varied as *Cinderella* (1950) and *The Jungle Book* (1967). In some, animals were the protagonists, such as *Dumbo* (1941) or *101 Dalmatians* (1961). Critics have noted Disney's tendency to focus on "cute" animals, whether in animated form or in his many live-action nature documentaries, in which the natural lives of animals are reduced to lively, fictionalized, and humanized plots to entertain audiences. In his biographical study *The Disney Version* (1968), the film historian Richard Schickel ascribed this to a reductive mind: "Wild things and wild behavior were often made comprehensible by converting them into cuteness, mystery was explained with a joke, and terror was resolved by a musical cue or a discreet averting of the camera's eye from the natural processes." Disney's treatment of animals was, in this view, linked to his drive to eradicate any hint of unhappiness, any irresolvable problem, in his films and theme parks.

While this point may be valid, it ignores arguably the most influential environmental film Disney ever produced, *Bambi* (1942). In that film about the life of a fawn, based on a German novel written in the 1920s, humans were presented as the implacable enemies of animals, burning the forest and killing Bambi's mother. The most ominous moments in the film occur when "Man" enters the forest. This encapsulated aspects of early 20th-century preservationist thought—WILDERNESS as a place free of humans and FIRE not as a natural occurrences but rather a terrible waste to be fought by foresters and conservationists. It may be merely a children's cartoon but is also perhaps the most effective antihunting film ever made.

If Disney shaped environmental attitudes in his films, his theme parks would shape the American landscape. This began with Disneyland, which opened in 1955 in Anaheim, California, surrounded by orange groves and accessible via a newly constructed freeway. Subsequently surrounded by Orange County sprawl, Disney's meticulously planned, carefully controlled park has been perceived by some academics as a critique of sprawling Southern California. Instead, with its encapsulation of Disney's films and Hollywood dreams in Fantasyland, its nostalgic recreation of Main Street, U.S.A., and its promises of future happiness through technology and American capitalism—from the Carousel of Progress to Autotopia—it represented Southern California as a hopeful model for the nation. Southern California, for better and for worse, would serve as a model for the SUNBELT, and in recent years themed environments—from outdoor malls to gentrified downtowns—have borrowed from Disneyland, using privatized and patrolled public space and themed, nostalgic architecture to draw shoppers and new residents.

As the park was surrounded by subsequent development, however, Disney began to look for a location where he could build a far larger park, where outside development could not encroach. The location selected for aptly named Disney World was 43 square miles of central Florida near Orlando. Here, Disney, his "imagineers," and, after his death, his corporation constructed a far larger park. In addition to the Magic Kingdom, Disney World would ultimately contain several different attractions. One was EPCOT, the Experimental Prototype Community of Tomorrow. As built, EPCOT serves as a kind of permanent world's fair, with pavilions and rides showcasing individual nations and technological themes, from agriculture to energy, not unlike the White City of 1893. However, Disney imagined an actual community of permanent residents, "living the life of tomorrow today." No such community was built until the 1990s, when the town of Celebration was founded near the park. The first residents arrived in 1996. This community espoused the principles of New Urbanism—walkable neighborhoods, houses with front porches for socializing, and nostalgic vernacular architecture—the kinds of homes built a century earlier in Marceline, or the then-new communities of Southern California, filled with midwestern migrants. Disney had imagined a community of the future, but by the end of the 20th century, some Americans were looking for a return to the past. The small-town, ruralist nostalgia Disney traded in ultimately overtook even his own vision.

Even so, Disney's influence remains pervasive. His films influenced how generations of audiences viewed nature, animals, and their relationships with humans. His theme parks have shaped the built environment, from urban planning and theming to new residential communities. Few individuals have wielded greater influence over the American landscape—cultural and physical—than Walt Disney. Disney died on December 15, 1966.

See also Los Angeles, California; suburbanization; Sunbelt; United States—California; United States—Deep South; urbanization.

Lawrence Culver

Further Reading
Findlay, John M. *Magic Lands: Western Cityscapes and American Culture after 1940.* Berkeley: University of California Press, 1992.
Gabler, Neal. *Walt Disney: The Triumph of the American Imagination.* New York: Knopf, 2006.
Marling, Karal Ann, ed. *Designing Disney's Theme Parks: The Architecture of Reassurance.* New York: Flammarion, 1997.
Schickel, Richard. *The Disney Version: The Life, Times, Art and Commerce of Walt Disney.* New York: Simon & Schuster, 1968.

dogs

Dogs *(Canis familiaris),* members of the family Canidae, are an assorted group of carnivores with extreme variations in diet, geographical habitat, and physical attributes. The most common usage of the word *dog* refers to a subspecies of domesticated wolves. The dog is one of the two most popular domesticated animals (the cat is the other), and as a result, its evolution has been strongly influenced by human interaction. The environmental history of domestic dogs reveals their complex roles in everything from hunting, guiding, transport, food sources, and military uses to a more modern utility of companionship.

The Canidae family is in the order Carnivora and includes dogs, wolves, jackals, foxes, and coyotes. They are characterized by large tails, nonretractable claws, large canines (teeth), and strong aural and olfactory senses. All species of the genus *Canis* can interbreed and have fertile offspring. Canines are found on every continent except Antarctica. Historically, scientists debated whether dogs were descendants of the wolf *(Canis lupus),* the golden jackal *(Canis aureus),* or perhaps both. Recent scholarship in morphology, vocalizations, and molecular biology, however, has narrowed the principal ancestor of dogs to the wolf.

The dog was probably the first domesticated animal. This domestication involves a chronologically long development, but the first true domestic dogs probably occurred near the end of the last ice age. The bones of wolves have been found with those of hominids as early as the middle Pleistocene period (ca. 300,000 b.c.e.). These tamed wolves were probably the precursors to the domesticated dog. The genetic social patterns of the wolf, in conjunction with those of humans, allowed for it to be separated from its feral breeding population. The successive breeding of these isolated tame wolves over several generations differentiated the species to that of the dog. These differentiations became more marked with the advent of sedentary subsistence agriculture. As human society became more specialized and hierarchical, so did the role of the dog. These defined roles, whether guarding, herding, hunting, or transport, began an even more selective process of breeding, enhancing the traits needed for these functions.

There is some confusion in the archaeological record regarding the first domestic dogs in North America. The earliest records are from Danger Cave in Utah. These deposits were dated to around 7000 to 8000 b.c.e. Because these finds are more recent than those in Europe and Asia, scientists speculate about whether dogs were transported over the Bering land bridge. DNA evidence of American canine bones shows that they are a closer genetic match to Asian and European canines than to North American gray wolves. To date, however, no confirmed remains of this "missing link" have been found.

Dogs are one of the few known animals to be domesticated by Native Americans. Because of the lack of written records, the majority of historical evidence regarding the Native Americans' relationship with dogs followed European contact. The Native Americans used dogs in a variety of roles. They were a food source for the Hidatsa tribe of present-day North Dakota and a spiritual guide in the afterlife for the Shoshone who inhabited portions of present-day Wyoming and Idaho. Dogs were certainly used as hunters in the Pacific Northwest and in Inuit lands. Spanish explorers witnessed Native Americans using dogs as beasts of burden. These dogs carried goods and equipment on their backs or pulled sleds called travois. These sleds eased movement for the migratory tribes. Thus, the role of the domesticated dog in Native American society ran the gamut of food, religion, transport, and hunter, making it an integral part of their livelihood.

The first dogs taken to North America by the post-Columbian Europeans were dogs of war and conquest. Later colonization introduced guarding, hunting, and working dogs. As the European settlers pushed Native Americans from their lands, indigenous North American dogs moved with them, were bred into the European lines, succumbed

Among the first domesticated animals, dogs are often bred for specific characteristics. Some Labrador retrievers, such as the one shown here, have been bred specifically for waterfowl hunting.   *(David E. Sharp, U.S. Fish and Wildlife Service)*

to disease, or became once again feral and interbred with wolves. Today, there are no true populations of the indigenous North American dog.

By the late 1700s, caring for small dogs in the household became common in America, particularly among well-to-do families. The keeping of dogs for company or pleasure followed trends in England and northern Europe and signified the development of another role of dogs—as pets. This development had significant consequences for the continued breeding of dogs.

Breeds of animals within a species occur when they are mated in a closed population. Over time, this mating leads to the development of specific sets of behavior and appearance. The breeding of lap dogs and pet dogs gave rise to the breeding of "purebloods." From the colonial period until the early 20th century in the United States, most dogs were of a

few types: hounds, terriers, mastiffs, spaniels, pointers, and bulldogs. The differences between these types arose from breeding in their utility, be it hunting, guarding, herding, or fighting. In the late 19th century, however, registries and stud books began documenting pedigrees as purebred dogs rose in popularity. This development further closed the genetic population for many breeds of dogs. Other purebreds were imported from different continents, most notably Europe. In 2008, the American Kennel Club, formed in 1884, recognized 156 breeds of dog.

Breeding within these tightly restricted populations has led to many inherited problems in dogs. The most well-known problem is canine hip dysplasia in large breeds, particularly German shepherds. Others include congenital heart defects, orthopedic faults, and thyroid problems in different breeds. The Orthopedic Foundation for Animals currently keeps a database for breeders relating to these problems.

The modern American dog still plays a large and varied role. Its traditional responsibilities in hunting, guarding, and transport remain, but the dog is now also used in many specialized fashions, such as assistance for the disabled, therapy, detection of illicit materials, and law enforcement. Nonetheless, the leading use of the dog in the contemporary United States has remained one of companionship. Moreover, the care, use, and upkeep of the modern domestic dog have become an annual business in excess of $1 billion. Much of this cost has resulted from problems associated with removing dogs from their natural habitat and adapting them to urban environments. The city poses numerous problems to dog care, including feeding, sanitation, loss, pest control, and attacks on humans. In the past three decades, urban officials have worked to counteract these difficulties by euthanizing unclaimed or dangerous dogs, building dog parks for canine exercise, and instilling civic responsibility toward waste, shelters, leash laws, and spaying and neutering.

The environmental impact of dog domestication has only recently begun to be studied in earnest. Some of the larger questions in the field include the processing and consumption of dog food, waste management, and the deterioration of the gene pool. In 2007, the American Veterinary Medical Association listed the domestic dog population in the United States as 72.1 million, representing 37.2 percent of all households. The sheer size of these numbers reflects a growing need to analyze their past and future environmental effects.

See also DISEASES, ANIMAL; VETERINARY MEDICINE.

Michael A. Ramey

Further Reading
Coppinger, Lorna. *Dogs: A Startling New Understanding of Canine Origin, Behavior, and Evolution.* New York: Simon & Schuster, 2001.
Serpell, James. *The Domestic Dog: Its Evolution, Behaviour, and Interactions with People.* Cambridge: Cambridge University Press, 1995.

dollar diplomacy

Coined during the presidency of William Howard Taft (1909–13), dollar diplomacy described the foreign policy objective of increasing the United States government's diplomatic influence through the promotion of U.S. commercial interests.

Dollar diplomacy emerged from the nation's relationship with its hemispheric neighbors. In 1822, the United States recognized the newly established American republics, such as Argentina and Mexico, after their wars of independence with Spain, three years before any European power did. U.S. leaders wanted to prevent the European mercantilist system of commercial restrictions from impeding U.S. trade with the new American republics. In what became known as the Monroe Doctrine, President James Monroe asserted, in December 1823, that the Western Hemisphere was henceforth closed to future European colonization and that any European threat to the new nations of the Americas would be viewed as a threat to the United States. U.S. hemispheric power increased throughout the 19th century, and U.S. financiers and industrialists pressed for a foreign policy that promoted a hospitable international commercial environment that safeguarded their investments.

Dollar diplomacy was an outgrowth of U.S. economic activity in the Dominican Republic. In 1893, the Santo Domingo Improvement Company, a U.S. firm, purchased the Dominican Republic's foreign debt in return for the right to collect the Dominican Republic's customs duties. Several company officers were connected to the highest circles of the U.S. government. Political instability following the assassination of the Dominican dictator Ulises Heureaux, in 1899, hindered the company's ability to collect duties, which provided funds for governmental administration and profits for foreign creditors. President THEODORE ROOSEVELT worried that European capitalists would continue to pressure their national governments to use military might to protect their economic interests in the Caribbean region, which was increasingly under U.S. influence after the 1898 SPANISH-AMERICAN WAR.

In December 1904, Roosevelt transformed Monroe's proscription against European incursion in the Western Hemisphere into an endorsement of U.S. intrusion. The Roosevelt corollary to the Monroe Doctrine declared that the United States would prevent European intervention in the hemisphere by itself intervening when nations of the Americas failed to meet international economic commitments. In 1905, by executive order, U.S. officials took over the customs houses of the Dominican Republic. This foreign policy decision reflected the expansion of state power and governmental interventionism of the PROGRESSIVE ERA that replaced GILDED AGE instrumental relationships between the U.S. DEPARTMENT OF STATE and specific business concerns such as the Santo Domingo Improvement Company.

Political and economic leaders in the United States had increasingly conceptualized their interests in global terms since the mid-19th century. As U.S. commercial interests invested abroad in order to create markets for U.S. goods and obtain distant natural resources such as rubber and sugar to satisfy U.S. manufacturing needs and U.S. consumer tastes, advances in transportation and communication created a more interdependent world. Many U.S. leaders believed that economic expansion helped avert domestic unrest and was therefore necessary for the stability of their nation.

Progressivism, the reform spirit of the early 1900s, permeated both domestic and foreign affairs. Believing the world was divided between civilized nations such as the United States and uncivilized or backward peoples, Roosevelt urged Americans to support their country's involvement in international affairs. During the Roosevelt administration, the United States intervened militarily in several parts of the world, including Cuba, Panama, and the Philippines. When William Howard Taft became president in 1909, he advocated "substituting dollars for bullets" in order to make the United States a global power. Secretary of State Philander C. Knox and Assistant Secretary of State for Latin America F. M. Huntington Wilson used the State Department to advance CAPITALISM generally abroad. The value of U.S. exports increased from $800 million in 1895 to $2.3 billion in 1914.

In Central America and the Caribbean, the United States pursued dollar diplomacy by exerting pressure on several nations to accept the U.S. government's supervision of their finances in exchange for loans from U.S. banks. The Taft administration believed the arrangement aided the U.S. economy by maintaining the political stability necessary in overseas markets for U.S. goods, but Taft's policy of managing other national economies without expensive military intervention failed. Many in the Americas accused the United States of economic IMPERIALISM, and frequent U.S. military interventions and occupations continued in nations near the PANAMA CANAL until the U.S. president FRANKLIN D. ROOSEVELT instituted a noninterventionist Good Neighbor Policy in 1933. Nevertheless, the promotion of private commercial interests, the exploitation of far-off natural resources to fill domestic manufacturing requirements and consumer demands, and the utilization of economic resources to achieve foreign policy goals became long-standing features of U.S. diplomacy in the 20th century and beyond.

See also MEXICO AND THE UNITED STATES.

David M. Carletta

Further Reading
Healy, David. *Drive to Hegemony: The United States in the Caribbean, 1898–1917.* Madison: University of Wisconsin Press, 1988.

Rosenberg, Emily S. *Financial Missionaries to the World: The Politics and Culture of Dollar Diplomacy, 1900–1930.* Cambridge, Mass.: Harvard University Press, 1999.

Scholes, Walter V., and Marie V. Scholes. *The Foreign Policies of the Taft Administration.* Columbia: University of Missouri Press, 1970.

Veeser, Cyrus. *A World Safe for Capitalism: Dollar Diplomacy and America's Rise to Global Power.* New York: Columbia University Press, 2002.

domesticated animals

Animal domestication is a process that humans have employed to change species of WILD ANIMALS so that their consecutive offspring improve human life. In this intimate relation with nature, humans have trained domestic animals to provide transportation, perform heavy work or transport goods, assist in the hunting and capture of other animals, be a dietary source of protein, or provide companionship. Animals also have served as subjects to test human medicines or surgical procedures.

Although the ancestors of modern humans did not possess scientific knowledge or laboratories, over time they effected neural modifications in certain animals' genetic code by inbreeding those animals that showed desirable traits in order to make animals tractable or trainable. In ancient societies, humans used animal products for FOOD and made their skins and fur into clothing and into large sheets for shelter. Humans domesticated the ancestors of modern DOGS approximately 15,000 years ago.

The earliest domestication of large animals occurred around 6000 B.C.E. In various parts of Europe and Asia, hunters lived in proximity to large game animals, and human migrations followed those of animals. After thousands of years of this hunting pattern, people discovered that once the herds were running, they could be forced into small spaces, where it was easier to slaughter them. This was probably the first alteration or at least the first attention to environment that facilitated domestication. The next step was to keep those captured animals alive until they were needed for food. Once animals were penned, they became dependent on human interaction for food and water. Since most large animals are herbivorous (vegetarians), plant domestication was closely related to ongoing processes of breeding and domesticating livestock. As humans and animals became more closely bonded, humans grew more sedentary because they no longer had to chase herds or forage for FOOD. They could grow their own crops, feed their animals, and remain in a modified environment instead of constantly moving.

Approximately 25,000 years ago, during the Pleistocene geological era, humans traveled across the Bering Strait from Asia into the Americas. Archaeologists, anthropologists, zoologists, and paleontologists believe that the dog was already a companion and accompanied the migrations to the Americas, but there is no concrete evidence of their existence in North America until about 8400 B.C.E. This first doglike animal in America is estimated to have migrated at that time, as evidenced by a canine-looking skeleton found in a cave in Idaho. This period was characterized by agriculture, pottery, the use of FIRE, and the ability to construct permanent shelters.

People continued to settle the northwest region of North America, and then traveled south through what is now California to Mexico and South America. As human social structures gained complexity, so did the incorporation of domestic animals in every aspect of life. Once settled in the Americas, societies changed from highly transient tribes to more sedentary groups that grew crops, lived in houses, and fabricated pottery with artistic modifications. Much of this pottery depicted animal images. Excavated artifacts demonstrate the use of animal bone, tooth, and sinew in implements, weapons, and decorative elements of early inhabitants. In Colima, Mexico, and areas of South America, an abundant array of bowls in the shape of dogs and statues of DOGS were found in tombs. However, these groups domesticated dogs for food rather than companionship.

The use of animals for companion animals, or pets, and for sports occurred much later in the history of the Americas as food sources became more abundant.

The horse, as people now know it, originated in Southwest Asia, where there are carvings and drawings of HORSES pulling chariots. In Iraq, tapestries show horses used as mounts for polo players. The ancient Greeks and Romans had horses that were used for racing and during battles. The horse arrived in the Americas with the Spanish conquistadores. When the indigenous people of Mexico first encountered the horse, they believed that it was a supernatural monster because it looked as if the human was attached. But later, after learning about the efficient way that horses could be used for transport of goods and transportation, they eagerly adopted those animals. North American Indians found the horse to be useful in warfare. For example, the Comanche Indians, a Plains Native American culture, adopted horses to pull their travois, a sledlike device used to transport goods, in place of dogs.

European colonization led to the introduction of a variety of domesticated animals, including horses, CATTLE, PIGS AND HOGS, poultry, oxen, and sheep. Horses, pigs, and cattle, in particular, quickly adapted to the North American environment. Grazing by these animals altered the landscape. In addition to eating the vegetation in FORESTS and PRAIRIES, these hoofed animals compacted the earth, depleting soil of nutrients and diminishing its ability to hold water. These changes in topography pushed out oaks and white pines in favor of red cedars and hemlock trees. The use of horses and oxen in farming allowed colonial and subsequent farmers to clear large swaths of forest and to plow a significantly greater amount of land than Indians had used in their SUBSISTENCE AGRICULTURE. Colonists and their American successors also introduced exotic GRASSES to feed these animals, driving out indigenous species.

Originally, the veterinary profession emerged to care for domestic animals used by farmers and a growing meat industry. When Professor Arthur S. Copeman gave the inaugural lecture for the New York College of Veterinary Surgeons in 1865, he emphasized that the goal of VETERINARY MEDICINE was to preserve the health of domestic animals and, by doing so, increase the wealth of the nation. By the end of the 19th century, an emerging veterinary profession played an important part in the U.S. economy. Veterinary schools were established at LAND GRANT INSTITUTIONS focused on agriculture. Professional veterinarians addressed many of the problems that accompanied the increase in numbers and importance of domestic animals. An epidemic of glanders (an infectious respiratory disease), for instance, was potentially devastating to a nation that depended on horses, mules, and donkeys for transportation and agriculture. Texas TICK FEVER was another disease that severely disrupted farms raising cows; an epidemic in 1907 in the American South necessitated bovine quarantines from Virginia to Southern California.

Domestic animals play an important part in keeping humans free of transmissible diseases. In 1894, scientists used horses to produce a diphtheria antitoxin, a vaccine against a disease that ravaged the lives of young children. Soon afterward, they employed sheep, goats, and dogs, but horses, because they were so large, remained the preferred animal. In addition to being able to use living animals to produce vaccines, scientists use animals in laboratories to provide models for certain human diseases and to develop and perfect surgical techniques such as skin transplants, pacemaker implants, and heart bypass operations. Certain animals, such as pigs, have tissues that are similar to human tissues and serve as predictors of success for particular procedures.

The proximity of animals and humans, however, threatened zoonoses—diseases that can be transmitted from animals to humans, such as rabies. Once discovered, however, vaccines have been developed to prevent such occurrences. Rabies, the most frequent animal-to-human disease, has lessened in humans since the 1940s because of vaccination programs that most states and municipalities adopted. Particularly threatening was the TUBERCULOSIS (TB) bacillus, which was transmissible from cows to humans. Although there was controversy over the mode of transmission, TB in domestic animals still required eradication. States, therefore, enacted sanitation measures to prevent the spread and acquisition of the disease.

By 1900, there were 72.8 domestic animals (not including cats, dogs, or poultry) per square mile in the United States. Cats, introduced to the United States in the 18th century, were valued as predators of RODENTS on both farms where GRAINS were stored and in crowded urban areas where rodents posed a threat to human health. There are now 90 million cats and 73 million dogs in the United States. Certain dog breeds such as German shepherds and golden and Labrador retrievers are extremely intelligent and tractable and are used by people with physical disabilities as companion animals.

By 2010, cats and dogs lived in almost 40 percent of all U.S. households. Called pets, many have been further genetically altered so that distinct breeds are recognizable. However, there has been a surplus of nonpedigreed cats and dogs, which often are uncared for and roam freely. The Humane Society of the United States estimates that there are six to eight million unwanted cats and dogs fending for themselves in urban environments. They pose a health problem because of the danger of rabies; animal bites;

spreading of viruses, worms, and infections; and uncontrolled breeding. In addition, since stray animals depend on GARBAGE and other waste to survive, they disrupt the process of food disposal and leave trash in alleyways, streets, and parking lots. Spay and neuter measures became popular in American cities as many pet owners recognized the problems involved with overpopulation and its effect on the environment. Certain animal shelters keep healthy strays so that they may be adopted, but shelters and government agencies have been forced to euthanize many animals for which there were no homes.

See also AGRICULTURE, COLONIAL; DEFORESTATION; DISEASES, ANIMAL; DISEASES, HUMAN; LAND GRANT INSTITUTIONS; POULTRY INDUSTRY; STOCKYARDS AND MEATPACKING.

Lana Thompson

Further Reading
Hough, Walter. "The Domestication of Animals." *Scientific Monthly* 39 (1934): 144–150.

Jones, Susan. *Valuing Animals: Veterinarians and Their Patients in Modern America.* Baltimore: Johns Hopkins University Press, 2003.

Markel, Howard. "Long Ago against Diphtheria, the Heroes Were Horses." *New York Times,* 10 July 2007.

Olsen, Stanley J. "Early Domestic Dogs in North America and Their Origins." *Journal of Field Archaeology* 1 (1974): 344–345.

Opie, John. *Nature's Nation: An Environmental History of the United States.* Fort Worth, Tex.: Harcourt Brace, 1998.

Swabe, Joanna. *Animals, Disease and Human Society: Human-Animal Relations and the Rise of Veterinary Medicine.* London: Routledge, 1969.

Dos Passos, John (1896–1970) *novelist*

John Dos Passos was a major American writer of the 20th century who took as his charge the task of defining America as a place and as a society in all of its complexity. In many books, he sought to capture the essence of the political, social, and cultural landscape of the United States; to plumb its depths; and to reveal its many strengths and frailties. Combining traditional narrative, stream of consciousness, and impressionist description of people, places, and experiences in entirely new ways, Dos Passos focused on the nation's struggles with the transformations and challenges of modernity and industrialization for society and the environment.

Most well known and regarded for his innovative, experimental style in highly political novels in the 1930s, Dos Passos produced some 42 books, including novels, essays, poetry, plays, travel writings, political treatises, histories, and even visual art. His politics shifted controversially after he witnessed firsthand the Spanish civil war

(1936–39) and after the death of his friend Jose Robles in that conflict. Dos Passos, who was initially enamored with Spanish anarchism, moved decisively from the left-leaning stance common to the major American writers of the 1920s and 1930s to a stridently conservative stance on the Right that he maintained for the rest of his life. Throughout this whole period, however, his political transformation did not change his goal of capturing and presenting the experience of Americans throughout the nation in all walks of life and in all regions, from coast to coast and in cities, towns, and the countryside.

John Dos Passos was born on January 14, 1896, in CHICAGO, ILLINOIS, to John Randolph Dos Passos and Lucy Addison Sprigg Madison, who was married to someone else at the time. The young John led a wide-ranging childhood, living in Virginia and traveling extensively in Europe with his mother before his birth parents eventually married. His international experiences as a child and the additional journeys to Europe he took as a young man had a profound influence on his writing. He gathered both political ideas and modernist techniques from a wide array of sources, particularly art and poetry. These perspectives and experiences also encouraged Dos Passos's decision to focus his writing on the American experience, America's national character, and the connections among place, identity, and outlook.

Dos Passos was educated at elite institutions from an early age while continuing to travel often, and after his education at Harvard University, he became a volunteer ambulance driver in WORLD WAR I (1914–18). This experience had a profound impact on Dos Passos's political views and his art, and the experience gave him the subject of his first two novels, *One Man's Initiation—1917* (published in 1920) and more successfully *Three Soldiers* (1921). Within two years, Dos Passos produced a volume of poetry *(A Pushcart at the Curb)* and a book of essays *(Rosinante to the Road Again)*. It was his novel *Manhattan Transfer* (1925) that revealed Dos Passos's developing mastery of experimental style. Influenced by the artistic insights of the cubists and expressionists, Dos Passos employed shifting and fragmented perspective and imagery to capture the chaos, verve, dynamism, and intense atmosphere of 1920s NEW YORK CITY. With this work, Dos Passos stood poised on the edge of literary greatness along with such contemporaries and friends as Ernest Hemingway and e.e. cummings.

Following up on this technique, and also deepening it and improving it, Dos Passos wrote his masterpiece: *U.S.A.,* a trilogy consisting of *The 42nd Parallel* (1930), *Nineteen Nineteen* (1932), and *The Big Money* (1936). It was for this body of work that Dos Passos is best remembered, and deservedly so. In *U.S.A.,* Dos Passos explores the many experiences, events, and transformation of the nation during the first two decades of the 20th century. These three novels were his document of the United States through the stories of the intersecting lives of a wide array of characters, through stream of consciousness sections called Camera Eye, through pastiches of popular media called Newsreels, and through pointedly political biographical sketches of famous and influential Americans. He discerned a commonality running through the American experience just as the 42nd parallel ran through the nation, despite the vastness and diversity of the land. "U.S.A. is the slice of a continent," wrote Dos Passos at the novel's start. Dos Passos was not a nature writer per se. However, concerned, in part, with the implications of industrialization for America, he explored how the new BUILT ENVIRONMENT of cities impoverished and endangered workers. At the same time, changes in COMMERCIAL AGRICULTURE and the use of rural land left the communities of the countryside in disarray. The exploitation of resources, his novels suggested, had led to an exploitation of workers.

This experimental and left-leaning novel gained Dos Passos wide critical acclaim, but this public approval was not destined to last. After his experience observing the Spanish civil war, and unlike many other prominent American novelists at the time such as Ernest Hemingway (1899–1961), Dos Passos began his journey to the political Right, which bewildered and alarmed many of his critics, friends, and readers. He continued to write prolifically on American topics, but most critics do not believe his later works match the intensity, innovation, or mastery of *U.S.A.* Dos Passos traveled widely and produced many more books, and throughout he remained a sharp and incisive interpreter of the United States. Dos Passos died on September 28, 1970.

See also GREAT DEPRESSION; LABOR, AGRICULTURAL; LABOR, EXTRACTIVE INDUSTRIES; LABOR, MANUFACTURING; LITERATURE; NATIONAL IDENTITY, FORMATION OF.

Daniel S. Margolies

Further Reading
Dos Passos, John. *Novels, 1920–1925: One Man's Initiation: 1917, Three Soldiers, Manhattan Transfer.* New York: Library of America, 2003.
———. *Travel Books and Other Writings, 1916–1941.* New York: Library of America, 2003.
———. *U.S.A.: The 42nd Parallel/1919/The Big Money.* New York: Library of America, 1996.
Ludington, Townsend. *John Dos Passos: A Twentieth-Century Odyssey.* New York: Carroll and Graf, 1980.

Douglas, Marjory Stoneman (1890–1998) *writer, environmental activist*

Marjory Stoneman Douglas was instrumental in the founding of EVERGLADES National Park and was the first president of the Friends of the Everglades. She was one of the most influential nature writers of the 20th century.

Born on April 7, 1890, Douglas was the daughter of Frank Bryant Stoneman, a judge, and Lillian Trefethen Stoneman, a violinist. Her parents separated when she was young, and six-year-old Douglas moved with her mother to Taunton, Massachusetts, to live with her maternal grandmother. Douglas's father moved to MIAMI, FLORIDA, and became the first editor of the *News Record,* a newspaper that later became the *Miami Herald.* In 1912, Douglas graduated from Wellesley College with a bachelor's degree in English composition. She married the newspaperman Kenneth Douglas, who was 30 years her senior, in 1914. She realized quickly that the marriage was a mistake, and within a year Douglas moved to Miami, where she reunited with her father and became a reporter for his newspaper. Her divorce was finalized in 1917.

During WORLD WAR I (1914–18), she served as a relief worker for the American Red Cross in Europe. In 1920, she returned to Miami and became an assistant editor at the *Miami Herald.* Douglas soon tired of the pressures of the newspaper business and left to become a short-story writer. Her work was published in prestigious journals, including the *Saturday Evening Post.* Her short story, "Peculiar Treasure of a King," won second place in the O. Henry Prize competition in 1928.

Douglas was an associate professor at the University of Miami from 1925 to 1929. She also developed an interest in the Florida Everglades in the 1920s. In 1927, she was invited to join a committee to promote the establishment of a national park to protect the Everglades's unique and fragile ecosystem. In 1941, Douglas decided to write an expansive study of the ecosystem of the Miami River and the Everglades. The result of her research was *The Everglades: River of Grass,* a natural and human history of the Everglades. Since the book's original publication in 1947, it has sold, on average, 10,000 copies per year.

After the Everglades National Park was founded in 1947, Douglas continued to be an advocate for the region. In 1969, she established the Friends of the Everglades, an environmental organization opposed to development and construction projects in the region.

Douglas was the book review editor for the *Miami Herald* from 1942 to 1949. She published her first novel, *Road to the Sun,* in 1951. In 1952, she received an honorary doctor of letters from the University of Miami. She also served as an editor for the University of Miami Press, from 1960 to 1963.

Douglas was active in her last years even though she was losing her hearing and was legally blind. With John Rothchild, she wrote her autobiography, *Marjory Stoneman Douglas, Voice of the River,* in 1987. President BILL CLINTON awarded her the Presidential Medal of Freedom in 1993. She died at her Coconut Grove home on May 14, 1998, at the age of 108. In 2000, Douglas was inducted into the National

Wildlife Federation Conservation Hall of Fame for her tireless effort in protecting the Everglades and for her leadership in the environmental movement.

See also CONSERVATION; ENVIRONMENTALISM, MAINSTREAM; MEDIA; NATIONAL PARK SERVICE; NATURE WRITING.

Kathy S. Mason

Further Reading

Breton, Mary Joy. *Women Pioneers for the Environment.* Boston: Northeastern University, 1998.

Douglas, Marjory Stoneman. *The Everglades: River of Grass.* 50th anniversary ed. Sarasota, Fla.: Pineapple Press, 1997.

——. *Florida: The Long Frontier.* New York: Harper & Row, 1967.

——. *Freedom River: Florida, 1845.* New York: Scribner, 1953.

——. *Nine Florida Stories.* Jacksonville: University of North Florida Press, 1990.

Douglas, Marjory Stoneman, and John Rothchild. *Marjory Stoneman Douglas: Voice of the River.* Sarasota, Fla.: Pineapple Press, 1987.

Sobel, Dava. "Marjory Stoneman Douglas: Still Fighting the Good Fight for the Everglades." *Audubon* 93 (July 1991): 31–39.

Douglas, William O. (1898–1980) *associate justice, U.S. Supreme Court*

An associate justice of the U.S. Supreme Court from 1939 to 1975, William O. Douglas contributed significantly to the American conservation movement by using his national prominence to draw attention to various CONSERVATION causes and to promote environmental ideas.

Born on October 16, 1898, in Minnesota, Douglas grew up in Yakima, Washington, where childhood illness weakened him. To strengthen himself, he hiked frequently in the CASCADE MOUNTAIN foothills. This time in the outdoors gave Douglas a great respect for the natural world and encouraged him to view nature as a place of independence and healing.

After graduating from Columbia University School of Law, Douglas rose quickly through the professional ranks. He joined the law faculties at Columbia and later Yale. Subsequently, Douglas served on the Securities and Exchange Commission beginning in 1934 and chaired it after 1937. President FRANKLIN D. ROOSEVELT appointed Douglas to the Supreme Court in 1939, the second-youngest justice ever appointed.

His meteoric rise to the court furnished Douglas an opportunity to distinguish himself legally. However, the Court did not contain his considerable energy and intellect, and among other things, Douglas soon became a prolific writer of books and articles. In 1954, he led his first public foray into conservation politics. The NATIONAL PARK SERVICE proposed building a scenic byway along the Chesapeake and Ohio Canal outside the nation's capital. The canal was a favorite hiking spot for Douglas, a place where he left his court duties behind and felt in touch with nature. Douglas led a protest hike with full MEDIA coverage that included many prominent individuals within the conservation community. Four years later, he led a similar hike to protest another proposed road, in Washington State's Olympic National Park. In both cases, Douglas furnished the cause a prominent spokesperson and drew attention to the value of roadless areas. From the 1950s on, Douglas frequently traveled to natural areas under threats from industrial, urban, highway, or resource development, gaining the attention necessary to rally conservationists throughout the nation to help preserve local landscapes.

Besides his activism, Douglas wrote many books that celebrated nature and articulated new ways of thinking about the environment. Books such as *My Wilderness: The Pacific West* (1960), *My Wilderness: East to Katahdin* (1961), and *Farewell to Texas: A Vanishing Wilderness* (1967) extolled diverse places, taught about ecological processes, and publicized various threats. In another book, *A Wilderness Bill of Rights* (1965), Douglas argued that nature possesses rights that deserve permanent legal protection. Furthermore, Douglas tapped into the emerging ideas of the day and insisted on democratic input to natural resource decisions and protection of minority interests. All of these ideas, presented clearly by a national figure, put the emerging environmental ideology into the common language of modern American politics and thus helped make ENVIRONMENTALISM part of the fabric of mainstream American culture.

Finally, as a member of the Supreme Court, Douglas argued for environmental protection. He consistently promoted the government's right to protect natural resources, such as SALMON in his 1967 opinion in *Udall v. FPC* (387 U.S. 428 [1967]), or the responsibility to follow new environmental mandates, such as his decisions in several cases involving the NATIONAL ENVIRONMENTAL POLICY ACT OF 1969 (1970). Most radically, Douglas dissented in *Sierra Club v. Morton* (405 U.S. 727 [1972]), arguing that natural systems themselves ought to have standing (the legal right to initiate a lawsuit). This extension of rights, though not adopted in law, announced a radical perspective and made Douglas the court's strongest backer of ENVIRONMENTAL LAW in history.

After suffering a debilitating stroke, Douglas retired from the Supreme Court, in November 1975. With a term of nearly 37 years, he is the longest-serving justice in the Court's history. Douglas died on January 19, 1980; in his lifetime, he effectively employed his national prominence to gain greater media attention for environmental causes and helped influence modern environmental thought and politics.

See also JUDICIARY; NATURE WRITING; OUTDOOR RECREATION; SIERRA CLUB; WILDERNESS.

Adam M. Sowards

Further Reading

Ball, Howard, and Phillip J. Cooper. *Of Power and Right: Hugo Black, William O. Douglas, and America's Constitutional Revolution.* New York: Oxford University Press, 1992.

Douglas, William O. *Farewell to Texas: A Vanishing Wilderness.* New York: McGraw-Hill, 1967.

———. *A Wilderness Bill of Rights.* Boston: Little, Brown, 1965.

———. *My Wilderness: East to Katahdin.* Garden City, N.Y.: Doubleday, 1961.

———. *My Wilderness: The Pacific West.* Garden City, N.Y.: Doubleday, 1960.

———. *Of Men and Mountains.* New York: Harper, 1950.

———. *The Three Hundred Year War: A Chronicle of Ecological Disaster.* New York: Random House, 1972.

Murphy, Bruce Allen. *Wild Bill: The Legend and Life of William O. Douglas.* New York: Random House, 2003.

Simon, James F. *Independent Journey: The Life of William O. Douglas.* New York: Harper & Row, 1980.

Sowards, Adam M. *The Environmental Justice: William O. Douglas and American Conservation.* Corvallis: Oregon State University Press, 2009.

———. "Modern Ahabs in Texas: William O. Douglas and Lone Star Conservation." *Journal of the West* 44 (Fall 2005): 39–46.

———. "William O. Douglas's Wilderness Politics: Public Protest and Committees of Correspondence in the Pacific Northwest." *Western Historical Quarterly* 37 (Spring 2006): 21–42.

———. "William O. Douglas: The Environmental Justice." In *The Human Tradition in the American West,* edited by Benson Tong and Regan Lutz, 155–170. Wilmington, Delaware: Scholarly Resources, 2002.

Wasby, Stephen L., ed. *"He Shall Not Pass This Way Again": The Legacy of Justice William O. Douglas.* Pitt Series in Policy and Institutional Studies. Pittsburgh: University of Pittsburgh Press for the William O. Douglas Institute, 1990.

Dissent in *Sierra Club v. Morton*
William O. Douglas (1972)

In 1965, the U.S. Forest Service, under its multiple-use policies, made the Mineral King Valley of Sequoia National Forest in California available to prospective developers of ski resorts. The Sierra Club filed a lawsuit hoping to block this activity. In Sierra Club v. Morton, *the U.S. Supreme Court ruled in 1972 that the Sierra Club, in its corporate capacity, lacked standing (the right or capacity to bring suit). However, the Court added that such an organization could sue on behalf of individual members who sustained an aesthetic or recreational loss. The case also is remembered for Associate Justice William O. Douglas's dissent, in which he argued that natural resources should have standing.*

❖

The critical question of "standing" would be simplified and also put neatly in focus if we fashioned a federal rule that allowed environmental issues to be litigated before federal agencies or federal courts in the name of the inanimate object about to be despoiled, defaced, or invaded by roads and bulldozers and where injury is the subject of public outrage. Contemporary public concern for protecting nature's ecological equilibrium should lead to the conferral of standing upon environmental objects to sue for their own preservation. This suit would therefore be more properly labeled as Mineral King v. Morton.

Inanimate objects are sometimes parties in litigation. A ship has a legal personality, a fiction found useful for maritime purposes. The corporation sole—a creature of ecclesiastical law—is an acceptable adversary and large fortunes ride on its cases. The ordinary corporation is a "person" for purposes of the adjudicatory processes, whether it represents proprietary, spiritual, aesthetic, or charitable causes.

So it should be as respects valleys, alpine meadows, rivers, lakes, estuaries, beaches, ridges, groves of trees, swampland, or even air that feels the destructive pressures of modern technology and modern life. The river, for example, is the living symbol of all the life it sustains or nourishes—fish, aquatic insects, water ouzels, otter, fisher, deer, elk, bear, and all other animals, including man, who are dependent on it or who enjoy it for its sight, its sound, or its life. The river as plaintiff speaks for the ecological unit of life that is part of it. Those people who have a meaningful relation to that body of water—whether it be a fisherman, a canoeist, a zoologist, or a logger—must be able to speak for the values which the river represents and which are threatened with destruction . . .

Mineral King is doubtless like other wonders of the Sierra Nevada such as Tuolumne Meadows and the John Muir Trail. Those who hike it, fish it, hunt it, camp in it, frequent it, or visit it merely to sit in solitude and wonderment are legitimate spokesmen for it, whether they may be few or many. Those who have that intimate relation with the inanimate object about to be injured, polluted, or otherwise despoiled are its legitimate spokesmen . . .

The voice of the inanimate object, therefore, should not be stilled. That does not mean that the judiciary takes over the managerial functions from the federal agency. It merely means that before these priceless bits of Americana (such as a valley, an alpine meadow, a river, or a lake) are forever lost or are so transformed as to be reduced to the eventual rubble of our urban environment, the voice of the existing beneficiaries of these environmental wonders should be heard.

Perhaps they will not win. Perhaps the bulldozers of "progress" will plow under all the aesthetic wonders of this beautiful land. That is not the present question. The sole question is, who has standing to be heard?

. . . Those inarticulate members of the ecological group cannot speak. But those people who have so frequented the place as to know its values and wonders will be able to speak for the entire ecological community.

Ecology reflects the land ethic; and Aldo Leopold wrote in *A Sand Country Almanac* (1949), "The land ethic simply enlarges the boundaries of the community to include soils, waters, plants, and animals, or collectively: the land."

That, as I see it, is the issue of "standing" in the present case and controversy.

Source: Sierra Club v. Morton, 405 U.S. 727 (1972), 741–744, 749–752.

drought

The word *drought* conjures images of dust storms and wilted leaves, of nearly skeletal, bony CATTLE and reservoirs drawn so low that docks stand on dry land. Extended periods of below-average precipitation, one definition of drought, have affected the lives of people in North America since the end of the last ICE AGE. Dry episodes lasting from months to multiple centuries occurred in all parts of the continent at various times, forcing the people, plants, and animals to adapt, innovate, and sometimes relocate.

TYPES OF DROUGHT

Multiple definitions of what exactly constitutes a drought exist. Throughout history and into modern times, most people knew the effects of too little moisture when they saw them, but "drought" has taken in many forms and has been described in several ways. Some descriptions are based on climatologic records, such as 30-year average precipitation. A meteorological drought indicates a certain percentage below the 30-year average, or a specific amount of precipitation, or even a set number of days without precipitation. One of the ways meteorological drought in the United States is described is the Palmer Drought Severity Index, a scale of percentages above or below a long-term precipi-

tation and evaporation average. Another definition is an agricultural drought, when precipitation is less than that needed for crops. Hydrologic drought relates to the effects of prolonged dry spells on bodies of water such as lakes, man-made reservoirs, streams, or even subsurface waters. A fourth view of drought considers the effects on people and can be called a socioeconomic drought. This definition incorporates multiple effects of dry weather, including increased food prices due to crop losses, reduced income for people who depend on water-based OUTDOOR RECREATION (no boating because the lake is low), or urban water-use restrictions. Some researchers believe that demand as well as supply should be considered when determining drought conditions.

DROUGHT IN THE PAST

Since the end of the last ice age, approximately 12,000 years ago, extended dry periods have affected parts and occasionally most of North America. Much of our information about these early droughts is gained from archaeological finds, pollen and sediment studies, and tree-ring data. One of the earliest and longest-lasting droughts occurred during a period called the Altithermal (highest temperature), or the Atlantic Climate Period, and extended from 7,500 to 3,000 years ago. Increased temperatures, decreased precipitation, or a combination of both led to the migration of animals and Native peoples out of the southern Great Plains into the ROCKY MOUNTAINS or east into moister areas and into river valleys during most severe parts of this period. The archaeological record from Blackwater Draw at Clovis, New Mexico, during this time shows that the Native people dug wells within stream channels to try to find water as the local groundwater levels dropped and springs and streams dried up.

Pollen records collected from the Chesapeake Basin on the eastern coast of North America show that long droughts are not restricted to the West. Drought, as shown by changes in composition of FORESTS, reduced freshwater inflow to the estuary and other markers, occurred from 50 to 350 C.E., 800 to 1200 C.E., 1320 to 1400 C.E., and 1525 to 1650 C.E. The last of these affected the English settlers on Roanoke Island in present-day North Carolina in the 1580s as well as the Native Americans, all of whose crops suffered. The dry period in the 1300s contributed to the collapse of the Mississippian cultural center at CAHOKIA by intensifying the effects of DEFORESTATION and population stress.

Drought, decreased local resources, and the arrival of Athapascan-speaking groups caused population shifts farther west, as well, during the 1200s–1300s. The people known as the Anasazi left their large settlements in the San Juan Basin of New Mexico and Arizona, moving first into the San Juan mountains at Mesa Verde and then relocating east to join groups already living along the RIO GRANDE. In the

Droughts strike the Great Plains approximately every 20 years. Despite the risks of farming in the region, farmers, with federal government support, moved to the area and suffered the effects of long-term drought.   *(Library of Congress)*

Texas Panhandle, the farmers growing CORN and beans along the Canadian River left the valley in the late 1300s, again as a result of an apparent combination of drought and pressure from new arrivals from the north.

After the arrival of European settlers, dry periods continued to cause problems and to affect settlement, especially as people moved west onto the Great Plains and beyond. Major Stephen Long (1784–1864) of the U.S. Army TOPOGRAPHICAL ENGINEERS crossed the central and southern plains during a dry period in the 1820s and named the area the GREAT AMERICAN DESERT. Drought affected the Southwest and southern plains in the 1850s, while the relatively wet 1870s drew homesteaders onto the plains only to suffer hardships during the dry 1880s, when rain failed to "follow the plow." A hot, dry summer and fall, combined with abundant fuel, contributed to the extensive forest fires in Wisconsin (Peshtigo) and the Upper Peninsula of Michigan and the Great CHICAGO, ILLINOIS, fire in October 1871.

The best-known droughts in North America are those of the 1930s (the DUST BOWL) and the 1950s, although they were not the only droughts. Many ranchers and farmers left West Texas and eastern New Mexico during the dry years between 1917 and 1920. Crop losses in the Upper Midwest between 1987 and 1989 reached into the billions of dollars,

while dry conditions contributed to the forest fires in the mountains of Montana and Wyoming, including the YELLOWSTONE fires. In 2000–01, the normally very damp Pacific Northwest suffered from lack of snowpack and rain both, although the years were not as dry as the record set in 1977. Cities including ATLANTA, GEORGIA, and Chattanooga, Tennessee, restricted water use as record-breaking drought affected the Southeast from 2006 to 2008.

While drought is in many ways a natural phenomenon reflecting below-normal levels of precipitation, its environmental consequences have been exacerbated by human choices. Extensive farming of marginal lands on the Great Plains in the early 1900s, for example, increased the scope of soil erosion in the 1930s. More Americans now live in or near the nation's deserts, since the movement of large segments of the U.S. population to the SUNBELT after WORLD WAR II (1941–45). Their increased demands on limited water resources for residences, businesses, and agriculture create problems at times of shortfalls in rain.

Drought has affected all of North America at some point since the end of the last ice age. European settlers, Native Americans, plants, and animals have dealt with drought in various ways over the centuries and will continue to face wet and dry times in the future.

See also ENGLISH EXPLORATION AND SETTLEMENT—
THE SOUTH; UNITED STATES—CENTRAL PLAINS; UNITED
STATES—MIDWEST; UNITED STATES—PACIFIC NORTHWEST;
UNITED STATES—SOUTHWEST.

Margaret Bickers

Further Reading
National Climate Data Center, National Oceanic and Atmo-
spheric Administration. "Drought: A Paleo-Perspective."
Available online. URL: http://www.ncdc.noaa.gov/paleo/
drought/drght_home.html. Accessed May 15, 2009.
Wilhite, Donald A., and Michael Glantz. "Understanding
Drought Phenomenon: The Role of Definitions." *Water
International* 10 (1983): 111–120.
Willard, Debra A., Thomas M. Cronin, and Stacey Verardo.
"Late Holocene Climate and Ecosystem History from Ches-
apeake Bay Sediment Cores, USA." *Holocene* 13 (2003):
201–214.
Wood, W. Raymond, ed. *Archaeology on the Great Plains.* Law-
rence: University Press of Kansas, 1998.

drugs, pharmaceutical

Since prehistoric time, humans have sought to utilize natural substances in order to improve overall health, extending
into modernity in the form of acupuncture, homeopathy,
and herbal medicine. The current pharmaceutical industry
represents a progression of this pursuit, seeking to develop
new drugs and modified biomolecules that improve human
health or disease management. While ingested drugs, such as
ANTIBIOTICS, pain relievers, and hormones, are biologically
effective in improving human health, the disposal of these
drugs has had a devastating impact on the subtle balance of
the ecological environment.

Pharmaceuticals are defined as medicinal drugs that
target a specific aspect of a symptom or disease. The pharmaceutical industry began in earnest during the 16th and
17th centuries with extensive cataloging of known drugs
and medicinal chemicals. Progress continued through the
19th century. Drugs such as morphine (from opium) were
extracted and quantified, reducing dosing errors and plant-
associated toxicity. Vaccines were created and implemented,
including the rabies vaccine that the French scientist Louis
Pasteur (1822–95) developed. The rabies vaccine was first
used in 1885.

The late 19th century yielded newly discovered classes
of drugs that continue to shape culture and society to this
day. These included artificial sweeteners, synthetic sedatives,
blood vessel dilators, fever reducers, pain relievers, and local
anesthetics. The 20th century saw a marked shift in professional training, from apprenticeships for physicians and
researchers to university-based science departments. Medical schools encouraged and recruited faculty to design pro-

grams of innovation, discovery, and rigorous training that
fueled a drug discovery boom. Importantly, antibiotics such
as penicillin and hormones such as insulin and estrogen were
described and first mass-produced during the 20th century.

In the 21st century, cheaper generic drug prescriptions
for antibiotics and hormones, in combination with pharmacy
shelves replete with over-the-counter pain-relieving medications, have led to a sharp increase in metabolic drug excretion. Whether it is through human metabolic excretory waste
down the drain or through excess or expired pills dumped
into LANDFILLS with leeching rainwater, human disposal
of drugs creates environmental problems. Many physicians
have recognized the often unnecessary overprescription of
the myriad antimicrobials—drugs that inhibit the growth
or spread of a microorganism—especially broad-spectrum
antibiotics. Environmentalists, accordingly, point to the
overuse of these "societal drugs" as the point of intervention
in reducing environmental impact of pharmaceuticals. After
excretion or disposal, the next intervention point is waste
treatment.

The same problems affect the United States and other
industrialized nations. Wastewater processing within sewage
treatment plants worldwide has improved dramatically over
the last century. A striking example of this is in Kristianstad,
Sweden, where stepwise treatment at a tertiary municipal
sewage treatment facility resulted in removal rates of almost
90 percent of multiple pharmaceuticals, metabolites, and
hormones. Unfortunately, untreated waste abounds from
facilities such as hospitals and the pharmaceutical plants that
manufacture drugs. A 2009 report on surface waters in Taiwan indicated that rivers and streams close to multiple pharmaceutical production facilities and hospitals experienced
unprecedented concentrations of both acetaminophen (common pain reliever) and erythromycin (common antibiotic) in
tested waters. The ecological impacts of estrogen-containing
wastewater on FISH populations around the world are well
documented; they include feminization of males and mal-
function of the fish immune system and filtration systems
of the kidneys and liver. Compounding the issue, the resulting mixture of different antibiotic or hormone compounds
within humans' excreted metabolic waste is not accounted for
or controlled by existing environmental impact assessment
in terms of ecological toxicity. Additionally, untreated broad-
spectrum antibiotics in wastewater are probably fostering an
evolutionary process within treatment facility tanks whereby
those microorganisms that are resistant to diverse antibiotics selectively flourish. When these "supermicroorganisms"
are released into the aquatic environment, humans acquire
infections that no longer respond to antibiotic treatment.

From metabolic drug waste to GLOBAL WARMING, it is
apparent that human innovation across a broad spectrum
of technologies resulting from the Industrial Revolution
has been at the expense of the environment. The challenge

for the future of the pharmaceutical industry, and for all humans, is to act responsibly in adopting stronger ecological assessment indices in disposal and in reducing consumption of easily accessible drugs. As humans move into the era of "personalized medicine," when treatment options for a range of illnesses will be determined according to an individual's unique genetic profile, it may be possible to curtail usage of pharmaceuticals and aid in restoring ecological balance.

See also DISEASES, HUMAN; EVOLUTION; HEALTH AND MEDICINE; WASTE DISPOSAL AND MANAGEMENT.

Isaiah G. Schauer

Further Reading

Blasco, M. D., et al. "Multiresistant Waterborne Pathogens Isolated from Water Reservoirs and Cooling Systems." *Journal of Applied Microbiology* 105 (August 2008): 469–475.

Filby, A. L., et al. "Health Impacts of Estrogens in the Environment, Considering Complex Mixture Effects." *Environmental Health Perspectives* 115 (December 2007): 1,704–1,710.

Lin, A. Y., and Y. T. Tsai. "Occurrence of Pharmaceuticals in Taiwan's Surface Waters: Impact of Waste Streams from Hospitals and Pharmaceutical Production Facilities." *Science of the Total Environment* 407 (June 1, 2009): 3,793–3,802.

Liney, K. E., et al. "Health Effects in Fish of Long-Term Exposure to Effluents from Wastewater Treatment Works." *Environmental Health Perspectives* 114 (April 2006): 81–89.

Sarkar, P., et al "Antimicrobial Agents Are Societal Drugs: How Should This Influence Prescribing?" *Drugs* 66 (2006): 893–901.

DuBois, W. E. B. (William Edward Burghardt DuBois) (1868–1963) *sociologist, author, civil rights activist*

One of the most important black civil rights leaders in the first half of the 20th century, W. E. B. (William Edward Burghardt) DuBois was known as one of the fathers of Pan-Africanism—a movement seeking to unify Africans and members of the African diaspora into a global community—a title earned through his numerous publications, speeches, and activities promoting black solidarity and social advancement. An outspoken opponent of RACISM AND DISCRIMINATION, DuBois is often cited for his thoughts on the "double consciousness" of African Americans, expressed in *The Souls of Black Folk* (1903), which he saw as a fracturing of racial identity enabling blacks variously to "act white" or "act black" as the situation required. Dedicated to the philosophy of "agitate and educate," DuBois was one of the founders of the NATIONAL ASSOCIATION FOR THE ADVANCEMENT OF COLORED PEOPLE (NAACP) in 1909 and served as editor in chief of the organization's publication, *The Crisis: A Record of the Darker Races,* pub-

lishing the works of HARLEM RENAISSANCE authors such as Langston Hughes and Jean Toomer.

Born in Great Barrington, Massachusetts, on February 23, 1868, DuBois worked odd jobs as a child to help his invalid mother; his father deserted the family when DuBois was two years old. Believing education offered him a chance to improve his family's situation and encouraged by teachers, DuBois attended Fisk University, a historically black college in Nashville, Tennessee, earning a degree in 1888. He then entered Harvard University, where he earned a bachelor's degree in 1890 and a doctorate in sociology in 1895—the first African American to receive a Ph.D. at Harvard. In his career, he taught at Wilberforce University in Ohio, the University of Pennsylvania, and Atlanta University in Georgia. In 1910, he became the publications director for the NAACP.

DuBois was a contemporary of the activists BOOKER T. WASHINGTON and William Monroe Trotter (1872–1934) in the United States and the global Pan-Africanists Marcus Garvey (1887–1940), Ahmed Sekou Toure (1922–84), and Edward Wilmot Blyden (1832–1912), though his conflicts with both Washington and Garvey over methods and ideologies became legendary. His major writings range from early sociological work on black communities, and the intersection of race and criminology in the United States, to later writings focused on peace issues and on African history. Additionally, DuBois authored countless articles and essays, as well as three autobiographies, during his long career.

One of DuBois's critical contributions to the study of African-American communities and ENVIRONMENTAL JUSTICE is *The Philadelphia Negro* (1899). Within this extensive study of the "condition of the forty thousand or more people of Negro blood now living in the city of Philadelphia," DuBois sought to understand the role of environment in what he termed "the many Negro problems of a great American city." The 15-month study of the social, political, and physical environments of African-American households in the Seventh Ward was a pathbreaking examination of the environmental context of these households, noted for its exploration of the urban environment's role in physical and social health, recreation, economics, resource use, and crime.

DuBois's study cited significant, complex environmental degradation in the Seventh Ward, in the form of overcrowding, poor ventilation, filth due to inadequate refuse disposal and the absence of sewer services, poor drainage, few private toilets, limited sunlight, poor public lighting, and little to no available space for recreation. According to DuBois, this constellation of environmental deficits was specific to the African-American community and was statistically significantly linked to social ills such as violence, crime, poverty, unemployment, and domestic instability, along with public health issues—making his study one of the earliest examinations of environmental injustice in African-American communities in the United States, as well as one of the earliest explorations of the interrelationships among race, degraded urban environments, civic demoralization, and widespread social ills.

Frustrated with persistent racism in the United States, DuBois moved to Ghana and became an expatriate. He died there on August 27, 1963.

See also GARBAGE; GHETTOS, SLUMS, AND BARRIOS; PHILADELPHIA, PENNSYLVANIA; URBANIZATION; WASTE DISPOSAL AND MANAGEMENT; WATER, DRINKING.

Cynthia J. Miller

Further Reading
DuBois, W. E. B. *The Philadelphia Negro.* New York: Lippincott, 1899.
———. *The Souls of Black Folk.* Chicago: A. C. McLurge & Co., 1903.
Lewis, David Levering. *W. E. B. DuBois, 1868–1919: Biography of a Race.* New York: Holt Paperbacks, 1994.

Ducks Unlimited

Established in 1937, Ducks Unlimited has emerged as a significant CONSERVATION group involved with WETLANDS and waterfowl protection in North America. The DUST BOWL that enveloped the central and northern plains in the 1930s served as a catalyst for this group's founding, as severe DROUGHTS in the breeding grounds in Canada's PRAIRIES resulted in a serious decline in the U.S. waterfowl population.

Joseph Knapp held the first organizational meeting of Ducks Unlimited in 1936, and the group was incorporated in WASHINGTON, D.C., one year later. Their Canadian chapter was founded in 1938. One of Ducks Unlimited's first projects was restoring the Canadian Big Grass Marsh, located in Manitoba. By the early 1940s, the water level in the Big Grass Marsh was at full supply, and waterfowl population in CANADA AND THE UNITED STATES significantly increased. From that point on, the organization grew in membership, size, and scope.

Ducks Unlimited primarily focuses on restoring grasslands, FORESTS, and WETLANDS. In some cases, Ducks Unlimited has purchased critical habitats in order to protect them. In addition, the organization provides incentives to landowners and farmers, encouraging wetlands restoration as well as reductions in carbon dioxide emissions and WATER POLLUTION. Ducks Unlimited's Conservation Easement program offers legal agreements between the organization and landowners, providing a plan for habitat protection as well as development opportunities for the landowners. Ducks Unlimited's primary focuses are waterfowl conservation and the SUSTAINABILITY of water-

fowl hunting, but their efforts have expanded over time to include broader environmental problems, such as climate change and water quality.

Ducks Unlimited prioritizes projects according to their severity. As of 2007, the most critical projects included the Prairie Pothole Region of southwestern Canada and the NORTHERN PLAINS in the United States, the Western Boreal Forest in Canada, the MISSISSIPPI RIVER's alluvial valley, the central coastal valleys of CALIFORNIA, and the Gulf coastal prairies of Texas and Louisiana. Besides encouraging land stewardship and conservation easements, Ducks Unlimited provides scientific data on habitat loss, through waterfowl inventories and the mapping of habitats through geographic information systems (GIS).

While much of the organization's work is done at the grassroots level, through local chapters and fund-raising, Ducks Unlimited also maintains a significant presence in Washington, D.C., as a traditional lobbying organization, meeting with members of CONGRESS, conferring with agencies, and filing amicus briefs for court cases, particularly those dealing with federal protection of wetlands. Besides lobbying for public policy, the organization regularly works with federal agencies, such as the FISH AND WILDLIFE SERVICE and the DEPARTMENT OF AGRICULTURE, and relies on federal funding through grants for part of its annual budget. Besides state and federal grants, Ducks Unlimited has developed several partnerships with major corporations for support, including Budweiser, GMC Trucks, Winchester Ammunition, and Pennzoil. These partnerships range from product licensing, which provides companies the right to sell products with the Ducks Unlimited logo, to major philanthropic projects, in which corporations provide funding for wetlands restoration. One criticism of this approach stems from preservationist and deep ecology environmentalists, who believe that habitats and species need to be absolutely protected by preventing all hunting. Ducks Unlimited's prohunting stance stands in sharp disagreement with the position of many animal rights activists. In 2006, Ducks Unlimited expanded its strategies and grassroots efforts. The organization sponsors Project Webfoot, a wetlands education program provided to schools, as well as Hunt & Home, a home party sales program, where consumers can purchase Ducks Unlimited spices, breads, and sauces, focusing on game cooking.

With chapters in every state, and a national headquarters in Memphis, Tennessee, Ducks Unlimited had nearly 800,000 members in North America as of early 2008. About 9 percent of its members are children, joining through their "Greenwing" program, which publishes the magazine *Puddlers* for children. Adult members receive a subscription to *Ducks Unlimited Magazine,* as well as decals and other benefits, in exchange for their 25 dollar membership fee. Ducks Unlimited also has international chapters in Canada, Mexico, parts of Latin America and the Caribbean, and Australia, where the group's name is Wetland Care Australia.

See also BIRDS; ECOLOGICAL RESTORATION; ENVIRONMENTALISM, GRASSROOTS; ENVIRONMENTALISM, MAINSTREAM; ENVIRONMENTALISM, OPPOSITION TO; GRASSES; HUNTING, RECREATIONAL; MEXICO AND THE UNITED STATES; NONGOVERNMENTAL ORGANIZATIONS; UNITED STATES—GULF COAST.

Melinda Mueller and Brittany Hoerdeman

Further Reading

Ducks Unlimited. "2006 Annual Report." Ducks Unlimited Web site. Available online. URL: http://www.ducks.org. Accessed April 26, 2007.

Environmental Protection Agency. "Wetlands, Oceans & Watersheds," EPA Web site. Available online. URL: http://www.epa.gov/owow/. Accessed April 30, 2007.

Lowery, David, and Holly Brasher. *Organized Interests and American Government.* Boston: McGraw-Hill, 2004.

Vaughn Switzer, Jacqueline. *Environmental Politics: Domestic and Global Dimensions.* 4th ed. Belmont, Calif.: Thomson Wadsworth, 2004.

dust bowl

In the 1930s, an ecological disaster known as the dust bowl engulfed North America's Great Plains. Caused by a confluence of human decisions and natural phenomena, the crisis also spurred greater federal intervention in American agriculture.

While many areas of the United States experienced unusually dry, hot weather during the 1930s, the Great Plains states bore the brunt of repeated DROUGHT and high temperatures. Farmers across the region faced withered crops and starving livestock, but the residents of the southern plains—in an oval-shaped area dubbed the dust bowl—suffered from persistent dust storms and severe wind erosion. In large part, they had arrived in the years just before and after WORLD WAR I, (1914–18) pushing onto arid lands where success was far from certain and hoping to cultivate large sections of WHEAT with the aid of gasoline tractors and combine harvesters. As wheat prices dropped in the 1920s, the settlers and speculators borrowed money for more machinery and broke sod for more wheat. They jettisoned more prudent forms of soil preparation such as listing, which left the soil in alternating ridges and better able to withstand the wind, and used a new form of AGRICULTURAL TECHNOLOGY, the disc plow, because it more quickly broke sod and destroyed WEEDS. The plows also laid bare large stretches of sandy soils that were particularly vulnerable to wind EROSION.

Drought, which prevented the wheat from growing and holding the soil intact, first appeared in summer 1931, when one-third of the Panhandle area of Oklahoma, Texas, western Kansas, southeastern Colorado, and northeastern New

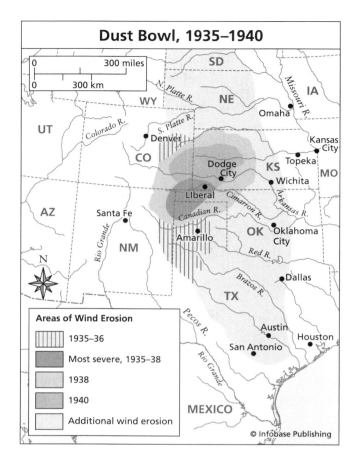

Mexico was plowed under and the soil exposed. Strong winds whipped the dirt into dust clouds that wreaked havoc for the next several years. Federal officials estimated that a single dust storm in May 1934 carried away 300 million tons of fertile topsoil, depositing some of it as far away as the Atlantic Ocean. Further government investigations in the 1930s revealed that in some dust bowl counties, wind had blown out more than half of the land planted to grain, and many farmers had abandoned their homes.

Arriving during the GREAT DEPRESSION, the drought and dust bowl highlighted the entwined scourges of soil erosion and rural poverty and drew the nation's attention to the plight of those suffering from both afflictions. Some of the era's most capable artists and documentarians captured the combined natural and social disaster with exceptionally memorable literature, photography, music, and film. Many dust bowl residents, weighted with poverty and desperation, indeed left their homes. However, most farmers remained in the area and weathered the emergency with help from government relief and reconstruction programs. The dust bowl area, in fact, received more federal funds per capita than any other agricultural region; drought-stricken farmers benefited from commodity support payments, emergency cattle purchases, emergency listing funds, soil conservation programs, relief grants, crop and seed loans, and jobs with NEW DEAL employment agencies such as the Works Progress Administration and the Public Works Administration.

The tragedy also provided an opportunity for a number of federal officials to denounce the "pioneer psychology" that had resulted in such degradation. New Deal agricultural administrators initially promoted the analysis that the Plains' conversion from rangeland to cropland had precipitated the disaster and contended that the only sure way to address both soil erosion and low farm incomes was to restore much of the region to grazing. The federal government subsequently acquired more than seven million acres on the northern and southern plains and in the Southwest; some of this was in the dust bowl area, and much became part of a new network of national grasslands. Though many dust bowl residents asked to be relieved of tax-delinquent and submarginal land, these purchases soon aroused fierce resistance from local inhabitants. Asking farmers to accept lower-density settlements, with fewer community amenities, struck at the very heart of FRONTIER ideology; many Plains residents and their political representatives feared that President FRANKLIN D. ROOSEVELT's administration ultimately intended to "depopulate" the Plains. Even the president appeared to be part of this conspiracy to restore the region to

grass: "Instead of using it for pastures," Roosevelt said of the dust bowl in 1936, "we are using it for wheat." Government officials soon backpedaled, however, reassuring Plains farmers that the federal government stood ready with an array of technical assistance programs and SOIL CONSERVATION techniques intended to help farmers retain their livelihoods and improve their yields. The return of rain in the early 1940s allowed Plains residents to imagine a future free of drought and—at least in theory—the federal government. Continued federal support, however, removed much of the risk from farming in the volatile climate, as did the increased use of pump IRRIGATION after WORLD WAR II.

Few environmental events have provoked as much scholarly debate as the origins and meaning of the dust bowl. For some historians, it remains the signature episode in the continental development of an industrial CAPITALISM heedless of ecological integrity and inevitably precipitating environmental disaster. For others, the dust bowl represents an unfortunate confluence of technological, cultural, and climatic conditions—a confluence Plains residents faced squarely, if stubbornly, eventually adapting to the fluctuating environment and to tremendous social and political change.

Blowing dirt from drought-stricken fields covered nearly everything in its path. Winds carried Great Plains topsoil as far as New York and Boston. *(Library of Congress)*

Recent research with meticulously gathered census data finds land use patterns in the Great Plains relatively stable over the 20th century, with the period from 1925 to 1940 marking a relatively mild course correction when crop farmers pushed a little too far onto marginal land and pulled back slightly. In this analysis, the factors of low rainfall and very high temperatures were more critical in triggering a county's dust storms during the 1930s than the amount of plowed acreage or its soil composition. Whatever the cause, for most Americans, the ferocity of the storms and the devastation left behind remained etched in their collective imagination and served as a cautionary tale about land conservation.

See also AGRICULTURE, COMMERCIAL; AGRICULTURE, DEPARTMENT OF; AQUIFERS; GRASSES; GUTHRIE, WOODY; SHARECROPPING; STEINBECK, JOHN; UNITED STATES—CENTRAL PLAINS; UNITED STATES—NORTHERN PLAINS; UNITED STATES—SOUTHWEST.

Sarah T. Phillips

Further Reading

Cunfer, Geoff. *On the Great Plains: Agriculture and Environment.* College Station: Texas A&M University Press, 2005.

Egan, Timothy. *The Worst Hard Time: The Untold Story of Those Who Survived the Great American Dust Bowl.* Boston: Houghton Mifflin, 2005.

Hurt, R. Douglas. *The Dust Bowl: An Agricultural and Social History.* Chicago: Nelson Hall, 1981.

Phillips, Sarah T. *This Land, This Nation: Conservation, Rural America, and the New Deal.* New York: Cambridge University Press, 2007.

Riney-Kehrberg, Pamela. *Rooted in Dust: Surviving Drought and Depression in Southwestern Kansas.* Lawrence: University Press of Kansas, 1994.

Worster, Donald. *Dust Bowl: The Southern Plains in the 1930s.* New York: Oxford University Press, 1979.

Dutch colonial settlements

In 1609, on behalf of the Dutch East India Company, the English explorer Henry Hudson (1565–1611) sailed up the river that would eventually bear his name. The Hudson River, known as the North River to the Dutch, would serve as the main artery for the eventual New Netherland colony. While the focus of New Netherland is often on the Hudson River and its settlements of Fort Orange, Beverwijck (present-day Albany), and New Amsterdam (present day NEW YORK CITY), at different times, the colony also included settlements on the Connecticut and Delaware Rivers. Much as in the water-based environment of the Netherlands, the life blood of New Netherland flowed along these rivers, but particularly along the waters of the Hudson. Although the colony was rather short-lived (1614–64) in comparison to its French and English neighbors, its effect on the lives and land within its proclaimed borders was significant.

TRADE COLONY

The name *New Netherland* first appeared on maps in 1614 when the New Netherland Company received a trade license from the Dutch government and established a FUR TRADE post on the upper reaches of the HUDSON RIVER at present-day Albany. In 1621, the Dutch government chartered the West India Company (WIC), which took over the colony in 1624. Settlement expanded beyond Albany to include the trade center of New Amsterdam at the southern tip of Manhattan Island, in 1626. It was these settlements that actually allowed the WIC to make a legal claim to the land. Without a physical presence on the land in the form of forts, trade centers, and, most importantly, people, a claim of possession would not stand against competing European claims. Therefore, more colonists would be needed.

Descriptions of New Netherland focused on trying to lure more colonists to the shores of the Hudson River by emphasizing the bounty of natural resources and the usefulness of those resources for the WIC and the Dutch homeland. Rivers were lauded for their navigability, soil for its fertility, hills for their mineral potential, and coastlines for their ports and abundant aquatic resources. All of these observations could be, and often were, made from the deck of a ship sailing the Hudson. The Dutch settlers and officials actually knew very little about the colony's interior. However, it was the animal resources of the interior lands that proved to be the economic boon for the WIC.

BEAVER pelts were the primary trade resource for most of New Netherland's existence, and because they were so valuable, the WIC maintained a monopoly in the trade until 1639, when it opened the beaver trade to other competitors. During the years of the WIC fur trade monopoly, the numbers of beaver pelts exported to Europe more than doubled from approximately 4,000 pelts in 1624 to about 8,800 pelts in 1633. The measured value of those furs in Dutch guilders more than tripled in that same period from 27,125 in 1624 to 91,375 in 1635. The volume of furs exported from Beverwijck downriver to New Amsterdam continued to rise, reaching just less than 38,000 pelts for 1657, after which the trade fell into decline.

While the Dutch exported the pelts, they relied on Native Americans actually to supply the beavers from farther and farther in the interior, particularly as local beaver populations declined as a result of overhunting. Competition among Indian tribes to control the trade led to what historians have described as the "Beaver Wars" in the 1640s and 1650s, when rival groups are said to have fought one another to control the trade and capture increasingly scarce pelts. However, there is little quantitative evidence to verify the validity of this argument. Another issue that could have led to a decline in the trade was a decline in the price Europeans were willing to pay for the pelts. After 1658, there appears to have been a drop in the price, which may have made fewer traders willing to participate in the beaver trade. It would seem that a combination of inter-Indian warfare, a decrease of the beaver population due to overhunting, and a drop in demand from Europe contributed to a decline in the trade.

SETTLEMENT COLONY

New Netherland, as a colony focused on trade, did not see the tremendous growth in population that its New England neighbors experienced during the mid-17th century. In the 1640s and into the 1650s, New Netherland also began to expand as a settlement colony with an interest in more sustained agriculture, particularly to feed the Dutch colonies in the West Indies. While New Netherland produced only limited amounts of GRAINS to send to its West Indian colonies, the local food supply did increase, and settlers began exporting TOBACCO as well as beaver pelts to the Netherlands. As the Dutch established new settlements, particularly along the Hudson River and on Long Island, the new demand for land caused tensions with local Indian populations. Much of the problem resulted from very different cultural understandings of land use and landownership. While Europeans viewed farming the land and holding a deed to the land as proper use and ownership, the area's Native populations viewed land as a source of resources to sustain life, both material and spiritual, and did not view it in terms of a commodity to be bought and sold. As the WIC approved more settlements, Native peoples and European settlers, and their worldviews, were increasingly in conflict.

THE END OF NEW NETHERLAND

In September 1664, the English took over New Netherland without firing a shot, thereby establishing the colony of New York. Although New Netherland lasted for only 50 years, it had a profound impact on the environment, not just within its claimed boundaries, but well beyond, as beaver populations were dramatically altered through the fur trade. Furthermore, as Indian peoples were forced off their lands to make way for European expansion, the Dutch, as did other Europeans, established not only European farming methods and crops but also the understanding that the land of North America, and by extension the resources on it, would be seen as a commodity to be bought, sold, and possessed.

See also AGRICULTURE, COLONIAL; ENGLISH EXPLORATION AND SETTLEMENT—THE MIDDLE COLONIES; INDIANS, NORTHEAST; UNITED STATES—NORTHEAST.

Holly A. Rine

Further Reading

Brandao, Jose A. *"Your Fyre Shall Burn No More": Iroquois Policy toward New France and Its Native Allies to 1701.* Lincoln: Nebraska University Press, 1997.

Burke, Thomas. "The New Netherland Fur Trade, 1657–1661: Response to Crisis." *Halve Maen: Magazine of the Dutch Colonial Period in America* 59, no. 3 (1986): 1–21.

Jacops, Jaap. *New Netherland: A Dutch Colony in Seventeenth-Century America.* The Atlantic World: Europe, Africa and the Americas, 1500–1830. Series edited by Wim Klooster and Benjamin Schmidt. Boston: Brill, 2005.

Starna, William A., and Jose A. Brandao. "From the Mohawk-Mahican War to the Beaver War: Questioning the Pattern." *Ethnohistory* 51 (2004): 725–750.

Learning from the Indians in New Netherland Adriaen van der Donck (1655)

Adriaen van der Donck (1618–55), a Dutch lawyer and landowner in New Netherland, promoted immigration to the colony (later known as New York) by extolling its topography, climate, waterways, vegetation, and animals. Arriving in 1641, he was impressed by the region's rich forests—particularly given the absence of such resources in the Netherlands. Initially employed as a kind of sheriff, van der Donck met with local Indians, learning and recording their language, customs, beliefs, and technology.

The Indians have a yearly custom (which some of our Christians have also adopted) of burning the woods, plains and meadows in the fall of the year, when the leaves have fallen, and when the grass and vegetable substances are dry. Those places which are then passed over are fired in the spring in April. This practice is named by us and the Indians, *"bush burning,"* which is done for several reasons; first, to render hunting easier, as the bush and vegetable growth renders the walking difficult for the hunter, and the crackling of the dry substances betrays him and frightens away the game. Secondly, to thin out and clear the woods of all dead substances and grass, which grow better the ensuing spring. Thirdly, to circumscribe and enclose the game within the lines of the fire, when it is more easily taken, and also, because the game is more easily tracked over the burned parts of the woods.

The bush burning presents a grand and sublime appearance. On seeing it from without, we would imagine that not only the dry leaves, vegetables and limbs would be burnt, but that the whole woods would be consumed where the fire passes, for it frequently spreads and rages with such violence, that it is awful to behold; and when the fire approaches houses, gardens, and wooden enclosures, then great care and vigilance are necessary for their preservation, for I have seen several houses which have recently been destroyed, before the owners were apprized of their danger. . . .

Frequently great injuries are done by such fires, but the burning down of entire woods never happens. . . .

Hence it will appear that there actually is such an abundance of wood in the New-Netherlands, that, with ordinary care, it will never be scarce there. There always are, however, in every country, some people so improvident, that even they may come short here, and for this reason we judge that it should not be destroyed needlessly. There, however, is such an abundance of wood, that they who cultivate the land for planting and sowing can do nothing better than destroy it, and thus clear off the land for tillage, which is done by cutting down the trees and collecting the wood into great heaps and burning the same, to get it out of their way. Yellow and white pine timber, in all their varieties, is abundant here, and we have heard the Northerners say (who reside here) that the pine is as good here as the pine of Norway.

❈

Source: Adriaen van der Donck. *Description of the New Netherlands.* Translated by Jeremiah Johnson. New York: New York Historical Society, 1841, 150–151.

Dutch elm disease

Dutch elm disease is a fungal disease spread by the elm bark beetle. Believed to be indigenous to Asia, the beetle was introduced into North America and Europe, where it devastated native elm trees that had not developed a resistance to the disease.

When the fungus *Ophiostoma ulmi* (also once known as *Ceratosystis ulmi*) attaches itself to a tree, it begins a parasitical relationship detrimental to the tree. This relationship is known as Dutch elm disease. Elm bark beetles *(Scolytus scolytus* and *Scolytus multistiiatus)* transmit the fungus between trees. The life cycle of the fungus begins when young beetles emerge from the bark of dead trees in spring. Carrying fungal spores with them, they fly to the young shoots of healthy elm trees nearby and begin to feed on the bark. Any damage to the underlying xylem vessels, which carry water and nutrients and strengthen the tree, facilitates the entry of the fungal spores. The fungus then spreads rapidly, causing yellowing of the leaves and the death of branches; eventually, the entire tree may die. The dead bark provides a suitable medium in which the fungus thrives and in which the elm bark beetle lays its eggs; the bark provides food as well as shelter and

the young beetles emerge in the spring to repeat the process. Gradually, entire woodlands or FORESTS can lose their elm populations through this process.

The first indication of a disease seriously affecting European elm trees (of the Ulmaceae family and *Ulmus* genus) occurred after 1910 in the Netherlands. Elm tree mortality became commonplace, and Dutch researchers undertook intensive studies between 1919 and 1934 that identified the culprit as the fungus *Ophiostoma ulmi.* Although Dutch researchers identified the disease, and thus the name, it probably originated in and was transported in logs from Central Asia to Europe and North America. In the latter two continents, elm tree mortality was high between 1920 and 1940. In European countries, losses of between 10 percent and 40 percent occurred. In Europe, the disease abated, but in North America, approximately half of the population of 77 million trees, notably of *Ulmus americana* (American elm), had been lost in the northeastern states alone by 1976. Dutch elm disease raged again in the mid-1960s to devastate British and Canadian elm populations. In Britain, for example, some 25 million elms, mostly native species of *Ulmus glabra* (Wych elm), *Ulmus minor* (smooth-leaved elm), and *Ulmus procera* (English elm), had been lost by the early 1990s out of a population of 30 million. On the basis of molecular studies and the failure of interbreeding, this more recent fungus strain has been identified as a new species and named *Ophiostoma novo ulmi.* Elm tree loss from Europe and North America has significantly altered landscape characteristics and woodland composition. People in North America widely planted elms in urban woodlands, parks, and gardens and along roads and substantially altered urban landscapes and temperate forests extending from eastern Canada to Florida.

The elm decline of the 20th century may not have been the only such phenomenon. The dynamics of the disease have led ecologists to speculate that the demise of elms between 8,000 and 4,500 years ago in Europe, as reflected in the pollen spectra of lake sediments and peats, may have been caused by an outbreak of Dutch elm disease as the first farmers and agriculture spread westward and opened up forests.

See also CHESTNUT BLIGHT; GLOBALIZATION; INSECTS; SPECIES, EXOTIC AND INVASIVE; SPECIES, INDIGENOUS.

A. M. Mannion

Further Reading

French, David W. *History of Dutch Elm Disease in Minnesota.* University of Minnesota Extension Service. Available online. URL: http://www.extension.umn.edu/distribution/natural resources/DD3765.html. Accessed September 8, 2008.

dying, death, and body disposal

Every culture has possessed a commitment to their dying and dead. Passage from life to death presented enormous challenges for the living. Where they deposited human remains and how they modified those remains before decomposition depended upon relatives, communities, and environments.

For pre-Columbian Native Americans, dying and the rituals associated with death varied as much as the geography. Many tribes let corpses decay naturally, either aboveground on a platform or buried in a shallow grave. Mississippian cultures (800–1500 C.E.), living from Florida to the Upper Midwest, buried bodies in earthen mounds. Some elaborate mounds remain extant in the OHIO RIVER and MISSISSIPPI RIVER watersheds. In extenuating circumstances, such as famines, survivors ate the flesh of the deceased to survive. These Indians regarded death as a normal, natural phase of the life cycle, although certain groups believed that malevolent spirits or forces caused death and disease. Early in the colonial period, Europeans attempted to force conquered indigenous groups to adopt Christianity and accompanying customs regarding body disposal. Many Native Americans acquiesced to practice Christianity after being tortured and accused of heresy.

RELIGION was an important element in several early American colonies. Christian services involved a religious service and burial. In some areas, churches denied Christian burials to "sinners" (unmarried pregnant women, adulterers, criminals, and non-Christians), disposing of their bodies in pits or unsanctified areas. Christians were often buried in yards adjacent to churches and set aside for burial. European American colonial grave markers were often flat with death's head images referred to as *memento mori* that served as reminders that death was imminent. By the late 18th and 19th centuries, ornate statuary of angels and heavenly subjects replaced skulls and frightening icons. Monuments increasingly expressed sentiment.

As urban populations grew in 19th-century America, towns located cemeteries close to populations but far from the main town activities. The "rural" cemetery movement coincided with the age of ROMANTICISM, and beautifully manicured cemeteries began appearing in scenic areas around urban centers. Building on European burial aesthetics, Mount Auburn Cemetery outside Boston was the first of a number of elevated and meticulously landscaped cemeteries near major urban areas that were closely related to an emergence of CITY AND SUBURBAN PARKS through the 19th and early 20th centuries.

By the mid-19th century, more public parlors began replacing family-oriented wakes. Embalming in the United States began at the time of the CIVIL WAR (1861–65), allowing armies to preserve dead soldiers and ship them home for burial services. Embalmers used various chemicals. One such formula required removal of the abdominal viscera before packing the cavity with potter's clay and crystallized carbolic acid. Over the next 100 years, embalming became standard practice.

Embalmers in the 1860s used heavy metals such as arsenic and antimony. When archaeologists exhumed mid-19th-century graves, they found well-preserved bodies that belie their 100-plus years of entombment. With the advent of refrigeration, the need for strong chemicals relaxed and more recent embalming practices use combinations of formalin and ethylene glycol (similar to antifreeze). The growing popularity of open caskets for viewing meant that faces and upper extremities required extensive embalming prior to cosmetic preparation. African-American embalmers developed superior techniques in the 20th century because many of their mortuaries lacked refrigeration.

Cremation in the United States was influenced by European customs. It began in France during the 18th century as a protest against existing funeral rites. Charles Nicolas de Beauvais, a physician and member of the National Assembly, was cremated in 1794. His ashes were put in an urn and placed in the national archives. A century later, a Belgian journal, *La Cremation*, begun in 1906, disseminated information about cremation throughout Europe. Cremation became quite popular in Europe as a supposedly more hygienic method of body disposal.

Although some Native Americans practiced forms of cremation, the first documented cremation of a European American occurred in 1792. Colonel Henry Laurens, a planter from South Carolina and president of the Continental Congress, was more fearful of being buried alive than of dying, so he specified in his will that unless he was burned, he would not bequeath his estate to his children. His family honored his wishes by cremating him on his estate.

Cremation gained popularity in the United States in the 20th century, particularly in urban areas where land for burial was getting scarce. In 1963, cremation followed some 4 percent of deaths. By 1999, the figure rose to 25 percent. Muslims, conservative Christians, African Americans, Jews, Mormons, and Catholics maintain certain religious or cultural objections to cremation. In 1970, African Americans were five times less likely than whites to choose cremation, but, by 1990, that figure decreased significantly. In 1996, the National Conference of Catholic Bishops requested a special dispensation to allow cremated remains at funeral masses. The Vatican granted it, provided that ashes remained in a worthy vessel or grave, mausoleum, or columbarium. Not all Catholic Americans followed that dictum. After John F. Kennedy, Jr., died in 1999, his family honored his wishes and scattered his cremated remains at sea.

In the latter part of the 19th century, an entire funeral industry emerged. Funeral homes assumed the role of caretakers of the dead from families. Public cemeteries on huge expanses of land emerged throughout rural America. Mausoleums allowed aboveground burials, especially important in coastal and low-lying areas and urban areas, where, to maximize space, bodies could be stacked vertically. Cremation also minimized the growth of cemeteries by allowing families to dispose of ashes or keep them in receptacles. By 2008, in the state of Florida, approximately 55 percent of dead bodies were cremated. High water tables partly account for this high percentage, but the large retirement population means people who die in Florida often have relatives who want the ashes sent to other states.

As Americans turned their sights toward environmental CONSERVATION and PRESERVATION in the 20th century, they addressed burial practices. Cremations reduced the decaying or preserved organic matter of the human body to inert sterile ashes, although residue from fillings, pacemakers, or other medical devices remained. Embalmed bodies gave cause for concern. Many people worried that over time, groundwater in cemeteries would become polluted, and eventually those embalming chemicals would leach into the environment.

In 2003, one of the first "green" cemeteries in the United States appeared in Marin County, California. The theory behind a green cemetery was that the dead should be buried without chemicals, cosmetics, or clothing. Instead of a casket inside a heavy concrete burial vault, green cemeteries dressed bodies in simple shrouds and placed them in wooden boxes.

These services reduced funeral costs by approximately 85 percent. The cemetery covered the land with native grasses or oak trees to be nourished by the bodies buried below. Survivors planted trees in memory of loved ones and marked graves with rocks instead of monuments or headstones.

See also CAHOKIA; HEALTH AND MEDICINE; INDIANS, PALEOINDIANS.

Lana Thompson

Further Reading

Dicum, Gregory. "Green Is the New Dead: Green-Burial Movement Gets More Ambitious." *Grist,* July 27, 2006.

Iserson, Kenneth V. *Death to Dust: What Happens to Dead Bodies.* Tucson: Galen Press, 1994.

Prothero, Stephen. *Purified by Fire: A History of Cremation in America.* Berkeley: University of California Press, 2001.

Sloane, David Charles. *The Last Great Necessity: Cemeteries in American History.* Baltimore: Johns Hopkins University Press, 1991.

Stroud, Ellen. "From Six Feet under the Field: Dead Bodies in the Classroom." *Environmental History* 8 (October 2003): 618–627.

E 🌿

eagle

The Second Continental Congress designated the bald eagle as the national emblem of the nascent United States, in 1782. Nonetheless, by the 20th century, overhunting, habitat loss, and PESTICIDES nearly drove the bald eagle to extinction while threatening other eagles as well. Federal laws and recovery programs subsequently helped restore populations.

Two eagles in the family Accipitridae primarily inhabit North America, the bald eagle *(Haliaeetus leucocephalus)* and the golden eagle *(Aquila chrysaetos);* the Steller's sea eagle *(Haliaeetus pelagicus)* and white-tailed eagle *(Haliaeetus albicilla)* are sometimes seen on the outer Aleutians and other Alaskan islands. Among the largest raptors in the United States, the golden eagle has a wingspan ranging from 80 to 88 inches (203–224 cm) and body length of 30 to 40 inches (76–102 cm), while the comparably sized bald eagle averages a wingspan of 70 to 90 inches (178–229 cm) and body length of 31 to 37 inches (79–94 cm). Although the golden eagle lives in parts of Asia and Europe as well as North America including Central America, the bald eagle is endemic to North America and inhabits the District of Columbia and every U.S. state except Hawaii.

Numbering up to a half-million individuals before European contact, the bald eagle declined in population as a result

A bald eagle at a dump in Adak Island, Alaska. Juxtaposing an iconic symbol of the United States with a trash pile, this image was chosen by the U.S. Fish and Wildlife Service as the winner of its 1976 photo contest. *(Robert H. Day, U.S. Fish and Wildlife Service)*

of competition with humans for food, loss of habitat, pollution, poisoning, and human hunting, reaching its nadir, in the 1960s, with only 417 nesting pairs recorded in the 48 contiguous states. Because of the eagle's substantial size and ability to hoist prey as large as a DEER fawn, early American stock growers feared predation to their herds and killed both bald and golden eagles defensively. Colonial residents threatened the bald eagle's survival also by usurping its main food source of FISH; as Euro-American settlement increased, human use of the eagle's food intensified, as did the appropriation of its once-abundant habitat. Gradual westward expansion, which accelerated rapidly in the second half of the 19th century, effected the same type of competition and habitat loss on a massive scale. Finally, relentless exploitation of natural resources in the service of American industrialization, including excessive LOGGING AND LUMBERING and the manipulation of rivers and streams, caused an abrupt deficit in what remained of suitable nesting, hunting, and scavenging areas for the raptor. By 1900, the bald eagle had suffered staggering losses.

The more solitary golden eagle (Mexico's national symbol) relies less than the bald eagle on low-lying areas that also support high concentrations of humans, preferring instead more remote and high-elevation habitat, where it uses its superior hunting skills to capture a variety of rodents and other mammals such as foxes and rabbits as well as BIRDS and reptiles. In addition, this raptor's standard selection of cliff faces or rocky crags for its aerie sites leaves its nest less vulnerable to the type of loss and molestation that the bald eagle's typically treetop aerie faces. Because of these factors, it escaped the same level of devastation caused by human population growth and industrialization in the United States that the bald eagle experienced, even as the European golden eagle's ranks steadily declined to the point of EXTINCTION in much of its former range.

Notwithstanding the proliferation of adversities that already threatened its survival, as the bald eagle entered the 20th century, it faced a new set of hazards in both the continental United States and Alaska. First, a sharp increase in commercial activity in the new U.S. territory of Alaska (purchased by the United States in 1867) led to the destruction of more than 100,000 bald eagles between 1917 and 1953 by SALMON fishers who feared competition for this valuable and abundant fish. Second, bald eagles faced direct slaughter as agricultural nuisances in the U.S. West—experienced also by golden eagles—which accompanied perhaps the greatest threat to the bald eagle's survival, the widespread use of DDT (dichlorodiphenyltrichloroethane) and other agricultural PESTICIDES after WORLD WAR II (1941–45). Because DDT and its related pesticides affect the eagle's metabolism in a way that causes it to produce thin eggshells that cannot support the weight of a brooding parent, hatchling recruitment plummeted, causing a final, precipitous decline in the popu-

lation of this species. The resulting plight of these raptors and other birds famously gained exposure in RACHEL CARSON's seminal 1962 book *Silent Spring*, which inspired a nearly complete ban of DDT in the United States 10 years later.

In response to the rapid disappearance of America's national symbol, the federal government enacted remedial legislation that began in 1940 with the Bald Eagle Protection Act, amended in 1962 to include golden eagles, which forcefully prohibited the possession and the direct or indirect disturbance of eagles or articles associated with them. Buoyed by the environmental movement, the Endangered Species Preservation Act of 1966 led to the official classification of the bald eagle in the coterminous United States as endangered, a status that was reinforced on July 4, 1976, under the more powerful ENDANGERED SPECIES ACT OF 1973 (ESA). After 19 years of recovery, the U.S. FISH AND WILDLIFE SERVICE changed the bald eagle's status to threatened and finally removed it from ESA protection by delisting the species, in June 2007. Although federal stewardship of both birds continues under the Bald and Golden Eagle Protection Act, only an isolated subpopulation of the bald eagle inhabiting the Sonoran Desert in Arizona maintains its threatened status under the ESA. The incidental destruction of bald eagles by human-imposed hazards such as power lines that ensnare or electrocute them and highly toxic LEAD pellets dispersed by waterfowl hunters continues to afflict the restored population of more than 70,000 individuals in North America. Nevertheless, both the bald eagle and the golden eagle now enjoy International Union for the Conservation of Nature and Natural Resources (IUCN) designations as species of least concern.

National emblems of the United States and Mexico, the bald eagle and golden eagle carry symbolic meaning for aboriginal peoples as well. To the Pawnee, for example, eagles signify fertility, while the Choctaw esteem the bald eagle as a symbol of peace for its link with the upper realm of the Sun. Because the raptors' feathers and talons historically have served as sacred and ceremonial objects, particularly among southwestern cultures, legal exceptions provide for their continued use by members of federally recognized tribes despite the restrictions imposed by protective laws. To accommodate this type of use, the U.S. Fish and Wildlife Service, in the early 1970s, established the National Eagle Repository in DENVER, COLORADO, as a collection and distribution facility for dead eagles. Permits issued to Native Americans allow holders to receive eagles or parts of eagles from the repository for use as religious or cultural objects, reducing the incidence of illegal taking of these raptors from the wild.

The bald eagle population has reflected the course of American history from its long use among Indian cultures, through centuries of agricultural and industrial developments, to the protective impulses of ENVIRONMENTALISM.

Their physical attributes and habits render bald and golden eagles, alternately vilified and highly esteemed, important members of the natural world that they share with humans.

See also BIRDS; CANADA AND THE UNITED STATES; ENDANGERED SPECIES; MEXICO AND THE UNITED STATES; ROCKY MOUNTAINS; UNITED STATES—ALASKA; UNITED STATES—COLUMBIA PLATEAU AND GREAT BASIN.

Wendy M. Zirngibl

Further Reading

DeMeo, Antonia M. "Access to Eagles and Eagle Parts: Environmental Protection v. Native American Free Exercise of Religion." *Hastings Constitutional Law Quarterly* 22 (1995): 771–813.

Ehrlich, Paul R., David S. Dobkin, and Darryl Wheye. *The Birder's Handbook: A Field Guide to North American Birds.* New York: Simon & Schuster, 1988.

Gerrard, Jon M., and Gary R. Bortolotti. *The Bald Eagle: Haunts and Habits of a Wilderness Monarch.* Washington, D.C.: Smithsonian Institution Press, 1988.

Earth Day

On April 22, 1970, some 20 million Americans participated in a nationwide demonstration to celebrate the Earth and to protest environmental destruction. Earth Day activities took place on more than 1,000 college campuses and in many thousands of parks, schools, and workplaces across the United States.

The Wisconsin senator Gaylord Nelson (1916–2005) first proposed the idea of a national demonstration against environmental harm in 1969 and recruited a Harvard Law School student, Denis Hayes (1944–   ), to organize the event. Instead of holding a mass march or rally, Hayes and the Earth Day organizers planned many small actions across the nation. They relied on participation by hundreds of campus-based student environmental groups, many of which had just been formed.

Earth Day did not center on traditional CONSERVATION issues, such as the preservation of scenic places and the protection of wildlife. Instead, many Earth Day events focused on pollution and other threats to human health and well-being. The demonstration was largely a reaction to well-publicized instances of environmental harm in the 1960s, such as OIL SPILLS, including in Santa Barbara; industrial chemicals burning on CLEVELAND, OHIO's Cuyahoga River; phosphates washing ashore from Lake Erie; polluted beaches; contaminated fish; and urban smog.

Established conservation groups, such as the SIERRA CLUB, the National AUDUBON SOCIETY, and the National Wildlife Federation, had only minor roles in Earth Day. Originally modeled after the anti–VIETNAM WAR (1955–75) movement's "teach-ins" (it was first called the "National

Teach-In on the Crisis of the Environment"), Earth Day had closer ties to 1960s student activism than to the mainstream conservation movement. The organizers, however, held ambivalent views about the confrontational rhetoric and tactics of the student New Left. Denis Hayes wanted Earth Day to have a critical edge, while not alienating the majority of Americans, and he sought official support for the event wherever it was available. The New Left, meanwhile, had mixed views of Earth Day and its ties to corporations and the government. Many thousands of student activists participated in the event, but just weeks before April 22, the New Left magazine *Ramparts* called Earth Day "the first step in a con game that will do little more than abuse the environment even further."

Earth Day turned out to be a mix of radical protest and moderate demonstration. Some activists used direct action tactics, vandalizing the headquarters of private corporations or public utilities with oil, soot, or dead animals. Others participated in sanctioned marches or rallies. Some public officials were heckled and booed off the stage, while others were received with applause and appreciation.

The legacy of Earth Day had as much to do with the way the MEDIA depicted the event as what speakers said and demonstrators did. Newspapers and magazines devoted many columns and pages to environmental issues and the emerging environmental movement in the weeks before and after Earth Day. Generally, the coverage presented environmentalism as a new cause, without connecting it to other 1960s social movements or exploring the points of overlap and contention between those social movements and environmental concerns. In this popular view, Earth Day became a sort of movement "big bang"—a single event separating a political vacuum from a wealth of activity.

Earth Day has been celebrated annually each year since 1970, generally through locally organized events aimed at raising environmental awareness. In the late 1980s, with concerns such as the hole in the OZONE LAYER and GLOBAL WARMING in the headlines, Denis Hayes began to talk with environmental leaders about another large-scale coordinated effort. The talks resulted in Earth Day 1990, an event celebrated by 200 million people in 140 countries. Major environmental groups, which had played a minor role in the first Earth Day, involved themselves in Earth Day 1990 from the beginning, helping to plan and carry out the international celebration. While the 20-year anniversary was, as was the original Earth Day, largely organized by ad hoc committees, it was a more top-down affair involving increased corporate funding and media influence. The scale of the event signaled the broad acceptance of environmentalism as a mainstream political movement.

See also ENVIRONMENTALISM, GRASSROOTS; ENVIRONMENTALISM, MAINSTREAM; ENVIRONMENTALISM, RADICAL; GREAT LAKES; POLLUTION, AIR; POLLUTION, WATER.

Keith Woodhouse

Further Reading

Christofferson, Bill. *The Man from Clear Lake: Earth Day Founder Senator Gaylord Nelson.* Madison: University of Wisconsin Press, 2004.

"Editorial." *Ramparts* 8, no. 11 (May 1970): 2–4.

Gottlieb, Robert. *Forcing the Spring: The Transformation of the American Environmental Movement.* Washington, D.C.: Island Press, 1993.

Rome, Adam. "'Give Earth a Chance': The Environmental Movement and the Sixties." *Journal of American History* 90, no. 2 (September 2003): 525–554.

Shabecoff, Philip. *A Fierce Green Fire: The American Environmental Movement.* New York: Hill & Wang, 1993.

earthquakes

Among the most frightening and devastating of natural DISASTERS, earthquakes strike without warning and pose significant threats to communities, buildings, and infrastructure. While popular knowledge of earthquakes in the United States often relegates violent seismic activity to the West Coast, there are, in reality, 39 states at risk for moderate to severe earthquakes. Scientists are unable to predict accurately where, when, or why an earthquake will strike. As a result, forecasters are unable to issue earthquake warnings, and larger shocks are often extraordinarily damaging.

One of the nation's most severe quakes was a series of three violent shocks centered near New Madrid, Missouri, in late 1811 and early 1812. Scientists speculate that each of the three tremors in question—two on December 16, 1811, and one on January 23, 1812—would have rated higher than 8.0 on the Richter scale, had the measurement system existed at the time. With epicenters located in a sparsely settled area, the quakes' overall damage and casualty tolls were minimal in comparison to their magnitude. Nonetheless, the seismic activity ravaged the small county of New Madrid. In addition, the quakes severely altered the region's topography, changing the course of the MISSISSIPPI RIVER, opening fissures in the earth, triggering mudslides, and creating new lakes, including Reelfoot Lake in Tennessee. Two years later, the region was still struggling to recover. In 1814, the territorial governor, William Clark, (1770–1838) issued the first ever request for federal disaster aid.

A massive 1964 earthquake flooded and sank much of Homer Spit, Alaska, the harbor for a large commercial fishing industry.   *(U.S. Fish and Wildlife Service)*

Approximately 70 years later, another truly devastating earthquake struck the United States. Affecting Charleston, South Carolina, on August 31, 1886, with an estimated magnitude of 7.3, the quake destroyed nearly half the city. It eventually cost the city more than $6 million in 1886 currency, terrified residents, and killed anywhere from 60 to 110 people. Survivors recounted the experience of fleeing buildings and watching the city crumble around them. Contemporaries created fantastic stories about the Charleston disaster. Throughout the southeastern United States, people suggested that Charleston and its environs had been swept away by a tidal wave; others argued that the Florida Peninsula had broken off and fallen into the ocean.

The next great quake was the 1906 San Francisco, California, earthquake. Modern estimates place the April 18, 1906, shock at a magnitude of 7.7–8.3 and suggest that the incident may have killed as many as 27,000 people. The quake set off a wave of fires throughout the city, burning much of it to the ground. The devastation drove nearly 300,000 people out of their homes, some of whom remained in makeshift "refugee camps" until 1908. Despite its severe consequences, the San Francisco earthquake was also the first incident to result in significant understanding of earthquakes and early attempts to mitigate their consequences. The quake was the first to be systematically documented and analyzed, thereby introducing scientists to the immense San Andreas Fault and allowing them to develop an understanding of seismic activity. The quake also gave birth to a wide range of emergency response improvements, including significant developments in the design of fire protection systems, earthquake-resistant architecture, and policies for postdisaster water distribution.

On April 1, 1946, a 7.4 magnitude earthquake struck the Aleutian Islands of Alaska. The quake triggered a Pacific-wide tsunami, and within an hour, a 100-foot tidal wave struck Unimak Island. The wave leveled a newly built U.S. Coast Guard lighthouse and killed more than 165 people. The damage was confined primarily to the Aleutian Islands, however, shielding the mainland from severe casualties. Nonetheless, as the 1906 earthquake had, the 1946 incident resulted in significant developments in emergency preparedness. Two years after the incident, 26 nations, including the United States, banded together to create the Seismic Sea Wave Warning System, eventually renamed the Tsunami Warning System, through which scientists monitored quakes throughout the Pacific Basin capable of causing a tsunami.

Less than 20 years later, a second enormous quake struck Alaska. This quake hit Prince William Sound on March 27, 1964, at a magnitude of 9.2, the largest recorded earthquake in U.S. history. It triggered a Pacific-wide tsunami as well as a series of devastating local tsunamis and mudslides throughout Alaska. At the Valdez Inlet, a large landslide triggered a tsunami that measured 200 feet high. The incident was the first to trigger such significant local tsunamis, and the Tsunami Warning System, housed in Honolulu, Hawaii, was unable to detect or warn of the oncoming waves in time to allow people to evacuate. As a result, officials and scientists made another significant leap in disaster preparedness. The inability to warn of localized tidal waves prompted federal and state officials to establish the locally run Alaska Tsunami Warning Center in 1967.

There were numerous earthquakes in the United States over the next three decades, but it was not until 1994 that the nation experienced an earthquake-related disaster to rival the aforementioned incidents. In the early morning hours of January 17, 1994, an earthquake struck Los Angeles, California. The earthquake's magnitude fell far short of the 1964 incident, registering 6.7, but the quake generated the highest ground acceleration ever recorded in a U.S. city. Known as the Northridge earthquake, the tremor killed 51 people, seriously injured more than 9,000, and caused major damage to critical infrastructure throughout Southern California. Freeways sustained significant damage as far as 20 miles from the epicenter, and portions of several highway systems collapsed. The quake also caused major damage to health care facilities, requiring the full-scale evacuation of eight acute care hospitals in the region.

The Northridge earthquake offered a number of lessons for emergency response. Despite large-scale damage across the region, the quake rendered relatively few structures other than single-family homes unsafe, a success many officials considered a validation of modern building codes. Postincident analysis revealed that of the large buildings that did collapse, several had been built without attention to earthquake-resistant architecture. Of the highway system damage, one collapsed portion had failed previously during a 1971 earthquake and had not been rebuilt with the necessary structural integrity. The California Department of Transportation also developed a model practice for disaster recovery, using an incentive technique to encourage contractors and builders to finish before scheduled, allowing the state to complete highway repair in approximately three-quarters of the time predicted.

Earthquakes are natural disasters that have the potential to disrupt both natural and built environments. Earthquake prediction remains in the nascent stages, and thus, more recent construction techniques and more stringent building codes have proven the most effective methods at diminishing the impact of these phenomena on the built environment.

See also engineering; Interstate Highway System; public works; United States—Alaska; United States—California; United States—Deep South.

Katherine Jenny Worboys

Further Reading

Bagwell, Joyce B. *Low Country Quake Tales.* Greenville, S.C.: Southern Historical Press, 1986.
Department of Transportation. *Effects of Catastrophic Events on Transportation System Management and Operations:*

Northridge Earthquake, January 17, 1994. Cambridge, Mass.: April 22, 2002.

Dougan, Michael Bruce. *Arkansas Odyssey: The Saga of Arkansas from Prehistoric Times to Present.* Little Rock: Rose, 1994.

Dudley, Walter C., and Min Lee. *Tsunami!* Honolulu: University of Hawaii Press, 1988.

Wallace, Robert E., ed. *The San Andreas Fault System, California.* Washington, D.C.: U.S. Geological Survey Professional Paper 1515, 1990.

eastern seaboard   *See* UNITED STATES—EASTERN SEABOARD.

ecofeminism   *See* FEMINISM AND ECOFEMINISM

ecological boycotts

Many observers believe that a major societal transformation will be required to realize the goal of an ecologically sustainable future. Moreover, this transformation, which will affect such areas as energy utilization, pollution control, and waste disposal, does not appear possible without the help of major corporations. Consumer activism in general, and consumer boycotts in particular, have been important motivators in securing corporate participation at times in the past. Organized consumer action in the form of boycotts has been an attractive approach available to ordinary people seeking to help secure a sustainable future. In theory, boycotts permit individuals to exercise "economic democracy" every day with their purchases in the marketplace by rewarding companies whose actions are ecologically sound and by punishing companies whose actions are not.

A critical question that naturally arises is how well economic democracy theory translates into practice. The findings of empirical research on consumer boycotts suggest that what works in theory often does not work in practice. Many ecological boycotts did not succeed in changing corporate behavior. Effective boycotts involved certain psychological properties not found for the ineffective boycotts. In particular, the objectives of the successful boycotts tended to be cognitively simple and emotionally appealing. Organizers persuaded consumers that the environmental good protected by the boycott is more important than the product they were asked to forgo. Some objectives took on the character of catchy slogans, such as "Save the dolphins" (from the nets of the tuna fishermen) or "Save the rabbits" (from the tests of the cosmetics developers). However, the complexities inherent in many ecological recommendations for corporate practices are not likely to be reducible to such simple slogans for energizing and directing boycott campaigns.

Successful ecological boycotts often have worked not only because consumers stopped buying the boycotted goods but also because the boycotters secured MEDIA coverage of the offending practices of the targeted companies; this bad publicity often embarrasses the firms into making corporate changes in the directions called for by the boycotters. Such boycott campaigns are often expensive, and indeed, it has been relatively large and well-funded organizations that have been able to initiate and sustain them. In 1988, the People for the Ethical Treatment of Animals (PETA) launched boycotts that secured an end to animal testing in cosmetics production by Avon, General Motors, Neutrogena, and Benetton. Well-publicized pressure and a two-year campaign from the Earth Island Institute and other environmental organizations forced tuna fishing interests to halt the wholesale killing of dolphins. In both cases, the NONGOVERNMENTAL ORGANIZATIONS targeted one industry leader. When the industry leader yielded, it created a domino effect, forcing other companies to comply. However, PETA has been less successful with protests against pharmaceutical companies producing drugs for human use where consumers value the end product more than the environmental good.

While the complexities of many ecological objectives have not lent themselves easily to the consumer boycott tactic, occasions have arisen that suggest the boycott as the approach to take, particularly when new corporate initiatives demonstrate insensitivity to ecological considerations. In the late 1980s and early 1990s, the Dow Chemical Corporation agreed to stop using the term *photodegradable* to describe its plastic bag products. The Environmental Action Foundation, the Environmental Defense Fund, and other nongovernmental organizations contended that the term was inappropriate because the bags did not degrade under normal consumer use and disposal. The publicity resulting from a boycott call from two environmental groups led to government inquiries and eventually to the end of the mislabeling practice.

In summary, while in theory consumer boycotts offer ecological change agents a powerful weapon for prompting corporations to work toward the realization of a sustainable future, in practice, the boycott tactic may have limited usefulness. It has worked most effectively under circumstances that permitted the ecological objectives of a boycott to be reduced to a simple message with wide appeal to consumers. Even in such circumstances, however, a major and sustained publicity campaign was required, one that was directed to the media as well as to consumers in the marketplace.

See also CONSUMERISM; CORPORATIONS, CHEMICAL; GREEN CONSUMERISM AND MARKETING.

Monroe Friedman

Further Reading
Cohen, Lizabeth. *A Consumers' Republic.* New York: Random House, 2003.

Friedman, Monroe. *Consumer Boycotts.* New York: Routledge, 1999.

Micheletti, Michele, Andreas Follesdal, and Dietlind Stolle, eds. *Politics, Products, and Markets.* New Brunswick, N.J.: Transaction, 2004.

Schmuck, Peter, and Wesley Schultz, eds. *Psychology of Sustainable Development.* Boston: Kluwer, 2002.

ecological footprints

An ecological footprint (EF) is a measure of ecological impact, which is based on the concepts of SUSTAINABILITY and carrying capacity. An ecological footprint analysis (EFA) is used to calculate the land area needed to sustain human consumption and absorb its ensuing wastes. It is a tool, entailing a complicated process, for determining whether human lifestyles are sustainable. By the end of the 20th century, there was wide agreement that the Earth's ecosystems could not sustain current levels of economic activity and material consumption. Many EFA measures have shown that humanity lives too heavily on Earth, that is, that human beings are too dependent on consumption.

The ecological footprint concept was developed in the mid-1990s at the University of British Columbia by the ecologist William Rees and one of his graduate students, Mathias Wackernagel. Their book, *Our Ecological Footprint: Reducing Human Impact on Earth* (1996), presented the concept. Studies about nature's capacity to support human life go back many centuries. GEORGE PERKINS MARSH's *Man and Nature* (1864) opened up a worldwide debate about human impact on environments. His study and others tried to quantify human reliance or overreliance on physical environments. Wackernagel and Rees, too, realized that human use of nature needed to be quantified before it could be reduced and developed an analytical tool for measurement. Their book was meant to stimulate thinking about human relationships to nature and each other and to stimulate public action in addressing the issue.

An ecological footprint is the land area, usually measured in global acres or hectares, that is required to support a defined human population and material standard indefinitely. The EF of a city, for example, is the total area that would have to be enclosed along with the city under a glass capsule to sustain the consumption and waste patterns of the people of that city. EFAs are commonly applied to specific populations and geographic areas, especially countries, and variables are based on income, prices, and social values. Although difficult, it is possible for an individual to calculate his or her own EF by monitoring personal and household consumption.

EF measurements of smaller geographic areas, such as cities and counties, are less common than those calculated for nations because current data are inconsistent and difficult to compare. However, calculation standards for subnational geographic units are being developed by organizations interested in achieving more accurate measures. A good example of a small-scale measurement was the 2001 County of Marin (California) Community Development Agency's EFA. Marin County's 2006 final report estimated that the county required

27 global acres per resident, three higher than the U.S. average. To reduce Marin County's EF, the Development Agency recommended changes in transportation patterns, energy efficiency, and conservation in buildings. To accomplish this goal, Marin set targets, for example, for reducing carbon dioxide emissions. Programs proposed to achieve this included allowing mixed use in commercial districts that keep residents closer to their places of business and thus doubling in 10 years the number of residents who walk or ride to work. Reducing waste included a proposal to require building projects to recycle or reuse a minimum of 50 percent of leftover or unused materials.

According to Redefining Progress, a nonprofit organization that works together with others to shift the economy and public policy toward sustainability, there are six exclusive uses that compete for the Earth's biologically productive space: growing crops; grazing animals; harvesting timber; fishing and other marine products; accommodating infrastructure for housing, transportation, industrial production, and capturing hydro energy; and burning fossil fuels. These categories are expressed in standardized global acres and then added up to determine the total footprint of a given population or geographic area.

The early analyses by Wackernagel and Rees failed to account for a number of variables and initially measured only about one-third of all biologically productive land. The shortcomings in their analyses led ecologists and others continually to refine and improve the methodology to make EF measurement more accurate and useful. This resulted in Footprint 2.0, developed by a team of researchers at Redefining Progress. The new version included a number of changes that created a more accurate analysis, by, for example, accounting for Earth's entire biocapacity surface, deducting 13.4 percent of biocapacity for other species, and incorporating carbon sequestration rates.

Footprint 2.0 data show that humans' impact on Earth is significantly worse than what was shown in version 1.0. The world's EF exceeds biocapacity by nearly 40 percent. According to the Ecological Footprint of Nations 2005 Update, at the present rate of consumption, humans would need nearly 1.4 Earths to ensure that future generations are at least as well off as people today. Because of affluence and consumption, including of FOSSIL FUELS, wealthier nations run a negative ecological balance. The 2.0 version shows the United Arab Emirates, Kuwait, and the United States as having the largest footprints. It also shows that if all the people of the world adapted the lifestyle of the top 42 consuming countries, there would simply not be enough carrying capacity to support the world's human population.

Ecological footprint also has become a successful slogan that helps market the idea of caring for the environment and is one of the most widely referenced sustainability analysis tools used around the world. The term provides a way to converse about lessening environmental damage by adopting the smallest ecological footprint possible. EF can lead to lighter footprints by encouraging renewable energy, locally grown organic FOOD, energy conservation, no-net (zero) waste, and many other ideas. Similar variations of the "footprint" term have developed, for example, *global footprint,* a more easily understood term for use in elementary and secondary schools, and *carbon footprint,* a measure of the output of carbon dioxide emissions. EF emphasizes that human activities are using the world beyond its long-term capacity and encourages humans to learn more, get involved, and do something about it.

See also CONSUMERISM; ECOLOGY; GLOBALIZATION; UNITED STATES—CALIFORNIA.

Byron Anderson

Further Reading

Global Footprint Network. Available online. URL: http://www. footprintnetwork.org. Accessed September 8, 2008.

Kitzes, Justin, and Steve Goldfinger. "Measuring Marin County's Ecological Footprint." February 2006. Available online. URL: http://www.co.marin.ca.us/depts/cd/main/pdf/planning/ footprint_final_report.pdf. Accessed August 28, 2008.

Venetoulis, Jason, and John Talberth. "Ecological Footprint of Nations: 2005 Update." Available online. URL: http:// www.ecologicalfootprint.org/pdf/Footprint%20of%20 Nations%202005.pdf. Accessed June 20, 2008.

Wackernagel, Mathias, and William Rees. *Our Ecological Footprint: Reducing Human Impact on Earth.* Gabriola Island, Canada: New Society, 1996.

ecological imperialism

The term *ecological imperialism* captures the idea that the exchange of species is one of the most important elements of the expansion of human settlement. Introduced as a concept by the historian Alfred W. Crosby, ecological imperialism originally focused on the biological exchange within and between Europe and the Americas. Subsequent applications of this term increased its focus to include the biological consequences of all human expansion, regardless of time or original geographic location.

Certain theories of ecological imperialism suggest that regions of dense animal and plant populations, such as Europe and parts of Africa and Asia, produce species that have a biological advantage because of greater competition and increased immunities that allow them to dominate indigenous species when they are introduced to new regions. Other theories suggest that various human attitudes toward the environment help to promote certain species while contributing to the decline of other species. Such theories help historians, ecologists, and others understand the extent of ecological imperialism and the importance of its impact on various environments.

EARLY EXCHANGES

Although the extent of early ecological imperialism is difficult to determine, human expansion into several regions coincided with noticeable changes in the biological diversity of the areas. The arrival of humans in both Australia and the Americas coincided with the decline of several species of large animals, although definitive causation linking human arrival and species decline during the Stone Age is still under study. Other early episodes of ecological imperialism occurred when humans migrated to previously unoccupied regions, such as the Guanches expansion before 1000 C.E. from the Canary Islands (off the coast of Morocco) to Madeira (an island southwest of Portugal) and the early Viking settlement of Iceland in the ninth century C.E.

EUROPEAN EXPANSION, 1400–1900
Pre-Columbian

The most well-known and studied cases of ecological imperialism were those caused by the rapid expansion of European empires between 1400 and 1900. With a desire to expand markets and political power and new technologies, several European countries initiated an age of exploration that resulted in contacts between previously separated regions of the world. Early settlement of the Madeira, Canary, and Azores archipelagos by Europeans introduced European livestock, crops, and pests to these islands, radically altering the existing ecology.

The Columbian Exchange

The best-known examples of ecological imperialism were the result of CHRISTOPHER COLUMBUS's arrival in the Americas in 1492 and the ecological exchanges made between those lands and Europe, Africa, and Asia. European explorers introduced a variety of different plants, animals, and diseases to the environments of the Americas. The introduction of diseases, particularly SMALLPOX, decimated the indigenous population, people who possessed little natural immunity to the diseases carried by the Europeans. The deaths and fear surrounding the introduction of these new diseases undermined Native governmental structures and facilitated European conquests.

Europeans also introduced a variety of plants to the environment of the Americas. Garden plants and fruit trees were some of the first European plants to prosper. European GRAINS, particularly WHEAT, took longer to become established and had to compete with indigenous grains including maize. The introduction of SUGAR cane resulted in dramatic changes to the environment of many regions, including several islands in the Caribbean Sea, parts of southeastern North America, and Brazil, as a result of production based on PLANTATIONS, which promoted DEFORESTATION and stripped soils of their nutrients. Certain species of flowering plants and grazing GRASSES were consciously imported to the Americas to help create a European atmosphere and to support livestock production. Several other plant species, including daisies, dandelions, and other WEEDS, were unintentionally introduced and overran indigenous ground cover.

The absence of numerous large carnivores and DOMES-TICATED ANIMALS in the Americas allowed introduced animals to succeed. Large European animals including CATTLE, PIGS AND HOGS, and HORSES flourished in the Americas with wild herds expanding throughout North America and South America. Cattle and pig herds provided sources of readily available meat and hide. The horse's migration into North America altered the power structures among various indigenous populations and allowed for more effective hunting of native animal species including the BISON. Other domesticated animals, including the donkey, the mule, and the sheep, also changed the animal population of the Americas. The unintentional introduction of various pests, including hundreds of species of INSECTS and rats, devastated native plants.

The introduction of diseases, plants, and animals from the Eastern Hemisphere altered the environments of the Western Hemisphere. Human populations in the Americas declined as a result of not only contact with foreign diseases but also the impact of these new species on traditional social structures and food sources. Dominant European attitudes toward the environment promoted various elements of ecological imperialism at the expense of local indigenous practices and beliefs.

The importance of American species to the environment across the Atlantic Ocean should not be ignored. Although syphilis was originally thought to be a disease introduced to Europe after Columbus's expeditions, further study suggests that this disease was already present in the population, although perhaps in a different form. Few, if any, other contagious diseases were transferred from the Americas to Europe.

The introduction of certain American plants is the most important contribution to the environment of Europe, Africa, and Asia from these exchanges. POTATOES, maize, manioc (or cassava), and various beans provided new sources of nutrition and became STAPLE CROPS in many regions. The introduction of these crops appears to be connected to the rise in the sustained population that Europe experienced after 1500. The political, social, and ecological importance of this demographic change is difficult to measure and still debated among scholars.

Other European Exchanges

The European discovery and settlement of Australia also involved dramatic episodes of ecological imperialism. European cattle and pigs quickly adapted to the environment of Australia, reproduced in the wild, and became a primary source of meat. European horses had difficulty adapting in Australia, although, by the middle of the 19th century, herds of "Brumbies" (wild horses) populated the interior of Australia. The introduction of the European rabbit to Australia proved to be devastating to the environment. The rabbit reproduced quickly and within 20 years became a pest, destroying numerous species of indigenous plants and dis-

placing the native RODENTS. New Zealand experienced a similar ecological encounter when the imported DEER repopulated until they became both a pest and a threat to INDIGENOUS SPECIES. The introduction of European diseases, such as smallpox, helped to decimate Native human populations of both Australia and New Zealand in much the same way they had in the Americas.

EASTERN EXPANSION

Europeans were not the only societies with the expansionist ambitions that promoted ecological imperialism. Both the Qing dynasty in China (1644–1912 C.E.) and the Sengoku and Tokugawa rulers (1467–1867 C.E.) in Japan contributed to more localized instances of ecological imperialism. The Qing dynasty's timber policy resulted in near-deforestation of parts of China. Similarly, the military competition during the Sengoku period in Japan created a heavy demand on local FORESTS, and the policies issued by the subsequent Tokugawa shogunate increased this pressure. Although both China and Japan subsequently took steps to protect existing forests and promote reforestation, the ecological devastation of these regimes still have an impact on their environments.

CONCLUSION

Initially introduced by Alfred Crosby to explain why Europeans conquered other parts of the world, creating "neo-Europes" where European species dominated, other scholars have extended the concept of "ecological imperialism" to encompass the biological consequences of other forms of human expansion over time. Ecological imperialism has involved intended introductions of crops and livestock; accidental introductions of diseases, pests, and weeds; and the often unconscious introductions of culture in the human prioritizing of species.

See also COLUMBIAN EXCHANGE; CORN; DISEASES, ANIMAL; DISEASES, HUMAN; DISEASES, PLANT; PEST CONTROL; SEXUALLY TRANSMITTED DISEASES; SPECIES, EXOTIC AND INVASIVE.

Brice E. Olivier

Further Reading
Crosby, Alfred W. *The Columbian Exchange: Biological and Cultural Consequences of 1492.* 30th anniversary ed. London: Praeger, 2003.
———. *Ecological Imperialism: The Biological Expansion of Europe, 900–1900.* Cambridge: Cambridge University Press, 1986.
Dunlap, Thomas R. *Nature and the English Diaspora: Environment and History in the United States, Canada, Australia, and New Zealand.* Cambridge: Cambridge University Press, 1999.
Griffiths, Tom, and Libby Robins, eds. *Ecology and Empire: Environmental History of Settler Societies.* Seattle: University of Washington Press, 1997.

ecological restoration

Human efforts to restore environments that have been degraded or destroyed can be called ecological restoration—a common activity in the United States after the 1980s. Scientific journals, professional societies, and wording in legislation all paid increasing attention to this activity in more recent years, when it was often viewed as the ultimate management strategy for transformed and exhausted sites. The more general pursuit of environmental restoration, which does not necessarily imply attention to ecological theory or insight, is a much older activity. It extends back to the 20th century and before, centering on changing notions of damaged and idealized natures and the processes by which the former is converted into the latter. Rehabilitating, renewing, replenishing, rewilding, and renaturing are all labels that suggest slightly different goals for restoration practitioners, from partial to complete replacement of former conditions.

Early wildlife biologists, environmental engineers, mining reclamationists, landscape architects, concerned gardeners, and conscientious farmers can all be considered to have practiced forms of restoration, whether by restoring single species or communities of species, improving soil composition or soil quality, or restoring ecosystem function or health. Members of the Society of Ecological Restoration International, founded in 1988, see themselves as "assisting the recovery of an ecosystem that has been degraded, damaged, or destroyed." The subtleties of definition and range of activities that qualify as ecological restoration, however, suggest that the activity has an enormously complicated past.

ALDO LEOPOLD is rightly considered an early voice of ecological restoration. In 1934, he called for restoring areas of the University of Wisconsin Arboretum, proclaiming that "the time has come for science to busy itself with the earth itself. The first step is to reconstruct a sample of what we had to start with." Yet even earlier, the range ecologist Arthur Sampson spent much of his career seeking ways to reestablish once-abundant grass and forage in western mountain pastures. Sampson concluded, in 1912, that "indigenous" (or native) species were the best choice for reseeding overgrazed ranges. Other notables, including FREDERICK LAW OLMSTED, SR., called for returning areas to their former conditions, such as at NIAGARA FALLS, where industrial development was transforming the character of the cataract. Olmsted's 1887 comments for managing this area echoed a planning commission's report that urged "preserving the scenery of the Falls of Niagara and of restoring the said scenery to its natural condition." Reforestation, as just one form of restoration with many precedents, was an important concern of the conservationist GIFFORD PINCHOT, who replanted forests at the Biltmore Estate, as did Frederick Billings at his Woodstock estate. FORESTRY laws and forestry practices, explained GEORGE PERKINS MARSH

Aldo Leopold examines tamarack, a small- to medium-sized deciduous coniferous tree, at his Sauk County, Wisconsin, retreat.   *(Library of Congress)*

in *Man and Nature* (1864), "divide themselves into two great branches—the preservation of existing forests, and the creation of the new." These brief quotations give an indication of how the modern pursuit of ecological restoration in North America grew out of the combined experience of early ecologists, landscape architects, foresters, and other natural resource experts.

Marcus Hall

Further Reading

Gobster, Paul H., and R. Bruce Hull. *Restoring Nature: Perspectives from the Social Sciences and Humanities.* Washington, D.C.: Island Press, 2000.

Hall, Marcus. *Earth Repair: A Transatlantic History of Environmental Restoration.* Charlottesville: University of Virginia Press, 2005.

Higgs, Eric. *Nature by Design: People, Natural Process and Ecological Restoration.* Boston: MIT Press, 2003.

Jordan, William, III. *The Sunflower Forest: Ecological Restoration and the New Communion with Nature.* Berkeley: University of California Press, 2003.

ecology

Environmental history frequently addresses issues of resource management and land-use development. The science of ecology offers environmental historians analytical tools for understanding the ecological consequences of such issues. Ecology has moved through several phases and branched into several subfields over the last 140 years, with shifting views on whether nature is harmoniously balanced or chaotically ordered and how the relations between humans and their physical environments should be defined and explained. Changing ecological theories, in turn, have influenced environmental historians who contemplated nature and the human ethical relationship to it.

HISTORY

In 1866, the German biologist Ernst Haeckel (1834–1919) used the term *ecology* (from Greek *oikos*—home, environment, and *logos*—studies or knowledge) to define the study of organic entities and the inorganic conditions upon which they depend. Inorganic conditions included physical and chemical properties such as climate, soil, and water. At the end of the 19th century, ecologists dealt with organism distribution and dynamics in connection with influence of separate factors of mainly climatic origin. As a result, an idea of organism communities (cenosis) has been put forward.

In the early 20th century, FREDERIC EDWARD CLEMENTS, a major American founder of scientific ecology, studied the evolution of plant relationships in the context of communities, believing the latter developed as living organisms do, under specific climatic conditions. Primary PLANT SUCCESSION was the process by which vegetation began to cover an area until it reached a mature climax formation. Plants determined which animals lived within a biome. Studying the Great Plains in the 1930s, Clements concluded that humans disrupted biomes.

Ecology developed rapidly in the 1920s and 1930s. The British ecologist Arthur Tansley (1871–1955) challenged Clements in 1935. He introduced the term ECOSYSTEMS and argued that the plant community was not greater than the sum of its parts; it was simply the sum of its parts. He described the quantifiable elements of ecosystems as biotic or abiotic and pushed ecology toward an approach in which humans managed nature to enhance productivity. CHARLES SUTHERLAND ELTON explained how species converge and interact in the food chain and described the number of animals present at each trophic (feeding) level. Elton recognized that there were relatively few predators compared with the number of intermediate species at lower levels. Elton

and Tansley considered the energy flows in and out of an ecosystem.

By the mid-20th century, the idea that organism complexes were mutually interrelated and deeply connected with their environment had gained recognition as a result of the work of these scholars and others. New studies focused on organisms' interaction and structural analysis of systems they formed. In such a framework, scientists conceptualized ecology as a science that explored the structure and function of the nature. Interpreted in such a way, ecology inevitably absorbed aspects of contemporary sciences, such as physics, chemistry, mathematics, cybernetics, geography, climatology, geology, oceanography, economics, sociology, psychology, and anthropology.

Rapid scientific and technological progress of the second half of 20th century forced Americans and other people to recognize the global consequences of anthropogenic intrusion into nature and natural processes. In this context, ecologists integrated their work with social and humanitarian sciences, such as demography, sociology, statistics, history, and anthropology. Ecology absorbed theory and methods of system approach and increasingly concentrated on multicomponent and multilevel systems in nature and society. In 1953, the American EUGENE PLEASANTS ODUM introduced the first ecology textbook, *Fundamentals of Ecology*. While most early ecological studies focused on smaller, isolated ecosystems, Odum argued ecologists needed to examine larger systems such as weather patterns, WATERSHEDS, and the human impact on otherwise balanced, homeostatic ecosystems. He believed that maximizing productivity degraded ecosystems.

By the 1980s, ecologists increasingly criticized the idea of a balanced nature. Chaos theory introduced the idea that natural disturbance, ranging in intensity and scale from beaver dams to earthquakes, disrupted ecosystems as much as humans. By the 1990s, nature appeared far more complex and disorderly than initially believed. These developments in turn influenced environmental history as they made it more difficult for historians to contemplate the disruptive force of human actions on nature in the past.

ECOLOGY SUBFIELDS

Over the course of the 20th century, ecology evolved as both a natural science concentrating on organisms and ecosystems and a humanitarian science defining the human place in nature. This dichotomy is reflected in the different but interrelated branches of ecology that emerged over time to study nature and society in mutually dependent development.

Human Ecology

Human ecology is the branch that deals with interrelationships of human being (population) and environment. First proposed by the American ecologists Ernest Burgess and

Robert Park at the University of Chicago in 1921, the field considered how urban environments shaped human behavior. The meaning of human ecology shifted over time and now focuses on detecting human adaptive potential in conditions of intensive industrial progress and deals in relationships between human beings and natural environments. As a result, a series of narrowly specialized disciplines has been formed on the border of ecology and anthropology in their broad understanding. Most widespread among them are palaeoecology in archaeology, physiological anthropology, and human behavioral ecology in biological anthropology, ethnoecology in linguistics, and others.

Social Ecology

A second branch of ecological science, social ecology, seeks explanations of economic and cultural features of human societies in frameworks of their natural environment; society and nature are regarded as biophysically linked systems. Social ecological studies work on different spatial and political levels, allowing them historical retrospection as well. Ecologists who prefer the label *social* to *human* stress sociocultural and economic behavior of human societies and human personalities in particular environments. Social ecology traces its roots, in part, to the so-called environmental philosophy of the second half of the 19th century, when the ideas of Karl Marx, John Ruskin, Peter Kropotkin, and other thinkers led economists and writers to assume there was a generally durable and stable interaction between human beings and natural environments.

Social ecologists later focused on environmental ethics, a subdiscipline in philosophy that emerged in the mid-1960s to replace anthropocentric interpretations of culture and environmental systems. Deep (or nature-centered) ecology and shallow (human-centered) ecology, a distinction proposed by the Norwegian philosopher Arne Naess (1912–2009) in 1973, contributed to further theoretical development of social ecological studies. In the late 1990s, social ecologists contemplated "radical ecology," which addresses how people change the physical world in accordance with a new social vision or ethic. Ecofeminism, for example, envisioned a more ecologically sustainable society based on male-female equilibrium instead of gender domination.

Cultural Ecology

Cultural ecology is an interdisciplinary field that concentrates on human adaptations and on the interdependence of cultural, economic, and environmental systems. It traces its roots to the work of Franz Boas (1858–1942) and Alfred Kroeber (1876–1960), early anthropologists who were concerned with variants of cultural elements and traits interpretation. Cultural ecologists address nature's impact on cultural evolution as mediated by technology, material culture, and forms of resource management, which, in their turn, depend on the availability, dynamics, and distribution of natural resources. By the mid-20th century, cultural ecology became a new sort of interdisciplinary study trying to integrate and synthesize creatively main ideas, concepts, and methods inherent in cognitive and behavioral anthropology, ecosystemology, geography, and economics. Cultural ecology encompassed local environmental knowledge, beliefs, values, and attitudes, including livelihoods, trying to connect environmental impacts with different kinds of human adaptive strategies.

By the mid-1970s, theoretical approaches that adopted the ecosystem as a model penetrated cultural anthropology, causing a "biologization" in this field. Cultural ecologists paid increasing attention to social and political variables of the human-environment interactive system. The label *ecological anthropology* often replaced *cultural ecology*, although they were sometimes used as synonyms. Scholars transitioned to small-scale studies of indigenous land use, often in tropical forests, and connected issues such as traditional ecological knowledge or indigenous production systems. Such studies involved forms of spatial analysis that could be elaborated by the geographic information system (GIS).

Spiritual Ecology

Spiritual ecology, or ecotheology, emerged as a transdisciplinary study occupied with cultures, lifestyles, and mythologies of indigenous peoples around the world. Its practitioners adopted a worldview based on the idea of sacredness of Earth and its inhabitants. Religion, they recognized, has been an important component for coping with different environmental challenges; most past and contemporary systems in the world referred to the human place in nature and potentially provided a sustainable environmental ethic. Christian ecology is an example of a subfield at the crossroads of ecotheology and environmental ethics.

Historical Ecology

Historical ecology, another branch of ecology, deals with the mutual influence and interdependence of culture and environment, as well as some limitations of human ecological reconstructions, in historical retrospection. Historical ecology often integrates aspects of ethnoecology, cultural and political ecology, and biological and regional ecology in a framework intimately linked with archaeology, sociocultural anthropology, geography, history, integrative biology, and general ecology.

Historical ecology assumes that since the earliest phases of their existence on Earth, humans interfered with nature while being deeply dependent on natural processes. The scale of human intrusion was mediated by many different agencies, which changed over time and space, such as the level of technology development, the modes of resource utilization, the character of the production system, and the level of pollution grade. Scholars elaborated three main theoretical concepts to comprehend dynamic of interactions between humans and nature over time. Geographical determinism concentrated on environmental impacts on human history. The second, "anthropogenic," concept concerned human agency in nature development and became popular alongside a global reconsideration of the human role in the universe at times of scientific revolution. Adepts of the third direction recognized that humans and nature shared mutual creativity and tended to interpret historical human-environment interactions as an integrated system in which all elements were of equal importance and engaged in complicated reciprocal influences. These three directions are represented in a wide spectrum of ideas, notions, and theories.

At the end of the 20th century, historical ecologists attempt to understand landscapes as a form of the ongoing dialectic between human acts and acts of nature. They saw cultural landscapes as sequent occupancies. For them, landscapes were texts that reflected the mental activity of their creators and thus could be deciphered and comprehended through the mental activity of other humans.

The latest theoretical gain of historical ecology is "two cultures" theory. It implies that representatives of social and humanitarian knowledge, on the one hand, and natural scientists, on the other, deal with deeply related issues but rarely communicate, preferring to examine their results within their respective genre. Historical ecology, which postulates the essentiality of the human species and its biosphere relations through time and space, proposes to bridge these "two cultures" in order to make possible fresh insights about the long-term construction and deconstruction of landscapes in which humans have lived.

Political Ecology

Political ecology emerged as an interdisciplinary field of study in the last decade of the 20th century as many political and environmental crises presented new questions about the deep interdependence of political, economic, technological, industrial, cultural, and environmental developments. It became especially acute in the discussions surrounding GLOBALIZATION and ongoing conditions associated with the reconsideration of modernity, socialism, and postsocialism. Political ecology originated as a curious synthesis of subject fields and investigation methods of ecology and political economy and resulted in attention to issues that traditionally remained outside frameworks of ecological investigations.

In particular, political ecology deals with political and economic relations of peoples exploring natural environments of large scale. Territorial frameworks of such studies have addressed state boundaries, but political ecologists also have used ethnic, national, and gender spatial units. Through these connections, political ecology contributes to general conceptualizations of place, identity, and nature as interdependent phe-

nomena. Political ecology has explored the ways state power and nonstate power shaped natural environments, often considering how science, ideology, and mass media contextualize and solve environmental problems. This field has also investigated environmental conflicts and disasters of scales ranging from the local to the global, working to develop optimistic approaches and alarmist approaches to understanding ecological crises in the second half of the 20th century.

One example of political ecological thought that emerged in the mid-1980s is the ENVIRONMENTAL JUSTICE movement. Environmental justice refers to the inequitable environmental burdens that racial and ethnic minorities, women, the poor, or citizens of developing nations have borne. It quickly became a worldwide movement dealing with local and global environmental issues. It influenced environmental history by forcing its scholars to contemplate how the benefits and costs of resource development had been dispersed within past societies.

SUSTAINABLE DEVELOPMENT is another conceptual model elaborated by political ecologists to define how civilization coexists with nature. The final report prepared by the World Commission on Environment and Development (WCED) in 1987 circulated the idea of sustainable development, defining it as development that meets the needs of the present without compromising future generations' ability to meet their own needs. Under this definition, sustainability became a goal for the purposeful regulation of individual and collective behavior designed to preserve natural resources.

Contemporary political ecologists pay special attention to the issues of environmental education aimed to alert young generations to emerging environmental problems and probable means of solving them, striving at the same time for the improvement of the urban and natural environments and against destruction of natural resources. Roots of environmental education can be traced as early as the period when Western industrialization began, and since that time, its content and methods have been gradually changing in accordance with the general environmental paradigm.

Biological Ecology

Biological ecology is a special field of biological science occupied with relationships of organisms and their environment. Sometimes it is defined as a science about relationships of organisms with other organisms and with their environment. Environmental historians rely on biological ecology to help them explain how relations between humans and their physical environments changed over time by expanding historians' understanding of the natural world. Biological ecology is divided into five branches. The first branch is autoecology, or factorial ecology. It deals with the ecology of organisms and the impact of natural agencies on organisms. An ecological factor is any element of the natural environment that directly influences organisms and their relations. There are three sorts of ecological factors: abiotic, biotic, and anthropogenic. Abiotic factors are conditions of nonorganic nature that influenced living species, adaptation over long periods. The most important abiotic factors include climatic and chemical conditions, temperature, humidity, solar radiation, and soil, among others. Biotic factors are living organisms. Biotic agencies influence organisms directly or indirectly throughout nonorganic nature. Anthropogenic factors refer to agency originating from and caused by human activity.

The second branch of biological ecology is demecology, or populational ecology. It studies populations and their inner connection and relationships with the environment. Population is regarded here as species's basic form of existence. Questions about the dynamics of population changes, the discernment of laws of population formation, and the self-regulation mechanisms of populations are at the center of this branch of ecology. Synecology, the third branch, deals with regularities that can be traced in multispecial groups of organisms interacting with and in relation to their environment.

A fourth branch, biogenocenology, or ecosystem studies, investigates regularities of origin, development, and normal functioning of ecological systems. Since Tansley introduced the term in 1935, ecosystems have been widely explored in Western science. The term *ecosystem* implies the flow of energy—a cycle of materials from the soil, water, and air through living organisms and back again. Concepts of succession, biome, community, food chain, trophic structure, and nutrient cycles are at the center of ecosystemology. At the end of the 20th century, questions of ecological equilibrium and ecological crises became acute in this field. Equilibrium implied relatively stable species composition and ecosystems progressing toward the formation of communities in the state of climax. An ecological crisis is a disturbance of the mutual relationships of elements inside an ecosystem or an irreversible phenomenon in a biosphere originated by anthropogenic activity that threatens human existence as a biological species. Contemporary ecological crises include gene pool changes, resource depletion, raw material and food shortages, environment pollution, species extinction, and tropical deforestation, among others.

The final branch is global ecology. Specialists in this field are occupied in studies of the biosphere, its organization and structure, functional aspects, evolution, and anthropogenic dynamics. Like the other four branches of biological ecology, global ecology is concerned with acute environmental issues affecting humans. Biological ecology involves a deep and mutual integration with geography, economics, sociology, demography, and other natural and social sciences.

The field of ecology has evolved and divided into subfields since the late 19th century in an effort to understand the complexities of life on Earth and the complicated relationships of humans with the natural world. Similarly, interdisciplinary, environmental history fosters dialogue between humanistic scholarship and environmental sciences such as ecology. Environmental history draws on the analytical tools used and research produced in ecology to understand better the history of human interactions with the environment.

See also CLIMAX THEORY; COWLES, HENRY; FEMINISM AND ECOFEMINISM; PLANT SUCCESSION; RICHARDS, ELLEN SWALLOW; UNITED NATIONS ENVIRONMENTAL CONFERENCES.

Olena Smyntyna

Further Reading
Anderson, E. N. *Ecologies of the Heart: Emotion, Belief, and the Environment.* New York: Oxford University Press, 1996.
Balee, William. *Advances in Historical Ecology.* New York: Columbia University Press, 1998.
Boyden, Stephen. *Western Civilization in Biological Perspective.* Oxford: Oxford University Press, 1987.
Crumley, Carole, ed. *Historical Ecology: Cultural Knowledge and Changing Landscape Systems.* Santa Fe, N.Mex.: School of American Research Press, 1994.
Ehrlich, Paul R., Anne H. Ehrlich, and John P. Holdren. *Human Ecology: Problems and Solutions.* San Francisco: W. H. Freeman, 1973.
Glaeser, Bernhard. *Environment, Development, Agriculture: Integrated Policy throughout Human Ecology.* London: UCL Press, 1995.
Netting, Robert. *Cultural Ecology.* Long Grove, Ill.: Waveland Press, 1977.
Odum, Eugene P. *Fundamentals of Ecology.* Philadelphia: W. B. Saunders, 1952.

ecosystems
An ecological system, or ecosystem, is a combination of all the living and nonliving elements in a defined area. It includes the biotic community—plants, animals, microorganisms—along with climate and soil, and their relationships with each other. All ecosystems are open systems where energy and matter are transferred in and out through the complex interactions of energy, water, carbon, oxygen, nitrogen, phosphorus, sulfur, and other biogeochemical cycles that occur within them. An obsolete hypothesis, the CLIMAX THEORY, stated that ecosystems developed through a process called "ecological succession," going through different growth stages until reaching a steady state, the climax state. This theory has been rejected, and nowadays ecosystems are considered to be autonomous and dynamic and to have self-regulating mechanisms that allow them to reach dynamic equilibriums. Ecosystems, however, are not completely independent; they are related and compose an entity called the biosphere—the sum of ecosystems.

Ecosystems include human activities, as people affect all parts of nature. Ecosystems offer goods and services of incalculable value to society, including food, water, timber, fiber, and genetic resources (BIODIVERSITY), along with regulation of climate, FLOODS, disease, and water quality. They also provide recreation, aesthetics, and spiritual benefits while supporting human productivity through soil formation, pollination, and nutrient cycling.

Ecosystems are not only what is seen in nature as forests or other kinds of places away from urban centers. They exist in the rivers where populations extract freshwater, in the soil under the pavement of the cities, and in the atmospheres of both urban and rural spaces. Within and through all these ecosystems flow all human activities, underlying the importance of understanding how their elements are interrelated in a complex way and in this way helping to conserve and preserve their important functions.

In all parts of the North American continent there has been ongoing degradation of ecosystems. The lack of scientific knowledge of how ecosystems work and how valuable and useful they are has led to misdirected management of ecosystems, resulting in habitat loss, ecosystem degradation and fragmentation, ENDANGERED SPECIES, and EXTINCTION with great losses in biodiversity. Currently, entire ecosystems are threatened. Though management efforts have led to the gradual recovery of some ecosystems, there is a need for citizens to gain a greater sense of their ecological connections and the long-term impacts of human activities. The active involvement of common citizens is a key feature to preserving ecosystems and achieving SUSTAINABLE DEVELOPMENT.

The tropical Amazon rain forest of South America is a prominent example of DEFORESTATION in a rich ecosystem. Brazilian business leaders and multinational corporations deplete biodiversity formed during centuries of evolution only to use those lands for CATTLE grazing or COMMERCIAL AGRICULTURE. Making short-term economic profits for a few without thinking of the consequences of the degradation of ecosystems, however, arises not only from the monetary ambitions of some but also from the lack of a general knowledge of the importance of ecosystems. Destruction is heightened by the lack of counteraction from committed citizens in both the developing and developed worlds. Given ecosystems' incalculable value for human beings, ecosystem management must be creative in combining conservation with economic activities to achieve true sustainable development worldwide.

See also ECOLOGY.

Diego I. Murguía

Further Reading
Golley, Frank. *A History of the Ecosystem Concept in Ecology.* New Haven, Conn.: Yale University Press, 1993.
Lewis Yaffee, Steven. *Ecosystem Management in the United States: An Assessment of Current Experience.* Washington, D.C.: Island Press, 1996.
World Resources Institute. Earth Trends. "Environmental Information." Available online. URL: http://www.earthtrends.wri.org. Accessed August 22, 2006.

ecoterrorism

Ecoterrorism (also known as eco-sabotage or monkey-wrenching) is a form of direct action that targets individuals, groups, and infrastructures believed to be antinature and, thus, harmful to the health of the environment. The purpose of what detractors know as ecoterrorism is to address by immediate action what is being ignored, stalled, or compromised through more mainstream measures—litigation, petitions, and the like. This direct action can include vandalism, arson, theft, firebombing, tree spiking, tree sit-ins, and protests. In theory, ecoterrorists target structures, not people. They set fire to research buildings, damage construction equipment, protest environmental degradation, and spike trees but do not directly injure people or animals.

Many radical environmentalists hold up EDWARD ABBEY's 1975 novel *The Monkey Wrench Gang* as a cornerstone of ecoterrorism. Although the book was a fictional narrative, Abbey himself advocated casual monkey-wrenching to people who happened, while backpacking or hiking, upon stakes, billboards, and the like. In reality, Abbey's book only attached a name to a concept that had been expressed a century earlier. The philosophy of eco-sabotage or monkey-wrenching appears first to have been suggested by HENRY DAVID THOREAU. In *A Week on the Concord and Merrimack Rivers* (1849), Thoreau expressed a belief that it might be worth taking a crowbar to the Billerica Dam in Massachusetts on behalf of the shad (a native FISH).

The no-violence-toward-people tenet does not, however, always transfer into reality. Ecoterrorists simultaneously argue against violence toward people and support doing whatever is necessary to protect the natural world from destruction via development. Moreover, there is some evidence that a few ecoterrorists have begun targeting individuals (such as corporate executives and research scientists). Ecoterrorists—or eco-warriors, depending on one's perspective—justify this action by arguing that an environmental crisis is looming, that traditional avenues have failed, and that humanity must immediately counteract the forces of overpopulation and overdevelopment if it hopes to survive.

Ecoterrorism generally does not result in death for bystanders or targets (the handful of deaths that have occurred appear to have been unintended, the result of a fire, for example). Yet, injuries are not uncommon. These injuries should perhaps be expected given that the participants, the ecoterrorists, are using direct action as their primary tool. Direct action is high-risk: It draws attention to a cause through violent—some would say desperate—actions. Destruction of property, for example, draws attention to the ecoterrorists' cause but necessarily endangers the lives of those people still working in the building, still using the equipment, or still occupying the hillside mansion.

An important component of the ecoterrorist identity, then, is violence. Ecoterrorists became the target of raids and sting operations in the 1980s and 1990s as the broader public and law enforcement officials decided that these activists boasted of dangerous antihuman beliefs. In fact, concerned outsiders continue to fill newspaper columns with discussions of ecologically oriented militant activity. The threat within the United States is real enough that CONGRESS has discussed the issue of ecoterrorism on multiple occasions. Furthermore, around the start of the 21st century, the Federal Bureau of Investigation (FBI) labeled ecoterrorism the top domestic terrorism threat, and an animal rights activist recently made the FBI's most wanted terrorist list—the first time a domestic terrorist has earned such recognition.

Ecoterrorism emerged as a tool during the 1970s, when part of the environmental movement became radical. Around the time of the first EARTH DAY in 1970, the movement began to gain support from a broader base, and the makeup of the movement changed. Nonviolent protestors from the CIVIL RIGHTS MOVEMENT era and scientific educators joined traditional conservationists in focusing on environmental problems. With this infusion of members, environmentalists began (with differing levels of success) to substitute federal intervention with action at the grassroots level and to pair WILDERNESS issues with survival and quality of life issues. One of the results of these shifts was ecoterrorism.

Ecoterrorism thus married RADICAL ENVIRONMENTALISM with political action to create an ecocentric philosophy (ecoterrorists are ecocentric in the sense that they believe that all things, rather than humans alone, share intrinsic value). These terrorists or warriors or activists consciously created an identity that reacted against the compromise policies of mainstream environmentalists, who focused on time-consuming litigation and were willing to sign away some natural features (such as Glen Canyon) if it meant saving other natural features (such as Dinosaur National Monument). These ecoterrorists thus sought to work outside the system of bureaucracy (which had failed them) and to undo the 1980s professionalization of the environmental movement (which had undercut the radicalism of the 1970s).

Ecoterrorists now operate across the globe and frequently, though not always, associate with radical environmental groups. The best known radical groups include the Sea Shepherd Conservation Society, Friends of Earth, the Animal Liberation Front (ALF), the Earth Liberation Front (ELF), and EarthFirst! These various groups, however, disagree about what qualifies as a radical environmental group. Members of ELF, for example, often accuse members of EarthFirst! of "going soft," and most of these groups view Friends of Earth as hardly radical at all. Yet, most if not all of these radical groups and individuals broke away from more mainstream groups—such as the WILDERNESS SOCIETY, GREENPEACE, and People for the Ethical Treatment of Animals (PETA). Radical and mainstream groups alike then can suffer accusations of spinelessness.

Whatever the intensity of radical action, all of these groups share a commitment to protecting a vulnerable environment. And it should be remembered that the term *ecoterrorism* is a label applied by outsiders to radical environmentalists. What concerned citizenry call ecoterrorism, insiders may know as monkey-wrenching, a semidesperate, unorthodox, and, occasionally, violent method of protecting the Earth where there is still land to protect.

See also DAMS, RESERVOIRS, AND ARTIFICIAL LAKES; ENVIRONMENTALISM, GRASSROOTS; ENVIRONMENTALISM, RADICAL; GLEN CANYON DAM; POPULATION.

Kenna Lang Archer

Further Reading
Abbey, Edward. *The Monkey Wrench Gang.* New York: HarperCollins, 1976.
Foreman, Dave. *Confessions of an Eco-Warrior.* New York: Crown, 1991.
Liddick, Don. *Eco-Terrorism: Radical Environmental and Animal Liberation Movements.* Westport, Conn.: Greenwood, 2006.
Shabecoff, Philip. *A Fierce Green Fire: The American Environmental Movement.* New York: Hill & Wang, 1994.

Edison, Thomas (1847–1931) *inventor, entrepreneur*
A scientist, inventor, and businessman, Thomas Edison held more than 1,000 patents in his lifetime. Edison helped developed the modern electrical industry in the United States and with other pioneers fostered the widespread distribution of electricity, changing how Americans and people around the world lived and how they interacted with their physical environments, although Edison also investigated renewable energy sources as well.

Thomas Alva Edison was born in Milan, Ohio, on February 11, 1847. At the age of 16, he became a telegrapher, working at various jobs in the Midwest. While he continued to work as a TELEGRAPH operator after moving to BOSTON, MASSACHUSETTS, in 1868, Edison also experimented with numerous inventions, mainly in the area of telegraphy but also in other fields. In 1876, he set up his "invention plant" at Menlo Park, New Jersey. Edison made many important advances, inventing the phonograph in 1877 and later perfecting the incandescent electric light bulb. In 1887, he moved his headquarters to West Orange, New Jersey, where he continued with his inventions as well as creating companies to sell them. These companies eventually became the General Electric Company. Edison's experiments with motion pictures in the 1890s helped give birth to the movie industry. At his winter home in Fort Myers, Florida, Edison established the Edison Botanical Research Laboratory. Edison married twice. With his first wife, Mary Stillwell, he had three children. He then had three more children with his second wife, Mina Miller. Edison died on October 18, 1931, in West Orange, New Jersey.

Edison's improvements of electrical generators allowed him to introduce direct-current electric light in 1879, establishing wiring methods for power distribution. He developed the first electric meter to record usage, allowing him to charge customers for their consumption and making the electric industry economically viable. In 1882, the first commercial power station went into operation in Manhattan, providing service within one square mile of the plant. Over the next few decades, Edison continued to develop systems to produce and distribute electricity, providing light, heat, and power for industry over increasingly larger swaths of land. Electrical distribution became big business. Various electric companies reorganized as Edison General Electric in 1889; however, given the large amounts of capital required to construct the infrastructure, Edison relied on investors and never had a controlling interest. The company combined with its largest competitor in 1892 to form the General Electric Company.

Edison was the best known of many innovators in electricity at the end of the 19th century and beginning of the 20th century. Convenient electricity meant that people enjoyed inexpensive and safe light at home, work, and play. It enabled construction of global economies and their industrial, communication, lighting, and transportation infrastructure. Americans' thirst for electrical power altered the way they interacted with the nation's environments. For example, after World War II, they increasingly moved to the SUNBELT as electrically powered AIR CONDITIONING made hot southern environments more tolerable. To satiate their thirst for electricity, they harvested ever-greater quantities of fossil fuels, polluted the air in the burning of those fuels, and blocked free-flowing rivers with large multipurpose DAMS, for hydroelectric power.

While many critics blame him, perhaps unfairly, for the massive electric consumption of the modern age, Edison in fact worked on many environmentally friendly projects. For example, Edison had an interest in promoting wind power. In an article published in 1901 in the *Atlanta Constitution*, Edison outlined a plan to use windmills and small electric generators to power rural households. He hoped to build on the work of the inventor Charles Brush, who had developed a wind-powered home in CLEVELAND, OHIO, in 1888. Edison sought to spread this concept by designing a windmill that would power a cluster of four to six homes. In 1911, he presented a prototype to manufacturers. Edison was ahead of his time, however, and his plans for wind power were never widely applied.

In addition to exploring wind power, Edison took an interest in developing energy-self-sufficient homes. His first attempt was in 1912 in West Orange, New Jersey. Edison designed the "Twentieth-Century Suburban Residence" to use numerous electric appliances. However, he created the home to be off of the electric grid. His first design utilized a gas-run motor that

charged 27 cells in the basement of the house. It seems, however, that Edison envisioned future versions of the home would use the wind power in which he had also taken an interest.

Edison also examined the practicality of electric AUTOMOBILES. He worked with his friend HENRY FORD to design an electric car that would be as affordable and practical as the Model T. He envisioned that such vehicles could be charged along the electric trolley lines found in many U.S. cities in the early 20th century.

When none of these schemes took off, Edison again showed that he was ahead of his time when in 1931 he told his friends Henry Ford and the RUBBER and tire entrepreneur Harvey Firestone (1868–1938), "I'd put my money on the sun and solar energy. What a source of power! I hope we don't have to wait until oil and coal run out before we tackle that."

Besides his attempts to develop more sustainable forms of energy, Edison liked to enjoy nature trips. In part, this was a reflection of the times. As a response to industrialization, many Americans sought to return to nature, whether it was through hunting, as was the case with THEODORE ROOSEVELT, or through CONSERVATION efforts such as those of JOHN MUIR and JOHN BURROUGHS. In addition, Edison's personality contributed to his desire to be close to nature, as he disliked the formality that dominated the circles of the rich and powerful. His second wife, Mina, contributed greatly to this aspect of Edison's life, as she had a great interest in nature, BIRDS, and GARDENS AND GARDENING. Furthermore, Edison saw nature trips in a practical light, as he could search for new plants to use as filaments in electric light bulbs.

In 1904, Edison began making nature trips by car in New Hampshire and Massachusetts. The following year, he ventured to North Carolina. During the 1910s, Edison spent much time exploring Florida from his winter home in Fort Myers. He was particularly fond of Florida's natural environment, making trips up the Caloosahatchee River, on which his winter estate was located. In 1914, he visited the EVERGLADES with Ford and Firestone, spending much time bird watching. Edison also carried out numerous experiments utilizing Florida's environment. He experimented unsuccessfully with making RUBBER from the goldenrod plant. He also worked on using bamboo fibers for filaments in incandescent bulbs. His friends Ford and Firestone encouraged Edison in many of his Florida experiments. Indeed, Ford bought a home adjacent to Edison's in Fort Myers.

Later, Edison continued his travels along with Ford, Firestone, and the naturalist John Burroughs. The "Four Vagabonds," as they called themselves, took camping trips to remote areas that Edison referred to as "Nature's Laboratory." These trips became circuslike MEDIA events that sometimes even included visits in the 1920s by Presidents Warren Harding (1865–1923) and Calvin Coolidge (1872–1933). Nevertheless, the excursions allowed Edison to relax and heal from his hectic professional life.

See also CORPORATIONS, UTILITIES; ENERGY, ELECTRICAL; ENERGY, RENEWABLE; HOUSEHOLD APPLIANCES; NIAGARA FALLS.

Ronald Young

Further Reading

Baldwin, Neil. *Edison: Inventing the Century.* New York: Hyperion, 1995.

Israel, Paul. *Edison: Life of Invention.* New York: John Wiley & Sons, 1998.

Millard, Andre. *Edison and the Business of Innovation.* Baltimore: Johns Hopkins University Press, 1990.

Rogers, Heather. "Current Thinking." *New York Times Magazine,* 3 June 2007.

Thulesius, Olav. *Edison in Florida: The Green Laboratory.* Gainesville: University of Florida Press, 1997.

Edwards, Jonathan (1703–1758) *theologian, philosopher*

Jonathan Edwards was a Calvinist minister and theologian and the first great American philosopher. In his religious and scientific writings, Edwards suggested that humans could discover God's glory in the beauty of nature, even in its smallest creatures.

Edwards was born in Northampton, Massachusetts, on October 5, 1703, to a family of ministers. His primary calling was to ministry, and he entered the new Yale College (founded in 1701), preparing for a career in the pulpit. Edwards also built a strong background in philosophy, however, and became especially influenced by the empiricism (a branch of philosophy emphasizing the role of individual experience in the acquisition of knowledge) of the English thinker John Locke (1632–1704). Edwards blended the Calvinist theology of God's predestination of human history and the salvation of the "elect" (those God chose from the beginning of time to save from eternal damnation) with the philosophical insights he gained from his reading of Locke, successfully integrating the belief in divine providence with personal, immediate religious experience. Both Edwards's writings and his sermons—most notably "Sinners in the Hands of an Angry God" (1741), for which he is best known—helped spark the first great American religious revival, generally referred to by historians as the first GREAT AWAKENING, in the mid-18th century. He died on March 22, 1758, shortly after assuming the presidency of the College of New Jersey (now Princeton University).

Edwards's reading of contemporary philosophy also fueled a strong interest in science. He produced several scientific papers, many of them providing detailed analyses of natural phenomena stemming from close observation and experimentation (Edwards died testing a SMALLPOX vaccine intended for American Indians). His scientific writings, as did his love of nature, arose from his religious fervor. In his brief spiritual autobiography, Edwards describes going into the woods to pray (a departure from the practice of most New England Calvinists) and delights in finding signs of God's handiwork in the natural world. Further, his scientific writings display an abundant confidence not only that God's creation is good but that God's love is so great for all of it that he extends his providence even to the smallest and (by human standards) most "vile" creatures. In his famous "Spider Letter" (1723), in which Edwards provides a theory about the way that "flying" spiders transport themselves in the wind, he sees God's love as a sort of safety valve built into nature, ensuring not only that the spiders may gain "enjoyment" by transporting themselves from tree to tree but also that the most "imprudent" spiders are swept on the wind out to sea, preventing creation from being overrun with them.

Despite his love of nature, Edwards always had humanity in mind and drew lessons with moral significance from his walks in the woods and his scientific observations. His example of the few prudent spiders who survive perdition in the fall is confirmation for him of the truth of predestination—that only the few elect will be saved. Further, in his posthumously published investigation of the theological significance of natural phenomena, *Images, or Shadows of Divine Things,* he compares such events as the ripening of fruit on a tree to the experience within the soul of the saved of sanctification, of the deepening of God's grace. Edwards's scientific and theological writings provide an overarching sense that God is in control of the cosmos, and that by appreciating the beauty of the natural world, humanity recognizes and heightens God's glory. Edwards's insight into the relationship between natural beauty and divine truth and his emphasis on the individual's spiritual experience—if not his Calvinism—influenced American transcendentalist writers such as RALPH WALDO EMERSON and HENRY DAVID THOREAU and poets such as Emily Dickinson (1830–86) and Robert Frost.

See also ENGLISH EXPLORATION AND SETTLEMENT—CANADA AND NEW ENGLAND, RELIGION.

Matt Stefon

Further Reading

Austin, Richard Cartwright. "Beauty: A Foundation for Environmental Ethics." *Environmental Ethics* 7 (Fall 1985): 197–208.

New, Elisa. *The Line's Eye: Poetic Insight, American Thought.* Cambridge, Mass.: Harvard University Press, 1996.

Smith, John E., Harry P. Stout, and Kenneth Mikema, eds. *The Jonathan Edwards Reader.* New Haven, Conn.: Yale University Press, 2004.

Ehrlich, Paul and Anne (1932– and 1933–) *authors, biologists*

The biologists Paul and Anne Ehrlich, who have been married since 1954, have authored separately, coauthored together, or coauthored with others more than 10 books and hundreds of scientific articles. Their best known works have predicted global problems of overpopulation and famine and helped raised awareness about the scarcity of natural resources and other environmental issues.

Born on May 29, 1932, in PHILADELPHIA, PENNSYLVANIA, Paul Ehrlich studied ZOOLOGY, earning a B.A. from the University of Pennsylvania and an M.A. and Ph.D. at the University of Kansas. He joined the faculty at Stanford University in 1959 and became the Bing Professor of Population Studies in the department of Biological Sciences in 1977. A well-regarded entomologist specializing in Lepidoptera (butterflies), Ehrlich is perhaps best known for his work on the subject of human overpopulation.

Paul Ehrlich's most popular and controversial book, considered a wake-up call for an entire generation, is *The Population Bomb,* published in 1968. In the book, Ehrlich predicted that exponential human population growth would exceed food sources and result in widespread famine within a few decades. When events did not come to pass as outlined in his books, critics of Ehrlich and the environmental movement argued that his research was characteristic of environmentalists' fearmongering claims of looming catastrophe. Ehrlich's book contributed to an antienvironmental backlash in the United States.

Ehrlich later conceded that the famines were averted through the GREEN REVOLUTION and a decline in the fertility rate, but he reminds his critics that his book described "various scenarios" and did not make specific "predictions." He points out that the total population of the planet has increased by "billions" since he began his work and that the world is in the midst of an ongoing population explosion, as confirmed by some 58 academies of science. Most serious researchers concede the preeminence of his scholarship, the importance of his conclusions, and the usual accuracy of his methodology.

Anne Ehrlich was born Anne Fitzhugh Howland on November 17, 1933, in Des Moines, Iowa. She attended the University of Kansas from 1952 to 1955. With her husband, she has conducted research on and authored several books on the subjects of overpopulation and ecology. In 1990, for example, the Ehrlichs published *The Population Explosion,* arguing that while Paul Ehrlich's most horrific conclusions had not been realized, some 600 million people in the world suffer from hunger or malnutrition. Other scholars, most notably the geographer and biologist Jared Diamond, have echoed the Ehrlichs' concerns, contending that overpopulation and overexploitation of resources have caused societies to collapse throughout human history.

Paul Ehrlich helped found the Zero Population Growth organization in 1968. Ehrlich has been president of the Center for Conservation Biology at Stanford University since its inception in 1984. Among many honors and awards, he is a fellow of the American Philosophical Society, the American Academy of Arts and Sciences, and the American Associa-

tion for the Advancement of Science. Anne Ehrlich has been an associate director and policy coordinator of the Center for Conservation Biology since 1987. At various times, she has served on the boards of the Federation for American Immigration Reform, the SIERRA CLUB, the New-Land Foundation, and the Pacific Institute for Studies in Environment, Development, and Security.

The Ehrlichs' recent books have focused on the preservation of genetic resources, environmental ethics, cultural evolution, and endangered species. Together Paul and Anne Ehrlich remain active leaders in environmental and scientific organizations. Through their positions in the Center for Conservation Biology, they work with international scholars to use science to help conserve humanity's "biological capital."

See also AGRICULTURE, COMMERCIAL; ENVIRONMENTALISM, MAINSTREAM; ENVIRONMENTALISM, OPPOSITION TO; ENVIRONMENTALISM, RADICAL; FOOD; POPULATION.

John V. O'Sullivan

Further Reading
Diamond, Jared. *Collapse: How Societies Choose to Fail or Succeed.* New York: Viking, 2005.

Ehrlich, Paul R. *Betrayal of Science and Reason: How Anti-Environmental Rhetoric Threatens Our Future.* Washington, D.C.: Island Press, 1998.

———. *The Population Bomb.* New York: Ballantine Books, 1968.

Ehrlich, Paul R. and Anne H. Ehrlich. *The Population Explosion.* New York: Simon & Schuster, 1990.

Einstein, Albert (1879–1955) *physicist*

Albert Einstein was one of the greatest physicists of all time and one of the most famous scientists to have ever lived. Einstein's fame is a direct outcropping of the fundamental problems of nature he solved and his presentation of new ideas that challenged established convention, especially the dogma of Newtonian mechanics. Einstein effectively changed the way humans view the physical world in which they live. As Einstein once said, "Unthinking respect for authority is the greatest enemy of truth."

Einstein was born on March 14, 1879, in the city of Ulm in the Kingdom of Württemberg within the German empire. His family moved to Munich that same year; there his father founded a firm that manufactured electrical equipment and Einstein later attended school. The family moved to Italy around 1894, and Albert continued his education at Aarau, Switzerland, entering the Swiss Federal Polytechnic School in Zurich in 1896 to be trained as a teacher. In 1901, the year Einstein gained his diploma, he acquired Swiss citizenship. Unable to get a job as a teacher, he accepted a position as technical assistant in the Swiss patent office. In 1905, he obtained his doctoral degree. During his stay at the Patent Office, and in his spare time, he produced much of his remarkable work.

In 1905, a watershed year for the scientist, Einstein published five papers—four of which addressed the photoelectric effect, Brownian motion, the special theory of relativity, and the interchangeability of mass and energy. In one paper, he dealt with the photoelectric effect, whereby photons of light cause metal atoms to release their hold on electrons. These freed electrons can be made to flow as electric current, the very basis on which solar energy panels produce electricity. Einstein explained that the photoelectric effect occurs because light is contained in discrete bundles of energy called quanta, known today as photons. His ideas in this area would be extended with the invention of the laser 55 years later. In another 1905 paper, Einstein explained Brownian motion, the irregular movement of microscopic particles suspended in a liquid or a gas, first observed by Robert Brown in 1827. Einstein's analysis stimulated research on Brownian motion that led to the first experimental proof that atoms exist.

Einstein's enormously influential June 1905 paper presented his special theory of relativity. Here he made a conceptual breakthrough. Einstein wrote that constant motion does not affect the velocity of light (an object's speed in a given direction)—the speed of light is a universal constant for all observers. Concurrent with this idea was the notion that the laws of physics are the same (invariant) for all observers moving at constant speed.

In his September 1905 paper, Einstein discussed one of the key results of the special theory of relativity—energy and mass are interchangeable. It was really an extension of the June paper that includes the world's most famous equation, $E = mc^2$. He argued that the speed of light is so great that the conversion of only a tiny quantity of mass releases a tremendous amount of energy, the principle upon which nuclear fission used in power plants is based and upon which nuclear fusion found in the heat of stars is observed. Einstein did not invent nuclear energy, but he transformed the way we think about space and time. The physicist's ideas led to dramatic changes in the ways humans used energy and were pivotal to the MANHATTAN PROJECT, which ushered in the atomic age.

Between 1908 and 1933, Einstein held various professorships at universities in Europe, returning in 1914 to the University of Berlin and Germany, where he again became a German citizen. In 1916, Einstein's paper on the general theory of relativity was published. Astronomers confirmed the theory in 1919 by observing the sun's gravitational field's bending light rays during a solar eclipse. Einstein showed that gravity affects time as well, in that the presence of a strong gravitational field makes clocks run more slowly. Gravity is not a force: It is the curvature of space and time. His theory also provided the basis for the existence of black holes, a region of space whose gravitational force is so strong that not even light can escape.

Einstein continues to be best remembered for realizing the inadequacies of Newtonian mechanics. His special theory of relativity stemmed from his attempts to reconcile the laws of mechanics with the laws of the electromagnetic field. The result is a grander theory, which treats Newtonian mechanics as a subset of the theory of relativity for speeds much slower than the speed of light. Einstein was a theoretician, not an experimentalist, and he popularized thought experiments.

Einstein received the 1921 Nobel Prize in PHYSICS for this work on the photoelectric effect. Shortly after the rise of Adolf Hitler and the Nazi Party in 1933, Einstein, a Jew, renounced his German citizenship for political reasons and immigrated to America to take the position of professor of theoretical physics at Princeton University, a post he held until 1945. He became a U.S. citizen in 1940. On August 2, 1939, shortly before the start of WORLD WAR II (1941–45), Einstein and other scientists advised President FRANKLIN D. ROOSEVELT of Nazi Germany's efforts to purify uranium-235, which could be used in an atomic weapon. Shortly thereafter, the U.S. government launched the Manhattan Project, which produced the atomic bombs that helped end World War II in 1945. The Germans did not succeed in their efforts. Ironically, the U.S. Army Intelligence Office deemed Einstein a security risk because of his leftist political views, denied him a security clearance to work on the Manhattan Project, and prohibited participating scientists from consulting him.

Einstein died on April 18, 1955, in Princeton, New Jersey. On December 31, 1999, *Time* magazine recognized him as the "person of the 20th century," believing that the 20th century would be remembered for its advancements in science and technology and that Einstein best symbolized the world's scientists. The physics community honored him during 2005 for the centennial of the year in which he produced his famous five papers.

See also ENERGY, NUCLEAR; NUCLEAR WEAPONS AND TESTING.

Robert Karl Koslowsky

Further Reading

Brockman, John, ed. *My Einstein: Essays by 24 of the World's Leading Thinkers on the Man, His Work, and His Legacy.* New York: Pantheon Books, 2006.

Crelinston, Jeffrey. *Einstein's Jury: The Race to Test Relativity.* New York: Princeton University Press, 2006.

Koslowsky, Robert K. *A World Perspective through 21st Century Eyes: The Impact of Science on Society.* Victoria, Canada: Trafford, 2004.

Eisenhower, Dwight D. (Ike) (1890–1969) *supreme commander of Allied Forces (World War II), 34th president of the United States (1953–1961)*

President Dwight D. Eisenhower and the officials of his administration did not rank protection of the environment as a high priority of domestic policy. Instead, throughout his presidency from 1953 to 1961, Eisenhower gave orders and pushed for laws that made the environment more accessible for business needs. Although many of his policies were later reversed by the subsequent administrations of Presidents JOHN F. KENNEDY, from 1961 to 1963, and LYNDON B. JOHNSON from 1963 to 1969, Eisenhower stood behind the idea that environmental health was second to national interests.

Eisenhower was born on October 14, 1890, in Denison, Texas, to David and Ida Stover Eisenhower. The family moved to Abilene, Kansas, in 1892. After graduating from high school, Eisenhower worked as a night foreman for two years to help pay his brother's college tuition. He then received an appointment to the U.S. Military Academy at West Point, graduating in the class of 1915. He moved up the ranks of the U.S. Army through various appointments, and in June 1942, six months after the attack on Pearl Harbor propelled the United States into WORLD WAR II (1941–45), he took command of all U.S. forces in Europe. In December 1943, Eisenhower became supreme allied commander in Europe, overseeing the D-day invasion in June 1944, the liberation of Western Europe, and the invasion and ultimate defeat of Germany in May 1945.

In 1948, Eisenhower assumed the presidency of Columbia University. In 1951, he took a leave of absence to assume command of the forces of the newly formed NORTH ATLANTIC TREATY ORGANIZATION. Although he had never served at the front, Eisenhower was a military hero for many Americans. Members of the REPUBLICAN PARTY persuaded him to be a presidential candidate in 1952, and he defeated the DEMOCRATIC PARTY nominee Adlai Stevenson (1900–65) that year and again in 1956.

Eisenhower was committed to reversing many of the policies established by President FRANKLIN D. ROOSEVELT's NEW DEAL. He wanted to remove power from the federal government and turn it over to the states. This position led him to oppose legislation that would have given more power to the federal government, including proposed laws to protect the environment. One of the major environmental questions during Eisenhower's administration concerned the preservation of forested lands. Eisenhower believed that local and state governments should have the final say over what do with forested lands in their jurisdictions. Eisenhower particularly opposed the further federal acquisition of forested land for preservation. Although his primary purpose was to limit the role of the federal government, this policy also helped him with another objective—trimming the federal budget.

As did many other Republicans, Eisenhower believed that the nation's resources should be utilized rather than preserved. His appointments to various federal bureaucracies reflected those views. To this end, the Eisenhower administration in 1954 supported building DAMS, RESERVOIRS, AND ARTIFICIAL LAKES in the COLORADO RIVER basin. One proposed dam was at Echo Park, a remote area within Dinosaur National Monument. After a vigorous MEDIA campaign by the SIERRA CLUB and other conservationists, CONGRESS and Eisenhower agreed to forgo the dam within the monument and instead built the GLEN CANYON DAM. Eisenhower agreed with the then-accepted wisdom of the BUREAU OF RECLAMATION and the U.S. ARMY CORPS OF ENGINEERS that free-flowing rivers were wasteful and needed to be dammed for control of FLOODS, IRRIGATION, and generating of electricity.

Eisenhower's administration launched another project that dramatically altered the American landscape—the INTERSTATE HIGHWAY SYSTEM. The proposed highway system greatly enhanced private and commercial transportation, and it also provided ground transportation routes for military supplies and troop deployments in case of emergency or foreign invasion. In many cases, however, the new highways and connecting roads destroyed outright or fragmented animal habitats. The highways also created new habitats for small mammals in medians, resulting in increased pressures on available food supplies. Engineers designed the system to move traffic efficiently, and adherence to this principal led to construction practices that added to soil EROSION, caused water drainage problems, and destroyed forests.

During Eisenhower's presidency, Americans also began to debate the safety and morality of nuclear energy, as concerns about nuclear war and the arms race with the Soviet Union influenced much of the national culture. Eisenhower supported additional research, believing that atomic energy for civilian use was the wave of the future. In 1953, Eisenhower called for the establishment of an international committee to discuss research issues and emphasized his desire that research be directed at civilian uses. The next year, nuclear fallout from an American test in the Pacific Ocean sickened the crew of a Japanese fishing boat, aptly pointing to the dangers posed by the expansion of nuclear energy. Even after this, the financial benefits of nuclear energy were too substantial to ignore, and research continued with Eisenhower's approval.

On January 17, 1961, on the eve of his departure from the presidency, Eisenhower gave a speech discussing what he called the MILITARY-INDUSTRIAL COMPLEX. In it, he noted the rise in prominence of the military and defense sector in society. While he believed that the military was essential to the nation's defense, he also worried about the effect on society of the sector's unprecedented growth since World War II. Eisenhower warned the people of the United States that although the military may grow in size, it should not be allowed to grow in power and influence. One worry that he left out was over the effect that the military-industrial complex would have on the environment. The DEPARTMENT OF DEFENSE and its subsidiaries are, and have been, some of the worst polluters in the United States, a concern that Eisenhower did not foresee or at least did not vocalize. Eisenhower died eight years after leaving office on March 28, 1969, in Washington, D.C.

See also ATOMIC ENERGY COMMISSION; ENERGY, NUCLEAR; NUCLEAR WEAPONS AND TESTING.

Chelsea Griffis

Further Reading
Andrews, Richard N. L. *Managing the Environment, Managing Ourselves: A History of American Environmental Policy.* New Haven, Conn.: Yale University Press, 1999.
Brooks, Karl Boyd. *Before Earth Day: The Origins of American Environmental Law, 1945–1970.* Lawrence: University Press of Kansas, 2008.
Eisenhower, Dwight D. "Military Industrial Complex Speech, January 17, 1961." Available online. URL: http://coursesa.matrix.msu.edu/~hst306/documents/indust.html. Accessed July 9, 2009.
Soden, Dennis L. *The Environmental Presidency.* Albany: State University of New York Press, 1999.

electrical energy   *See* ENERGY, ELECTRICAL.

Elton, Charles Sutherland (1900–1991) *ecologist, author*

The British ecologist Charles Sutherland Elton was one of the leaders in developing an economic approach to ECOLOGY—the idea of ecology as a science that investigates the economy of nature. In this approach, organisms are characterized as producers and consumers while nature maximizes efficiencies and yields.

Elton was born in Withington, England, on March 29, 1900. After his schooling at Liverpool College, Elton began his academic career at New College, University of Oxford, in 1919. Influenced by his mentors at Oxford, Edwin S. Goodrich and Julian S. Huxley, Elton pursued his interest in ZOOLOGY, while eschewing the traditional emphasis on laboratory-based embryology and anatomy for the emerging field-based discipline of ecology. The early 20th century was an exciting time in scientific research associated with the environment and most notably with the birth of this discipline, which applied scientific method to NATURAL HISTORY.

During his university years, Elton participated in three scientific expeditions to Spitzbergen in the high arctic in 1921, 1923, and 1924 to collect ecological data. This work strengthened his view that fieldwork was a vital component of ecological studies because it allowed scientists to study animals in relation to their environment and its plants and other animals. Graduating with first-class honors in 1922, he was appointed a departmental demonstrator the next year at Oxford, where he remained throughout his career. Elton's first book, *Animal Ecology* (1927), became a seminal work and remains an important text today, in part, because of its recognition of a concept that became known as the Eltonian niche, which is discussed in the following.

Elton's arctic experience focused on the population dynamics of arctic mammals, an emphasis that led to his appointment as a consultant to the Hudson's Bay Company (1926–31). This position gave him access to company records dating from 1736, which, in turn, facilitated his research on the population fluctuations of fur-bearing animals. Subsequently, he wrote *Voles, Mice and Lemmings* (1942). Elton was responsible for a long-term ecological project between 1945 to 1967 at Wytham Wood, Oxfordshire. These investigations of animal communities and population fluctuations culminated in *The Pattern of Animal Communities,* published in 1966, the year before he retired from full-time service at Oxford, although he remained affiliated with the university until his death.

Elton's various studies on food webs and food chains continue to be referred to today, notably the concept of the "Eltonian niche" and the pyramid of numbers. The Eltonian niche emphasizes how individual species converge and interact (e.g., through food chains) to form communities. The pyramid of numbers describes the number of organisms that are present at each trophic (feeding) level in a community; generally there are few top predators compared with many more primary producers and intermediate numbers of intermediate species. Both concepts contribute to the understanding of how communities and ecosystems function, notably through energy flows.

Elton's embrace of the issue of biological invasions led to another classic work, *The Ecology of Invasions by Animals and Plants* (1958). He recognized problems associated with the invasiveness of introduced plants and animals in natural ecosystems and their capacity to cause environmental change. His work established invasion ecology as a subdiscipline of ecology.

In addition to publishing several other books and research papers, Elton founded and directed, from 1932 to 1967, the British Bureau of Animal Population. He helped found and edited, from 1932 to 1952, the *Journal of Animal Ecology.* Elton's many contributions to ecology received recognition throughout the scientific world and included an honorary membership in the New York Zoological Society in 1931, election to the Royal Society in 1953, inclusion as a life member and eminent ecologist of the Ecological Society of America in 1961, presidency of the British Ecological Society from 1948 to 1950, an honorary membership in 1959 and the gold medal in 1967 from the Linnean Society, and the Darwin Medal of the Royal Society in 1970. In addition to his research, Elton was involved in ecosystem management and conservation and helped to establish the Nature Conservancy Council in the United Kingdom. He died on May 1, 1991, in Oxford, England.

See also ANIMALS, WILD; ODUM, EUGENE PLEASANTS; RODENTS; SPECIES, EXOTIC AND INVASIVE; SPECIES, INDIGENOUS.

A. M. Mannion

Further Reading
Crowcroft, Peter. *Elton's Ecologists: A History of the Bureau of Animal Population.* Chicago: University of Chicago Press, 1991.

Elton, Charles S. *Animal Ecology*. London: Sidgwick and Jackson, 1927.

Sheail, John. *Seventy-Five Years in Ecology: The British Ecological Society*. Oxford: Blackwell, 1987.

Worster, Donald. *Nature's Economy: The Roots of Ecology*. San Francisco: Sierra Club Books, 1977.

emancipation

In the context of U.S. history, emancipation involved the abolition of African chattel slavery. It occurred in two periods and places. The first emancipation happened in the northern states largely in conjunction with the AMERICAN REVOLUTION (1775–83). The second emancipation took place during the CIVIL WAR (1861–65) and applied to the remainder of the country. This second phase of emancipation substantially altered agricultural practices and the environments of the American South.

In the northern colonies before the Revolution, slave labor did not account for a high percentage of the total workforce, and it is therefore often overlooked by historians. Emancipation in these colonies (later states) occurred in a wave rather than at a precise moment. Starting in northern New England and pushing its way south, emancipation in the North was characterized by two approaches, immediate and gradual emancipation. In New England during the 1770s and 1780s, Massachusetts, Connecticut, Rhode Island, New Hampshire, and Vermont witnessed a quick and immediate emancipation of the small numbers of slaves found there. The Mid-Atlantic region, containing higher numbers of slaves, moved more slowly to abolish slavery. The state of Pennsylvania set the example in 1780, when its new state government instituted a gradual emancipation. This style of emancipation was slowly adopted by New York and New Jersey, with the effect of slavery lingering in the North until the mid-19th century.

The southern case of emancipation is strikingly different. While the northern colonies or states enacted their own emancipation legislation, the federal government mandated emancipation in the rebelling states of the CONFEDERACY (Virginia, North Carolina, South Carolina, Georgia, Florida, Alabama, Mississippi, Tennessee, Arkansas, Louisiana, and Texas). During the Civil War, on January 1, 1863, President ABRAHAM LINCOLN issued the Emancipation Proclamation—an executive order—freeing all slaves in the rebelling states. In the border states of Kentucky, Maryland, Missouri, West Virginia, and Delaware, emancipation waited until 1865 and the ratification of the Thirteenth Amendment to the U.S. CONSTITUTION, which legally abolished slavery in the United States.

The emancipation of some four million slaves over the short period of two years had a profound effect on the southern landscape. The steep decline in agricultural production during the Civil War was primarily attributable to military disruptions rather than slaves' gaining freedom. Emancipation for most did not occur until the arrival of the Union Army in their particular region. While the Union general William Tecumseh Sherman (1820–91), in Special Field Order 15, briefly attempted to redistribute land to former slaves along the Georgia coast, the infamous "FORTY ACRES AND A MULE" was actually more myth than reality. Agriculture continued to dominate the southern economy after the war, and COTTON remained king, but changes did occur.

The first effect of emancipation was the internal migration of large numbers of freedmen and freedwomen throughout the South. Many former slaves moved across the land testing their freedom and searching for lost family members. Southern cities swelled as thousands of African Americans fled the horrors of the field. However, most freed black men and women stayed near their old PLANTATIONS and homes and continued performing agricultural work, although they did not continue their old lives as slaves. Instead, they forced the southern economy to adjust to wage labor. African Americans bargained for shorter hours, better working conditions, and real wages through the FREEDMEN'S BUREAU, a government agency established to assist former slaves. The immediate effect was a labor shortage. The RICE plantations along the coasts of South Carolina and Georgia felt this labor shortage most sharply as their extensive drainage systems crumbled and washed away during the postwar years; slave labor previously provided the demanding maintenance these systems required.

White landowners, searching for an effective way to increase cotton production in the cash-strapped South, leased land to tenants in a SHARECROPPING system. Sharecropping is an agricultural practice in which the farm and SEED are owned by the landholder and the tenant farmer receives half of the product at harvest in return for labor. In the South, this agricultural system focused almost exclusively on cotton.

Sharecropping dramatically changed southern agriculture. In a period of 10 years, from 1860 to 1870, the size of farms was greatly reduced while cotton production greatly increased. In 1860, for example, 81 percent of southern farms were more than 100 acres. By 1870, only 30 percent of farms were that large. During this decade, the number of smaller farms, from three to 49 acres, increased from 7 percent to 20 percent. African Americans worked nearly all of these smaller farms through sharecropping.

Required to grow cotton by both landlords and local moneylenders, sharecropping further added to the South's dependence on the MONOCULTURE production, the growing of a single crop. The small amount of land available to African-American sharecroppers meant an increased demand for field productivity. Harvesting nearly twice the amount of cotton per acre of white landowners, African-American sharecroppers in the South depleted soil fertility at high rates yet remained in debt to white landowners in a system that strongly favored the landowner.

In the 1850s and 1860s, the southern states' production of food crops exceeded 35 bushels per person; this number fell below 20 bushes by 1870. Consequently, before the war, southern states generally produced enough food to feed their populations; after the war, farmers in the region increasingly bought food to feed their families rather than growing it themselves. Seven out of 10 sharecroppers relied on local store credit to supplement food production from their own land.

From generations of working the southern landscape, African Americans developed an intimate knowledge of their environment. With emancipation and the new demands of sharecropping, this relationship changed. For slaves, there was a marked division between the oppression of the agricultural lands and the freedom found in swamps and FORESTS. Emancipation nullified the freedom once associated with marginal lands and gave new meaning to agricultural land. With even the limited sense of ownership found in sharecropping, African Americans began associating field productivity with personal identity. Thus African Americans' reappraisal of land narrowed their perception of its use. Previously valued natural spaces containing native plants and animals gave way to capital-driven agricultural production, which was not sustainable. The result left southern soils nutrient deficient and susceptible to insect infestations and plant pathogens, common side effects in monocultural farming.

See also AGRICULTURE, COMMERCIAL; BOLL WEEVIL; SECTIONALISM; UNITED STATES—DEEP SOUTH; UNITED STATES—GULF COAST; UNITED STATES—TIDEWATER.

Bob Watson

Further Reading

Berlin, Ira. *Generations of Captivity: A History of African-American Slaves.* Cambridge, Mass.: Belknap Press of Harvard University, 2003.

Holzer, Harold, et al. *The Emancipation Proclamation: Three Views.* Baton Rouge: Louisiana State University Press, 2006.

Ransom, Roger L. *Conflict and Compromise: The Political Economy of Slavery, Emancipation and the American Civil War.* New York: Cambridge University Press, 1989.

Stewart, Mart A. *What Nature Suffers to Groe: Life, Labor and Landscape on the Georgia Coast, 1680–1920.* Athens: University of Georgia Press, 1996.

Emerson, Ralph Waldo (1803–1882) *philosopher, theologian, essayist*

A leading philosopher and essayist of the transcendentalist school of thought, Ralph Waldo Emerson believed that the human soul corresponded to a universal oversoul, allowing people to find larger truths through self-examination. He believed that nature embodied this universal spirit. Unlike

The essayist Ralph Waldo Emerson was one of the leading voices of the transcendentalist movement in the 19th century. *(Library of Congress)*

other transcendentalists, Emerson also eagerly embraced the commercial spirit of an industrializing United States in the 19th century.

Born in Boston, Massachusetts, on May 25, 1803, into a family of ministers, Emerson graduated from Harvard University with the intention of maintaining the tradition. Yet while serving as pastor to Boston's Second Church, Emerson grew to feel that the Unitarian Christianity he was preaching ran contrary to a truly religious life because it was too concerned with reason and ritual rather than with a life open to the spirit of God. Resigning his post because of a disagreement about the significance of the Lord's Supper, and inheriting money after his young wife's death, Emerson moved to nearby Concord, Massachusetts, studying philosophy, including non-Western (especially Indian) thought, and launching a career as an essayist and public speaker.

His first essay, a long piece entitled "Nature" and published in 1836, proposed the "correspondence" between natural and spiritual facts, a resonance between human religiosity and the greater world of which human society is only a small part. This was Emerson's call to Americans to find spiritual truths not from human institutions but from a more immediate source, which he identified with nature. His essay attracted the attention of other younger writers—including the recent Harvard graduate and Concord native HENRY DAVID THO-

REAU—inspired by Emerson's essay to link both religious and social reform. Many of Emerson's subsequent essays—including "Experience" and "Fate"—took a less optimistic, darker view of any possible affinities between nature and the oversoul. Thoreau, who spent much time observing natural phenomena and meditating on their spiritual and moral significance for humanity, arguably put Emerson's philosophy into practical use more effectively than Emerson did himself. Yet as the effective spokesperson for the so-called transcendentalist movement, Emerson influenced a tradition of writers and thinkers seeking in the individual experience of nature spiritual and moral rejuvenation, an eminence he continued to enjoy long after his death on April 27, 1882, in Concord.

Emerson invigorated the notion held by New England Puritans of the 17th and early 18th centuries of the "Book of Nature," the notion that the natural world had some spiritual and moral significance for human destiny. Puritans themselves were generally wary of the natural world; in the 18th century, the Puritan theologian and philosopher JONATHAN EDWARDS provided a more positive interpretation of the idea, stressing creation's goodness and arguing for God's providence. Emerson adapted the notion further, moving away from Calvinism (a theological approach that emphasized an omnipotent God, a depraved humanity, and an alien nature) and adopting a view of a transcendent divinity that was also immanent, present within the natural world and within one's own soul. To Emerson, nature was more than woods and trees. Nature was an active and dynamic power that shaped humans and the world around them. Further, Emerson's nature is not a text upon which God, as the supreme author of the universe, has written his intention for humanity to read in nature. Rather, as he wrote in "The Poet" (1844), spiritual facts must be interpreted through the ingenuity of the poet, who promotes "health" among the human community by "reattaching" the things of nature to "the whole" dynamic soul animating it.

Emerson saw the natural world as a dynamic, unfolding, vital process of which human beings were a part and to which they needed to attune in order to fulfill their spiritual as well as their intellectual capacities. He gradually distanced himself—especially after the advent of the Darwinian view of EVOLUTION through unceasing competition and strife rather than benign providence and design—from the optimism of his earlier writings. Yet the "evanescence and lubricity" characterizing the natural world of which humans were part and parcel still did not entail pessimism, he wrote in "Experience" (1844). Subsequent thinkers influenced by Emerson—most notably Thoreau but also the naturalist and preservationist JOHN MUIR—extended regard for this natural dynamism into a reverence, echoed by their own followers, for the WILDERNESS.

See also DARWIN, CHARLES; NATURE WRITING; TRANSCENDENTALISM.

Matt Stefon

Further Reading

Buell, Lawrence. *Emerson.* Cambridge, Mass.: Harvard University Press, 2003.

Gura, Philip. *American Transcendentalism: A History.* New York: Hill & Wang, 2007.

Richardson, Robert D., and Barry Mosner. *Emerson: The Mind on Fire.* Berkeley: University of California Press, 1996.

Robinson, David M., ed. *The Spiritual Emerson.* Boston: Beacon Press, 2003.

"Nature"
Ralph Waldo Emerson (1836)

The transcendentalism of Ralph Waldo Emerson and Henry David Thoreau challenged both literal readings of the Bible and the Enlightenment idea that nature could be understood simply through empirical observation and scientific organization. Emerson's essay "Nature," published anonymously in 1836, was foundational in the development of this uniquely American philosophy, which emphasized a mystical union with nature unencumbered by layers of history.

In the woods, we return to reason and faith. There I feel that nothing can befall me in life,—no disgrace, no calamity (leaving me my eyes), which nature cannot repair. Standing on the bare ground,—my head bathed by the blithe air and uplifted into infinite space,—all mean egotism vanishes. I become a transparent eyeball; I am nothing; I see all; the currents of the Universal Being circulate through me; I am part or parcel of God. The name of the nearest friend sounds then foreign and accidental: to be brothers, to be acquaintances, master or servant, is then a trifle and a disturbance. I am the lover of uncontained and immortal beauty. In the wilderness, I find something more dear and connate than in streets or villages. In the tranquil landscape, and especially in the distant line of the horizon, man beholds somewhat as beautiful as his own nature.

The greatest delight which the fields and woods minister is the suggestion of an occult relation between man and the vegetable. I am not alone and unacknowledged. They nod to me, and I to them. The waving of the boughs in the storm is new to me and old. It takes me by surprise, and yet is not unknown. Its effect is like that of a higher thought or a better emotion coming over me, when I deemed I was thinking justly or doing right.

Yet it is certain that the power to produce this delight does not reside in nature, but in man, or in a harmony of both. It is necessary to use these pleasures with great temperance. For nature is not always tricked in holiday attire, but the same scene which yesterday breathed perfume and glittered as for the frolic of the nymphs is overspread with melancholy to-day. Nature always wears the colors of the spirit. To a man laboring under calamity, the heat of his own fire hath sadness in it. Then there is a kind of contempt of the landscape felt by him who has just lost by death a dear friend. The sky is less grand as it shuts down over less worth in the population.

⟨◆⟩

Source: Nature; Addresses; and Lectures. Ralph Waldo Emerson. Boston and New York: Houghton, Mifflin, 1903, 10–11.

emissions trading

Emissions trading is an incentive-based alternative to direct, across-the-board regulation of pollution sources. The latter approach, by virtue of its uniform application, tends to impose higher compliance costs on some firms relative to others due to variations in technical, geographical, or other circumstances.

Emissions trading addresses this deficiency by allowing firms with high compliance costs to transfer their pollution-reduction obligation to others in exchange for payment. Under one prominent version of this approach (known as cap-and-trade), regulatory authorities first set a limit on the aggregate amount of pollutants to be emitted by a group of polluters over a given period and next allocate to each of the sources within that group a specified amount of pollution "allowances," or "permits," consistent with the achievement of the aggregate pollution target. The permits are tradable in a fashion that offers plants a choice between two modes of compliance. The first is to restrict their emissions to levels equal to or lower than the amount authorized by their permits. The second is to emit above the initial permit quota through the purchase of additional permits from sources that find it economical to create surplus pollution reductions. This flexibility allows for differential levels of pollution control across regulated sources, in contrast to across-the-board demands for uniform reduction by all relevant sources. The benefits and drawbacks of this approach are at the heart of current environmental policy debates.

The theoretical foundations for emissions trading were laid out during the 1960s in parallel with growing political pressure for environmental regulation. Ronald Coase, Thomas D. Crocker, and John H. Dales are the three prominent economists whose work is most often cited in this connection. The passage of the 1970 CLEAN AIR ACT prompted

the first practical applications of the trading concept when the U.S. ENVIRONMENTAL PROTECTION AGENCY (EPA) instituted a number of trading schemes in order to ease the burden of compliance with the act. The first nationwide emissions trading system was put into place by the 1990 Clean Air Act Amendments with the goal of further reductions in electric utility emissions that contributed to acid rain. Under that program, the EPA capped, and reduced in two phases, the total amount of sulfur dioxide that power plants were allowed to emit. Under the Kyoto Treaty adopted in 1997 (but never ratified by the United States), the European Union (EU) agreed to establish a cap-and-trade system to limit carbon dioxide emissions from large industrial sources. This emissions trading system took effect on January 1, 2005.

AIR POLLUTION has been the primary target of emissions trading programs, but a number of early programs geared at water pollution have recently been put into place in the United States and elsewhere. Moving beyond pollution to natural resources, trading-based instruments have been used to allocate access to FISHERIES, FORESTS, and land use. Invented and first implemented in the United States, emissions trading was slow to gain followers elsewhere in the world. Recent years have shown a change in this respect, with the establishment of the EU program as well as national trading schemes in other countries including China and the Netherlands.

Advocates of emissions trading argue that they provide both cost savings and better incentives for technological innovation relative to direct regulation. Empirical evidence on the actual performance of these markets is limited, however, because of their relatively short history. Evaluations of the EPA's sulfur dioxide program thus far credit the program with significant reductions at relatively low cost. There is little evidence to date, however, that the program spawned technological innovation. Because pollution trading allows some sources to forgo controls, the result may be localized pollution "hot spots" in the vicinity of plants that opt to buy pollution credits rather than reduce the emissions themselves. Efforts to institute trading in toxic pollutants have encountered strong opposition on this ground. Overall, it is somewhat early to assess the impact of emissions trading from the standpoint of environmental history. While no idea of the past four decades has influenced discourse on environmental regulatory reform more, the actual capacity of emissions trading to deliver promised environmental benefits remains to be seen.

See also FEDERAL LAW—ENVIRONMENTAL REGULATIONS; FEDERAL LAW—INDUSTRIAL REGULATIONS; UNITED NATIONS ENVIRONMENTAL CONFERENCES.

Noga Morag-Levine

Further Reading
Dales, John H. *Pollution, Property, and Prices.* Toronto: University of Toronto Press, 1968.

Gorman, Hugh S., and Barry D. Solomon. "The Origins and Practice of Emissions Trading." *Journal of Policy History* 14, no. 3 (2002): 293–316.

Tietenberg, T. H. *Emissions Trading: Principles and Practice.* Washington, D.C.: Resources for the Future, 2006.

endangered species

An endangered species is a population of organisms either so few in numbers or threatened by changing environmental or predation parameters that it is at risk of EXTINCTION. According to a survey conducted by the American Museum of Natural History in 2004, the planet is presently suffering a mass extinction process, which is the fastest in Earth's 4.5-billion-year history and, unlike prior extinctions, is mainly the result of human activity. In order to hinder, or better yet, to deter, this fast extinction process, organizations and governments list endangered species in the International Union for the Conservation of Nature's (IUCN) Red List of Threatened Species. This register is the world's most comprehensive inventory of the global conservation status of plant and animal species, so that they receive special protection.

When referring to endangered species, many people only think of panda bears in China, tigers in India, or rhinoceroses in Africa. Conservationists present these mammals as "charismatic species" or "ambassadors for conservation" and thus deserving protection. Worldwide, however, there are thousands of endangered species, both plants and animals, whose value within ECOSYSTEMS is not often widely known. Loss of species provokes disruptions in food chains and ecosystems with serious consequences for human beings. Some less well-known examples are, for instance, jaguars *(Panthera onca)* in the areas of Arizona, Texas, and New Mexico or the Florida perforate cladonia *(Cladonia perforata),* a lichen.

Endangered species need protection because they are integral to functional ecosystems. Species become endangered because of the human consumption of resources, depletion of natural habitats, hunting, and other reasons. The diversity of species, including endangered ones, is the key to stability of ecosystems, food chains, and other interchanges of energy and matter—all of which are crucial for a "system" to work correctly. Additionally, multiplicity of species constitutes the basis of BIODIVERSITY. If biological diversity decreases, the richness of the world diminishes, as well. The chances of finding new genetic pools, cures for diseases, relationships between organisms, and many other amazing discoveries may disappear if extinctions continue. It becomes important, therefore, to stop processes that cause rapid depletion of species and habitats, a process that accelerated with the Industrial Revolution in the 18th century.

In the United States, the ENDANGERED SPECIES ACT OF 1973 (ESA) passed by the Congress was the most wide-ranging of dozens of environmental laws passed in the 1970s. It represented an effort to halt or reverse species endangerment. The act was designed to protect critically imperiled species from extinction stemming from "the consequences of economic growth and development untempered by adequate concern and conservation." The stated purpose of the ESA was not only to protect species but also to conserve "the ecosystems upon which they depend." At the species level, it protects all plants and animals; previous laws protected only vertebrates. The ESA forbids federal agencies to authorize, fund, or carry out actions that would jeopardize endangered species. It also bans any government agency, corporation, or citizen from taking, harming, or killing endangered animals without a permit. At the ecosystem level, the ESA requires that endangered species be granted "critical habitats" that encompass all areas necessary for their recovery. Federal agencies are forbidden to authorize or carry out any action that "destroys or adversely modifies" a critical habitat area.

The ESA is administered by two federal agencies, the FISH AND WILDLIFE SERVICE (FWS) and the National Oceanic and Atmospheric Administration (NOAA) Fisheries (formerly the National Marine Fisheries Service). NOAA Fisheries handles marine species, and the FWS has responsibility over freshwater and land species. The FWS established an Endangered Species Program involving habitat conservation plans intended to coordinate corporate and private owners of essential species's habitats. The ESA was passed in the wake of a 1973 conference that led to the signing of the Convention on International Trade in Endangered Species of Wild Fauna and Flora (CITES), the most important international convention that currently restricts international commerce in plant and animal species believed to be actually or potentially harmed by trade.

In the United States, before a plant or animal species can receive protection under the ESA, it must first be placed on the federal list of endangered and threatened wildlife and plants. Currently in the United States, 746 species of plants and 586 species of animals are listed as threatened or endangered, according to the Threatened and Endangered Species System (TESS). Recovery plans made by the Fish and Wildlife Service are designed to reverse the decline of threatened or endangered species and eventually set populations at self-sustaining levels. Currently, 1,074 species are subject to approved recovery plans.

On a global scale, the number, taxonomic name, and register of endangered species (along with threatened and vulnerable species) are kept by the IUCN, which regularly updates its Red List of Threatened Species to provide information on species in each country and region worldwide. The IUCN, however, not only provides conservation status but also works on several projects along with other NONGOVERNMENTAL ORGANIZATIONS, such as the World Wildlife Fund (WWF) or Conservation International (CI), to support research and projects helping to restore the populations of most endangered species.

Although efforts by organizations like IUCN, WWF, CI, and many others, are remarkable, preventing the disappearance of endangered species is a global need with local obligations requiring many more contributions. Similarly to biodiversity, present diversity of species, including those threatened and endangered, is the result of millions of years of evolution of life on Earth and as such requires urgent protection.

See also CONSERVATION; ECOSYSTEMS; FOREST SERVICE, U.S.; HUNTING, COMMERCIAL.

Diego I. Murguía

Further Reading

Czech, Brian, and Paul R. Krausman. *The Endangered Species Act: History, Conservation Biology, and Public Policy.* Baltimore: Johns Hopkins University Press, 2001.

Foreman, Paul, ed. *Endangered Species: Issues and Analysis.* New York: Nova Science, 2002.

U.S. Fish and Wildlife Service. "Species Information. Threatened and Endangered Animals and Plants." Available online. URL: http://www.fws.gov/endangered/wildlife.html. Accessed August 22, 2006.

Endangered Species Act of 1973

The Endangered Species Act of 1973 has roots that began in the dramatic surge of public and political awareness of species endangerment in the late 1950s and early 1960s. The law is distinctive in its clarity and strength in protecting listed species from harm—characteristics that have made it both a centerpiece for environmentalists and a source of great controversy over its 35-year history.

In 1964, the U.S. FISH AND WILDLIFE SERVICE (FWS), which is part of the DEPARTMENT OF THE INTERIOR, established the Committee on Rare and Endangered Wildlife Species and produced the first official list of endangered species, commonly known as the "Red Book." Although the list was ostensibly impartial with regard to economics and politics, it focused on mammals and BIRDS—no plants or INSECTS were included in the 63 species listed.

Under pressure from both the committee and the general public, CONGRESS passed the Endangered Species Preservation Act of 1966. The law specifically addressed trade-related causes of EXTINCTION, particularly of high-profile birds and mammals. Three years later, Congress enacted the Endangered Species Conservation Act (ESCA). The new statute authorized the Interior Department to establish a list of species threatened worldwide and to prohibit their importation to the United States. It also amended existing domestic laws to prohibit the sale or purchase of any ENDANGERED SPECIES, broadened the range of species protected to include certain invertebrates, and facilitated development of the Convention on International Trade in Endangered Species (CITES) of Wild Fauna and Flora.

Congressional hearings on the Endangered Species Act of 1973 suggested that efforts to strengthen the ESCA continued to focus on individual species and worries about overhunting, rather than changes in habitat or landscapes. The record is littered with speeches about "charismatic megafauna" like bald EAGLES, alligators, and whooping cranes. Few legislators paid much attention to economic and political impacts that might result from the act's sweeping language and objectives. The Endangered Species Act of 1973 (ESA) was enacted into law with nearly unanimous approval in December 1973, just a few months after the signing of the CITES agreement.

Although the primary concern of the legislators drafting the ESA may have been the overexploitation of specific, high-profile species, they wrote the act as a comprehensive approach to species protection. They did this primarily by prohibiting the "take" of endangered or threatened species on both public and private lands, and by extending the law's protection to species beyond those directly threatened by hunting and trade. *Take* is defined in the ESA as any action that would "harass, harm, pursue, hunt, shoot, wound, kill, trap, capture, or collect" a listed species. Listing is based on nominations by the public or the agencies themselves and is to be decided on the basis of scientific information alone. The ESA also required federal agencies to designate critical habitat for all listed species, and to consult the FWS to ensure their actions are unlikely to "jeopardize the continued existence of any endangered species and threatened species."

The ESA's controversial nature became apparent in two significant court cases of the late 1970s and early 1980s. In *TVA v. Hill* (437 U.S. 153 [1978]), the U.S. Supreme Court ruled that construction of the nearly complete multimillion-dollar Tellico Dam on the Little Tennessee River violated the ESA by jeopardizing the only known habitat of an endangered three-inch fish, the snail darter. Besides confirming the act's disregard for economic costs, the case reaffirmed the biologically important relationship between a species and its habitat; take in this case was not a direct harm to the snail darter itself but rather the elimination of its critical habitat. *Palila v. Hawaii Department of Land and Natural Resources* (639 F. 2d 495 [9th Cir. 1981]) went further on the habitat issue, ruling that the destruction by livestock of nesting sites for an endangered Hawaiian bird was also a take in violation of section 9. As a result of the *Palila* decision, the FWS extended its own regulatory definition of take to include "significant habitat modification or degradation where it actually kills or injures wildlife by significantly impairing essential behavioral patterns including, breeding, feeding, or sheltering."

In response to these controversies, an alternative emerged from a development conflict in San Mateo County, California, in the early 1980s. Construction of a new multi-million-dollar housing project on the local San Bruno Mountain had been delayed by the discovery of a population of the endangered Mission Blue butterfly. A committee of relevant parties, including the private landowners, San Mateo County, several nearby city governments, and a local organization called Save San Bruno Mountain, sought a compromise, retaining the services of an environmental consulting firm, Thomas Reid Associates, to help craft a biologically sound alternative. The result of this collaboration was the first Habitat Conservation Plan (HCP). The San Bruno plan designated only 368 acres of the mountain (11 percent) for development, while preserving the remainder as habitat.

There was only one catch to this apparent win-win solution: Under the terms of the ESA, the San Bruno HCP was illegal. There was no provision under the law for the permitted loss of habitat in violation of the no-take regulations issued after *Palila*. Thus, after local negotiators finalized the plan, it was presented to Congress as the basis of an amendment that would save the ESA from the threat of expiration or legislative evisceration. Congress went along, amending the ESA in 1982 to include section 10, which creates the incidental take permit (ITP) as a new exception to the no-take rule in cases where mitigating factors arise and the ITP will not "appreciably reduce the likelihood of the survival and recovery of the species in the wild." ITPs are granted once an HCP has been written and approved by FWS.

Initially, HCPs got off to a slow start—only 14 were approved during the first 10 years of the program, and most were modest in scale, addressing areas of less than 1,000 acres and only a single species. Among the reasons offered for this initial lack of enthusiasm were uncertain guidelines for producing HCPs (no formal handbook was published by FWS until 1990), the large amount of time and money required to design and receive approval for a plan, and the inherent uncertainties that accompanied all endangered species protection. And soon after the 1992 election, President BILL CLINTON's new administration faced another reauthorization battle over the ESA. The prior authorization had expired in October 1992. As with many federal laws, the authorization for funding must be renewed periodically, although the law remained in force. As in 1982, there was strong political pressure for change, especially in light of the high-profile "train wreck" of SPOTTED OWL conservation versus economic development in the Pacific Northwest. Indeed, Congress has been unable to resolve this issue since 1992 and has relied instead on annual interim renewals, meaning that the funding for the ESA, most of which goes to the FWS, has varied from year to year.

HCPs seemed to be a promising way to lower the level of conflict, but developers were not taking full advantage of them. So instead of trying to amend the ESA further (for fear that introducing any ESA legislation during the 104th Congress would prove disastrous for environmentalists), the new president turned to administrative fixes, in the form of new regulations that provided HCP applicants with greater security. A "no surprises" rule stipulated that landowners would no longer have to change their approved HCPs if "unforeseen circumstances" were to occur in the future. It also stipulated that in the case of an "extraordinary circumstance" whereby further mitigation steps were required, the additional financial responsibility would fall not on the landowner but rather on the "federal government, other governmental agencies, private conservation organizations, or other private landowners who have not yet developed an HCP." Soon thereafter, a related "safe harbor" policy, based on ideas from the advocacy group Environmental Defense Fund, emerged. This initiative discouraged a "scorched earth" approach to development to prevent future ESA problems by stipulating that if landowners voluntarily agreed to maintain or develop more attractive habitat for endangered species on their land (thus providing a "safe harbor"), they could preserve the future right to return the land at any time to its previous baseline condition without penalty.

These regulatory reforms seemed to provide landowners and developers with the incentives and assurances they required. By the end of 2003, there were roughly 440 approved HCPs (some with multiple Incidental Take Permits) covering more than 39 million acres of land and protecting more than 500 endangered and threatened species. Concentrated in a few states with major ESA conflicts, especially Texas, Florida, and California, HCPs are nonetheless now in operation in every Fish and Wildlife Region except Alaska.

See also DAMS, RESERVOIRS, AND ARTIFICIAL LAKES; ECOSYSTEMS; FEDERAL LAW—ENVIRONMENTAL REGULATIONS; INSECTS; SPECIES, INDIGENOUS; TENNESSEE VALLEY AUTHORITY; TREATIES AND INTERNATIONAL LAW; UNITED STATES—CALIFORNIA; UNITED STATES—GULF COAST; UNITED STATES—PACIFIC NORTHWEST, WILD ANIMALS.

Laura A. Watt

Further Reading
Czech, Brian, and Paul R. Krausman. *The Endangered Species Act: History, Conservation Biology and Public Policy.* Baltimore: Johns Hopkins University Press, 2001.
Petersen, Shannon. *Acting for Endangered Species: The Statutory Ark.* Washington, D.C.: Island Press, 2002.
Scott, J. Michael, Dale Goble, and Frank Davis. *The Endangered Species Act at Thirty: Renewing the Conservation Promise.* Washington, D.C.: Island Press, 2005.
Stanford Environmental Law Society. *The Endangered Species Act.* Stanford, Calif.: Stanford University Press, 2001.
Watt, Laura A., Leigh Raymond, and Meryl L. Eschen. "On Preserving Ecological and Cultural Landscapes." *Environmental History* 9 (October 2004): 620–647.

Tennessee Valley Authority v. Hill (1978)

The Tennessee Valley Authority (TVA) began building the Tellico Dam on the Little Tennessee River in 1967, six years prior to the passage of the Endangered Species Act of 1973. Shortly after its passage, the secretary of the interior reported that the inundation of the reservoir would destroy the habitat of the snail darter, an endangered species of small fish. Environmental groups sued to enjoin the TVA from completing the dam. In Tennessee Valley Authority v. Hill *(1978), the U.S. Supreme Court confirmed that the Endangered Species Act prohibited the TVA from impounding the river and reiterated the importance of habitat protection regardless of the financial loss.*

In shaping legislation to deal with the problem thus presented, Congress started from the finding that "[the] two major causes of extinction are hunting and destruction of natural habitat." . . . Of these twin threats, Congress was informed that the greatest was destruction of natural habitats. . . .

As it was finally passed, the Endangered Species Act of 1973 represented the most comprehensive legislation for the preservation of endangered species ever enacted by any nation. Its stated purposes were "to provide a means whereby the ecosystems upon which endangered species and threatened species depend may be conserved," and "to provide a program for the conservation of such . . . species. . . ."

It is against this legislative background that we must measure TVA's claim that the Act was not intended to stop operation of a project which, like Tellico Dam, was near completion when an endangered species was discovered in its path. While there is no discussion in the legislative history of precisely this problem, the totality of congressional action makes it abundantly clear that the result we reach today is wholly in accord with both the words of the statute and the intent of Congress. The plain intent of Congress in enacting this statute was to halt and reverse the trend toward species extinction, whatever the cost. This is reflected not only in the stated policies of the Act, but in literally every section of the statute. All persons, including federal agencies, are specifically instructed not to "take" endangered species, meaning that no one is "to harass, harm, pursue, hunt, shoot, wound, kill, trap, capture, or collect" such life forms. One might dispute the applicability of these examples to the Tellico Dam by saying that in this case the burden on the public through the loss of millions of unrecoverable dollars would greatly outweigh the loss of the snail darter. But neither the Endangered Species Act nor Art. III of the Constitution provides federal courts with

authority to make such fine utilitarian calculations. On the contrary, the plain language of the Act, buttressed by its legislative history, shows clearly that Congress viewed the value of endangered species as "incalculable." Quite obviously, it would be difficult for a court to balance the loss of a sum certain—even $100 million—against a congressionally declared "incalculable" value, even assuming we had the power to engage in such a weighing process, which we emphatically do not. . . .

Here we are urged to view the Endangered Species Act "reasonably," and hence shape a remedy "that accords with some modicum of common sense and the public weal." But is that our function? We have no expert knowledge on the subject of endangered species, much less do we have a mandate from the people to strike a balance of equities on the side of the Tellico Dam. Congress has spoken in the plainest of words, making it abundantly clear that the balance has been struck in favor of affording endangered species the highest of priorities, thereby adopting a policy which it described as "institutionalized caution."

Our individual appraisal of the wisdom or unwisdom of a particular course consciously selected by the Congress is to be put aside in the process of interpreting a statute. Once the meaning of an enactment is discerned and its constitutionality determined, the judicial process comes to an end.

Source: Tennessee Valley Authority v. Hill *437 U.S. 153 (1978).*

Energy, Department of

The Department of Energy (DOE) was established on October 1, 1977, when President JIMMY CARTER signed into law the Department of Energy Organization Act. As the 12th cabinet-level department of the U.S. government, the DOE was charged with coordinating national energy policy and the management of federal energy programs, including production, distribution, research and development, regulation, pricing, and conservation.

Prior to the formation of the DOE, the responsibility for U.S. energy policy was scattered among different agencies, administrations, and commissions throughout the federal government. Until the energy crisis of the 1970s, when the rising cost of crude oil prompted fuel shortages and rising prices, the federal government played a limited role in meeting the nation's energy needs. Although the DOE was established in response to these crisis, its origins can be traced to WORLD WAR II (1941–45) and the MANHATTAN PROJECT's development of the atomic bomb. In 1946, CONGRESS created the ATOMIC ENERGY COMMISSION (AEC) to guarantee that the civilian government maintained authority over atomic research and development. In 1954, exclusive government control over atomic energy ended when the Atomic Energy Act permitted nongovernment entities to establish research programs in atomic energy. The Atomic Energy Act required, however, that the AEC regulate the newly created nuclear power industry.

By the early 1970s, both supporters and critics of nuclear power believed that the promotional and regulatory responsibilities of the AEC should be divided between different agencies. In 1974, the Energy Reorganization Act dissolved the Atomic Energy Commission and created the Nuclear Regulatory Commission (NRC) and the Energy Research and Development Administration (ERDA). The NRC was assigned the responsibility of regulating the nuclear power industry in order to protect public health and safety. ERDA was created to manage the programs that involved nuclear weapons, naval reactors, and nuclear energy development. During the energy crisis of the 1970s, it became clear that the U.S. government was not prepared for the economic and political upheaval created by the changes in crude oil prices or embargoes by oil-producing countries. Several officials within the federal government suggested that a single department was needed to develop and implement a comprehensive energy program. In 1977, Congress responded by creating the Department of Energy. DOE became responsible for the Federal Energy Administration, the Energy Research and Development Administration, the Federal Power Commission, and several other energy programs that were housed in different agencies throughout the federal government. The DOE also became responsible for much of the long-term, high-risk research and development of energy technology conducted in the United States, federal power supplies and marketing, the NUCLEAR WEAPONS AND TESTING program, energy conservation and regulatory programs, and a central energy database. By 2005, the DOE had a budget of more than $22 billion and had more than 116,000 employees working to maintain a secure and affordable energy supply.

The energy crisis of the 1970s demonstrated the vulnerability of the American economy to disruptions in the energy supply. Between 1977 and 1980, DOE focused primarily on ensuring the supply of inexpensive energy from abroad and working to develop domestic resources such as COAL, nuclear energy, and hydropower. Responding to requests by the Carter administration, the DOE also established price controls and energy conservation programs. Alleviating the economic impact of the energy crisis was the priority, not environmental stewardship. Except for restoring contaminated nuclear weapons development facilities, the DOE lacked any cohesive environmental management plan.

While campaigning for president in 1980, RONALD REAGAN often attacked President Carter's energy policy and even suggested that the Department of Energy should be dismantled. Reagan argued that the DOE increased the threat to the nation's energy security by allowing the development of a dangerous dependence on imported oil. Energy issues, however, never became a central part of Reagan's presidential agenda. Instead, his campaign focused primarily on the economy and national defense. After winning the 1980 presidential election in a landslide, Reagan appointed the former South Carolina governor James B. Edwards as secretary of energy. Edwards was a well-known advocate of nuclear energy and a strong proponent of a free market for energy. His appointment indicated how clearly Reagan's energy policy differed from Carter's belief that government should play a central role in energy development. The Reagan administration wanted to reduce or, when possible, eliminate government activities in areas where private industry and the free market might set energy priorities. The new strategy focused on ending government regulations that the administration believed prevented domestic energy production. In 1981, Reagan released his energy plan, titled *Securing America's Energy Future: The National Energy Policy Plan,* which stated that the primary responsibility of federal energy policy was to promote increased energy production and improve access to energy resources located on federal land. President Reagan's energy plan acknowledged that energy conservation and environmental protection were important goals, but that they should not be the primary goals of the Department of Energy.

Although Reagan threatened to dismantle the department, the DOE actually expanded during his administration from 1981 to 1989. The National Renewable Energy Laboratory (NREL) in Golden, Colorado, was created to help diversify America's energy supply by conducting research in solar energy. In addition, the 1992 Waste Policy Act called for the DOE to construct a geologic storage facility for spent nuclear fuel, which has yet to be constructed. During Reagan's administration, budgets at the DOE also experienced some growth, leveling out around $13 billion by 1985.

By 1988, the issue of GLOBAL WARMING was receiving growing attention. Although scientists and the MEDIA showed increasing concern over the potential effects of global warming, the Reagan administration cautioned against making any hasty judgments before global warming and the role of humans in its causation were scientifically proven. If global warming could be confirmed, the DOE's official position was that any action would appropriately occur on a global rather than a national scale. However, several high-ranking DOE officials under Reagan insisted that global warming was part of a larger natural cycle immune to human interference.

During the administration of President GEORGE H. W. BUSH from 1989 to 1993, the DOE's main priority was the continued cleanup of the massive quantities of waste generated by

SECRETARIES OF ENERGY AND THEIR ACCOMPLISHMENTS

Secretary of Energy	Term	Appointed by President	Accomplishments
James Schlesinger	1977–79	Carter	Assisted in drafting legislation to create Department of Energy (DOE) and coordinated energy conservation policies during the 1970s energy crisis.
Charles Duncan	1979–81	Carter	Stressed the importance of market forces in regulating energy prices.
James Edwards	1981–82	Reagan	Wanting the government out of energy policy, Reagan hoped to eliminate DOE and appointed Edwards to oversee a dismantling that ultimately failed.
Donald Hodel	1982–85	Reagan	Taking a more nuanced position on DOE's role in energy policy than his predecessor, he advocated tax credits for energy conservation.
John Herrington	1985–89	Reagan	Linking energy policy and national security, he advocated further development of domestic power sources including nuclear, oil, and coal. He sparked controversy by advocating oil exploration and production in the Arctic National Wildlife Refuge and plans to store nuclear waste at Yucca Mountain, Nevada.
James Watkins	1989–93	G. H. W. Bush	Called for a comprehensive national energy strategy that stressed increased production of energy and conservation efforts.
Hazel O'Leary	1993–97	Clinton	Championed research into global warming.
Federico Pena	1997–98	Clinton	Pushed for further deregulation of the utilities industry.
Bill Richardson	1998–2001	Clinton	Furthered plans to store nuclear waste at Yucca Mountain and advocated greater deregulation of the utilities industry.
Spencer Abraham	2001–05	G. W. Bush	Stridently antiregulatory, he promoted increased domestic production while denying the existence of global climate change.
Samuel Bodman	2005–09	G. W. Bush	Worked to clear final obstacles to opening Yucca Mountain to nuclear waste.
Steven Chu	2009–	Obama	Advocate of alternative energy sources and further nuclear energy research.

Source: Department of Energy Web site. Available online. URL: http://www.energy.gov/news/4757.htm. Accessed May 30, 2009.

four decades of nuclear weapons research and development. In addition to nuclear waste cleanup programs, the Bush administration desired to increase nuclear power generation. In order to expand production, construction of the YUCCA MOUNTAIN facility in Nevada to store nuclear waste was necessary. However, opposition by the state of Nevada and environmental groups prevented any significant movement on the issue. As did his predecessor, President Bush focused on diversifying America's energy supply. Rather than address energy efficiency and conservation, President Bush's 1991 *National Energy Strategy* called for expansion of domestic oil production and nuclear power and increased research into alternative fuels. Environmentalists criticized this strategy for its continued emphasis on energy production at the expense of environmental protection.

In the 1990s, the election of BILL CLINTON, who was president from 1993 to 2001, and growing concerns over global warming finally prompted the DOE to take a more active role in environmental protection. The newly appointed DOE secretary, Hazel O'Leary, directly linked energy policy decisions to human health and the quality of the environment. Global warming quickly became a focal point for the Clinton administration. The White House formed the Interagency Climate Change Mitigation Group, which subsequently directed the DOE and other key agencies to develop an emissions action plan. With energy playing a pivotal role in any attempt to reduce greenhouse gas emissions, the DOE emerged as the lead agency. However, the administration's *Climate Change Action Plan* only requested the voluntary reduction of greenhouse gas emissions by industry and electric utilities. The voluntary increases in energy efficiency and conservation were expected to account for nearly 70 percent of the plan's reduction in harmful emissions.

Emphasis on energy efficiency, conservation, renewable energy, and natural gas formed the core of the DOE's energy strategy. During the Clinton administration, the DOE's annual budget increased by nearly 30 percent. This new funding was mostly due to the new requirements of the 1992 Energy Policy Act. With large annual funding increases, environmental management (headed by the Office of Environmental Restoration and Waste Management) emerged as the DOE's largest single program area. With the responsibility for cleaning up the nations' nuclear weapons complex, environmental management accounted for nearly one-third of the department's budget.

The conclusion of the COLD WAR in the early 1990s and the resulting changes in America's nuclear weapons policy allowed the DOE to embark on a new agenda that combined economic growth and environmental protection. In 1994, the Department of Energy issued its first comprehensive strategic plan. The new plan provided the DOE with more focused goals of fueling a comprehensive economy, improving the environment through WASTE DISPOSAL AND MANAGEMENT

and POLLUTION prevention, and reduction of the nuclear danger. Acknowledging that energy plays a crucial role in the nation's economic success, the strategic plan identified five new mission areas: industrial competitiveness, energy resources, national security, environmental quality, and science and technology.

The election of President GEORGE W. BUSH in 2000 produced several changes to the Department of Energy. The Bush administration shifted the priorities of the DOE from a balance between economic growth and environmental protection to one that focused primarily on energy development. The Bush administration's desire to expand the nation's commercial nuclear power infrastructure and develop the crude oil reserves located under the frozen tundra of the ARCTIC NATIONAL WILDLIFE REFUGE generated a backlash from environmental organizations. The Bush administration also directed the DOE to focus more of its research on science and technology rather than on energy efficiency and conservation. This new direction expanded research in advanced technologies such as alternative fuels, clean coal, coal gasification, hydrogen fuel cells, and advanced nuclear reactors.

Over its first three decades, the Department of Energy has continually evolved in order to meet the changing demands of each new administration. Its priorities have shifted from energy crisis of the 1970s to nuclear weapons disposal in the 1980s and concerns about global warming in the 1990s. Through this work, the Department of Energy has remained at the center of some of the most important and controversial environmental issues in the United States.

See also BUREAU OF LAND MANAGEMENT; DEMOCRATIC PARTY; ENERGY, ELECTRICAL; ENERGY, FOSSIL FUEL; ENERGY, HYDRAULIC; ENERGY, RENEWABLE; GORE, ALBERT, JR.; GREENHOUSE EFFECT; PUBLIC DOMAIN; REPUBLICAN PARTY.

Roger J. Flynn

Further Reading

Fehner, Terrence R., and Jack M. Holl. *Department of Energy, 1977–1994: A Summary History.* Washington, D.C.: Government Printing Office, 1994.

NetLibrary, Inc. *Renewable Power Pathways: A Review of the U.S. Department of Energy's Renewable Energy Programs.* Washington, D.C.: National Academy Press, 2000.

Stelzer, Irwin M., and Robert Patton. *The Department of Energy: An Agency That Cannot Be Reinvented.* Washington, D.C.: AEI Press, 1996.

energy, electrical

The widespread use of electricity drove what historians have called the second Industrial Revolution, from 1870 to 1940, and remains critical to everyday life in the 21st century. In the 1800s and early 1900s, electrical energy was applied to

factories to lower manufacturing costs and achieve economies of scale. Power was initially gained through water, or
hydroelectric, power. Large civil ENGINEERING projects, such
as the HOOVER DAM, were built to harness the power of
moving water. As the electrical grid expanded and demand
for power grew, new prime movers had to be found. Some

Electricity began reaching many homes and businesses in the late 1800s. Since then, electricity generation has stemmed from various
sources, including hydroelectric dams, coal, oil, nuclear power, solar energy, and wind. Pictured here is a power plant along the Mississippi River, Minneapolis, Minnesota, 1939.   *(Library of Congress)*

of these prime movers included COAL, NATURAL GAS, and nuclear energy to heat water for steam and to drive turbines to generate electricity. This centralized utility model was balanced on a smaller scale by a distributed model of electrical energy generation embodied by wind, solar cells, and a variety of other forms of renewable energy generation. Regardless of the power source, the globalization of industry accelerated with electricity as a major catalyst.

Electric energy is abundant. It can be produced from almost any source and at any scale. Flowing water is harnessed to convert its mechanical energy into electrical power. Heat generated by burning coal or natural gas changes water into high-pressure steam, and spinning gas turbines convert the attendant mechanical energy into electricity. Radioactive energy in nuclear power plants converts water into high-pressure steam, and gas turbines again transform their rotational energy into electric energy. In all of these applications, selection of the prime mover is based on a complex analysis of geographical and regulatory factors that have evolved over the past 100 years.

Many sources of electrical energy have environmental drawbacks. Large hydroelectric projects are considered a source of renewable energy. They cause environmental damage, however, through regulating water flow feeding a power plant. The lakes or reservoirs formed behind DAMS often destroy natural habitats. Burning fossil fuels to produce electricity has contributed to AIR POLLUTION from sulfur and nitrogen oxides that produce acid rain while accelerating global warming through the emission of carbon dioxide into the atmosphere. Nuclear power is often heralded for its lack of carbon dioxide emissions. Many people, however, fear radiation poisoning or death from radioactive leaks. This concern has dampened U.S. nuclear ambitions but also led to making a new generation of nuclear power plants safer for other countries around the world. Aside from nuclear dangers, heating water for steam to drive turbines is a form of thermal pollution that damages marine life as local water temperatures are affected by nearby cooling towers.

Abundant generation of energy does not mean it is used efficiently; nor does electricity production completely account for its hidden costs. Many studies suggest that improving the efficiency of Western homes, for example, would cut energy consumption in half without sacrificing personal comfort. Extracting nonrenewable fossil fuels such as coal and natural gas from the earth to generate electricity has an associated replacement cost that cannot be calculated. Storage of radioactive nuclear waste products for 100,000 years, until they become safe through radioactive decay, are costs rarely considered in the cost-benefit analysis when governments consider approval of a nuclear power plant.

As a result of environmental concerns, many utility companies have tried to augment their centralized generation model with distributed components. In this model, businesses and homeowners can choose to generate their own electricity and feed the power grid with any excess capacity, while watching their power meter run backward. Customers use renewable energy technologies including photovoltaic cells that convert sunlight into electricity and wind turbines that convert the mechanical energy of flowing air into electricity. Solar energy is of particular interest to larger utility companies. Since peak energy loads are most often generated when the hot sun bears down on a region, distributed solar cells, which are then producing their maximal power, offset the demand stressing the utility's generating facilities. Consequently, dirty, polluting "peaker plants" occasionally remain inactive as solar production handles these peak power periods.

While engineers developed a variety of prime movers to generate electricity, others looked for ways to distribute power. The two primary distribution methods are alternating current and direct current. An alternating current is a current that reverses direction in a circuit at regular intervals; direct current flows in only one direction. Electrical innovation, marked by the invention of the motor and generator, gave rise to alternating current—ideal for long-distance transmission. Electricity in America experiences 60 reversal cycles every second. In fact, this alternating current can produce direct current for those devices that operate better without voltage variations. Furthermore, to overcome the mass of electric batteries needed for power, engineers perfected electric motors and generators for continuous, reliable operation. Since direct current motors are easier to run at a variety of speeds, they are commonly found on subway and light-rail systems.

THOMAS EDISON pioneered the modern electrical power system in the United States. In 1879, he introduced direct current electric light by improving generators, establishing wiring methods for power distribution, and developing the first electric meter for recording customer consumption. With this end-to-end approach, Edison knew what to charge customers. Electrical distribution soon became big business. Edison's contemporary and sometimes competitor Nikola Tesla (1856–1943) was able to visualize working inventions, and his persistence to see them developed led to the alternating current motor, a revolutionary way to generate and distribute electrical power. The Edison approach to electricity favored direct current generation with distribution limited to about a mile from a noisy generating plant, and suitable only for lighting. Tesla foresaw these pitfalls and fought to introduce the alternating current approach, whereby electrical power could be transmitted over hundreds of miles with little power loss. In addition to lighting, alternating current could be used for powering residential appliances and industrial machinery. Tesla's vision for alternating current power was ultimately realized during the 20th century, but Tesla was a poor businessman and died in poverty.

Electricity supplied inexpensive and safe light to homes and businesses, replacing unsafe flame from candles and noxious fumes from gas. New businesses formed both to drive and to serve the demand for increasing consumption of electricity. Westinghouse, founded in 1886, and General Electric, founded in 1892, focused primarily on kitchen appliances. Convenience bolstered consumption, and these corporations thrived by serving the customers' demands for more leisure time.

Electrical energy began to define the way humanity consumed physical energy, totally transforming American society in the 20th century. It made possible the construction of global economies and their industrial, communication, lighting, and transportation systems. The science of electricity drove the second Industrial Revolution. Electricity changed the way in which Americans lived and related to their most immediate environment. At the same time, Americans' thirst for electrical power has led them to alter landscapes in the harvesting of fossil fuels, block free-flowing rivers, and pollute the skies.

See also AIR CONDITIONING; CORPORATIONS, UTILITIES; ENERGY, NUCLEAR; ENERGY, RENEWABLE; HOUSEHOLD APPLIANCES; HOUSING, PRIVATE; MASS TRANSIT; THREE MILE ISLAND; YUCCA MOUNTAIN.

Robert Karl Koslowsky

Further Reading

Grob, Bernard. *Basic Electronics.* 8th ed. Westerville, Ohio: McGraw Hill, 1997.
Jonnes, Jill. *Empires of Light: Edison, Tesla, Westinghouse and the Race to Electrify the World.* New York: Random House, 2003.
Koslowsky, Robert K. *A World Perspective through 21st Century Eyes: The Impact of Science on Society.* Victoria, Canada: Trafford, 2004.

energy, fossil fuel

GLOBAL WARMING and CLIMATE CHANGE present the major environmental crises in the 21st century. They are largely attributable to the emission of greenhouse gases and particulate black carbon in the atmosphere. These greenhouse gases primarily occur in energy production through burning fossil fuels. In general, humans increased greenhouse gas production exponentially in the 20th century to satisfy soaring industrial and household energy needs. Many environmentalists and scholars believe that this reckless fossil fuel–based civilization is ecologically unsustainable and creates uninterrupted environmental damage, which is perhaps unrepairable in the future, such as incessant air pollution in all megacities; acid rains that have decimated lakes and river ecologies, crops, and forest environment; oil spills in many parts of the world; and, above all, change in the global climate.

Humans have used fossil fuels for 4,000 to 6,000 years, primarily for heat until the era of industrialization. Fossil fuels are carbon or hydrocarbon found in the earth's crust. Fossil fuels formed millions of years ago, in the Carbonifer-

ous period, from the organic remains of prehistoric plants and animals. Preserved remains of organisms such as phytoplankton, zooplankton, and terrestrial plants transformed into fossil fuels under high levels of heat and pressure. Three major forms of fossil fuels that help in energy production are COAL, oil or petroleum, and NATURAL GAS. Researchers have investigated other fossil fuel sources such as bituminous sands and oil shale, but these remain very costly to process in comparison to coal, oil, and gas.

Coal is a hard, rocklike substance composed of carbon, hydrogen, oxygen, nitrogen, some amount of sulfur, and traces of radioactive materials. Anthracite coal contains the maximal amount of carbon and has higher energy content. Bituminous-type coal has a medium energy content, while the lignite coal is the softest and of low energy content. The major use of coal is power production in coal-fired power plants. Almost all countries in the world have coal reserves. Petroleum is the liquid form of fossil fuel. Unlike coal, petroleum is found in pockets of the earth's crust. Like coal, petroleum is very carbon rich. Humans use petroleum to power AUTOMOBILES and to heat commercial buildings and houses. Natural gas is the gaseous form of the fossil fuel. It is mainly made up of METHANE (CH_4), which consists of carbon and hydrogen. It is toxic and highly flammable. Natural gases are used for heating buildings, running automobiles (compressed natural gas is used in cars to reduce air pollution), and producing electricity in gas power stations.

Primary energy production in the world and in the United States in the 21st century depends heavily on fossil fuels. In 2006, the Energy Information Administration of the U.S. DEPARTMENT OF ENERGY reported that approximately 86 percent of the world's primary energy is produced from fossil fuels, in which petroleum contributes 36.8 percent, coal 26.6 percent, and natural gas 22.9 percent. World energy usage increases annually by 2.3 percent.

According to the Department of Energy report, total energy production in the United States is around 71 quadrillion (10^{15}) British thermal units (BTU), which is 1.5 times the production of all of Europe and, by a small amount, exceeds the entire production of Eurasia. Energy consumption by the United States in 2006 was around 85 quadrillion (10^{15}) BTU, representing almost 20 percent of total world energy consumption. The consumption of petroleum in the United States in 2006 was 20.7 million barrels per day, which was about 24 percent of the world's total consumption of 85 million barrels per day. In 2006, the United States consumed 21.65 trillion cubic feet of natural gas, more than one-fifth of total world consumption. Although China exceeded the United States in coal consumption by 2006, the United States still consumed 1.1 billion tons of coal for energy production, which is 16 percent of the world's usage.

This ever-increasing consumption of fossil fuels presents significant environmental dangers. The burning of fossil fuels around the world produces some 21.3 billion tons of carbon dioxide (CO_2) per year, constituting approximately 47 percent of greenhouse gases. It is the primary contributor to global warming. The level of atmospheric CO_2 has risen from the 19th-century level of 280 parts per million (ppm) to the present level of 387 ppm. According to scientists working in Mauna Loa Observatory and confirmed by the U.S. National Oceanic and Atmospheric Administration, since the start of the Industrial Revolution, this level has increased almost 40 percent and is now at the highest level in at least the last 650,000 years. The CO_2 level since the 19th century, the nascent industrialization era in the United States, started with an upward swing until the present era of massive industrialization. Although 387 ppm is not dangerous for humans or animals, it is detrimental to the environment, causing global warming and climate change. It is also estimated that emissions of CO_2 by all human activities (including the burning of fossil fuels plus other activities) are presently around 130 times greater than the quantity emitted by VOLCANOES, or approximately 25 billion tons per year.

In addition to CO_2, the coal burned in power stations produces sulfur dioxide (SO_2), an acidic gas. When SO_2 is released into the atmosphere, it contributes to the formation of ACID RAIN. A technique called flue gas desulfurization is used in many power plants to clean up SO_2 gas before it is released. This method involves using limestone to clean up SO_2 and creates gypsum, which is used in the building industry, as an end product. Coal burning also produces carbonic and nitric acid gases, which are among the worst contributors to global warming and climate change. Fossil fuels also contain radioactive materials such as uranium and thorium, and in the burning process, these are released in the atmosphere. Power generated with natural gas produces lower levels of atmospheric pollution than that with coal and oil.

Because they took millions of years to form, fossil fuels are nonrenewable resources. Contemporary consumption rates are depleting them significantly faster than new sources can form. Some experts predict that the world's oil reserves will last only for 40 to 50 more years given current consumption rates. Natural gas reserves will last for perhaps 170 years, and, being more abundant, coal will last for another 400 years or so, but some reserves are more difficult and expensive to reach. These estimates of dwindling reserves suggest that prices for fossil fuels will increase unless demand substantially abates. These facts have contributed to an intensified search for economically affordable and environmentally beneficial renewable energy sources for power generation. Solar, wind, ocean, hydropower, biomass, geothermal resources, biofuels, and hydrogen derived from renewable resources presently appear to be the most viable options.

In the interim, there are technologies that assist in cleaning the exhaust gases from fossil fuel burning. For example, clean coal technologies potentially reduce the environmental

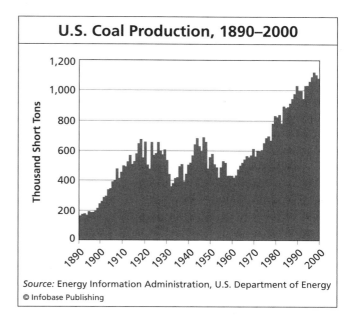

U.S. Coal Production, 1890–2000

Source: Energy Information Administration, U.S. Department of Energy
© Infobase Publishing

impact of energy generation from coal. These technologies include chemically washing the minerals and impurities from coal, flue gas desulfurization, dewatering of low-carbon-content coals, and, above all, carbon capture and sequestration. The carbon capture and sequestration is perhaps the best suggested technology because the emitted gases from the coal-powered plants are captured and buried permanently underground. In 2000, a coal-fueled synthetic natural gas plant in Beulah, North Dakota, became the world's first coal plant to capture and sequester CO_2, proving the potential for industrial economics and future clean coal technology. Carbon sequestration has other added advantages that would compensate some of its application cost. In the United States, since 1972, sequestrated CO_2 is extensively being used for enhanced crude oil recovery. Even sequestered CO_2 is helping coal recovery from deep mines.

Nonetheless, the continuing high levels of energy consumption from fossil fuel sources in the United States and around the world continue to present significant problems. Global warming and climate change are ongoing and worsening environmental crises.

See also ENERGY, RENEWABLE; GREENHOUSE EFFECT; OIL, DOMESTIC; OIL, IMPORTED; OIL REFINING.

Sudhanshu Sekhar Panda

Further Reading
Adam, David. "World CO_2 Levels at Record High, Scientists Warn." *Guardian*, 12 May 2008.
Campbell, C. J., and J. H. Laherrere. "The End of Cheap Oil." *Scientific American* 78 (March 1998): 80–86.
Energy Information Administration. "World Energy Overview: 1996–2006." Available online. URL: http://www.eia.doe.gov/iea/overview.html. Accessed February 12, 2009.

McNeill, J. R. "*Something New under the Sun*": An Environmental History of the Twentieth Century World. New York: W. W. Norton, 2000.

Oil & Gas Journal 105 (December 24, 2007): 48.

Panda, S. S. "Carbon Sequestration." In *Encyclopedia of Global Warming and Climate Change*, edited by S. G. Philander. Los Angeles: Sage, 2008.

———. "Energy, Renewable." In *Encyclopedia of Global Warming and Climate Change*, edited by S. G. Philander. Los Angeles: Sage, 2008.

United States Department of Energy. "Green House Gases, Climate Change, and Energy." Available online. URL: http://www.eia.doe.gov/bookshelf/brochures/greenhouse/Chapter1.htm. Accessed February 12, 2009.

United States Geologic Survey. "Volcanic Gases and Their Effects." Available online. URL: http://volcanoes.usgs.gov/hazards/gas/index.php. Accessed February 12, 2009.

energy, hydraulic

Hydraulic energy, the power extracted from moving water, has been essential to settlement and development of North America since the earliest colonial days. From small waterwheels to larger commercial mills to hydroelectric power plants, hydraulic energy infrastructure has figured continuously in the American landscape and economy. The technologies used to harness waterpower also have reshaped streams, rivers, and valleys. Waterpower, while considered a "clean" source of energy, has effected change in local and regional ecologies across the United States.

SHIFTING TECHNOLOGY

Hydraulic energy is derived from moving water through the use of wheels and turbines in combination with a mechanical or electrical transmission system. The simplest waterwheels used only a few gears to shift energy from water to millstone, while more complex mills and hydroelectric plants include a variety of wheels, turbines, gears, pulleys, shafts, and belting to transfer energy to mechanical processes and to transform it to electricity. Until the technologies of electrification allowed transmission of energy over long distances, end users had to be fairly close to the energy source. In colonial America, single-purpose waterwheels powered gristmills, sawmills, iron works, and some cloth-making processes, mostly serving local communities. By the late 18th century, larger commercial mills emerged in conjunction with the expansion of markets. With the development of turbines that could power larger and more complex mechanical processes, industrial-scale production expanded from the mid-19th century. Finally, with the advent of hydroelectric power at the end of the 19th century, hydraulic energy was transmitted over long distances to power residences, farms, commercial centers, and all forms of modern industry.

HISTORICAL USES

Historically, waterwheels have been in use for more than 2,000 years in Europe and Asia. They were a significant element of early European settlement in North America. The earliest reference to a rotary, water-powered mill dates to 85 B.C.E. in Greece. Similar mills existed across the American colonies. By 1840, there were 66,000 water mills across the United States, with the highest concentration in the Northeast. Water mills provided a ready source of energy as the young United States moved to increased regional and international trade and greater commercialization of products. By 1850, the introduction of turbines to American manufacturing facilitated growth of industrial centers. Lowell, Massachusetts, famous as a major textile production center, was founded in 1822 on a stretch of the Merrimac River. Within 60 years, the river boasted 900 mills and factories. At the same time, access to steam power changed the geographic limitations to the location of commercial manufacturing.

Through the late 19th century, the water features of the Northeast had been well suited to early industrial development. Before 1880, industries were distributed among sites that provided good water mill seats. The introduction of steam power during the 19th century enabled industries to move away from favorable water locations and concentrate in areas convenient to labor and transportation. By 1880, steam power constituted more than half of all energy generated in the United States, and nearly 90 percent by 1890. URBANIZATION, industrialization, and shifts in energy sources occurred hand in hand in the late 19th century. Access to attractive waterwheel seats no longer determined the geographic distribution of industry, and waterpower receded in importance to American manufacturing.

ELECTRIFICATION

The advent of electrification provoked renewed interest in hydraulic energy. THOMAS EDISON demonstrated the efficacy of central station electrical service with the lighting of Wall Street in NEW YORK CITY on September 4, 1882. A waterwheel on the Fox River in Wisconsin supplied energy to the country's first hydroelectric plant that same year. With the development of cost-effective electricity transmission systems was the opportunity to exploit very large water energy resources and transmit the power to urban and industrial centers. In 1896, 100,000-horsepower turbines installed at NIAGARA FALLS began generating electricity transmitted 20 miles away to Buffalo, New York. In the early 20th century, progressive politicians and engineers began to promote comprehensive river development for electric power generation, control of FLOODS, navigation, and IRRIGATION. Revenues from electric power sales would finance the large-scale improvements envisioned.

In 1920, the Federal Power Act put the U.S. government in the role of regulating and investing in hydroelectric facilities on navigable waterways. The federal government began investing in large-scale hydroelectric dams that sent electricity across hundreds of miles to customers in cities and on farms. These power plants also attracted industries that could benefit from economical access to both water and power. Both the Tennessee River valley and the Columbia River valley saw extensive growth of metal- and chemical-processing industries in conjunction with the construction of federal hydroelectric dams.

Use of waterpower to fuel electrification grew rapidly in the early 20th century. In 1912, waterpower provided 39 percent of the nation's energy. By 1920, hydroelectric plants generated 6 million horsepower of energy and that quadrupled in another 35 years. Hydroelectric power continued to supply 40 percent of the nation's energy through the middle of the century. By 1950, the hydroelectric share of power generation had dropped to 30 percent, and it continued to drop to 16 percent in 1970, 10 percent in 1990, and only 7 percent in 2000. Yet, the United States is still the fourth-largest producer of hydroelectric power in the world. More than half of the country's hydroelectric capacity is in the western United States, and the majority of that resides in Washington State.

RENEWABILITY

Hydroelectric power offers many benefits to an energy-dependent nation. Waterpower is renewable, although it is not always reliable. Through the water cycle, rivers are replenished annually, but water levels vary from year to year. Reservoir systems can regulate flow in high- and low-water years. Hydroelectric plants are "clean"—they emit no greenhouse gases and discharge no polluted waste to waterways. And hydroelectric facilities do not rely on fossil fuel extraction since the source of energy is moving water. Yet, the use of hydraulic energy also exacts an environmental cost.

ENVIRONMENTAL IMPACTS

All types of waterpower installations, from the simplest waterwheels to the largest and most complex hydroelectric dams, involve modifications to waterways in order to function. Dams, races, ponds, and reservoirs are all employed to manage the flow of water and maximize the power potential at the energy site. From the very earliest days of colonial settlement and construction of cooperative mills, waterpower initiatives have resulted in modifications to waterways and the ECOSYSTEMS they support. As waterpower installations have grown in scale, so, too, have alterations to the surrounding ecosystems. The environmental effects of hydropower development have ranged from minor adjustments to stream flow to major inundations of valleys, relocation of settlements, covering of cultural and archaeological artifacts, loss of wildlife, and dramatic changes to river flow patterns.

Dams intentionally alter river flow, causing significant ecological changes up- and downstream. As reservoirs form behind dams, dry-land habitat is covered, local species of plants and animals may be eliminated, migratory BIRDS lose feeding and nesting grounds, water temperatures change, and aquatic life is transformed. Below dams, stream flow rates are altered, water temperature may be lowered and dissolved oxygen depleted, and often silt flow is blocked, leading to erosion. Dams cause major problems for natural FISHERIES, particularly for salmon. Reservoirs literally cover fisheries and render them inaccessible to fishermen. This is a special problem for Native Americans, who historically relied on fishing for their livelihood and whose access, guaranteed under federal treaties, disappeared when the fisheries were covered.

Hydropower installations result in a variety of other river changes affecting aquatic life. Dams effectively block annual upstream fish migration, thus interrupting spawning cycles, while turbines harm the fish that do pass through the works. Changes in water temperature above and below dams create further problems in the reproduction cycle. The results are evident in the large loss of anadromous fish populations (those that move between oceans and rivers during their life cycles) along the Atlantic and Pacific coasts. Because fisheries are of great importance to the U.S. economy, especially in the Pacific Northwest, dam designs have incorporated features such as ladders and bypasses since the early 20th century. Federal and state governments have also experimented with projects to move fish up and down rivers artificially at key points in the spawning cycle, with limited success. In addition, industrial and agricultural development near hydroelectric dams contributes agricultural and industrial waste and, in some cases, hydrothermal pollution, further harming fish populations.

Dams also pose a safety risk for downstream residents. The St. Francis Dam was constructed on the Owens River in California in 1924 under the direction of WILLIAM MULHOLLAND to provide a reservoir for both a downstream hydroelectric plant and LOS ANGELES, CALIFORNIA's water supply. When the dam broke on March 12, 1928, the floodwaters devastated several towns and killed more than 500 people. Large-scale dams have resulted in large-scale effects on human populations—displacement of communities, loss of fisheries, and future risks of flooding. Yet they have also created new recreation resources, encouraged the establishment of industrial centers, and supported economic development.

Hydroelectric projects and related dams have attracted controversy over potential damage to the surrounding region throughout the 20th century, as a few examples illustrate. Proposals to flood the HETCH HETCHY VALLEY in California in 1906 pitted conservationists against preservationists. JOHN MUIR led the opposition to the hydroelectric and water supply project, while a progressive Congress passed the Raker Act, allowing flooding of the valley. Environmental groups continue to advocate removal of the dam. In order to preserve Dinosaur National Monument, the SIERRA CLUB led a successful campaign against the proposed Echo Park dam in 1956. Nine years later, the Scenic Hudson Preservation Coalition opposed the construction of a pumped storage hydroelectric plant at Storm King Mountain on the basis of potential damage to local fish populations and destruction of aesthetically valuable resources. Con Edison eventually abandoned the project.

By the end of the 20th century, opposition to hydroelectric dams expanded to include initiatives to decommission active facilities. For example, in 2007, Portland Gas and Electric (PGE) completed removal of the nearly 100-year-old Marmot Dam on the Sandy River in Oregon. Built in 1913 as part of a complex of hydroelectric improvements, the dam and its system of canals and tunnels routed and managed river flow to a downstream powerhouse. Fish screens were added in 1951 to improve salmon and steelhead migration. In 1999, PGE announced plans to decommission the project. PGE and 22 environmental groups and government agencies developed a decommissioning and resource protection plan that is still in effect.

CONCLUSION

Hydraulic energy was essential to the early development of the United States, and access to waterpower resources shaped patterns of growth throughout the nation's history. From waterwheels to hydroelectric dams, use of this clean fuel source has also caused extensive ecological disruption. Each waterpower project embodies the conflict between efficient use of natural resources for maximal economic benefit and preservation of ecological systems for the long-term health of the environment.

See also BONNEVILLE POWER ADMINISTRATION; CENTRAL ARIZONA PROJECT; CENTRAL VALLEY PROJECT; FISHING, SUBSISTENCE; GLEN CANYON DAM; HOOVER DAM; LOWELL-WALTHAM SYSTEM; MILL TOWNS; PROGRESSIVISM; TENNESSEE VALLEY AUTHORITY; TEXTILES.

Julie Cohn

Further Reading

Hindle, Brooke, ed. *America's Wooden Age: Aspects of Its Early Technology.* Tarrytown, N.Y.: Sleepy Hollow Restorations, 1975.

Hunter, Louis C. *A History of Industrial Power in the United States, 1780–1930.* Vol. 1, *Water Power in the Century of the Steam Engine.* Charlottesville: University of Virginia Press, 1979.

Hyman, Leonard S., Andrew S. Hyman, and Robert C. Hyman. *America's Electric Utilities: Past, Present, and Future.* 8th ed. Vienna, Va.: Public Utilities Reports, 2005.

Melosi, Martin V. *Coping with Abundance: Energy and Environment in Industrial America.* Philadelphia: Temple University Press, 1985.

Reisner, Marc. *Cadillac Desert: The American West and Its Disappearing Water.* Rev. ed. New York: Penguin Books, 1993.

energy, nuclear

Nuclear energy has both fascinated and terrified scientists, engineers, politicians, and citizens since the mid-20th century. Nuclear energy is released when an atom is split, and through technical manipulation, nuclear energy can be used to fuel a variety of processes. Developed first for a bomb and later for electrification, transportation, and industrial uses, nuclear energy has been a controversial part of American life for more than 60 years, raising concerns about human and environmental health.

THE MANHATTAN PROJECT

During WORLD WAR II (1941–45), President FRANKLIN D. ROOSEVELT directed the army secretly to assemble a team of physicists, chemists, mathematicians, and engineers to build an atomic bomb. Called the MANHATTAN PROJECT, the team worked from several sites around the country to manufacture nuclear fuel, design a weapon, and test the world's first atom bomb. After the successful test in the New Mexico desert on July 16, 1945, the United States dropped atomic bombs over Hiroshima, Japan, on August 6, 1945, and Nagasaki, Japan, on August 9, 1945, to devastating effect, ending the war. Although the Manhattan Project was decommissioned after the war, the federal government continued to develop military and civilian uses of nuclear energy. With passage of the Atomic Energy Act of 1946, creating the ATOMIC ENERGY COMMISSION (AEC), CONGRESS established a firm commitment to nuclear power.

POST–WORLD WAR II DEVELOPMENTS

While weapons development continued to be a top priority, the federal government invested in other uses of nuclear energy as well. In 1951, an AEC test reactor generated electricity for the first time in the United States. Two years later, President DWIGHT D. EISENHOWER called for creation of an "Atoms for Peace" program, expanding the focus on civilian uses of nuclear energy. In 1954, Congress amended the Atomic Energy Act, permitting commercial development of nuclear power. During that same year, under the leadership of Admiral Hyman G. Rickover (1900–86), who had worked at the Oak Ridge (Tennessee) site of the Manhattan Project, the navy launched the *Nautilus,* its first nuclear submarine.

The light-water reactor that powered the *Nautilus* became the model for future American nuclear power stations. Congress passed the Price Anderson Act in 1957, providing partial indemnification for private industry against nuclear accident claims. In 1958, the AEC dedicated the country's first commercial nuclear power station at Shippingport, Pennsylvania. Funded by the federal government and built by Westinghouse, the Shippingport reactor served as a prototype for future light-water power plants throughout the country.

Nuclear power plants in use today, such as Pennsylvania's Three Mile Island Generating Station shown here, use nuclear fission reactions. Electric utility reactors heat water to produce steam, which is then used to generate electricity. (Dobresum/Shutterstock)

ELECTRIFICATION

Shippingport demonstrated the technical feasibility of the use of nuclear energy for electrification and launched two decades of commercial investment in nuclear power. Between 1958 and 1978, utilities ordered 259 reactor units, and the number of operating units reached a peak of 112 in 1990. By 1988, nuclear energy provided approximately 20 percent of the electricity generated in the United States, and it has continued to do so through the beginning of the 21st century. By 2009, nuclear plants operated in 31 states, and the 55 oldest plants have been operating for nearly 30 years. During this time, nuclear plants have also demonstrated the challenges of using a complex, potentially hazardous, and militarily useful technology for civilian purposes.

At first, nuclear energy held out great promise as a nearly limitless supply of energy at very low cost. Yet in the process of designing, building, and operating nuclear plants, the industry learned that nuclear energy was not yet cheaper than fossil fuels for generating power. In addition to complex technical challenges related to controlling nuclear reactions, plant designers and operators were faced with escalating costs associated with the very large size of power plants and equipment changes and retrofits resulting from ever-changing regulations.

ENVIRONMENTAL ISSUES

From the earliest days of nuclear energy development, the safety of those working with and living near nuclear materials has been an issue. Engineers and regulators designing nuclear reactors have had to address safe handling of fuel, management of the nuclear reaction, and safe disposal of waste to protect against radiation exposure. Engineers employed an approach known as "defense in depth" that depended upon multiple layers of technical and operating protections to prevent radiation exposure. Accidents at the Browns Ferry power plant in Alabama in 1975 and the THREE MILE ISLAND plant in Pennsylvania in 1979 demonstrated that the defense in depth design approach failed to incorporate sufficient protections against human error. Further, the Three Mile Island accident revealed the insufficiency of emergency response plans.

Scientists continue to debate the health effects of long-term exposure to low levels of radiation that may be emitted from nuclear power plants. Safety regulations, first under the aegis of the AEC and later under the Nuclear Regulatory Commission, have changed dramatically since the 1940s as scientists have increased their understanding of the risks associated with radiation exposures and the public has demanded greater protection. In the United States, there have been no major releases of radiation resulting from an accident at a nuclear power plant.

Early on, nuclear power plants posed a more tangible environmental risk in the form of thermal pollution. Located near lakes, rivers, and oceans, nuclear power plants use vast quantities of water to cool reactors and spent fuel. Wastewater from nuclear plants heats the receiving water and causes significant changes in the local ecology. Overheated water can have adverse effects on fish spawning cycles, growth of algae and water plants, and overall health of the nearby aquaculture. While thermal pollution was a problem shared by other types of power plants, in the 1960s it became a lightning rod for activists opposed to nuclear power. By the early 1970s, the Congress granted the AEC regulatory authority over thermal pollution and the utility industry invested in cooling equipment to reduce the discharge of waste heat.

The disposal of nuclear waste has been by far the most intractable environmental problem associated with nuclear energy. Spent fuel from nuclear power plants will remain radioactive for tens of thousands of years. Thus, disposal strategies must address concerns about both exposure to radiation and access to potential fuel for nuclear weapons. In the United States, nuclear power plants generate nearly 2,000 metric tons of spent fuel annually, most of which is currently stored on the sites of the generating facilities. The DEPARTMENT OF ENERGY is responsible for ultimate disposal of this waste and is considering development of a long-term storage site under YUCCA MOUNTAIN in Nevada. This site has the advantages of being relatively distant from major population centers and sitting on a geologic configuration favorable to nuclear waste storage. However, opponents to this site see it as both environmentally risky and culturally insensitive, as Yucca Mountain has served as a spiritual center for Indian populations for hundreds, if not thousands, of years.

In addition to managing spent fuel from power plants, nuclear waste treatment and disposal strategies in the United States must address low-level nuclear waste generated by medical and industrial facilities, as well as millions of gallons of waste stored at military nuclear production sites, and thousands of acres of land and water contaminated during decades of nuclear weapons testing. The long-term handling of waste products from nuclear power sites thus forms only one component of a complex nuclear waste scenario.

ANTINUCLEAR ACTIVISM

Those living and working near nuclear power facilities have been concerned about a wide range of issues affecting health and livelihood. Environmental activists, neighboring citizens, unions, and politicians have protested nuclear power for reasons of safety, hydrothermal pollution, aesthetic values, ethical opposition to any use of nuclear energy, and economics.

A few examples illustrate the range of antinuclear activities over the past several decades. The Union of Concerned Scientists organized in 1969 to debate the scientific basis of findings about nuclear energy publicly. The group regularly challenged the government to strengthen safety standards at nuclear power plants. In 1971, a citizens committee sued the AEC for failing to include environmental considerations under the NATIONAL ENVIRONMENTAL POLICY ACT (NEPA) OF 1969 when it issued a license for a nuclear power plant at Calvert Cliffs, Maryland. The ruling, favorable to the citizens group, gave judicial teeth to NEPA and forced AEC to expand environmental considerations in licensing.

In 1976, activists organized the Clamshell Alliance to protest permitting of the Seabrook nuclear plant in New Hampshire. This alliance opposed nuclear power altogether and through civil disobedience sought unsuccessfully to prevent Seabrook from ever opening. In the late 1970s and early 1980s, utility customers in Washington State refused to accept accelerating rate increases to finance construction of five nuclear power plants. Plant costs rose astronomically, but no electric power was produced. In 1982, the Washington Public Power Supply System (WPPSS) stopped construction on two plants and defaulted on $2.25 billion in bonds, the largest municipal bond default in history. Today, WPPSS still operates one nuclear power plant that provides electricity to the Northwest Power Pool. Similarly, citizen objection to the Shoreham Nuclear Power Plant in Long Island, New York, led the state to acquire the licensed plant from the private utility that had built it and shut the plant down before it ever generated electricity. The plant was fully decommissioned in 1994.

The nuclear power industry experienced a decline in popularity, political support, and economic feasibility beginning in the late 1970s. A drop in demand due to the economic recession and inflation made nuclear power less attractive to the public. Further, the combination of low energy prices, expanding access to oil and NATURAL GAS, technical challenges in building and operating nuclear plants, stricter regulatory requirements, public fears related to nuclear accidents at Three Mile Island and Chernobyl (in the former Soviet Union on April 26, 1986), and increasing environmental opposition to nuclear power led to a halt in industry expansion. Orders for new plants dropped after 1974, and many utilities canceled scheduled construction projects in the following years. During this period, the environmental community embraced another global problem as scientists provided increasing evidence for a link between the use of fossil fuels, which generate greenhouse gases, and CLIMATE CHANGE. Thus, a new, hopeful future for nuclear power, which does not contribute to greenhouse gases, emerged at the end of the 20th century. On September 24, 2007, the South Texas Nuclear Project submitted the first license request received by the Nuclear Regulatory Commission since the 1970s.

CONCLUSION

Nuclear energy has demonstrated technical feasibility as an alternative to fossil fuel power generation. Yet, nuclear power plants have failed to offer an inexpensive, safe, environmentally sound alternative fuel source to the degree originally expected. Electric power consumption is still on the rise in the United States, despite efforts to invoke conservation principles and to shift to renewable sources of energy. In the 21st century, the future of nuclear power rests upon the technical safety of plants, the stability and security of long-term waste disposal options, and the willingness of the public to trade the risks and costs of fossil fuels for the risks and costs of nuclear energy.

See also DEFENSE, DEPARTMENT OF; ENERGY, FOSSIL FUEL; ENERGY, HYDRAULIC; ENERGY, RENEWABLE; GREENHOUSE EFFECT; NUCLEAR WEAPONS AND TESTING; OIL, DOMESTIC; TENNESSEE VALLEY AUTHORITY.

Julie Cohn

Further Reading

Garwin, Richard L., and Georges Charpak. *Megawatts + Megatons: The Future of Nuclear Power and Nuclear Weapons.* Chicago: University of Chicago Press, 2002.

Rhodes, Richard. *The Making of the Atomic Bomb.* New York: Simon & Schuster, 1986.

Walker, Samuel J. *A Short History of Nuclear Regulation, 1946–1999.* Washington, D.C.: U.S. Nuclear Regulatory Commission, 2000.

———. *Three Mile Island: A Nuclear Crisis in Perspective.* Berkeley: University of California Press, 2004.

Wellock, Thomas R. *Critical Masses: Opposition to Nuclear Power in California, 1958–1978.* Madison: University of Wisconsin Press, 1988.

energy, renewable

"Renewable energy" popularly refers to sources of energy, such as wind energy and biofuels, perceived as inexhaustible. This quality differentiates renewable energy from energy technologies based on the consumption of preexisting fuels such as PETROLEUM, COAL, and uranium. Advocates of renewable energy argue that humanity will eventually exhaust the Earth's reserves of nonrenewable fuels and that renewable energy sources do not have the same environmental costs as competing technologies. Renewable energy has grown in popularity, if not in practice, as nations such as the United States attempt to respond to the problem of GLOBAL WARMING by reducing their use of carbon-dioxide-creating FOSSIL FUELS.

In 2008, the U.S. Energy Information Agency (EIA), which is part of the DEPARTMENT OF ENERGY, specified "renewable energy" as naturally replenished, but flow-limited, meaning that such sources, while virtually inexhaustible, could provide only a limited amount of energy per unit of time. The EIA identifies the most commonly recognized renewable energy resources as including biomass fuel, hydropower, and geothermal, solar, and wind energy. According to the EIA, renewable sources provided 7 percent of the total energy consumed in the United States in 2007; this figure includes both electricity and other energy uses.

Descriptions of "renewable" energy that focus on the generation of electricity or the production of liquid fuels reflect modern ideas about energy, and the concept of "renewable" versus "nonrenewable" energy is a 20th-century idea. The scientific discipline of PHYSICS, however, defines energy as "the capacity for doing work." By this definition, the United States has, throughout its history, depended heavily on renewable energy.

Animal labor is one important source of renewable energy that has served the United States across most of its history. Prior to the advent of the steam engine and the railroad, horses, donkeys, and oxen provided by far the largest source of energy for overland transportation, both by carrying riders and by pulling carts and wagons. Beasts of burden provided the energy for much of the agricultural work in the early United States, pulling plows to break up the land in preparation for planting. Animals also provided energy in a variety of other settings—donkeys, for example, were used to haul ore carts to the surface in many early mines.

Historically, hydro energy has been one of the most popular renewable energy sources used in the United States. *Hydro* refers to using water-based sources of energy to do work. This category includes hydroelectric dams built on rivers, but it also includes power plants that harness the power of tides or wave action or ocean thermal sources to produce electricity. Prior to the 20th century, Americans harnessed many non-electricity-generating forms of hydropower. The famous Lowell textile mills built in the early 19th century used the energy of the water flow in the Merrimack River to run power looms, and waterwheels provided power for sawmills and gristmills throughout the United States. In the form of canals, hydropower was also one of the major sources of transportation energy in the early United States. The Erie Canal system, for instance, allowed for the shipment of large loads of grain and agricultural products throughout New York. Some of these systems combined hydropower and animal power—in the early years after it opened, freight traveled along the Erie Canal on mule-drawn barges.

Wind energy uses technological concepts similar to those of hydropower, but in this case moving air, rather than moving water, does work for humans. The most common form of wind energy involves the use of windmills—machines with blades that spin when wind blows across them. Modern windmills spin electricity-generating turbines; historically, windmills in the United States have provided energy for activities such as grinding grain and sawing lumber. In dry parts of the country, farmers often relied on water pumped from wells by small windmills. Wind energy also provided an important source of transportation energy in the early United States, driving sail-powered shipping.

Solar energy technology encompasses a variety of strategies for harnessing the Sun's output to do work. Some solar technologies capture the warmth of sunlight, using it to heat homes, to heat water for residential use, or to boil liquids for electricity-generating steam turbines. Photovoltaic (PV) cells convert light energy (rather than heat) directly into electricity by taking advantage of the photoelectric effect.

Biofuel describes fuel sources derived from the recent transformation of organic products, such as plants, animal waste, and algae (as opposed to FOSSIL FUELS, which result from the transformation of organic products over long periods, ranging from centuries to millennia). The indigenous peoples of North America burned wood to heat their residences and cook food long before the arrival of Europeans on the continent, making wood one of the earliest and most commonly used biofuels. Animal waste, such as cow and bison chips, also served as an important biofuel, providing burnable fuel for Indians and white settlers in parts of the United States that lacked wood. Modern biofuels such as ethanol, a liquid fuel produced from plant matter, may eventually replace petroleum products as the primary source of energy for transportation in the United States.

Despite their collective reputation as environmentally friendly and safe sources of power, renewable energy technologies have remained less popular in the United States than other energy sources. The most common criticism of renewable energy centers on cost, with opponents citing the high cost of renewable energy, especially in comparison to fossil fuel technologies. Additionally, renewable energy technologies have had unexpected environmental and social costs. Local residents have fought against the construction of wind farms in several parts of the United States on the grounds that wind turbines are eyesores, and the conversion of agricultural crops such as CORN into fuel production has contributed to worldwide spikes in food prices.

In spite of these difficulties, it seems likely that renewable energy sources will grow in popularity and importance in the 21st century as the U.S. government attempts to respond to the problem of global warming by reducing the nation's dependence on fossil fuels. The percentage of the nation's energy provided by renewable energy sources has grown steadily since 2001. If renewable energy consumption continues to grow, the 21st century will begin to look more and more like the 19th, as the United States returns to new versions of the technologies that powered America long before the introduction of the internal combustion engine.

See also AGRICULTURE, COMMERCIAL; AGRICULTURE, SUBSISTENCE; ANIMALS, DOMESTICATED; ENERGY, ELECTRICAL; ENERGY, FOSSIL FUEL; ENERGY, HYDRAULIC; LOWELL-WALTHAM SYSTEM; UNITED STATES—CENTRAL PLAINS; UNITED STATES—NORTHERN PLAINS.

Jeffrey Womack

Further Reading
Berinstein, Paula. *Alternative Energy: Facts, Statistics, and Issues.* Westport, Conn.: Oryx Press, 2001.
Energy Information Administration. "Energy Information Administration: Official Energy Statistics from the U.S. Government." Available online. URL: http://www.eia.doe.gov/. Accessed October 10, 2008.
Greene, Ann. *Horses at Work: Harnessing Power in Industrial America.* Cambridge, Mass.: Harvard University Press, 2008.

engineering

Engineers apply scientific and mathematical theory to practical ends such as the design, manufacture, and operation of efficient and economical structures, machines, processes, and systems. They turn ideas into reality to solve the practical problems of contemporary society. The field of engineering is the artful work of professionals, delivering practical applications with the knowledge of science. In the 21st century world of technological evolution, engineering is essential for the survival and health of civilization. The field of engineering is mandatory for the planning, design, execution, and maintenance of a host of products and projects from large dams that regulate water flow to the intricate electronics used in zero gravity environments such as the International Space Station.

ORIGINS AND EVOLUTION OF ENGINEERING

Since the days of ancient Rome, humans have valued the use of technology and application of engineering. Romans built some of the best roads ever constructed, as well as aqueducts, which carried millions of gallons of water to Rome and other cities daily. Those roads and aqueducts are examples of state support given to the engineering discipline. These early civil works projects taught humanity that the use of LEAD piping was toxic and revealed the need to use safer materials to ensure health would not be compromised. As centuries went by, the engineering role was shaped by guilds in which apprentices and their skills were nurtured. The transition from the master-and-apprentice relationship of passing down unique skills to a common pool of technical knowledge was accelerated after the scientific revolution of the 17th century. With THE ENLIGHTENMENT and its emphasis on reason as the source of authority, engineering solutions often provided the means by which humans attempted to shape, control, or dominate nature so as to be less susceptible to changing or unpredictable environmental conditions.

By the 19th century, academic training increasingly became the norm for engineers, and specialties within engineering began to emerge. Innovators such as Ernst Werner von Siemens (1816–92) of Germany coined the German term *Elektrotechnik* for electrical engineering. Other engineers have hailed him as the father of this field. Others followed in his footsteps around the world, and a new class of engineers in all disciplines received formal education by the 19th century. The practicing engineer had replaced the traditional self-educated amateur with a technical degree in a specific field from a reputable university.

Civil engineering, with its roots in antiquity, delivered ROADS AND TURNPIKES, bridges, DAMS and IRRIGATION systems, water collection and purification facilities, plants and pipelines, and much more. It is considered the oldest of the engineering disciplines. Civil engineers plan, design, and build infrastructure and continually make incremental improvements with each new breakthrough in materials and processes. Massive projects such as HOOVER DAM, dedicated in 1935, are more than a triumph of civil engineering. Its sheer size and graceful lines reinforced the power of the American dream to a nation struggling through the darkest days of the GREAT DEPRESSION. This incarnation of civil engineering became a monument to the material and spiritual values of a country. The discipline was central to building the country's infrastructure.

The field of mechanical engineering contributed innovations necessary to power the increasingly complex infrastructure of society—to generate new forms of energy. Engines and turbines enabled the work of civilization to be done without relying on human labor and animal toil. Advances in mechanical engineering led to the use of machine tools, construction of large-scale chemical and power plants, AUTOMOBILES for mobility, refrigeration for urbanization of society, and robotics for further mechanization of repetitive human tasks, to name a few. Machines often have performed their programmed tasks better, more reliably, and faster than people. Today, this continues to be done, but with an eye on reducing pollution and developing sustainable processes that power human activity.

Chemical engineering necessarily appeared during the 18th century when industrialists sought to scale laboratory advances to the consumer market. Dyes, soaps, perfumes, and medicines had to be produced in volume to satisfy the public demand for colored fabrics, cleanliness, luxuries, and health, respectively. Demand was high for engineers who possessed technical knowledge related to chemical reactions, controls, and processes and could apply their skills to leverage distillation, evaporation, absorption, and drying techniques.

In concert with a shift to more ecologically friendly products at the end of the 20th century, CHEMISTRY and its effect on the environment and biological entities played a key role in their formulation. Terms such as *toxicity, precious metal mitigation,* and the like, are becoming part of our daily language. People protest finding benzene in their sodas or drinking water, citizens demand better wastewater treatment facilities, and cities legislate the disposal of batteries and fluorescent lights be done in newly created hazardous material recycling centers. Chemists and environmental engineers work in close collaboration to address these issues on a global scale.

As the population rapidly grew in the United States and around the world, the discipline was reinvigorated late in the 20th century as many institutions, such as the University of Florida and the University of Washington, augmented their civil engineering programs with environmental engineering. If, in the past, engineering serviced dramatic and subtle transformations of nature, environmental engineering, as a discipline, has attempted to apply scientific principles to improve or restore healthy environments for humans and other organisms. Environmental engineers, for example, crafted technology to control air and water pollution or build systems for the safer handling of sewerage and industrial wastewater. Engineered solutions increasingly took into account the impact on the air, water, or land. This approach embraces the philosophy of the late father of the environmental movement, ALDO LEOPOLD, who wrote in *A Sand County Almanac* (1949), "We abuse land because we regard it as a commodity belonging to us. When we see land as a community to which we belong, we may begin to use it with love and respect."

AMERICAN INNOVATORS

Electrical engineering emerged as a new discipline after the discovery of a reliable source of power when the Italian physicist Alessandro Volta (1745–1827) invented the battery in 1800 and with the extensive electrical investigations of the English physicist Michael Faraday (1791–1867) in the 1830s. Initially, the power of electricity allowed for new forms of personal communications engineered by American inventors in the 19th century: the TELEGRAPH invented by Samuel F. Morse (1791–1872), the TELEPHONE by Alexander Graham Bell (1847–1922), and the phonograph by THOMAS EDISON. These innovations shrank time and distance, realtering human relations with their physical world. At the same time, power engineers such as Nikola Tesla (1856–1943), Samuel Insull (1859–1938), and George Westinghouse (1846–1914) saw to the production, distribution, and utilization of electricity to power industry and illuminate residences.

One of the greatest engineers of this era was Thomas Alva Edison, who patented 1,093 inventions, earning him the nickname "The Wizard of Menlo Park" (Menlo Park is the New Jersey town in which he established his industrial research laboratory). Edison's most famous contribution was the incandescent light bulb, which extended the length of the day by illuminating the night. He also developed the phonograph and improved upon the original designs of the stock ticker, the telegraph, and the telephone. From these basic tools of communication, the vacuum tube was developed and created the field of electronics embodied in the form of broadcast radio and TELEVISION. The breakthrough of the transistor and its miniaturization in the form of integrated circuits led to the proliferation and ubiquity of COMPUTERS. Engineering accelerated and expanded at a feverish pace in the 20th century.

NEW AREAS OF SPECIALIZATION AND INCREASED PROFESSIONALIZATION

As areas of specialization increased, the number of engineering disciplines increased in conjunction with the notion of division of labor. Aeronautical engineering appeared after the success of the Wright brothers to work with aircraft and ultimately spacecraft designs. The field of bioengineering emerged to address the need for medical instruments and artificial organs, the synthesis of biology with mechanical and electrical engineering. Geological engineering separated itself from civil engineering to focus on mineral exploration and mining. Similarly, material engineering left the fold of chemical engineering to develop ceramics, metal alloys, plastics, and a whole host of artificial materials for new products used in exotic applications. Increasing industrialization of the world economy led to the field of industrial engineering, which yielded productive factory layouts and improved ergonomics and increased quality control of products, while ensuring a safer operating environment. Most recently, marine engineering and nuclear power engineering emerged from the established fields of mechanical and electrical engineering. With such a diversity of engineering fields, an emphasis on increasing the scientific component of an engineer's training began in the 1950s.

Higher institutions of learning chartered to train future engineers were accredited to ensure consistent excellence in the profession. Today, these same institutions have begun to help the engineering mind think beyond the simple black-and-white terms with which it is most comfortable. Engineers are encouraged to develop a solution to a problem and innovate such that the solution does not degrade the environment. Engineering schools have ample examples and experience to provide background for engineering students to consider the potential social impact of new products and processes. Even with constraints such as time schedules and low cost targets imposed by the business world to ensure profits, the role of the engineer is to transcend such artificial limitations and highlight a set of solutions that honors human health, resource preservation, and environmental sustainability. The best engineer in his or her chosen professional discipline is that unique individual possessing the ability to think about problems independently and then become a skeptic by asking lots of questions to arrive at the closest solution to perfection possible.

Engineering contributes to society in another way. The process of scoping a problem, developing the solution, examining associated risks and costs, and testing, implementing, and maintaining the chosen solution gives humanity the tools for making decisions concerning social values. This estab-lished procedure allows politicians and citizens to understand a range of new technologies and debate their impact on society. Engineering processes make society more organic, enabling change for the better. The engineering profession must play a leading role in this debate to ensure the right thing is done in an increasingly technologically complex society.

Today, most engineers are employed in industry. They provide support for basic research, component development, subassembly packaging, product testing, manufacturing process development, total project design, quality control initiatives, technical support of sales and marketing organizations, development of training and maintenance programs, and technical management. These functions are in high demand where businesses invest capital to satisfy customer demand or serve government initiatives. Engineering progress has been most rapid in such environments and is viewed more favorably today when new products or services support a green philosophy. Marketplace and government needs require engineers to move scientific theory or novel ideas to reality. Evidence of this dots the historical landscape of Western civilization, from the Industrial Revolution to modern warfare, from the electronic age to the nuclear age, and from the space age to the emergence of the environmental age.

CONCLUSION

Engineers have augmented the work of colleagues in other disciplines and built upon engineering contributions from previous generations. They did so to ensure power was available to fuel the society they belonged to while maintaining a competitive advantage over other societies. From the Dutch engineers who used wind power to enable the Netherlands to dominate the 16th and 17th centuries to the English engineers who used COAL-driven steam power to ensure the British Empire dominated the 18th and 19th centuries of the industrial era, engineers toiled to produce the machines and processes to support the nation state. In the 20th century, American engineers helped the United States leverage the synthesis of a petroleum-based and an electrically connected republic to dominate the globe. As the 21st century begins, winds of change continue to buffet the direction of engineered solutions.

See also AIRPLANES; CORPORATIONS, CHEMICAL; CORPORATIONS, UTILITIES; ENERGY, ELECTRICAL; ENERGY, FOSSIL FUEL; ENERGY, HYDRAULIC; ENERGY, NUCLEAR; ENERGY, RENEWABLE; GREEN CONSUMERISM AND MARKETING; NATIONAL AERONAUTICS AND SPACE ADMINISTRATION; PUBLIC WORKS.

Robert Karl Koslowsky

Further Reading
Florman, Samuel C. *The Civilized Engineer.* New York: St. Martin's Press, 1987.
Lienhard, John. *The Engines of Our Ingenuity: An Engineer Looks at Technology and Culture.* New York: Oxford University Press, 2000.

Shute, Nevil. *Slide Rule, Autobiography of an Engineer.* New York: William Morrow, 1954.
Wozniak, Steve, with Gina Smith. *iWoz: Computer Geek to Cult Icon.* New York: W. W. Norton, 2006.

English exploration and settlement—Canada and New England

When the Separatists, later known as Pilgrims, landed at Plymouth, Massachusetts, in 1620, they found a land of plenty, with a greater diversity of plant and animal resources than they had known in Europe. They arrived with a belief that their God had given them dominion over those resources to subdue them and make the land "productive." While the Pilgrims, and the Puritans who followed, are primarily known for their desire to improve their spiritual world, this desire to give order to a "howling wilderness," to create a garden from what they saw as chaos, was also a part of their mission. This was quite unlike the relationship the Algonquian Indian populations of the area had with the land. They stressed subsistence and restraint. Instead of dominion over the land, Algonquian belief required a responsibility to the land and its resources to ensure the continual presence of those resources. Moreover, the Pilgrims, and the many English settlers who followed, introduced their technology, diseases, and plant and animal life, all of which permanently altered the ecosystems of the land that would be called New England.

BEGINNINGS—DIFFERENT CONCEPTS OF THE LAND

Such stark differences in European and Algonquian attitudes toward the land can also be seen in their contrasting ideas of ownership of land, which is illustrated in early land transactions between the two groups. When Indians signed over land to New England settlers, they typically believed they were allowing the newcomers user rights to the resources of the land, while the New Englanders believed they were gaining ownership in perpetuity. Such fundamental differences in attitudes and understandings would lead to conflict between the two groups, with the colonists' system eventually being imposed on the New England landscape.

NEW ENGLAND FARMING

Although the English colonists viewed this new land as an untamed WILDERNESS, despite the presence of a substantial Native population, there was plenty of it for them to subdue and put under European forms of cultivation. This was a stark reversal from their experience in England, where land was scarce and expensive. After the initial "starving times" in which the colonists survived because of Indian assistance, the New England colonies quickly began to thrive. Furthermore, their population grew dramatically, particularly during the 1630s, when thousands of Puritans and others settled the region. From a handful of colonists in 1620, New England was home to about 33,000 Europeans by 1660. Conversely, the population of Native peoples declined as they fell victim to European DISEASES to which they had no immunity. With ever increasing numbers of colonists was an increasing demand for land.

New England never produced a staple crop such as TOBACCO or SUGAR with which to make the landowners, as well as the English Crown, wealthy. The soil was too rocky and the growing season too short to support a MONOCULTURE such as those practiced in the West Indies or the region around the CHESAPEAKE BAY. However, the Puritan emphasis on hard work as a way to glorify God allowed the colonists to succeed in this "howling wilderness."

The New Englanders established farming communities that produced imported English crop species such as WHEAT and rye, as well as beans, POTATOES, and maize (CORN) that they adopted from the Indians. The English settlers much preferred to maintain their familiar agricultural practices instead of following the Indian examples, which were less taxing on the land. Indians intermingled their crops of beans, maize, and squash, thereby providing for natural support and control of WEEDS in a smaller space. The Indian system was also much less labor intensive. However, the New Englanders maintained their practice of planting single crops in a field, thereby using more land and labor. The New England system also exhausted the nutrients in the land faster, reinforcing the need for more land for more and more people.

The New Englanders also introduced their livestock with them. Cows, oxen, HORSES, and particularly PIGS AND HOGS foraged through the countryside and FORESTS of New England until their owners tracked them down. This was an inexpensive and relatively labor-free way of maintaining livestock. However, the pigs invaded Indian fields, which were not fenced, as well as oyster banks where Indians gathered shellfish for their own food stocks. Now livestock and Native peoples were in direct competition for a once-abundant food source.

NEW ENGLAND FORESTS

The commoditization of the land was accompanied by the commoditization of the forests as well. Barrels made from New England trees transported goods throughout the British Empire. Trees were also cut to supply the growing lumber industry. In the 1630s, the white pine forests of Maine and New Hampshire had the largest concentration of commercial lumbering in New England. Much of this lumber served the shipbuilding industry centered in and around BOSTON, MASSACHUSETTS, which had 15 shipyards by 1700. Between 1674 and 1714, the shipyards of New England produced more than 1,200 ships. At this time, Boston was second only to London, England, as a British shipbuilding center.

With the forests of England depleted, royal officials needed to ensure a sufficient supply of lumber for the English navy. In the 1690s, the Broad Arrow Policy was enacted in New England, reserving all white pine trees with a 24-inch diameter (as measured one foot from the ground) for use as masts in the royal navy. These trees were marked with the King's Broad Arrow symbol, indicating they were reserved for use in His Majesty's Royal Navy, when needed.

New Englanders' appetite for land and timber also led to clearing of forest lands in much greater amounts than the Indians had previously cleared for their SUBSISTENCE AGRI-CULTURE. After a century of English dominion over the land, this clear-cutting led to actual climate change. Both the air and the soil became warmer and drier. Clear-cutting also led to more numerous and more destructive FLOODS as nothing stopped the spring melt runoff from quickly filling streams and rivers. Furthermore, clear-cutting also led to decreased habitat for DEER and turkeys, other Native food sources.

NEW ENGLAND FISHING

Whereas the inland forests of northern New England provided the lumber, the ports of the area north of Boston became fishing centers. In fact, it was the abundance of FISH in the coastal waters of New England that had led European ships to visit the area in the 15th century. Cape Cod, Massachusetts, received its name from the experiences of early fishermen, who caught so many fish that they had to throw some overboard. Interior waterways were filled with the great spawning runs of alewives, smelts, and sturgeons. Along with the fish resources in freshwater, fishermen from the North Shore, New Hampshire, and Maine exploited the abundant fish resources of the Georges and Grand Banks regions of the Atlantic Ocean. In 1641, New England fishermen caught and sold 600,000 pounds of fish. In 1675, more than 1,000 New England fishermen on 440 ships caught upward of six million pounds of fish. The higher-quality fish were sent to Europe, while the lower grades were sent to West Indian PLANTATIONS to feed slaves.

While the bounty of the sea seemed inexhaustible, the colonial period saw significant declines in fish populations in inland waters. With increased agriculture and lumber industries arose the need for dams for mills and IRRIGATION ponds. Damming rivers prevented spawning fish from swimming upstream. Rivers that were filled with alewives, sturgeons, and SALMON in the early years of English colonization became depopulated. Salmon were gone from the Piscataqua River of New Hampshire by 1750, and the upper reaches of the Connecticut and Salmon Fall Rivers were depopulated by the early 19th century.

CANADA

New England also participated in the BEAVER fur trade, but on a limited basis in comparison to their agriculture, timber, and fishing industries. The FUR TRADE was centered in the towns along the Connecticut River, which provided easy access to interior lands of northern New England. By the time of Metacom's War between the Indians and the colonists in 1675–76, the New England fur trade was in decline, and it never recovered. Therefore, the English looked farther north, into what was then French-controlled Canada. It was in the year 1670 that London merchants created the Hudson's Bay Company. The Hudson Bay, while accessible by ship only two months of the year, provided access to more than a million square miles of land with an abundant beaver population and much more direct transportation to England, which translated into lower costs in comparison to their French competition. Through the late 17th century, the Hudson's Bay Company established trading posts, or "factories," as they were called, along the western shore of the bay at the mouths of principal rivers, such as the Albany and Nelson Rivers, to ensure easy access to traders and ships.

The fur trade required very different attitudes toward the land and the Indian peoples who populated it. Englishmen intent on success in the beaver trade were not interested in gaining rights to land in perpetuity but in gaining control of the animal resources of the land. Because the English of the Hudson's Bay Company were in direct competition with French traders to their south, they needed to make sure they maintained strong alliances with Indian traders, particularly the Cree, who supplied most of the furs. Moreover, Canada did not experience the explosion of English population along the lines of the Great Migration to New England. In fact, the Hudson's Bay Company employed fewer than 200 British subjects, many of whom were orphaned teenage boys hoping to make money in order eventually to return home. So while the fur trade activities of the Hudson's Bay Company altered the population of fur-bearing animals in northern and central Canada, the English stationed at the factories along Hudson Bay did not create the same alterations of land use seen in New England farming and forestry areas.

CONCLUSION

As the AMERICAN REVOLUTION (1775–83) approached, it was evident that a century and a half of English colonization had drastically transformed the landscape of New England. Colonists' concepts of order and land use, such as fenced and clear-cut fields, mill ponds, and lumberyards, dominated the landscape. The animal population had dramatically decreased, and the land and its resources had been fully commoditized. Still, the New England population clamored for more land and continued to push west into Vermont, New York, and the newly opened lands of the OHIO RIVER valley.

See also AGRICULTURE, COLONIAL; COLUMBIAN EXCHANGE; ECOLOGICAL IMPERIALISM; ENGLISH EXPLORATION AND SETTLEMENT—THE MIDDLE COLONIES; ENGLISH EXPLORATION AND SETTLEMENT—THE SOUTH; FENCES AND FENCE LAWS; FISHERIES; INDIANS, NORTHEAST; LOGGING AND LUMBERING; MERCANTILISM; NAVAL STORES.

Holly A. Rine

Further Reading

Anderson, Virginia DeJohn. "King Philip's Herds: Indians, Colonists, and the Problem of Livestock in Early New England." *William and Mary Quarterly* 51 (October 1994): 601–624.

Cronon, William. *Changes in the Land: Indians, Colonists and the Ecology of New England.* 20th Anniversary ed. New York: Hill & Wang, 2003.

Eccels, W. J. *The Canadian Frontier, 1534–1760.* Albuquerque: University of New Mexico Press, 1983.

Krech, Shepard. *The Ecological Indian: Myth and History.* New York: W. W. Norton, 1999.

Merchant, Carolyn. *Ecological Evolutions: Nature, Gender, and Science in New England.* Chapel Hill: University of North Carolina Press, 1989.

Salisbury, Neal. *Manitou and Providence: Indians, Europeans, and the Making of New England, 1500–1643.* New York: Oxford University Press, 1982.

Vickers, Daniel. *Farmers and Fishermen: Two Centuries of Work in Essex County, Massachusetts, 1630–1850.* Chapel Hill: University of North Carolina Press, 1994.

Religion and Land Rights
John Cotton (1630)

John Cotton, an early New England minister, looked to Christianity to justify expansion of English settlements into Indian lands. Envisioning the American landscape as "vacant," he argued that Puritans introduced culture and husbandry to the region and thus owned title to the land. As the English moved into local Indians' "uninhabited" old fields and hunting areas, Cotton believed that growing Puritan populations and diminishing Indian populations, weakened by smallpox epidemics, were part of God's plan for North America. He wrote the following treatise in 1630.

Now God makes room for people 3 wayes:

First, when he casts out the enemies of a people before them by lawfull warre with the inhabitants, which God calls them unto: as in *Ps.* 44. 2. *Thou didst drive out the Heathen before them.* But this course of warring against others, & driving them out without provocation, depends upon speciall Commission from God, or else it is not imitable.

Secondly, when hee gives a forreigne people favor in the eyes of any native people to come and sit downe with then either by way of purchase, as *Abraham* did obtain the field of *Machpelah;* or else when they give it in courtesie, as *Pharaoh* did the land of *Goshen* unto the sons of *Jacob.*

Thirdly, when hee makes a Country though not altogether void of Inhabitants, yet void in that place where they reside. Where there is a vacant place, there is liberty for the sonnes of *Adam* or *Noah* to come and inhabite, though they neither buy it, nor aske their leaves. *Abraham* and *Isaac,* when they sojourned among the *Philistines,* they did not buy that land to feede their cattle, because they said There is roome enough. And so did *Jacob* pitch his Tent by *Sechem, Gen.* 34. 21. There was roome enough, as *Hamor* said, *Let them sit downe amongst us.* And in this case if the people who were former Inhabitants did disturbe them in their possessions, they complained to the King, as of wrong done unto them: As *Abraham* did because they took away his well, in *Gen.* 21, 25. For his right whereto he pleaded not his immediate calling from God, (for that would have seemed frivolous among the Heathen) but his owne industry in digging the well, verse 30. Nor doth the King reject his plea, with what had he to doe to digge wells in their soyle? but admitteth it as a Principle in Nature, That in a vacant soyle, hee that taketh possession of it, and bestoweth culture and husbandry upon it, his Right it is. And the ground of this is from the grand Charter given to *Adam* and his posterity in Paradise, *Gen.* 1. 28. *Multiply, and replenish the earth, and subdue it.* If therefore and sonne of *Adam* come and finde a place empty, he hath liberty to come, and fill, and subdue the earth there.

Source: John Cotton. *Gods Promise to His Plantation.* London, 1630, 4–5.

English exploration and settlement—the Middle Colonies

In the 17th and 18th centuries, the British referred to New York, New Jersey, Delaware, and Pennsylvania as the Middle Colonies because of their geographic location between New England to the north and the Chesapeake to the south. The most socially diverse of the English settlements in North America, the Middle Colonies developed a more egalitarian economy based on YEOMAN agriculture and artisan trades that drew on the rich natural resources and rivers of the region.

Dutch and Swedish colonists first settled parts of New York and New Jersey, in the early 17th century, with little interference from British colonists in the Chesapeake and New England. The Protestant countries of the Netherlands, Sweden, and England were allied against Catholic Spain in a race to colonize North America. By midcentury, the European political climate changed as Spain's imperial power waned and the commercial competition between Britain and

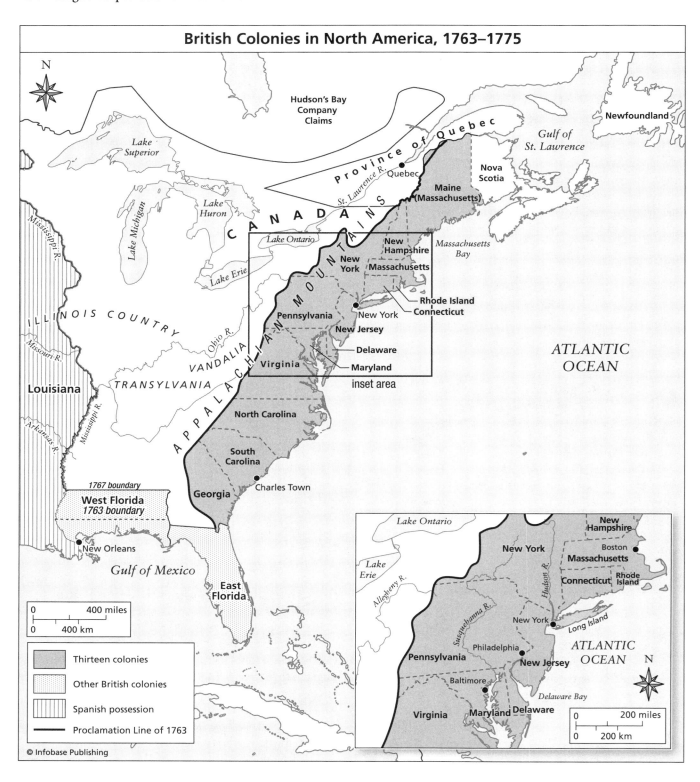

British Colonies in North America, 1763–1775

the Netherlands intensified. Britain and the Netherlands vied for control in the North American and Caribbean colonies in a bid to become the dominant European power in the Atlantic world. Within the context of this larger struggle for colonial territory, Britain wrested from the Dutch, in 1664, the territory that became the Middle Colonies and consolidated its holdings in North America.

Three geographical elements combined to make the Mid-Atlantic colonies especially attractive to the European settlers. The first was the vast river system that allowed trading ships to travel upriver to inland trading posts. The Dutch established forts on the HUDSON RIVER as far inland as 160 miles. The river system also included the Delaware and Susquehanna Rivers. The second element was the region's temperate climate. It was not as cold, allowing for a longer growing season than in New England. However, it was cooler, and thus healthier and less deadly for Europeans, than the hot, humid Chesapeake. Finally, there was a cornucopia of natural resources: fertile soil, dense hardwood FORESTS, deposits of stone and iron ore, large populations of game and fowl, and freshwater streams teeming with FISH.

HUDSON RIVER VALLEY

After Henry Hudson's voyage upriver from New Amsterdam (NEW YORK CITY) in 1609, the Dutch explored and settled the Hudson River region, establishing the first settlements in New Netherland under the auspices of the Dutch West India Company for the purpose of monopolizing the valuable FUR TRADE with the Iroquois. They dispersed trading centers along rivers so that traders could contact Indian hunters who traveled by canoe. The success or failure of the outermost trading posts depended on the Dutch traders' demonstration of respect for the power of the Iroquois. Fort Orange was located at present-day Albany, and Fort Nassau was located at the mouth of the Delaware River. New Amsterdam, the commercial center for the West India Company, stood at the mouth of the Hudson River. The Iroquois proved fierce, competitive traders who took advantage of the lucrative Dutch market in furs, thus causing the Dutch West India trading monopoly to falter.

With the Dutch West India Company unable to control the market, independent Dutch traders competed in the fur trade and diversified commercial ventures. Dutch merchants integrated the extensive river system into the global shipping network. As the fur trade grew, farming communities developed in the Hudson River valley and Long Island and New Jersey. Agricultural production supported the trading settlements in the Hudson River valley and SUGAR PLANTATIONS in the Caribbean.

New Netherland was religiously and ethically diverse. European settlers immigrated to New Netherland from Belgium, France, Germany, and Scandinavia, usually after first immigrating to Holland. A policy of tolerance, maintained by colonial governors in the interest of good business, attracted people seeking religious freedom and economic opportunity. Farmers, artisans, and merchants all contributed to the colonial economy. Jews, in particular, invested a significant amount of capital, enjoying more freedom in New Netherland than in any other American colony.

DELAWARE RIVER VALLEY

Plans to settle the Delaware River valley began in 1626 as Dutch traders sought to undermine the monopolistic hold of the Dutch West India Company. The traders secured the backing of Swedish investors to establish a colony in the name of the Swedish Crown. Colonists emigrated with instructions to collect BEAVER pelts, grow TOBACCO, raise silkworms, and search for valuable woods and minerals. Unsuccessful at all tasks, the colony failed. The traders relinquished control to the Swedish Crown. New Sweden occupied both sides of the Delaware River and included parts of New Jersey, Delaware, and Pennsylvania. The Delaware River linked scattered farms and trading centers. The colony, however, never fully developed because the Swedish investors failed to provide arms, building materials, tools, and clothing. The predominance of males created social friction that hindered economic development. The Crown's control was short-lived and too weak to fend off the encroachment of the Dutch from the north and the English from the south.

Independent Swedish settlers, however, adapted well to heavy forests, employing practices that later defined the American FRONTIER. SUBSISTENCE HUNTING and FISHING supplemented agriculture, and they moved frequently when resources became depleted. The Swedes combined indigenous crops and European agricultural techniques, producing maize (CORN) and WHEAT for the market. Farmers cleared forests by girdling trees and burning underbrush. They planted grain among the dead trees and used the logs for houses and barns. Swedish farmers built fences to protect fields and orchards from free-ranging livestock. Their woodland farming techniques suited the topography of the Delaware River valley.

English Quakers soon made the furthest-reaching changes in the landscape. In 1672 and 1675, King Charles II gave land to the duke of York after the Anglo-Dutch War. The duke divided it into smaller colonies. Quaker investors purchased East Jersey and attracted a multiethnic mix of yeoman farmers from Scotland, Ireland, New Netherland, and New England. The Scottish settlers clustered together, keeping their distance from others. Large groups of Quakers settled West Jersey. Before 1675, Quaker immigrants to North America tended to be individual missionaries and itinerant evangelists. Between 1677 and 1681, the number of Quakers in the two colonies reached 1,400. Religious beliefs influenced these early Quaker migrations; they faced persecution in England. Migration allowed Quakers to demonstrate that their belief system worked if freed from a restrictive English society. For many, migration was a pilgrimage, a calling to do God's work. These Quakers did not seek economic benefits nor fear economic losses. They wanted a society defined by religious tolerance and social pluralism.

In 1682, 23 ships arrived at the mouth of the Delaware, carrying more than 2,000 Quakers with provisions, tools, and livestock. One vessel carried WILLIAM PENN, the aristocratic founder of Pennsylvania Colony. Penn received 45,000 square miles west of the Delaware River from the duke of York to settle a debt owed to Penn's father. The sizable land grant to Penn solved a nagging problem by removing religious dissidents from England. Approximately 23,000 colonists immigrated to the Delaware Valley, between 1675 and 1715. During the early 18th century, the number of Quakers doubled with each generation. By 1750, the Quakers were the third-largest religious group in the British colonies.

The Lenape Indians, also known as the Delaware, inhabited the land claimed by Penn. The Algonquin-speaking Lenape lived in small autonomous bands along the Delaware and subsisted on horticulture, gathering, hunting, and fishing. Weakened by epidemics, raids by the Iroquois, and alcoholism stemming from trade with the Dutch, the Lenape posed little threat to the Quakers. Initial relations between Penn's agents and the Lenape were peaceful; the English and the Indians incorporated the needs of each group into their political arrangements. By 1737, the English turned against the Lenape Indians with the signing of the Walking Purchase, a fraudulent transaction that effectively expelled the Lenape.

During the 1680s, Penn used capital from investors to organize and support the most rapid and efficient colonization

This wood engraving from an 1856 edition of *Ballou's Pictorial* newspaper shows Henry Hudson and his companions trading with Native Americans on shore in the early 1600s. *(Library of Congress)*

in the British Empire. He viewed his colony as a "holy experiment" and an "example to nations." Penn also sought to enhance his fortune by selling real estate and collecting annual fees from the colonists. Most Quakers emigrated from the North Midland counties of Cheshire, Lancashire, Yorkshire, Derbyshire, and Nottinghamshire. Those who settled the Delaware River valley created small communities that reflected their places of origin. Colonists from the Peake Districts of Derbyshire and Nottinghamshire settled in Trenton, New Jersey. Colonists in the farming counties of Chester and Bucks were generally from Yorkshire, Lancashire, and Cheshire. More than 80 percent of the Quakers who immigrated to PHILADELPHIA, PENNSYLVANIA, between 1682 and 1687 were from London.

From the founding, settlers of the Delaware Valley enjoyed ethnic diversity and social equality. Quakers from Ireland and Wales and many non-Quakers settled the region. Penn attracted, and sometimes subsidized, French, Dutch, Germans, Swedes, Danes, Finns, Scotch, French, and English. Most non-Quaker immigrants to Pennsylvania migrating in family groups and as free laborers of lower to middling rank—similar to the social status of English Quakers themselves—were important to the development of society and culture in colonial Pennsylvania.

Quaker colonists had eyed the Delaware River valley as early as 1660 because the region's ecology was well suited for their agricultural, commercial, and industrial purposes. The soil was fertile. Near Philadelphia were deposits of stone, COAL, COPPER, iron ore, and dense forests of oak, walnut, and chestnut. Towns lined the rivers and bays and supported a booming trade among watermen. Colonists included husbandmen, craftsmen, small shopkeepers, laborers, and servants. With sound credit and reputations, Quaker merchants and artisans maintained extensive trading connections throughout the British Empire. Their faith underwrote Pennsylvania's success because it afforded Quaker merchants a measure of trust.

Penn devised an efficient and equitable land distribution scheme. First, land sales funded his "holy experiment." Second, Penn wanted an agrarian community without the extremes of poverty and wealth experienced by Quaker communities in the Midlands. Penn sold land in blocks of 5,000–10,000 acres to wealthy English buyers with restrictions. Penn required residency by landowners for continued possession and demanded that absentee owners subdivide property into smaller parcels for sale to individual "underpurchasers." Between 1681 and 1685, Penn sold 715,000 acres to 589 "First Purchasers," mostly wealthy Quakers from London or Bristol. Half moved to America. Others forfeited purchases for nonpayment or nonresidence. Most underpurchasers held between 100 and 500 acres. By 1715, there was no unsettled land within 50 miles of Philadelphia. Pennsylvania, tax records revealed, was the most egalitarian British colony.

Penn envisioned single-family farmsteads that worked independently but did not live in isolation. He wanted the houses close together in clusters separated by agricultural fields while town centers held common lands for grazing livestock. This settlement pattern supposedly combined material autonomy with spiritual community. By 1685, some 50 small towns existed. Colonists, however, resisted Penn's nuclear towns in favor of farms scattered across the countryside. As colonists spread across Pennsylvania away from the coast, settlements with their own distinctive cultural characteristics appeared in fertile valleys.

Except for their treatment of the Lenape Indians, ethnic and religious diversity marked the Middle Colonies and distinguished them from the Chesapeake and New England colonies. This diversity fostered culture that resisted deference to political and social elites and created a diversified economy grounded in agriculture and trade. Diverse groups avoided violence because of wealth drawn from bountiful natural resources. They used political rhetoric to air grievances, developing a political and social culture that anticipated a distinct form of American DEMOCRACY.

See also AGRARIANISM; AGRICULTURE, COLONIAL; ARTISAN TRADITIONS; ATLANTIC WORLD, POST-1500; COLUMBIAN EXCHANGE, DUTCH COLONIAL SETTLEMENTS; ECOLOGICAL IMPERIALISM; ENGLISH EXPLORATION AND SETTLEMENT—CANADA AND NEW ENGLAND; ENGLISH EXPLORATION AND SETTLEMENT—THE SOUTH; INDIANS, EASTERN SEABOARD; MERCANTILISM; RELIGION; RIVER TRANSPORTATION.

Mary Richie McGuire

Further Reading
Balmer, Randall H. *A Perfect Babel of Confusion: Dutch Religion and English Culture in the Middle Colonies.* New York: Oxford University Press, 1989.

Dennis, Matthew. *Cultivating a Landscape of Peace: Iroquois-European Encounters in Seventeenth Century America.* Ithaca, N.Y.: Cornell University Press, 1993.

Fischer, David Hackett. *Albion's Seed: Four British Folkways in America.* New York: Oxford University Press, 1989.

Goodfriend, Joyce D. *Before the Melting Pot: Society and Culture in Colonial New York City, 1664–1730.* Princeton, N.J.: Princeton University Press, 1992.

Harper, Steven Craig. *Penn's Promised Land: Penn's Holy Experiment, the Walking Purchase and the Dispossession of the Delawares, 1600–1763.* Bethlehem, Pa.: Lehigh University Press, 2006.

Pencak, William A., and Daniel K. Richter, eds. *Friends and Enemies in Penn's Woods: Indians, Colonists, and the Racial Construction of Pennsylvania.* University Park: Pennsylvania State University Press, 2004.

Rink, Oliver. *Holland on the Hudson: An Economic and Social History of Dutch New York.* Ithaca, N.Y.: Cornell University Press, 1986.

Taylor, Alan. *American Colonies.* New York: Viking, 2001.

English exploration and settlement—the Pacific Rim

The Pacific Rim comprises lands that border the Pacific Ocean. These lands include the western coasts of North America and South America, the eastern Asian coast, Australia, New Zealand, the Philippines, Malaysia, and all Pacific Islands. English exploration of the Pacific Rim began in the 16th century but was most pronounced in the 18th century, followed by colonization in the 19th century. The importation of English diseases, trading practices, and modes of production often devastated the indigenous peoples and altered the ecologies of the Pacific Rim.

English exploration of the Pacific Rim began in 1577, when Queen Elizabeth I (1533–1603) sent Sir Francis Drake (1540–95) to explore the Pacific coast of South America. Drake's voyage was notable for his pirating of Spanish ships and his landing on the western coast of North America. Drake sailed from Plymouth, England, aboard the *Pelican,* later renamed the *Golden Hinde,* around the Straits of Magellan at the tip of South America and entered the Pacific Ocean in September 1578. He then turned north up the present-day coast of Chile and Peru, attacking Spanish ports. Loaded down with Spanish gold, Drake continued north, possibly looking for an eastern passage to the Atlantic Ocean. In June 1579, Drake landed the *Golden Hinde* somewhere on the coast of North America, north of Point Loma (present-day San Diego), for repairs and provisions. Drake kept this exact location a secret, but it was in all probability just north of present-day SAN FRANCISCO, CALIFORNIA. He claimed the land for the English Crown, calling it Nova Albion (New Britain). Drake returned to England in 1580, the first Englishman to circumnavigate the globe.

Despite the financial success of Drake's mission, Spain's increased naval security, European warfare, and the futile search for a NORTHWEST PASSAGE from Hudson Bay to the Pacific hindered England's immediate ambitions in the Pacific. Until the middle of the 18th century, English exploration in the Pacific focused on the search for the mythical Terra Australis, also known as the Great Southern Continent, a hypothetical landmass in the South Pacific that European scientists believed had to exist to counterbalance the large landmasses of the Northern Hemisphere. Despite these setbacks, England mapped many lands in the Pacific throughout the 18th century, including Tahiti, New Zealand, Australia, Tasmania, and Antarctica.

English exploration of North America's Pacific Rim was resumed during Captain James Cook's (1728–79) third and final voyage into the Pacific in 1776. Cook's voyage was largely an attempt to find the famed Northwest Passage, a sea route through the North American arctic that could connect the Atlantic Ocean to the Pacific Ocean. In January 1778, Cook became the first European to explore the Hawaiian Islands. Two months later, he sighted the Oregon coast and continued north, repairing and replenishing his stores at Nootka Sound on Vancouver Island. The English traded iron tools for sea otter fur with the indigenous people. Cook mapped the coastline of Alaska north through the Bering Strait and near the Arctic Ocean. Finding no navigable passage, he returned in 1779 to Hawaii, where he was killed in a dispute with the islanders. Cook's expeditions explored large regions of the Pacific, increased the accuracy of English cartography, and further opened the northwest coast of North America to the FUR TRADE.

English exploration continued with George Vancouver (1757–98), who had sailed on James Cook's third expedition. Vancouver thoroughly charted the west coast of present-day Oregon, Washington, British Columbia, and Alaska. Many cities and geographic features in these areas bear his name. Sir Alexander MacKenzie (1764–1820), a Scottish employee of the fur-trading North West Company founded in 1779 in British Canada, led an expedition that searched for the Northwest Passage. His travels led him overland through western Canada, eventually reaching the Pacific near the mouth of the Bella Coola River in southern British Columbia in July 1793. His journey preceded the LEWIS AND CLARK EXPEDITION by more than a decade.

English settlement on the western shores of North America was primarily along the British Canadian coast of present-day British Columbia. These settlements were mostly fur trading posts and forts under the authority of the Hudson's Bay Company (founded in 1670) after its merger with the North West Company in 1821. Further English settlement in this area occurred with the discovery of GOLD in Fraser Canyon in 1858. Prior to European contact, British Columbia was populated by many indigenous groups, including the Nisga'a, Tsimshian, Haisla, Kwakwaka'wakw, Nuu-chah-nulth, and Coast Salish. Trading furs and fish for metal tools, guns, and alcohol in British Columbia, as well as Russian Alaska and the U.S. Pacific Northwest, sponsored friendly relations with the indigenous people, but it also altered the traditional social and economic roles of the Natives. Many of these indigenous communities became dependent upon this trade, destroying their conventional community structure and methods of subsistence. The growing competition and scale of the fur trade also decimated sea otter and BEAVER populations in the Pacific Northwest.

European contact and settlement severely damaged the indigenous populations of North America. Prior to English contact, some 200,000 Native people lived on the northwest coast of North America. Within 100 years, these populations had been reduced by roughly 80 percent. This devastation was due in large part to the introduction of new HUMAN DISEASES into the indigenous populations, which had no natural immunities. SMALLPOX, INFLUENZA, measles, whooping cough, MALARIA, and scarlet fever reached epidemic proportions. Further losses were incurred by increased tribal warfare over control of the regional fur trade. This warfare was augmented by the introduction of European firearms. A similar pattern of decimation emerged in Hawaii, where conservative estimates show that indigenous populations decreased by 80–90 percent within 70 years of Cook's landing.

The Pacific coast of North America was initially considered unsuitable for European agriculture. Therefore, the actual colonization and settlement of the mainland did not occur until the 1830s and 1840s. Land clearing, timber industries, increased travel, and the desire for colonial landscapes that resembled those of England created niches into which invasive plant and animal species could proliferate. These invasions of nonindigenous flora and fauna were not as destructive in Pacific North America as they were in other regions settled by England (namely, Australia and New Zealand), but they still had a detrimental impact on native species. European species of Scotch broom, cheatgrass, lilacs, and roses flourished, often at the expense of native plants. English settlement decreased species of WOLVES, grizzly BEARS, and mountain lion, while nonindigenous English sparrows and starlings still compete against native BIRD species. Invasive species continue to be a problem in the North American Pacific Rim. For example, the endangered Pacific SALMON populations are being threatened by nonindigenous aquatic predators.

By the turn of the 20th century, English settlement spanned the globe, prompting the phrase "The sun never sets on the British Empire." British imperial exploration and colonization in the Pacific Rim provided strategic naval bases and trading communities, as well as vital commodities, including wool, timber, cotton, and fur. Many of these gains were achieved at the expense of the indigenous people and wildlife that had occupied the land prior to English contact. English settlement decimated many of these populations by disease, warfare, and the introduction of invasive plants and animals.

See also CANADA AND THE UNITED STATES; 54°40' OR FIGHT; INDIANS, PACIFIC NORTHWEST; INDIGENOUS PEOPLES, PACIFIC ISLANDS; OCEANS; RUSSIAN EXPLORATION AND SETTLEMENT; SPECIES, EXOTIC AND INVASIVE; SPECIES, INDIGENOUS; UNITED STATES—HAWAII AND THE PACIFIC ISLANDS; UNITED STATES—PACIFIC NORTHWEST; WEEDS.

Michael A. Ramey

Further Reading
Crosby, Alfred W. *Ecological Imperialism: The Biological Expansion of Europe, 900–1900.* New York: Cambridge University Press, 1986.
Obeyesekere, Gananath. *The Apotheosis of Captain Cook: European Mythmaking in the Pacific.* Princeton, N.J.: Princeton University Press, 1992.
Williams, Glyndwr. *Buccaneers, Explorers, and Settlers: British Enterprise and Encounters in the Pacific, 1670–1800.* Variorum Collected Studies Series. Coventry, England: Variorum, 2005.

English exploration and settlement—the South

In 1584, Sir Walter Raleigh attempted to establish a colony at Roanoke Island, in present-day North Carolina, but failed after three disastrous years. Among the reasons for the failure of his attempts, according to dendrochronologists, were seasonal DROUGHTS, indicated by observations of tree rings from the period. The English, in the meantime, introduced diseases such as SMALLPOX that devastated local Indian populations and spread inland to other communities. The first successful English North American colony was at Jamestown in 1607. Building in a Virginia swamp on CHESAPEAKE BAY, the colonists were subject to disease and starvation for decades, and relations with the local Powhatan Indians broke down quickly. Ultimately, however, the English transplanted a South American TOBACCO varietal, both valuable in European markets and suitable to the Virginia environment, to their farms, thus making the colony financially viable. A combination of settlers' economic ambitions and English law soon created a system of plantation agriculture that depended upon a hierarchical social structure. Virginians first used white indentured labor to plant tobacco but soon adopted African slave labor. The hierarchical social structure and colonial extractive economy based on one crop spread quickly throughout the Chesapeake with the founding of Maryland in 1634.

In order to farm tobacco profitably, colonists fundamentally altered the landscape. Tobacco planters pursued massive deforestation as they cut down walnut, oak, and cedar trees to plant fields. In addition, tobacco quickly depleted the ground of nutrients, at which point colonists would plant CORN or move on to new lands. Livestock also altered the local landscape and created further tensions with local Indians, whose unfenced fields provided ready sustenance for cattle. The FUR TRADE also led to the depletion of regional BEAVER and DEER populations as Indians searched for new hunting grounds. The same sort of effects occurred in Maryland and Carolina.

With the restoration of Charles II to the throne in 1660, the English began to create colonies farther south, granting Carolina to eight lords proprietors in 1663. Individuals leaving Virginia had settled Albemarle, a coastal county in what is today North Carolina, far earlier. The proprietors developed the southern portion, founding Charles Town (later Charleston) in 1669. The Crown eventually took control of the southern portion in 1719. King George II created Georgia, the most southern British colony (and last of the thirteen colonies), in 1732. The colony under General James E. Oglethorpe pursued a series of utopian measures to better the lives of the first Georgia colonists—many of them prisoners. In larger imperial terms, Georgia's purpose was to serve as a buffer against Spanish Florida to the south. The original policies of the colony that barred slavery and alcohol were quickly abandoned, and settlers pursued the same sort of landholding and slave policies as other southern colonies. The social system itself owed a great deal to English SUGAR colonies in the West Indies. Many of the English colonists, particularly in the Lower South, which ultimately had a slave majority, were from the Caribbean Islands. The southern colonies all shared a system of government based on counties. Most areas were predominantly rural and the few cities were ports—the centers for resource shipment to the metropole after extraction.

The economies of the Carolinas were first developed by whites from the West Indies and the Chesapeake and involved trading with Indians, primarily the Cherokee, Creek, Chickasaw, and Tuscarora. The Europeans traded guns, tools, and rum in return for deerskins that they would transform into items of clothing. The dominant Indian trading partners also did a lucrative business in trading Native American slaves. The British-allied tribes began hunting DEER and other game in interior tribes' traditional hunting grounds, a practice that led to the disruption of Indian boundaries and the depletion of native species. In the resulting tribal wars, the British-allied tribes with access to superior weapons proved more successful, and many of their prisoners were then sold to the British as slaves for use in both the southern colonies and the West Indies.

The Carolinas eventually turned to the cultivation of RICE along the tidal plains, the knowledge of which may have been gained from African slaves. In order to produce rice, land had to be cleared and CANALS cut, then flooded with freshwater while guarding against entry of seawater. Rice cultivation could also rob the land of nutrients, such as nitrogen, within 10 years, thus requiring more and more land clearing. INDIGO was cultivated in the more inland areas, also leading to deforestation in part from building the large tubs necessary to collect the residue from the plant. This is not to say that the changes being made were cavalier: Once land was worn out, it would be flooded for years to restore it to production. Later, the colonists also engaged in the cultivation of sugar.

After the AMERICAN REVOLUTION (1775–83) and the introduction of the COTTON gin, cotton production spread throughout the southern states in the 19th century. Georgians and South Carolinians on the coastal plain, however, continued to grow RICE and INDIGO. All the southern states additionally exported lumber and livestock to Europe and the West Indies. Other major exports from southern longleaf pine forests included NAVAL STORES such as tar, pitch, and turpentine. The southern states' extractive plantation economies established by early English settlers and colonial officials lasted long after the collapse of the British Empire.

See also AGRICULTURE, COLONIAL; ATLANTIC WORLD, POST-1500; COLUMBIAN EXCHANGE; ECOLOGICAL IMPERIALISM; ENGLISH EXPLORATION AND SETTLEMENT—CANADA AND NEW ENGLAND; ENGLISH EXPLORATION AND SETTLEMENT—THE MIDDLE COLONIES; PORT TOWNS.

Michael Kelly Beauchamp

Further Reading

Hatfield, April Lee. *Atlantic Virginia: Intercolonial Relations in the Seventeenth Century.* Philadelphia: University of Pennsylvania Press, 2004.
Horn, James. *Adapting to a New World: English Society in the Seventeenth-Century Chesapeake.* Chapel Hill: University of North Carolina Press, 1994.
Wood, Peter H. *Black Majority: Negroes in Colonial South Carolina from 1670 through the Stono Rebellion.* New York: Knopf, 1974.

English Agriculture in Early America Thomas Hariot (1588)

As an important member of Sir Walter Raleigh's Roanoke Colony, the first English settlement in North America, Englishman Thomas Hariot lived along the present-day North Carolina coast during 1585 and 1586. Hariot urged further English settlement and wrote favorably about the region's commercial and agricultural prospects. Perhaps his most important contribution to English colonization of the Americas was his encouragement of cultivating indigenous American plants such as corn and tobacco.

I thought also good to note this unto you, you which shall inhabite and plant there, maie know how specially that countrey corne is there to be preferred before ours: Besides the manifold waies in applying it to victuall, the increase is so much that small labour and paines is needful in respect that must be used for ours. For this I can assure you that according to the rate we have made proofe of, one man may prepare and husband so much grounde (having once borne corne before) with lesse the foure and twentie houres labour, as shall yeelde him victuall in a large proportion for a twelve moneth, if hee have nothing else, but that which the same ground will yeelde, and of that kinde onelie which I have before spoken of: the saide ground being also but of five and twentie yards square. And if neede require, but that there is ground enough, there might be raised out of one and the selfsame ground two harvestes or ofcomes; for they sowe or set and may at anie time when they thinke good from the middest of March untill the ende of Iune: so that they also set when they have eaten of their first croppe. In some places of the countrey notwithstanding they have two harvests, as we have heard, out of one and the same ground.

For English corne nevertheles whether to use or not to use it, you that inhabite maie do as you shall have farther cause to thinke best. Of the grouth you need not to doubt: for barlie, oates and peaze, we have seene proof of, not beeing purposely sowen but fallen casually in the worst sort of ground, and yet to be as faire as any we have ever seene here in England. But of wheat because it was musty and hat taken salt water wee could make no triall: and of rye we had none. Thus much have I digressed and I hope not unnecessarily: nowe will I returne againe to my course and intreate of that which yet remaineth appertaining to this Chapter.

There is an herbe which is sowed a part by it selfe & is called by the inhabitants Uppowoc: In the West Indies it hath divers names, according to the severall places & countries where it groweth and is used: The Spaniardes generally call it Tobacco. The leaves thereof being dried and brought into powder: they use to take the fume or smoke thereof by sucking it through pipes made of claie into their stomacke and heade; from whence it purgeth superfluous fleame & other grosse humors, openeth all the pores & passages of the body: by which meanes the vse thereof, not only preserueth the body from obstructius; but also if any be, so that they haue not beene of too long continuance, in short time breaketh them: wherby their bodies are notably preserued in health, & know not many greeuous diseases where withall wee in England are oftentimes afflicted.

This Uppowoc is of so precious estimation amongst then, that they thinke their gods are marvelously delighted therwith: Wherupon sometime they make hallowed fires & cast some of the pouder therein for a sacrifice: being in a storme upon the waters, to pacifie their gods, they cast some up into the aire and into the water: so a weare for fish being newly set up, they cast some therein and into the aire: also after an escape of danger, they cast some into the aire likewise: but all done with strange gestures, stamping, sometime dauncing, clapping of hands, holding vp of hands, & staring up into the heavens, uttering therewithal and chattering strange words & noises.

⬦

Source: Thomas Hariot. *A Brief and True Report of the New Found Land of Virginia.* London, 1588.

Enlightenment, the

The Enlightenment was an intellectual movement caused in part by conjunctures of environmental, social, and political events in Western Europe and throughout the world, in the late 17th through the 18th centuries, that profoundly affected how humans thought about and interacted with the natural environment. The Enlightenment has been characterized as a period in European history when leading intellectuals, scientists, and politicians started to believe that the world could be understood through reason and empirical philosophies instead of relying upon classical religious, philosophical, and scientific texts. Developing first in France, the Enlightenment spread through Scotland, England, the Netherlands, Germany, and North America during the 18th century.

Perhaps the two best known products of the Enlightenment are the all-encompassing French *Encyclopédie* published in 1751 and the American DECLARATION OF INDEPENDENCE drafted in 1776. These two documents highlight the Enlightenment emphasis on the universality of knowledge, the rationality and goodness of humans, and the possibility of technological and moral progress. Enlightenment philosophers and politicians saw it as their goal to understand the historic and social forces driving the world in order to harness them for progress and the diffusion of liberty. THOMAS JEFFERSON, the primary author of the Declaration of Independence, was among the most brilliant and vociferous proponents of Enlightenment philosophy in the Americas. He argued that natural rights formed the basis for all states and that when the British government violated those rights, the American colonists had the right to "dissolve the political bonds" that tied them to England.

Jefferson also became an accomplished amateur scientist, using his Monticello estate in Virginia to record meteorological data and to study the success of indigenous and alien plants empirically under different weather conditions or in different soils. As president, Jefferson oversaw the LOUISIANA PURCHASE and launched the LEWIS AND CLARK EXPEDITION. While the expedition's primary purpose was to locate the famed NORTHWEST PASSAGE, Jefferson also ordered his explorers to document and catalog the climates, topography, plants, animals, and peoples they met along the way.

Enlightenment science was characterized by the belief that the world could be manipulated through a rational understanding of its constituent parts, its organization, and its dynamics. Some of the leading Enlightenment thinkers were avowed atheists and agnostics, and they actively disavowed the religious dogmas of the organized churches. The Enlightenment period saw increasing concern with temporal realities across broad areas of European society, from religion to society to science.

The causes of the Enlightenment remain a hot topic of debate. Historians have argued that a variety of environmental factors contributed to this intellectual shift. Some argue that the ending of the deadly European plague in the 18th century was one of the main reasons for the increasingly progressive

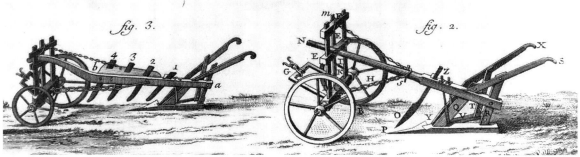

Titled *Agriculture, Labourage*, this engraving is the first plate in volume 1 of the *Encyclopédie*, 1751. *(Library of Congress)*

and positive outlook that characterized much Enlightenment thought. Others argue that the increased destruction of plants and animals in continental Europe and throughout tropical islands around the world led humans to begin realizing that God did not regulate nature, and that universal rules applied to plants and animals around the globe. The increased importation of new commoditized plants—tea, SUGAR, TOBACCO, and coffee—from the plantation economies of the Western Hemisphere helped spur many philosophical and political discussions in the coffee shops in London and the salons (large parties where the elite met) in Paris. The publication of anthropological texts from the Americas inspired Europeans to begin reassessing humans' place in the world. In France, the philosopher Jean-Jacques Rousseau (1712–78) argued in the *Social Contract* (1762) that Native Americans were "noble savages" who knew no conception of property and thus lived harmoniously among the land and each other. Regardless of debates about the exact importance of events causing the Enlightenment, it is clear that it had many environmental origins.

Many of the ideas formulated during the Enlightenment shaped our modern scientific perceptions of the environment. Scientists sought to classify the world according to universal principles. The most influential Enlightenment classifier was the Swedish botanist and doctor, Karl von Linnaeus (1707–88). In his *Species Plantarum* (1753), Linnaeus created a system of classifying plants according to *binomial nomenclature,* which sorted animals according to a genus and a species. As botanists created a common language, the various European empires more rigorously utilized the natural products of their subject colonies in the Americas and elsewhere because of the ease of diffusing knowledge about the various properties of plants.

Throughout the 18th century, travelers, scientists, politicians, and philosophers increasingly viewed the actions of the environment as driven by material forces instead of by God. This secular view led to an increased interest among some to discover the material forces of nature. The belief that the entire world was a secular, constituent whole with particular parts was wholeheartedly adopted by Enlightenment explorers, such as the German aristocrat and explorer Alexander von Humboldt (1769–1859), who helped create the fields of biogeography, ECOLOGY, and comparative climatology, after the publication of his book *Personal Narrative of Travels to the Equinoctial Regions of America, during the Year 1799–1804* (1807).

The Enlightenment strongly influenced the development of modern science and environmental movements. Modern science is pervaded with the belief in a secular view of the world that attempts to understand the world rationally in universal terms. The Enlightenment also affected how humans manipulated the environment. Scientists during the 19th and 20th centuries—especially foresters, soil experts, and climatologists—who were influenced by Enlightenment universalist assumptions argued that states should strongly regulate the way humans interact with the physical environment. This belief in the universality of European science has led to increasing state control over many of the FORESTS, rivers, plants, and animals around the world.

There were also backlashes against the Enlightenment. In the late 18th and early 19th centuries, a group of poets and authors who called themselves "romantics" openly assailed the universalist and rational assumptions of Enlightenment thinkers. A variety of leading American protoenvironmentalists such as JOHN MUIR and ALDO LEOPOLD patterned many of their thoughts and writing upon these romantics. By the 21st century, many people criticized the state appropriation and control of natural resources as being heavy-handed and ultimately destructive to nature. The division between those who sought to understand nature through its "sublime" forces and aesthetic experiences and Enlightenment rationalists continues today among different strains of environmentalists. Yet the division between the Enlightenment and ROMANTICISM is often overstressed among present-day academics and environmentalists: Almost anyone who believes that the world can be understood through reason and scientific empiricism owes much of his or her thought to the Enlightenment. For good or bad, the Enlightenment has shaped the way humans think about and interact with the natural environment from the 18th century until today.

See also BOTANY; FORESTRY; NATURAL HISTORY; SOIL CONSERVATION; ZOOLOGY.

Brett Bennett

Further Reading
Beinart, William, and Lotte Hughes. *Environment and Empire.* Oxford: Oxford University Press, 2007.
Grove, Richard. *Green Imperialism: Colonial Expansion, Tropical Island Edens and the Origins of Environmentalism, 1600–1860.* Cambridge: Cambridge University Press, 1995.
Mintz, Sidney. *Sweetness and Power: The Place of Sugar in Modern History.* New York: Penguin, 1985.
Radkau, Joachim. *Nature and Power: A Global History of the Environment.* New York: Cambridge University Press, 2008.
Worster, Donald. *Nature's Economy: A History of Ecological Ideas.* 2d ed. Cambridge: Cambridge University Press, 1994.

environmental art

The term *environmental art* is generally used to describe any artwork that is intimately involved with or interacts with the elements of nature: water, air, land, and biota. In environmental art, nature is not just a subject represented through an artwork, such as a landscape painting. Instead, nature is the art, and nature is as important as, or more important than, the individual artist. Environmental art is any physical artistic method used to utilize, explore, educate about, or repair natural sites.

Sam Bower, the director of the online virtual art museum Green Museum (greenmuseum.org), uses the name *environmental art* as an umbrella term encompassing more specific artistic practices. Earthworks, land art, art in nature; and site-specific art emerged from the postmodern art movement. Postmodern art is the creative proliferation of artistic styles and mediums that emerged in the 1960s and 1970s. Postmodern artists built on, but also broke the boundaries of, modern art, in particular the idea of art's being defined as items found in galleries and museums, art as a fashionable investment, as well as artistic styles defined by critics rather than artists.

Earthworks and *land art,* two terms that are used interchangeably, as well as art in nature, are aesthetic forms of art that utilize items in nature, such as trees, twigs, or stones to create the works. Robert Smithson's 1970 *Spiral Jetty,* built of black rock and earth in Utah's Great Salt Lake, is a good example of earthworks or land art. Purely ornamental, photographs of the work emphasize its abstract beauty. Art in nature is exemplified by the artist Andrew Goldsworthy, who photographs his creations of twigs, leaves, water, and ice before they are destroyed by natural processes.

Site-specific art focuses attention on the particular attributes of the piece of land they are situated on but often imports materials into the site rather than using items in the landscape. Nancy Holt's 1976 *Sun Tunnels,* large concrete tubes pierced with holes corresponding to constellations, is a good example of site-specific art. Holt's intention to make people aware of natural processes is an interface between art concerned mostly with the beauty of nature and activist art.

Social sculpture, ecological art, and ecoventions are activist art forms that use ideas for promoting social change articulated by the feminist and environmental movements. Social sculpture, ecological art, and ecoventions utilize the feminist philosophy that if the personal is political, then daily activity must be motivated by personal belief systems, and these actions have the potential to produce change in their society. Environmental activist-artists attempt to create ecosystem awareness, educate about environmental problems, and restore or remediate an ecosystem through their interdisciplinary, collaborative artworks.

Ecological art is specifically created to help people reenvision their relationship to nature and to inform people about environmental issues and the ecological processes of the natural world. Ecoartists sometimes combine aesthetics with a utilitarian function, creating works that either remediate or repair ECOSYSTEMS. Ecological art is focused on the processes, interactions, and interdependencies of ecosystems. A good example of remediative ecoart is Patricia Johanson's 1981 *Fair Park Lagoon* in Dallas, Texas. Johanson built a flowing sculptural pathway over the lagoon, planted vegetation, and persuaded landscapers not to wash FERTILIZERS into the lagoon to stem EROSION, kill off the lake's suffocating algae, and create a generative habitat. The lagoon is currently a healthy ecosystem and popular park.

The term *ecovention* (ecology and invention) is used to describe an artist-initiated, collaborative project that combines an artwork with an invention, usually scientific, to help heal or maintain an ecosystem. In 1980, Betsy Beumont completed *Ocean Landmark,* laying 17,000 recycled coal-ash bricks in Long Island Sound to reconstitute a degraded marine environment. To achieve this work, she drew in and collaborated with biologists, chemists, oceanographers, and engineers. A good example of ecovention artwork, today it is a flourishing ecosystem, documented periodically in film and photographs.

Social sculpture is a term coined by the activist-artist Joseph Beuys. He defines society as a large artwork in which every person is a participatory artist. Any artwork that demands participation of many people to heal, repair, remediate, or maintain an ecosystem can be described as a social sculpture. In 1982, Beuys enlisted hundreds of people to plant 7,000 trees in his social sculpture work *7000 Trees,* which took five years to complete.

Environmental art, in all its various disciplines, pushes the definition of art to new boundaries. Nonactivist, early postmodern works were primarily countercultural impulses, a reaction against the gallery-driven commodification of artworks. Activist artworks are proactive, creatively advancing social change. All the disciplines that fall under the umbrella term *environmental art* push the definitions of art to accommodate unique practices, and all of them have engendered multiple discussions on the nature and reason for creating art, the separation of art and life, art as a contemplative pleasure, art as a commodity, and art as a form of social activism.

See also ART; ENVIRONMENTALISM, MAINSTREAM; ENVIRONMENTALISM, RADICAL; LANDSCAPE ART, AMERICAN.

Susan Birchler

Further Reading

Bower, Sam. "A Profusion of Terms." Available online. URL: http://www.greenmuseum.org. Accessed June 1, 2009.

Grande, John K. *Art Nature Dialogues: Interviews with Environmental Artists.* Albany: State University of New York Press, 2004.

Kastner, Jeffrey, and Brian Wallis. *Land and Environmental Art.* London: Phaidon Press, 1998.

environmental conferences   *See* UNITED NATIONS—ENVIRONMENTAL CONFERENCES.

environmental education

Environmental education seeks to explain the ways that natural systems operate and how human beings can interact with those systems in a more equitable and sustainable manner. Environmental education occurs in schools throughout the United States and in government agencies. More informally, environmental education takes place in MUSEUMS, ZOOS, nature clubs, camps, and outreach programs conducted by environmental interest groups.

Although environmental education as a distinct pedagogic practice emerged with the environmental movement of the 1960s, its roots reach back to the great ENLIGHTENMENT philosophers of education. The Swiss philosopher Jean-Jacques Rousseau (1712–78), the Swiss educator Johann Pestalozzi (1746–1827), and the German educator Friedrich Froebel (1782–1852) all posited that sound education depended upon interaction with the natural world.

Progressive educators read those theorists as the United States industrialized in the 19th century, and concerns about the relationship between humans and nature became acute. Liberty Hyde Bailey (1858–1954), ANNA BOTSFORD COMSTOCK, Wilbur Jackman (1855–1907), and others responded with the NATURE STUDY movement, which sought to develop sympathy between people and nature. Proponents of nature study advocated that a broad knowledge in basic NATURAL HISTORY was the foundation for good living and advanced work in science.

Nature study education took a utilitarian turn with the rise of governmental bureaucracies and the environmental crisis engendered by the DUST BOWL. Efforts at scientifically minded CONSERVATION education—not the broad sympathy advocated by nature study—proliferated because governments needed professionals who could staff and manage conservation bureaucracies.

Modern environmental education is a central part of the environmental movement. In 1969, the U.S. CONGRESS passed the NATIONAL ENVIRONMENTAL POLICY ACT (NEPA) OF 1969, signed into law on January 1, 1970, by President RICHARD NIXON, which encouraged a "productive and enjoyable harmony between man and his environment," achieved, in part, by enriching the "understanding of ecological systems and natural resources." Environmental education was central to these goals, and Congress passed the first National Environmental Education Act the same year.

The international community quickly adopted similar objectives. The 1972 United Nations Conference on the Human Environment held in Stockholm, Sweden, proposed environmental education as a central means to address the global ecological crisis. The recommendations from the conference sought to instill environmental teaching from preschool through doctoral education. Three years later, delegates at a UNESCO (United Nations Educational, Scientific and Cultural Organization) conference in Belgrade, Yugoslavia, ratified the Belgrade Charter, which outlined the fundamental structure of environmental education. These goals, which continue to provide a foundation for current practices, were updated at a 1977 UNESCO conference held in Tbilisi, Republic of Georgia.

American educators quickly implemented environmental education. Environmental education combines the nature study emphases on observation, discovery, and moral reflec-

tion with the conservation education emphasis on responding to current environmental crisis. Environmental education thus uses environmental science leavened with moral deliberation to create its unique pedagogy. These trends were further institutionalized when Congress passed the National Environmental Education Act of 1990.

Contemporary environmental education continues to build upon these achievements, with added emphasis on the social effects of ecological problems. The wide-ranging goals of environmental education make sure that its practice varies widely. This variety makes it hard to specify but also enables it to thrive in diverse forms.

See also BURROUGHS, JOHN; ECOLOGY; ENVIRONMENTAL JUSTICE; UNITED NATIONS ENVIRONMENTAL CONFERENCES.

Kevin C. Armitage

Further Reading

Johnson, E., and M. Mappin, eds. *Environmental Education and Advocacy: Changing Perspectives of Ecology and Education.* Cambridge: Cambridge University Press, 2005.

Louv, Richard. *Last Child in the Woods.* Chapel Hill, N.C.: Algonquin Books, 2006.

Palmer, J. A. *Environmental Education in the 21st Century: Theory, Practice, Progress and Promise.* New York: Routledge, 1998.

Wilke, Richard J. *Environmental Education Teacher Resource Handbook.* Millwood, N.Y.: Kraus International, 1993.

How to Make Home and City Beautiful
H. D. Hemenway (1911)

In his 1911 book, How to Make Home and City Beautiful, *H. D. Hemenway, a horticulturalist and advocate of nature education, challenges readers to make their homes attractive and the city a better place in which to live by cultivating green plants and trees. Gardening, he believes, nurtures a "better American citizen" by teaching patience and the value of community cooperation, while providing children, particularly young boys, with a sense of responsibility and a civil alternative to delinquency. In this excerpt, he offers his support of the School Garden movement.*

Several institutions in the country have already begun to train teachers and the School Garden movement is making rapid progress. The time is not far distant, when practical, elementary agriculture and gardening will be taught in many schools. It develops the children physically as well as mentally and in the open air often creating a love for things which keep the city boy off the street corners during the summer, and teaches the country child the business-like, up-to-date methods in agriculture and gardening.

It not only educated the head, the heart, and the hand, but it aids in the practical application of reading, writing, and arithmetic. Gardening increases and develops the power of observation. It makes a person quick to grasp ideas and to put these ideas into action. These are important foundations for success in any line of business. It develops moral character. . . .

Establishing a School Garden may change the entire healthfulness of a neighborhood. The school grounds, themselves may be better planned and more healthful, but the best effect may be at the homes. No matter how small the yard, there is room for a garden for the boy or girl, even if it has to be established in a soap-box. There is much waste room often used for ashes, tin cans, or rubbish in many yards. What was once unsightly, unsanitary, and unproductive, becomes a resort of beauty, of health and utility for a whole family. It opens up a source of revenue, creates a love of industry, and respect for a property, and is often the beginning of better things. The gardener becomes a better American citizen.

Source: Herbert Daniel Hemenway. *How to Make Home and City Beautiful.* Northampton, Mass.: H. D. Hemenway, 1911, 7, 9.

environmentalism, grassroots

Grassroots environmentalism refers to actions taken by local groups of citizens to address and remedy specific environmental problems. Grassroots activism can be distinguished from mainstream environmental politics in several ways. Although grassroots activists may seek to influence state and federal legislative and regulatory action, they generally operate outside the lobbying/policy system. Most grassroots activists focus upon the protection of the use value of a specific local environment, such as a workplace, neighborhood, or wetlands preserve. Last, although grassroots activists typically have more flexibility in tactical approaches than do mainstream organizations, they often struggle to achieve visibility and impact. As a result, the success of grassroots campaigns has often depended upon forming alliances with mainstream environmental organizations, civil rights activists, and professional associations.

The decades following WORLD WAR II (1941–45) witnessed an expansion in grassroots actions by neighborhood associations, local and national unions, recreational hunters and fishers, and ENVIRONMENTAL JUSTICE coalitions. Activists responded to dramatic changes in the American landscape that resulted from the specific path of postwar economic recovery. Construction of tract-home developments boomed, as builders developed techniques for building on WETLANDS, floodplains, and steep slopes. A plethora of synthetic FERTILIZER, PESTICIDES, cleaners, cosmetics, and household products entered the domestic and agricultural landscapes. COAL miners, autoworkers, and farmworkers were exposed to harmful unregulated chemicals in the workplace. Combined industrial and domestic runoff increasingly contaminated groundwater and waterways. As a result, Americans became increasingly convinced that their total landscape was awash in synthetic harmful substances. Labor environmentalism, residential activism, and the environmental justice movement constitute three key aspects of the grassroots struggle against environmental pollution. Through the matrix of human health and safety, union health and safety committees, antisprawl activists, homeowners' associations, and environmental justice activists each addressed specific aspects of the toxic postwar landscape.

LABOR ENVIRONMENTALISM

Labor environmentalism is the solidly proenvironmental stance taken by the United Autoworkers (UAW), the United Steel Workers of America (USWA), the United Mine Workers (UMW), the United Farm Workers (UFW), and the Oil, Chemical and Atomic Workers (OCAW), between 1945 and the early 1970s. In response to increasingly hazardous work conditions, air and water pollution in workers' neighborhoods, and the growing participation by workers in recreational hunting and fishing, these unions espoused the belief that environmental protection could proceed hand in hand with economic growth and worker safety.

Labor's postwar engagement with environmental issues began with the Donora smog of 1948. The air inversion (a change in temperature that trapped smog close to the ground) killed 20 and sickened 7,000 in Donora, Pennsylvania. It was widely, though never legally, attributed to the sulfur dioxide emissions of the U.S. Steel Corporation's Donora Zinc Works. The USWA, several of whose members were victims of the smog, conducted an independent investigation into the incident, intending to prove the responsibility of U.S. Steel.

Unions frequently targeted industries whose practices threatened the health of humans and the environment. As the OCAW citizenship-legislative director Anthony Mazzocchi (1926–2002) stated in 1973, "A degraded work environment ultimately affects the general environment." During the 1950s, the UAW protested the construction of a fast-breeder nuclear reactor in Detroit, and the UMW undertook an educational campaign regarding the hazards of atomic energy. The UAW created a Conservation and Resource Development Department in 1962, which testified in support of increased emissions requirements for automobiles. It went on to establish the Down River Anti-Pollution League (DAPL) to address the threat posed by local DETROIT, MICHIGAN, industry to residential and recreational health. In 1965, the National Farm Workers' Association, under the leadership of CÉSAR CHÁVEZ, organized a strike against California grape growers, protesting both worker pesticide poisoning and exploitive labor conditions.

In 1967, the UMW began a nationwide boycott of General Electric and Westinghouse products and lobbied Congress to restrict funding to the Atomic Energy Commission. The United Active Women, a group of UAW wives, organized in 1971 against high-phosphate detergents. In 1973, the OCAW launched a strike and consumer boycott of Shell Oil, protesting the threats posed by workplace chemicals to the health of both workers and consumers. In each of these campaigns, unions framed their opposition through concern for the health of workers, nearby residents, and the broader environment. Labor's consistent victories against polluting industries stimulated an alliance with mainstream environmental organizations, culminating in the Urban Environmental Conference (1971).

Labor environmentalists also advocated WILDERNESS conservation. Growing numbers of industrial workers—particularly Detroit autoworkers—participated in recreational hunting and fishing. These workers formed a dense network of sportsmen's clubs, which consolidated into the Michigan United Conservation Clubs (MUCC) in 1937. The MUCC expanded its initial emphasis on CONSERVATION into an active campaign against municipal and industrial WATER POLLUTION, a petition campaign against a cyanide-induced fish kill in the Kalamazoo River, a network of summer camps for workers' children, and educational programs in conservation of FORESTS and wildlife.

RESIDENTIAL ACTIVISM

Labor environmentalism directly links the pollution of the environment to exposure to hazardous substances at work. Residential grassroots activism addresses environmental problems—suburban sprawl, water and AIR POLLUTION, and the placement of toxic waste facilities—which directly threaten the health and safety of living conditions. Open space and antisprawl activists identify suburban expansion as an environmental problem. Beginning in the early 1960s, open space preservationists used suburban sprawl—the expansion of a city and its suburbs into the surrounding rural areas—to dramatize issues of water pollution and population growth. Many preservationists formed neighborhood associations to save specific features of the landscape, either through lobbying local representatives or collectively purchasing the land in question. The Sudbury Valley Trustees (1953) began in Massachusetts as a small group of neighbors pooling funds to preserve the state's eastern wetlands from development. California's People for Open Space (1958), New York's Open Space Action Institute (1964), and the St. Louis Open Space Council (1965) also began as local land trusts.

In several instances, residents pursued more direct action against development. Starting in 1959, the Grand Canyon Defenders felled more than 500 billboard advertisements for housing developments along the highway connecting Flagstaff, Arizona, with the GRAND CANYON. One decade later, the

Tucson Eco-Raiders added construction-site vandalism and survey-stake disruption to the repertoire of antisprawl direct action.

In LOVE CANAL, a neighborhood in Niagara Falls, New York, neighbors organized to protest the presence of 21,000 tons of buried chemical waste under and around their homes and local school. Love Canal achieved national notoriety in 1977, when, after a heavy rainy season, residents began to complain of noxious chemicals bubbling from the ground into their swimming pools, sinks, and gardens. Residents soon discovered that the Niagara Falls School Board had constructed the 99th Street School on a toxic waste dumping site knowingly purchased from Hooker Chemical in 1953, and that the city of Niagara Falls had allowed developers to construct the Love Canal neighborhood immediately adjacent to the site.

LOIS GIBBS, a resident whose son, Michael, fell ill shortly after entering the 99th Street School, helped to organize her neighbors into the Love Canal Homeowners Association (LCHA), which mounted a continuous lobbying and media campaign to elicit government action and to require Hooker Chemical to admit its responsibility. The LCHA connected elevated rates of illness and mental retardation among neighborhood children, as well as high rates of miscarriage among neighborhood women, to the buried waste. Despite numerous scientific studies documenting the presence of high levels of dioxin and benzene in Love Canal backyards and basements, and the ENVIRONMENTAL PROTECTION AGENCY's findings of chromosomal damage among 33 percent of area residents, Hooker Chemical was never held responsible. The government responded to the LCHA's prolonged media campaign by relocating 800 families and passing the Comprehensive Environmental Response, Compensation, and Liability Act (CERCLA), popularly known as the SUPERFUND Act, in 1980. Gibbs soon organized the Citizens Clearinghouse for Hazardous Wastes (1981), a grassroots antitoxics campaign that helped stimulate the nascent environmental justice movement.

ENVIRONMENTAL JUSTICE

The ENVIRONMENTAL JUSTICE movement constitutes one of the strongest elements of present-day grassroots activism. Environmental justice seeks to remedy the disproportionate burden of environmental pollution borne by economic and ethnic minorities. The movement is widely considered to have begun in the early 1980s in Warren County, North Carolina. In summer 1978, the Ward Transformer Company contaminated 240 miles of road shoulder with polychlorinated biphenyls (PCBs). North Carolina, held responsible for the cleanup, proposed to construct a landfill in Warren County, a rural area with a high percentage of poor African-American residents.

Initially, Warren County's white landowners, organized into the Warren County Citizens Concerned about PCBs (Concerned Citizens), agitated to construct the landfill in Alabama. Concerned Citizens' primary focus was local control over land use; when Warren County refused to bend to popular protest, Concerned Citizens reached out to local CIVIL RIGHTS MOVEMENT activists in 1982. With the involvement of the United Church of Christ Commission on Racial Justice (UCC), the Southern Christian Leadership Conference (SCLC), and the NATIONAL ASSOCIATION FOR THE ADVANCEMENT OF COLORED PEOPLE (NAACP), they began a six-week direct-action campaign focused on the racial discrimination at the heart of the decision to locate the landfill in Warren County. During the protest, Warren County residents lay on the highway to block the North Carolina Department of Transportation trucks, held prayer and candle vigils, and led marches to local government offices.

Although unsuccessful in halting the construction of the landfill, the Warren County campaign's purposeful rejection of any identification with mainstream, "elitist" organizations, its reliance upon a repertoire of actions developed by the civil rights movement, and its research into the connection between race and the location of environmental hazards formed the backbone for the continued strength of the environmental justice movement today. Other campaigns include the MOTHERS OF EAST LOS ANGELES (1984), who have successfully organized against the building of a hazardous waste incinerator, an oil pipeline, and the construction of further penitentiaries in Los Angeles County; the work of the Ohio Valley Environmental Coalition's (1987) and the West Virginian organization Coal River Mountain Watch (1998) to end mountaintop removal mining in Appalachia; Louisiana's Concerned Citizens of Norco (1987), which sought compensation for the explosion of a Shell Oil pipeline in 1973; and the Kentucky Environmental Foundation's (1990) fight for the safe disposal of chemical weapons.

See also CORPORATIONS, CHEMICAL; ENERGY, NUCLEAR; ENVIRONMENTAL LAW; FEDERAL LAW—ENVIRONMENTAL REGULATIONS; FISHING, RECREATIONAL; HEALTH AND MEDICINE; HOUSING, PRIVATE; HUNTING, RECREATIONAL; INCINERATION; LABOR, AGRICULTURAL AND MIGRANT; LABOR, EXTRACTIVE INDUSTRIES; LABOR, MANUFACTURING; LABOR MOVEMENTS; SUBURBANIZATION; URBAN SPRAWL.

Jennifer Thomson

Further Reading
Blum, Elizabeth D. *Love Canal Revisited.* Lawrence: University Press of Kansas, 2008.
Burnham, John C. "How the Discovery of Accidental Childhood Poisoning Contributed to the Development of Environmentalism in the United States." *Environmental History Review* 19 (1995): 57–81.
Dewey, Scott. "Working for the Environment: Organized Labor and the Origins of Environmentalism in the United States, 1948–70." *Environmental History* 3 (January 1998): 45–63.
Gordon, Robert. "'Shell No!': OCAW and the Labor-Environmental Alliance." *Environmental History* 3 (1998): 460–487.
Hays, Samuel P. *Beauty, Health and Permanence: Environmental Politics in the United States, 1955–1985.* New York: Cambridge University Press, 1987.
McGurty, Eileen. "From NIMBY to Civil Rights: The Origins of the Environmental Justice Movement." *Environmental History* 2 (1997): 301–323.
Montrie, Chad. "Expedient Environmentalism: Opposition to Coal Surface Mining in Appalachia and the United Mine Workers of America, 1945–1975." *Environmental History* 5 (2000): 75–98.
———. *Making a Living: Work and Environment in the United States.* Chapel Hill: University of North Carolina Press, 2008.
Rome, Adam. *The Bulldozer in the Countryside: Suburban Sprawl and the Rise of American Environmentalism.* New York: Cambridge University Press, 2001.

environmentalism, mainstream

Mainstream environmentalism is an umbrella term that refers to environmental action by groups and individuals that focuses on enacting environmentally positive change within the political, economic, and cultural constructs of human society. Mainstream environmentalists use any legal, legislative, and political means, including lobbying, rallies, and petitions, to achieve their goals. American environmentalism is a broad continuum of theory and practice. Mainstream environmentalism can be seen as the middle of the environmental continuum in opposition to RADICAL ENVIRONMENTALISM on one end and OPPOSITION TO ENVIRONMENTALISM on the other. The diversity within environmentalism arises from the extent to which each environmentalist or group believes humans are part of the natural world and how much, or how little, intervention and manipulation of the natural world humans should undertake. Moral beliefs range from the biocentric idea that nature is sacred, and humans are not the center of the world (and thus should exist harmoniously within ECOSYSTEMS), to the more anthropocentric belief that humans are the most important but need to act responsibly as stewards of nature. Mainstream environmentalism generally occupies the latter category.

The mainstream environmental movement is characterized by the environmental groups most recognizable in the United States. The big 10 are the National Wildlife Federation, Izaak Walton League, AUDUBON SOCIETY, SIERRA CLUB, WILDERNESS SOCIETY, NATURAL RESOURCES DEFENSE COUNCIL, Environmental Defense Fund, Environmental Policy Center, Friends of the Earth, and the National Parks and Conservation Association, although membership in the big 10 has changed over time, and other groups have been part of the mainstream movement as well. The aims of these big 10 and other mainstream groups have become increasingly legislative, aimed at either securing passage or preventing the gutting of environmental legislation. A large part of their efforts involve lobby-

Created by the artist Charles Saxon, this poster was sponsored by the Environmental Protection Agency, ca. 1970.   *(Library of Congress)*

ing and maintaining a large membership base that contributes through donations.

ORIGINS

Mainstream environmentalism shares the roots of the environmental movement as a whole. An environmental movement was identifiable in the United States as early as the 19th century, although in the 19th century and first half of the 20th, Americans did not use this term. The environmental movement has not been a static, homogeneous movement. Instead, many diverse movements have existed and sometimes coalesced. PRESERVATION, CONSERVATION, WILDERNESS, rural, and urban movements all existed under the rubric of environmentalism.

The catalysts for the major transformation in the 19th century were the Industrial Revolution and the growing concern about how the increased industrialization affected the environment. Americans had not seen themselves as having a major impact on nature since the Puritans and other colonists arrived and cleared the land. This separation became magnified in the 19th century. Three American thinkers, HENRY DAVID THOREAU, GEORGE PERKINS MARSH, and JOHN MUIR, helped initi-

ate one of the key transformations of the 19th century: that of awareness, and a new way of perceiving humans' relationship to their natural surroundings.

Marsh wrote *Man and Nature* (1864) as a warning against overexploitation of resources. He had seen the devastation of Europe's natural world and was concerned that the same process was occurring in America. While Marsh was not calling for preservation, he did sound the alarm on the costs of unregulated exploitation. At the same time, Muir was leading people into the Sierras in the Far West in an attempt to illustrate that nature had intrinsic value. Some thinkers such as Thoreau had been writing and thinking about these issues earlier, but it was in the 1880s and 1890s that this line of thought manifested itself into actions such as the formation of the Sierra Club in 1892. In the case of John Muir and the Sierra Club, it was the threat of development within the Sierra Nevada that spurred them into action. One of the key transformations was simply awareness spurred on by the rapidly increasing incursions by humans into previously pristine places. This awareness helped create a new way of perceiving humans' relationship with nature, which enabled other transformations to take place. It was concern about increasing alienation from nature and other industrial phenomena, such as the factory and industrial waste, that spurred on the creation of an actual movement in the last quarter of the 19th century.

Industrialization was also a catalyst for urban environmental movements. Smoke abatement groups formed at the beginning of the Progressive Era. Although many historians of the environmental movement overlook the urban movement in favor of the wilderness side of environmentalism, urban reform movements served equally as forerunners of modern environmentalism.

Within the burgeoning movement there was also a break between preservationists, who wanted to keep natural places as "pristine" as possible, and conservationists, who wanted "wise use" of resources. The divide between preservationists and conservationists has been personified by Muir and Gifford Pinchot (Theodore Roosevelt's chief forester in the early 1900s) in most histories of the environmental movement, but it went beyond those two personalities. President Roosevelt, who could accurately be called a conservationist president, did much to harness and protect American resources but did not embrace preservation. Within the Roosevelt administration (1901–09) and in the early decades of the 20th century, the tension between the call for wise-use resource extraction and demands for preservation increased. Conservationists were proponents of what they called the rational management of resources. Government agencies, such as the U.S. Forest Service, increasingly advocated multiple uses of the nation's resources, opening forests, for example, to mining, logging, and other commercial interests.

EARLY TWENTIETH-CENTURY ENVIRONMENTALISM

Threaded throughout what could be called the mainstream historical narrative was a more class-conscious environmentalism in urban areas. Alice Hamilton, arguably the first urban industrial environmentalist in the United States, was at the forefront of investigating industrial diseases and their effects in the workplace and the community. She wrote *Industrial Poisons in the United States* (1925) and helped found the Workers Health Bureau. The bureau put forward a program that integrated labor and the environment. This sort of activism moved parallel to the wilderness advocacy of groups such as the Sierra Club. Although it did not initially become part of the mainstream environmental movement, this urban activism was the forerunner of the environmental justice movement that increasingly moved toward mainstream environmentalism in the late 20th and early 21st centuries.

The election of President Franklin D. Roosevelt in 1932 provided a return to a more balanced approach between conservation and preservation. Roosevelt and his New Deal used legislation to advance the cause of conservation much as Theodore Roosevelt had a generation earlier. However, the New Deal was concerned about more than just conservation. Instituted

during the Great Depression, the New Deal managed to create jobs that were conservation-minded and used public works as way to contribute to the conservation effort. For example, President Roosevelt created the Civilian Conservation Corps (CCC) in 1933. The CCC was designed to provide employment for the masses of unemployed in the cities by putting them to work planting trees, building dams for flood control and roads in public parks, as well as restocking rivers and even draining swamps to prevent the spread of malaria. As well as the CCC, initiatives such as the Tennessee Valley Authority (TVA) made utilities public instead of private. The TVA built dams to provide electricity, control floods, and improve irrigation in a region that had been overused and its soils depleted. Roosevelt also created a new kind of national park, Kings Canyon National Park in California, which preserved wilderness and excluded roads and hotels.

During this period, Robert Marshall (1901–39), who founded the Wilderness Society in 1937, began to argue that social liberation and the liberation of nature from exploitation were intrinsically linked. Marshall's advocacy through the years of the Great Depression provided a link to the post–World War II environmental thinkers and activists who took the idea of rights of nature to a new level.

POST–WORLD WAR II ACTIVISM

Aldo Leopold emerged as a key figure in reshaping environmentalism in the United States. His book *A Sand County Almanac* (1949) redefined how we understand the relationship between humans and nature. Leopold was already influential because of his groundbreaking book about wildlife management, *Game Management* (1933), which led the University of Wisconsin to create a new department, the Department of Game Management, with Leopold as chair. However, it was the posthumous publication of *A Sand County Almanac* that provided his greatest legacy. In this book, he offered the idea of an ecological community in which humans were not separate but a part of nature. Leopold argued that human ethics could no longer be human-centered but must be enlarged to include all of nature. He believed it was critical that people have a close personal connection to the land.

Rachel Carson also made an influential contribution to this changing perception of humans' relationship to nature. With the publication of *Silent Spring* (1962), she illustrated that failure to see humans as a part of nature had devastating consequences. The publication of *Silent Spring* sounded the alarm about the devastating consequences of the pesticides such as DDT (dichlorodiphenyltrichloroethane). Its publication helped make environmentalism a mainstream phenomenon. *Silent Spring* was one of the catalysts for the creation of the Environmental Protection Agency (EPA) in 1970 and for the first celebration of Earth Day that same year.

The federal government created the EPA in 1970 in response to growing concerns about the negative impacts of industrial activity on our water, air, and land. Its twofold purpose was to protect the environment from further degradation and to remedy damage already done. During the following decade, Congress enacted more laws designed with environmental protection in mind: the CLEAN AIR ACT of 1970, the Water Pollution Control Act of 1972, the SAFE DRINKING WATER ACT of 1974, the Resource Conservation and Recovery Act of 1976, and the SUPERFUND Act of 1980. In 1972, the Club of Rome, an international think tank, published a report authored by scientists from the Massachusetts Institute of Technology and entitled "The Limits to Growth." Translated into 30 languages, with more than 30 million copies sold over time, the report explored the tensions between a growing world population and finite resources and stressed the choices open to human society in reconciling sustainable progress within environmental constraints.

OTHER VARIANTS

The 1980s witnessed a backlash against the growing environmental movement. President RONALD REAGAN, elected in 1980, sought to undo many of the environmental policies generated by the federal government in the 1970s and earlier. In large part, his administration's actions led to the breakaway movements from mainstream environmentalism. New, more radical environmental groups such as Earth First! emerged. Mainstream environmental groups increasingly focused on preventing the gutting of standing environmental legislation in addition to their other goals.

The 1980s also saw a resurgence of grassroots groups who formed the backbone of new types of environmentalism such as the antitoxic movement, ENVIRONMENTAL JUSTICE, and urban environmentalism, among others. Grassroots movements often emerged as a reaction to specific and immediate environmental problems. However, many groups did not disband when the immediate problem was solved but rather created networks uniting similar groups who battled hazards in their neighborhoods and beyond. This type of activism was labeled "Not in My Backyard," or NIMBY, but the groups that continued and expanded resisted the label and made it more inclusive to "Not in Anyone's Backyard." These grassroots efforts were increasingly subsumed within mainstream environmentalism.

The fight at LOVE CANAL in the late 1970s epitomizes this phenomenon. Residents created the Love Canal Homeowners Association to force local, state, and federal governments to respond to high levels of toxicity discovered in their neighborhood near Niagara Falls, New York. Their successful fight forced the federal government to aid in their relocation and forced the Hooker Chemical Company to rectify the conditions at its dumpsite. Their success confirmed the potential strength and effectiveness of grassroots activism and citizen action. LOIS GIBBS, one of the main organizers of the homeowners' association, later founded the Citizens Clearinghouse on Toxic Waste.

The antitoxics movement, along with the antinuclear movement and environmental justice groups, have redefined what environmentalism means.

CONCLUSION

The continual emergence of new groups, new tactics, and new focuses of struggle reveal the dynamic nature of American environmentalism. It has evolved over time to include new issues and new groups of activists. Mainstream environmentalism has tended toward the anthropocentric side of the continuum of environmentalism, representing the majority of activists. Over time, mainstream environmentalism has created an environmental ethos embraced by the majority of Americans, who express that ethos in activities ranging from recycling to driving fuel-efficient vehicles and visiting national parks.

Environmentalism has had an enormous impact on U.S. history, altering how people live, work, and spend leisure time. It has also transformed American industry and changed the nation's economy and business practices. As environmentalism enters the 21st century, the definition of who and what are accorded rights continues to change as well. The idea that other animals and even inorganic life have rights has been the latest step in an expanding moral view of environmentalism. With more people and groups entering into the discourse around extreme GLOBAL WARMING, CLIMATE CHANGE, energy independence, and other issues, mainstream environmentalism will remain a dynamic force.

See also ENVIRONMENTALISM, GRASSROOTS; ENVIRONMENTALISM, RADICAL; PROGRESSIVISM; SAGEBRUSH REBELLION.

John-Henry Harter

Further Reading
Gottlieb, Robert. *Forcing the Spring: The Transformation of the American Environmental Movement.* Washington, D.C.: Island Press, 1993.
Hays, Samuel P. *Conservation and the Gospel of Efficiency: The Progressive Conservation Movement, 1890–1920.* Cambridge, Mass.: Harvard University Press, 1959.
Leopold, Aldo. *A Sand County Almanac: and Sketches Here and There.* New York: Oxford University Press, 1949.
Nash, Roderick. *The Rights of Nature: A History of Environmental Ethics.* Madison: University of Wisconsin Press, 1989.
Pepper, David. *Modern Environmentalism: An Introduction.* London: Routledge, 1996.
Shabecoff, Phillip. *A Fierce Green Fire: The American Environmental Movement.* Washington, D.C.: Island Press, 2003.

environmentalism, opposition to

Early critics of post–WORLD WAR II (1941–45) environmentalism cast the movement's supporters as pagan worshippers of the land for their advocacy of land preservation, as irrational and antihuman for their efforts to create a cleaner environment, and as opposed to progress and capitalism in their insistence that business fund efforts to clean and abate the pollution it produced.

An early form of this ideological opposition to environmentalism is seen in Ayn Rand's essay "The Anti-Industrial Revolution" published in 1971. Rand argued that environmentalism represented a return to primitivism; that environmentalists really wanted to return society to a Dark Ages distopia. "Make no mistake about it: it is *technology* and *progress* that the nature-lovers are out to destroy." To Rand, ecologists were anti-technology because they criticized AUTOMOBILES and attacked power plants and industrial development. In short, they were against progress. Pollution, Rand believed, was a technological problem to be solved by technology and not politics. "Even if smog were a risk to human life," she writes, "we must remember that life in nature, without technology, is wholesale death." That ecologists have sought political solutions was evidence, Rand suggested, that ecologists were really after the destruction of capitalism and the establishment of a global dictatorship.

Building on this critique, environmentalists were also painted as elitists, or "limousine-liberals," who sought to retard economic progress and the advancement of working-class Americans so that they could enjoy a greener environment. This view saw environmentalism as part of a larger liberal agenda of social revolution and framed environmental regulation as the enemy not of big business but of blue-collar workers.

While these arguments could, at times, be marshaled by organized labor fearing that the costs of environmental protection could cost jobs, they were more often the result of organized business. By the 1970s, business groups began vigorously responding to the challenges and costs created by environmental reform by organizing trade associations that filed court challenges and lobbied state and federal officials. These efforts have succeeded in greatly affecting the administration of environmental policy.

More contemporary critiques of environmentalism focus indirectly on the role it prescribes for government. Legislators in the 1970s wrote pollution control legislation that mandated specific environmental results. While effective, these "command and control" measures became identified with a heavy-handed, big government approach that appeared increasingly outdated in the 1980s and 1990s. Through this time, successive presidential administrations promised to reduce the burden of government regulation on the economy as free-market mechanisms for effecting public policy became increasingly popular.

The willingness to employ government to produce a cleaner environment also partly explains how and why environmentalism became an issue increasingly associated with liberalism. As a result, political solidarity has made large numbers of Republicans suspicious of the movement's claims and goals.

The politicized nature of the split between environmentalists and those opposed to the movement is also a reflection of how different regions have embraced or rejected the environmentalists' claims. Opinion polls and voting records indicate that the most environmentally conscious voters are found in New England and along parts of the East and West Coasts. Environmentalism was an issue enjoying broad bipartisan support in the middle decades of the 20th century in part because these regions voted into office significant numbers of representatives from both parties. Since the 1970s, however, a broad realignment in American politics has made these regions increasingly the province of the Democratic Party.

This regional disparity in the reception of environmentalism owes something to the existence of large federal landholdings in the West. In the 1960s and 1970s, the federal government began instituting policies that considered the ecological health of environments when making land-use decisions. This development in part helped spark what became known as the SAGEBRUSH REBELLION, peaking with the effort by the state of Nevada to expropriate the federal land within its borders. The "wise-use" movement, also centered in the American West, was inspired by the experience of the Sagebrush Rebellion and consists of a coalition of state and local groups formally organized against the claims and goals of the environmental movement. Critics of these opposition groups have long pointed out that both the Sagebrush Rebellion and the wise-use movement were largely funded by industry and trade groups associated with western resource extraction.

In the early 21st century, the success and reach of anti-environmental groups and ideas were not to be found in the American West but in WASHINGTON, D.C. For it is in the nation's capital that environmental laws and regulations have been most effectively watered down through litigation, administrative hearings, and appointments. The power and reach of antienvironmental ideas and organizations are perhaps best exemplified by the increasing absence of American leadership on global environmental issues. In the 1970s, the United States was widely admired and acknowledged as a world leader for tackling its environmental problems and for encouraging and advising other nations to do the same. In the early 2000s, across a range of issues, the United States worked to prevent the international community from addressing a number of problems, most famously global climate change.

See also ENVIRONMENTALISM, GRASSROOTS; ENVIRONMENTALISM, MAINSTREAM; ENVIRONMENTALISM, RADICAL; ENVIRONMENTAL LAW; ENVIRONMENTAL PROTECTION AGENCY; FEDERAL LAW—ENVIRONMENTAL REGULATIONS; FEDERAL LAW—INDUSTRIAL REGULATIONS; FEDERAL LAW—LAND POLICIES; NATIONAL ENVIRONMENTAL POLICY ACT (NEPA) OF 1969; UNITED NATIONS ENVIRONMENTAL CONFERENCES.

Robert Lifset

Further Reading

Arnold, Ron. *Ecology Wars: Environmentalism as If People Mattered.* Bellevue, Wash.: Free Enterprise Press, 1987.

environmentalism, radical   **489**

Cawley, R. McGreggor. *Federal Land, Western Anger: The Sage-brush Rebellion and Environmental Politics.* Lawrence: University Press of Kansas, 1993.

Helvarg, David. *The War against the Greens: The "Wise-Use" Movement, the New Right and the Browning of America.* Revised updated ed. Boulder, Colo.: Johnston Books, 2004.

Rand, Ayn. *Return of the Primitive: The Anti-Industrial Revolution.* New York: Meridian, 1999.

Switzer, Jacqueline Vaughn. *Green Backlash: The History and Politics of Environmental Opposition in the U.S.* Boulder, Colo.: Lynne Rienner, 1997.

environmentalism, radical

Radical environmentalism is a strain of the American environmental movement, originating in the 1970s. Radical environmentalism grew less out of a specific agenda than out of reaction against two things: modern, technological, and industrial society and the reform, or mainstream, environmental movement.

Radical environmentalists reject what they see as the basic values of modern society; they believe that industrial society tends to view nature only in terms of its usefulness to people, and they argue instead that nature has intrinsic worth, apart from—and possibly greater than—human interests. Radical environmentalists object to the strategies and tactics of reform environmental organizations; they criticize mainstream groups as favoring political negotiation over confrontation, and as compromising with corporations and the government rather than taking a firm stance in defense of the environment. They favor direct-action tactics, often including "ecotage" (the destruction of property to prevent environmental harm).

HISTORY

In many ways, reform environmentalism and radical environmentalism developed alongside each other. The modern environmental movement emerged in the late 1960s, buoyed by major legislative successes, overwhelming public participation in the first EARTH DAY in April 1970, and President RICHARD NIXON's declaration that the 1970s would be the "environmental decade." During this new decade, the major environmental organizations grew increasingly prominent in WASHINGTON, D.C., and their strategies shifted from organizing public pressure to protecting the environment through legislation and lawsuits. Environmentalism's rise to power sparked criticism from within the movement, as many activists grew frustrated with the professionalization and bureaucratization of groups such as the SIERRA CLUB, the NATURAL RESOURCES DEFENSE COUNCIL, and the WILDERNESS SOCIETY. Some of the more notable critics were DAVID R. BROWER, the onetime executive director of the Sierra Club, and Dave Foreman, a Wilderness Society staff member who left the society to found the radical group Earth First!

A handful of environmental activists were already engaging in direct action and ecotage in the 1970s. In 1971, an anonymous saboteur attacked heavy equipment owned by Peabody Coal to fight the construction of a mine on Black Mesa, in Arizona. At around the same time, a vigilante called "The Fox" plugged the drains and capped the chimneys of soap companies in the Midwest to protest water and air pollution. Between 1971 and 1973, a group calling themselves the "eco-raiders" took down billboards, pulled up survey stakes, and damaged bulldozers in Tucson, Arizona, in an attempt to slow urban sprawl. Also early in the decade, the "bolt weevils"—a group of rural activists—tried to sabotage the construction of new power lines in the Minnesota countryside.

The best-known radical environmental group was Earth First!, which for many friends and foes of the environmental movement defined radical environmentalism in the 1980s. Throughout that decade, Earth First! focused on WILDERNESS as the key issue for protecting nature from industrial society. The group began, in part, as a reaction to the second Roadless Area Review and Evaluation (RARE II). In 1977, the U.S. DEPARTMENT OF AGRICULTURE began an inventory of 62 million acres of national FORESTS eligible for wilderness protection, to determine what areas would receive protection and what areas would be opened to LOGGING. The department recommended that less than a quarter of the forestland under consideration receive protection, and the JIMMY CARTER administration accepted this recommendation. For some environmentalists, the mainstream environmental organizations' measured advocacy during RARE II, and limited response after, demonstrated the movement's diminishing effectiveness as it became more entrenched in Washington politics.

Soon after RARE II, Dave Foreman, Howie Wolke, Mike Roselle, Bart Koehler, and Ron Kezar—most of whom were former staffers of established environmental organizations—founded Earth First! as a group that would promote ecotage and civil disobedience in protecting the environment and push the environmental movement as a whole toward more extreme positions. Earth First! was an anarchistic group, and so it had little overall structure and only an outline of a formal program. Throughout the 1980s, however, activists affiliated with the group staged sit-ins and tree-sits, blockaded and sabotaged road-building equipment, and organized protests to protect wilderness or potential wilderness and to focus public attention on environmental issues.

PHILOSOPHY

Earth First! and many other radical environmentalists subscribe at least in part to the philosophy of deep ecology. The Norwegian philosopher Arne Naess (1912–2009) introduced deep ecology in 1972 as a critique of reform environmentalism (which he called the "shallow" ecology movement). Since then, deep ecologists have argued that the reform environmentalism of the 1970s and 1980s relied on legal and institutional approaches to protecting nature and natural resources, instead of challenging the ways people think about the natural world. Deep ecology is rooted in the idea that nature has intrinsic value, beyond its importance to humans, and that only when people embrace this ethic will they be able to address the root causes of environmental problems. Deep ecologists question the benefits of technology and industrialization and promote a vision of society as decentralized and less technologically dependent.

The deep ecologists' vision of an ideal society has been described in more specific terms by the bioregionalists. Bioregionalism is a version of deep ecology, but with a concrete plan. Bioregionalists share the belief that people must fundamentally change the way they understand nature and begin to value the natural world for its own sake. They also argue that the people who live in an ecological region are best fit to care for and build sustainable relationships with that region. Locals know the land best, and so bioregionalists advocate decentralized, democratic communities, based in regions determined according to natural, instead of political, contours.

CRITICS

Radical environmentalism has attracted criticism from across the political spectrum. Those whom radical environmentalists often target for direct action—officials and employees of federal agencies such as the U.S. FOREST SERVICE and officials and employees of corporations involved in resource extraction—have called their radical antagonists "criminals," or even "terrorists." In 2001, the Federal Bureau of Investigation designated the radical environmental group Earth Liberation Front the top domestic terrorism threat in the United States.

On the Left, radical environmentalism has been criticized mainly for its narrow focus on wilderness and the nonhuman. Social justice activists have argued that this focus ignores the ways that harm to the natural world is wrapped up in injustice against humans. Inequities of power and wealth within society, these critics contend, lead directly to environmentally destructive practices, and a more egalitarian society would therefore be a more environmentally sustainable society. The social ecologist Murray Bookchin and the anarchist David Watson have been especially vocal in their complaints about deep ecology, accusing it of glossing over issues of race, class, and gender and of being fundamentally antihuman.

Some radical environmentalists, in response, argue that paying heed to social issues inevitably leads to compromises in protecting nature. They see human interests in the modern world as fundamentally at odds with nature's interests and believe that at some point, people must make a choice between protecting the environment and advancing industrial society. In the 1990s, this debate fractured Earth First!, as many newer Earth First!ers argued for a broader agenda, including alliances with leftist movements such as organized labor. As early as 1990, Dave Foreman, the most public figure

in Earth First!, left the group in part because he felt it was losing its uncompromising focus on wilderness.

THE BROADER MOVEMENT

A broad definition of radical environmentalism can include movements as diverse as ecofeminism, animal liberation, social ecology, antiglobalization, and a variety of indigenous movements around the world. These various movements share a strong critique of industrialized society and its values, and a commitment to promoting the interests of the natural world. What those interests are, however, is open to debate, even among these different branches of environmentalism. Social ecologists have accused ecofeminism of essentializing both nature and gender, antiglobalization activists have tried to push radical environmental groups to adopt a more inclusive agenda, and some indigenous movements have resisted the imposition of American-style environmentalism.

Radical environmentalism remains a movement in flux. However, it continues to offer an important counterpoint to reform environmentalism and an influential critique of industrial society.

See also ECOTERRORISM; ENVIRONMENTALISM, MAIN-STREAM; ENVIRONMENTAL JUSTICE; FEMINISM AND ECO-FEMINISM; GLOBALIZATION; MEDIA; NONGOVERNMENTAL ORGANIZATIONS; SUSTAINABILITY.

Keith Woodhouse

Further Reading
Bookchin, Murray, and Dave Foreman. *Defending the Earth: A Dialogue between Murray Bookchin and Dave Foreman.* Boston: South End Press, 1991.
Manes, Christopher. *Green Rage: Radical Environmentalism and the Unmaking of Civilization.* Boston: Little, Brown, 1990.
Merchant, Carolyn. *Radical Ecology: The Search for a Livable World.* New York: Routledge, 1992.
Taylor, Bron, ed. *Ecological Resistance Movements: The Global Emergence of Radical and Popular Environmentalism.* Albany: State University of New York Press, 1995.
Zakin, Susan. *Coyotes and Town Dogs: Earth First! and the Environmental Movement.* New York: Viking, 1993.

environmental justice

Environmental justice is an environmental and social movement concerned with how people are affected by industrial pollution, toxins, and other modern environmental hazards that enter ECOSYSTEMS. The environmental justice movement is interested in how pollutants entering ecosystems make their way into human bodies and is particularly concerned with whether social groups are affected by these processes differentially along lines of class, race, ethnicity, and gender. Issues surrounding environmental injustice can be found throughout American history, occurring when and where groups of people have been denied equal access to healthy environments or unequally exposed to environmental risks. Nascent forms of the environmental justice movement emerged with the intensive industrialization and responsive social reform movements of the Progressive Era in the early 20th century. However, it was not until the social and environmental movements of the 1960s and 1970s that environmental justice became conceptually and firmly rooted into America's social consciousness.

ENVIRONMENTAL JUSTICE AND LABOR MOVEMENTS

While social and environmental movements during the 1960s and 1970s cannot be characterized as always mutually supportive of each other, alliances between these two movements were central in establishing the concept of environmental justice in the American social consciousness, political structures, and social structures. The United Farm Workers (UFW) led by CÉSAR CHÁVEZ, for example, attempted to form alliances with environmental groups during the late 1960s and early 1970s to gain more control over the economic and human conditions of California's powerful agribusiness industry. Chávez viewed an alliance between the United Farm Workers and environmental groups as a means to combat agribusinesses' increasing use of PESTICIDES, which put immigrant workers, who constituted the majority of California's agribusiness labor, as well as soils, WATERSHEDS, and wildlife habitat at risk. Chávez was successful in gaining the backing of some environmental groups, such as Environmental Action, Environmental Defense Fund, the Environmental Policy Center, and Friends of the Earth.

Other social and environmental coalitions emerged in the early 1970s. Labor organizations, such as the United Auto Workers (UAW), the United Mine Workers (UMW), and the Oil, Chemical, and Atomic Workers (OCAW), increasingly began to link industrial pollutants that threatened the safety of workers to the same pollutants that affected natural ecosystems. The OCAW, for example, was successful in forging an alliance with 11 of the largest environmental organizations, including the SIERRA CLUB, to support a massive strike in 1973. Concerned with health and safety conditions in five Shell refineries and three Shell chemical plants—located near the West Coast, the Gulf Coast, and inland western areas—4,000 to 5,000 workers went on strike. Workers were primarily concerned with the thousands of toxins found in the chemical plants and refineries that might cause cancer or other serious health problems. At the same time, environmental groups contended that Shell emitted toxins into natural ecosystems, which put both wildlife and humans at risk, and joined this labor movement, which was focused on improving health and safety conditions within the workplace.

LOVE CANAL

Environmental justice was also expressed in social and environmental movements led by women during the 1970s. One good example of the centrality of gender in an environmental justice movement is LOVE CANAL. The Hooker Chemical Company had used a long-abandoned shipping canal in Niagara Falls, New York, as a landfill for toxic waste chemicals between 1942 and 1952. The company sold the land including the chemical dump to the city of Niagara Falls, New York, in 1953 for a single dollar, with the city's assuming responsibility for the toxic waste with the purchase. The city constructed a new school and cheap housing developments over the buried chemical waste, and working-class and minority communities moved into the area.

Beginning in the 1970s, members of the community noticed chemical waste seeping into their yards, homes, and surrounding property, which residents, particularly mothers, connected to miscarriages, birth defects, and diseases in children. Lois Gibb, a mother whose child attended a school built on the Love Canal toxic waste site, emerged as a leading voice of the community. Gibb and other working-class women, emphasizing their roles as mothers, worked with experts to link the contaminated environment of Love Canal to the health of fetuses, infants, and children. Working-class, African-American, and middle-class groups expressed various and sometimes differing concerns with the chemical contaminants at Love Canal. However, women were central to raising public consciousness about this issue and eventually securing federal compensation to relocate their families. Finally, in 1988—10 years after women became active in the Love Canal communities—Occidental Petroleum Corporation (the successor of Hooker Chemical) was forced to pay multimillion-dollar fines to both the state of New York and the federal government. Another 10 years later, in 1997, Occidental settled the last of the residents' lawsuits.

ENVIRONMENTAL JUSTICE AND GRASSROOTS AND NONGOVERNMENTAL ORGANIZATIONS

Environmental justice movements, as in the case of Love Canal, are fundamentally grassroots movements that center on environmental health and social equality. Increasingly throughout the 1980s and 1990s, local communities began consciously to form environmental justice movements. These movements ranged from community-based resistance groups to incorporated nonprofit organizations concerned with environmental hazards within their communities. Two of the oldest, best established, and most prominent environmental justice organizations are the WEST HARLEM ENVIRONMENTAL ACTION, COMMITTEE (WEACT) and MOTHERS OF EAST LOS ANGELES (MELA).

WEACT emerged in NEW YORK CITY during the mid-1980s and early 1990s from community resistance against the building of the North River Sewage Treatment Plant on portions of the Hudson River located within African-American communities living in West Harlem. In 1993, WEACT and the city of New York settled a lawsuit for building the flawed sewage facility in Harlem. With the funds from the lawsuit, WEACT became institutionalized as a nonprofit organization that focuses on environmental justice, which has been operating for more than 20 years.

MELA also emerged as an environmental justice organization during the mid-1980s. This women-led grassroots group in Los Angeles focuses on environmental justice issues for Latino and African-American communities. MELA initially formed to protest the building of a prison within their community, a plan that the state of California dropped in 1992. MELA later became active in opposing and stopping the planned construction of the Vernon INCINERATOR and the Chemclear plant—two toxin-producing industries—within their community. While MELA and WEACT are relatively prominent and established environmental justice organizations, similar grassroots environmental justice organizations have formed and are forming throughout the country where private industries and governmental facilities pose environmental and health hazards to their communities.

ENVIRONMENTAL JUSTICE AND THE FEDERAL GOVERNMENT

Paralleling the intersection of social and environmental movements was an increase in government attention to how environmental hazards disproportionately affect certain social groups. In 1971, the president's COUNCIL ON ENVIRONMENTAL QUALITY conducted a study to look at social disparities in environmental hazards. Some 12 years later, in 1983, a Government Accounting Office study found that three-quarters of all hazardous waste LANDFILLS were located near minority communities. This increasing governmental awareness of and concern for environmental justice culminated with the establishment of the Office of Environmental Equity (now the Office of Environmental Justice) in 1992 and President Clinton's Executive Order 12898 in 1994, which required federal agencies to develop a plan that addresses human health and environmental effects of its programs, policies, and actions. The Office of Environmental Equity became the Office of Environmental Justice branch of the U.S. ENVIRONMENTAL PROTECTION AGENCY. This office defined environmental justice in 2009 as "the fair treatment and meaningful involvement of all people regardless of race, color, national origin, or income with respect to the development, implementation, and enforcement of environmental laws, regulations, and policies."

ENVIRONMENTAL JUSTICE AND THE ACADEMY

Environmental justice also became more firmly rooted in academic disciplines during the late 1980s and early 1990s. Sociology, geography, political science, environmental history, and other disciplines have investigated the contours of environmental justice to understand better the social and environmental contexts in which injustices arise. These academic studies arose in the wake of two pivotal studies that took place in the late

1980s and early 1990s. The first of these was a report published in 1987 by the United Church of Christ's Commission for Racial Justice entitled, "Toxic Wastes and Race in the United States." This study looked at 18,000 landfills throughout the United States and found that 75 percent of all African Americans and Hispanic Americans lived near hazardous waste sites. Coining the term *environmental racism,* the study concluded that social racism and the federal government were complicit in population's being unequally exposed to hazardous waste dumps.

The sociologist Robert Bullard, in his book *Dumping in Dixie: Race, Class and Environmental Quality* (1990), suggested that African-American communities in the South were less able to stop toxic industries and hazardous wastes from entering their communities because they were excluded from both the political process and the mainstream environmental movement. A number of recent studies have specifically examined the issue of intentionality—that is, whether or not there is or has been intentionality in polluting and toxic industries being disproportionately located in communities consisting of specific racial, ethnic, or class groups. Environmental history and historical geography are useful for looking at the issue of intentionality, as well as less overt social processes that lead to environmental injustice, because these fields historicize the social and environmental organization of a given community and trace the way it develops through time. These studies reveal the importance of examining cases of environmental injustice within their specific social and historical contexts because the forms of environmental injustice change through time.

A study of Gary, Indiana, for example, shows that African Americans were disproportionately exposed to environmental hazards from the U.S. Steel plant prior to the 1970s. The company's racist labor system, for example, placed African Americans in the most hazardous jobs. Although civil rights and labor organizations ameliorated the racial inequalities within the steel industry throughout the late 1960s and 1970s, the social patterning of Gary outside the steel mills became more and more organized in ways that left African-American communities bearing the brunt of the steel industry's pollution. High suburban property prices and discriminatory practices in real estate prohibited most African Americans from moving into outer city suburbs. The study of Gary, Indiana, suggests that environmental inequalities were linked to racist social processes, such as unequal access to political processes and property, rather than polluting and hazardous industries directly targeting specific social groups. The study, however, does not address cases of environmental injustice in which hazardous waste or toxic-producing industries are located within already existing minority communities.

Although environmental justice has become embedded in modern political and social structures, such as the federal government and academia, it is important to realize that this issue has remained a central concern for a number of modern social and environmental movements. That is, environmental justice is a real concern that affects real people living in real communities. One recent example of a community facing an environmental justice issue was the Skull Valley Goshute Indian tribe located in western Utah. The Goshute and other tribes were targeted by Public Fuel Storage (PFS), a consortium of 11 eastern and midwestern utility companies, to store 44,000 tons of irradiated nuclear waste on their reservation. The Skull Valley tribal government and community both considered and contested the proposal for storing nuclear waste from 1990 to 2006, when the U.S. DEPARTMENT OF THE INTERIOR finally rejected the proposal. The issue created a major schism in the tribe, with some people aligning with PFS as a means of economic survival and others aligning with environmental groups and the state government to oppose the storage of nuclear waste on the reservation. Probably PFS's intention was not simply to expose Native Americans to radioactive waste; rather, the corporation was interested in exploiting the sovereign status of tribal lands and a relatively small tribal government as a way to expedite the regulatory process for storing nuclear waste. The fact that tribal government members themselves wanted to store nuclear waste on their reservation complicates this case for those concerned about environmental injustice. Nonetheless, the fact that PFS, under the auspice of the Nuclear Regulatory Commission, attempted to store nuclear waste on Indian reservations is another example—this one taking the shape of environmental racism—in a long history of dominant powers' exploiting Indian peoples and lands for their own benefit.

CONCLUSION

Environmental justice offers a strong framework to make corporations and governmental agencies accountable for exposing both people and natural ecosystems to risks. Environmental justice is also a powerful framework for the field of environmental history as it bridges social and environmental issues. In turn, the field of environmental history holds much potential for further illuminating the processes that lead to environmental injustice. Environmental histories focusing on environmental justice—and other disciplinary studies that look at environmental justice—have largely addressed urban contexts. However, environmental injustice is equally applicable to nonurban contexts, such as rural communities and Indian reservations where extraction and agricultural industries are found—and where industrial production, energy production, and hazardous waste dumping are increasingly common. Although the concept of environmental justice is now embedded within our governmental and academic structures, environmental toxins and hazards continue to threaten communities and ecosystems today. By better understanding the historic processes underlying environmental injustice, people may better recognize and form resistance to environmental injustice within our own communities.

See also AGRICULTURE, COMMERCIAL; CARCINOGENS, POISONS, AND TOXINS; ENVIRONMENTALISM, GRASSROOTS; ENVIRONMENTALISM, MAINSTREAM; GARBAGE; HUMAN BODY; LABOR, AGRICULTURAL AND MIGRANT; LABOR MOVEMENTS; LOS ANGELES, CALIFORNIA; NEW YORK CITY; NUCLEAR WEAPONS AND TESTING; RACISM AND DISCRIMINATION; SUPERFUND.

Spencer Wakefield

Further Reading

Blum, Elizabeth D. *Love Canal Revisited: Race, Class, and Gender in Environmental Activism.* Lawrence: University Press of Kansas, 2008.

Bullard, Robert D. *Dumping in Dixie: Race, Class, and Environmental Quality.* Boulder, Colo.: Westview Press, 1990.

Flanagan, Maureen A. "Environmental Justice in the City: A Theme for Urban Environmental History." *Environmental History* 5 (2000): 159–164.

Gordon, Robert. "Poison in the Fields: The United Farm Workers, Pesticides, and Environmental Politics." *Pacific Historical Review* 68 (1999): 51–71.

Harkin, Michael E., and David Rich Lewis, eds. *Native Americans and the Environment: Perspectives on the Ecological Indian.* Lincoln: University of Nebraska Press, 2007.

Hurley, Andrew. *Environmental Inequalities: Class, Race, and Industrial Pollution in Gary, Indiana, 1945–1980.* Chapel Hill: University of North Carolina Press, 1995.

Pulido, Laura. "Rethinking Environmental Racism: White Privilege and Urban Development in Southern California." *Annals of the Association of American Geographers* 90 (2000): 12–40.

environmental law

Americans use environmental law to structure their individual and social relationships with the natural world. Environmental law, as do all legal rules, enables people to order their relationships with each other, with those yet unborn, and with people in other countries. Even though people make environmental law to govern themselves, its commands both affect and reflect nonhuman ecological imperatives.

ORIGINS

Environmental law displays characteristic strengths and weaknesses of American law in general. It secures individual rights while enforcing public obligations, primarily by regulating use of private property. It blends majority preferences with personal liberty, giving the common good some traction on the pursuit of economic freedom. American law's nondemocratic English origins, as well as constitutional traditions enshrined in the federal and state bills of rights, restrain governmental power from reordering basic economic and social relations. Environmental law has not, therefore, substantially eroded transcendent American beliefs in market capitalism, economic profit, and material security. Nor has it dethroned human privilege to act the superior over nonhuman life. Environmental law has, however, at certain times and in particular places, slowed the rate of environmental transformation and encouraged people at least to consider other species' claims to some kind of justice.

Property and contract rules demarcated the contours of American environmental law for the first 300 years after Europeans first arrived on the continent. They defined nature as "resources," enabling their conversion into private property or national assets. By the middle of the 20th century, widespread public-health problems and aesthetic anxieties prompted a collective reappraisal of this long quest to own nature. By treating nature solely as property, Americans had bequeathed themselves and their progeny a precarious legacy: polluted air and water, denuded forests, vanishing species, and diminished recreation opportunities. Environmental law emerged as a response to these undeniable problems. New legislation and judicial decisions, occurring fairly quickly after 1945, recast legal precedents into new methods to accomplish new goals. Americans began using law to slow the rate, and ameliorate the ecological consequences, of treating nature simply as a commodity warehouse.

Americans after WORLD WAR II (1941–45) turned to federal environmental lawmaking because, first, their municipalities and then their states had proved unable, when not actually unwilling, to safeguard either public health or natural systems on which human life depends. Nascent environmental sciences were revealing that human alteration of most biotic systems produced results that rendered political map lines meaningless in any legal or ecological sense. Even when local or state governments did overcome political resistance to stronger controls on enterprise, a single jurisdiction could not effectively address environmental transformations, such as air and water pollution, that ignored boundaries.

National markets, created and served by great industries, actually facilitated the growth of environmental law after 1945. Ecological damage, as did the economic activity that caused it, crossed state lines with impunity. The U.S. CONGRESS, encouraged by generous U.S. Supreme Court interpretations during the NEW DEAL in the 1930s, extended national law to the very limits of the CONSTITUTION's interstate commerce clause (Article I). In essence, the commerce clause empowers Congress to make federal law regulating nearly any form of human activity that involves or causes economic behavior in two or more states. Nearly all purposeful human actions that produce or consume affect the natural environment, so the U.S. Supreme Court has consistently held that Congress enjoys nearly plenary authority to make federal law affecting the natural environment. And when federal law has encountered conflicting state and local rules, the Constitution's supremacy clause (Article VI) usually ensures federal primacy. Only very recently has the Supreme Court suggested constitutional boundaries to "commerce clause environmental lawmaking," but Congress and the future presidents may not take its hints, and future justices might withdraw even its suggestion. National primacy to make environmental laws shaping the 700 million acres of public lands—national FORESTS and rangelands, defense facilities, Indian reservations—has never been doubted, given the Constitution's expansive federal property clause (Article IV).

FEDERAL ADMINISTRATIVE LAW

Until the 1890s, state and federal courts made most legal rules affecting nature while deciding private legal disputes about contracts and property through common-law adjudication. After 1900, progressive reformers, at both the state and national levels, began grafting important new branches onto private law's old roots: legislative statutes administered by executive branch or independent agencies staffed by expert civil servants. By the 1920s, legal commentators had begun to recognize that this new pattern of lawmaking by administrators posed both new opportunities and unresolved challenges. Many political liberals praised administrative law's flexibility, impartiality, and expertise, while conservatives, especially lawyers who represented regulated business, feared an erosion of democratic accountability. Despite the debates, administrative law would become the most influential form of environmental lawmaking after the middle of the 20th century.

The GREAT DEPRESSION, New Deal, and World War II cemented the "administrative state" into the framework of American law between 1930 and 1950. Administration typically involved enactment of broad statutes by elected legislators and actual application of the statutes to real-world behavior by executive branch agencies in the form of rules, permits, and adjudicatory decisions within the agencies. Administration became the preferred legal method to handle the complex array of problems caused by adapting private action to public needs. Measured by their sheer output, administrative agencies, some directly responsible to the executive and others formally independent, now make the most influential, and problematic, environmental law. For example, the U.S. Department of Agriculture's conservation agencies help manage farmers' fields, the NATIONAL PARK SERVICE cares for natural treasures, and the BUREAU OF LAND MANAGEMENT superintends millions of private permittees who demand their share of the PUBLIC DOMAIN.

Even before enactment of the major federal environmental statutes around 1970, administrative law undergirded environmental law. Few Americans know of the most influential federal environmental statute: the 1946 Administrative Procedure Act (APA). The APA established a rough but flexible framework to ensure elected representatives make basic policy choices, professional administrators execute those choices in everyday matters, and federal judges protect constitutional rights to liberty and property by reviewing both agency action and congressional statute writing. Today, nearly every celebrated environmental legal dispute turns on application of the APA. When a federal agency makes rules to execute a congressional statute, a regulated business decides how or whether to comply with a rule, or a judge resolves a lawsuit against an agency, the APA does far more than sketch mere "procedures." Many states have now also enacted "little APAs," with equally significant impact, over time, on the shape and direction of state-based environmental law.

American environmental law today resembles a massive legal temple. Federal statutes compose its central pillars: the NATIONAL ENVIRONMENTAL POLICY ACT (NEPA) OF 1969, CLEAN AIR ACT of 1970 (CAA), CLEAN WATER ACT of 1972 (CWA), ENDANGERED SPECIES ACT OF 1973 (ESA), and waste-management laws established by the Resource Conservation and Recovery Act of 1976 (RCRA) and Comprehensive Environmental Response, Compensation, and Liability Act of 1980 (CERCLA, or SUPERFUND). Agency-made rules cap these pillars to form pediments baroque in their complexity but essential to accomplishing the temple's ambitious purposes.

So lofty stands the federal legal temple that most Americans believe only governmental actors at the national level—Congress, executive branch agencies, federal judges—make environmental law. Although misleading, an exclusively federal focus reveals environmental law's basic architecture, as states and localities usually replicate or modify national practices. Federal environmental lawmaking and enforcement involve all three branches of the government established by the U.S. Constitution. Citizen activism mixes with legal professionals' expertise, illuminating American law's symbiotic relationship with politics. Environmental law is more the product of power and emotion than of reason and order. Thus, it rarely displays the settled certainty of legal principles governing contracts, torts, commercial paper, or other areas of law.

Elected representatives exercise legislative power by enacting broad environmental statutes to achieve constitutional objectives, such as regulating interstate commerce. Executive branch agencies accomplish statutes' general purposes by promulgating administrative rules, additional forms of law that translate statutes' general language into real-world specifics. Citizens, and corporations that can assert the rights of citizens, may contend the rules, as applied to their conduct, violate rights secured by the Constitution or transgress the legislature's intent. An aggrieved citizen who fails to change the agency's position, after exhausting remedies within the administrative process, may seek redress from the courts. Judicial review of agency action resolves the dispute by providing an authoritative interpretation of the disputed law, often by applying precedents established earlier in similar cases. A judicial decision, if affirmed on appeal to the highest relevant court, may prompt a regulated citizen, an administrative agency, or a legislative body—or even all three, depending on the nature of the environmental issue and the public temper—to initiate the making of new statutes or rules.

Environmental law displays American lawmaking's interconnected tensions and creative opportunism. Blunt power politics and shrill rhetoric infuse careful, even mundane rule parsing. Legal professionals joust with scientific experts. And occasionally, a group of ordinary citizens—whether a legislative committee working on a bill or a jury weighing a claim for money damages—must decide the meaning of the nation's foundational legal document, the U.S. Constitution.

Federal enforcement of national statutes has dominated environmental-law headlines for at least 40 years, but all 50 states and nearly every size and type of local government have created a complex body of rules that adjust citizens' relationships to land, air, water, and life-forms. Of the major federal environmental statutes, only NEPA does not depend on substantial state lawmaking power. American FEDERALISM, an uneasy and often unpredictable blend of national authority with residual state (and local) sovereignty, requires not only the lawyer but the citizen to heed environmental law made and enforced beyond WASHINGTON, D.C.

STATE AND LOCAL LAW

Environmental law's state and local heritage makes federalism more than a ritualistic nod toward American political history. Local law bears a powerful, though often unrealized, potential to do "equal justice under law" by recasting human relationships with each other and with nature. American law was once English law, for the most part. Embedded deep within the fabric of Anglo-American law rests the "police power." Essentially, the police power entitles governments to restrain private liberties—such as property ownership and individual action—to protect the public welfare. For more than three centuries, local and state governments have deployed their police powers to keep drinking water pure, to make workplaces safer, and to abate nuisances that threaten both owners' rights quietly to enjoy their property and the public's right to quality of life. Given the sanctified status of liberty and property in American law, the police power's capacity to restrain private conduct can protect environmental quality in the real places where people live and work.

Today, a basic knowledge of environmental law is nearly mandatory for entry into, and success in, the legal profession. Yet until about 1970, environmental law composed neither a distinctive subject of legal education nor a practice specialty. As with labor law during the period 1930–50, environmental law emerged as a contested creation amid vivid political and social struggles between 1960 and 1980. As does labor law, therefore, environmental law reflects both new rules specific to the conditions of its birth and internal evolution of older legal principles. Still visible and vital are environmental law's heritage in the law of property and contract, nuisance and tort, business corporations, and municipal government. Labor and environmental law share another paradoxical trait: Born amid strife as a means of restraining CAPITALISM's relentless expansion, both kinds of law pacified early battlefields by turning political conflict into routine dispute resolution. Daily, routine practice by government agencies and regulated business has largely defanged environmental law's original critical bite.

Even as its overriding objective of slowing the rate of human-caused change has become more imperative, American environmental law has gradually become less confrontational.

See also BUREAU OF INDIAN AFFAIRS; ENVIRONMENTALISM, GRASSROOTS; ENVIRONMENTALISM, MAINSTREAM; FEDERAL LAW—ENVIRONMENTAL REGULATIONS; FEDERAL LAW—INDUSTRIAL REGULATIONS; FEDERAL LAW—LAND POLICIES; NUISANCE LAW; POLLUTION, AIR; POLLUTION, WATER; TREATIES AND INTERNATIONAL LAW.

Karl Brooks

Further Reading

Andrews, Richard N. L. *Managing the Environment, Managing Ourselves: A History of American Environmental Policy.* New Haven, Conn.: Yale University Press, 1999.

Brooks, Karl Boyd. *Before Earth Day: The Origins of American Environmental Law, 1945–1970.* Lawrence: University Press of Kansas, 2008.

Environmental Policy Act   *See* NATIONAL ENVIRONMENTAL POLICY ACT (NEPA) OF 1969.

Environmental Protection Agency

The Environmental Protection Agency (EPA) was created under Title I of the NATIONAL ENVIRONMENTAL POLICY ACT (NEPA) OF 1969, signed into law by President RICHARD NIXON on January 1, 1970. Its mission and scope were enumerated under the Reorganization Plan No. 3 of July 9, 1970, a statute that consolidated and unified the efforts of key departments and agencies with direct responsibility for human health and environmental protection. These acts made a clear and unambiguous statement of the federal government's intent to remediate and reverse the harmful effects of the polluting activities of the 19th and early 20th centuries. These activities included invasive federal land policies, aggressive industrialization with subsequent demands for hydroelectric and nuclear power and a rapidly developing transportation and communications network, the mass and increasingly industrial production of agricultural products, an unprecedented demand for urban and suburban residential communities, and a growing appreciation for the aesthetic and recreational values of undeveloped tracts of land.

The primary tool for guaranteeing this commitment to ecological reform is the Environmental Impact Statement (EIS), a process governed by the EPA that reviews in detail potential environmental impacts of federal programs and possible alternatives to lessen any dangers. This procedure substantively altered the policy process of all federal agencies, enforcing closer interagency cooperation and public participation on behalf of human health and the environment. Today, the EPA is one of the nation's largest regulatory entities, employing nearly 18,000 people and commanding a budget of nearly $8 billion invested in research, standardization, oversight, and the enforcement of 15 specific legislative acts addressing air and water pollution, waste disposal and cleanup, the effects of radiation, and pesticides. Those standards and practices have been adopted by more than 80 countries worldwide; they serve as the foundation for international environmental regulation including requirements for World Bank funding projects.

THE LIMITS OF COMMON LAW

Students of U.S. environmental law refer to the evolution of environmental regulation in six stages. In the post–WORLD WAR II period, dissatisfaction with the limits of common law to determine equity in the PUBLIC DOMAIN and a growing concern for the quality of the common environment ushered in sweeping changes in intergovernmental policies and practices. Key legislation before and during World War II included the Rivers and Harbors Act (1899), the Federal Food, Drug and Cosmetic Act (1938), and the SAFE DRINKING WATER ACT (1944). The established traditions of nuisance and trespass proved inadequate in the face of the unanticipated and far-reaching effects of industrialization. The pollution activities of some parties were increasingly difficult to balance against the harm done to others and were complicated by the accelerated pace of land development, aggressive industrialization, MASS TRANSIT, and CONSUMERISM. The waste products of postwar economic prosperity were evident along the littered roadsides, in the polluted air, and in the contaminated waterways that flowed into the water systems of the nation's cities and neighborhoods.

Turn-of-the-20th-century common law and the Progressive Era CONSERVATION of public resources gave way to a post–World War II dependence on federal assistance to the states to initiate pollution control measures. These state and local pollution abatement efforts revealed the ubiquitous nature of interstate air and water pollution as traditional local, state, and national relationships broke down in addressing widespread issues of contamination and ecological damage. Key legislation of the second period included the Federal Water Pollution Control Act and CLEAN WATER ACT (1948), the Air Pollution Control Act and CLEAN AIR ACT (1955), the National Emission Standards Act (1955), and the Federal Hazardous Substances Act (1960). A third wave of heightened public awareness of the deteriorating environment opened with the 1962 publication of RACHEL CARSON's book *Silent Spring,* a classic best seller that helped fan widespread concern for the cumulative effects of toxins on ecological systems. This period, corresponding with the presidential administrations of DWIGHT D. EISENHOWER, JOHN F. KENNEDY, and LYNDON B. JOHNSON, ushered in a series of landmark legislation, setting the stage for the enactment of the NEPA in 1970. Critical acts of Congress addressed natural resource preservation, air and water pollution control, and consumer protection. To do this,

This 1975 poster was sponsored by the Environmental Protection Agency, founded in 1970, the same year Earth Day was first celebrated. *(Library of Congress)*

advisory committees were formed to present substantive evidence and analysis on subjects requiring scientific, technological, and economic expertise. These committees also provided a forum for public response.

Under Johnson's administration in the mid-1960s, the public base was broadened to assess the diversity of opinion on policy issues more accurately. The incorporation and expansion of the Bill of Rights and the broad sweep of civil rights legislation, initiated during the 1950s and enacted during his administration, helped level the political playing field for many, allowing new voices to be heard from local communities nationwide. Broadening public support for environmental initiatives created a mandate for grassroots community action on a scale unimagined during the early postwar period. This was reinforced by increased federal participation in urban affairs. These efforts endured during the second half of the century, connecting quality of life issues to questions of social equity and participation. During the 1980s, Community Based Environmental Planning (CBEP) was introduced to strengthen stakeholder participation in the protection of human health and the environment. In response to a polychlorolphenol (PCP) landfill protest in North Carolina, the ENVIRONMENTAL JUSTICE movement took root, culminating in the creation of the Office of Environmental Justice within the Environmental Protection Agency in 1992, the creation of the National Environmental Justice Advisory Council on September 30, 1993, and the enactment of the environmental justice statutes signed into law on February 11, 1994, by President BILL CLINTON under Executive Order 12898.

The remarkable legislation enacted during the 1960s reflected the qualitative values of an optimistic and affluent society, one that questioned poverty, civil rights, urban decay, consumerism, and industrialism, all in an effort to define equitable standards of living appropriate to a free society. The WILDERNESS ACT OF 1964, the Land and Water Conservation Act (1965), the Water Quality Act (1965), the Solid Waste Disposal Act (1965), the Shoreline Erosion Protection Act (1965), the NATIONAL HISTORIC PRESERVATION ACT (1966), the Freedom of Information Act (1966), the Clean Water Restoration Act (1966), and the Air Quality Act (1967) established enduring legislative precedents for the role of the EPA in the years to come. Other precedents were established with the enactment of new consumer protection laws including the National Traffic and Motor Vehicle Act, the Fair Packaging and Labeling Act, the Federal Hazardous Substances Act, the Federal Meat Inspection Act, the Natural Gas Pipeline Safety Act, the Flammable Fabrics Act, the Child Protection Act, and the Hazardous Materials Transportation Act. Subsequent federal environmental legislation, including clean air and water amendments, is grounded in these efforts, whose public roots extend back to the Progressive Era reform movements of the late 19th and early 20th centuries.

NEPA: ESTABLISHING THE STATUTORY FRAMEWORK FOR ENVIRONMENTAL REFORM

Senator Henry Jackson (D-Wash.) and Professor Lynton Caldwell successfully guided the landmark National Environmental Policy Act through both houses of Congress. On January 1, 1970, President Nixon signed the bill, one of the nation's first laws establishing federal statutory and regulatory guidelines for protecting the environment. Its implementation included mandatory environmental impact assessment requirements administered by the Environmental Protection Agency as directed in Title I of NEPA. Title II established the COUNCIL ON ENVIRONMENTAL QUALITY, an advisory group approved to help develop and clarify NEPA's regulatory and procedural guidelines.

The EPA was created in 1970 as a direct response to the damaging environmental effects of federal actions that included clear-cut logging of forests, dam construction, highway construction, nuclear power development, strip mining, and oil extraction within fragile ECOSYSTEMS. Its primary mission was to draw together the interagency efforts of those managing the nation's environmental interests and programs including wildlife, recreation, conservation, agriculture, human health, and economic development. This objective was explicated in NEPA's opening declaration to preserve the harmony of man and nature for present and future generations. The primary tool for guaranteeing this commitment was a requirement that prior to any federal action affecting the quality of the human environment, the initiating agency must complete an Environmental Impact s (EIS), reviewing in detail potential environmental impacts of that program and possible alternatives to lessen those dangers. This procedure, the result of efforts by the political scientist Keith Caldwell and Senator Jackson, chairman of the Senate Committee on Interior and Insular Affairs, substantively altered the policy process of all federal agencies, enforcing closer interagency cooperation and public participation on behalf of human health and the environment.

NEPA was followed by the Reorganization Plan No. 3 of July 9, 1970, whose purpose emphasized the importance of interpreting the environment as a single, interrelated system. To reflect that reality, interagency changes were made, unifying the federal government's efforts by putting key departments and activities under the direction of the Environmental Protection Agency. These included the Federal Water Quality Administration (previously within the Department of the Interior); the National Air Pollution Control Administration (from the Department of Health, Education and Welfare [HEW]); pesticide registration, research, and control (moved from the DEPARTMENT OF AGRICULTURE, the DEPARTMENT OF THE INTERIOR, the FOOD AND DRUG ADMINISTRATION, and HEW); the Bureau of Solid Waste Management; the Bureau of Water Hygiene; the administration of studies on ecological systems (previously administered by the newly formed Council on Environmental Quality), radiation criteria and standards (previously established by the ATOMIC ENERGY COMMISSION and Federal Radiation Council), and related functions administered by the HEW Bureau of Radiological Health of the Environmental Control Administration.

The EPA opened its doors in WASHINGTON, D.C., on December 2, 1970 under the direction of WILLIAM RUCKELSHAUS. Ruckelshaus served two noncontiguous terms as administrator; his first term, ending in April 1973, was a time of organizational formation, immediate attention to the nation's most polluted cities and industries, enforcement of emissions standards for six pollutants and automobile emissions, the communication and enforcement of air quality standards applicable to the states, and the end of the use of DDT (dichlorodiphenyltrichloroethane) as a pesticide. Five days after assuming office, Ruckelshaus gave the keynote address to the second International Clean Air Congress. On December 11, 1970, he gave the mayors of CLEVELAND, OHIO; DETROIT, MICHIGAN; and ATLANTA, GEORGIA, six months to enter into compliance with the nation's water pollution standards. Ruckelshaus served until April 1973 and then returned to office in 1983 and served for two years at White House Chief of Staff James Baker's request. Other administrators include Russell E. Train (1973–77), Douglas M. Costle (1977–81), Anne M. Gorsuch (1981–83), Lee M. Thomas (1985–89), William K. Reilly (1989–93), Carol M. Browner (1993–2001), Christine Todd Whitman (2001–03), Michael O. Leavitt (2003–05), Stephen L. Johnson (2005–09) and Lisa P. Jackson (2009–   ).

PROTECTING HUMAN HEALTH AND THE ENVIRONMENT

The fourth phase of U.S. environmental law, corresponding with the administrations of Presidents Richard Nixon, Gerald Ford, and JIMMY CARTER, is noted for the extensive volume of legislation that was implemented, setting into motion a new and complex federal regulatory infrastructure whose practices were imitated and adopted throughout the 50 states and, later, in countries all over the world. This phase coincided with the growing participation of the courts, which conducted judicial reviews of the decisions of federal agencies, providing citizens the legal framework needed to challenge agency programs. It also reflected the ethos of the EPA under the direction of its early directors Ruckelshaus and Train, who used the momentum of the times to position the EPA as a proactive and exclusive innovator of environmental policy, regulation, and reform.

With the enactment of the Clean Air Act of 1970, the fledgling EPA was charged with the enormous and unprecedented task of setting ambient air quality standards to be enacted by the states, national emissions standards for hazardous air pollutants, and auto emissions standards. In 1971, standards were set for emissions of sulfur dioxide, particulate matter, carbon monoxide, photochemical oxidants, and nitrogen dioxide. Congress mandated that national ambient air standards were to be met by 1975, including a 90 percent reduction in auto-

mobile emissions, and that a list of hazardous pollutants was to be published within 90 days of enactment. Levels of nitrogen oxides were to be similarly reduced by 1976. Final emissions standards were to be published within a year and to include a listing of categories of stationary sources of pollution. In real time, these directives required the scrupulous regulation of tens of thousands of major stationary sources of air pollution and millions of cars and the reduction of hundreds of toxins.

The Clean Water Act of 1972 drove home an equally daunting list of requirements, setting a standard of zero discharge of pollutants by 1985 and requiring that the EPA set technology-based effluent limits on dischargers. It also established a national permit system to be administered by the agency. Setting acceptable standards for potable water was complicated by the scientific uncertainties of measuring and regulating the physical properties of water and its substrata ecologies, and the converging and overlapping influences of its multiple uses by industry, agriculture, recreation, wildlife, and residences.

Other legislation followed in rapid succession, catapulting the EPA into the limelight to begin piecing together a regulatory infrastructure for the nation. These included the Environmental Quality Improvement Act (1970), the Resource Recovery Act (1970), the Occupational Safety and Health Act (1970), the Federal Water Pollution Control Act (1972), the Federal Insecticide, Fungicide and Rodenticide Act (1972), the Marine Protection, Research, and Sanctuaries Act (1972), the ENDANGERED SPECIES ACT OF 1973, the Safe Drinking Water Act (1974), the Toxic Substances Control Act (1976), the Resource Conservation and Recovery Act (1976), and the Comprehensive Environmental Response, Compensation, and Liability Act (1980).

Of these statutes, the Toxic Substances Control Act (TSCA) is considered to be the one that gives the EPA much of its regulatory power. This act authorizes the agency to regulate more than 75,000 chemicals throughout their "life cycle" from manufacture to disposal. It is assisted by the Administrator's Toxic Substance Advisory Committee, which provides assistance related to policy. The 1976 Resource Conservation and Recovery Act strengthened the EPA's control of the production and disposal of hazardous wastes, putting under government regulation the nation's hazardous waste generators and treatment, storage, and disposal facilities. In 1986, Title III of the SUPERFUND Amendments and Reauthorization Act put into law the Emergency Planning and Community Right-to-Know Act (EPCRA). Under this act, the toxics release inventory and the hazardous chemical inventory were created, requiring specific parties publicly to disclose an annual listing of the toxins they have released. In the decades to follow, governments all over the world would adopt Agenda 21, accepted at the 1992 UNITED NATIONS Conference on Environment and Development, encouraging the international creation and publication of pollutant release and transfer registries.

The advances in environmental law during the 1970s occurred against a background of increasing public disillusionment and dissent following the VIETNAM WAR; the assassinations of John F. Kennedy, MARTIN LUTHER KING, JR., and Robert Kennedy; and as real wages began to decline and new worries about the environment surfaced. The battle for Echo Dam, the Cuyahoga River conflagration, EARTH DAY, the Organization of Petroleum Exporting Countries (OPEC) oil embargo, the Santa Barbara and other OIL SPILLS, the THREE MILE ISLAND meltdown, and the LOVE CANAL scandal shocked the nation into a growing awareness of resource scarcity and the need to address the polluting activities of the past to protect the limited resources of the future. These public concerns hardened into a firm resolve with the Chernobyl meltdown in Russia in 1986 and the *Exxon Valdez* oil spill in Alaska in 1989.

Three events ushered in the fifth phase of environmental law: the Three Mile Island meltdown in Pennsylvania in 1979, the Love Canal scandal in New York in 1979, and the enactment of the Comprehensive Environmental Response, Compensation and Liability Act (CERCLA) of 1980, which created the Superfund program. The intent and practice of this unprecedented statute extend the EPA's regulatory powers beyond the prospective management of hazardous wastes to include the remediation of sites despoiled by toxic releases and disposals. While RCRA controls the life cycle release of toxins into the environment, CERCLA provides for the redress of pollution and toxic waste activities that occurred in the past. CERCLA also differs from other environmental statutes in that it is site specific and is applied to any hazardous substance of concern at a particular facility regardless of its environmental medium.

CERCLA authorizes the common law practice of strict liability in cases of harmful release and contamination by hazardous substances. Modeled on the principles established under the Clean Water Act of 1972, CERCLA enjoins the EPA to use the Superfund for removal and remediation of site-specific contaminants. These sites are formally recognized by placement on a National Priority List, where facilities presenting the greatest risk to health and the environment are ranked on a regular basis. Strict liability serves as a deterrent to future contamination of the environment while cleanup serves to preserve and restore resources for future generations. Liability is determined by the cost of cleanup. More than 5,000 sites were approved for contaminant removal by 1998 at an average cost of $500,000. Remediation is much more extensive and costs run an average of $30 million per site. All potentially responsible parties (PRPs) are identified; they include past and present property owners, shippers of the harmful substances under removal or remediation, their manufacturers, and those who stored them. Liability is joint and individual and subject to contentious and complicated litigation, which is why this statute has a critical prominence in legal practice and review. The international export, marketing, and trade of hazardous wastes (frequently of substances banned in the United States and purchased by developing countries) and the global dumping of toxins in unprotected LANDFILLS and waters are loophole issues outside U.S. legal protection that have forced continuing international cooperation and environmental regulation.

BROWNFIELDS are another subject of interest under CERCLA. Their remediation demonstrates the EPA's growing understanding and oversight of the revitalization of urban environments. As environmental reform evolves, practitioners are seeking to address the harmful effects of past urban planning and design, including the unregulated disposal of wastes, unregulated development, inadequate and aging infrastructure, unequal housing and municipal services due to discrimination and the displacement of people of color, and unequal levels of risk due to landfills, industrial releases, and contaminated land sites. Many of these valuable properties, designated as brownfields and grayfields, include contaminated residences and places of business in need of demolition, remediation, and restoration for future development. The EPA established the Brownfields Initiative in 1995 to begin revitalizing and restoring the nation's estimated 450,000 properties for reinvestment. Similar programs address the futures of port cities and obsolete shopping malls and business centers.

Stages five and six in the growth of the environmental statutory and regulatory framework included the broad extension and refinement of legislation designed to address waste management and pollution control, health and safety, and resource management. Issues addressed included data management, information disclosure, technology implementation, product design, performance standards, emissions control, negotiated rule making, planning, taxation, and subsidization. These concerns are shared by countries all over the world united under a variety of international protocols and conventions to share technology and expertise in addressing common problems. The Office of International Affairs was established within EPA in 1970 to affirm the nation's commitment to work with Canada and Mexico to develop effective transboundary policies and practices. It also serves as a forum for engaging international agencies such as the World Trade Organization and the North American Commission for Environmental Cooperation, whose economic and political clout can be brought to bear on issues of climate change, sustainability, hazardous waste transfers, acceptable air and water pollution standards, the remediation of polluted industrial sites, and the remediation and protection of marine and agricultural landscapes.

POLITICIZATION OF THE EPA

Over the course of its 40-year history, the EPA has seen its influence wax and wane, depending upon who sits in the White House. Although Richard Nixon generally approached the environment as a bipartisan issue, he also wanted the EPA to serve as a model for his new federalism and placed more than half of the agency's staff in 10 regional offices across the nation. While regional autonomy allowed each office to address

EPA ADMINISTRATORS AND THEIR ACCOMPLISHMENTS

EPA Administrator	Term	Appointed by President	Accomplishments
William D. Ruckelshaus	1970–73	Nixon	Banned general application of the pesticide DDT as well as set standards for air quality and automobile emissions.
Russell E. Train	1973–77	Nixon	Supported approval of automobile catalytic converters to meet requirements of the Clean Air Act of 1970, worked to balance environmental issues with energy crisis, and led the Alaska Pipeline Intergovernmental Task Force.
Douglas M. Costle	1977–81	Carter	An original founder of EPA, he was administrator during the Three Mile Island partial nuclear meltdown but held mixed views on the efficacy of nuclear power plants.
Anne M. Gorsuch	1981–83	Reagan	Reduced EPA's role in limiting pollution. Gorsuch cut the environmental regulation agency's budget by 22 percent and eventually resigned after a fight with Congress over executive privilege and illegal dumping of waste.
William D. Ruckelshaus	1983–85	Reagan	Restored some funding to EPA as well as the agency's tarnished image after Gorsuch.
Lee M. Thomas	1985–89	Reagan	An advocate of risk assessment in regard to pollution and waste, Thomas was responsible for two of the largest and most important EPA programs, the Comprehensive Environmental Response Compensation and Liability Act and the Resource Conservation and Recovery Act.
William K. Reilly	1989–93	G. H. W. Bush	Faced with growing global challenges, including global warming, the ozone layer, and oceanic pollution, he advocated domestic and international environmental protection. Reilly helped revise the Clean Air Act of 1970.
Carol M. Browner	1993–2001	Clinton	Advocate of environmental justice, Browner helped craft amendments to the Safe Drinking Water Act and the Food Quality Protection Act and tackled the issue of global warming. Faced scrutiny from a Republican Congress that wanted to undermine EPA's role in environmental protection.
Christine Todd Whitman	2001–03	G. W. Bush	Resigned from her position after numerous confrontations with the Bush administration, especially over the administration's refusal to acknowledge a relationship between carbon emissions and global warming.
Michael O. Leavitt	2003–05	G. W. Bush	Followed the administration's belief that environmental regulation was tied to economic success, opening public land to new development.
Stephen L. Johnson	2005–09	G. W. Bush	The first career employee to hold the position of administrator and the first scientist to head the agency, he argued against state control of greenhouse gas emissions.
Lisa P. Johnson	2009–	Obama	The first African American to hold this position, she has focused on protecting children, the elderly, and low-income communities particularly susceptible to environmental threats.

Source: U.S. Environmental Protection Agency Web site. Available online. URL: http://www.epa.gov/history/administrators/index.htm. Accessed May 28, 2009.

the specific needs of its locale, it also left the offices in a poorly defined middle ground between federal and state governments, where the enforcement of standards was less clear. Given the patchwork of complex regulations that had emerged in the preceding decades, Nixon, Gerald Ford, and Jimmy Carter increased presidential control over EPA regulatory actions in the 1970s, creating White House offices that reviewed the quality of analysis and economic effectiveness of the agency's proposals.

Ronald Reagan, however, reversed more than three decades of legislation and political activity by making the environment a partisan issue. After his 1980 election, he worked to reduce the federal role in environmental protection by relaxing regulations, cutting the budgets of regulatory agencies, and turning over many functions to state and local governments, although most were unwilling or unable to assume them. To achieve these ends, he first appointed an ideological loyalist, Anne Gorsuch, with no management experience as the EPA's administrator. The Reagan White House regularly undermined the agency's work. For example, as a substitute for regulation, the EPA adopted voluntary testing and self-certification for chemical manufacturers. Reagan caused permanent damage to the EPA and undermined the public consensus that had emerged to support environmental regulation in the 1960s and 1970s. At the same time, outrage over certain actions strengthened the nation's environmental movements.

As president, George H. W. Bush initially tried to distance himself from Reagan's harsh environmental policies in 1989 and 1990 by supporting various EPA efforts, including the fostering of research and international cooperation on global warming and participation in the upcoming United Nations Earth Summit in Rio de Janeiro in 1992. However, Bush became increasingly noncommittal in public statements while courting conservative business interests to support his reelection campaign in 1992, and in the end, under his leadership, the United States was the only developed country that did not sign the Biodiversity Convention from the UN conference. Domestically, for example, the Bush administration created a "safe harbor" rule that allowed utilities to upgrade old coal-fired facilities and increase production indefinitely without triggering new emission standards. Bush utilized a "cap-and-trade" system for sulfur emissions from power plants, allowing plants with higher pollution to operate by buying permits from other facilities.

Under Bill Clinton, the EPA reversed these policies and aggressively enforced emissions standards for sulfur and mercury for utilities. During his first term (1993–97), his EPA administrator, Carol Browner, tightened air-quality standards for fine particulates and nitrogen oxide. While she promoted place-based approaches to watershed management, she also centralized the agency's enforcement program to ensure consistent and regular initiatives against high-pollution industries, particularly as scientific evidence accumulated in support of tighter restrictions. Clinton's environmental agenda, however,

was truncated by various scandals and opposition from a Republican-controlled Congress during his second term (1997–2001).

After his 2000 election, President George W. Bush and the Republican-controlled Congress aggressively changed much of the federal environmental policy by removing restrictions on industry. His administration introduced strong new regulations for diesel engines but pushed the EPA to lower air pollution standards for utilities and industry. His administration reduced citizens' rights to participate in the judicial review mandated by many federal statutes, narrowed the application of many environmental laws, and eliminated policies for interagency review created in the 1970s. Bush's White House exercised greater political control over the scientific information the EPA provided the public. For example, in an EPA report in 2004 assessing the state of the U.S. environment, agency officials chose not to address global warming rather than include language from the White House that suggested uncertainty on the issue despite the consensus of the scientific community.

CONCLUSION

On May 20, 2008, the Environmental Protection Agency released its 2008 Report on the Environment, a resource designed to help educate and inform the nation's citizens about the condition of the environment and its effect on human health. This report was the culmination of an effort begun in 2001 to assemble for the first time a rigorously tested set of scientific indicators that could be used accurately to gauge the nation's success at setting and meeting effective environmental standards. Two preliminary documents were prepared in 2003. The final 2008 document was updated and refined after intensive peer review and established a sound national benchmark for measuring and analyzing indicator trends in the years to come. Five key chapters provide a comprehensive coverage of the vast national inventory of emissions and toxins currently under regulation by the EPA to safeguard the nation's air, water, land, human health, and ecologies. The report was also segmented into 10 regional reports detailing key indicators such as air pollutants, acid deposition, drinking water quality, land-use patterns, population, fertilizer use, forestland, carbon storage, and others for particular sites.

This report stands at the crossroads of environmental reform in the United States. It documents the results of the EPA's efforts over the past 40 years to comply with the unprecedented national mandate to safeguard the nation's health and environment. In doing so, EPA officials hope to set a workable standard for environmental reform in the 21st century, ensuring that protection of the environment remains an influential factor in national life and politics in the decades to come.

See also CARCINOGENS, TOXINS, AND POISONS; EMISSIONS TRADING; ENVIRONMENTALISM, GRASSROOTS; ENVIRONMENTALISM, MAINSTREAM; FEDERALISM; FEDERAL LAW—ENVIRONMENTAL REGULATIONS; FEDERAL LAW—INDUSTRIAL REGULATIONS; FEDERAL LAW—LAND POLICIES;

INTERSTATE HIGHWAY SYSTEM; NUISANCE LAW; PESTICIDES; POLLUTION, AIR; POLLUTION, WATER; UNITED NATIONS ENVIRONMENTAL CONFERENCES.

Victoria M. Breting-Garcia

Further Reading

Andrews, Richard N. L. *Managing the Environment, Managing Ourselves.* 2d ed. New Haven, Conn., and London: Yale University Press, 2006.

Collin, Robert W. *The Environmental Protection Agency: Cleaning Up America's Act.* Westport, Conn., and London: Greenwood Press, 2006.

Hays, Samuel P. *Explorations in Environmental History: Essays by Samuel P. Hays.* Pittsburgh: Pittsburgh University Press, 1998.

Lazarus, Richard J. *The Making of Environmental Law.* Chicago and London: University of Chicago Press, 2004.

Percival, Robert V., Christopher H. Schroeder, Alan S. Miller, and James P. Leape. *Environmental Regulation: Law, Science, and Policy.* 4th ed. New York: Aspen, 2003.

Rothman, Hal K. *The Greening of a Nation? Environmentalism in the United States since 1945.* Fort Worth, Tex.: Harcourt Brace College Publishers, 1998.

U.S. EPA. "U.S. EPA's 2008 Report on the Environment (Final Report)." U.S. Environmental Protection Agency, Washington, D.C., EPA/600/R-07/045F. Available online. URL: http://www.epa.gov/roe. Accessed August 20, 2008.

environmental regulations   *See* ENVIRONMENTAL LAW; FEDERAL LAW—ENVIRONMENTAL REGULATIONS.

erosion

Erosion is the process of detachment, transportation, and deposition of soil material by wind or water. As such, it is a natural process that has been going on for millions of years, creating natural wonders such as the GRAND CANYON and Bryce Canyon in the American West as well as fertile river valleys with deposited silt. Erosion does not have a single cause, and factors such as the type of soil, slope, precipitation, soil moisture, temperature, and plant cover all have an impact on the erosion potential.

Apart from the problems of COASTLINE EROSION AND STABILIZATION, the environmental debate over soil erosion has mostly focused on the destruction of agricultural land. The most pertinent symbol of the hazards of soil erosion were the dust storms that ravaged the Great Plains in the 1930s, but the DUST BOWL, immortalized in JOHN STEINBECK's *The Grapes of Wrath,* was only the most visible of a multitude of erosion problems on American soil. Indications are strong that soil erosion is a typical side effect of high-intensity industrialized farming, as soil compaction through heavy machinery, deep plowing, growing field size, and plants such as CORN tend to increase the hazard. In regions such as the Palouse in Washington State, soil cultivation without erosion is next to impossible.

Erosion control did not become a major part of CONSERVATION policy until the 1930s. Earlier efforts by farmers and agricultural advisors were usually haphazard ineffective and, in fact, nonexistent in large parts of the country. In 1928, the soil conservationist HUGH HAMMOND BENNETT secured the first federal appropriation for soil erosion research. In 1933, Bennett organized the Soil Erosion Service within HAROLD ICKES's DEPARTMENT OF THE INTERIOR, which was renamed the Soil Conservation Service (SCS) and transferred to the U.S. DEPARTMENT OF AGRICULTURE in 1935. The dust bowl gave fodder to popular concerns, generating generous appropriations and expansion of the SCS, but the fight against soil erosion was always conceived as a nationwide endeavor. In fact, the early SCS gave more attention to the water erosion problems of the South than to wind erosion in the Midwest, with Bennett's roots in North Carolina playing an important role in this notable choice of priorities. In recognition of its additional duties in fields such as water conservation, mined resources, and pollution control, it was renamed Natural Resources Conservation Service in 1995.

Early concepts of SOIL CONSERVATION focused on comprehensive land-use planning. However, these concepts, born out of the NEW DEAL penchant for planning, were quickly abandoned for lack of support, leaving the Soil Conservation Service without a clear political direction. With field personnel struggling to enlist the support of often reluctant farmers, monetary incentives became the instrument of choice. Subsidies such as cheap lime and equipment with low leasing rates attracted farmers to the SCS. Early work often focused on ground-moving activities as many SCS officials had to create labor for Civilian Conservation Corps camps.

The SCS increasingly worked through regional (often countywide) Soil Conservation Districts, of which there were more than 300 by 1940, more than 2,000 a decade later, and more than 3,000 by 1969, constituting 99 percent of all U.S. farms and 97 percent of the agricultural land by then. At the same time, a network of research stations began to study the many open questions about the causes of erosion and means of control. Since the second Agricultural Adjustment Act of 1936 provided for payments to farmers who reduced "soil depleting" crops, there were actually two federal programs side by side that sought to fight erosion, resulting in a significant amount of friction and ill-fated attempts to coordinate the two lines of activity.

After Bennett's retirement in 1951, federal soil conservation policy became even more diffuse, though the fight against erosion ultimately remained the agency's prime mission. The general trend was for the campaign against erosion to merge with efforts to boost agricultural production. An especially controversial part of SCS work was the cultivation of WETLANDS. To their consternation, SCS officials found themselves under fire from environmentalists in the late 1960s and early 1970s even though they saw themselves as legitimate heirs of the conservation tradition.

Cotton planting in the South expanded rapidly after the Civil War. Poor farming practices, followed by topsoil erosion, by the early 20th century led to massive gullies in several counties in Georgia. *(Library of Congress)*

In general, erosion problems have received rather little attention from environmentalists, especially compared with other problems of industrialized agriculture such as genetically modified organisms and the use of chemicals. Erosion emerged as a political issue in the 1970s, as did many other environmental concerns, only to disappear from the headlines when the Reagan administration's policies of OPPOSITION TO ENVIRONMENTALISM galvanized environmentalists' attention. Nonetheless, erosion continues to be a problem of astounding proportions. The 1997 National Resources Inventory found that the United States is losing 1.9 billion tons of soil per year through erosion, while estimates of the annual costs of soil erosion for the U.S. economy vary between $30 billion and $44 billion. Stopping this trend and preserving the fertility of America's farmland remain a major challenge for environmental policy in the 21st century. Recent trends toward more soil-sensitive farming techniques such as conservation tillage may provide a glimpse of hope. At the same time, these practices are a reminder that erosion control has the best prospects when it enlists the farmers' personal interest, as conservation tillage often saves the farmer time and energy.

See also AGRICULTURAL TECHNOLOGY; AGRICULTURE, COMMERCIAL; UNITED STATES—DEEP SOUTH; UNITED STATES—MIDWEST; UNITED STATES—TIDEWATER.

Frank Uekoetter

Further Reading

Helms, Douglas, and Susan L. Flader, eds. *The History of Soil and Water Conservation.* Washington, D.C.: Agricultural History Society, 1985.

Simms, D. Harper. *The Soil Conservation Service.* New York: Praeger, 1970.

Troeh, Frederick R., J. Arthur Hobbs, and Roy L. Donahue. *Soil and Water Conservation for Productivity and Environmental Protection.* 4th ed. Upper Saddle River, N.J.: Prentice Hall, 2004.

eugenics

Coined by the British statistician Sir Francis Galton in 1883 to describe a new scientific approach to the improvement of society through the study and control of human heredity, eugenics attracted a wide spectrum of adherents from the late 19th to the mid-20th century. Ranging from the far Left and the far Right, eugenicists included biologists, physicians, industrialists, psychologists, socialists, feminists, and traditionalists. Eugenic societies appeared in nations as diverse as Japan, Italy, Brazil, and Romania. What this heterogeneous group shared was the conviction that social maladies could be addressed through scientific solutions and the application of biological models, especially those derived from the burgeoning field of

GENETICS. By the early 1900s, a eugenics movement was forming in America, propelled by organizations such as the Race Betterment Foundation, founded by the Michigan physician and cereal promoter John Harvey Kellogg, and the Eugenics Record Office, established by the prominent biologist Charles B. Davenport, who defined eugenics in 1911 as "the science of the improvement of the human race by better breeding."

Concomitant to the creation of national and local eugenics organizations in the first several decades of the 20th century, CONGRESS approved eugenically inspired immigration bills, most notably the highly restrictive 1924 National Origins Act. Moreover, during this period, states passed marriage bans and laws for the segregation and sterilization of the "unfit," who included persons who today would be considered developmentally or physically disabled as well as those disenfranchised through racial prejudice, poverty, or illiteracy. Indiana was the first state to pass a eugenic sterilization law, in 1907, followed two years later by Washington and California. In 1927, the U.S. Supreme Court upheld the right of the state forcibly to sterilize inmates and patients in public institutions in the notorious *Buck v. Bell* (274 U.S. 200 [1927]) ruling, which declared Virginia's 1924 sterilization law constitutional. In his oft-quoted majority opinion in this case, Justice Oliver Wendell Holmes declared in reference to the supposedly feebleminded Carrie Buck, her mother, and daughter, all of whom had been forcibly sterilized: "Three generations of imbeciles are enough." By the late 1920s, approximately 30 states had passed eugenic sterilization and marriage laws, most of which were not repealed until the 1960s and 1970s, when a new generation of legislators realized, often with dismay, that such discriminatory and biased statues remained on the books. By that time, more than 60,000 Americans had been sterilized in 33 states.

Beholden to the principle of better breeding, many American eugenicists were as interested in humans as in plants and animals. Indeed, eugenicists often sought to apply lessons from the cultivation of crops and livestock to humans. Applying findings about genetic selection from lower- to higher-order organisms was the aim of the Eugenics Section of the American Breeders' Association, formed in 1906 by Davenport, the Stanford University chancellor and ichthyologist David Starr Jordan, and the renowned "plant wizard" Luther Burbank. Eugenicists believed they could guide the processes of natural selection and adaptation to improve and even perfect a wide range of species. Initially, eugenicists believed that betterment could be achieved largely through positive environmental inputs. For plants, this meant hybridization and horticulture to produce vigorous organisms, examples of which were Burbank's daisy and potato orchards. For humans, betterment included good nutrition, disciplined calisthenics, and well-selected mating and marriage, which were promoted by Kellogg at the Battle Creek Sanitarium in Michigan. Over time, however,

Mendelian theories of hereditary inheritance, which posited that genetic traits were inalterably transmitted from parent to offspring, became the central tenets of American eugenics. Thus, by the 1920s, the American eugenics program revolved around efforts to prevent the propagation of those labeled "unfit" and encourage the procreation of those identified as "fit." Because many eugenicists thought there were strong associations between defectiveness and race or ethnicity, they supported controlling the entry of immigrant groups, such as Italian, Poles, Eastern European Jews, and Mexicans, just to name a few, whom they considered biologically inferior.

Often overlooked in historical scholarship is the strong link between the environmental movement and eugenics. Yet, leading eugenicists were charter members of several of the country's most important conservationist and preservationist organizations, such as the SIERRA CLUB, founded 1891, and the Save-the-Redwoods League, founded in 1918. These early environmentalists saw the protection of particular plants and animals, usually species categorized as native, ancient, or endangered, as crucial to the maintenance of a pristine and unpolluted WILDERNESS. Furthermore, they often equated the choicest plants, such as the *Sequoia sempervirens*, California REDWOODS, with white American stock, both of which eugenicists thought were imperiled by infiltrating inferior and foreign types and in grave need of biological preservation. After WORLD WAR II, this relationship endured as an alliance between environmentalist groups and population control advocates. Although the era of coercive eugenics, exemplified by compulsory sterilization, closed in the 1970s, questions related to better breeding, species superiority, and the genetic modification of living organisms remain central to the way Americans think about the environment and MAINSTREAM ENVIRONMENTALISM. For example, in recent years, the Sierra Club has been criticized for supporting xenophobic policies that blame environmental degradation on undocumented immigrants, particularly those hailing from Mexico and Central America.

See also BIOTECHNOLOGY; DARWIN, CHARLES; EVOLUTION; FRUIT AND VEGETABLE PRODUCTION; IMMIGRATION; RACISM AND DISCRIMINATION; SPECIES, ENDANGERED; SPECIES, EXOTIC AND INVASIVE; SPECIES, INDIGENOUS.

Alexandra Minna Stern

Further Reading
Brechin, Gray. "Conserving the Race: Natural Aristocracies, Eugenics, and the U.S. Conservation Movement." *Antipode* 28, no. 3 (1996): 229–245.

Kevles, Daniel J. *In the Name of Eugenics: Genetics and the Uses of Human Heredity.* Rev. ed. Cambridge, Mass.: Harvard University Press, 1995.

Kimmelman, Barbara. "The American Breeders' Association: Genetics and Eugenics in an Agricultural Context, 1903–13." *Social Studies of Science* 13 (1983): 163–204.

Stern, Alexandra Minna. *Eugenic Nation: Faults and Frontiers of Better Breeding in Modern America.* Berkeley: University of California Press, 2005.

Everglades

The Everglades is the largest subtropical WILDERNESS in the United States. It is a green, flat, mostly treeless complex of marshes extending from Lake Okeechobee on the north to Florida Bay on the south, an area of more than 7 million acres across five Florida counties. This unique and delicate ecosystem serves as a habitat for diverse species of plant and animal life.

The story of the Everglades is one of conflict between economic development and ecological preservation. Human penetration of the Everglades began in the mid-19th century as the U.S. military sought to drive out the Seminole Indians who had taken refuge in the South Florida interior. Throughout the 1800s, settlers tried to drain and reclaim the land in order to put it to profitable uses. Reclaimed lands were found to be very fertile and particularly well adapted to the growing of sugarcane, oranges, and garden vegetables. Economic development was further encouraged by mining, road building, and railroad interests. Barron G. Collier (1873–1939) made the Everglades the headquarters for his Tamiami Trail Roadbuilding Company in the 1920s. The Tamiami Trail linked Tampa and MIAMI, FLORIDA, crossing the state through the Everglades. Roads themselves functioned as dams of a kind, impeding the water flow from north to south. As roads improved, more people ventured inland. Burgeoning land development and speculation schemes caused great damage to the natural environment. After 1928, engineering projects shifted from drainage and land reclamation to flood control. New CANALS were dug, old canals deepened, and dikes, levees, and pumping stations added.

These projects made it possible for cities to grow, but natural areas were severely affected by reduced and arbitrary water flow. Farms and cities threatened the existence of the Everglades, taking the water this complex ecosystem needs to survive. Most damaging was the impact of heightened SUGAR cultivation. The water table was lowered to stimulate sugarcane growth, and nutrient-laden water that flowed south from the fields altered the vegetation. Massive doses of phosphorus-based FERTILIZER used on the sugarcane fields caused extensive damage to the ecosystem. Phosphorus causes algae blooms in waterways and decreases the dissolved oxygen for aquatic life. Human control of the water supply had adverse effects on animal life, especially those creatures with specific adaptations to alternating wet and dry seasons.

The dangers of unfettered development and the harmful effects of dredging and draining became apparent by the early 20th century. Members of the Florida Federation of Women's Clubs spearheaded early preservation efforts. In the 1920s, the landscape architect Ernest Coe (1866–1951) began a campaign to convince CONGRESS to designate the Everglades as a national park. He was joined by the journalist MARJORY STONEMAN DOUGLAS, who, in her 1947 book, *Everglades: River of Grass,* encouraged Americans to view the Everglades as much more than "just a swamp." Their goals were realized in 1947, when President HARRY TRUMAN set aside more than 2 million acres as Everglades National Park.

Today, much of the Everglades is protected as a national park, a national wildlife refuge, and water conservation areas. Restoration and protection ventures are complex joint initiatives among a variety of federal, state, local, and tribal partners. The largest of all initiatives is known as the Comprehensive Everglades Restoration Plan, or CERP, a 30-year, $10.5 billion joint federal-state partnership that is the world's largest ecosystem restoration project of its kind. CERP has more than 60 major components. Its goals are to improve and sustain the distribution of water throughout the Everglades, to protect natural wildlife and plants, to reintroduce native species, to provide flood control and water supply for a growing population, and to maintain the quality of life for South Florida residents.

See also ECOLOGICAL RESTORATION; ENGINEERING; FRUIT AND VEGETABLE PRODUCTION; NATIONAL PARK SERVICE; SPECIES, ENDANGERED; UNITED STATES—DEEP SOUTH; UNITED STATES—GULF COAST; URBANIZATION; WETLANDS.

Marie Marmo Mullaney

Further Reading
Douglas, Marjory S. *Everglades: River of Grass.* Rev. ed. Sarasota, Fla.: Pineapple Press, 1988.
Grunwald, Michael. *The Swamp: The Everglades, Florida, and the Politics of Paradise.* New York: Simon & Schuster, 2006.
Public Affairs Office. "Evolution of Ecosystem Restoration Efforts." National Park Service. Available online. URL: http://www.nps.gov/archive/ever/eco/restore.htm. Accessed October 8, 2008.
SFWMD. "CERP/Everglades Restoration." South Florida Water Management District. Available online. URL: http://www.sfwmd.gov/site/index.php?id=20. Accessed October 8, 2008.

evolution

Although many American fundamentalists continue to reject the theory of evolution, it has remained essential to scientific understandings of the natural world in the 20th and 21st centuries. The theory of evolution has underpinned environmentalists' arguments for increased BIODIVERSITY and SUSTAINABLE DEVELOPMENT.

Over long periods, life has slowly branched out from its beginning as a collection of single-celled organisms to represent what we now recognize as a diverse tree of life. Evolution is the scientific fact that life-forms have descended from a common ancestor, diversifying through mutation and the inheritance of successful adaptations. Most genetic mutations are harmful, but some have the potential to help an organism survive longer and, therefore, reproduce more successfully. Successful reproduction allows the organism to pass its genes to future generations. An example of a helpful mutation could be a gene that increases the length of a gazelle's legs, which makes it a faster runner that more easily escapes predators.

Although theories of evolution have existed since the Greek philosopher Anaximander (ca. 610–ca. 546 B.C.E.) conceived of the various species springing forth from the seas to dwell on land, it was not until the mid-19th century, when CHARLES DARWIN introduced the mechanism of evolution, that the idea was raised from speculation in the field of natural philosophy to scientific theory. That mechanism is natural selection. It states that through the process of descent with modification, species are able to increase their ability to survive in their environments. Life-forms are able to produce many more offspring than their habitats will support, but in a competitive environment, only the fittest are able to live long enough to breed. Competition occurs on various levels: Within a species, individuals compete for territory; at the level of sexual selection, males (usually) compete to secure female mates; and within an ecosystem, various species can compete for the same food source. Thus, the struggle for existence ensures that only the best adapted life-forms are able to carry on their lines, passing their genetic traits to their offspring.

THE THEORY OF EVOLUTION AND MODERN SCIENCE

The noted geneticist Theodosius Dobzhansky (1900–75) once remarked, "Nothing in biology makes sense except in light of evolution" (1973). Similarly, the advancement of modern evolutionary theory owes many debts to the field of genetics. Inspired by experiments by Gregor Mendel (1822–84) on the hereditary traits of peas, later scientists identified the genetic basis of transmission and inheritance, allowing them to compile vast amounts of experimental data to support Darwin's theory.

Most notable in the history of modern evolutionary theory is the discovery of DNA by James Watson (1928–   ) and Francis Crick (1916–2004) in 1953. This insight allowed scientists to explain the mechanism of genetic transmission—that is, how information is passed from the individuals of one generation to their offspring. With the publication of *The Selfish Gene,* in 1975, the Oxford ethologist Richard Dawkins (1941–   ) completed the synthesis of these two fields in regard to evolutionary theory by promoting the idea that natural selection occurs as a function of genes attempting to replicate, and that their ability to do so depends greatly on the successful survival and reproduction of the "machines" (life-forms, including humans) they inhabit.

After publishing his landmark *On the Origin of Species* in 1859, Darwin theorized the common descent of man and ape

Darwin's theory of natural selection—that the survival and reproductive success of individuals or groups best adjusted to their environment led to the perpetuation of genetic qualities best suited to that particular environment—argued in his 1859 book *On the Origin of Species,* sparked many antievolutionist sentiments. Titled *The Darwin Club,* this 1915 India ink–over-pencil drawing by Rea Irvin is set inside a grandly decorated men's club where distinguished-looking, elderly gentlemen interact with monkeys.   *(Library of Congress)*

in his second major work, *The Descent of Man* (1871), but it was not until the human genome was sequenced, in 2003, that scientists could be absolutely certain, no matter how staggering the amount of observational evidence, that human beings shared a common ancestor with other hominids. Through this study and those that followed it, we have learned that while humans share about 99.5 percent of the same genes with humans of other "races," making the idea of race a dubious one at best, we also share about 98.5 percent of our genes with chimpanzees. Evidence this strong allows scientists to feel certain that the idea of a common ancestor in the recent (evolutionary) past did indeed link humans and chimpanzees.

"CONTROVERSY" IN THE UNITED STATES

Some Americans have objected to the theory of evolution because it makes humans only one species among the approximately 50 million that have been fortunate enough to survive through successful adaptation and reproduction. This view makes it difficult to argue for the special status some religious believers feel humans deserve. Some criticisms of evolution involve the term *theory* itself, mistaking the general use of the word (representing a common opinion) as interchangeable with a scientific theory (which has not been falsified by contradictory evidence). Other objections refer vaguely to a controversy over evolution's existence. However, no such controversy exists within reputable scientific circles.

In the United States, antievolutionist sentiments stem primarily from the views of fundamentalist Christian groups, who seek legal restrictions against the teaching of evolution in public schools. The most famous attempt at suppressing evolutionary theory occurred in 1925, with the passage of the Butler Act in Tennessee, forbidding the teaching of any theory that contradicts biblical creationism. The SCOPES TRIAL represent the conflict this act caused between American evolutionists and creationists, moving the debate into public view nationwide.

Although the U.S. Supreme Court ruled that teaching creationism (that a God or gods created the species as they now exist) in public schools violated the First Amendment and was unconstitutional in *Edwards v. Aguillard* (482 U.S. 578 [1987]), many school boards have felt pressured to introduce religious ideas into their science curricula. This pressure is primarily from the intelligent design movement—an attempt by those who believe in the literal truth of the book of Genesis in the Bible to pass creationism off as legitimate science.

Arguments for intelligent design rest primarily on discredited scientific and philosophical theories of the past. One such argument repeats what William Paley (1743–1805) put forth in his *Natural Theology* (1802) regarding a hypothetical watch one finds while hiking. Put simply, because the watch is so complex, Paley argued that it must be designed. Nature is much more complex than the watch; therefore, the best explanation for nature's existence is that it, too, is designed. However, this does not follow. When arguing from likelihood, evolution by means of natural selection is the best explanation for the complexity of life on Earth, because it corresponds with all of the available physical evidence.

Other arguments for intelligent design presuppose the perfection of bodily organs, such as the human eye, in order to necessitate the existence of a designer (God), but the human eye in fact represents a shoddy "design." The retina, for instance, developed in a way that forces us to look through the wiring that carries visual signals, causing a blind spot in our vision. Intelligent design advocates also frequently refer to a supposed lack of transitional forms—fossil remains that link the evolution of earlier species to a later form—but paleontological museums display many transitional forms for public viewing. One example is the *Archaeopteryx,* a feathered, gliding lizard whose discovery provides a clear example of how dinosaurs evolved into birds.

ENVIRONMENTAL AND ECOLOGICAL IMPLICATIONS

Rarely in history has North America seen such a wide variety of life-forms as it now holds. So why are environmentalists concerned with the potential extinction of a few species? The desire to maintain BIODIVERSITY stems from the acknowledgment that all species are a part of wider ECOSYSTEMS. One might imagine an ecosystem as a spider's web. Were one strand of the web suddenly to disappear, the structure of what remains would be made weaker, possibly causing other strands to break. If too many strands snapped, the entire structure could collapse. In terms of this analogy, the impending collapse of the web would represent sudden mass extinctions within that ecosystem.

EXTINCTION in the United States has occurred mainly through loss of habitat, the primary cause of which is the encroachment of humankind. Humanity has many reasons for its interference in fragile ecosystems, including LOGGING, MINING, and farming. Other pressures result from phenomena such as URBAN SPRAWL and toxic waste longevity. A well-known example of species extinction in the United States is the heath hen, whose range spread south from New Hampshire to Virginia. The heath hen was hunted to extinction on the mainland; the last surviving group, located on the island of Martha's Vineyard, Massachusetts, came under government protection in 1908, with the establishment of a heath hen reserve there. However, a combination of circumstances, including a fire, in-breeding, and disease, completed the human-initiated destruction of a population once ubiquitous in the eastern United States.

At face value, it would seem that extinction due to human encroachment would be most troubling in the Tropics, where biodiversity is highest. However, the extinction of one species has an even greater impact at higher latitudes, where the loss of a single life-form can cause a great blow to an ecosystem's stability. While a solitary species might compete with many others in the Tropics to fulfill similar roles, there is often only one species in colder climates that is adapted to do a necessary job.

There are various reasons to be concerned about the extinction of species in the United States, not least of which is aesthetic. Many Americans worry that without some CONSERVATION they will be unable to share the experience and wonders of the natural world with future generations. More pressing to politicians and business leaders is the economic cost of extinction. One can reasonably argue that beyond intrinsic value, all life has financial value as well. This value is expressed in various forms: medicine, building material, and FOOD, to name a few.

Some environmental lobbies argue in WASHINGTON, D.C., that there must be a sustainable way to exploit natural resources that would not be as destructive as the short-term gains sought today. Sustainable practices would promote greater levels of global health than current schemes to extract value from nature. A growing number of politicians and government leaders now recognize that the continued use of unsustainable practices in extracting value from nature could not only cause mass extinctions of other plant and animal species but also lead to the downfall of our own.

See also AGRICULTURE, COMMERCIAL; AGRICULTURE, SUBSISTENCE; BOTANY; BRYAN, WILLIAM JENNINGS; CARCINOGENS, POISONS, AND TOXINS; ECOLOGY; ENVIRONMENTALISM, MAINSTREAM; HEALTH AND MEDICINE; SUSTAINABILITY; WASTE DISPOSAL AND MANAGEMENT; ZOOLOGY.

Alex C. Parrish

Further Reading
Bates, Marston, and Philip S. Humphrey, eds. *The Darwin Reader.* New York: Scribner, 1956.
Dawkins, Richard. *The Selfish Gene.* 30th anniversary ed. Oxford: Oxford University Press, 2006.
Leakey, Richard, and Roger Lewin. *The Sixth Extinction: Patterns of Life and the Future of Humankind.* New York: Doubleday, 1995.
Smith, John Maynard. *The Theory of Evolution.* Cambridge: Cambridge University Press, 1993.
Wilson, Edward O. *Sociobiology: The Abridged Edition.* Cambridge, Mass.: Harvard University Press, 1980.

exotic and invasive species   *See* SPECIES, EXOTIC AND INVASIVE.

extinction

The term *extinction,* as it relates to biological organisms, refers to the termination or dying out of a species. Mass extinction refers to the termination of a number of species over a relatively short period over a large, even global, area.

A number of factors directly or indirectly may cause a species to become extinct, including genetic change, habitat loss, and human influence. Genetic change may occur through genetic drift, inbreeding depression, or interbreeding and hybridization. The population size of a species influences genetic change. Small populations risk genetic drift or inbreeding depression, both of which make a species more susceptible to loss in the event of natural DISASTERS. With genetic drift, a random gene may not be passed from parent to offspring, or the gene may mutate and be passed on to progeny. Although larger populations can more easily recover from the gene loss through reproduction, smaller populations may lose the gene permanently because there are fewer individuals to pass it on. The gene loss and gene mutations may contribute to a species's extinction if the characteristics of the species are weakened. With inbreeding depression, recessive genes are more likely to be passed on in small populations because of inbreeding. If the gene passed on is deleterious to the species's survival, the species becomes more vulnerable to extinction. Genetic change in a species can also occur through interbreeding or hybridization with a nonnative species, where the species cross or hybrid eventually replaces the original species in the habitat.

Habitat loss or modification also influences whether a species becomes extinct. A species whose habitat becomes unsuitable for its continued existence may die out unless it finds other suitable habitat or adapts to the change. Although habitat loss or modification may result from natural causes (e.g., destruction by FIRE or other natural disaster), human impact is a large cause. Human development worldwide plays a major role in the loss of species habitat. For example, the construction of highways and other roadways often fragments habitat, dividing species populations and making harmful genetic changes in the species more likely. Habitat is also destroyed by DEFORESTATION—the clearing of wooded areas for residential or commercial development, agricultural use, or timber products—and by pollution, which can make a species's habitat become toxic and unable to support the species.

Humans can also directly or indirectly cause the extinction of species by overhunting and by introducing alien species into other species' habitats. Overhunting can lead to extinction where populations are reduced to such an extent that recovery is impossible. For example, the passenger pigeon was once the most common bird in the United States. It became extinct by 1914 through overhunting and habitat loss. Alien species (nonnative animals or plants) can doom native species in a habitat to extinction in several ways. Because alien species generally do not have any natural predators in the new habitat, the alien species may outcompete the native species and take over the habitat. Introduced from Asia in the 19th century as a decorative plant and for EROSION control in the American South, KUDZU flourished, crowding out FORESTS and farms as it now covers some 7 million acres in the region. Finally, native species may become prey for the alien species or be detrimentally impacted by disease carried by the alien species.

Extinction is a part of the natural progression of a species. Species not affected by human activity generally die out at "background" extinction rates—that is, random species dying out at low rates. However, as shown by the fossil record, throughout its geologic history, Earth has undergone a number of periods when the extinction rate has gone up in both frequency of extinctions and number of species affected. These "mass extinctions" were widespread, with species across the globe dying out. Although there were several more episodes of high levels of extinctions (minor or lesser extinction events), scientists generally agree on the existence of five major mass extinctions: the End-Ordovician, the Late Devonian, the End-Permian, the End-Triassic, and the End-Cretaceous. Theories for each of the mass extinctions vary, but they generally include climate change or sea-level fluctuations, asteroid impacts, volcanic eruptions, and continental drift and plate tectonics.

The End-Ordovician event, sometimes known as the Ordovician-Silurian extinction event, saw two periods of extinction during a 10-million-year period beginning about 450 million years ago. The event had a massive impact on the diversity of marine organisms, including graptolites, conodonts, brachiopods, and trilobites, with losses of 26 percent of marine families and about 60 percent of marine genera. The Late Devonian extinction involved a number of minor extinction events followed by a major mass extinction at the boundary between the Frasnian Age and the Famennian Age, around 375 million years ago. As did the End-Ordovician event, the Late Devonian event affected many warm-water species, especially the bottom-dwelling corals and reefs, brachiopods, trilobites, and a variety of other marine organisms including fishes. In all, the Late Devonian event saw the loss of about 22 percent of all families and more than 57 percent of all genera. The End-Permian event is the largest mass extinction event in geologic history, occurring about 251 million years ago, at the end of the Permian Period. The event affected marine and land species, extinguishing 51 percent of all families and about 82 percent of all genera. Scientific estimates of species-level extinctions during this event range as high as 95 percent of marine species and 70 percent of land species. Particularly affected were the rugose and tabulate corals, which died out completely, and other marine organisms affected in previous events. Land species affected by the End-Permian event included all large herbivores, some insects, and some plants. The End-Triassic (or Triassic-Jurassic) extinction event occurred about 200 million years ago. This event affected about 22 percent of all families and 53 percent of all genera, with significant impacts to bottom-dwelling bivalves and brachiopods. On land, important regional extinctions of plants have been documented as well as of some insects. Importantly, a number of REPTILES and large amphibians became extinct, to be ecologically replaced with dinosaurs. Finally, the End-Cretaceous (or Cretaceous-Tertiary or K-T) extinction occurred 65 million years ago. During this event, the Earth lost 16 percent of all families and 47 percent of all genera. Marine extinctions included two planktonic groups and several marine invertebrates. On land, all dinosaurs and some plant species became extinct.

Many scientists believe that Earth is now suffering a human-caused sixth mass extinction event since extinction rates have become highly elevated since the appearance of humans on Earth. Megafauna have been particularly affected, but extinctions of species of all sizes have occurred. An accurate count of modern extinction loss is impossible because the full number of species is unknown; however, estimates of the current extinction rate range from 1,000 to 1,500 times the background rate. Although many scientists believe this elevation is due to humans, other factors such as CLIMATE CHANGE may have an impact as well.

To combat the increased number of extinctions, a number of countries have enacted laws and treaties to protect species that are endangered with extinction. In the United States, the federal law enacted to protect and help endangered species recover is the ENDANGERED SPECIES ACT OF 1973. Most states also have laws designed to protect native species. ECOLOGICAL RESTORATION projects have increased some populations, such as the BISON and gray WOLVES, on the brink of extinction, but other human activities continue to leave extinction rates at high levels.

See also BIODIVERSITY; DARWIN, CHARLES; ENDANGERED SPECIES; EVOLUTION; GENETICS; NATURAL HISTORY; SPECIES, EXOTIC AND INVASIVE; SPECIES, INDIGENOUS; VOLCANOES.

Francesca Ortiz

Further Reading

Ehrlich, Paul, and Anne Ehrlich. *Extinction: The Causes and Consequences of the Disappearance of Species.* New York: Random House, 1981.

Erwin, Douglas H. *Extinction: How Life on Earth Nearly Ended 250 Million Years Ago.* Princeton, N.J.: Princeton University Press, 2006.

Hallam, A., and P. B. Wignall. *Mass Extinctions and Their Aftermath.* Oxford: Oxford University Press, 1997.

Hallam, Tony. *Catastrophes and Lesser Calamities: The Causes of Mass Extinctions.* Oxford: Oxford University Press, 2004.

Martin, Paul S. *Twilight of the Mammoths: Ice Age Extinctions and the Rewilding of America.* Berkeley: University of California Press, 2005.

The Passenger Pigeon
John James Audubon (1844)

Once one of the most common birds in North America, the passenger pigeon moved from abundance toward extinction during the 19th century. Most scholars attribute their disappearance to two factors: the loss of habitat and, more importantly, the targeted hunting of the pigeons as a cheap food source for slaves and the poor. In 1844, the noted painter and ornithologist John James Audubon described the bird and its "astonishing" movements as they filled the sky "in countless multitudes." The last passenger pigeon is thought to have died in 1914.

Their great power of flight enables them to survey and pass over an astonishing extent of country in a very short time. This is proved by facts well known. Thus, Pigeons have been killed in the neighbourhood of New York, with their crops full of rice, which they must have collected in the fields of Georgia and Carolina, these districts being the nearest in which they could possibly have procured a supply of that kind of food. As their power of digestion is so great that they will decompose food entirely in twelve hours, they must in this case have travelled between three and four hundred miles in six hours, which shows their speed to be at an average of about one mile in a minute. A velocity such as this would enable one of these birds, were it so inclined, to visit the European continent in less than three days. . . .

The multitudes of Wild Pigeons in our woods are astonishing. Indeed, after having viewed them so often, and under so many circumstances, I even now feel inclined to pause, and assure myself that what I am going to relate is fact. Yet I have seen it all, and that too in the company of persons who, like myself, were struck with amazement. In the autumn of 1813, I left my house at Henderson, on the banks of the Ohio, on my way to Louisville. In passing over the Barrens a few miles beyond Hardensburgh, I observed the Pigeons flying from north-east to south-west, in greater numbers that I thought I had ever seen them before, and feeling an inclination to count the flocks that might pass within the reach of my eye in one hour, I dismounted, seated myself on an eminence, and began to mark with my pencil, making a dot for every flock that passed. In a short time finding the task which I had undertaken impracticable, as the birds poured in in countless multitudes, I rose, and counting the dots then put down, found that 163 had been made in twenty-one minutes. I travelled on, and still met more the farther I proceeded. The air was literally filled with Pigeons; the light of noon-day was obscured as by an eclipse; the dung fell in spots, not unlike melting flakes of snow; and the continued buzz of wings had a tendency to lull my senses to repose.

Source: John James Audubon. *The Birds of America*, Vol. 5. New York: J. J. Audubon, 1844, 26–27.

extractive industries   *See* LABOR, EXTRACTIVE INDUSTRIES.

exurbia

Exurbia describes the communities that are located beyond suburban areas and often outside city boundaries. Coined by Auguste C. Spectorsky in his 1955 book *The Exurbanites*, the term originally referred to small communities that developed in rural areas, which allowed wealthy residents to build large homes and commute from home to work. Exurbia, although not easily definable visually, is now generally considered the small, outer-edge communities that are neither fully suburban nor fully rural but that in time may become fully suburban as the outlying areas of cities continue to grow.

Exurban areas are noted for lower-cost housing, often populated with middle-class families with children. This classification, however, is not absolute, as exurban areas also include higher-priced homes for more wealthy residents. Although some residents commute to city centers for work, many exurban areas now include office parks. Other exurban characteristics include the nearby location of discount chain stores and shopping malls. Exurbia often lacks open space, community meeting centers, and other places for cultural activities.

Estimates from the Brookings Institution indicate that about 10.8 million people lived in the exurban areas of large metropolitan areas of the United States in the year 2000, with exurban areas growing at more than double the rate of cities in the previous decade. Not all regions of the United States, however, are as exurban as others. Southern populations, for example, tend to be more exurban than those in other areas of the country.

Exurban growth is often seen as poor planning that may have negative environmental consequences. Building practices tend to include low-density development that converts agricultural lands to residential use and fragments or destroys habitats. In addition, because of greater reliance on automobile transportation for commuters, higher exhaust emissions can adversely affect air quality. Metropolitan areas may also suffer with exurban development because the increased infrastructure and public service costs are not always offset by the tax revenues garnered by newly developed areas. These negative impacts will probably increase as populations continue to move outward from city centers, converting former exurban areas into suburban areas and pushing new lines of exurbia even farther into rural areas.

See also HOUSING, PRIVATE; SUBURBANIZATION; URBAN SPRAWL; ZONING.

Francesca Ortiz

Further Reading
Berube, Alan, Audrey Singer, Jill H. Wilson, and William H. Frey. "Finding Exurbia: America's Fast-Growing Communities at the Metropolitan Fringe." Brookings Institution. Available online. URL: http://www.brookings.edu/metro/pubs/20061017_exurbia.pdf. Accessed October 18, 2006.
Daniels, Tom. *When City and Country Collide: Managing Growth in the Metropolitan Fringe.* Washington, D.C.: Island Press, 1999.
Gillham, Oliver. *The Limitless City: A Primer on the Urban Sprawl Debate.* Washington, D.C.: Island Press, 2002.

F

Faulkner, William (1897–1962) *author*

Hailed by many critics as one of the 20th century's greatest novelists, William Faulkner is best known for experimental classics such as *The Sound and the Fury* (1929), *As I Lay Dying* (1930), and *Absalom, Absalom!* (1936). These works display his modernist hallmarks, including stream-of-consciousness narration, long sentences, multiple perspectives, and time shifts. Throughout his career, however, the Mississippi author used many styles and genres, ranging from American

Portrait of William Faulkner taken by the photographer Carl Van Vechten, December 11, 1954 *(Library of Congress)*

gothic in *Sanctuary* (1931) to "who done it" detective fiction in *Intruder in the Dust* (1948). As did Shakespeare, he often successfully blended the tragic and the comic.

Faulkner also created one of American LITERATURE's most famous fictional landscapes—Yoknapatawpha County, the setting for most of his works. Yoknapatawpha is the literary derivative of Lafayette County, Mississippi, where Faulkner spent most of his life. Before the U.S. CIVIL WAR (1861–65), Lafayette was concurrently prosperous and undeveloped; cotton PLANTATIONS and slave labor buoyed a wealthy planter class, and the "Big Woods" stretching east from the Mississippi Delta constituted a vast WILDERNESS. War and RECONSTRUCTION crushed the county's economy, however, as did COTTON's deleterious effects on the soil. Extensive timbering and industrialization, alongside exploitative SHARECROPPING practices and corrupt politics, contributed to Lafayette's decline.

In the Yoknapatawpha novels, Faulkner captures this aura of decay. He chronicles his fictional county's history from the antebellum period to the GREAT DEPRESSION and beyond. Environmental destruction often provides a backdrop for his explorations of evil, racism, dishonesty, and greed. In *Go Down, Moses* (1942), the aging hunter Ike McCaslin reflects on a "land across which there came now no scream of panther but instead the long hooting of locomotives." In *Light in August* (1932), Lena Grove wanders across a South pockmarked by abandoned lumber mills, scenes "of profound and peaceful desolation, unplowed, untilled, gutting slowly into red and choked ravines." Faulkner's fiction often intertwines the decay of society and nature. In interviews, he frequently described his works' philosophical core as man's struggle between his conscience and his environment.

William Faulkner, the eldest son of Murry and Maud Falkner, was born on September 25, 1897, in New Albany, Mississippi. He added the *u* to his last name when he became a published author. Faulkner's family moved to Oxford—the Lafayette County seat and home of the University of Mississippi ("Ole Miss")—in 1902. Despite lengthy stays in Europe; LOS ANGELES, CALIFORNIA; NEW ORLEANS, LOUISIANA; and NEW YORK CITY, Faulkner maintained a residence in Oxford for the rest of his life. He never finished high school and indeed showed little interest in formal academics, but he read widely and began writing at a young age. Near the end of WORLD WAR I (1914–18) Faulkner briefly enlisted in the Royal Air Force, training in Toronto, Canada, and receiving a discharge that same year.

After an unsuccessful stint as a student at Ole Miss, and an even less successful career as its postmaster, Faulkner left for Europe in 1925 and returned late that year. The time abroad further stimulated his imagination and desire to write, and he published his first novel, *Soldier's Pay,* in 1926. This began a prolific period in Faulkner's intellectual career, during which he published nearly a book a year until 1942. It also began a busy time in his personal life. He married Estelle Oldham Franklin—a former childhood sweetheart—in 1929 and purchased Rowan Oak, an estate near Oxford, the following year. He later purchased a large farm in Lafayette County, with agriculture joining hunting, horseback riding, sailing, and flying as his primary pastimes. While Faulkner's marriage proved unhappy, aggravating lifelong problems with alcoholism, the couple never divorced. Critics were initially wary of Faulkner's experimental style, but he eventually gained their respect and its attendant financial security. When needed, however, he bolstered his income by working as a Hollywood screenwriter.

Later in life, Faulkner became more of a public intellectual, representing the United States on diplomatic trips to South America and Japan. He received the Nobel Prize in literature in 1949, optimistically claiming in his speech accepting the award that "man will not merely endure: he will prevail." He continued sporadically to publish fiction, which while still formidable, was not of his previous quality. In 1957, he became writer in residence at the University of Virginia in Charlottesville. His daughter and grandchildren lived there, and he enjoyed fox hunting in surrounding Albemarle County. On July 6, 1962, in Byhalia, Mississippi, Faulkner died of a heart attack. He left behind a significant literary legacy, influencing writers ranging from Flannery O'Connor and Toni Morrison to Jose Luis Borges and Albert Camus.

See also MISSISSIPPI RIVER; UNITED STATES—DEEP SOUTH.

Steven E. Knepper

Further Reading
Blotner, Joseph L. *Faulkner: A Biography.* 2 vols. New York: Random House, 1974.
Buell, Lawrence. *Writing for an Endangered World: Literature, Culture, and Environment in the U.S. and Beyond.* Cambridge, Mass.: Harvard University Press, 2001.
Kartiganer, Donald, and Ann J. Abadie, eds. *Faulkner and the Natural World.* Oxford: University Press of Mississippi, 1999.
Parini, Jay. *One Matchless Time: A Life of William Faulkner.* New York: HarperCollins, 2004.
Urgo, Joseph, and Ann J. Abadie, eds. *Faulkner and the Ecology of the South.* University Press of Mississippi, 2005.

federalism

Federalism is the division of powers between the federal and state governments under the U.S. Constitutional system. As a general matter, the federal government has only the limited powers provided by the U.S. CONSTITUTION, while the states have more general powers. The balance of powers between the federal and state governments has shifted back and forth throughout American history.

Throughout the late 18th and 19th centuries, the balance of powers tilted in the direction of the states, while the federal government remained limited in both authority and resources. A shift began in the early 20th century, and President FRANKLIN D. ROOSEVELT's NEW DEAL grew the federal government into a major spending and regulatory force during the 1930s. The New Deal also changed Americans' expectations, as they began to rely on the federal government, rather than their state governments, to solve economic and social problems. The CIVIL RIGHTS MOVEMENT of the 1960s, followed by other social movements in the 1970s, continued to focus on the federal government to cure society's ills. However, with the election of President RONALD REAGAN in 1980 and the growth of CONSERVATISM in the latter decades of the 20th century, the expansion of the federal government was questioned on legal, political, and social grounds.

Federalism is an important concept in American environmental policy. The U.S. Constitution presumes that regulatory power will rest primarily with the states, and until the 1970s, states were the primary source of environmental policy. However, the landmark environmental laws of the 1970s, such as the CLEAN AIR ACT and CLEAN WATER ACT, gave the federal government a central role in environmental protection. These laws rely heavily on cooperative federalism to achieve their goals. Cooperative federalism uses a federal-state partnership, in which the federal government sets national environmental standards for the states to administer and enforce. The federal government also provides research, funding, and expertise to assist the states in their administration of the federal environmental laws.

The concept of federalism suggests that state governments, not the federal government, should be the primary source of environmental law. However, there are three generally cited justifications for a strong federal role in environmental protection. First, the federal government needs to set minimal standards to prevent states from lowering their environmental standards to attract businesses and economic growth, creating a race to the bottom. Second, many environmental problems cross state lines, and some environmental problems (for example, ozone depletion) are international in scope and, thus, beyond the capacity and jurisdiction of states. Finally, it is argued that the federal government is more sympathetic to environmental protection than the states. These justifications are hotly debated, as there is conflicting evidence on the subject. The debate is also ideological, shaped by conflicting fundamental preferences for federal versus state and local governance that date back to the founding of the republic and the drafting of the U.S. Constitution.

Noah D. Hall

Further Reading

Adler, Jonathan H. "Jurisdictional Mismatch in Environmental Federalism." *New York University Environmental Law Journal* 14 (2005): 130.

Esty, Daniel C. "Revitalizing Environmental Federalism." *Michigan Law Review* 95 (1996): 570.

Hall, Noah D. "Political Externalities, Federalism, and a Proposal for an Interstate Environmental Impact Assessment Policy." *Harvard Environmental Law Review* 32 (2008): 49–94.

Lazarus, Richard J. *The Making of Environmental Law.* Chicago: University of Chicago Press, 2004.

Revesz, Richard L. "Federalism and Environmental Regulation: A Public Choice Analysis." *Harvard Law Review* 115 (2001): 553.

federal law—environmental regulations

On January 1, 1970, President Richard M. Nixon signed the National Environmental Policy Act (NEPA) of 1970 on national television, declaring that the 1970s would be the "decade of the environment." This event precipitated an explosion of legislative activity that ushered in the modern environmental regulatory era. From the signing of NEPA through the end of 1980, Congress enacted virtually all of the major legislation that continues to constitute the modern federal environmental regulatory system in the United States.

The earliest federal environmental legislation focused on the nation's natural resources. During the 18th and 19th centuries, federal legislation primarily promoted development and economic exploitation of natural resources. Public concern for preservation and conservation of natural resources induced a shift in congressional legislative efforts during the late 19th and early 20th centuries. By the mid-20th century, congressional policies favoring preservation, conservation, and management of natural resources were reflected in such statutes as the National Park Service Organic Act of 1916, the Migratory Bird Treaty Act of 1918, the Mineral Leasing Act of 1920, the Taylor Grazing Act of 1934, the Bald and Golden Eagle Protection Act of 1940, and the Submerged Lands Act of 1953.

During the 1960s, Congress continued to advance a strong national interest in resource preservation through enactment of statutes designed to preserve water, land, and wildlife. Particularly important legislation included the Refuge Protection Act of 1962, the Land and Water Conservation Act of 1964, the Wilderness Act of 1964, the National Wildlife Refuge Administration Act of 1966, and the National Wild and Scenic Rivers Act of 1968.

Environmental challenges beyond natural resource preservation proliferated with the growth of major population centers and industrialization in the latter part of the 19th century. By the mid-20th century, Congress began to address threats to environmental quality and public health posed by urban and industrial pollution by enacting statutes encouraging state and local governments to pass regulatory laws to control such problems on their own. The first such statute, the Water Pollution Control Act of 1948, provided financial assistance to states for creation of state water pollution control programs.

Congress increased federal involvement in environmental protection through a series of statutes enacted during the 1950s and 1960s. The Air Pollution Control Act of 1955 and the Water Pollution Control Act Amendments of 1956 authorized additional financial and technical assistance to the states in combating pollution control problems. The Clean Air Act of 1963, the Water Quality Act of 1965, the Clean Water Restoration Act of 1965, and the Air Quality Act of 1967 were among statutes creating an expanded federal role in pollution control by authorizing federal research and the issuance of advisory standards. Despite this substantial increase in federal legislation relating to pollution concerns, congressional policy continued to view direct regulation of urban and industrial pollution as primarily a state and local responsibility.

The decade of the 1960s witnessed a dramatic increase in public concern for the environment. Public environmentalism has roots in the conservationist and preservationist movements of the late 19th and early 20th centuries. However, the modern environmental movement first emerged during the broad national social unrest of the 1960s. Events such as the publication in 1962 of Rachel Carson's *Silent Spring,* which critiqued public health and environmental risks related to pesticide use, and several well-publicized environmental disasters, such as the burning of the Cuyahoga River in Cleveland, Ohio, and oil spills, including the massive Santa Barbara oil spill off the coast of California, energized public alarm over the perceived threats of industrial activities and pollution. By the end of the decade, pollution concerns were at the forefront of public consciousness, and environmental protection had become an important issue in national electoral politics. This increase in public concern, combined with a perception that state laws were ineffective to address pollution problems of interstate dimensions, encouraged the sweeping changes in the federal regulatory role in environmental protection that occurred during the subsequent "environmental decade" of the 1970s.

The signing of NEPA on New Year's Day 1970 mandated that federal governmental agencies begin to consider environmental concerns in making decisions on major federal activities. Creation of the United States Environmental Protection Agency (EPA) and enactment of the Clean Air Act of 1970 followed later that year. Over the next 10 years, Congress enacted more than a dozen additional major fed-

FEDERAL ENVIRONMENTAL LAWS

Title of Act	Year of Passage
National Park Service Organic Act	1916
Migratory Bird Treaty Act	1918
Mineral Leasing Act	1920
Taylor Grazing Act	1934
Bald and Golden Eagle Protection Act	1940
Water Pollution Control Act	1948
Submerged Lands Act	1953
Air Pollution Control Act	1955
Water Pollution Control Act Amendments	1956
Refuge Protection Act	1962
Clean Air Act	1963
Land and Water Conservation Act	1964
Wilderness Act	1964
Water Quality Act	1965
Clean Water Restoration Act	1965
National Wildlife Refuge Administration Act	1966
Air Quality Act	1967
National Wild and Scenic Rivers Act	1968
National Environmental Policy Act	1969
Clean Water Act	1972
Coastal Zone Management Act	1972
Federal Environmental Pesticide Control Act	1972
Endangered Species Act	1973
Safe Drinking Water Act	1974
Resource Conservation and Recovery Act	1976
Toxic Substances Control Act	1976
Comprehensive Environmental Response, Compensation and Liability Act (Superfund)	1980
Emergency Planning and Community Right-to-Know Act	1986
Safe Drinking Water Act	1986
Clean Water Act	1987
Oil Pollution Act	1990
Pollution Prevention Act	1990
Clean Air Act	1990

Note: Over the course of the 20th century, the federal government's laws expanded from the conservation of resources to the preservation of wilderness and animals separate from human interests, to the control and cleanup of pollution and toxic substances.

eral environmental regulatory programs, including notably the CLEAN WATER ACT of 1972, the Coastal Zone Management Act of 1972, the Federal Environmental Pesticide Control Act of 1972, the ENDANGERED SPECIES ACT OF 1973, the Safe Drinking Water Act of 1974, the Resource Conservation and Recovery Act of 1976 (RCRA), the Toxic Substances Control Act of 1976, and the Comprehensive Environmental Response, Compensation and Liability Act of 1980 (CERCLA or SUPERFUND). The vast majority of major environmental legislative programs enacted during this period were passed with broad bipartisan support.

These programs dramatically transformed the federal role in regulating environmental pollution. Instead of primarily providing assistance to state and local governments to control pollution, these statutes mandated a federal framework of national minimal pollution control standards, stringent regulation, permitting requirements, and enforcement. Congress authorized the EPA to oversee the creation, implementation, and enforcement of most of these federal regulatory mandates, with assistance from individual states delegated the authority to administer and enforce the federal standards. Within this federal framework, state and local governments may establish pollution control standards that are more stringent, but not less so, than the federal minimal standards.

Congress expanded and strengthened the federal environmental regulatory system over the course of the following decade, adding new major programs, such as the Emergency Planning and Community Right-to-Know Act of 1986, the Oil Pollution Act of 1990, and the Pollution Prevention Act of 1990, and enacting comprehensive amendments to RCRA in 1984, to the Safe Drinking Water Act and CERCLA in 1986, to the Clean Water Act in 1987, and to the Clean Air Act in 1990. During the decade of the 1990s, federal environmental regulation became a divisive political issue in Congress with aggressive but ultimately unsuccessful pushes to repeal many major federal environmental programs. Federal environmental regulation remains a politically divisive issue in the early 21st century, but the system largely constructed during the 1970s remains in place and is credited with substantial success in reducing pollution and improving environmental quality in many areas around the nation. Critics of federal environmental regulatory programs argue that many critical problems continue to flourish and are insufficiently addressed by the current system.

The current political divisiveness over federal environmental law and regulation is in stark contrast to the bipartisan outlook that largely prevailed during the "environmental decade" of the 1970s. The sources of this divisiveness are numerous and complex. Notable differences include disagreement over such issues as whether the substantial costs of pollution controls on regulated industry outweigh the attendant benefits in environmental protection, whether

more authority over environmental regulation should be shifted from the federal government to state and local control, and the extent to which laws governing natural resource conservation and preservation should interfere with private property rights.

See also ENVIRONMENTAL LAW; JUDICIARY.

David W. Case

Further Reading

Andrews, Richard N. L. *Managing the Environment, Managing Ourselves: A History of American Environmental Policy.* 2d ed. New Haven, Conn.: Yale University Press, 2006.

Coglianese, Cary. "Social Movements, Law, and Society: The Institutionalization of the Environmental Movement." *University of Pennsylvania Law Review* 150, no. 1 (November 2001): 85–118.

Lazarus, Richard J. *The Making of Environmental Law.* Chicago: University of Chicago Press, 2004.

Percival, Robert V., Christopher H. Schroeder, Alan S. Miller, and James P. Leape. *Environmental Regulation: Law, Science, and Policy.* 5th ed. New York: Aspen, 2006.

federal law—Indian policies

Federal Indian law is the set of laws that have developed over the course of U.S. history to define the legal relationship between American Indian tribes and the U.S. government. This body of law includes several lines in the U.S. CONSTITUTION, more than 700 treaties between the United States and tribes (of which CONGRESS ratified 371), and thousands of court decisions, executive orders, congressional acts, and administrative decisions. Included in this vast body of law are numerous legal principles and regulations that define how environmental protection and management are to be administered in Indian Country. In order to understand how federal environmental policy and law apply to Indian tribes and their lands, it is first necessary to understand the historical evolution of the legal relationship between Indian nations and the U.S. government.

U.S. GOVERNMENT– AMERICAN INDIAN RELATIONS

Since its founding, the United States has formally recognized American Indian tribes as independent sovereign nations with whom it has direct government-to-government relationships. Codifying this recognition in the late 18th and early 19th centuries in the U.S. Constitution, numerous treaties, legislative acts, and court decisions, the U.S. government acknowledged that tribes have inherent rights to self-government and that neither individual states nor any other political entity may infringe on their political sovereignty or pass laws affecting their lands and resources. Aside from Indian nations themselves, only the federal government may engage in making and enforcing laws that pertain to tribes. And it

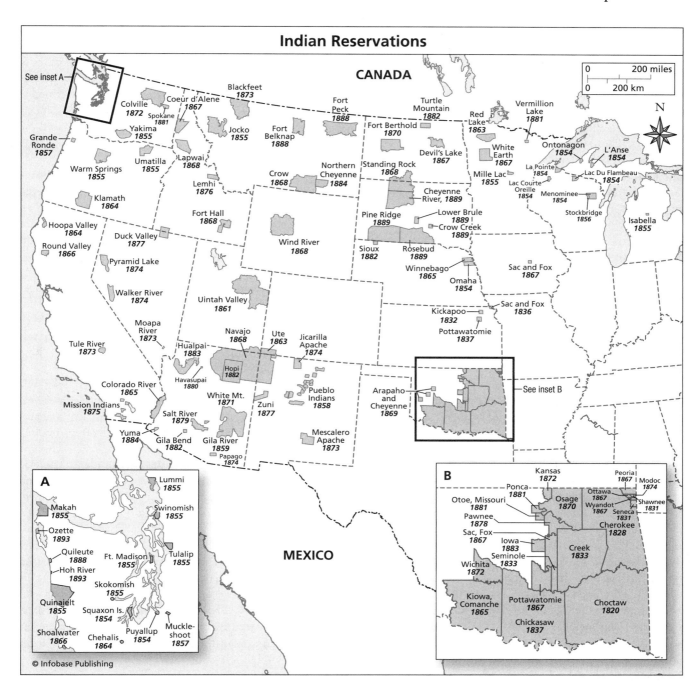

Indian Reservations

may only do so insofar as it honors the legal boundaries that define the U.S. government's unique relationship with these nations. How this relationship is defined has varied greatly throughout different policy eras in U.S. history, and it is constantly being redefined and negotiated through ongoing changes in federal law.

Changes in federal Indian policy over the past two centuries have had profound impacts on Indian nations' relationships with the land and the quality of their environments. Although the federal government ostensibly recognized

these nations' sovereignty in the late 1700s and early 1800s, it also supported expansion into their territories. In the 1820s and 1830s, the U.S. military waged wars against and forcibly relocated several southeastern tribes. As westward expansion increased in the 1840s, the United States sought to open lands and resources for settlers by removing Indians from their lands and relocating them to federal reservations. During the following decades, horrific violence and irrevocable alterations of many of the West's ecosystems accomplished these goals. By the 1870s, the United States adopted a formal policy of assimilation aimed at transforming Native peoples' lifeways, including their belief systems, material cultures, and subsistence. Coupled with assimilation policies, Congress passed the 1887 Dawes Act, which sought to break up communal Indian lands and transform Native peoples into individual landowning farmers. By the turn of the 20th century, the combined effects of these policies left hundreds of tribes depopulated and severely impoverished, without access to land and resources, and dependent on government services and food rations.

By the 1920s, it was clear to many in the U.S. government that 19th-century federal Indian policies had failed. In 1934, Congress authorized the Indian Reorganization Act, popularly known as the "Indian New Deal," which put an end to allotment under the Dawes Act and sought to revitalize Indian cultures, to return governing powers to tribes, and to support their economic development. This period of government support was relatively short-lived as political backlash in the 1940s and 1950s led to policies once again aimed at mainstream assimilation of Native peoples and the termination of tribal lands and sovereignty. However, the rise of the CIVIL RIGHTS MOVEMENT and increased presidential support for poverty alleviation under the JOHN F. KENNEDY and LYNDON B. JOHNSON administrations in the 1960s gave way in the 1970s to a new era in federal policy aimed at supporting tribal self-determination. Since then, tribes and the federal government have worked cooperatively to reverse harmful policies and their effects, to restore tribal self-government, and to revitalize Native cultures and land bases.

In 2008, the U.S. government recognized government-to-government relationships with 562 American Indian nations and provided direct federal services to more than 1.7 million Indian people. This included 336 tribes in the lower 48 states and 226 Alaska Native entities. These federally recognized tribes possess the right to enact tribal codes governing a wide range of issues, including those affecting the environment on the 55.7 million acres within these nations' territories. This includes setting environmental standards as well as regulating and assessing penalties for activities that affect the quality of tribal lands, water, air, BIODIVERSITY, and human health. Local tribal courts and agencies have jurisdiction to enforce these codes with tribal members, though the extent to which they can be enforced with nonmembers or outside tribal lands remains highly contentious and contested.

ENVIRONMENTAL RIGHTS AND LAWS

In addition to rights to environmental self-government, many individual tribes have specific environmental rights that have been recognized through treaties, statutes, executive orders, and other agreements with the federal government. Many of these rights involve access to specific resources in territories that were ceded by tribes or otherwise alienated from their ownership. These include rights to land and water as well as to fish, hunt, and gather resources outside current tribal political boundaries. In many cases, tribes specifically reserved fishing, hunting, and gathering rights in the treaties or other agreements through which they ceded portions of their lands to the United States. In other cases, federal courts have recognized that tribes retained implied rights to these resources, as well as to water, even if they were not explicitly mentioned in these treaties or agreements.

Under federal law, these rights are protected and cannot be infringed upon by any state or other entity. However, because of historical policies that sought to destroy Indian nations' self-government, most tribes have had to fight for these rights in federal courts. As a result, there is a significant body of federal case law concerning Indian fishing, hunting, gathering, and water rights. In the case of land rights, many tribes lost portions of their aboriginal homelands and places of cultural significance through illegal takings by the federal government and encroachment by private citizens. Hundreds of lawsuits and other federal actions have led to the successful reinstatement of tribal ownership or payment for these losses.

As delegated by the U.S. Constitution and acknowledged by federal courts, Congress has ultimate decision-making power over federal Indian affairs. As such, it enacts and amends federal legislation that affects both individual nations and all federally recognized tribes as a whole—including legislation regarding the environment. The U.S. president also has the authority to issue executive orders and policies that provide guidance to federal agencies on how to carry out their mandates. In the 1990s, President BILL CLINTON issued a number of important executive proclamations affecting environmental policy in Indian Country, including an executive order and memorandum on ENVIRONMENTAL JUSTICE (Executive Order 12898 of February 11, 1994), a memorandum on government-to-government relations with tribal governments (Presidential Memorandum of April 29, 1994), and an executive order concerning how federal agencies consult and coordinate with tribes (Executive Order 13084 of May 14, 1998).

Congress has delegated a significant portion of its authority over Indian affairs to the U.S. DEPARTMENT OF THE INTERIOR (DOI). This executive agency and its BUREAU OF INDIAN AFFAIRS (BIA) have been responsible for providing services to federally recognized tribes and for administering Indian lands held in trust by the federal government since 1849. Among its many duties, the DOI plays a critical role in managing how Indian lands and resources are used, leased, and transferred, and it acts as an important liaison agency between tribes and the federal government. Other executive agencies, including the U.S. DEPARTMENT OF HOUSING AND URBAN DEVELOPMENT, the Indian Health Service in the DEPARTMENT OF HEALTH AND HUMAN SERVICES, and the

ENVIRONMENTAL PROTECTION AGENCY (EPA), also administer federal policies that concern environmental and human health in Indian Country. Among them, the EPA has been the primary agency responsible for researching, establishing, and enforcing national environmental protection regulations related to clean air, water, and land and the control of toxic pollutants. The EPA administers these laws, as set forth by Congress, through the principle of cooperative FEDERALISM. It does so by establishing national base standards and by providing guidance and resources to individual states and tribes to support their implementation of environmental laws and programs.

Since the mid-1980s, the EPA has increasingly recognized and Congress has amended several environmental statutes (including the SAFE DRINKING WATER ACT, CLEAN WATER ACT, and CLEAN AIR ACT) to acknowledge that tribes have primary authority over the implementation of federal environmental programs within their territories. These amended laws contain language that allows the EPA to treat tribes "in the same manner as states" by delegating regulatory control to tribal governments. In order for tribes to qualify, however, they must go through a lengthy administrative review process proving to the EPA that they have the capacity to implement these programs effectively. The EPA has also interpreted these amendments in such a way as to allow tribes to develop and enforce standards that are more stringent than those set forth by the federal government. Although the legality of allowing tribes to set more stringent standards has been contested by surrounding states, federal courts have upheld the rights of tribes to do so.

REGULATORY AUTHORITY

A number of federal environmental laws do not mention or contain less concrete language regarding tribal regulatory authority. However, the EPA has interpreted them or used its discretion to treat tribes in the same manner as states for the purposes of implementing these statutes and developing tribally run programs. These laws include the Comprehensive Environmental Response, Compensation and Liability Act (SUPERFUND); Emergency Planning and Community Right-to-Know Act; Federal Insecticide, Fungicide and Rodenticide Act; Hazardous Material Transportation Act; Nuclear Waste Policy Act; Oil Pollution Act; Toxic Substances Control Act; and Resource Conservation and Recovery Act.

With regard to the ENDANGERED SPECIES ACT OF 1973, tribes may request and work with the U.S. FISH AND WILDLIFE SERVICE and the National Marine Fisheries Service to list ENDANGERED SPECIES; to comment on proposed listings, critical habitat designations, and recovery plans; as well as to enter into conservation agreements. Under the NATIONAL ENVIRONMENTAL POLICY ACT (NEPA) OF 1969, the federal government must prepare environmental impact assessments when undertaking or approving actions that may affect environmental health. The BIA is responsible for preparing these assessments when the proposed action occurs on Indian lands. Furthermore, the federal government must consult and solicit comment from tribes when any proposed action may affect tribal nations and their environments.

In cases when federal environmental statutes have not specifically allowed tribes to assume regulatory authority or tribes have been unable or unwilling to do so, the EPA generally has retained responsibility for implementing these laws. In order to enforce such laws, the agency may request that the U.S. DEPARTMENT OF JUSTICE take enforcement actions such as filing criminal or civil lawsuits against polluters on Indian lands. The Indian Resources Section within the Environment and Natural Resources Division of the Department of Justice is primarily responsible for such litigation. Because many tribes lack the human, technical, and financial resources required to implement and enforce environmental programs, many tribes continue to rely on the federal government to carry out these duties.

Before the mid-1980s, the federal government made little effort to assist tribes with environmental protection. Combined with the effects of past federal Indian policies that led to severe poverty, poor infrastructure, and unsustainable exploitation of tribes' natural resources, many Indian nations continued to struggle with serious human and environmental health problems and lacked the capacity to address them alone. Beginning in 1984, the EPA adopted a formal Indian policy aimed at addressing environmental issues in Indian Country, and in 1994, the agency established an American Indian Environmental Office (AIEO) to assist tribes with these issues. Since then, the EPA has increasingly recognized its responsibility to interact with tribes on a government-to-government basis and has worked cooperatively with them to inventory environmental conditions and set management priorities and goals. To assist tribes with implementation, the AIEO has acted as a facilitator by helping to remove legal and procedural barriers at the federal level, fostering cooperation with other federal agencies (and when possible with states), and providing tribes with information, technical assistance, training, and funding.

The struggle to protect the environmental health and well-being of American Indian nations' peoples and ECOSYSTEMS continues. Federal policies aimed at destroying these nations in the past continued to shape their relationships with the federal government in the 21st century. Since the 1970s, the U.S. government has reversed many of its more harmful policies and made significant strides in restoring governing powers to tribes. Programs and laws have been reformulated and developed to recognize the sovereignty of these nations and to facilitate their political, economic, and cultural self-determination. Since the 1980s, the federal government has also worked more cooperatively with tribes to meet their environmental needs. However, in the 21st century, there remains a need for increasing federal responsiveness and cooperation and greater allocation of resources to tribes. As such, the tribal-federal relationship will continue to evolve, and Indian nations will continue to work to protect their environments now and into the future.

See also FEDERAL LAW—ENVIRONMENTAL REGULATIONS; FEDERAL LAW—LAND POLICIES; INDIANS, APPALACHIA; INDIANS, CALIFORNIA; INDIANS, CENTRAL PLAINS; INDIANS, COLUMBIA PLATEAU AND GREAT BASIN; INDIANS, DEEP SOUTH; INDIANS, EASTERN SEABOARD; INDIANS, GULF COAST; INDIANS, MIDWEST; INDIANS, NORTHERN PLAINS; INDIANS, PACIFIC NORTHWEST.

Melanie A. Stansbury

Further Reading

Calloway, Colin G. *First People: A Documentary Survey of American Indian History,* 2d ed. Boston: Bedford/St. Martins, 2004.

Cohen, Felix. *Cohen's Handbook of Federal Indian Law, 2005 Edition.* Edited by Nell Jessup Newton. Newark, N.J.: LexisNexis, 2005.

Environmental Protection Agency. "American Indian Tribal Portal." Available online. URL: http://www.epa.gov/tribal-portal/index.htm. Accessed March 1, 2006.

Getches, David H., Charles F. Wilkinson, and Robert A. Williams, Jr. *Federal Indian Law: Cases and Materials.* 5th ed. St. Paul, Minn.: West Group, 2005.

Prucha, Francis Paul. *The Great Father: The United States Government and the American Indians.* 2 vols. Lincoln: University of Nebraska Press, 1984.

Royster, Judith V., and Michael C. Blumm. *Native American Natural Resources Law: Cases and Materials.* 2d ed. Durham, N.C.: Carolina Academic Press, 2008.

federal law—industrial regulations

Industrial regulation in the United States began slowly but accelerated as the economy, new technologies, and the population exploded in the 19th and 20th centuries. The authors of the U.S. CONSTITUTION envisioned a system of FEDERALISM in which the central government had minimal authority over the nation's businesses. Yet, by the 21st century, federal law had an all-encompassing influence on the American workplace. Through tariffs, trade agreements, restrictions on interstate commerce, and wartime emergency actions, presidents and the CONGRESS created an increasingly expansive regulatory structure that affected the size, location, and functioning of a wide variety of industries. Many laws, while not specifically designed to change the way individuals and organizations interacted with their surroundings, have left a profound environmental legacy.

THE FEDERAL ROLE—AN OVERVIEW

From no regulation to deregulation, the national government has played a changing role in health, safety, welfare, and production. Before the CIVIL WAR (1861–65), federal officials were primarily concerned with protecting domestic industry and agriculture, as reflected by tariffs imposed on foreign goods and a laissez-faire approach to most interstate trade. After the Civil War and until the GREAT DEPRESSION, the federal government experimented with laws that addressed market fairness, public health and safety, corporate monopolies, and management of natural resources.

The first major expansion of federal regulation took place during the NEW DEAL, the collection of socioeconomic measures crafted by the FRANKLIN D. ROOSEVELT administration and Congress in response to the depression in the 1930s. Congress enacted laws and created agencies to govern particular industries, establish Social Security, and protect labor in the workplace. During WORLD WAR II (1941–45) and the following two decades of economic expansion, industries grew within the framework of the established regulatory structure. In the 1960s and 1970s, Congress enacted a series of new types of cross-industry regulation to achieve social, environmental, and civil rights goals. The end of the 20th century was marked by efforts to deregulate industries, especially in the transportation, communication, and energy sectors, while liberalizing international trade agreements.

The three branches of government—executive, legislative, and JUDICIARY—each play a role in regulating industry in the United States, while a de facto fourth branch—the regulatory bureaucracy—has emerged over time. Under the commerce clause of the Constitution (Article I, Section 8.3), Congress may enact laws that affect interstate and international trade. The executive carries out legislative requirements. The judiciary considers the constitutionality of laws, regulations, and executive orders—at times undoing efforts to limit industrial activity and at other times upholding pathbreaking protections for workers, consumers, and the environment. Most significantly, federal agencies and commissions, created either by law or through executive action, have administered most of the regulatory rule making and enforcement. There are now hundreds of agencies and commissions performing regulatory functions. These entities administer statutes, make rules, and adjudicate disputed cases. In 1946, Congress passed the Administrative Procedures Act to ensure that regulatory agencies carry out their duties in a fair, open, and consistent manner.

REGULATION OF COMMERCE

Congress took early steps to protect domestic manufactures and agriculture through tariffs. Until the enactment of the federal income tax in 1913, tariffs on foreign goods provided the primary source of income for the country. The earliest such measure, the 1789 Hamilton Tariff, was also the second statute ever enacted by Congress. Levied against particular imports, the tariffs of the early 19th century, which peaked at 50 percent in 1828, served to encourage and protect a wide variety of manufactures, which in turn transformed the ecology, economy, and social life of regions within the United States. In 1800, for example, Great Britain dominated the COTTON textile trade while there were fewer than two dozen cotton mills operating in the United States. With the help of protective tariffs, this number grew to more 800 mills by the 1830s, the majority located along the major rivers of New England. By midcentury, New England's textile industry had attracted a large labor force, transformed villages into cities, reconfigured and polluted rivers, purchased cotton from the South, and provided finished goods to the rest of the country.

The effects of tariffs on different geographic and economic sectors led to regular debates over rates until the 1930s. Tariff rates generally fell until the outbreak of the Civil War, rose during the war, and were hotly contested during the presidential elections thereafter. In the late 1930s, the United States ended the practice of instituting unilateral tariffs and participated in reciprocal trade agreements both to protect domestic industries and to promote sales of American goods in international markets.

Accelerating industrialization in the mid-19th century was characterized by a variety of problematic business practices including corruption, unfair pricing, and a tendency toward monopolistic control of major economic sectors. Congress created the Interstate Commerce Commission (ICC) in 1887 in an attempt to regulate rates and quality of service of the RAILROADS. The federal government already played a role in railroad development through land grants, route surveys, and lower tariffs on iron. As railroad ownership concentrated in fewer hands, and companies colluded on rates and schedules, farmers and ranchers formed organizations such as THE GRANGE to increase their own bargaining power and lobbied at the state and national levels for regulatory intervention. With the creation of the ICC, the federal government entered a new phase of regulatory activity intended to protect the public interest. To mitigate the harmful effects of industrial monopolies, Congress also passed the 1890 Sherman Antitrust Act and, in 1914, the Clayton Act and Federal Trade Commission Act. While some monopolies, such as the Sugar Trust, successfully fought the antitrust laws in court, others, most famously Standard Oil, were forced to break up into smaller companies.

During the 1930s, Congress expanded the federal government's authority over trusts, rates, routes, and quality of service in a variety of industries including NATURAL GAS, electricity, TELEPHONE and TELEGRAPH service, trucking, transocean freight shipments, and commercial air travel. The agencies implementing these laws exerted significant control over the growth of these industries, affecting physical expansion, location, profitability, cost of goods and services, and response to consumer demand.

CITIZEN HEALTH AND SAFETY

By the end of the 19th century, as the federal government tentatively undertook direct regulation of commerce, Congress also began to address the health and safety of citizens. Under the influence of PROGRESSIVISM, Congress began to pass industry-specific laws that affected conditions in the workplace, the outdoor environment, consumer products, and some industrial practices. FOOD safety was an early concern, especially with the introduction of refrigerated railcars in the 1870s. Congress considered more than 100 bills to regulate food and drugs between 1865 and 1906 and passed several to control the import and use of diseased animals in the food supply. First, the Treasury Department and, later, the U.S. DEPARTMENT OF AGRICULTURE enforced quarantines and inspected both live animals and certain salted meats. With the passage of the Meat Inspection and Food and Drug Acts in 1906, Congress signaled a more serious attempt to regulate food production practices. The government focused on both the quality and the safety of products and the sanitary conditions of slaughterhouses and processing plants.

During this same period, Congress also began to regulate the conditions of harbors and navigable waterways. Since 1824, when the U.S. Supreme Court confirmed federal authority over navigable waterways, federal law addressed commerce and safe passage on lakes and rivers. In the 1880s, scientists persuasively demonstrated that many HUMAN DISEASES were waterborne, giving impetus to laws that also proscribed dumping. In the 1899 Rivers and Harbors Act, Congress banned waste discharges into federal waterways. With the creation of the Public Health Service in 1912, the federal government began monitoring WATER POLLUTION and set standards for DRINKING WATER quality. The 1924 Oil Pollution Control Act prohibited discharge of oil into coastal waters. These pieces of legislation provided a foundation for much of the ENVIRONMENTAL LAW and regulation that proliferated later in the 20th century.

NATURAL RESOURCE EXTRACTION

Throughout the 19th century, Congress encouraged private LOGGING and MINING, often in PUBLIC DOMAIN areas, as an essential component of national expansion. The 1872 Mining Act was designed to facilitate the removal of minerals by supposedly clarifying the right of ownership for various claims and did nothing to halt the environmentally destructive practices from hydraulic mining to slag heaps and cyanide processing of ores. In 1891, Congress passed the first mining safety statute, covering only facilities in the U.S. territories. In 1910, Congress created the Bureau of Mines to investigate mining safety in all states and territories and reduce the growing number of mining fatalities. The bureau, however, had no inspection authority until 1941 and did little to address ecological damage.

Likewise, laws related to FORESTRY, river usage, and oil and gas drilling did not significantly proscribe industrial activity until later in the 20th century. At the turn of the 20th century, Progressive Era CONSERVATION, as reflected in federal policy, focused on the more efficient use of FORESTS rather than their preservation, for example. The Reclamation Act of 1902, which created the agency later known as the BUREAU OF RECLAMATION, established federal management of water resources, especially in the western states, but the law still assumed that rivers, particularly in the arid West, were wasted if they flowed freely rather than providing urban drinking water, irrigating farms, or powering factories. The Federal Power Act of 1920 created the Federal Power Commission (FPC) to regulate the location of hydroelectric DAMS.

During the New Deal years, federal laws began to manage energy industry practices, as well as the location and rate of natural resource extraction on public land. For decades, oil companies had competed to develop oil fields as quickly as possible, rapidly depleting reserves and flooding the market with cheap oil. First by executive order, and then under the 1935 Connolly Hot Oil Act, the federal government regulated interstate sales of oil to control oil field depletion. A series of acts established regulatory control over the business structure of electric utilities and the rates charged for interstate sales of electricity, while federally funded power plants and transmission lines competed with private providers. Similarly, under the Natural Gas Act of 1937, the FPC began to regulate the size, location, and rates of natural gas pipelines.

WARTIME ECONOMIES

During WORLD WAR I (1914–18) and World War II, the two major wars of the 20th century, presidents requested and Congress provided unprecedented authority to direct the economy from WASHINGTON, D.C., leading to rapid growth of industries and lax enforcement of rules that would slow production. These intervals marked a stark change in government policy toward the private sector, as the demand for massive quantities of armaments, food, clothing, vehicles, and fuel dominated national priorities. During World War I, for example, the War Industries Board regulated 57 different commodity groups, while other agencies managed imports and exports, the railroads, investments in munitions production, coal pricing, and food distribution. Industrial regulation took place without specific enabling legislation, and agencies relied upon the cooperation of the private sector. In the years immediately following the war, the federal government retreated from strong management of the economy.

During World War II, the federal government once again exerted extensive industrial authority, imposing wage and price controls, setting production and distribution quotas, rationing goods, and, in some instances, building entire industries, including the nuclear power industry, first created under the MANHATTAN PROJECT. Federal agencies erected dams on rivers, authorized construction of huge gas and oil pipelines, and diverted fuel and electric power to war-related factories. After the war, the federal government retained authority over nuclear energy, closely regulating private industries that worked with nuclear materials, including utilities building nuclear power plants. For the most part, however, the end of the war restored earlier regulatory relationships, while a new, growing, and federally supported MILITARY-INDUSTRIAL COMPLEX emerged in the 1950s.

WORKPLACE PROTECTIONS

During the country's early years, local and federal governments provided few protections for the workplace, but industrialization presented increasing hazards to the American labor force. Factory conditions in MILL TOWNS were exploitive and dangerous, and workers organized periodically during the first decades of the 19th century to protest, albeit to little avail. By the end of the century, factory deaths were as high as 35,000 annually, and more than 500,000 workers were injured each year. Labor groups organized, often went on strike to protest dangerous workplaces, and pushed for protective legislation. Congress passed a series of laws, between 1888 and 1933, addressing the methods for resolving labor disputes, the length of the workday, and the rights of laborers to self-organize. For the most part, however, efforts to establish safer and healthier work conditions in industrial settings were unsuccessful and often left to ineffective state laws until the New Deal. In the 1930s, Congress enacted laws that protected and empowered organized labor. The 1936 Walsh-Healy Act specifically addressed the workplace conditions of federal contractors, although 24 years passed before a secretary of labor issued the first safety code under the act.

By 1960, the American workplace had been transformed by mass production, the assembly line, successful labor activism, and an increased understanding of the risks associated with exposure to an array of chemicals and materials used in manufacturing. The rapid mobilization of industry for World War II led to an increase in industrial accidents that continued through the 1950s and 1960s. After a West Virginia mine explosion in 1968 in which 78 workers were killed, labor concerns about the conditions of the workplace gained prominence. Congress responded in 1973 by creating the Occupational Health and Safety Administration (OSHA) and the National Institute for Occupational Safety and Health. In addition to establishing a mechanism for adopting workplace standards, a process for inspections, a system of penalties for noncomplying employers, and a research program, this legislation included a general duty clause that required employers to maintain safe and sanitary work environments.

OSHA regulations have led to a significant drop in workplace deaths and injuries and a reduction of worker exposures to hazardous chemicals and materials. OSHA inspectors visit more than 35,000 workplaces every year, and OSHA has set exposure limits for about 500 chemical hazards, including well-understood toxic substances such as asbestos, cotton dust, and vinyl chloride. Critics argue that OSHA is slow to update workplace standards, workers are still exposed to thousands of unregulated chemical substances, and the number of federal inspectors has fallen. Thus, federal law has reshaped the environments in which Americans labor, yet the health and safety conditions of the workplace are still contested.

Moreover, the federal government passed a series of laws in the 1960s and 1970s that regulated and restricted how factories and other places of production interacted with the natural environment. A series of CLEAN AIR ACTS and CLEAN WATER ACTS forced industry to reduce its pollution. Other federal environmental laws limited where and how industry could dump its toxic wastes, while the SUPERFUND law attempted to hold individual corporations accountable for the cleanup costs associated with hazardous wastes.

DEREGULATION

By the 1960s, a variety of factors led to a dramatic shift in government regulatory programs. The CIVIL RIGHTS MOVEMENT, the women's movement, and the environmental movement all influenced policy makers to consider sweeping changes to the role of the central government. From President Lyndon Johnson's GREAT SOCIETY to the NATIONAL ENVIRONMENTAL POLICY ACT (NEPA) OF 1969, federal law influenced the way Americans lived, worked, and played in new ways. Even as Congress introduced an array of regulations that reached across industries to address social concerns, rising electricity prices, fuel shortages, frustrated consumers, and new technologies prompted questions about the efficacy of older industrial controls. Beginning with the transportation sector, Congress loosened rules for trucking, rail transportation, and air travel in the 1970s. In 1978, Congress deregulated interstate sales of NATURAL GAS, and in 1979, Congress opened the door to competition in the electricity market. These changes and others in the next decades led to restructuring in a number of industries, including expansion of natural gas exploration, increased air traffic, and new markets in energy trading. The industrial deregulation trend in the late 20th century had mixed results for the environment, in some cases accelerating depletion of natural resources and increasing sources of pollution and in other cases increasing opportunities for cleaner manufacturing.

Over the past 200 years, federal law has played an expanding role in shaping industrial activity and its environmental consequences. Tariffs and trade agreements have fostered domestic manufacturing growth and, joined with efforts to manage natural resource extraction, have influenced regional concentration of industrial activity. Worker protections as well as efforts to improve public health, limit the spread of animal-borne diseases, and address food quality have resulted in cleaner workplaces and safer consumer products. More recently, deregulation of specific industries has reversed some environmental gains while increasing a number of creative endeavors to produce more ecologically protective goods and services. A wide array of federal regulations has influenced the growth and practices of American industries in ways that continue to have profound environmental consequences outside the marketplace and beyond the shop floor.

See also AGRICULTURE, FEDERAL POLICIES; CATTLE; FEDERAL LAW—ENVIRONMENTAL REGULATIONS; FEDERAL LAW—LAND POLICIES; FOOD AND DRUG ADMINISTRATION; HEALTH AND MEDICINE; ISOLATIONISM; LABOR MOVEMENTS; OIL, DOMESTIC; PIGS AND HOGS; SINCLAIR, UPTON; TREATIES AND INTERNATIONAL LAW; WATER RIGHTS—PRIOR APPROPRIATION; WATER RIGHTS—RIPARIAN.

Julie Cohn

Further Reading
Andrews, Richard N. L. *Managing the Environment, Managing Ourselves: A History of American Environmental Policy.* 2d ed. New Haven, Conn.: Yale University Press, 2006.
Breyer, Stephen G. *Regulation and Its Reform.* Cambridge, Mass.: Harvard University Press, 1982.
Hall, Kermit, Paul Finkelman, and James W. Ely. *American Legal History: Cases and Materials.* 3d ed. New York: Oxford University Press, 2005.
Nester, William R. *A Short History of American Industrial Policies.* New York: St. Martin's Press, 1998.
Northrup, Herbert Roof, Richard L. Rowan, and Charles R. Perry. *The Impact of OSHA: A Study of the Effects of the Occupational Safety and Health Act on Three Key Industries, Aerospace, Chemicals, and Textiles.* Labor Relations and Public Policy Series. Philadelphia: Industrial Research Unit, Wharton School, University of Pennsylvania, 1978.
Vietor, Richard H. K. *Energy Policy in America since 1945: A Study of Business Government Relations.* Studies in Economic History and Policy Series. Cambridge and New York: Cambridge University Press, 1984.

federal law—land policies

Land has long been one of the North American continent's most plentiful natural resources, and its management has presented one of the great challenges to the continent's inhabitants. Many of the first European immigrants to North America were pulled to the Americas by the abundance of land, and the possibility of landownership has drawn millions of immigrants into the United States since. Over the centuries, land policies evolved alongside the nation, ranging from the distributive ambitions of a Confederation Congress overwhelmed by the size of the new nation to the conflicts over management of shrinking natural resources that characterize 21st-century federal-state relations.

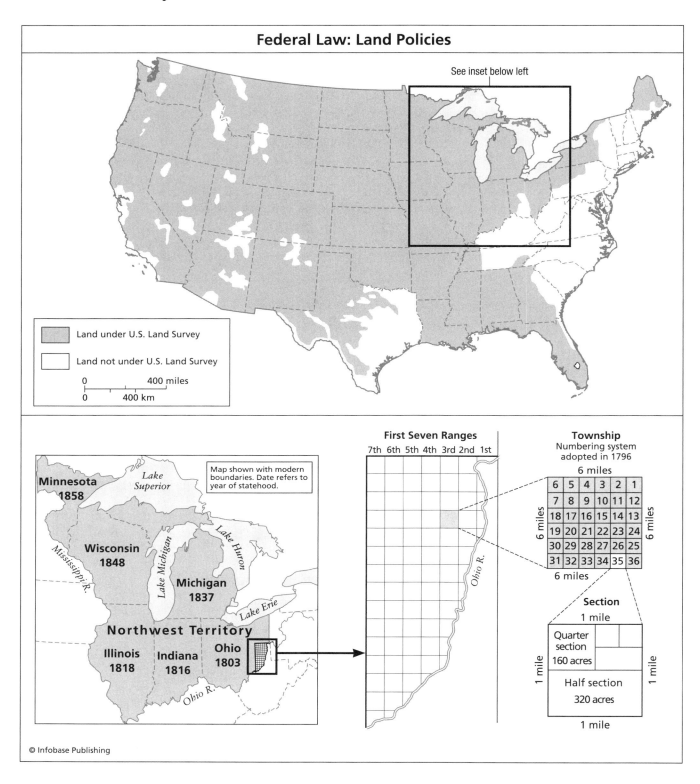

Federal Law: Land Policies

See inset below left

Land under U.S. Land Survey

Land not under U.S. Land Survey

0   400 miles

0   400 km

Minnesota 1858

Lake Superior

Map shown with modern boundaries. Date refers to year of statehood.

Wisconsin 1848

Lake Michigan

Lake Huron

Mississippi R.

Michigan 1837

Lake Erie

Northwest Territory

Illinois 1818   Indiana 1816   Ohio 1803

Ohio R.

First Seven Ranges

7th 6th 5th 4th 3rd 2nd 1st

Ohio R.

Township

Numbering system adopted in 1796

6 miles

6	5	4	3	2	1
7	8	9	10	11	12
18	17	16	15	14	13
19	20	21	22	23	24
30	29	28	27	26	25
31	32	33	34	35	36

6 miles

6 miles

6 miles

Section

1 mile

Quarter section
160 acres

1 mile

Half section
320 acres

1 mile

1 mile

© Infobase Publishing

Since the first decades of the colonial period, the question of how to manage the land best to promote American development and democracy has concerned the American people and their government. In the first years of the new nation, CONGRESS conceptualized a grand project of land surveys and distribution that established a model for future development. Then, in the mid-19th century, Congress sought to democratize access to the land, even as it subsidized commercial projects, and by the late 19th century, the federal government moved into a conservationist framework that dominated legislation in the 20th century. Each of these eras of land policy reflects conditions that had emerged in the nation, and they all spoke to shifting American ideas about the land and its best use.

FORMULATING A NATIONAL SYSTEM

From the creation of the United States in 1776, land was a primary concern for the nation, and the new government, in one of its few accomplishments under the ARTICLES OF CONFEDERATION, established a program for land distribution in the 1780s. Land speculation and competing land claims threatened the viability of the nascent United States. Many national leaders believed that access to land would help to promote a nation of small farmers, whom they envisioned as the guardians of democracy. Consequently, the first plans for federal land policy embraced an agrarian vision for the expansion of YEOMAN farmers across the nation.

The first design for U.S. land policy detailed a program for the organization and rationalization of the natural landscape. The Ordinance of 1785 provided a system for managing the territory controlled by the national government. This legislation established a plan for managing the vast western landscape; Congress designed a land survey to divide the area west of the Ohio River into equal-sized, quantifiable plots of land. The Land Ordinance directed federal surveyors to mark natural features on each section of land, and, after the territory had been cataloged and measured, the PUBLIC DOMAIN was auctioned off to the people. Under the terms of this legislation, federal lands would be sold for a minimum of one dollar per acre, in townships of 36 square miles or sections of 640 acres (one square mile). The ordinance set aside four sections within each township for the federal government. It also granted to the secretary of war one-seventh of the townships of the first seven ranges for distribution to veterans. Congress intended to use the proceeds from land auctions to help repay the national debt and to provide a principal source of funding for the national government, and the Ordinance of 1785 envisioned a system that would allow national growth while ensuring the establishment of an independent yeoman citizenry.

This legislation provided a model for the expansion of the United States across its territory, and it offered a clear strategy for land distribution. Its disadvantages were related to its scale: The minimal parcel size, 640 acres, was too large for a family to manage; the purchase price was too high even for wealthy investors; and the plan for distributing whole townships to settlement companies had little appeal for many prospective settlers who sought independence on their own farms. Over the subsequent decades, Congress revised the Land Ordinance to address many of its shortcomings. These revisions provided the basis for an early federal subsidy to landowners. The Land Law of 1800 adjusted federal policy to permit purchases on credit, with a fourth of the purchase price due within 40 days and the remainder due in the second, third, and fourth years. This revision also reduced the parcel size to 320 acres and set the minimal price at two dollars an acre. The system of liberal credit was an attractive feature for settlers who could purchase with a down payment on the property, but few purchasers were able to repay the federal treasury even after several years had passed, creating a large cohort of perpetually indebted landowners.

The evolution of federal land policy demonstrates Congress's adaptations to public and national needs. Some innovations enjoyed less success than others, and the provision of credit created several unanticipated problems, allowing small farmers to overextend themselves by purchasing as much land as possible in the expectation of a quick profit. Credit provisions also fueled speculation, because buyers could acquire large acreages with a down payment of 25 percent and then resell it to later arrivals. Speculators frequently bought large parcels of land and marketed it at higher prices, or they loaned money so that prospective settlers could pay cash. Others claimed public lands for a minimal price and then stripped it of timber or mineral resources, abandoning the claim before making additional payments. In reaction against the injustices of speculation, another land law in 1804 reduced minimal parcel sizes to 160 acres, and Congress shrank the minimal size again in 1820 to 80 acres. The act of 1820 responded to widespread defaults by once again requiring full payment in cash and dropping the minimal price per acre to $1.25, with the intention of stabilizing western communities.

During the late 18th and early 19th centuries, economic growth and decline repeatedly influenced land policy. In a further attempt to systematize land surveys and land distribution, Congress created the General Land Office within the Treasury Department in 1812. In 1849, these land management functions were transferred into the new DEPARTMENT OF THE INTERIOR; the growing federal infrastructure reflected the increasing complexity of land management.

PUBLIC DEMANDS FOR EXPANDED ACCESS TO LAND

From the beginning of Euro-American settlement, people moved to the margins of settlement in search of new opportunity, and in the period after 1785, their advance often preceded the process of Indian cession, survey, and public auction. SQUATTING had roots in early American history, and after the institution of federal land laws, aspiring profiteers and those without access to cash sought to avoid land sales by squatting on land that had not yet been surveyed. Squatters would typically travel to unsurveyed areas, build houses and improve the land, and then insist on their claims to that land. Many squatters opted to settle on the most desirable lands, particularly those with strategic or productive potential, such as mill sites, alluvial lands, and areas clearly rich in minerals or valuable woodlots. These settlers argued that they should have the right of first refusal to land they had put into production. They increasingly demanded the right of preemption, which gave preference to the squatter who desired to purchase land in advance of a public auction. During the 1820s and 1830s, squatters defended their claims through vigilante action during land sales, and they developed community organizations and occasionally enacted local and territorial laws to support their cause.

Congress eventually began to acknowledge squatters' claims and passed the Preemption Act of 1830 in response to the demands of the western states for squatters' rights. This statute gave sole first rights to squatters who sought to purchase their land directly from the federal government, with up to 160 acres at a minimal price of $1.25/acre. This was the first of a series of temporary preemption laws, and it was renewed until the passage of a general preemption act in 1841. Other legislation of the 1830s concerned financing land acquisition—especially the 1836 Specie Circular, a reaction to rampant speculation in public land. This federal mandate required that payment for nonresident purchases of public lands totaling more than 320 acres be made in specie, rather than in the often-unreliable notes of local banks. It led to a dramatic decline in land sales for almost a decade. The 1841 Distribution-Preemption Act offered preemptors permanent protection, permitting settlers to stake a claim on surveyed land. After 14 months of residency, the preemptor could purchase the land, prior to public sale. The "distribution" provision of this 1841 law allotted 500,000 acres to each new state to support the construction of internal improvements, an incentive that set a precedent for later federal aid for the development of western infrastructure.

During the early 1850s, Congress passed a number of additional laws to encourage settlement in areas still undeveloped within the Midwest and Southeast. With the Illinois Land Grant Act of 1850, the federal government promoted transportation development, offering land grants to build RAILROADS within Illinois, a state with a great deal of fertile farmland that remained unsold because of its inaccessibility to markets. This legislation spurred the donation of 21 million acres to develop railroads in the Mississippi Valley over the following seven years, and it precipitated a new era of land cessions intended to support the development of western railroads. By 1871, when federal grants to the railroads ceased, the national government had granted a total of 129 million acres of land—an area larger than the state of California—to support railroad construction. In 1850, Congress also passed the Swamp Lands Act, responding to settlers' hesitancy to inhabit large swaths of the Mississippi Valley because of fears of FLOODS. This legislation granted to states the swamp and flood-prone lands within their boundaries; state legislatures could use the proceeds from selling this land to reclaim swamplands from flooding; the act thus encour-

aged settlers and speculators to gamble on the erratic hydrology of western lands.

Congress sought to correct the uneven distribution of population through the Graduation Act of 1854, another response to the slow rate of settlement on significant swaths of the midwestern landscape. This legislation reduced the selling price on lands that had been on the market for 10 years or more, adjusted according to the amount of time that had passed since the land was first offered for public sale, from $1.00/acre for land on the market more than 10 years down to $0.125/acre for land on the market longer than 30 years. The law precipitated rapid land sales at sharply reduced prices, and, unsurprisingly, since these lands had often been passed over as "less desirable," settlers confronted significant challenges with developing these farms. The era of controlled distribution was slowly eroding, and congressional support for graduation boded well for the growing number of advocates of free land in the West.

FEDERALLY SPONSORED EXPANSION

Calls for "free land" emerged alongside other plans for making landownership more democratic, and as early as the 1840s, Congress had begun to discuss homestead legislation. Proponents of the homestead principle argued that the hardships and privations of establishing farms and developing the region's natural resources entitled settlers to land that they could turn into a home. The future president Andrew Johnson introduced the first homestead bill in the House of Representatives in 1845, followed by Stephen Douglas in the Senate in 1849. By 1859, Congress passed a homestead bill, but President James Buchanan vetoed it in June 1860. Once the southern states seceded in 1860 to 1861, however, Congress passed the legislation again, and with President Abraham Lincoln's signature, this law opened access to land in designated areas after January 1, 1863.

The 1862 Homestead Act provided that anyone who headed a family, had reached the age of 21, or had served in the nation's military; was a citizen or had filed the intention of becoming a citizen; and had not borne arms against the U.S. government was entitled to 160 acres of land, a parcel known as a "quarter section" because it was a quarter of a square mile. From the date of filing a claim, the homesteaders had six months to move onto the property and begin to cultivate and improve the land. The land had to be for personal use, and it had to serve as a permanent residence for the five years following the date of application. Fees and taxes for the final title carried a total cost of between $13 and $22.

The Homestead Act spurred a significant increase in rates of migration to the trans-Missouri West; by 1870, the rush of settlers had reached central Kansas and Nebraska. In some areas, competition for land grew so fierce that prospective homesteaders were encouraged to indicate that the land was claimed before setting off for the land office—some

Homesteaders stand before their home in Alaska in the early 20th century.   *(Library of Congress)*

people broke the sod, dug a well, or started to construct a dwelling in order to signal their intention to occupy a particular piece of land. Those improvements indicated a prior right, recognized in the case of competing claims to the same quarter section.

By the 20th century, difficult conditions for homesteaders, particularly in the arid West, had led to widespread resentment in the face of natural obstacles and the lack of government aid. As Senator William Borah (R-Idaho) observed in 1912, "The government bets 160 acres against the entry fee of $14 that the settler can't live on the land for five years without starving to death." In many cases, the homesteaders lost the bet, and across the United States, although 141,446 homestead entries were made between 1863 and 1900 for 19 million acres, homesteaders only carried half of the claims through to the final patent.

The Homestead Act encouraged many people to move west on the assumption that their farms would provide success and security. However, many aspiring farmers traveled out to their land without money to buy supplies, without agricultural experience, or without an understanding of local climate and weather. Sometimes, prospective farmers were plagued by all three of these disadvantages. Environmental dangers west of the 100th meridian—DROUGHTS, destruc-

tive storms, and pests—further undermined the would-be homesteaders.

The congressional session of 1862 that passed the Homestead Act spawned several other dynamic laws intended to develop the West. Through the Morrill Act, Congress granted land to support public education in those states and territories that remained in the Union, with 30,000 acres allotted for each senator and representative. States were expected to take their share from land within their boundaries, although those states with no public lands remaining were entitled to scrip for public lands elsewhere, which the state could sell in order to fund the establishment of colleges offering liberal and practical education in the military, agricultural, and mechanical arts.

The 1862 Pacific Railroad Act also donated public land to support the development of western infrastructure—in this case, the transcontinental railroad. This legislation granted between 20 and 40 sections per mile to the Union Pacific and Central Pacific Railroads to encourage the rapid construction of new railroad routes. In addition to land sales, RAILROADS spurred settlement by opening vast new areas to prospective settlers at unprecedented speeds; the locomotive soon replaced the slow and tedious wagon trains. Congressional railroad grants in states such as Kansas, Iowa, and

In 1863, the Union Pacific Railroad company began westward construction of a transcontinental line from Omaha, Nebraska. The flat western plains facilitated quick progress toward the Central Pacific track, which was advancing eastward from Sacramento, California. The Plains Indians were the greatest obstacle to the Union Pacific project. Distressed by uninvited construction on their lands, they attacked workers, ambushed trains, and destroyed supplies. Construction was completed May 10, 1869, when the two lines met in Utah.   *(Library of Congress)*

Minnesota constituted huge swaths of the states, and some of these withdrawals endured for decades; in the early 1870s, for example, more than 20 percent of Kansas remained reserved by railroad grants.

Although the idea of homesteading captivated prospective settlers in the West, the majority of land acquired during the late 19th century was purchased through federal and state land sales, preemption, graduation, swamp lands, railroad land sales, sales of Indian lands, and the use of Morrill Act scrip. Between 1863 and 1870, at the height of the rush for new homesteads, only a quarter of new farms in the West were claimed through the Homestead Act. In the 1870s, homesteaders registered 300,000 new claims, but land purchasers established an additional 1.3 million new farms. The Homestead Act had its greatest impact on the tier of states and territories crossing the 100th meridian, west of central Kansas, Nebraska, and the Dakotas. Due to a number of factors, those areas opened for homesteading were frequently less desirable, and often on land distant from railroad lines and services. The federal government opened the richest and most fertile sections of the West to

cash purchase, even after the enactment of the Homestead Act. When scholars conducted a final accounting of land acquisition in the West, they discovered 84 million acres of the public domain opened to homesteading, 125 million acres granted to railroads, 140 million acres granted to the states, 100 million acres sold as Indian lands, and another 100 million acres offered by federal sale. In sum, land sales constituted the vast majority of land transactions in the West, contrary to the myth of a vast western frontier of independent homesteads.

Indian land policies also influenced western development. Until 1871, most federal Indian land policies were enacted through treaties, but in that year Congress resolved to stop dealing with Indian tribes as sovereign nations. The 1887 Dawes Severalty Act opened up vast swaths of formerly reserved Indian lands for sale to settlers. This legislation authorized the allotment of 160 acres to each head of family, with incrementally less acreage for other family members. The Dawes Act intended that the remaining reservation lands would be sold off, and proceeds from sales placed in an Indian education fund, and many of the former reservation lands were later opened up to white settlement through Indian land sales.

The late 19th century introduced additional adjustments to federal land policy, including several revisions to the Homestead Act, adapting the provisions of the legislation to the climate and terrain west of the 100th meridian. As Americans expanded into the Far West, they discovered that ranching required much more than 160 acres, while irrigated agriculture required less. The 1873 Timber Culture Act granted land to settlers who planted and protected 40 acres of timber for 10 years. The Desert Land Act of 1877 offered 640 acres for $800 in improvements if settlers began to develop an IRRIGATION program within three years. Later recommendations for altering the Homestead Act appeared in several other legislative actions: The 1904 Kincaid Homestead Act granted 640 acres in western Nebraska to people who farmed for five years and implemented $800 worth of improvements. The 1909 Enlarged Homestead Act expanded this provision to the rest of the West, granting 320 acres to those who pledged to farm for five years and make improvements on their land. These modifications to the Homestead Act emerged in spite of a contradictory impulse that emerged in the federal government in the late 19th century—the move toward comprehensive federal land management and conservation policies.

THE AGE OF CONSERVATION

In response to growing concerns about land fraud, speculation, the difficulty of farming, and slow relinquishments of railroad grants, Congress created the first Public Land Commission in 1879 to analyze the prospects for further development of the public domain. This commission sought to classify land as either agricultural or nonagricultural, and it divided areas not suited to agriculture into mineral and timber zones. The commissioners recommended repealing the Preemption, Timber Culture, Desert Land, Timber and Stone, Swamp Land Indemnity, and cash sale acts because of the widespread fraud associated with land acquisitions through these laws. The commission's report also acknowledged that agricultural land accessible to the small farmer was nearly gone, and it proposed that Congress replace the Homestead Act with legislation geared to facilitating ranching and resource development on the remaining western lands. Many of the Public Land Commission's recommendations were implemented by the 1891 General Revision Act, which repealed the Preemption Act and Timber Culture Act, clarified commutation policies, amended the policy for desert land entries, ended the process of land auctions, and gave the president power to designate forest preserves.

In 1934, after almost 150 years of revision and adjustment, the Taylor Grazing Act retracted the Ordinance of 1785's model for surveying and selling western lands. This NEW DEAL legislation placed the remaining western public lands into permanent federal holdings, primarily organized into grazing districts that contained a maximum of 80 million acres of land (amended in 1936 to an expanded size of 142 million acres). Congress granted the Department of the Interior responsibility for managing the grazing districts and for developing waterpower, carrying out soil conservation programs, and disposing of any land not needed for grazing districts. Through executive orders in 1934 and 1935, President FRANKLIN D. ROOSEVELT withdrew the remaining public domain, totaling 165,695,000 acres, from sale as part of a nationwide conservation program—most of this land was put into additional grazing districts, national FORESTS, parks, game reserves, and hydropower developments. The 1930s was the age of SOIL CONSERVATION programs and plans for revising land utilization nationwide, and for a period the federal government envisioned a widespread intervention in land use, though many of these policies never became law.

In 1946, Congress merged the functions of the General Land Office and the Grazing Service to create the BUREAU OF LAND MANAGEMENT (BLM), which thereafter oversaw the 778 million acres of the public domain not controlled by other federal agencies. Today, the BLM manages a vast territory in the Far West through a mixed-use regime. In 1976, Congress passed the Federal Land Policy and Management Act, repealing the Homestead Act in the continental United States but granting a 10-year extension to claims in Alaska. The federal homestead era ended formally in 1986 with the expiration of that provision.

Reactions against federal land policy have been a regular part of American culture, from assaults on surveyors to SQUATTING, to sabotage. Building on this long tradition, in 1979 the Nevada legislature passed a bill wresting control of BLM lands within the state, spawning the SAGEBRUSH REBELLION, a local protest against federal land management. This Nevada initiative gave voice to the frustration of many westerners with their lack of control over local resources on the federal lands that they deemed essential to their state economies. The attempt to seize federal lands had no impact on federal policy, but the "rebellion" expressed western legislators', taxpayers', and resource users' hostility to federal land policies within their states, policies that the Sagebrush rebels felt did not represent their needs or ambitions for local development.

It is clear from the last two centuries of American history that the broad sweep of federal land policies will continue to shift alongside changing national needs. From the early efforts of a national government driven to spread its population over a seemingly endless territory to the more recent, and urgent, attempts of federal policy makers to rein in abuses of the public lands, the changes in federal land policy have reflected the mind-set of the nation. As land policies shifted from distribution to conservation over the past century, they have expressed the evolving need for control over natural resources in first an agricultural, then an industrial, and now a postindustrial nation. In the process, the land and its resources have repeatedly been the focus of contests for power and profit, and the future of American land management will continue to depend upon an ever-changing vision of a profitable and sustainable future.

See also AGRICULTURE, COMMERCIAL; FEDERAL LAW—INDIANS POLICIES; KANSAS-NEBRASKA CONTROVERSY; LAND GRANT INSTITUTIONS; LOGGING AND LUMBERING; MANIFEST DESTINY; MINING AND SMELTING; POWELL, JOHN WESLEY; UNITED STATES—ALASKA; UNITED STATES—CENTRAL PLAINS; UNITED STATES—COLUMBIA PLATEAU AND GREAT BASIN; UNITED STATES—MIDWEST; UNITED STATES—NORTHERN PLAINS; UNITED STATES—PACIFIC NORTHWEST; UNITED STATES—SOUTHWEST.

Sara M. Gregg

Further Reading

Dick, Everett. *The Lure of the Land: A Social History of the Public Lands from the Articles of Confederation to the New Deal.* Lincoln: University of Nebraska Press, 1970.

Gates, Paul W. *The History of Public Land Law Development.* Washington, D.C.: U.S. Government Printing Office, 1968.

Opie, John. *The Law of the Land: Two Hundred Years of American Farmland Policy.* Lincoln: University of Nebraska Press, 1994.

Robbins, Roy M. *Our Landed Heritage: The Public Domain, 1776–1936.* Princeton, N.J.: Princeton University Press, 1976.

The Land Ordinance of 1785

Adopted by the Congress in 1785, the Land Ordinance laid the foundation of federal land policy prior to the Homestead Act of 1862. Lacking the power of taxation, Congress, under the Articles of Confederation, hoped to raise revenue through the sale of land in U.S. territory west of the original thirteen colonies. The ordinance also created a system of surveying that divided the land into geographical square miles—a pattern still evident in the modern American landscape.

An ORDINANCE for ascertaining the Mode of disposing of LANDS in the WESTERN TERRITORY.

BE IT ORDAINED BY THE UNITED STATES *IN* CONGRESS ASSEMBLED, THAT the territory ceded by individual states to the United States, which has been purchased of the Indian inhabitants, shall be disposed of in the following manner. . . .

The surveyors as they are respectively qualified shall proceed to divide the said territory into townships of six miles square, by lines running due north and south, and others crossing these at right angles, unless where the boundaries of the late Indian purchases may render the same impracticable, and then they shall depart from this rule no farther than such particular circumstances may require.

The first line running north and south as aforesaid, shall begin on the river Ohio, at a point that shall be found to be due north from the termination of a line which has been run as the southern boundary of the state of Pennsylvania; and the first line running east and west shall begin at the same point, and shall extend throughout the whole territory. The geographer shall designate the townships or fractional parts of townships, by numbers progressively from south to north, always beginning each range with No. 1; and the ranges shall be distinguished by their progressive numbers to the westward. The first range extending from the Ohio to the lake Erie, being marked No. 1. The geographer shall personally attend to the running of the first east and west line, and shall take the latitude of the extremes of the first north and south line, and of the mouths of the principal rivers. . . .

The plats of the townships respectively, shall be marked by subdivision into lots of one mile square, or 640 acres, in the same direction as the external lines, and numbered from 1 to 36. . . .

As soon as five ranges of townships, and fractional parts of townships, in the direction from south to north, shall have been surveyed, the geographer shall transmit plats thereof to the board of treasury, who shall record the same with the report, in well bound books to be kept for that purpose.

Source: The Library of Congress. "American Memory." Available online. URL: http://memory.loc.gov/cgi-bin/query/r?ammem/bdsdcc:@field(DOCID+@lit(bdsdcc13201)). Accessed November 11, 2008.

feminism and ecofeminism

For more than 160 years, feminists have addressed inequities between men and women in politics, economy, and society. More recently, a new form of feminism, known as ecofeminism, has challenged the patriarchy's shared domination of women and nature.

Although the exact origins are difficult to find, feminism is a relatively new term first coined in France during the 1880s and eventually adopted in the English-speaking world. American definitions of feminism varied as cultural, historical, and social conditions changed. One definition positioned feminism as a movement concerned with achieving equality between the sexes. Many feminists started with the observation that the perspectives of men have been historically privileged over those of women. Feminists described this systematic and cultural inequity as *patriarchy*. Feminism as a social and political movement has fought patriarchy in all of its forms to achieve equality between men and women. Later feminists broadened their definition to challenge the unjust distribution of power in all human relations, linking the struggle for equality between men and women to struggles for social, racial, political, environmental, and economic justice.

In the United States, feminism developed in three historical "waves." First-wave feminism began in the mid-19th century. Women voiced concerns about the inequities between men and women and struggled for political equality, especially securing the right to vote. Elizabeth Cady Stanton (1815–1902) helped launch the first wave of feminism with her 1848 Declaration of Sentiments endorsed by the first women's rights convention in Seneca Falls, New York. Centrally tied to the suffrage movement, first-wave feminism ended in 1920 with the passage of the 19th Amendment to the U.S. Constitution, which secured women's right to vote.

In the 1960s, second-wave feminism emerged and first-wave feminism, in hindsight, gained its name. Second-wave feminism built on the rights gained by the preceding generations and engaged a broader range of issues, addressing discrimination in social, cultural, and economic contexts and challenging women's cultural confinement to the domestic sphere. Scholars point to the publication of Betty Friedan's *Feminine Mystique* in 1963 as the beginning of second-wave feminism. Friedan questioned the stereotype that women were happiest as homemakers. She discouraged women from losing their identities to the men in their lives by seeing themselves only in relation to their families. Friedan cofounded and became the first president of the National Organization for Women (NOW). NOW quickly established a reputation as a women's civil rights organization and remains active in the 21st century.

Second-wave feminists engaged burgeoning women's health issues. The FOOD AND DRUG ADMINISTRATION approved birth control pills in 1960. In 1972, the U.S. Supreme Court ruled in *Eisenstadt v. Baird* (405 U.S. 438) that all people had the right to obtain contraception. However, the most controversial Supreme Court case was *Roe v. Wade* (410 U.S. 113 [1973]), which ruled that first-trimester abortions were legal. The second wave of feminism also addressed economic rights. Feminists advocated equal pay for equal work and equal opportunities for advancement. In *Corning Glass Works v. Brennan* (417 U.S. 188 [1974]), the Supreme Court ruled that it was illegal to pay women less than men for the same work if gender was the only differentiating factor. Nonetheless, women have struggled to obtain equal pay even in the 21st century.

Second-wave feminism has not ended. However, if second-wave feminism was largely an extension of first-wave feminism, third-wave feminism is a reaction against the perceived shortcomings of second-wave feminism. Beginning in the 1990s, third-wave feminists contended that white middle-class women overdetermined the second-wave feminist agenda. Poor or working-class women and minority women did not necessarily experience the world in the same way. Gender, class, and race were inseparable; there was no singular feminist identity. Black third-wave feminists were some of the most vocal in their objections, and their attempts to talk about race within feminism are often identified as the starting point for third-wave feminism.

Third-wave feminists faced criticism for being too scattered and for depriving the movement of a clear goal, although many women found the cacophony of voices a welcome change from the monotone voice of the past. Today, second- and third-wave feminists categorize themselves in a number of ways. Lesbian feminists focus on questions of sexuality and gender; Marxist feminists fight for economic equality; black feminists see racism and sexism as intimately linked. Feminism also intersected with the environmental movement in a unique perspective known as ecofeminism.

Ecofeminists argue the subordination of women and the abuse of nature by men are inherently connected; the same attitudinal practices that allow men to dominate women lead them to try to control nature. In other words, patriarchy must be resisted as an oppressive force that dominates humans and nature. The exact origins of ecofeminism are difficult to identify. The French feminist Françoise d'Eaubonne (1920–2005) was perhaps the first to use the phrase *ecological feminism*, in 1974. Although d'Eaubonne's use of the term *ecofeminism* coincided with the second wave of feminism in the United States, ecofeminists have more in common with third-wave feminists.

Many ecofeminists believe that patriarchal language illustrates the connection between domination of women and domination of nature. Many terms in the English language feminize nature and the Earth. Phrases such as "Mother Nature" and "Mother Earth" construct a clear connection between women and nature. The role of patriarchal domination becomes clearer in phrases such as "the rape of the land." However, the linguistic link is not unidirectional. In the same way wild nature became feminized, many ecofeminists argue, language use allowed women to be seen as naturally wild in need of "taming." Patriarchal language positions both women and nature as passive objects open to men's control and manipulation.

Although many ecofeminists believe language links domination of nature with that of women, others begin from a more materialist point of view. Some ecofeminists contend men abuse nature because patriarchy has allowed men to be the main possessors of the land. In addition, because women have been systematically and institutionally oppressed, their traditional economic roles have not given them the opportunity to engage in proper stewardship. If patriarchy were dismantled, and women were given equal say in the human-nature relationship, many ecofeminists contend, humans would no longer abuse the natural world.

Ecofeminism also has a spiritual dimension. Many ecofeminists believe there is an intuitive and spiritual link between women and nature that patriarchy has stifled. Ecofeminists who subscribe to this view argue the Earth is sacred and should not be desecrated by unsustainable and irresponsible use. Likewise, many ecofeminists see the divine in all living creatures; for a man to harm a woman or an animal is also to harm the sacred. Because all things are sacred, they all have inherent value. This strand of ecofeminism often links the concerns of feminism with that of deep ecology and the animal rights movement.

Today, the future of the feminist movement remains uncertain. The United States may be approaching a time when feminism loses a significant portion of its societal relevance. While some women choose not to call themselves feminists, they remain concerned with equality between men and women. Many feminists believe feminism will be needed until those in power understand the interconnected relationships that exist among men, women, nature, animals, and all things sacred.

See also ENVIRONMENTALISM, GRASSROOTS; ENVIRONMENTALISM, MAINSTREAM; ENVIRONMENTALISM, RADICAL; ENVIRONMENTAL JUSTICE; HEALTH AND MEDICINE; MOTHERS OF EAST LOS ANGELES.

Richard D. Besel

Further Reading

Freedman, Estelle B. *No Turning Back: The History of Feminism and the Future of Women.* New York: Ballantine Books, 2002.

Gaard, Greta, ed. *Ecofeminism: Women, Animals, Nature.* Philadelphia: Temple University Press, 1993.

Mellor, Mary. *Feminism and Ecology.* New York: New York University Press, 1997.

Warren, Karen J., ed. *Ecofeminism: Women, Culture, Nature.* Bloomington: Indiana University Press, 1997.

fences and fence laws

Throughout the history of North America, boundaries between different societies, cultures, and nations have been marked in a variety of ways. Since 1492, one such boundary took the physical form of fences and the legal form of fence laws. The building of fences required a lot of hard work in order to hew or saw logs from trees, lift stones uncovered from the soil, dig holes for posts, and maintain the integrity of fences over years of weather, decay, and invasion by predatory animals. Building fences was an attempt to arrange the lands of North America in rational order, domestic neatness, economic efficiency, or legal division, all of which accorded with European cultural norms.

Fences separated Europeans from Native Americans both physically and culturally. Beginning in the early 1500s, European settlers and their descendants introduced notions of property ownership, which were foreign to the Native Americans who first inhabited North America. For the most part, Native Americans had not built fences for two reasons—because they had other methods of protecting their food crops of maize, squash, and beans from animal predators or other competing Indian groups, and because Native Americans did not have the kinds of domestic livestock that were introduced by Europeans to North America. Without CATTLE, HORSES, sheep, PIGS AND HOGS, and poultry owned as property, Native Americans had little need for fences to separate animals from fields and gardens. To ward off DEER and other animal foragers, Native peoples used FIRE and traps.

Fence laws were mainly a creation of European settlers, who allowed their livestock, specifically cattle and hogs, to roam freely through the woods and backcountry. Fence laws established rules about how high fences should be and how many rails they should contain. The first fence law in the English colonies was established in Virginia in 1632; it stated that "every man shall enclose his ground with sufficient fences upon their own peril." After the Virginia fence law, fence laws before the mid-1800s placed the burden on the owner of the fields to erect strong and sturdy fences to prevent wandering livestock from entering planted fields. Food crops were fenced in rather than animals. Native Americans, however, objected when the Europeans' livestock wandered and ate the CORN, beans, and squash planted in the unfenced fields of Native peoples.

This English style of agriculture, adapted to the North American WILDERNESS, led to conflicts between the English, who wished to farm with cattle, pigs, and sheep, and the Indians, who saw little need for keeping and managing such domestic animals. Such cultural conflicts were most frequent in the eastern temperate forests from Canada to Georgia. By the 1850s, Europeans, Canadians, and Americans had asserted their dominance over the eastern Indians through a new agricultural landscape marked by farms, fields, livestock, and fences. West of the MISSISSIPPI RIVER, however, it was not until the 1870s and 1880s that the Great Plains were conquered by the Euro-American ecology of agriculture, cattle, swine, and sheep, as well as the adoption of fences and fence laws.

Fence construction changed over the centuries. Before the industrial manufacture of fences, fences were made of local materials found in great abundance. Fences were often built from the seasonal labor of farmers. Preindustrial fences reflected individuality among farmers, as well as the ecological variety among regions of North America. Most European settlers in the 1600s and 1700s, for example, began by building worm fences made of trees cut to clear the forest. By the 1800s, however, New England was defined by walls built from stones that farmers had plowed up in their fields over the generations. Because New England had a unique amount of rocky glacial soils, no other region took to stone walls to the extent that New England did. Other regions, such as the South and West, relied upon stumps or hewn wood from the 1600s well into the 1800s. Wood for fences, however, became scarcer in some eastern states by the 1820s. Innovative farmers in Delaware tried the use of English-style hedges, or "live fences," to replace wooden fences. When the PRAIRIES of Indiana, Illinois, Iowa, and Missouri were stripped of riverbank trees during the 1850s, farmers experimented with Osage orange, a plant whose thorny growth separated animals from fields. Farm reformers of the 1830s, 1840s, and 1850s argued that farmers would reduce the amount of fencing materials necessary to enclose fields if they just fenced in their livestock.

During the Industrial Revolution in the mid-1800s in the United States, the materials with which fences were made became specialized and standardized. The invention and manufacture of fences made of metal wire and barbed metal wire by the 1870s were the best examples of specialization and standardization. Barbed wire had many different metal twists, yet it proved to be the most versatile of all fencing materials ever manufactured. Barbed wire, however, did not end conflicts over fencing. Texas cattlemen who wished to drive their longhorn cattle northward to railcars without encountering the barriers of barbed wire fences along the cattle trails bitterly disputed the building of fences. Deadly conflicts erupted among white Americans in the 1870s over fences on the Plains.

Fences are not only boundaries between groups of human beings; they are also technologies used to separate humans from the natural environment. When the early environmental philosopher HENRY DAVID THOREAU criticized his neighbor's "puny" fences in the 1840s, he argued that fences domesticated and cheapened the land. Fences had dramatically changed the North American landscape by turning a "vast and untamed wilderness" into farms owned by individual farmers. To Thoreau, fences had helped to disrupt humans' organic and divine connection to nature. Still, most Americans at the time disagreed with Thoreau. They insisted that the building of good fences ensured not only the separation of animals and plants but also the cultural division between civilized and uncivilized land use.

See also ENGLISH EXPLORATION AND SETTLEMENT— CANADA AND NEW ENGLAND; ENGLISH EXPLORATION AND SETTLEMENT—THE MIDDLE COLONIES; ENGLISH EXPLORATION AND SETTLEMENT—THE SOUTH; UNITED STATES— CENTRAL PLAINS; UNITED STATES—DEEP SOUTH; UNITED STATES—MIDWEST; UNITED STATES—SOUTHWEST.

Eric Stoykovich

Further Reading

Bourcier, Paul G. "'In Excellent Order': The Gentleman Farmer Views His Fences, 1790–1860." *Agricultural History* 58, no. 4 (October 1984): 546–564.

Cronon, William. *Changes in the Land: Indians, Colonists, and the Ecology of New England.* New York: Hill & Wang, 1986.

Danhof, Clarence. "The Fencing Problem in the Eighteen-Fifties." *Agricultural History* 18 (1944): 168–186.

Hayter, Earl. "Livestock-Fencing Conflicts in Rural America." *Agricultural History* 37, no. 1 (January 1963): 10–20.

Valentine, J. O., ed. *Thoreau on Land: Nature's Canvas.* Boston: Houghton Mifflin Company, 2001.

"Mending Wall"
Robert Frost (1914)

Robert Frost's poem "Mending Wall" (1914) is set in the countryside outside Boston. The narrator retells how he and his neighbor repair a stone wall dividing their properties. While the narrator questions the metaphorical meaning of erecting barriers between people, his neighbor recognizes that the exercise is a New England ritual and part of a larger American tradition. The neighbor reminds the narrator that "good fences make good neighbors."

Something there is that doesn't love a
    wall,
That sends the frozen-ground-swell
    under it,
And spills the upper boulders in the sun,
And makes gaps even two can pass
    abreast.
The work of hunters is another thing:
I have come after them and made repair
Where they have left not one stone on a
    stone,

But they would have the rabbit out of
   hiding,
To please the yelping dogs. The gaps I
   mean,
No one has seen them made or heard
   them made,
But at spring mending-time we find
   them there.
I let my neighbor know beyond the hill;
And on a day we meet to walk the line
And set the wall between us once
   again.
We keep the wall between us as we go.
To each the boulders that have fallen to
   each.
And some are loaves and some so nearly
   balls
We have to use a spell to make them
   balance:
"Stay where you are until our backs are
   turned!"
We wear our fingers rough with
   handling them.
Oh, just another kind of out-door game,
One on a side. It comes to little more:
There where it is we do not need the
   wall:
He is all pine and I am apple orchard.
My apple trees will never get across
And eat the cones under his pines, I tell
   him.
He only says, "Good fences make good
   neighbors."
Spring is the mischief in me, and I
   wonder
If I could put a notion in his head:
"Why do they make good neighbors?
   Isn't it
Where there are cows?
But here there are no cows.
Before I built a wall I'd ask to know
What I was walling in or walling out,
And to whom I was like to give
   offence.
Something there is that doesn't love a
   wall,
That wants it down." I could say "Elves"
   to him,
But it's not elves exactly, and I'd rather
He said it for himself. I see him there
Bringing a stone grasped firmly by the
   top

In each hand, like an old-stone savage
   armed.
He moves in darkness as it seems to me~
Not of woods only and the shade of
   trees.
He will not go behind his father's saying,
And he likes having thought of it so well
He says again, "Good fences make good
   neighbors."

Source: Robert Frost. *North of Boston.* New York: Henry H. Holt and Company, 1915, 11–13.

fertilizer

Fertilizers are chemical compounds given to plants to promote growth; they are usually applied either through the soil, for uptake by plant roots, or by foliar feeding, for uptake through leaves. Fertilizers can be organic (composed of organic matter) or inorganic (made of simple, inorganic chemicals or minerals). They can be naturally occurring compounds such as peat or mineral deposits or manufactured through natural processes (such as composting) or chemical processes. Americans use fertilizers in agriculture, landscaping, and recreation (golf courses, for example). The misuse of fertilizers can damage groundwater and waterways.

All ECOSYSTEMS, including natural agricultural, forest, and aquatic ecosystems, depend upon various systems of fertilizer nutrients. The functional components of the ecosystem are producers (plants), consumers (animals and microbes), and reducers, or decomposers (animals and microbes). The total system is driven by the sun's energy.

Plants require carbon, hydrogen, oxygen, nitrogen, phosphorus, potassium, calcium, and several other fertilizer nutrients to function. Solar energy is used along with these elements to construct the needed chemicals for growth, development, and reproduction for the plants. The dependent animals and microbes require the same elements for growth, development, and reproduction but derive nutrients from plants either directly or indirectly.

All the nutrients mentioned are essential, but some are utilized in greater quantities than others. Water is one of the largest quantities required by plants and in turn animals and microbes. A plant such as CORN requires about 6 million liters of water per hectare (a hectare equals 2.47 acres) just during the three-month growing season, roughly for each kilogram of corn or other plant biomass, about 1,000 liters of water is needed. The water provides

LIVESTOCK NUMBERS AND MANURE AND NITROGEN (N) PRODUCED PER YEAR IN THE UNITED STATES

Livestock	Number ($\times 10^6$)	Manure produced per head lb./year	Manure tons ($\times 10^6$)	N produced per head (lb.)	Total N lb. ($\times 10^9$)
Cattle	100	22,000	1,000	600	60 (18)[a]
Hogs	60	2,700	90	136	8.2
Chickens	9,000	68	61	0.21	18.9
Total					45.1

Total = 20.5 million metric tons of nitrogen per year.

[a]Only the quantity of manure collected for use.

Source: U.S. Department of Agriculture. *Agricultural Statistics.* Washington, D.C.: U.S. Government Printing Office, 2004; NRAES. "Manure Characteristics: Natural Resource, Agriculture, and Engineering Service." Available online. URL: http://www.nraes.org/nra_order.taf?_function=detail&pr_id=88&_UserReference=9F83B8273CC7F1784628E275. Accessed April 20, 2007.

the essential hydrogen and oxygen required by plants. The animals and microbes that feed on the plants may also require additional water for their growth, development, and reproduction.

About 20 percent of the water that falls on the earth as rain is from evaporation from the oceans. About 14 percent of the water evaporation is from the terrestrial systems. In fact, large quantities of water are released by plants during their metabolism. Approximately 68 percent of the water that is released into the atmosphere in terrestrial systems is from plant physiology or evapotranspiration.

Plants require carbon dioxide, which provides the plants with their needed carbon and more oxygen. Actually, plants release large quantities of oxygen, which is required by animals and microbes for their survival. There can be too much carbon dioxide in the atmosphere, as is the current situation, and this excess carbon dioxide is contributing to the GREENHOUSE EFFECT.

Nitrogen, an essential element for plants and animals, is difficult to maintain in ecosystems at sufficient quantities for plants and, in turn, animals and microbes. After nitrogen, the other nutrients required by the biological systems include phosphorus, potassium, and calcium, plus several other elements. Plants obtain these fertilizing nutrients from decomposing animals, microbes, and plants. For agricultural purposes, most of the phosphorus, potassium, and calcium elements are mined from large concentrations that have accumulated over millions of years.

Nitrogen fertilizer is easily lost from ecosystems, whether agricultural or natural ecosystems. Nitrogen is lost by several means: From 30 percent to 50 percent is used by plants, approximately 30 percent is lost by leaching, from 20 percent to 30 percent is lost by dinitrification, and 1 percent to 30 percent is lost by soil EROSION. These losses explain why nitrogen fertilizer is one of the scarcest nutrients for plants in both agricultural and natural ecosystems.

Nitrogen, after carbon, hydrogen, and oxygen, is one of the major limiting resources for plants. Although the Earth's atmosphere is 80 percent nitrogen, plants cannot use this nitrogen directly. Plants obtain their nitrogen primarily from four sources: decomposing animals, microbes, and plants; wastes, such as manure, from animals; nitrogen-fixing microbes that are fed by plants; and nitrogen fertilizer produced from fossil energy (primarily NATURAL GAS).

Nature, with the objective to conserve the basic elements required for life systems, has evolved a system of recycling the nutrients in plants, animals, and microbes. No organism is immortal or can survive indefinitely; all organisms die and their nutrients are recycled in the ecosystem. The dead organisms decompose, and their nutrients are picked up by plants and reused for their growth, development, and reproduction. Then, the plants are fed upon by animals and microbes dependent upon the nutrients provided by plants, either while alive or once dead.

For centuries, people used manure, cinder, and iron making slag to improve crops. Agricultural advancements in the 19th century depended, in part, on the substantially greater use of fertilizers in the United States and other industrialized nations. These advancements minimized the need for agricultural labor and produced enough food to feed the growing populations of America's industrial cities. By midcentury, factories emerged to produce and sell chemically processed fertilizers. After WORLD WAR II (1941–45), agricultural intensification and the use of fertilizers spread across the globe as part of the GREEN REVOLUTION. Many new types of seed possessed increased nitrogen-absorbing potential, particularly the high-response varieties of maize, WHEAT, and RICE.

The use of fertilizers on a global scale, in turn, contributed to increased emissions of greenhouse gases. Additionally, when fertilizers have been used in excessive quantities, runoff has carried nitrogen and phosphorus into waterways. Both of these are needed for healthy plant growth but in large amounts are toxic. Excess phosphorus, for example, spurs the growth of algae and WEEDS in lakes. Another ecological problem is the accumulation of arsenic, cadmium, and uranium in fields treated with phosphate fertilizers.

In the United States today, one of the largest quantities of fertilizer nutrients is obtained from wastes such as manure from animals including agricultural livestock. In 2006, the 100 million CATTLE, 60 million PIGS AND HOGS, and nine billion poultry maintained in the United States (*see* table on page 535) produced an estimated 45 million metric tons of nitrogen per year. Most of this nitrogen is produced by cattle. However, of the 45 million metric tons produced, only an estimated 20.5 million tons of nitrogen per year could be used in crop production. To collect and manage this nitrogen require special attention, as approximately 50 percent of the nitrogen is lost as ammonia within 24 to 48 hours, if the animal waste is not immediately buried in the soil or placed in a lagoon under anaerobic conditions. The liquid nutrient material in the lagoon must be buried in the soil immediately after it is applied to the land, or again the nitrogen will be lost to the atmosphere.

Some 70 percent of cattle manure is dropped in pasture or rangeland. Using this estimate, the amount of nitrogen theoretically collected per year is 18 million metric tons that could be effectively used in agriculture.

Almost an equal amount of nitrogen is provided in the United States via biological nitrogen fixation. The amount produced by nitrogen fixation is estimated to be 14 million tons each year. This compares favorably with the annual amount of 12 million tons applied as commercial nitrogen, which is produced from natural gas.

See also AGRICULTURAL TECHNOLOGY; AGRICULTURE, COMMERCIAL; CHEMISTRY; CORPORATIONS, CHEMICAL; FOOD; GARDENS AND GARDENING; GREEN REVOLUTION; LAWNS; MEXICO AND THE UNITED STATES; SOIL CONSERVATION.

David Pimental

Further Reading
Pimentel, David, and Marcia Pimentel. *Food, Energy and Society.* 3d ed. Boca Raton, Fla.: CRC Press (Taylor and Francis Group), 2008.

David Pimental, et al. "Water Resources: Agricultural and Environmental Issues." *Bioscience* 54 no. 10 (2004): 909–918.
Troeh, Frederick R., J. Arthur Hobbs, and Roy Donahue. *Soil and Water Conservation for Productivity and Environmental Protection.* Upper Saddle River, N.J.: Prentice Hall, 2004.

54°40′ or Fight

The odd expression "54°40′ or Fight" ("Fifty-four-forty or Fight") is from the 19th century; it refers to a conflict between the United States and the British Empire related to the border separating the United States, Russian America (Alaska), and Canada. The 54°40′ latitude still corresponds to the southern limit that separates the southern part of the Alaskan strip from the Canadian province of British Columbia along the Pacific Ocean. The 19th-century dispute involved the Oregon country, which many Americans believed included all of the land that makes up Oregon, Washington State, Idaho, parts of Wyoming and Montana, and a section of British Columbia. The expression also reflected the idea of MANIFEST DESTINY that many Americans evoked to justify their claims to territorial expansion. The United States was eager to extend its borders from the Atlantic Ocean to the Pacific Ocean and to acquire territories such as the Pacific Northwest that were rich in natural resources such as timber, minerals, FISHERIES, good soils, and natural harbors.

In the early 19th century, four countries, Spain (Mexico after 1821), Russia, Britain (for Canada), and the United States claimed rights to the Oregon country. Russia and the United States agreed to the 54°40′ border between Russian America and the Oregon country in 1824 and 1825, but neither consulted Canada or the British Empire, which protected the FUR TRADE interests of the Hudson's Bay Company, the oldest corporation in North America. Russia and Britain also signed a treaty setting the boundary between their territories along the coast at the 56° parallel. Little, if any attention was paid by any of these parties to the interests of Native Americans in the region.

Britain and the United States jointly occupied the Oregon country from 1818 until 1844. JOHN JACOB ASTOR's American Fur Company increasingly competed with the Hudson's Bay Company for the region's resources. Other American settlers followed and by the late 1830s began to dominate the region, particularly the land south of the 49° parallel. In 1844, the expression "54°40′ or Fight" became a political slogan for the Democratic presidential candidate JAMES POLK. Using ruse and demagogic strategies, candidate Polk even threatened war with Great Britain in order to gain U.S. control of the entire region. During this era of expansion, many U.S. borders were disputed or contested. Polk won the election and became the 11th U.S. president in March 1845.

In the end, a war over the Oregon boundary dispute never materialized. Instead, the United States found itself in a war with Mexico. The U.S. annexation of Texas in 1845 helped launch the MEXICAN-AMERICAN WAR (1846–48) a year later. By the end of the war in 1848, the United States acquired more than half of Mexico's national territory, including land that eventually became the states of California, New Mexico, Arizona, and Nevada, and parts of Utah, Colorado, and Wyoming.

The Polk administration and the British Empire chose diplomacy to resolve the controversy over Oregon and reached a final agreement in 1846. The Oregon Treaty established the 49° latitude (except for special cases such as Vancouver Island) as the international border west of the Rocky Mountains, as it remains today. Many U.S. critics thought President Polk had compromised on his campaign promise, while Canadians argued that from the beginning, the ambitious U.S. claims overreached. Decades after the treaty, many Canadians believed that the British Crown sacrificed too large a portion of Canadian territory in order to maintain a harmonious relationship with the United States. Local conflicts periodically exploded, such as the 1859 dispute over San Juan Island in PUGET SOUND. Sometimes ironically labeled the "Pig War," this conflict began with the shooting of a pig, the only casualty, and resulted in both sides' engaging in a military occupation of the island until an international commission in 1872 ruled that the island belonged to the United States.

A similar border dispute over the 54°40′ limit occurred among Canada, the British Empire, and the United States, after the Russian-American Convention of 1867. Before 1867, Russia still claimed Alaska, then known as Russian America, as one of its territories. The United States purchased the territory in 1867 for $7.2 million and renamed it Alaska. With the new Canadian confederation in 1867, Canada wanted to survey the Pacific coast boundaries to confirm the extent of its territory, but this did not occur until the Klondike GOLD rush at the end of the century flooded the region with prospectors and gave it a new importance. In 1903, the Alaska Boundary Tribunal (made up of three Americans, two Canadians, and one British member) ruled in favor of the Americans and set the border at the 54°40′ parallel, a decision that left a general sentiment of bitterness and created a source of anti-Americanism in western Canada.

The slogan and the tension it revealed continued to resonate after the border was resolved. In 1909, *54°40′ or Fight* became the title of a novel by the U.S. writer Emerson

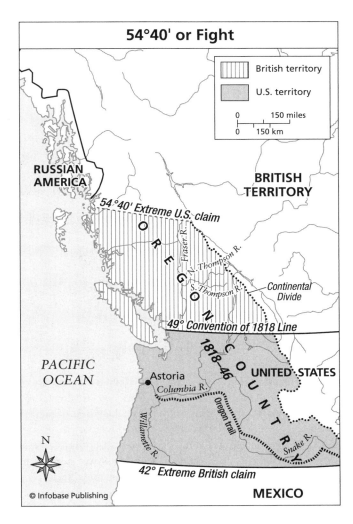

Hough (1857–1923). In the beginning of the 12th chapter, he wrote: "But sometime, one way or another, the joint occupancy of England and the United States in the Oregon country must end." This epic book can be found online today. More recently, in the early 21st century, 54°40′ or Fight even became the name of an independent record company.

To strengthen their relationship as good neighbors, the Canadian and U.S. governments jointly created, in 1908, a permanent bilateral treaty organization, the International Boundary Commission/Commission de la frontière internationale, to define and mark the longest unprotected border in the world. Until June 2009, citizens from both countries crossed the physical border at the 49th parallel without having to show a valid passport. However, since 2009, a valid passport is mandatory.

See also CANADA AND THE UNITED STATES; ENGLISH EXPLORATION AND SETTLEMENT—CANADA AND NEW ENGLAND; LEWIS AND CLARK EXPEDITION; RUSSIAN

EXPLORATION AND SETTLEMENT; UNITED STATES—ALASKA; UNITED STATES—PACIFIC NORTHWEST.

Yves Laberge

Further Reading

Heyes, Derek. *Historical Atlas of the American West with Original Maps.* Berkeley: University of California Press, 2009.

International Boundary Commission. Available online. URL: http://www.internationalboundarycommission.org/products.html. Accessed June 4, 2009.

Munro, John A. *The Alaska Boundary Dispute.* Toronto: Copp Clark, 1970.

Nugent, Walter. *Habits of Empire: A History of American Expansion.* New York: Alfred A. Knopf, 2008.

Penlington, Norman. *The Alaska Boundary Dispute: A Critical Reappraisal.* Toronto: McGraw-Hill Ryerson, 1972.

film   *See* DISNEY; HOLLYWOOD; NATURE FILMS.

fire

Fire is a reaction, not an element: It is what its circumstances make it to be. Those circumstances were broadly created by the living world, beginning in the early Devonian (ca. 425 million years ago), when oxygen spawned by marine life met land-colonizing plants. What remained to complete fire's chemical triangle—fuel, oxygen, and heat—was a spark to initiate the process. Lightning assumed that role.

The geography of fire thereafter followed from gross rhythms of wetting and drying. Lands had to be wet enough to grow plants and dry enough to allow them to burn. Some places experienced this cycle annually, some by decades, some over centuries. Some places had ideal environments for fire, save the presence of proper ignition. The arrangement of fire was thus lumpy in space and time. Some places never burned. Some burned yearly. During the Carboniferous, an immense quantity of biomass was buried rather than burned.

All this changed when the Earth, a uniquely fire planet, acquired a uniquely fire creature capable of manipulating ignition and establishing a species monopoly. Probably *Homo erectus* could maintain fire, but not until *Homo sapiens* could hominids make fire at will. Only people have thus had fire all their existence. Increasingly, the geography of fire became what humans made it.

Still, humanity's firepower had limits. The power to kindle fire was only as good as a landscape's capacity to spread it. To move beyond that barrier required control over fuel. Slashing, draining, loosing grazers and browsers, growing, and fallowing—such practices amplified the combustibles available to burn and defined the essence of agricultural fire. Again, there were limits on how much biomass people could coax or coerce from land before a place degraded. An escalation of firepower demanded a more unbounded cache of fuel, which people found in fossil biomass: COAL, lignite, gas, oil.

Here is the pith of industrial fire, as humanity routed its fire practices through the internal combustion of machines. The Earth today is dividing into two combustion realms, one devoted to burning surface biomass; the other, fossil biomass. Save during a period of transition, there is little overlap between them. Industrial fire's limits reside less in the availability of combustibles than in problems of waste disposal, especially the liberation of greenhouse gases, and in the growing appreciation that fire's removal can be as ecologically powerful as fire's presence.

FIRE'S AMERICAN NARRATIVE

That, concisely, is the grand narrative of fire, to which America, as everywhere else, has subscribed. Natural regimes concentrate in the arid West, with a secondary core in Florida. The epicenter of lightning fire is the mountainous Southwest, subject to annual barrages; a wider range of episodic ignitions spread from the Sierra-Cascades to the Rockies, with fires kindling according to varied rhythms and regional conflagrations two or three times a century. Shortgrass plains, too, burn according to a cadence set by rainy spells, grazing, and dry lightning.

Aboriginal fire practices altered patterns by imposing a new, mobile matrix, characterized by lines of fire and fields of fire. The former refers to routes of seasonal travel, and the latter, to patches where burning assisted foraging and hunting and otherwise sculpted the landscape into a habitat favorable to people. Moreover, there undoubtedly occurred substantial fire littering, of fire left or accidentally scattered, some of which propagated widely. Burning generally occurred prior to the natural season; areas people wanted protected or burned were treated before lightning arrived.

In some places, such as the Southwest, the outcome meant the transfer of already extensive burning from the bolt to the torch; aboriginal burning added to the mix and locally restructured its cadences. In other places, such as mediterranean California, aboriginal practices made fire routine where conditions for burning were ideal but ignition rare. Elsewhere, by keeping some flame almost constantly on the land, people contributed to the episodically eruptive fire that would not otherwise have occurred. Overall, the thrust was to encourage grass, forbs, and useful shrubs at the expense of dense FORESTS and brushlands. The mosaic effects were both intricate and coarse. Extensive tallgrass PRAIRIES were probably created by a combination of climatic drying and aboriginal burning but were almost certainly maintained by anthropogenic fire. The removal of that flame quickly yielded landscapes overrun by woody plants.

In pre-Columbian times, agricultural fire thrived too, primarily throughout the eastern Mississippi Valley and Southeast, but punching north into New England and around parts of the GREAT LAKES. The onset could be sudden: Excavations in the Tennessee Valley, for example, show a sharp increase in soil charcoal along with pollen from introduced crops. Farmed sites warped other fire practices, with cropping often in floodplains and uplands burned for hunting, gathering, and travel. This fire geography existed under human auspices and rapidly disintegrated when people left.

European colonization initially adopted and added heft to such practices, then overwhelmed them. Early legislation banned fire hunting; logging and land clearing associated with settlement bulked up indigenous patterns of slash-and-burn agriculture; livestock, both grazers and browsers, upset fuels that powered old burning regimens; new plants were stirred into the cauldron, some more fire-prone, some less. Yet, ultimately, fire remained universal: The hearth was the center of the home; corridors of traffic remained well fired; the burned field endured as the mark of farmed and pastured landscapes. The magnitude of American burning swelled. The FRONTIER was a flaming front.

Three 19th-century reports captured the sense of fire's pervasiveness. In its 1878 *Arid Lands* treatise, the Powell Survey, sponsored by the U.S. GEOLOGICAL SURVEY, mapped burned land in Utah, ranging from the thickening edge of the desert to the rim of the high plateaus. The deep cause, JOHN WESLEY POWELL reasoned, was the West's seasonal aridity; the proximate cause, Native burning. Damage to local forests far exceeded the levies made by settlement. Charles Sargent's survey "Forests" for the 1880 census expanded that map to include the entire country's fire geography. The distribution of fires corresponded with the character of settlement. The most extensive burning lay in the Southeast (as it still does); the most damaging fires occurred around the Great Lakes, where railways were fast opening the North Woods, and in the Northeast, where a renewal of LOGGING sparked a wave of wildfires. For 60 years, the lake states endured a train of holocaust burns—fires that commanded attention amid a political groundswell for state-sponsored CONSERVATION. In 1882, Franklin Hough published the fire volume of *Report upon Forestry,* in which he also recorded an almost universal recourse to folk burning along with a nearly universal shrug from practitioners. In its fires, the United States in the 1880s resembled Brazil in the 1980s, responding to similar causes and provoking comparable outrage from intellectuals. Bernhard Fernow (1851–1923), then head of the Bureau of Forestry, dismissed the American fire scene as one of "bad habits and loose morals."

The nation's rapid industrialization aggravated the situation. This pyric transition follows a rude trajectory in which the population of fires first multiplies wildly as new sources of fuel and ignition compound with the old until, over 50–60 years, the number of open fires shrinks below what might be called replacement values. (The primary exception are arid grasslands, where the rail link to markets encourages the mass introduction of sheep and CATTLE that crop the fuels into oblivion and fire with them.) The cycle moves from a surplus of bad burns to a deficit of good ones.

Thoughtful observers concluded that fire was out of control—promiscuous, abusive, dangerous, embarrassing. Flame seemed the universal element in America's wanton exploitation of its environment, a cause, a catalyst, a consequence. Without fire control, no other reform could succeed.

LANDSCAPES OF INDUSTRIAL FIRE

The working out of the industrial transformation—the switch from living to fossil biomass as dominant fuel—is the story of American fire since the late 19th century. As pervasive as fire was in vernacular life, as equally pervasive has been its extinction. It is gone nearly everywhere in domestic life. Fireplaces are largely ceremonial; an occasional candle is the most combustion an average citizen sees. Fire is gone or going from agriculture, as fallowing vanishes and agriburning conforms to air-quality statutes and urban standards. It is gone from industrial manufacturing—the furnace as antiquarian as the hearth. Only reserved public wildlands have been spared. Consider how fire has fared in three critical landscapes: agricultural lands, cities, and wildlands.

Agricultural lands

Fire does in agricultural settings what it does in nature: It fumigates and fertilizes. It temporarily allows exotic flora and fauna to occupy a site otherwise denied to them. With agricultural fire, people redirected basic fire ecology to their own ends, just as they did with domesticated plants and animals. The effect was most pronounced in pioneering, but it was recycled periodically, and had to be, to freshen field and pasture. Such fires required fuel, and in a farmed landscape, fuel was obtained from fallow.

All this was well known to practitioners—and condemned by officials and intellectuals. Especially European agronomic thinking had, since antiquity, anathematized fallow and fire as wasteful and dangerous and denounced those who migrated through landscapes with a torch, from swiddeners to shepherds. European FORESTRY was grafted on this rootstock; foresters joined in scorning all fire practices. Almost from the beginning, a chasm existed between those who lived off the land and found fire necessary and beneficent and those who lived in cities and saw fire as an expression of violent disorder and waste. As America underwent its pyric transition, this fissure widened.

Industrialization found surrogates for open flame. Internal-combustion-powered tractors; artificial FERTILIZER, PESTICIDES, and herbicides replaced fire's purgative and promotive force. Fallowing disappeared, and with it the flames it had fed. Burning became subject to ever more restraints, not the least of which was air quality. Economic logic and public-safety considerations compelled agriculture to find alternatives to fire as a tool. By the 1980s, the fire geography recorded in Sargent's 1880 map was disappearing.

Cities

For a long time, American cities burned much as their surrounding landscapes did. They were composed of similar materials, subject to the same patterns of DROUGHTS and wind, and likewise littered with point sources of fire that, when conditions warranted, bolted free. As with rural outlands, firefighting relied on local residents, more or less organized. To argue for fire's abolition was pointless: Humans could not survive without controlled combustion. Cities burned and rebuilt in a macabre urban swidden.

After the great London fire of 1666, the ENLIGHTENMENT thinkers argued that such fires might be controlled through smarter urban design, more fireproof construction materials, improved apparatus, and better behavior, helpfully directed by fire insurance. Such reforms entered America slowly, aggravated by the urban frontier's constantly unsettled state. Eventually, however, the world of industrial fire supplanted that of open burning.

The usual explanation is that professional fire departments replaced volunteer brigades and multiplexed engines their predecessor man- or horse-drawn hand pumps; that modern materials such as iron and kiln-dried brick substituted for wood and thatch; that open flames disappeared from stoves, furnaces, fireplaces, and lighting in favor of coal, electricity, and NATURAL GAS; that steam- (and later petroleum-) powered transportation pushed the urban fringe into more thinly settled, less fire-prone suburbs; that fire insurance companies demanded reforms to reduce hazard.

All this happened, but the details argue for a more complicated narrative. Most professional departments initially absorbed the volunteers they succeeded. Insurance companies worried whether their income exceeded losses and only became alarmed when general burning patterns became so unsafe and widespread that they threatened those insured. A sense of civic reform—that it was time to end such senselessness—brought political pressure to bear during the Progressive Era (1890–1920) at a time when similar perceptions shaped public response to wildland fire.

In modern cities, fires became progressively rarer and less likely to ramble. Major outbreaks accompanied wars, EARTHQUAKES, or riots when fire-suppression infrastructures and general social order collapse. The last citywide American conflagrations occurred in BALTIMORE, MARYLAND, in 1904 and SAN FRANCISCO, CALIFORNIA, in 1906, following the earthquake. Serious fires were associated with race riots in LOS ANGELES, CALIFORNIA (1965), and DETROIT, MICHIGAN (1967); with megahotels such as LAS VEGAS, NEVADA's MGM Grand (1980); and most spectacularly with the terrorist attack on NEW YORK CITY's World Trade Center (2001). More and more urban fire services have evolved into all-hazard emergency services, of which medical calls account for most responses.

In recent decades, the proliferation of a fractal urban fringe and of exurban enclaves slammed against wildlands or planted on abandoned farmland grown feral became a major concern. This intermixed landscape, or wildland/urban interface, has preoccupied wildland fire agencies more than urban fire departments since most of EXURBIA lies outside municipal jurisdictions. Distinct cultures of urban arid wildland firefighting have been forced together in curious ways, particularly in California.

Wildlands

As America industrialized, it did not abolish fire on all lands, save for accident or arson, because the country elected to reserve permanently large swaths of the PUBLIC DOMAIN. National parks, beginning with YELLOWSTONE in 1872; state preserves, announced by the Adirondacks in 1885; national forests, from 1891—all set aside large chunks of the American scene that were not farmed, urbanized, or otherwise converted apart from contract logging, grazing, and OUTDOOR RECREATION. Reserving such lands meant little without fire protection, which became the first order of business and a public display of administrative effectiveness. Foresters were particularly rabid fire abolitionists.

Initially, there were many fire protection models from which to choose. The most powerful emanated from Yellowstone, where the U.S. Cavalry assumed control in 1886 (it administered other major parks until 1916). In 1905, oversight of the forest reserves was transferred from the General Land Office in the DEPARTMENT OF THE INTERIOR to the Bureau of Forestry (renamed the U.S. FOREST SERVICE) in the DEPARTMENT OF AGRICULTURE. The modern era of American wildland fire dates from this event.

In 1910, a defining moment occurred when all issues swirling around wildland fire crystallized into policy and practice that defined American procedures through most of the 20th century. In August 1910, massive wildfires swept over the West, culminating in the fabled Big Blowup of August 20–21, which scorched more than three million acres in the northern Rockies, killed 78 firefighters, and plunged the Forest Service into an almost-million-dollar debt. That same month, a public debate flared about whether the service's strategy was correct: Critics argued that "light burning" (the "Indian way" of forest management), in which surface fuels were routinely burned away by "light" surface fires, was a more sensible alternative, and that adherence to a paramilitary suppression policy only led to overgrown, diseased, unhealthy woods prone to ever-larger fires.

In the wildfires' aftermath, CONGRESS upheld a 1908 act that allowed for deficit spending during fire emergencies, confirming a pattern of almost unchecked expenditures, and then passed the Weeks Act, which promoted Forest Service expansion by purchase (primarily in the East). Salvage logging, emergency rehabilitation of burned lands, the transfer of personnel across boundaries, a debate over how to honor (and bury) dead firefighters, a renewed commitment to full-bore fire suppression—the whole suite of modern fire issues was suddenly manifest. Until 1940, successive chief foresters had all personally weathered the Big Blowup. They resolved never to allow another such conflagration and fought light burning unremittingly. Although the Forest Service was one federal land agency among many, it dominated the discourse for 50 years and beyond.

While the Forest Service sought to beat down wildfire and folk burning, it could do little beyond the front country landscape and programs with cooperators. Prospects improved in 1924 as the Clarke-McNary Act expanded the Weeks Act and eventually embraced all the states. Nonetheless, much backcountry remained inaccessible before the President FRANKLIN D. ROOSEVELT administration, the appearance of the Civilian Conservation Corps (CCC), and serious funding for emergency rehabilitation. In 1935, the Forest Service announced a universal policy that every fire should be controlled by 10 A.M. the day after its report, or, failing that, controlled by 10 A.M. the next day, ad infinitum. The CCC's presence and expanded emergency funds (for presuppression) made the scheme plausible. Although WORLD WAR II stripped staffing, fire protection became bonded with national defense, a policy that persisted through the decades as a kind of COLD WAR on fire bolstered by war-surplus equipment to which the Forest Service and its cooperators had priority access and by the creation of three fire laboratories under its direction. The Forest Service became a fire hegemon.

This state of affairs began unraveling during the 1960s. The Leopold Report (1963) for the NATIONAL PARK SERVICE, the WILDERNESS ACT OF 1964 for public lands, and a series of fire ecology conferences under the auspices of the Tall Timbers Research Station redefined fire suppression, not fire, as the problem and urged controlled burning (or prescribed fire) as the solution. The NPS reformed its fire policy in 1968; the Forest Service followed a decade later. In 1969, the nucleus of what became the National Interagency Fire Center was established in Boise, Idaho, fragmenting the Forest Service monopoly over crews and equipment. The NPS sponsored research to advance its own, distinctive ends; the National Science Foundation began funding fire ecology. By 1976, a National Wildfire Coordinating Group assumed responsibility for setting standards and merging practices.

Overall, agencies recognized that suppression, as a singular policy, was self-defeating. Fire's removal had huge ecological and economic costs. Continued suppression in the face of mounting wildland combustibles was insupportable. Free-burning fire ought to be reintroduced. Only a confederation of agencies could cope with the variety and complexity of the American fire scene. The reforms that followed sought to protect against wildfires and promote prescribed fires. Experimentation flourished, but fire's restoration proved difficult, not unlike reintroducing a lost species. The era climaxed with the Yellowstone conflagrations of 1988, which vividly announced the policy to the public while underscoring the confused methods behind its implementation.

A decade of telegenic fires followed, beginning with the 1993 fires around Los Angeles and ending with San Diego's Cedar fire in 2003. In 1995, a consolidated federal fire policy declared that fire management should plan for "appropriate response." Three years later, a Joint Fire Science Program received major funding. The 2000 season advertised the magnitude of the task, amid drought and a landscape of overgrown wildlands. Agencies struggled feebly to contain wildfires that swept the northern Rockies, while the NPS lost control of two major prescribed fires in the Southwest. A National Fire Plan followed later that year, succeeded by fire provisions contained within a Healthy Forest Initiative. The televised backdrop, however, remained a flaming exurban landscape that annually displayed burning houses and evacuated communities.

The American fire community was never better financed, staffed, equipped, coordinated, and informed by scientific research and never seemed further from the goal of managing fire to its own ends. One half-century revealed the irony that establishing reserves did not abolish fire but created a permanent habitat for it. The next half-century demonstrated that fire was not a simple phenomenon but a creature of its setting. Goals had to be many, methods plural, and the core politics one of cultural choices about what Americans wanted their public lands to be and how to reconcile those desires with fire's logic.

CONCLUSION: FIRE'S FUTURE

The immediate future promised more of the same. Prescribed fire has become more cumbersome and expensive, while continued suppression has sustained ecological insurgency. Proliferating exurbs, invasive species, and GLOBAL WARMING have aggravated this scene. Industrial fire has spread around the globe; the future offers more combustion and less fire. Open fire, like a threatened species, is retiring to reserves or hunted down as a hazard.

See also INDIANS, CALIFORNIA; INDIANS, MIDWEST; INDIANS, NORTHEAST; INDIANS, SOUTHWEST; NEW DEAL; SMOKEY BEAR; SPECIES, EXOTIC AND INVASIVE; WILDERNESS.

Stephen J. Pyne

Further Reading

Carle, David. *Burning Questions: America's Fight with Nature's Fire.* New York: Praeger, 2002.

Goudsblom, Johan. *Fire and Civilization.* New York: Penguin Group, 1993.

Hazen, Robert, et al. *Keepers of the Flame: The Role of Fire in American Culture, 1775–1925.* Princeton, N.J.: Princeton University Press, 1992.

Hoffer, Peter-Charles. *Seven Fires: The Urban Infernos That Reshaped America.* New York: Public Affairs, 2006.

Pyne, Stephen. *Fire: A Brief History.* Seattle: University of Washington Press, 2001.

——. *Fire in America: A Cultural History of Wildland and Rural Fire.* Seattle: University of Washington Press, 1995.

——. *Year of the Fires: The Story of the Great Fires of 1910.* New York: Viking, 2001.

Tebeau, Mark. *Eating Smoke: Fire in Urban America, 1800–1950.* Baltimore: Johns Hopkins University Press, 2003.

fish and game laws and poaching

SUBSISTENCE HUNTING represents one of the oldest forms of human interaction with the North American environment. Indeed, while there remains considerable debate as to when the first humans arrived in North America, there is little question that these early peoples supported themselves through hunting, as even the latest date proposed for human arrival on the continent (12,000 years

A U.S. Game Management agent holds 121 mink pelts taken illegally in Alaska, 1951.   *(D. C. Freimuth, U.S. Fish and Wildlife Service)*

ago) precedes the rise of SUBSISTENCE AGRICULTURE by several millennia.

For much of hunting's long history in North America, rules governing the chase occupied the realm of custom, being enforced via community censure, taboos, or other forms of informal practice. But the COLUMBIAN EXCHANGE that the arrival of non-Indians in the Americas set in motion in 1492 was more than simply material. Just as Europeans carried with them new plants, animals, and diseases, they also introduced new ideas of how to relate to nature, including the idea that government had the right to enforce laws governing hunting and fishing.

SUBSISTENCE VERSUS RECREATION

This idea was not uncontested in Europe, and as it evolved in North America, it proved contentious in its new habitat as well. In Great Britain, the chase had been limited to property holders since medieval times. This class privilege left in its wake both an elite tradition of sports hunting and a peasant tradition of poaching, complete with folklore about such famous "environmental bandits" as Robin Hood.

In contrast, in colonial America, hunting became associated with subsistence rather than upper-class recreation. Colonists were free to hunt on any unfenced land on the principle of *ferae naturae:* WILD ANIMALS were the property of those who took them in the chase, not of those on whose land they might be found. Other regulations were slight. A few colonies outlawed Sunday hunting or limited the chase to certain seasons of the year. The most prevalent game laws at the time, however, were not those designed to protect wildlife but rather designed to exterminate "vermin" via the payment of bounties on WOLVES, foxes, and other predators.

Given the association of Great Britain's game laws with aristocratic privilege, universal access to game became a potent way, after the AMERICAN REVOLUTION (1775–83), for the new United States to distinguish itself from its former home country. This impulse was especially apparent in the new state constitutions of Pennsylvania and Vermont. The 1776 Pennsylvania Constitution, for example, stated that "the inhabitants of this state shall have liberty to fowl and hunt in seasonable times on the lands they hold, and on all other lands therein not inclosed." Court cases in several states, during the early 1800s, resolved the latent conflict between property in game and property in land that this republican legacy created by asserting that landowners who had not fenced their property could not restrict hunting on it. Indeed, as late as 1886, the sportsman George Putnam Smith wrote, "The sportsman in America runs much less risk of . . . trespass than he would in England. Not only are there in this country large tracts of uninclosed land belonging either to the state or private owners, who do not exclude the sportsman there from, but the 'custom of the country' in most localities is to permit him to enter on any unposted land in pursuit of game."

During the antebellum period, wildlife remained a state rather than federal responsibility, resulting in considerable variation in game laws across the United States. In some states and territories, especially in the West and South, there were no game laws on the books at all prior to the CIVIL WAR (1861–65). In those locations where laws did exist, they tended to be sporadically enforced, and responsibility for implementation usually fell to local police. These forces often proved unwilling to arrest fellow community members for hunting or fishing out of season. Consequently, game laws remained more of a legal fiction than a lived reality for much of this period.

CONSERVATION MOVEMENT AFFECTS HUNTING

The watershed moment in making game laws a tangible presence in the American countryside did not take place until the closing decades of the 19th century with the rise of the CONSERVATION movement. The changes produced by conservation proceeded along two parallel tracks. The first was a far more comprehensive set of rules governing hunting and fishing. If before, most game laws had placed only modest restrictions as to when and, in a few cases, how one could take game, the 1880s and 1890s witnessed a flurry of new laws limiting the chase. Legislatures imposed bag limits (restrictions on how many animals one could kill in a season), set age and gender regulations (often outlawing the killing of female or young animals), required the purchase of hunting licenses, and further tightened the rules over hunting practices. Many states, for example, limited the use of hounds or FIRE to drive game animals or outlawed the use of nets to catch fish.

The second change that occurred with conservation was far more effective enforcement of game laws. As R. W. Williams of the U.S. BIOLOGICAL SURVEY suggested at the turn of the 20th century, "As methods of game protection develop, the local system becomes more and more inadequate, and most States have replaced it with the stronger one in which the duties are committed to a board of commissioners or to a State game warden." Given its commercial value, fishing usually attracted the first such oversight. Massachusetts and New Hampshire created fish commissions in 1865, followed two years later by Connecticut and Vermont and the next year by New York. In 1878, New Hampshire reorganized its bureau into the nation's first fish and game commission. By the early 1900s, some 39 states and territories had similar offices.

As these new state agencies made game wardens fixtures of rural life for the first time in U.S. history, the response of the inhabitants of the American countryside was one of profound ambivalence. At one pole were those who welcomed the new regulations as a way of protecting an often vulnerable local game supply. At the other extreme were those who saw the heightened restrictions as undermining local subsistence and, with it, the enduring American ideal of self-sufficiency. Those who adopted this latter position were often quick to point out what they perceived to be a none-too-subtle class bias in the new game laws that often seemed to favor the growing numbers of urban sportsmen who hunted for pleasure over the rural working class who hunted for food. "Times is different now," grumbled one inhabitant of Upstate New York in 1897. "In them days nobody said a word if a poor man wanted a little meat an' killed it, but now they're savin' it until the dudes [sports hunters] get time to come up here an' kill it . . . an' they'd put me in jail if I killed a deer when I needed meat." Given such sentiments, one outcome of the creation of new game laws was the creation of new criminals, as some rural residents continued to hunt and fish as they wanted despite changes in regulations.

Perhaps the community most affected by these new game laws and enforcement efforts was Native Americans. Given the import of hunting and fishing for Indian subsistence, a number of treaties between the federal government and Indian nations had reserved for specific indigenous communities the right to engage in such activities off their reservations. In the 1805 Treaty of Fort Industry, for example, signed with representatives of Ohio's Munsee, Delaware, Ottawa, Shawnee, Wyandot, and Potawatomi nations, the federal government agreed that "said Indian nations . . . shall be at liberty to fish and hunt within the territory and lands which they have now ceded to the United States, so long as they shall deman themselves peaceably." By the turn of the century, however, conservationists found such rights an unwanted interference in their plans to manage wildlife populations and sought to place limits on Indian off-reservation hunting. As WILLIAM HORNADAY, director of the New York Zoological Park, argued in 1913, "The Indian should have no game advantages whatever over a white man."

The legal foundation for restricting Indian hunting and fishing occurred in the 1890s, when the Bannock Indian chief Race Horse was arrested some 100 miles away from his reservation for killing seven elk in violation of Wyoming's game law. Race Horse maintained that his hunting was permissible under the Treaty of Fort Bridger, which granted the Bannock "the right to hunt on unoccupied lands of the United States so long as game may be found thereon." The case proceeded all the way to the U.S. SUPREME COURT. In 1896, the justices ruled that upon its admission as a state, Wyoming had acquired the right to regulate hunting on its lands regardless of preexisting Indian treaties. This decision established a precedent that Wyoming and many other states used to restrict Indian off-reservation hunting and fishing well into the 20th century.

As the ultimate venue of the Race Horse case suggests, although game laws had originally been a state matter, they had increasingly entered the federal realm by the turn of the century. In 1894, the U.S. CONGRESS passed the National Park Protective Act, which created penalties for hunting in an expanding network of national parks. Six years later,

in 1900, Congress endorsed the Lacey Act, forbidding the interstate shipment of wildlife killed in violation of state game laws. In 1918, Congress approved the MIGRATORY BIRD TREATY in an attempt to stop the devastating commercial trade in BIRDS and feathers by proclaiming all migratory and insectivorous birds subject to federal oversight. In addition to these measures, the federal government negotiated international wildlife treaties in the early 20th century with Russia, Canada, Mexico, Great Britain, and Japan that pledged it to regulate the hunting of American waterfowl and fur-bearing seals.

To a remarkable extent, hunting operates today within the parameters established during the conservation era. Not only do most of the institutions (bag limits, licenses, closed seasons, game wardens, and the like) remain; so, too, do debates over Native American hunting rights as well as the sense that hunting is fundamental to American notions of masculinity and freedom. At the same time, paradoxically, the actual number of hunters in the United States has decreased over the past half-century. According to a 2001 survey done by the U.S. FISH AND WILDLIFE SERVICE, only 6 percent of Americans hunted that year, a decline of 7 percent over the previous decade.

See also BUREAU OF INDIAN AFFAIRS; CANADA AND THE UNITED STATES; FEDERAL LAW—INDIAN POLICIES; FENCES AND FENCE LAWS; FISHERIES; FISHING, COMMERCIAL; FISHING, RECREATIONAL; FISHING, SUBSISTENCE; FUR TRADE; HUNTING, COMMERCIAL; HUNTING, RECREATIONAL; INDIANS, APPALACHIA; INDIANS, CALIFORNIA; INDIANS, CENTRAL PLAINS; INDIANS, DEEP SOUTH; INDIANS, COLUMBIA PLATEAU AND GREAT BASIN; INDIANS, NORTHERN PLAINS; INDIANS, PACIFIC NORTHWEST; MEXICO AND THE UNITED STATES; NATIONAL IDENTITY, FORMATION OF; NATIONAL PARK SERVICE; TREATIES AND INTERNATIONAL LAW.

Karl Jacoby

Further Reading

Jacoby, Karl. *Crimes against Nature: Squatters, Poachers, Thieves, and the Hidden History of American Conservation.* Berkeley: University of California Press, 2001.

Lund, Thomas A. *American Wildlife Law.* Berkeley: University of California Press, 1980.

Spence, Mark. *Dispossessing the Wilderness: Indian Removal and the Making of the National Parks.* New York: Oxford University Press, 1999.

Tober, James A. *Who Owns the Wildlife? The Political Economy of Conservation in Nineteenth-Century America.* Westport, Conn.: Greenwood Press, 1981.

U.S. Department of the Interior, U.S. Fish and Wildlife Service, and U.S. Department of Commerce, U.S. Census Bureau. *2001 National Survey of Fishing, Hunting, and Wildlife Associated Recreation.* Washington, D.C.: Department of the Interior, 2001.

Warren, Louis. *The Hunter's Game: Poachers and Conservationists in Twentieth-Century America.* New Haven, Conn.: Yale University Press, 1997.

fish and other aquatic organisms

Fish, waterfowl, mammals, mollusks, crustaceans, and other aquatic organisms have long supplied humans with resources including FOOD, FERTILIZER, feathers, fur, shells, and pearls. Many aquatic populations, in both freshwater and salt water, have been decimated by heedless exploitation or by human-induced changes to their habitats. Charismatic fishes, particularly SALMON, have been the focus of many struggles over river management. Today, a wide range of aquatic species are protected under the ENDANGERED SPECIES ACT OF 1973, and they are increasingly valued as a source of information about the fragile ECOSYSTEMS they inhabit.

The Atlantic cod was a critical resource for the early settlements of New England and Maritime Canada. In 1497, the British explorer John Cabot discovered great schools of cod off the east coast of present-day Canada. Cod was already a major commodity in Europe, where Christian customs prohibited the consumption of "meat" on Fridays and during Lent. Over the next century, Basque, Portuguese, French, and British fishermen mobilized to harvest cod by hand line from open boats. The boats arrived in April or May and returned in July, laden with salted or dried cod for sale in European markets. Starting with a Salem-based fishery in 1628, coastal settlements in present-day Canada and New England became heavily dependent on market fishing for cod as a source of trade goods and income. British, French, and other colonial interests vied for control of the fishing grounds. British tariffs created tensions among the cod fishermen of Boston, which, by the mid-1700s, was a major cod fishing and trade center. Thus the cod fishery figured prominently in the taxation controversy that sparked the Boston Massacre, BOSTON TEA PARTY, and other events leading up to the AMERICAN REVOLUTION (1775–83).

Well into the 20th century, many coastal communities remained economically dependent on the harvest, processing, and marketing of cod. Canadian and American fleets were joined by fishing vessels from Britain, the Soviet Union, Germany, and other nations. By the 1960s, modern trawlers dragged giant nets across the seafloor on the fishing grounds off Newfoundland. A single ship could harvest 100 tons of fish, an entire season's catch for a 16th-century cod boat, in a single hour. The peak total annual catch was recorded at more than 800,000 metric tons in 1968, and then catches began to decline. Continued overfishing led to a collapse of the population in the early 1990s. Government agencies closed large parts of the fishery in 1992, 1994, and 2003. The industry's collapse produced a rash of bankruptcies, rampant unemployment, and severe social problems in many coastal communities. In recent decades, this story has become sadly familiar: Similar declines have devastated many FISHERIES throughout the world's oceans.

Even before impacts on marine fisheries began to materialize, several freshwater fishes and mussels were threatened by habitat change and overexploitation in the United States. Salmon are anadromous fishes. They spawn in fast, clear headwater streams; swim down to the ocean as juveniles; grow in the ocean for several years; and then return upstream to spawn. This lifestyle becomes nearly impossible in river systems that are transformed by human activity. Spawning streams are damaged by DEFORESTATION and other land disturbances that clog spawning beds with sediment. Dams produce formidable obstacles between spawning grounds and the sea for juveniles traveling downstream and for adults on the return trip. Recreational, commercial, and tribal fisheries harvest salmon in the ocean and in rivers. Today, salmon symbolize the plight of the nation's wild rivers, and their CONSERVATION is central to several high-profile controversies about water use, dam management, and land use.

The story of the big-river fisheries of the Midwest is less well known. Fisheries were key industries in the Midwest in the 1800s and early 1900s. In particular, native river-dwelling mussels were heavily exploited. In 1857, a New Jersey man made the chance discovery of a $1,500 pearl in a mussel pulled from a small creek. Mussels were harvested by fortune hunters throughout eastern North America for the next 50 years. Mussel shells were also valuable as a raw material for button making. Industrial harvest began with the establishment of a button factory in Muscatine, Iowa, in 1891. Eventually, the industry supported about 20,000 mussel gatherers and button-factory workers throughout much of the Mississippi basin. Between 1914 and 1920, about 35,000 tons of shells were harvested, and billions of buttons were produced each year. By the early 1930s, mussels were scarce and the fishery collapsed.

We have recognized individual species of food and game fish but have used catchall terms like *minnow* or *bait fish* to describe the preponderance of aquatic BIODIVERSITY. Thus, many people were incredulous when the three-inch-long snail darter delayed the construction of the Tellico Dam in Tennessee. The fish was discovered just upstream of the dam site in 1973 and thereafter figured in several antidam lawsuits brought by environmentalists. In 1978, the U.S. Supreme Court ruled that the snail darter, despite its obscurity, was entitled to the full force of protection under the Endangered Species Act of 1973 (ESA). Senator Howard Baker (R-Tenn.) made his disdain for the snail darter clear in a statement before CONGRESS in 1979: "We who voted for the Endangered Species Act with the honest intentions of protecting such glories of nature as the wolf, the eagle, and other treasures have found that extremists with wholly different motives are using this noble act for meanly obstructive ends." He secured passage of an amendment that exempted the Tellico Dam from the provisions of the ESA, and the project was completed. But the legal precedent set in the 1978 Supreme Court strongly reinforced the ESA. Over the next two decades, hundreds of plant and animal species were listed and received strong federal protection.

Today, communities of aquatic invertebrates and fish are widely studied as indicators of ecosystem health. We have a better appreciation for and knowledge of the small and obscure species. We continue to prize a few species above the others, but in practice we find our favored "targets" to be inseparable from the greater whole of which they are a part. This ecosystem awareness is a foundation for many new approaches to the management and conservation of aquatic resources.

See also DAMS, RESERVOIRS, AND ARTIFICIAL LAKES; ENDANGERED SPECIES; TENNESSEE VALLEY AUTHORITY; WHALING.

Jon D. Hoekstra

Further Reading

Ellis, Richard. *The Empty Ocean.* Washington, D.C.: Island Press, 2003.

McPhee, John. *The Founding Fish.* New York: Farrar, Straus & Giroux, 2002.

Outwater, Alice. *Water: A Natural History.* New York: Basic Books, 1996.

Postel, Sandra, and Brian Richter. *Rivers for Life.* Washington, D.C.: Island Press, 2003.

Fish and Wildlife Service, U.S.

In the late 1930s, under President FRANKLIN D. ROOSEVELT's administration, Secretary of the Interior HAROLD ICKES proposed the creation of a new federal Department of Conservation, which would include all government agencies dealing with natural resources. Ultimately, the plan failed. Instead, in 1940, CONGRESS merged two agencies, the U.S. BIOLOGICAL SURVEY (in the DEPARTMENT OF AGRICULTURE) and the U.S. Fish Commission (in the Department of Commerce), into one entity. Placed within the DEPARTMENT OF THE INTERIOR (DOI), the new agency became the U.S. Fish and Wildlife Service (FWS).

Ira Gabrielson (1889–1977), former chief of the Biological Survey, became the director of the new enterprise, holding the position for the next six years. In contrast to the Biological Survey, which engaged in state and regional animal studies, the FWS pursued management and regulatory issues. Under the Interior Department's policies, all scientific research needed to fulfill specific mission objectives. In the FWS's first decade, its efforts included studies on the effects of federal water-control efforts on fish and detailing of the migratory pathways of birds for waterfowl hunting management.

Biological Survey sections still lived on within the new agency, but its specimen collections fell under the jurisdiction of the Denver Wildlife Research Center. The specimens themselves continued to be housed, as they had been since 1910, in the National Museum of Natural History in WASHINGTON, D.C. As the parent service grew, however, the section languished, with little staff and poor funding. When the centennial of the old Biological Survey's founding was celebrated in 1985, the *Washington Post* described the Biological Survey section, with a staff of 16 people (out of 6,400 FWS employees), as "a struggling, dispirited bureaucratic waif, far from the center of power."

The Federal Aid in Fish Restoration Act, often referred to as the Dingell-Johnson Act (1950), was intended to accomplish for fish what the Pittman Robertson Wildlife Restoration Act (1937) had done for game species of BIRDS and mammals. The Pittman Robertson Act provided federal aid to states for the management and restoration of wildlife. It passed just prior to the founding of the FWS; the federal government funded hunting habitat restoration under the 1937 law through taxes on firearms, ammunition, bows, and archery equipment. Likewise, a tax on rods and reels underwrote funding for implementation of the Dingell-Johnson Act. Between 1952 and 1988, the FWS spent $873 million in Dingell-Johnson initiatives, with the federal government funding state fish management and restoration projects. A generation later, the Forsythe-Chafee Act (1980) extended federal protection to nongame fauna and flora as part of U.S. membership in the Convention on International Trade in Endangered Species, or CITES. Under the law, both the FWS and the National Marine Fisheries Service enforce provisions against the importation, export, sale, or possession of animals protected by the act. FWS designed and implemented recovery plans for INDIGENOUS SPECIES in cooperation with individual states.

Along with these laws, enforcement of provisions of the ENDANGERED SPECIES ACT OF 1973 (ESA) has led to conflict. Proponents of ENVIRONMENTAL RESTORATION and CONSERVATION have been dogged by advocacy groups unhappy with their effects on private property, by questions about their efficacy, and by business and other groups whose construction and other projects have been blocked or delayed by environmental legislation. Farmers, for example, demanded continued poisoning of prairie dogs, yet prairie dogs were the principal prey species for the black-footed ferret, a predator in danger of extinction. In response to public objections over Compound 1080, a poison employed in so-called coyote getter traps, its use was discontinued through President RICHARD NIXON's 1972 executive order, but pressure from unhappy ranchers prompted its reintroduction in modified form in 1975. President RONALD REAGAN's administration reauthorized use of Compound 1080 in 1982.

Conservation advocates and western ranchers have repeatedly clashed over the reintroduction of WOLVES, an endangered

Established in 1940, the U.S. Fish and Wildlife Service monitors and manages fish and wildlife populations in the United States. To check migration habits of the swordfish, these sportsmen are cooperating with the Fish and Wildlife Service by tagging and throwing back the smaller fish caught. Only larger swordfish will be kept aboard and later eaten. *(Library of Congress)*

species that had been largely extirpated from the West by the late 1970s. Wolves reestablished themselves in Glacier National Park in 1982. The FWS reintroduced them into YELLOWSTONE National Park in 1994–95 because agency officials believed wolves had an important role to play in the regional ecosystem. Opposition to this decision has not abated. Wolves have continued to receive federal protection, although the Rocky Mountain gray wolf was dropped from protection under the ESA for several months in 2008, but ranchers or hunters illegally kill dozens of wolves every year. Another source of conflict between the FWS and ranchers arises from government regulations that determine where and how ranchers may graze their animals— on both wildlife refuge and national forest land. The amount of the grazing fees the government may charge has been a persistent issue of contention. On other fronts, difficulties arose when gas or oil was discovered in or near wildlife refuges. The Department of Interior must determine whether drilling can take place under various conditions or whether such operations are too threatening to the fish and wildlife.

The National Biological Survey (later National Biological Service [NBS]), a federal initiative during President BILL CLINTON's administration in the 1990s, was intended to protect and manage wildlife populations and ECOSYSTEMS but proved highly controversial when established in 1993. The NBS objective was to map, inventory, and monitor biotic resources and conduct—and apply—research on individuals and groups of species, populations, and ecosystems. The goal was to provide the scientific support and technical assistance required for the Department of the Interior to make appropriate management and policy decisions. The NBS's 1,360 employees were drawn from five agencies within DOI, the great majority of them from FWS.

The NBS was a late 20th-century version of the old Biological Survey. The Clinton administration used a study from the National Academy of Sciences that called for a National Partnership for Biological Survey to justify the new project. The NBS planned to integrate federal, state, and local agencies in the collection and assessment of scientific information on the nation's biological resources and the explanation of changes in the resource inventory. Secretary of the Interior BRUCE BABBITT envisioned the NBS as a "world-class science agency," which would, among other things, address the nation's critical ecosystem losses. Anticipating possible objections raised by conservatives, he stressed that the NBS was not a regulatory agency and was not empowered to seize private property from individual citizens. Indeed, as envisioned, the NBS employees could not even enter private property without the owner's permission.

Before and after the midterm elections of 1994, however, private property advocates voiced strong objections to the NBS, which had been created by DOI reorganization rather than congressional approval. Foes of the NBS feared that the organization's studies might be used to designate a wider range for the protection of ENDANGERED SPECIES. Many members of the new REPUBLICAN majority in Congress were not convinced of the ESA's importance to wildlife conservation. Other congressional members favored elimination of NBS as a deficit-cutting measure. Congressional objections reflected some Americans' continuing ambivalence regarding the proper role of government in the management of the nation's resources. In 1996, after just three years of existence, Congress integrated the NBS into the U.S. GEOLOGICAL SURVEY (USGS). Some 1,600 NBS personnel assigned to 40 NBS field stations around the nation were transferred to a newly created Biological Resources Division of the USGS. There, its advocates hoped, some of the original ECOLOGY and BIODIVERSITY objectives might still be realized.

By 2010, the FWS's 7,500 employees were spread between the WASHINGTON, D.C., headquarters, 520 National Wildlife Refuges and thousands of other conservation sites, eight regional offices, more than 200 fishery-related sites, and more than 50 field offices around the country. Most marine zoological research takes place in Patuxent, Maryland, regarded by many as a ninth regional office. Wildlife under FWS protection are found in dozens of coordination sites, thousands of conservation sites and refuges, and more than 150 waterfowl protection areas. However, other federal agencies have specific, often overlapping responsibilities at many of these sites. To confuse the picture further, the individual states in which the FWS facilities are located have their own state programs to pursue. Finally, federal research units operate at numerous state universities, carrying out projects that potentially affect other wildlife initiatives.

See also ANIMALS, DOMESTICATED; ANIMALS, WILD; BUREAU OF LAND MANAGEMENT; FISH AND OTHER AQUATIC ORGANISMS; LAND GRANT INSTITUTIONS; NATIONAL WILDLIFE REFUGE SYSTEM; RODENTS; SPECIES, EXOTIC AND INVASIVE.

Keir Sterling

Further Reading

Babbitt, Bruce. "Transfer of the National Biological Service to the United States Geological Survey as a New Biological Services Division." Order No. 3202, News Release, U.S. Geological Survey, U.S. Department of the Interior. Washington, D.C., September 30, 1996.

Dunlap, Thomas E. *Saving America's Wildlife.* Princeton, N.J.: Princeton University Press, 1988.

Kallman, Harmon, et al. *Restoring America's Wildlife, 1937–1987: The First 50 Years of the Federal Aid in Wildlife Restoration (Pittman-Robertson) Act.* Washington, D.C.: U.S. Department of the Interior, 1987.

National Research Council. *A Biological Survey for the Nation.* Washington, D.C.: National Academy of Sciences, 1993.

Sterling, Keir B. "Zoological Research, Wildlife Management, and the Federal Government." In *Forests and Wildlife Service in America: A History,* edited by Harold K. Steen, 19–65. Durham, N.C.: Forest History Society, 1999.

Watkins, T. H. *Righteous Pilgrim: The Life and Times of Harold L. Ickes.* New York: Henry Holt, 1990.

fisheries

According to the National Marine Fisheries Service, the federal agency in charge of managing U.S. fisheries, consumers spent an estimated $68.4 billion for fishery products in 2007. While a significant portion of those products was imported, the commercial marine fishing industry in the United States contributed $34.2 billion to the country's gross national product.

U.S. fisheries, however, are a shadow of what they once were. When the Italian explorer and navigator John Cabot (ca. 1450–ca. 1498) returned to England after a 1497 voyage to North America, he reported schools of cod so thick a person "could walk across their backs." However, as of the mid-1990s, the cod, haddock, and flounder stocks have all but disappeared from the Grand Banks, a shallow fishing region of the North Atlantic Ocean, lying off the southeastern coast of Newfoundland, Canada. Historically, the Grand Banks supported some of the world's most productive fisheries. While landings of cod peaked in the late 1960s, Canada and the United States continued to encourage the expansion of their domestic fishing industries. By 1988, fisheries scientists were sounding the alarm, but neither country had the political will to curtail COMMERCIAL FISHING severely until the Canadian government closed the Grand Banks cod fishery in 1992.

In 2008, U.S. fisheries managers closed the Pacific SALMON fishery in Oregon and California. Scientists estimate that only 66,264 adult Chinook salmon returned to the Sacramento River in fall 2008 to spawn. That was the lowest number of returning salmon in history, and the speed of the decline was quite dramatic. As recently as 2002, some 768,388 adult salmon returned to the rivers of California's Central Valley. The population crash probably resulted from a combination of factors, including climatic changes, increasing water withdrawals from the California Delta, and a reliance on poorly adapted hatchery fish to supplement wild stocks.

CAUSES OF DECLINE

Decades of technological advances and ineffective management have driven many U.S. fish stocks to the brink of collapse. While there are signs of improvement, 16 percent of U.S. commercial fish stocks are subject to overfishing. Under federal law, *overfished* means the harvest level exceeds the target quota set by federal fisheries managers. Fisheries are under strain not only in the United States. The UNITED NATIONS Food and Agricultural Organization (FAO) estimates that a quarter of the world's commercial fish stocks are overexploited or depleted, meaning fishers are removing more fish than can be replenished.

Fish are a common-pool resource, traditionally subject to the "rule of capture," meaning that no individual owns a fish until he or she captures it. The first person to hook a fish on a line or capture it in a net "owns" it and has a right to profit from it either through use or through sale. Thus, the rule of capture encourages overharvesting. There is no incentive for individuals to restrict harvest. The profits forgone by conservation-minded fishers simply will be reaped by others. Until recently, the rule of capture governed most U.S. fisheries. While fishing licenses were often required by federal and state governments, there were few restrictions on the issuance of such licenses. Anyone with a boat could obtain a license and begin participating in the "race to the fish."

Until the late 19th century, the "race" for the fish was more like an arduous, slow crawl. For much of human history, fish were caught from shore or small oar- or sail-powered boats in coastal waters with nets or baited lines. Conditions were dangerous, and harvests per individual fisherman or vessel relatively small. However, by the end of the 20th century, the race had become an all-out sprint.

Technological advances, which began in the late 1800s, made it possible for fishing vessels to travel farther, stay out on the water longer, locate fish more efficiently, and process their catch on board. With steam engines, and later gasoline and diesel engines, fishers traveled hundreds of miles from home in search of new fishing grounds. After the installation of onboard refrigeration and freezing systems, fishing vessels remained at sea for weeks or even months without sacrificing the quality of the catch. Refrigeration and freezing also increased demand for fish and seafood products by opening new inland markets served by the expanding RAILROADS. After WORLD WAR II (1941–45), fishermen increased harvests and saved precious money and time by using sonar, developed by the U.S. Navy to detect enemy submarines, to locate schools of fish. Today, global positioning systems aid fishermen in charting and scouting fishing trails and schooling patterns.

A pattern of boom and bust soon emerged. As yields dwindled in one area, fishermen sought new grounds. If the species found in that new area proved profitable, more fishermen followed and fishing pressure increased exponentially until yields decreased and the fishery crashed. Oyster fisheries along the U.S. East Coast expanded and collapsed in a linear fashion from New York to Georgia as harvesting spread. As yields decreased in coastal fisheries in the 1960s and 1970s, U.S. fishermen invested in bigger boats and more powerful engines and moved into deeper waters farther offshore.

For a while, the technological improvements masked the resource depletion that was taking place. Total catch levels remained stable, or even increased, as new areas and species were exploited. Species of deep-water fish never heard of before, such as orange roughy, were marketed to American consumers. Species of fish once discarded by fishermen as trash, such as spiny dogfish and monkfish, became primary targets as cod, haddock, and flounder disappeared. Today, with some stocks continuing to decline, U.S. fishermen are turning to jellyfish and other less-desirable species.

Throughout history, scientists and fishermen have periodically raised concerns about the impact of fishing on fish stocks. By 1716, for example, England had imposed minimal mesh sizes for nets and minimal size limits for a variety of fish species. In the late 1800s, the states of Washington and Oregon enacted seasonal and gear restrictions to control salmon harvests on the COLUMBIA RIVER; however, their efforts proved ineffective. In 1902, the scientific community formed the International Council for the Exploration of the Sea to advance scientific understanding of human impacts on fisheries and marine ECOSYSTEMS. Regulation, however, remained negligible until the middle of the 20th century, driven in part by the misguided belief that fisheries could not be depleted. Most fisheries managers agreed with the famous statement by the English biologist Thomas Huxley (1825–95) in 1883 that "all the great sea-fisheries are inexhaustible."

PUSH TO ENCLOSE THE SEAS

During the 20th century, U.S. fisheries management became entwined with U.S. foreign policy. Just as technology helped U.S. fishermen advance into new fishing grounds, Japanese, Russian, Spanish, and other European fishing fleets were freed from their home waters by engines and refrigeration. Prior to World War II, Japanese fishing vessels were operating around the world in waters that many countries, including the United States, viewed as their own. In 1936, for example, Japanese fishing vessels began harvesting salmon in Bristol Bay, Alaska, an area previously only fished by U.S. and Canadian fishermen. U.S. fishermen viewed the Japanese presence as an "invasion" of their fishing grounds and pressured CONGRESS and the U.S. government to protect their interest. Both Canada and the United States were concerned that Japanese vessels would intercept the salmon on their way to the spawning grounds, reducing both the number of salmon available for U.S. and Canadian fishermen to harvest and the number of eggs spawned.

At the time, under INTERNATIONAL LAW, coastal nations had exclusive jurisdiction over a belt of waters extending three nautical miles from shore, known as the territorial sea. The United States had a right to control who harvested fish within this zone but had no authority to restrict harvests beyond three miles. Concern for the fishermen's livelihoods and the salmon's health led President HARRY TRUMAN to take the extreme step of unilaterally asserting jurisdiction over offshore fish stocks. In September 1945, President Truman issued a proclamation claiming authority to declare "conservation zones" outside U.S. territorial waters where fisheries had been exploited historically by the United States and when additional entrants into the fishery might endanger the stocks. Within these conservation zones, the United States would control all fishing.

The Truman Proclamation launched an international fisheries management revolution. In the years that followed the proclamation, nations around the world claimed jurisdiction over fish stocks located beyond the territorial sea. Some countries, such as Chile, went so far as to claim sovereignty over all waters within 200 nautical miles (nm) of the shore. In 1976, the U.S. Congress passed the Magnuson Fishery Conservation and Management Act (Magnuson Act) to assert exclusive jurisdiction to explore, exploit, conserve, and manage all fish located within 200 nm from shore and establish a management regime for such fisheries. This assertion of jurisdiction enabled the United States to evict, once and for all, foreign fishing fleets from waters frequented by U.S. fishing vessels. The U.S. jurisdictional claims were accepted by the international community and incorporated into the 1982 UN Convention on the Law of the Sea. Under the convention, coastal nations have the right to declare 200-nm Exclusive Economic Zones (EEZ) within which they have "sovereign rights for the purpose of exploring and exploiting, conserving and managing the natural resources." Although the United States has yet to ratify the Law of the Sea Convention officially, President RONALD REAGAN claimed a 200-nm EEZ for the United States by presidential proclamation in 1983.

CONTINUED DEPLETIONS

Extending coastal nations' jurisdiction into the ocean, however, did little to prevent the depletion of marine fisheries. Several factors contributed to the continuing decline of fish stocks. First, coastal nations wanted more control over offshore fisheries resources, not to conserve them, but to ensure that their fleets, as opposed to foreign fleets, would profit from the exploitation. As a result, after the passage of the Magnuson Act, the U.S. government offered low-interest loans and other subsidies to help U.S. vessels fill the gap left by foreign fishing fleets. Harvesting continued to increase in many fisheries during the 1980s, eventually resulting in devastating fishery losses, such as the North Atlantic groundfish depletion.

Science and management were also partially to blame. Fisheries in the United States are managed in terms of "maximum sustainable yield" (MSY). In theory, MSY is the harvest level at which fishermen are removing exactly as many fish as the stock recruits every year. As long as fishermen do not remove more fish than the stock can replace, the stock can be fished forever. In practice, MSY has been almost impossible to calculate accurately and, thus, to enforce. The number of fish born each year is influenced by more than the number of breeding adults that remain at the end of a fishing season. Seasonal variations in climate and water temperature, pollution, and other environmental factors can affect spawning cycles and juvenile survival rates. Furthermore, managers must rely on catch reports submitted by fishermen to determine when MSY has been reached.

New management regimes for marine fisheries are beginning to emerge. Increasingly, fisheries managers are considering alternative management techniques, such as "individual fishing quotas" (IFQs), to replace the traditional methods such as seasonal closures and gear restrictions, which limit the type, amount, or use of a particular type of fishing gear. In the United States, an IFQ is a federal permit that authorizes the holder to harvest a particular quantity of fish. IFQs can eliminate the "race to the fish" because each fisher has a right to catch only a certain percentage of the overall harvest. As long as the IFQ is enforced effectively, fishermen in a fishery with IFQs no longer have to worry about another fisherman's "stealing" their fish. However, because IFQs are designed primarily to increase the economic efficiency of the fishery, the success of the system still depends on the establishment of a total allowable catch at a sustainable level. The National Marine Fisheries Service manages a number of U.S. fisheries, including Alaska halibut and GULF OF MEXICO red snapper, utilizing IFQs.

See also CANADA AND THE UNITED STATES; CLIMATE CHANGE; DAMS, RESERVOIRS, AND ARTIFICIAL LAKES; FOOD; GLOBALIZATION; MARITIME COMMERCE; OCEANS; STATE, DEPARTMENT OF; TREATIES AND INTERNATIONAL LAW; UNITED STATES—ALASKA; UNITED STATES—CALIFORNIA; UNITED STATES—EASTERN SEABOARD; UNITED STATES—GULF COAST; UNITED STATES—NORTHEAST.

Stephanie Showalter

Further Reading
H. John Heinz III Center for Science, Economics, and the Environment. *Fishing Grounds: Defining a New Era for American Fisheries Management.* Washington, D.C.: Island Press, 2000.
Kurlansky, Mark. *Cod: A Biography of the Fish That Changed the World.* New York: Penguin Books, 1998.
McEvoy, Arthur F. *The Fisherman's Problem: Ecology and Law in the California Fisheries, 1850–1980.* New York: Cambridge University Press, 1986.

Rose, Alex. *Who Killed the Grand Banks? The Untold Story behind the Decimation of One of the World's Greatest Natural Resources.* New York: John Wiley & Sons, 2008.

fishing, commercial

Commercial fishing, also known as the fishing industry, harvests, processes, and markets fish. Economically and environmentally, the industry differs significantly from traditional fishing, as practiced by aboriginal peoples for subsistence or ritualistic purposes, as well as from RECREATIONAL FISHING, in which fish are captured for sport and are not intended for sale. Unlike traditional and recreational fishing, commercial fishing operates within an international market; moreover, the scale of its impact upon marine and freshwater species and ecosystems is profound and potentially irreversible.

HISTORY

Catching, trading, consuming, and preserving fish were central to the lifestyle of indigenous North American tribes in many of the coastal regions of the present-day United States, most particularly in the Pacific Northwest and Southeast Alaska. Oregon country tribes, including the Chinook, the Nez Perce, and the Kathlamet, practiced SALMON subsistence along the COLUMBIA RIVER basin for thousands of years. They used a variety of technologies, including spears, gill nets, seines, and weirs. The Tlingit and Haida of Southeast Alaska hunted Pacific salmon, varying their catch technologies to match the different ECOSYSTEMS of the salmons' migratory cycle. For winter sustenance and trade, the salmon were preserved by smoking and drying.

The fishing practices of European settlers differed significantly from those of indigenous North Americans. Colonial New England's economy depended upon ground fishing—the catching of fish that swim close to the ocean floor. Communities such as Gloucester and New Bedford, Massachusetts, thrived upon harvesting Atlantic halibut, ocean perch, haddock, cod, redfish, and yellowtail flounder. European settlers supplemented subsistence farming with seasonal fishing of shad, salmon, alewives, and sturgeon. By the early 19th century, fish stocks—most notably the salmon population of the Connecticut River—had been severely depleted by the construction of dams and lumber mills along the river. Migratory runs were increasingly affected by coastal weir fishing, which allowed for year-round harvesting.

Europeans arrived in the American West in the late 18th century but did not begin settling in significant numbers until the 1840s. Along the Oregon coast and the Columbia River, fur trappers traded with local tribes for salmon; in the 1820s, the Hudson's Bay Company, a chartered British company, began employing tribesman to catch and cure salmon for resale at Fort Vancouver.

As in the East, the economic and environmental impact of Europeans on the salmon population of the Northwest was profound. Economically, Europeans established a dense and far-reaching trading network. Unlike local tribes, who harvested large quantities of salmon for local consumption, Europeans supplied a market economy centered in the eastern seaboard and Western Europe. Environmentally, Europeans' exploitation of a wide range of natural resources profoundly affected the health of the salmons' ecosystem. In the Pacific Northwest, MINING, LOGGING, trapping, grazing, and farming polluted, diverted, and warmed the salmons' waterways. Increased settlement exerted demands upon the remaining open land and water; by the 1860s, the cities of Portland and Salem, Oregon, and Spokane, Washington, engaged the U.S. ARMY CORPS OF ENGINEERS to improve the extant rail and water transportation networks. Portland General Electric built a hydroelectric dam at Willamette Falls in 1888, impeding the salmons' migration. The drastic effect of these human activities on the salmon population was such as to prompt an army engineer, in 1886, to assert proof of "an enormous reduction in the numbers of spawning fish."

THE MODERN FISHING INDUSTRY

The key characteristics of the present-day fishing industry—the harvesting of fish for an international market, the use of capital-intensive extractive technologies, the construction of canning and processing facilities, and "slash and burn" single-species harvesting—emerged in the mid-19th century. Along the Oregon coast, fishers introduced the stationary technologies of the fish trap, pound-net, and fish-wheel. In addition to allowing more efficient harvests, these technologies did not require continuous labor. Canneries were established on the Sacramento (1864) and Columbia (1866) Rivers by Hapgood, Hume & Company; by 1884, West Coast canneries were processing 42 million pounds of salmon. By the 1870s, Pacific salmon was regularly available in NEW YORK CITY; CHICAGO, ILLINOIS; London; Berlin; Australia; and India. Given consumer preferences for Chinook and sockeye salmon, commercial fishers concentrated on these two species. By 1880, the Lower Columbia River had become a dense network of FISHERIES and canneries, fully integrated into an international transportation network, supplying an international appetite.

In Alaska, acquired by the United States in 1867, fishing corporations battled throughout the 1870s for control of the territory's ample fishing grounds. From this competition, the Alaska Packers Association (APA), a consortium of 29 canneries, formed. It produced nearly 70 percent of Alaska's total output of canned fish between 1893 and 1903. The APA encouraged the spread of more efficient catch technologies of the gill net, the purse-seine, and the fish trap. The trap, a stationary device, allowed the APA to monopolize prime fishing sites, acquire immense volumes of fish, and consolidate its market edge. It also occasioned widespread condemnation for the waste it incurred: Snared fish not intended for consumption were left ashore to die.

In the Northeast, fishing was largely controlled by fishermen's cooperatives until the early 20th century. The introduction of the capital-intensive, steam-powered trawler in 1906 displaced small-scale cooperatives that relied upon schooner fleets. Furthermore, the trawlers harvested significantly more fish than were marketable. The excess fish were discarded at sea: In 1930, 37 million haddock were caught around BOSTON, MASSACHUSETTS, while an additional 70 million were left dead at sea.

While the key elements of commercial fishing were established in the late 19th century, several innovations were initiated in the 20th century to meet rising consumer demand despite the decline in fish stocks engendered by commercial practices. The impact of trawl fishing, in which a net is drawn through the water or along the ocean floor by one or more boats, was increased through the introduction of heavier, stronger gear, and its reach expanded through advanced navigation technology. Aquaculture, or fish farming, which involves raising fish in tanks or enclosures for consumption, began to be practiced on a large scale in both oceanic and freshwater ecosystems.

REGULATION

The growth of commercial fishing was facilitated by the federal government, in particular its progressive dispossession of coastal tribes. Although there was no significant public uproar regarding the government's treatment of indigenous North Americans, citizens, government officials, and fishers in the Pacific Northwest and New England began complaining as early as the 1860s about the depletion of fish stocks and the disappearance of certain species. Although responsibility for the declining fish runs was initially attributed solely to industrial fisheries, by the 20th century, regulatory attention was expanded to include any activity, whether industrial, governmental, residential, or recreational, that affected fish habitat.

The first attempts to regulate the fishing industry were made in the 1860s, with the creation of fishing commissions in Connecticut, New Hampshire, Vermont, and Massachusetts. These commissions, which met jointly in 1867, sought to address the rapid decline in fish stocks due to increased POPULATION and industrial activity. The commissions aimed to restore New England's fish stocks by restricting the time and manner of fishing, prohibiting pollution of waterways, constructing fishways around dams, and empowering the commissions to enforce conservation legislation.

In 1871, President Ulysses S. Grant (1822–85) established the United States Commission of Fish and Fisheries (U.S. Fish Commission), under the leadership of the American ichthyologist Spencer Fullerton Baird (1823–87). As an independent organization, the commission was tasked with investigating why inland and coastal fish stocks had decreased, presenting recommendations to CONGRESS and local governments, and managing restoration efforts. To accomplish these tasks, the commission worked closely with marine biologists to reassess extant fishing technologies, as well as to establish the National Fish Hatchery System (NFHS). The first of these hatcheries was the Baird Hatcher, established on California's McCloud River in 1872. The initial focus of the NFHS was on the restoration of lake trout, rainbow trout, cutthroat trout, paddlefish, and sturgeon; it has since expanded to the rehabilitation of Atlantic salmon, Atlantic striped bass, and Pacific salmon.

In 1902, the commission was renamed the United States Bureau of Fisheries and incorporated into the Department of Commerce and Labor. By 1940, the federal government divided responsibility for national fish stocks between land-based and oceanic fish populations, with the U.S. FISH AND WILDLIFE SERVICE (FWS), part of the DEPARTMENT OF THE INTERIOR, responsible for the former, and the U.S. National Marine Fisheries Service (NMFS), part of the National Oceanic and Atmospheric Administration and the Department of Commerce, responsible for the latter. The FWS oversees the NFHS, which by 2009 comprised 70 hatcheries in the coastal and lake regions of 35 states, nine fish health centers, and seven fish technology centers. The NMFS, which regulates marine life and habitats from 3.72 miles (6 km) to 230 miles (370 km) offshore, operates under the Magnuson-Stevens Fishery Conservation and Management Act (Magnuson-Stevens Act) of 1976. The agency works with local communities to manage fisheries sustainably. Although the central offices of the FWS and the NMFS dictate CONSERVATION and restoration policy, the regional branches exert significant control over implementation and play a central role in mediating conflict with local communities.

OPPOSITION

Criticism of commercial fishing stretches back to the mid-19th century. Early criticism focused upon collapsing fish populations, as well as monopolistic practices such as use of fish traps. Until the mid-20th century, the federal government was the primary recipient and investigator of these complaints.

Since the mid-20th century, significant opposition to commercial fishing has been expressed by environmental protection groups. These groups criticized industrial fisheries, industries responsible for polluting marine ecosystems, as well as federal and regional regulatory bodies. They targeted a range of environmental and health issues, including elevated MERCURY levels in fish, the use of ANTIBIOTICS and coloring agents in farmed fish, the international transportation of fish, industrial pollution of the OCEANS and waterways, destruction of CORAL AND CORAL REEFS and deep-sea habitats by trawling, and the lack of adequate catch and bycatch limits (limits on the number of fish that can be caught, as well as limits on the aquatic animals such as turtles, dolphins, and sharks that are ensnared in fishing nets).

A sea lion drowned after becoming entangled in a fishing net.   *(© Specialist Stock/Corbis)*

Among environmental groups, GREENPEACE has waged a prominent campaign against the commercial fishing industry. Greenpeace's notable actions include a recent campaign to require the North Pacific Fisheries Management Council to mitigate the overfishing of Alaskan pollock, as well as its Bering Witness campaign against bottom trawling and single-species management in the Bering Sea. Oceana, Food and Water Watch, and the Coastal Alliance for Aquaculture Reform (CAAR) are also active in the struggle against commercial fishing. Many environmental groups, such as the World Wildlife Foundation (WWF) and the NATURAL RESOURCES DEFENSE COUNCIL (NRDC), have allied with consumer groups such as Seafood Watch and the Seafood Choices Alliance to criticize the adverse health effects of commercially harvested fish on the consumer. Through publications like the *Sustainable Seafood Guide,* they aim to redirect consumer habits with information about which fish species are most vulnerable to pollution and overfishing.

Environmental advocates have experienced some success in changing commercial fishing practices, as well as in securing increased federal protection for fish spawning grounds. Created by President GEORGE W. BUSH in 2006, the Northwestern Hawaiian Islands Marine National Monument, managed jointly by the FWS and the NOAA, is the largest marine conservation area under U.S. jurisdiction. Furthermore, small-scale fishermen have been instrumental in advocating alternatives to commercial fisheries. Fishing cooperatives, such as Massachusetts's Cape Ann Fresh Catch and Maine's Midcoast Fishermen's Association, practice sustainable fishing and implement low-impact technologies.

See also ENGLISH EXPLORATION AND SETTLEMENT—CANADA AND NEW ENGLAND; FISHING, SUBSISTENCE; FOOD; GLOBALIZATION; INDIANS, ALASKA; INDIANS, PACIFIC NORTHWEST; SPECIES, INDIGENOUS; SUSTAINABILITY.

Jennifer Thomson

Further Reading

Arnold, David F. *The Fishermen's Frontier: People and Salmon in Southeast Alaska.* Seattle: University of Washington Press, 2008.

Cumbler, John T. "The Early Making of an Environmental Consciousness: Fish, Fisheries Commission and the Connecticut River." *Environmental History Review* 15 (1991): 73–91.

Judd, Richard. *Common Lands, Common People: The Origins of Conservation in Northern New England.* Cambridge, Mass.: Harvard University Press, 2000.

McEvoy, Arthur F. *The Fisherman's Problem: Ecology and Law in the California Fisheries, 1850–1980.* New York: Cambridge University Press, 1986.

Taylor, Joseph E., III. "Burning the Candle at Both Ends: Historicizing Overfishing in Oregon's Nineteenth-Century Salmon Fisheries." *Environmental History* 4 (1999): 54–79.

———. *Making Salmon: An Environmental History of the Northwest Fisheries Crisis.* Seattle: University of Washington Press, 1999.

fishing, recreational

Fishing, of some form or another, has been a part of the American landscape for as long as humans have inhabited North America. In its earliest manifestations—both for the indigenous peoples residing here for thousands of years and the swarm of European settlers who began arriving more than 500 years ago—fishing was a matter of life and death. Fish was often the only FOOD available in areas scarce of game or edible plants. As Americans migrated across the continent and industrialized North America, fishing experienced a transition. It became a largely recreational activity, especially for affluent white males who wanted to escape urban congestion and find refuge in the ever-diminishing areas of remote and pristine WILDERNESS. They traded nets and spears for rods and reels, while the nation's attitude changed toward this new sport. Beginning in the 19th century, fishing became one of America's most popular and enduring outdoor activities. It spawned thousands of sporting competitions and contests, a multibillion-dollar "rod and reel" industry, countless publications, a literature and lore unrivaled by most other American pastimes, hundreds of governmental regulatory divisions, and one of the country's most effective CONSERVATION movements.

Charles F. Waterman's encyclopedic and illustrated work *Fishing in America* (1975) described some indigenous American fishing practices. After wading into water, Indians stirred up mud from the bottom until it clogged the gills of nearby fish. Seeking relief, the fish moved to the surface, where the Indians easily caught them, by hand or with a flat wooden tool. Archaeologists commonly find ancient American Indian settlements near lakes, rivers, and streams, suggesting these indigenous people sought a constant supply of freshwater and what those waters contained. Ceremonial Indian

mounds of the Upper MISSISSIPPI RIVER reveal a variety of shell spoons, fishhooks, and effigies of fish carved in stone. Similar examples are found at archaeological sites throughout the United States, including artifacts probably used during SALMON runs in the Northwest or ice-fishing equipment utilized by the earliest inhabitants of the Arctic. From coast to coast, fishing was a substantial part of many indigenous cultures well up to the time of European contact. Early European and American explorers, from Hernando de Soto (c. 1496–1542) to Father Jacques Marquette (1637–75) to Meriwether Lewis (1774–1809) and William Clark (1770–1838), all reported witnessing the fishing exploits of the indigenous Americans they encountered.

When Europeans began arriving on the North American continent in large numbers in the 16th and 17th centuries, fishing was a fairly reliable way to acquire nourishment, often by borrowing Indian techniques. At this time, "angling" became a popular leisure activity in Europe, especially in England. Izaak Walton's *The Complete Angler,* published in 1653, demonstrated the growing popularity of recreational fishing. Some early colonists transported this pastime to the Americas. They found enjoyment by venturing into the wilderness to find food for the family, although wilderness still carried negative connotations. It represented the unknown and the locus of possible attacks by Indians. The quasi-religious belief that the wildlands of America were home to evil and temptation kept most people away from colonial FORESTS. After the AMERICAN REVOLUTION (1775–83), Euro-American attitudes toward the outdoors began to change. OUTDOOR RECREATION, including fishing, emerged as a highly desirable pursuit for affluent urban men.

At the end of the 18th century, cultural shift spurred the growth of fishing as a leisurely activity. First and foremost, the onset of industrialization caused a substantial reconsideration of humanity's place within the natural world. No longer was wilderness seen as a threat or place of evil. Americans increasingly believed that they must conquer nature and replace it with civilization. By the 19th century, writers such as HENRY DAVID THOREAU and artists of the HUDSON RIVER SCHOOL began depicting a natural world that was open to human encounters with it, even serving as a place of refuge for urbanites tired of the daily grind of city life. Instead of destroying nature, wilderness advocates insisted, Americans should appreciate the nation's wild places, in whatever form—including fishing for leisure. Moreover, with the rise of industrialization, the upper and middle classes experienced an economic boom and enjoyed more leisure time. Thus, many turned to outdoor activities such as fishing.

Industrialization also wrought severe consequences on the nation's waterways. It increased pressure on many native fish species and the habitats in which they resided. This development helped solidify fishermen in efforts to preserve local fishing spots. Some of the first acts of environmental

Using intricately tied lures, fly-fishing in rivers and streams, often stocked by local or national organizations, is typically practiced by refined or advanced anglers. *(Luther Goldman, U.S. Fish and Wildlife Service)*

activism were taken by anglers angered by industrial pressures on cherished fishing holes. It is perhaps at this point in American history that clear distinctions can begin to be made among subsistence, commercial, and recreational fishing.

Like many American pastimes or sporting activities, recreational fishing was welcomed into mainstream culture with the establishment of fraternal clubs for affluent male anglers. The first such club, the Schuylkill Fishing Company of Philadelphia, was established in 1732 and continues today. Similar clubs emerged in cities throughout the country, most of them not until the 19th century. Although these organizations often favored the social nature of the sport over the actual practice of it, they still influenced the earliest and most widely accepted codes, guidelines, and mores. These organizations, for example, emphasized the qualitative aspects of fishing—the techniques involved in casting and catching, the challenge of using a rod and reel over a net, the preference for fish rarer and more difficult to land, the respect one should hold for the fish themselves, and an overall appreciation for the outdoors—over the quantity of fish caught. Indeed, until CONGRESS created the U.S. Fish Commission in 1871, which formally regulated fishing practices, the sport was largely self-regulated. This reality commonly led to unethical behavior by poachers and others, including overfishing key areas and the inhumane treatment of both fish and recreational anglers.

As fishing became more egalitarian in the latter half of the 19th century, the attitudes of elite fraternal organizations sparked debates about how the sport should be enjoyed. As fishing expanded throughout the country, for example, anglers contested types of tackle and bait. Older, more traditional—and wealthy—anglers favored fishing with flies, preferably those made by hand. Fly-fishing required great skill, not only to cast but to make fake flies look real enough to appeal to a fish. Of course, as manufacturing and industrialization spread into the sporting world, it became easy to manufacture mass quantities of believable-looking flies, a practice frowned upon by purists. Many less affluent anglers preferred utilizing live bait—frogs, minnows, and worms being the most popular—that could be used once, lost, and easily replaced. The blood and grime associated with live bait were, however, unappealing to upper-class anglers. With the boom of cheaply produced rods and reels, artificial bait and lures, and ever-larger containers for hauling this equipment, such distinctions became even more commonplace. As the 19th century closed, the standard image of the American angler—wealthy, dignified, professional—was challenged by the image of kids lazily lounging by the side of a stream, little attention being given to their cheaply made fishing poles and equally modest concern for the catch.

Another debate arose over which species to pursue. Northeastern elites often preferred lakes, rivers, and streams filled with "refined" species such as trout and bass, while anglers in the South, Midwest, and West found just as much worth in less "dignified" species such as catfish, pike, and walleye. As adventurous anglers on the coasts took up offshore and deep-sea sport fishing in the early 20th century, a number of saltwater species joined the list of "sport fish." Today, largemouth bass retains its notoriety as the fish most sought after, although anglers pursue dozens of other species in nearly equal numbers. In the 21st century, geography more than class standing dictates the species fishers seek, although the politics of stocking lakes with particular species remains a point of contention. Such debates go back to the founding of the sport and constitute part of its traditions, lore, and lure.

According to a report by the U.S. Fish and Wildlife Service, in 2006, more than 30 million Americans participated in some form of recreational fishing annually, roughly a tenth of the population. Men and women spent more than $40 billion in fishing-related expenses. More than 80 percent of this activity involved freshwater fishing, a significant portion of the Great Lakes region. Freshwater anglers most often pursued black bass. Walleye was the most popular fish in the Great Lakes region. Flatfish and redfish were the most desired saltwater species.

At the dawn of the 21st century, fishing remains a popular activity on both coasts and along any body of water in between, even while other "blood sports"—like hunting—see declines. The less expensive cost of equipment and supplies, relatively easy access to fishing sites, an increase in the stocking of desirable freshwater fish, "family-friendly" marketing campaigns, and the tradition of passing the sport from generation to generation have reinforced the popularity of fishing.

See also FISH AND GAME LAWS AND POACHING; FISHERIES; FISHING, COMMERCIAL; FISHING, SUBSISTENCE; LEWIS AND CLARK EXPEDITION.

Matthew Low

Further Reading
Grover, Kathryn, ed. *Hard at Play: Leisure in America, 1840–1940.* Amherst: University of Massachusetts Press, 1992.
Murphy, Brian, comp. *The Angler's Companion: The Lore of Fishing.* New York: Paddington Press, 1978.
Popkin, Susan A., and Roger B. Allen. *Gone Fishing! A History of Fishing in River, Bay, and Sea.* Philadelphia: Philadelphia Maritime Museum, 1987.
Schullery, Paul. *American Fly Fishing: A History.* Manchester, Vt.: Nick Lyons Books and the American Museum of Fly Fishing, 1987.
Schulz, Ken, and Dan D. Gapen. *The Complete Book of Freshwater Fishing.* New York: Penguin Books, 1989.

fishing, subsistence

Also known as artisan fishing, subsistence fishing involves rods and tackle, nets, fish wheels, harpoons, and arrows to take fish for creating and selling of handicrafts, trade or barter, and sharing for personal and family consumption. Historically, subsistence fishing was essential to Native Americans across North America, and it remains integral to the preservation of the traditional ways of life of indigenous peoples but has led to numerous controversial legal and political challenges.

State and federal governments often work at odds regarding subsistence fishing. Washington and Oregon, for example, states that generate income from COMMERCIAL FISHING and RECREATIONAL FISHING, in the 1950s followed the lead of white anglers in blaming American Indians for declining SALMON runs. Although American Indians typically took less than 5 percent of the states' salmon harvests, Washington and Oregon banned subsistence fishing on the COLUMBIA RIVER and PUGET SOUND and its tributaries. When a number of individual states repeatedly eroded subsistence fishing rights, several groups of Washington Indians in the 1960s reasserted their rights from an 1854–55 treaty by practicing "fish-ins." They openly harvested salmon outside reservation boundaries in protesting antisubsistence fishing laws. After scores of arrests, the fish-ins culminated in a 1974 ruling by U.S. District Court Judge George Boldt that restored traditional fishing rights to Washington's American Indian tribes. The U.S. SUPREME COURT largely affirmed the Boldt decision in 1979 in *U.S. v. Washington* (443 U.S. 658).

In 1990, following precedent set by the Boldt decision, several Chippewa bands in Minnesota asserted their rights to subsistence fish under an 1837 treaty. Citing a negative impact on walleye fishing tourism, the state legislature ruled against Chippewa fishing rights, but in 1998 the U.S. Supreme Court ruled 5-4 in support of the 1837 treaty rights. Subsistence fishers, however, still adhere to numerous restrictions in the name of CONSERVATION while provoking new arguments to limit or stop subsistence fishing in the name of FEDERALISM.

Subsistence fishing is most common in Alaska and creates numerous fights among Alaskans and between the state and federal agencies. In 1964, the Alaska Board of Fisher-

Fish wheel used by indigenous Alaskans. The rotating baskets catch fish traveling upstream. *(U.S. Fish and Wildlife Service)*

ies and Game prohibited subsistence fishing at several traditional American Indian fisheries along the Copper River. In 1980, President JIMMY CARTER signed the Alaska National Interest Lands Conservation Act, which created a national park in the Copper River region and gave rural residents priority in fishing on federal lands. The Alaska Supreme Court, however, declared that the act violated a state guarantee of equal access to fish and game and in 1989 ruled against the rural preference. In response, the federal government, which owns 60 percent of all land in Alaska, took over SUBSISTENCE HUNTING on its lands, and in 1990, the federal government began managing hunting, trapping, and fishing on nonnavigable waters and federal lands. After a series of lawsuits, U.S. District Court Judge H. Russel Holland ruled, in 1994, that Native American fishing rights were not being upheld by the state of Alaska and placed lakes, streams, and waterways within or alongside federal lands under federal jurisdiction.

The state, however, continued to regulate American Indian sport hunting and fishing.

Through ongoing legal and political challenges, in 1999, the federal government took control of fisheries on all federal lands and navigable waters to safeguard subsistence fishing rights for Eskimos, Indians, and other Native peoples. The federal action was unpalatable to those who recalled that federal practices before statehood had greatly diminished the salmon catch by being overly generous to commercial fishers. Opponents further contended that the rules discriminated against urbanites who hunted and fished for FOOD. The federal government acted after eight state senators blocked an effort to call a vote on a constitutional amendment giving rural subsistence fishers priority. The priority applied to roughly 20 percent of the population, 120,000 rural Native Alaskans—Aleuts, Indians, and Eskimos. Subsistence rather than sport fishing meant that they could catch more fish through more efficient methods, and the new rule reduced the volume taken by sport and commercial hunters and fishermen, leaving more for the subsistence fishermen. After Sarah Palin (1964–   ) became governor of Alaska in 2006, however, she attempted to overturn laws regarding tribal sovereignty, including various laws dealing with subsistence hunting and fishing, but failed when the courts in 2007 upheld federal jurisdiction dating to 1980.

Beyond rights to subsistence fish, in the 1990s, states began issuing health warnings for pollutants in their waters, including MERCURY, DDT, chlordane, and other CARCINOGENS, POISONS, AND TOXINS, causing concern about the health risks of fish consumption. Many Asian immigrants, in particular, rely on subsistence fishing to provide food. With diets traditionally high in fish consumption, poor Asians, especially throughout the Southeast, fish frequently and often eat mercury-laden fish because warning signs are not commonly written in their languages. Poor Asian, Hispanic, and African Americans are especially vulnerable to polluted waters as a majority of these populations live near toxic sites. High mercury levels in fish, however, are typically attributed to COAL-burning power plants that affect insects and move up the food chain. Mercury, therefore, is not localized and even affects ocean fish.

GLOBAL WARMING is expected to change subsistence as well as commercial fishing by warming rivers, melting ice, and reducing populations of salmon and other fish; in 2006, the pink salmon harvest, for example, was 40 million fish below estimate as a result of warmer temperatures. Warming will change environments and force subsistence populations to relocate, altering migratory patterns and life cycles.

See also ENVIRONMENTAL JUSTICE; FEDERAL LAW—INDIAN POLICIES; FISH AND OTHER AQUATIC ORGANISMS; INDIANS, PACIFIC NORTHWEST; INDIGENOUS PEOPLES, ALASKA; UNITED STATES—ALASKA; UNITED STATES—PACIFIC NORTHWEST.

John H. Barnhill

Further Reading

Taylor, Joseph E., III. *Making Salmon: An Environmental History of the Northwest Fisheries Crisis.* Seattle: University of Washington Press, 1999.
Washington, Sylvia Hood, Heather Goodall, and Paul C. Rosier. *Echoes from the Poisoned Well: Global Memories of Environmental Justice.* Lanham, Md.: Lexington Books, 2006.

floods

Floods have compelling power as a natural force in human history. Human settlements are often concentrated along rivers, which serve as sources of water, fish, and game and provide routes for trade and travel. Rich alluvial soils also attract farming cultures to river floodplains. Rivers, however, are naturally dynamic, and their pulsing cycles of flood and DROUGHT have sometimes exacted a terrible toll on human life and property. Myths describing epic, global floods are common in oral histories from diverse cultures worldwide. These accounts reflect a shared historical experience of the destructive power of floods, but they also point to another theme—that floods can be an agent of renewal.

Floods happen for many reasons. They may occur when artificial or natural dams fail suddenly, releasing impounded water in a sudden rush. In coastal regions, catastrophic floods can be generated by tsunamis or storm surges. Typical stream and river floods are generated by heavy precipitation or rapid snowmelt. Floods occur when water is delivered to the land's surface much faster than it can be absorbed or retained by soils. As a result, excess water pools on the earth's surface and flows directly into drainage channels. Water enters stream or river channels faster than it can be carried downstream and overtops channel banks. In smaller streams, floods rise and dissipate quickly, generally within a few hours. Flash floods occur in extreme cases, and the leading edge of the floodwater may sweep down stream in a roiling wave. In recently burned or logged areas with steep slopes, floodwaters often pick up large quantities of soil, gravel, cobbles, wood, and other objects to form highly destructive "debris flows." Floodwaters rise more slowly in big rivers, but floods also subject much larger areas to days or weeks of inundation.

Minor floods that barely exceed channel capacity occur routinely in rivers and streams, about once every year or two on average. Bigger floods occur less frequently. In most rivers, truly massive floods occur quite rarely in response to unusual climatic conditions. These rare events, however, are critically important in shaping river landscapes. Flood energy can dramatically rework river channels, cause banks to collapse, and destroy built structures such as bridges, levees, and roads. Subsiding floodwaters typically drop a heavy load of sediment to create new islands and sandbars. In large lowland rivers, floods shape the adjoining landscape to produce broad, flat floodplains with seasonally flooded WETLANDS.

Among the great floods of recorded history, the worst killers have occurred in China, where vast numbers of people live in RICE farming villages within the floodplains of extremely flood-prone rivers such as the Huang He (Yellow) River. A flood there in 1887 took an estimated 6 million lives; floods in 1931 and 1938 killed a combined total of nearly five million people.

In the United States, federal sources place floods as the top natural hazard in the nation and estimate that floods kill 140 people and cause $6 billion in property damage each year. Localized flood damage occurs regularly in almost every region. Storm surges threaten coastal areas, and large regional floods have regularly struck the Ohio, Mississippi, Missouri, and Red River basins and parts of the Northeast and Pacific coast states. One such regional flood occurred in the OHIO RIVER basin in 1913, when two March rainstorms dumped a total of more than 10 inches of rain on saturated soils over a four-day period. Record high-flood stages were measured in several cities and towns along the Ohio and Wabash Rivers. Damage of $100 million and nearly 500 deaths were attributed to this regional flood. Similar spring-time deluges flooded parts of Pennsylvania, Ohio, Kentucky, and West Virginia in 1907, 1908, and 1912.

The 1907 floods in Pennsylvania, Ohio, West Virginia, and Kentucky played a particularly important role in shaping federal environmental policy. These floods coincided with an ongoing congressional debate about the role of FORESTS in flood prevention. Conservationists argued, with some justification, that intact forests promote infiltration of water into the soil and reduce the severity of flooding and EROSION. The science, however, was uncertain. The floods of 1907 occurred in a region where mountains had recently been stripped bare by clear-cut logging. Thus, the floods were seen as a vindication of conservationists' warnings and helped prompt passage of the Weeks Act, a 1911 law that authorized the federal purchase of "forested, cut-over, or denuded lands . . . necessary to the regulation of the flow of navigable streams." These lands were to be managed scientifically as forest reserves and eventually formed the core of the southeastern National Forests. Congress continued to expand the federal role in soil and land management through the early part of the 20th century. In these efforts, flood prevention was often cited as a key goal.

A heavy federal emphasis was placed on river-channel engineering in the early 20th century. From the 1900s through 1936, piecemeal legislation authorized investments in specific regional dam-building and levee projects. The TENNESSEE VALLEY AUTHORITY, for example, was established in 1933 and still manages a network of major reservoirs in the Southeast. Flood disasters of the late 1920s and 1930s helped spur passage of the Flood Control Act of 1936. This ambitious law declared floods "a menace to national welfare" and authorized 211 flood-control projects in 31 states. Hundreds of additional projects were authorized subsequently. The U.S. ARMY CORPS OF ENGINEERS and the federal BUREAU OF RECLAMATION constructed and managed the majority of these developments. Federal projects were undertaken to straighten river channels, thus increasing the rate at which water is carried downstream. Levee projects on the MISSISSIPPI RIVER and other river systems were built to contain floods within main channels, protecting floodplains and freeing them for settlement. Upstream reservoirs, particularly in regional flood-control networks, served to store water during storms and release it gradually after flood risks had subsided. Taken together, these efforts did yield clear benefits under a range of conditions and mitigated flood hazards in many regions. Yet, attempts to engineer great rivers have also produced many ill effects.

In the United States today, most of the rivers that are suitable for channel engineering have already been dammed, contained within levees, straightened, or otherwise regulated. Few new projects are proposed, and even efforts to maintain existing structures face stiff opposition on environmental grounds. Dams and other channel structures can damage and alter river ecology in myriad ways. Moreover, many of the nation's dams are now nearing the end of their useful lifetimes. As a result, dams are now regularly being decommissioned and dismantled to restore rivers to more free-flowing conditions.

Increasingly, critics are shifting their focus away from specific tactics, such as dams and levees, and instead are calling into question the entire enterprise of flood control. Flood control itself, no matter how it might be accomplished, is now emerging as a major threat to river ECOSYSTEMS. Working in a range of systems from small streams to the Earth's biggest rivers, ecologists have demonstrated the vital and positive role of flooding in supporting the productivity of aquatic habitats, shaping and renewing the structure of river channels, and maintaining habitat for native species. Big-river ecologists developed the flood-pulse concept to describe the effects of annual floods on river and floodplain ecosystems. Through many complementary processes, natural seasonal fluctuations in flow maintain high degrees of diversity and productivity in big rivers. The life histories of native species are closely matched to the natural-flow pattern, and disruptions tend to interfere with their reproduction and growth. Floods also play a key role in physically reshaping river-bottom and floodplain landscapes, and artificially constant flow patterns deprive rivers of the energy and sediments required to do this work.

Today, nearly all big temperate-zone rivers are highly engineered and regulated, and it is no simple matter to recover the lost natural functions of flooding. Yet, there is some leeway to modify river management to emulate natural floods, thus balancing ecological concerns against the competing demands for navigation, power generation, and flood control. In the GRAND CANYON, agency scientists and managers have recently begun a program of intentional experimental flooding. When the COLORADO RIVER ran free, annual floods scoured vegetation from the canyon bottom. Receding floodwaters dumped large sandbars along the channel margins, producing ideal camping beaches for rafters and other canyon users. Today, the Colorado is a regulated river. Downstream of GLEN CANYON DAM, routine dam releases are unnaturally steady, cold, and sediment-free. As a consequence, sandbars have disappeared and exotic vegetation has established itself in previously flooded areas. Experimental floods in 1996 and 2004 were intended to correct these and other problems caused by flow regulation. The artificial floods did not duplicate the magnitude and duration of natural spring floods. But the experimental floods far exceeded the normal flow rate and did produce at least temporary expansion of sandbars and other favorable effects. Each flood has been heavily studied; managers use the term *adaptive management* to describe the steep learning curve involved in this strikingly novel endeavor.

Flood control remains a hot-button issue for environmentalists, most of whom adamantly oppose the large-scale engineering efforts exemplified by the Glen Canyon Dam. Dam proponents steadfastly remind us of the benefits engendered by flood control projects and suggest that ecological repercussions may be an unavoidable cost of progress. But experience has warned against simplistic optimism and wishful thinking when it comes to floods. A key point expressed by many engineers and risk analysts is that levees and other control systems are built to function only within limits. The system is built to handle what is sometimes termed the *design flood*—which is by no means the largest of all possible floods. The situation presents a devil's bargain. Flood control prevents harm from minor, routine floods. As a result, floodplain areas become more attractive for settlement and development. As William G. Hoyt and Walter B. Langbein wrote in 1955, the frequent benefits of protection against routine floods are "bought at the price of occasional great harm." When a flood a little bigger than the "design flood" becomes a reality, disastrous results generally occur.

Two recent events demonstrate this situation all too well. One is the extensive flooding in the central Mississippi River basin in summer 1993 after a protracted period of heavy rainfall in the region. This flood overwhelmed many levee and containment systems, costing 48 lives and an estimated $20 billion in property damage. The affected communities were protected from routine flooding but dangerously vulnerable to extreme events. Similarly, Hurricane Katrina's flood surge along the Gulf Coast and in New Orleans, Louisiana, in 2005 was the main factor responsible for the loss of 1,464 lives, the displacement of more than 200,000 residents, and property damage that exceeded $80 billion. The storm was at or near the design limit of the levee system. Furthermore, levee-design flaws and ecological damage to coastal marshes may have worsened the situation.

Immediate rebuilding and stubborn optimism have been a traditional refuge in the aftermath of disaster, but many people are calling for a reassessment of development patterns to avoid flood-prone areas. In the wake of the 1993 Mississippi flood, federal and state authorities bought about 25,000 properties from floodplain dwellers who agreed to move to higher ground. The vacated lands were restored to wetlands. These wetlands dissipate and store floodwaters, thus reducing the severity of downstream flooding in the process. After a century of mixed experience with "flood-control" policy, the freshest alternatives emphasize flood avoidance, flood accommodation, and even intentional restoration of flooding to our river landscapes.

See also DAMS, RESERVOIRS, AND ARTIFICIAL LAKES; DISASTERS, MISSOURI RIVER.

Jon D. Hoekstra

Further Reading
Hoyt, William G., and Walter B. Langbein. *Floods.* Princeton, N.J.: Princeton University Press, 1955.
Leopold, Luna B. *A View of the River.* Cambridge, Mass.: Harvard University Press, 1994.
Postel, Sandra, and Brian Richter. *Rivers for Life.* Washington, D.C.: Island Press, 2003.

food
Cycles of food production and consumption dominate much of American environmental history and are inextricable from the nation's natural resources and its history of industrialization. One way to trace changes in the environmental history of food in the United States is to examine the shifting geographies of its foodsheds.

As do WATERSHEDS, foodsheds encompass the landscapes from which food for human consumption is generated. Well into the 19th century, Native American populations frequented and managed resources across a range of regions in order to source their foodstuffs. European settlers from the 17th century onward, however, tended to settle in particular locations, where they established communities in which they transformed local natural resources into food and energy and for export to European nations. Throughout the colonial era and into the early national period, settlers moved on to new lands as farmlands wore out, but their practices of sourcing the majority of their foods from local foodsheds remained. Over the past two centuries, developments stemming from the Industrial Revolution and the transformation from a rural to an urban nation have expanded consumers' foodsheds from the local to the global.

Since WORLD WAR II (1941–45) in particular, farmers in different climatic and geographic regions have responded to economic incentives and legislative imperatives to specialize in MONOCULTURE, the production of single crops. Although a national system of monoculture provides consumers with food year-round, the shifts from mixed, seasonal, and local agriculture to specialized agriculture produced for national markets have altered relationships between Americans and their environments in profound ways. These changes have also unleashed significant debates over how best to balance environmental capacities to produce the foodstuffs required of growing populations.

EARLY NATIONAL FOODSHEDS
In the 1780s and 1790s, the population of the United States was overwhelmingly rural. The majority of Americans lived in farming communities, where they worked local plots of land in close exchange with other individuals and, at least for free white families, according to particular gendered divisions of labor. In the most efficient practices, male farmers sowed fields with GRAINS for household consumption, rotated crops from season to season, manured their lands, and paid close attention to cycles of the Moon and to almanac wisdom for crop management. Farm holdings passed from a father to

his sons or, as land in a given community became scarce, to the oldest son. Meanwhile, farmers' wives, daughters, and mothers milked cows, gathered spring eggs, tended garden vegetables and herbs, baked bread, killed chickens, and set aside seeds for future years. Throughout any given year, farm families relied on their close relationships to nature and their own labor for the majority of their sustenance, which they gleaned from local foodsheds.

While families provided most of the labor required for their food consumption, their foodsheds extended outward for certain purposes. Not infrequently, neighbors traded meat animals (such as lambs) for others' goods or services. In addition, old recipes contained in "receipt books" show that many Americans incorporated ingredients such as coffee, tea, sugar, Madeira wine, and nutmeg into their diets. These products required extensions of the families' local foodsheds via trade networks and others' labor in faraway climates. But before the 19th century, these items were consumed in relatively small quantities. More often than not, families' labor on individual plots of land within local foodsheds defined the production and consumption of food in the new nation.

The Land Ordinance of 1785, passed by CONGRESS under the ARTICLES OF CONFEDERATION, laid the groundwork for the new nation's transformation of its foodsheds and the landscapes on which its foods were produced. Designed to foster a democracy of small farmers, the ordinance imposed a grid of sections and townships onto vast expanses of the trans-Appalachian frontier. As farmers purchased 160-acre plots of land from the government, their new agricultural communities formed 640-acre sections within 36-square-mile townships. By laying the legislative basis for the nation's future agricultural and geographical mobilization, the act established an important framework for the future expansion of national foodsheds. At the same time, it provided a clear incentive for farmers to transform woodlands, marshes, and PRAIRIES into fields dedicated to agricultural production.

FOODSHEDS IN AN INDUSTRIALIZING NATION BEFORE THE CIVIL WAR

Alongside early legislative acts encouraging western settlement and landscape transformation, revolutions in transportation and technology, as part of the Industrial Revolution, transformed the local foodsheds of the late 18th century into the interregional, national, and global foodsheds of the 19th and 20th centuries. In the early 1800s, steamboats opened a new era of waterborne transportation. As their floating engines harnessed the energy contained in wood, water, and steam in ambitious ways, they enabled those in western settlements such as the Genesee River and OHIO RIVER valleys to move people, goods, and heavy foodstuffs upriver as well as down. Expanding trade infrastructures, in turn, encouraged increased levels of emigration and agricultural production, which put greater quantities of foodstuffs produced in

one climate or geography into others. These bounties gravitated toward lucrative urban markets.

As new transportation technologies facilitated the movement of foodstuffs and the dedication of landscapes to agricultural production, additional sets of knowledge, tools, and technologies enabled farmers and planters to work their lands with greater efficiency and to extract more food from them. In the late 18th century, for example, West African slaves imported by southern RICE planters showed planters how to control tidal watersheds through more efficient systems of ditches. New modes of tidal IRRIGATION dramatically increased rice planters' yields. Farther north in the first decades of the 19th century, farmers began to replace moldboard wood plows with cast-iron plows. John Deere (1804–86) revolutionized their tentative adoption of this technology in 1837, when he patented his steel plow. His new tool allowed settlers in Illinois and other prairie states to cut through the deep roots of bluestem and other GRASSES and plant the sod to CORN and WHEAT. Similarly, Cyrus McCormick's (1809–84) mechanical reaper, patented in 1831 and improved over a series of decades, enabled farmers to automate the difficult tasks of cutting, curing, and binding grains. Because the reaper freed laborers from the arduous work of cradle harvesting, it enabled more extensive cultivation of land, which in turn prompted the transformation of soil and water resources into lands suitable for cultivation.

Technology was a boon for many farmers and urban consumers at the turn of the 19th century because it allowed a growing commoditization of foodstuffs for sale and trade. However, changing resource uses transformed foodsheds in unexpected ways for other groups. Settlers moving into new territories sought access to waterpower for their saw and grist mills. By a similar token, New England's MILL TOWNS harnessed ponds, streams, and waterways as they transformed the regional economy into an economic powerhouse. Yet when mills and factories dammed streams and delivered water to the giant wheels that powered their industries, they blockaded SALMON and shad runs that had long provided protein for inland inhabitants, especially poorer farmers, thereby destroying natural rhythms of fish migration and collapsing key elements of regional foodsheds.

Collapses in local foodshed availability were important markers in the industrializing nation's shift toward national foodshed reliance. As the nation continued its path toward industrialization and as growing urban populations began to rely on foods produced farther afield, the twofold development of transportation and technology continued to expand American foodshed geographies. Toward this end, the 1825 completion of the Erie Canal revolutionized the movement of people and goods in the Northeast and inaugurated an era of canal transit. Steamboats permitted north-south transfers of foodstuffs; western farmers used CANALS to ship foodstuffs to lucrative eastern markets. Farmers along the Erie Canal, meanwhile, responded to the new route by transforming their grain fields into more perishable but highly lucrative vegetable crops.

By the mid-19th century, farmers, merchants, and grain dealers in and around the city of CHICAGO, ILLINOIS, began a wholesale transformation of the grain industry, the prairie lands in the surrounding hinterland, and national habits of food consumption. Reaping the combined benefits of rich loess soils laid down by glacial activity millennia before, the Ordinance of 1785, the plow, the reaper, steam transit, early RAILROADS, and increased emigration and IMMIGRATION, greater numbers of farmers in the West put more acres under the plow to produce larger quantities of crops for sale. In the 1830s through the 1840s, farmers in the West sold sacks of their excess wheat and corn to Chicago storekeepers. Dealers, in turn, shipped the sacks to ports south and east in steamboats' oddly shaped holds. Containing the product of one farmer's given field or fields, distinct sacks of grain could be bought and sold so as to connect the consumer directly to the nature of the producer's land. When someone bought the sack of grain in Manhattan, he or she could knowingly purchase the fruits of one farmer's labor and the environmental conditions through which that grain was grown. Three new technologies of the late 1840s and 1850s, however—the steam-operated grain elevator, the grain grading system, and the futures market—transformed the earlier system into one in which grain formed a interchangeable "stream" of capital that could be bought and sold. This transformation of the grain industry encouraged more extensive land cultivation and facilitated a new industrial system of feeding CATTLE and PIGS AND HOGS for the market. It also played a vital part in replacing local foodsheds with those that were national in scope and obscured the connection between consumers and any given crop of grain, its grower, and the particular soil or climate in which it grew.

FOODSHEDS IN AN INDUSTRIALIZING NATION AFTER THE CIVIL WAR

After the CIVIL WAR (1861–65), the completion of the transcontinental railroad in 1869 further expanded the foodsheds of the nation's citizens, moving foods sourced from remote farms and wilderness areas alike across the continent with record speed. As evocative symbols of America's fruitful nature, WILD ANIMALS such as PASSENGER PIGEONS were esteemed in the 12-course feasts strewn on the tables of the nouveau riche, especially at places like Delmonico's restaurant in NEW YORK CITY. Yet just as consumers of grain in the second half of the 19th century no longer sourced their wheat from a given plot of land or created under known geographic or climatic conditions, so, too, upper-class diners consumed a commoditized nature and lacked a direct connection to the life or death of the pigeon lying on their plate. Moreover, the inclusion of midwestern game birds in coastal foodsheds, a

prime example of foodshed expansion as part of industrialization, contained a recipe for the species's EXTINCTION.

The commoditization of nature as food thrived in the railroad industry's postbellum growth. Having become the primary medium of transportation, RAILROADS moved people and products across space and time. Their prevalence enabled the industry to incubate a host of companies that applied ever-more innovative technologies to the question of how to transform nature into food, and how to move foodstuffs from field, sea, or air to consumers' tables. Whereas earlier generations had driven western beef to market on the hoof, for example, companies such as the Chicago-based Swift & Co. perfected "disassembly lines" and meat distribution networks. In the slaughterhouse factories of the 1870s, immigrant laborers turned corn-fed cattle into cuts of beef, which in turn were shipped to consumers in eastern and western cities in iced railroad cars. The invention of this meat disassembly line, along with the railroads' systems for harvesting and guarding winter ice for summer use, meant that consumers could sidestep the messiness of working with living animals and slaughtering those destined for the table. These industrial innovations also meant that urban and rural families no longer had to rely upon their own labor for preserving meat. Whereas housewives of the late 18th or early 19th centuries salted or pickled their families' pork supplies after killing hogs in winter, new modes of transportation and food production enabled consumers to access meat without an equivalent investment of time, labor, or regard for season.

As the system of harvesting winter ice for summer meat preservation suggests, new technologies of preservation further enabled the expansion of foodsheds from the local to the national and the global. Corporations such as Heinz poured large sums of money and effort toward developing new technologies for preserving and canning berries, vegetables, meats, and sauces. These technologies enabled consumers to access foods from a range of locales in nearly any season, with the end result that they experienced diminishing relationships to living and growing foodstuffs. By the turn of the 20th century, companies such as the United Fruit Company and Sunkist began to ship delicate citrus from California, Florida, and Hawaii to urban centers across the nation. Consumers, meanwhile, broadened their palates and their foodshed geographies as they transitioned, for instance, from the once-yearly Christmas orange to a daily serving of the blemish-free fruit.

Yet as consumers grew to expect oranges in Iowa in February, their demands prompted growers in California to produce fruit on a massive scale. Producers turned to monoculture, FERTILIZER, and PESTICIDES in order to meet consumers' demands at minimal economic costs. Yet cost savings required a host of inputs with long-term ecological consequences. To maintain soil fertility and grow beautiful oranges at low costs, growers turned to fertilizer rather than practicing crop rotation or fallowing. They first relied on nitrogen-laden guano, which was mined from ancient sources on islands located off the coast of Peru.

After WORLD WAR I (1914–18), they turned to chemical fertilizers, which were produced via the Haber-Bosch method. This process synthesizes ammonia from atmospheric nitrogen and enables farmers to grow nitrogen-dependent cash crops without reverting to less-remunerative crops of nitrogen-fixing legumes. While extra nitrogen augments farmers' yields and boosts available food supplies, nitrogen runoff remains a problem for waterways, where it feeds algae and chokes marine life and contaminates DRINKING WATER. Later generations have turned to FOSSIL FUELS, which provide the key inputs for fertilizers and pesticides, as the basis for maintaining land fertility. Those fuels, moreover, provide the energy to run farm machinery, irrigate fields, and transport crops to market.

As does nitrogen runoff, fields containing row after row of the same crop, no matter how cheap they may have been to operate, created a host of problems for fields' ECOSYSTEMS. In the past, seasonal crop rotations and fields holding a variety of crops might have stymied the spread of any given pest. Now flies, bugs, and fungi flourished where only one crop was cultivated. Responding to those pests, 20th-century farmers turned to pesticides. While chemical sprays and mists were effective, at least until pests grew resilient, many early pesticides were laden with arsenic. Given that a new generation of advertising told consumers to expect nothing more potent than pure sunshine from their morning orange, consumers did not respond to arsenic-laden fruit with glowing approval. On the contrary, though foods of the nation were available at urban consumers' corner grocers, they did not anticipate that their morning produce would be so *unnatural*.

NATIONAL FOODSHEDS AND CONSUMER ACTIVISM

If there is one major consequence of foodsheds that are national in scope, it is that consumers no longer have knowledge of the ways in which foods are produced, transported, or preserved. Fallout from expanded foodsheds, namely, the knowledge of unsavory slaughterhouse conditions, suspicion of the nature packed inside tins of processed foods, and reticence at monoculture crop production and its concomitant pesticide use, has, however, inspired legions of consumer activists. UPTON SINCLAIR's *The Jungle* (1906), for example, raised public awareness of slaughterhouse conditions and brought about the passage of the 1906 Pure Food and Drug Act. Similarly, the food reformer Harvey J. Wiley (1844–1930) fought for consumers' rights against the unknowable nature of canned and refined foodstuffs in the second decade of the 20th century. Jerome Irving (J. I.) Rodale (1898–1971) told consumers, in the 1930s and 1940s, that they could in fact lead healthier lives by caring for the health of their soil through organic gardening. More recent generations of activists have responded to challenges posed by national and global foodsheds by invoking the benefits of organic and local farming, by seeking to change Farm Bill policies promoting excessive corn-and-soybean cultivation, and by highlighting the links between industrial agriculture and GLOBAL WARMING.

CONCLUSION

The expansion of foodsheds from the local to regional, national, and global scales encompassed a great deal of social and environmental change. As new technologies have altered the nature of agricultural production, the industrialization of transportation and packing industries continue to facilitate the movement of foodstuffs from one location to many. Today, rather than locally producing a variety of produce, grains, meat, and dairy for home use, the majority of individual households rely on an enormous system of specialized producers and costly external inputs to source their food.

In addition, the spread of geographic foodsheds has distanced consumers from knowing the nature of their food. Infrastructure and distance have, in turn, prompted new cycles of legislation and consumer activism. While advances in agricultural production, storage, processing, and transportation have made it possible to eat New Zealand apples in New York in May, Chilean peaches in Michigan in February, and fresh pork or beef year round, the first decade of the 21st century has seen a surge of consumer interest in eating organically and locally. Restaurants, GROCERY STORES, and urban farmers' markets have become hubs of a revitalized interest in connecting consumers to small-scale producers, seasonal crop cycles, and legislative policies, including debates over annual farm bills and which crops the federal government subsidizes. Similarly, Web sites, books, and newspapers have formed communities of individuals who connect questions of food procurement and availability to issues of public health, social justice, and global climate change. As consumers become more aware of the environmental issues connected to food production and consumption, organic farming practices, and public health, new chapters will be added to the environmental history of food in the United States.

See also AGRICULTURAL TECHNOLOGY; AGRICULTURE, COLONIAL; AGRICULTURE, COMMERCIAL; AGRICULTURE, DEPARTMENT OF; AGRICULTURE, ORGANIC; AGRICULTURE, SUBSISTENCE; AGRICULTURE, SUSTAINABLE; CHICAGO BOARD OF TRADE; ENERGY, HYDRAULIC; FEDERAL LAW—INDUSTRIAL REGULATIONS; FEDERAL LAW—LAND POLICIES; FOOD AND DRUG ADMINISTRATION; GLACIERS; HEIRLOOM FRUITS AND VEGETABLES; LAND GRANT INSTITUTIONS; RIVER TRANSPORTATION; STOCKYARDS AND MEATPACKING; YEOMAN.

Kelly J. Sisson

Further Reading

Cronon, William. *Changes in the Land: Indians, Colonists, and the Ecology of New England*. New York: Hill & Wang, 1983.

———. *Nature's Metropolis: Chicago and the Great West.* New York: W. W. Norton, 1991.

Knobloch, Frieda. *The Culture of Wilderness: Agriculture as Colonization in the American West.* Chapel Hill: University of North Carolina Press, 1996.

Pollan, Michael. *The Omnivore's Dilemma: A Natural History of Four Meals.* New York: Penguin Press, 2006.

Price, Jennifer. *Flight Maps: Adventures with Nature in Modern America.* New York: Basic Books, 1999.

Sackman, Douglas C. *Orange Empire: California and the Fruits of Eden.* Berkeley: University of California Press, 2005.

Steinberg, Ted. *Down to Earth: Nature's Role in American History.* New York: Oxford University Press, 2002.

Stoll, Steven J. *The Fruits of Natural Advantage: Making the Industrial Countryside in California.* Berkeley: University of California Press, 2002.

———. *Larding the Lean Earth: Soil and Society in Nineteenth-Century America.* New York: Hill & Wang, 2002.

Vileisis, Ann. *Kitchen Literacy: How We Lost Knowledge of Where Food Comes From and Why We Need to Get It Back.* Washington, D.C.: Island Press, 2008.

White, Richard. *The Organic Machine.* New York: Hill & Wang, 1995.

Food and Drug Administration, U.S.

The U.S. Food and Drug Administration (FDA) is an agency in the U.S. DEPARTMENT OF HEALTH AND HUMAN SERVICES that mediates Americans' relationship to the natural environment by regulating the safety of the FOOD, PHARMACEUTICAL DRUGS, and related products on which they rely for sustenance and bodily health. Before nature's raw materials, as processed by the food and pharmaceutical industries, reach Americans' bodies as food and medicine, they undergo a series of checks by the FDA, an agency in the federal government created expressly to protect American citizens as consumers.

Throughout the 19th century, concerns about the safety of food produced in the United States grew as the economy industrialized. Agricultural production of individual farms increased, and more Americans moved to towns and cities. Consequently, far fewer Americans were growing their own food, milking their own cows, and slaughtering their own CATTLE. They were instead relying on large agricultural producers and processing plants to supply them with food. The expanding network of RAILROADS and the improvement of the refrigerated railroad car facilitated these changes.

The burgeoning system of mass production and mass consumption, left largely unregulated, led to unhealthful practices and abuses by industry. For example, dangerous copper and zinc salts were added as preservatives to canned foods. Some dairies put chalk in milk to improve its appearance. Soldiers fighting in the SPANISH-AMERICAN WAR of 1898 complained of spoiled canned beef, leading to an army court of inquiry into the production process the following year.

Drugs also raised concerns, and it was with medicine that the federal government made attempts at regulation. The short-lived Vaccines Act of 1813 and the spottily enforced Drug Importation Act of 1848 proved to be inadequate, however. The need for effective measures ensuring drug safety became more evident in the early 20th century, when 13 children in ST. LOUIS, MISSOURI, and nine children in Camden, New Jersey, died after being injected with contaminated diphtheria antitoxins. These episodes led to the passage of the Biologics Control Act in 1902, which empowered the Hygienic Laboratory of the Public Health and Marine Hospital Service to evaluate and license manufacturers of vaccines, serums, and antitoxins. The laboratory was the precursor to the FDA's Center for Biologics Evaluation and Research.

Frightening incidents involving tainted food and drugs, as well as a growing public awareness of contagion and the need for large-scale hygienic measures, caused fears to grow in intensity, but passing federal legislation proved to be a long and arduous process. One of the main proponents of pure food and drugs was Harvey Washington Wiley (1844–1930), who began serving as chief chemist in the Division of Chemistry in the U.S. DEPARTMENT OF AGRICULTURE (USDA) in 1883. From 1887 to 1902, his division published a 10-part study entitled *Food and Food Adulterants* that detailed how manufacturers had mishandled, mislabeled, and tainted a variety of food products, including spices, condiments, alcoholic beverages, coffee, and canned meat. Wiley and other public health advocates organized a number of meetings and testified before Congress many times during the 1890s and early 1900s, but their research and revelations could not get legislation enacted by Congress, where producers held considerable sway.

The publication of UPTON SINCLAIR's novel *The Jungle* in 1906 provided the catalyst for federal pure food and drug legislation. Sinclair spent seven weeks in the STOCKYARDS AND MEATPACKING plants in CHICAGO, ILLINOIS, researching his tale of exploited immigrant workers. His novel proved popular, but instead of promoting socialism as he had hoped, it called attention to the filthy conditions in packinghouses. President THEODORE ROOSEVELT, following Sinclair's advice, appointed independent investigators to confirm the charges in *The Jungle*. They found that most of the incidents dramatized in the novel had actually occurred. Roosevelt used the report as leverage and leaned on the meatpackers and legislators to push through legislation. After intense debate, on June 30, 1906, Congress passed and Roosevelt signed both the Pure Food and Drug Act and the Meat Inspection Act.

The acts gave the USDA's Division of Chemistry responsibility for enforcing the laws with the intention of curbing adulteration and misbranding of food and medicine. Its tasks were to oversee meat produced for interstate and foreign commerce, perform antemortem and postmortem examinations of animals slaughtered for meat, inspect processed food and drug products, and control hygienic conditions in plants. In 1927, the Bureau of Chemistry was reorganized into two separate entities: the Food, Drug, and Insecticide Administration, responsible for legislation, and the Bureau of Chemistry and Soils, responsible for research. Three years later, the name of the former administration was shortened to the Food and Drug Administration. Wiley and his successors aggressively pursued violators of the law, but its scope remained limited and thus elicited vociferous criticism.

In 1933, the FDA recommended a complete revision of the 1906 Food and Drug Act, initiating a five-year fight over new legislation. Once again, a dramatic occurrence helped spur action in WASHINGTON, D.C. In 1937, some 107 people died after being injected with elixir sulfanilamide contaminated with a poisonous solvent. The following year, President FRANKLIN D. ROOSEVELT signed the Food, Drug, and Cosmetic Act, which required new drugs to undergo a system of checks before being approved for public consumption, expanded the FDA's authority to regulate cosmetics and therapeutic devices, provided that safe tolerance levels be set for unavoidable toxic substances, authorized new standards of identity and quality for foods, approved factory inspections, and added new penalties for violators of the law.

The Food, Drug, and Cosmetic Act significantly increased the FDA's responsibilities, and over the ensuing decades, the agency has taken on many more. A 1954 amendment to the 1938 act set safety limits for residue of PESTICIDES on agricultural products, a concern for many Americans and one that environmentalists would take up in the years that followed. In fact, when the ENVIRONMENTAL PROTECTION AGENCY was established in 1970, it took over the FDA's program for setting pesticide tolerances. Also in 1954, the FDA began its first large-scale inspection of foods feared to be radioactive, in response to reports of radioactive tuna being imported from Japan. The Kefauver-Harris amendments of 1962 declared for the first time that drug manufacturers had to prove the efficacy of their medicines to the FDA before marketing them, beginning the system of review that still exists today. In 1979, the FDA responded to the near nuclear meltdown at THREE MILE ISLAND by providing potassium iodide to those threatened with thyroid cancer from radiation exposure. The Food and Drug Administration Modernization Act of 1997 represented the most significant attempt to reorganize the FDA by improving the agency's regulation capacities and adjusting its role for changes in production and medical technologies. As an example of the agency's flexibility, beginning in 2004, the FDA began regulating living organisms: leeches and maggots used in medical treatments.

In 1988, the FDA became an agency in the Department of Health and Human Services. It monitors the quality of not only food, drugs, and cosmetics, but also dietary supplements, vaccines, biological medical products, blood prod-

ucts, medical devices, veterinary products, and, as a result of 2009 legislation, TOBACCO products. American consumers have entrusted the FDA with protecting their health from products that may become contaminated on their way from the natural environment to their bodies.

See also AGRICULTURE, COMMERCIAL; CARCINOGENS, POISONS, AND TOXINS; CONSUMERISM; FEDERAL LAW—INDUSTRIAL REGULATIONS; DISEASES, HUMAN; HEALTH AND MEDICINE; PROGRESSIVISM; SALT.

Jonathan Anzalone

Further Reading
Hilts, Philip J. *Protecting America's Health: The FDA, Business, and One Hundred Years of Regulation.* New York: Alfred A. Knopf, 2003.
Jackson, Charles O. *Food and Drug Legislation in the New Deal.* Princeton, N.J.: Princeton University Press, 1970.
Temin, Peter. *Taking Your Medicine: Drug Regulation in the United States.* Cambridge, Mass.: Harvard University Press, 1980.
Young, James Harvey. *Pure Food: Securing the Federal Food and Drugs Act of 1906.* Princeton, N.J.: Princeton University Press, 1989.

Ford, Henry (1863–1947) *business executive, industrialist*

Henry Ford helped to revolutionize the automobile industry in the United States during the first half of the 20th century. His founding of the Ford Motor Company and perfection of the assembly line allowed for the mass production of high-quality, inexpensive AUTOMOBILES that were accessible to the masses. Thus, Ford contributed to the birth of the modern consumer economy. Throughout his life, Ford struggled both to tame and to preserve the natural environment, both in the United States and abroad.

Born on July 30, 1863, in Dearborn, Michigan, Ford trained as a machinist and learned how to build and repair steam engines. In 1891, he began working as an engineer for the Edison Illuminating Company while he experimented with gasoline engines and self-propelled vehicles. Although he was not the first or the only engineer to develop an automobile, he proved to be one of the most successful. In 1903, after two unsuccessful ventures, he launched the Ford Motor Company. Five years later, he introduced the Model T. Reliable, easy to operate, and reasonably priced, this car helped initiate a new era of personal transportation. By 1918, more than half of all cars in the United States were Model Ts.

During the 1920s and 1930s, Ford was instrumental in the push to use an alternative fuel to replace gasoline in automobiles. There had been some attempts in the early 20th century to develop other fuels. However, the automobile had largely relied on gasoline to power vehicles. In 1925, Ford told a *New*

York Times reporter that ethanol was the fuel of the future. One reason was that General Motors had been developing tetra-ethyl LEAD and government officials had quietly approached Ford to find other alternatives. A second reason was the economic crisis in the farming sector. Ford hoped that ethanol would create new markets for farm products. He thus gave his political and financial backing to the movement to open industrial markets for farmers. This movement became known as the Farm Chemurgy movement.

Ford also sought to implement what has sometimes been called industrial pastoralism, in which he attempted to establish sustainable sources of raw materials and humane living conditions for workers. His first attempt was in Michigan's Upper Peninsula, in the early 1920s. Ford purchased vast tracts of land to supply the lumber used in his Model T automobiles. Seeing himself as a conservationist and wanting to have a future supply of lumber, Ford tried to prevent DEFORESTATION in the Upper Peninsula.

During the 1920s, Ford also looked for ways to acquire more natural RUBBER for the U.S. automobile industry. The growing number of cars combined with the Goodyear Company's new tires that required 30 percent more elastic material led to an increased demand for rubber in the United States. However, the British and the Dutch monopolized the Southeast Asian sources of natural rubber, leading American industrialists to look elsewhere for the material. In 1923, the Brazilian government approached Ford about a rubber venture in South America, but Ford initially declined. Two years later, in 1925, with rubber prices rising, Brazil again contacted Ford, offering a vast estate with tax remission and police protection. By 1927, Ford reached an agreement to acquire 2.5 million acres of land in the Amazon region of Brazil, where natural rubber had long grown. The agreement allowed Ford to import equipment and export rubber duty-free. After 12 years, Ford would pay a 7 percent tax on any profits. The Brazilian government imposed few restrictions on the way Ford could alter the environment, granting him the right to build dams, RAILROADS, or airports in the Amazon.

By 1929, Ford's Brazilian scheme cleared about 1,500 acres of rain forest and planted rubber trees. However, within five years, leaf blight had severely hindered the project. Rubber trees had naturally evolved and survived by growing in a scattered fashion to avoid fungal problems. Ford had planted his rubber trees in neatly controlled rows to make cultivation easier and thus allowed the fungus to spread easily and destroy the trees. Ford moved his rubber project to a new site, but a drought in 1938 and swarms of caterpillars in 1942 led him to withdraw from Brazil in 1945.

On a personal level, Ford increasingly sought to enjoy nature and the environment as he aged. As a child, Ford had been interested in BIRDS. After enjoying success as an entrepreneur, Ford purchased large tracts of farmland and forest around his birthplace to use not only for experiments with tractors but also as bird sanctuaries. Ford even kept a bird-watching telescope in his office at the Ford Motor Company.

Ford also admired the work of the naturalist JOHN BURROUGHS. Noting his interest in ornithology, Ford's wife, Clara, bought him a complete set of Burroughs's books. Burroughs worried about the pace of industrialization in the United States and was especially concerned that automobile use would hurt the way that Americans appreciated nature. Hoping to change Burroughs's mind, Ford presented the naturalist with an automobile as a gift. Burroughs began to enjoy the car, as he could use it to get closer to nature by driving throughout the countryside to bird-watch. In June 1913, Ford and Burroughs met in DETROIT, MICHIGAN, and the naturalist was impressed by Ford's knowledge of birds. Ford's friendship with Burroughs soon led to regular camping trips that also included THOMAS EDISON and the tire and rubber entrepreneur Harvey Firestone (1868–1938). This "gathering of geniuses" captivated the MEDIA and the public. Starting in 1914 and continuing through the 1920s, the so-called Four Vagabonds sought inspiration in nature. While Ford sometimes complained of the media attention given to his back-to-nature trips, the journeys helped to solidify his status as an American folk hero. The fact that industrial giants such as Ford, Edison, and Firestone traveled with the likes of the naturalist Burroughs illustrated the growing leisure and recreation ethic of an increasingly urban and industrial United States, as people from all walks of life began to reconnect with the natural environment. Ford died in Dearborn, Michigan, on April 7, 1947.

See also CONSUMERISM; INTERSTATE HIGHWAY SYSTEM; ROADS AND TURNPIKES.

Ronald Young

Further Reading
Collier, Peter, and David Horowitz. *The Fords: An American Epic.* New York: Simon & Schuster, 1992.
Grandin, Greg. *Fordlandia: The Rise and Fall of Henry Ford's Forgotten Jungle City.* New York: Metropolitan Books, 2009.
Kovarik, Bill. "Henry Ford, Charles F. Kettering and the Fuel of the Future." *Automotive History Review* 32 (Spring 1998): 7–27.
Nevis, Allan, and Frank Hill. *Ford: The Times, the Man, the Company.* New York: Scribner, 1954.
Tucker, Richard. *Insatiable Appetite: The United States and the Ecological Degradation of the Tropical World.* Berkeley and Los Angeles: University of California Press, 2000.
Watts, Steven. *The People's Tycoon: Henry Ford and the American Century.* New York: Alfred A. Knopf, 2005.

forest products

Forest products are items manufactured from materials produced by forests for use by people. They are classified into two categories: timber products, such as lumber, plywood, paper, and pulp; and nontimber forest products (NTFPs), including foliage, fungi, medicinal herbs, mushrooms, berries, oils, and even game. Yet, in another sense, forests produce more than material for "products" that people can use. Forests provide numerous ecosystem services, which include sequestering carbon, conserving BIODIVERSITY, and protecting WATERSHEDS.

Since prehistory, humans have harvested NTFPs to maintain physical strength and cultural traditions. Before their encounter with Europeans, Native Americans used FIRE in hunting, but the impact on forests was not severe. With the arrival of Europeans, there were increasing needs for timber, pitch, and tar for shipbuilding, which caused DEFORESTATION along the Atlantic coast. Europeans expanded westward with minimal care for FORESTS. Along the way, lumber has been widely used for heating homes and supplying material for mining and smelting and the construction of RAILROADS and waterways.

It was not until the last decade of the 19th century that systematic efforts to study and halt deforestation took place. Bernard Fernow (1851–1923), a Prussian-born and trained forester, became chief of the Division of Forestry in 1886. He assembled staffs and started research in silviculture (the care and cultivation of forest trees), pathology, and wood technology. Fernow's special interest in the physical properties of wood laid the groundwork for forest products research, but he was unsuccessful in persuading the CONGRESS to increase the division's funding and expand its personnel.

His successor, GIFFORD PINCHOT, gained support from Congress and the DEPARTMENT OF AGRICULTURE, expanded the "division" to the "bureau" in 1901, established the U.S. FOREST SERVICE in 1905, and inherited the Forest Reserve (soon renamed the National Forest) from the DEPARTMENT OF THE INTERIOR.

Even though Fernow and Pinchot showed interest in specialized research on forest products, it was not until the formation of the Forest Products Laboratory (FPL), in 1910, that efforts to secure sources for systematic research were stabilized. McGarvey Cline, chief of the Office of Wood Utilization, suggested that all wood product scientists work under one roof and chose Wisconsin State University (now the University of Wisconsin) as the office's partner. The U.S. Forest Service provided a staff of 14 technicians and six assistants with a payroll of $28,000 per year, testing equipment, and materials. In return, the university provided 13,000 square feet of floor space, special foundations for the testing machines, heat, utilities, and administrative offices. Citing the appalling waste between the stump and the consumer, the new chief forester, Henry Graves (1871–1951), who held the position from 1910 to 1920, emphasized better utilization, less waste, and more products.

The main goal of FPL was to study methods to reduce LOGGING AND LUMBERING waste and to improve lumber production in sawmills. FPL also studied and tested the physical properties of wood, developed wood preservation techniques, and devised new uses for wood fiber. In addition to research and development, they distributed wood product information to the public and cooperated with the wood products industry. As a result, FPL contributed to increased use of forest products from private and public forests.

As with the U.S. Forest Service, FPL did not have many women researchers. Among the very few, Eloise Gerry (1885–1970), its first female research scientist, contributed greatly to the study of southern pines and turpentine production. Gerry specialized in microscopic observation of wood and trees for physiological characteristics. Audrey Richards (1888–1953), a wood products pathologist, for example, studied the effect of fungi on the wood decking of aircraft carriers.

During WORLD WAR I, needs for lumber increased as the military needed to produce barracks, warehouses, hangars, shipyards, and portable docks. Wood in solid, laminated, and plywood forms was used in land vessels, patrol boats, and minesweepers and provided decking on aircraft carriers and battle ships. FPL expanded its workforce from fewer than 100 to 450. It produced lightweight but strong material for AIRPLANES. As paper was in short supply, research began on tree species not commonly used for paper production, such as southern pines and hardwoods.

WORLD WAR II (1941–45) increased FPL employees to 700. Wartime needs for airplanes, ships, buildings, and containers skyrocketed. Special papers were developed for greater wet strength and stability. Adhesives for wood became common. FPL also trained wood processors, users, and inspectors.

The post–World War II home construction boom demanded large quantities of timber for framing, paneling, plywood, fiberboard, particleboard, and furniture. Timber access roads were built near populated areas, and chainsaws, war surplus trucks, and tractors were applied there. The industry revived clear-cutting practices, raising concern among environmentalists and other citizens. By this time, the timber industry had used up most private forests' timber and now turned to National Forests to meet housing and other consumer needs. They pressured Congress to raise annual timber harvest limits within National Forests. The Forest Service continued to maintain its guidelines, but lobbying from the National Lumber Manufacturers Association (NLMA) was strong enough to compel Congress to increase the annual harvest.

Meanwhile, the FPL began shifting emphasis to lesser-used species and to more efficient uses of existing timber supplies. At the same time, the private sector funded small laboratories to conduct research on wood products and manufacturing techniques. The Timber Engineering Company, a research affiliate of the NLMA, established a product research and development laboratory in WASHINGTON, D.C., in 1943 and initiated the study of wood sugar production and fundamental research on lignin.

The use of facilities declined except for some supported by Weyerhaeuser, Georgia-Pacific, and other companies. Industrial research was mostly restricted to applied research of short-term use. In contrast, universities received grants from federal and state governments as well as industry and expanded their research scope and workforce. The McIntire-Stennis Act of 1962 authorized federal support for FORESTRY and forest products research at LAND GRANT INSTITUTIONS and provided a more stable situation for the forest products research.

Growing concerns about clear-cutting and the emergence of multiple use–sustained yield forest ideas introduced new approaches to forest products. The training of NTFPs entrepreneurs, the reduction of the environmental effects of pulp and paper mills, and RECYCLING attracted more attention. However, timber production is still the main concern of the Forest Service in terms of revenue and workforce. International cooperation to reduce chemical pollution of the lumber and paper industries and the development of environmentally friendly manufacturing processes are becoming increasingly important.

See also CANALS; FUEL WOOD; HOUSING, PRIVATE; HUNTING, SUBSISTENCE; NAVAL STORES; POLLUTION, WATER; WEYERHAEUSER, FREDERICK.

Jongmin Lee

Further Reading
Lewis, James G. *The Forest Service and the Greatest Good: A Centennial History.* Durham, N.C.: Forest History Society, 2005.
Steen, Harold K. *Forest Service Research: Finding Answers to Conservation's Questions.* Durham, N.C.: Forest History Society, 1998.
———. *The U.S. Forest Service: A History.* Seattle: University of Washington Press, 1976. Reprint, Durham, N.C.: Forest History Society, 2004.
Williams, Gerald. *The Forest Service: Fighting for Public Lands.* Westport, Conn.: Greenwood Press, 2007.
Williams, Michael. *Americans and Their Forests: A Historical Geography.* Cambridge, Mass.: Cambridge University Press, 1989.

forestry

Forestry involves the art and science of developing, cultivating, and managing forested areas and all of their resources. The management of FORESTS and their ECOSYSTEMS has been a source of great debate in American history. Foresters, conservationists, environmentalists, industries, and federal, state, and local governments, and the general public have long grappled with questions and issues related to forest policy. Particularly since the mid-19th century, the competing interests of these groups have dictated how forests have been owned, preserved, and used. As a result, forest management has been characterized by fragmentary policies.

Before the 1850s, forest management was largely nonexistent. Early European settlers in North America used the continent's forests and their resources for survival. They industriously cleared forests to build towns, roads, ships, farms, and factories. Until the mid-1800s, early Americans' approach to forestry was based on consumption rather than protection or maintenance. The American belief of MANIFEST DESTINY and westward expansion further bolstered consumption of forested areas. Forest loss tapered off around the turn of the century, and forested areas began to increase slightly in acreage until the 1920s. This increase resulted, in part, from Americans' abandoning farmland to move to urban areas, beginning in the 1880s. Many farms reverted to forests. The temporary cessation of forest loss was also due to technological changes. COAL and oil replaced wood as fuel, and motorized machinery superseded animals. Advances in AGRICULTURAL TECHNOLOGY also led to considerable increases in productivity, which decreased the amount of farmland needed. Nevertheless, new challenges surfaced and old questions remained concerning forestry.

In France and Germany, forestry education first began in the 1820s. American schools first established forestry programs in 1898. Some early U.S. foresters such as GIFFORD PINCHOT trained in Europe. In response to more than 300 years of DEFORESTATION, Pinchot joined conservationists and early foresters such as Franklin B. Hough (1822–85) to confront issues about forest management in the late 19th century. Along with the federal, state, and local governments and the businesses that utilized FOREST PRODUCTS, they posed important questions: Who owns the nation's forests? Who decides how forests are managed? Who decides how and which forests are used and for what purposes? These questions proved difficult to answer because the divergent groups' views and positions often conflicted. This conundrum led to years of failed or exploited congressional acts, lobbying from timber and lumber companies and conservationists, and general stagnation in forest management.

Early forest management efforts were limited to creating committees of inquiry that documented the extent of deforestation or to establishing weak state forestry associations. These groups were hampered by untrained staff and inadequate financial resources. Early foresters and conservationists advocated government control of forests. Sharing some of the Progressive Era's concerns about monopolies, they sought to protect the PUBLIC DOMAIN from the control of the timber barons and lumber industries. Foresters decried these corporations' extractive practices and domination of forest resources.

CONGRESS first responded to pressures for forest management in 1872 by creating YELLOWSTONE National Park in Wyoming and subsequently passed the ill-fated Timber Culture Act of 1873 to persuade homesteaders to protect forests. This act, which resulted in extensive land fraud, was replaced with the Forest Reserve Act of 1891, which sought to retain forest lands under federal control. This act authorized the president to "reserve" millions of acres of land from public sale. In theory, the reserves protected land from exploitation and allowed for a more sustained yield of timber, that is, the amount of timber that can be perpetually produced from a forest without degradation. The idea behind the reserves was that new forest growth would replace the timber that was cut.

Many foresters endorsed the creation of reserves, including Bernard Fernow (1851–1923), who headed the U.S. Bureau of Forestry from 1886 to 1898. He authored the Forest Management Act (commonly known as the Organic Act of 1897), which established management principles for the reserves, including protection of WATERSHEDS (drainage basins) and provision of a timber supply for the country. Under the leadership of Gifford Pinchot, perhaps the most well-known forester of the period, the names of the reserves and the Bureau of Forestry changed in 1905 to the National Forests and U.S. FOREST SERVICE, respectively.

As head of the U.S. Forest Service, Pinchot proved adept as both a forest steward and a businessman. He sought to ensure continued prosperity of the country's LOGGING AND LUMBERING, agricultural, MINING, and livestock interests through an ample supply of timber. Pinchot and other foresters were thus more concerned with using rather than protecting the National Forests. Pinchot, however, actively enforced sustained-yield guidelines, whereby timber industries practiced selective logging and cutting, as opposed to clear-cutting. Along with industries that profited from forest consumption and timber production, foresters became a formidable and persuasive pressure group. CONSERVATION-minded organizations and individuals such as the SIERRA CLUB and JOHN MUIR often challenged consumption practices, expressing their concern for protecting forests, ecosystems, and other natural resources. Forestry in the late 19th century and early 20th century became a balancing act among groups who believed that National Forests were not to be managed for any one industry or to yield a single product but for a variety of benefits.

In the decades after the establishment of the U.S. Forest Service, commercial timber companies did not want the products from the National Forests to be sold and to compete with their sales. By 1950, however, a concern about a timber famine emerged as a result of forest loss from private harvesting during WORLD WAR II (1941–45). After the war, the Forest Service shifted from sustained-yield management to industrial forest management. By 1970, timber industry pressure on the Forest Service and Congress had mounted. Whereas 1.5 billion board feet per year of timber had been cut in National Forests in the 1940s and 3.5 billion in the 1950s, the number had increased to around 13 billion in the 1970s and remained at that rate through the 1990s.

In reaction to environmental pressure groups that feared the timber industry would infringe on the nation's remaining wild lands, Congress passed the WILDERNESS ACT OF 1964. The act secured public lands from industrial

With each car carrying a huge load of lumber, this logging train winds down from the fir forests of the Cascade Mountains in the Pacific Northwest in the 1940s.   *(Library of Congress)*

extractive practices and other exploitative uses. During the 1970s, Congress passed several acts, including the Forest and Rangeland Renewable Resources Planning Act of 1974 (RPA), the Federal Land Policy and Management Act of 1976 (FLPMA), and the National Forest Management Act of 1976 (NFMA), to improve forest and land planning and management. Since the 1970s and into the 21st century, many of the forest management policies, however, continue to vacillate between plans espoused by environmentalists and conservationists and those of the industries that profit from forests.

See also AGRICULTURE, DEPARTMENT OF; FEDERAL LAW—LAND POLICIES; FUEL, WOOD; HOUSING, PRIVATE; HOUSING, PUBLIC; MARSH, GEORGE PERKINS; OIL, DOMESTIC; PROGRESSIVISM.

Jordan Bauer

Further Reading
Williams, Michael. *Americans and Their Forests: A Historical Geography.* Cambridge: Cambridge University Press, 1989.

Forestry
Gifford Pinchot (1898)
When Gifford Pinchot attended Yale University in the late 1880s, neither Yale nor any other university in the United States offered courses or a degree in forestry. Pinchot and other interested Americans were forced to study abroad in France and Germany. Upon returning home in 1893, he took a number of positions, overseeing forests at the Biltmore Estate in North Carolina and in the Adirondacks in New York, among others, before joining the federal government in 1898 and becoming chief of the newly formed U.S. Forest Service in 1905. Pinchot and other foresters called for "conservative lumbering," in which scientific principles dictated

profitable plans for cultivating, maintaining, and developing forests. In his opinion, expressed in his 1898 book The Adirondack Spruce, *commercial lumbermen were necessary partners in preventing the destructive waste of forest resources.*

THE owners and operators of Spruce lands in the Eastern United States will find within the covers of this little book a collection of facts and figures which is intended first of all to be of practical use. The information it contains is the product of a prolonged investigation conducted throughout with that intention. If its results have any merit, therefore, it must be because they are capable of assisting American lumbermen to get better returns from their investments in Spruce lands through conservative lumbering and successive crops than they could by considering the productiveness of these lands as of merely temporary interest. In the attempt to be of use in, this way, some departures from established methods of study and statement have been necessary. Such changes are inevitable. As yet forestry in America is young. In its progress toward maturity it must develop new methods to meet the unfamiliar conditions with which it has to deal. Rules and practices which were devised without reference to American forests cannot always be counted on to fit American needs. Perhaps nothing has done more to retard the progress of forestry in America than the disregard of its intimate and friendly relation to lumbering—a relation which was almost wholly overlooked for years after the advocates of forest protection first brought their cause to public attention. In the eyes of many of its early friends the lumberman was a vandal whose inordinate greed called for constant denunciation, while to the lumberman the ideas of the forest reformer had no relation whatever to the affairs of practical life. Since that early day lumbermen and foresters have been drawing together, and much progress has been made toward the right opinion, which may be expressed by saying that lumberman and forester are as needful to each other as the ax and its helve. Without the ax the helve has little weight; without the helve the ax is lacking both in reach and in direction.

Source: Gifford Pinchot. *The Adirondack Spruce: A Study of the Forest in Ne-Ha-Sa-Ne Park.* New York: Critic Co., 1898, iii–iv.

forests

American forest historians have tended to focus on LOGGING AND LUMBERING, particularly logging driven by Euro-American settlement and industrial FORESTRY. Yet, the key question in forest history should not be what kills trees, for trees grow back when given a reasonable chance. What really matters should be the factors that affect forest resiliency. The history of forests depends not just on people but on trees' ability to regenerate after disturbances, whether those are anthropogenic disturbances such as logging, ecological disturbances such as herbivory and FIRE, or biophysical disturbances such as glaciation, EROSION, and CLIMATE CHANGE.

SHAPING THE FORESTS

The biophysical template of climate and soils sets the stage upon which the drama of forest history plays out. Repeated glaciation has determined the possible trajectories for forests in much of North America. GLACIERS repeatedly scoured forests off the face of much of the continent during the Pleistocene, so the forest communities that now exist across much of the continent are young—often only 10,000 years old—and still evolving as communities. People have been part of those forests for as long as they have existed; no natural or pristine state has ever existed for these communities. The greater forest diversity in tropical America exists in significant part because of the absence of glacial activity and the greater time for coevolution and development of complex communities. Upon the stage set by soil, climate, and glacial history, ecological disturbances such as fire, wind, DROUGHTS, herbivory, competition, and disease shape the patterns of forest death and rebirth. People influence all these processes, but often in ways that are invisible to historians. For example, few forest historians have paid much attention to the interconnections between forests and the sea, except to note that the sea trade between European powers created a great demand for American timber to build the ships. Yet, for thousands of years, the critical vertebrates shaping western forests were not people but SALMON.

Ecologists long wondered how the nutrient-poor soils of the West could have supported massive conifer forests. The answer lay in the ways that the rotting bodies of salmon connected forest and sea. Billions of salmon spawned each year in tiny headwater streams, swam out to sea, gathered energy from solar-powered oceanic cycles, then returned to their natal streams, where they spawned and died. Their corpses were washed in annual FLOODS into the forest, and BEARS helped too, by dropping half-gnawed salmon bodies over upland forest floors. This influx of energy from the ocean had

Area of Original Forest, 1620–1920

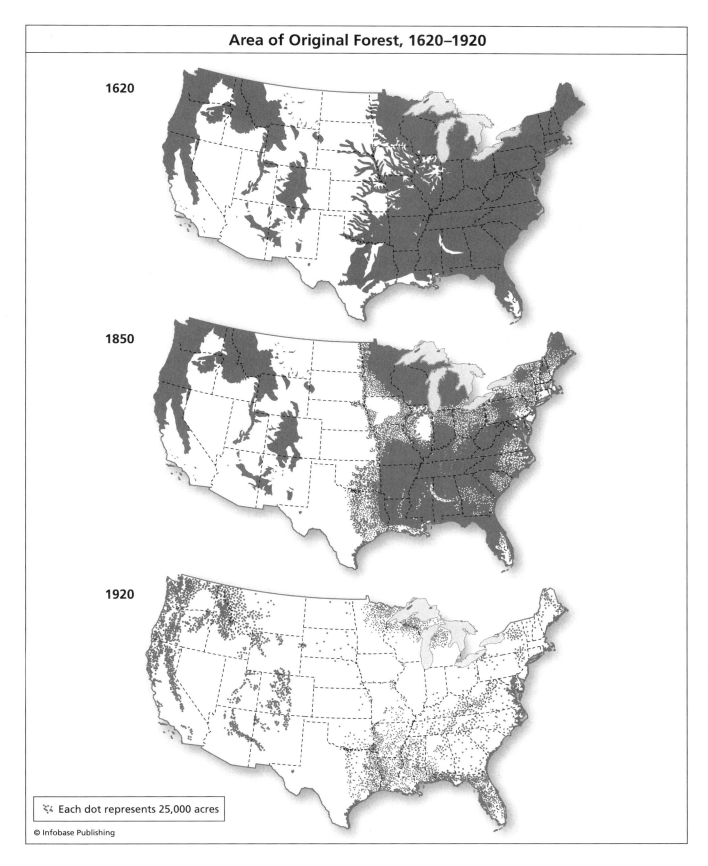

1620

1850

1920

Each dot represents 25,000 acres

© Infobase Publishing

an extraordinary effect on forest systems because the nutrient composition of the fish and their densities are so great. When people interrupted those cycles either by depleting salmon, killing bears, removing logs from streams, or blocking rivers, both the forest and the sea lost ecological structure and diversity.

As Michael Williams argues in *Deforesting the Globe*, DEFORESTATION is not just a product of corporate GLOBALIZATION; it is as old as human occupation of the Earth. The story of deforestation is also the story of the development of farming systems, and it is fundamentally driven by growth in human numbers. Native Americans were crucial in shaping forest disturbance processes and plant communities across the Americas. Indian nations did not evenly distribute themselves across the country, and the intensity of human disturbances varied a great deal from one forest to another, helping to create varied patterns across the forest landscape.

Fishing, hunting, wild ricing, gardening, location of village sites, and trade networks all shaped forests. In most of the northern forests, extensive clearing for farming was rare, and hunting pressures and fire manipulation were the major effects of Indian peoples on forests. Fire patterns determined the location of the border between forests and PRAIRIES across much of the American continent. Indian manipulations of fire, often to provide better hunting, helped restrict the extent of forests across the center of the continent.

EUROPEAN COLONIZATION

European exploration, FUR TRADE, and the various wars from the 1600s to the 1800s altered Indian effects on American forests in myriad ways. Tribes who entered into trade relations with the Europeans, particularly with French fur traders, changed the intensity and seasonal timing of hunting and trapping. Seasonal movements of people changed as well; as Indian contact with the French increased, they became located in larger, higher-density, and more persistent settlements around trading points, a pattern that led to local reduction in forests.

Disease and famine quickly devastated American Indian populations, however, and wars exacerbated these processes. The Iroquois War in the eastern GREAT LAKES in the mid-17th century led to a ripple effect across the Great Lakes region, as the Iroquois were the first to acquire guns and pushed westward; massive migrations resulted, leading to new social relations, population pressures, and effects on local and regional forests. By 1750, after disease had decimated Indian cultures, the forest was probably denser and more widespread than it had been for centuries.

European sea trade soon put an end to the 18th-century expansion of the forests. Before the advent of iron ships, European trade depended on wood because massive timbers were needed for shipbuilding. An intricate interplay developed between the military and commercial power of the British, and the raw materials such as timber, pitch, and tar of North America. Europeans who traveled to North America were awed and often overwhelmed by forests that appeared inexhaustible. Immigrants hacked and sawed their way through forests that soon proved to be anything but limitless. By 1900, half of the original forest cover in the United States had been eliminated, much to many people's surprise.

AMERICAN LUMBER INDUSTRY

White pine (*Pinus strobus*) was the foundation of the American lumber industry for more than two and a half centuries. White pine rarely grew in pure stands, but it was a key component of mixed forests from west of the Great Lakes to the Atlantic coast. Commercial logging of white pine at first focused on Maine, which had large stands of pine, plus swift rivers and good lake connections. With excellent sources of waterpower for sawmills and good water access to ocean ports, Maine was the first region in North America to develop a profitable large-scale export industry.

The demands of new technologies and new markets led to new stresses on American forests in the early 19th century. The combination of two factors, large capital investment into steam-powered sawmills and the constant threat of fires, meant Maine lumber barons, in order to stay in business, needed a rapid return on investments, since neither the forest nor the mill was expected to be around for long. The demand for quick returns meant that efficient logging operations needed to run night and day, with lands logged in the fastest and cheapest way, with little thought for future regeneration.

As Maine's pine forests declined, lumbermen and loggers headed west to the pineries of the Great Lakes states. The first step in the development of the Midwest logging industry was the removal of Indian title to the land. Treaties negotiated in 1830s and 1840s began the process of dispossessing Ho Chunk, Chippewa, and Sioux from tribal forest lands. Speculation in timberlands quickly followed, marked by the migration of the Maine timber baron Isaac Stephenson to Wisconsin in 1845. Stephenson found amazing stands of white pine growing on sandy soils that had been deposited by the glaciers. One Wisconsin acre could yield as much as 94,000 board feet of white pine, compared to Maine, where 10,000 board feet had been considered a nice stand.

Before 1845, logging in the Great Lakes region had been driven by farming, not by an export market for timber. Wood had been cut largely for local farm consumption, and logging had provided farmers with cash to buy farming supplies. But by the 1860s, the rate of forest clearing for farming sharply declined as farmers pushed onto the fertile prairies. Those farmers needed lumber, as did a growing industrial economy, and the rate of cutting for industrial logging skyrocketed. By the beginning of the CIVIL WAR (1861–65), 153 million acres of forests was cleared for agriculture and more than 12 times that area had been cleared for industrial logging. As William Cronon notes in *Nature's Metropolis,* CHICAGO, ILLINOIS, became the center of industrial transformations of the northern forests. In 1847, the Illinois-Michigan canal was completed. With the shorter, cheaper route for lumber, prices soon dropped by 50 percent, and a substantial deterrent to settlement on the prairies was removed.

Lumber production grew from 5 billion board feet in 1850 to 13 billion board feet in 1870, a rate of production the vast pineries of the Great Lakes states could hardly sustain for long. Wisconsin sawmills processed 60 billion board feet of lumber between 1873 to 1897, and by 1898, the federal forester Filbert Roth estimated only 13 percent of the white pine originally in Wisconsin was still standing. The ecological and human effects of this deforestation were devastating, particularly for the Great Lakes Indian peoples.

By the end of the 19th century, lumbermen began a second migration, turning their sights both south and west. It proved far more profitable for them to relocate to regions where timberland was as cheap as $1.25 an acre than to stay put and attempt reforestation. Timber barons moving on to the next frontier had little interest in future forests, regeneration, or sustained yield. Loggers left behind piles of waste timber 10 to 15 feet high that turned brown and dry in summer. Sparks set them alight, and intense fires followed. Immense tracts of clear-cut land burned, often when settlers were beginning to try to farm it. The worst forest fires in American history took place in the cutover, in Wisconsin, Michigan, and Minnesota. In 1871, a spark caught near Peshtigo, Wisconsin, and swept across thousands of acres, trapping entire towns and trains filled with people trying to escape. By the time the fire died down, more than 1,500 people were dead.

Logging changed wildlife habitat and, in the short term, eliminated access to many of the mammals and plants on which Indians had relied. Logging also changed the composition of the forest. Harvests eliminated much of the seed source for white pine, while slash fires killed many pine seedlings. Logging affected WATERSHEDS and FISHERIES in complex and poorly understood ways. Logging dams eliminated much riparian habitat, while poor harvest practices and slash fires increased erosion and siltation of streams. Tremendous quantities of sawdust were dumped in creeks and rivers, blocking fish passage and destroying their habitat. Stream temperatures rose as forest cover was removed, probably reducing spawning habitat for cold water fish. The reduction in spawning habitat and fish passage occurred simultaneously with intensive fishing harvests and invasion by sea lampreys and alewives. The cumulative effects of these pressures led to a collapse of many Great Lakes fisheries, an economic disaster for Native peoples and Anglo-American settlers alike.

NATIONAL FORESTS AND FORESTRY

The devastation of the Great Lakes forests became a galvanizing issue for the emerging American environmental movement. Most American settlers had thought forests were so abundant that loggers could never reach the end of them. When the white pines, a seemingly limitless resource, vanished in less than four decades, fears of a timber famine soon spread. In response to concerns about a timber famine, CONGRESS created the federal forest reserve system in 1891, withdrawing millions of acres of federal land from settlement and placing it under the control of the General Land Office of the DEPARTMENT OF THE INTERIOR. The legislation, however, provided no means for administration or management of those areas; nor did the law designate what activities could take place within the reserves. It was increasingly unclear whether the reserves were intended for use, which most people interpreted as grazing and logging, or for protection. In 1897, Congress passed the Organic Act, which clarified the purposes of the reserves: to protect water flow and to ensure a continuous supply of timber. The Organic Act gave the government the authority to use the forests and made it clearer that the forests were not preserves. Different federal agencies, however, struggled for control of the forests, and corruption was rampant during this era.

Finally, in 1905, GIFFORD PINCHOT, the most charismatic forester of his generation, won control of the forest reserves within the DEPARTMENT OF AGRICULTURE. Pinchot created a U.S. FOREST SERVICE that, he believed, would put an end to wasteful exploitation of resources by the rich for private gain. He set out to protect the forests, not for eternal preservation, but for fair, conservative, sustainable use. He believed that the government had an obligation to put an end to wasteful exploitation of resources, and scientific forestry was the tool the federal agencies would use to do this.

Early government foresters had several strong articles of faith. First, the point of forestry was to reduce waste and make forests more efficient, which meant making them produce more timber, as quickly as possible. Second, America needed wood, and demands would continue to increase as quickly as they had after the Civil War. Third, if harvesting continued as usual, the country would run out of timber within several decades. Fourth, forests ought to be used, but scientifically, to assure a perpetual supply of timber for a growing nation. Finally, scientists were best at solving land-management problems, so they, rather than politicians, should control the Forest Service. Professional foresters would redesign the old-growth forests, to improve them and so ensure a perpetual supply of timber for a growing nation.

Armed with their conviction that old growth was decadent and wasteful, foresters set out to clean up the forest, hoping to make it as productive as possible. Foresters believed that disease, dead wood, old growth, and fire all detracted from efficient timber production. In other words, they were assuming that the role of the forest was to grow trees as fast as it could, and any element that was not directly contributing to that goal was bad. Any space that a dead tree took up, any light that a fir tree used, any nutrients that an insect chewed up: These were all judged to be stolen from productive trees. If timber trees did not use all the available water, that water was wasted. If young, vigorous pines did not get all the sun, that sun was lost forever. These assumptions made it difficult for foresters to imagine that insects, waste, disease, and decadence were essential for forest communities; indeed, that the productive part of the forest might depend on the unproductive part.

WOMEN AND FORESTS

With the professionalization of forestry, women lost many of their customary rights to forest access in the United States. As federal foresters transformed complex forest communities into professionally managed, sustained-yield forests, the diversity of women's work vanished in the forests, just as did much of the diversity of plant and animals that had supported their work. With the increasing growth of scientific, sustained-yield forestry, "working forests" had room only for timber, not for medicinal plants, mushrooms, firewood, fish insects, and herbs. Working forests became the province of working men: of loggers, professional foresters, and corporate accountants. In the process, women were increasingly defined as peripheral to the concerns of forestry.

Changing tenure relations structured these changes in women's access to forests. Across the world, it is a reasonable generalization to state that, before the 18th century, most forests were traditionally some form of common property, with no single person owning all the rights to a forest. Unlike agricultural fields, which were often private property in many cultures, forests had broader, but not unrestricted, access. Customary tenure systems traditionally regulated access to common property resources. Women's work was critical in shaping forests under these customary tenure regimes, through gathering, fishing, and other activities that altered forest disturbance processes and plant communities. In turn, even as women changed forests, forests changed women as well, affecting their family's health, welfare, and food.

These links between women and forests were often invisible to the cadre of professional foresters who emerged in the late 19th century. As forestry developed into a profession, its practitioners defined their work in explicitly gendered terms. In trying to transform a chaotic, disorderly wild nature into a regulated forest, professional foresters saw themselves doing the work of men. As noted by the historian James Lewis, the U.S. Forest Service described the job of forester as a combination of lumberjack, frontiersman, and explorer, giving men the opportunity to live the strenuous, masculine life.

During its first six decades, the Forest Service resisted hiring women as professional foresters. An agency leaflet from circa 1950 insisted that fieldwork with the Forest Service was solely a man's job because of the physical requirements, the arduous nature of the work, and the work environment. By the mid-20th century, the Forest Service found itself facing a conundrum: If forestry was man's work, then hiring a woman for the job would change the very way forestry was defined.

Even though the profession defined itself as man's work, women were important in the development of forestry, but their contributions have remained largely invisible. Women's clubs in the late 19th and early 20th centuries spearheaded American forest CONSERVATION efforts. The Forest Service would have had fewer forests to manage if it were not for the determined efforts of such women's clubs. Just as men defined forestry in gendered terms, women defined their conservation interests in equally gendered terms. Clubwomen both led campaigns to protect wild areas and managed forests, justifying their public efforts by calling attention to their domestic interests in health, children, and education.

POST–WORLD WAR II DEVELOPMENTS

In the decades following WORLD WAR II (1941–45), global timber trade shifted toward the south, as recreation pressures on American forests increased and an environmental constituency concerned about logging grew. Increasing protections on forests in the Northern Hemisphere were accompanied by a shift in timber production toward the south, not by a decrease in wood consumption. Net deforestation in the temperate developed world declined to almost zero, while nearly 555 million hectares in the Southern Hemisphere was harvested. With this shift to the south industry consolidation, loss of jobs, increase in chipping and pulping, intensive capital investments, and ecological changes brought about by the massive planting of eucalyptus and *Pinus radiata* PLANTATIONS across the globe for pulp production resulted.

People affect all forests, but humans are not the only important agents of forest history. Livestock, farming, trade, droughts, competition from other plants, insects, ice, and fire all weave together into a complex tapestry of forest change. Since industrialization, people have transformed climate processes in unprecedented ways, with lasting effects on forest disturbances. Insect and disease outbreaks, fire frequency and intensity, drought, winter snows, and human demands on forests are all changing with GLOBAL WARMING. What this will mean for American forests is controversial. Some modelers predict that the conifers of the Great North Woods will be gone by the mid-21st century and will be replaced by scraggly hardwoods. Others predict the boreal forest will soon be lost to fire and insect outbreaks sparked by warming summers. Forests will persist, but they will be very different forests. For all the uncertainty, one point remains constant: People are radically changing forest histories.

See also DISEASES, HUMAN; DISEASES, PLANT; ECOLOGY; FISHING, COMMERCIAL; FISHING, RECREATIONAL; FISHING, SUBSISTENCE; FUEL, WOOD; HUNTING, COMMERCIAL; HUNTING, RECREATIONAL; HUNTING, SUBSISTENCE; INDIANS, MIDWEST; INDIANS, NORTHEAST; PIGS AND HOGS; UNITED STATES—DEEP SOUTH; UNITED STATES—MIDWEST; UNITED STATES—NORTHEAST.

Nancy Langston

Further Reading

Cronon, William. *Nature's Metropolis: Chicago and the Great West.* New York: Norton, 1992.

Flader, Susan, ed. *The Great Lakes Forest: An Environmental and Social History.* Minneapolis: University of Minnesota Press, 1983.

Hayes, Samuel P. *Conservation and the Gospel of Efficiency: The Progressive Conservation Movement, 1890–1920.* Cambridge, Mass.: Harvard University Press, 1959.

Hirt, Paul. *A Conspiracy of Optimism: Management of the National Forests since World War Two.* Lincoln: University of Nebraska Press, 1994.

Langston, Nancy. *Forest Dreams, Forest Nightmares: The Paradox of Old Growth in the Inland West.* Seattle: University of Washington Press, 1995.

Lewis, James G. "The Applicant Is No Gentleman: Women in the Forest Service." *Journal of Forestry* 103 (2005): 259–263.

Williams, M. *Deforesting the Earth: From Prehistory to Global Crisis.* Chicago: University of Chicago Press, 2003.

Forest Service, U.S.

The U.S. Forest Service (USFS) is the largest agency in the DEPARTMENT OF AGRICULTURE. Stewards of 193 million acres (an area larger than the state of Texas) of national FORESTS and national grasslands, the Forest Service manages forest, grazing, recreation, WILDERNESS, WATERSHEDS, and wildlife resources under the mandate of sustainable multiple use.

ORIGINS AND GROWTH

The Forest Service traces its origins to the establishment of the Division of Forestry within the Department of Agriculture, in 1881. Although the division had no forests to supervise, its employees initiated scientific research and a professional approach to FORESTRY. Responding to lobbying by Division Chief Bernard Fernow (1851–1923) and the American Forestry Association (established in 1875), CONGRESS passed the General Land Revision Act of 1891 (often referred to as the Forest Reserve Act) to address concerns about destruction of forests on the PUBLIC DOMAIN that threatened timber supplies and watersheds. It allowed the president to withdraw by proclamation public lands from entry and sale under the land laws administered by the General Land Office. In the 1890s, Presidents Benjamin Harrison (1833–1901) and Grover Cleveland (1837–1908) withdrew from the public domain nearly 50 million acres of land as forest reserves.

The enactment of the 1897 Forest Organic Law answered a broad range of questions about forest access and use. It declared as its purposes "to improve and protect the forest within the reservation or for the purpose of securing favorable conditions of water flows, and to furnish a continuous supply of timber for the use and necessities of citizens of the United States." The act made direct mention of permitting MINING activities while indirectly approving livestock grazing. Western resource users welcomed the new law, which opened the forests to a broad range of enterprise.

When GIFFORD PINCHOT replaced Fernow as chief of the Division of Forestry in 1898, the American CONSERVATION movement gained momentum. Having studied forestry in France and Germany, Pinchot shared similar outlooks with the Prussian-trained Fernow. Pinchot had already practiced forestry on George Vanderbilt's Biltmore Estate in North Carolina in the early 1890s. When THEODORE ROOSEVELT assumed the presidency in 1901, Pinchot's friendship with him served the cause of professional forestry. He collaborated with the president to initiate a broad-ranging conservation movement emphasizing utilitarian resource use, or "the greatest good of the greatest number in the long run."

In 1905, Congress, with the prompting of Pinchot and Roosevelt, passed the Transfer Act. It reassigned administration of 63 million acres of forest reserves from the DEPARTMENT OF THE INTERIOR to the Department of Agriculture (USDA). Under the USDA, a new U.S. Forest Service emerged with Pinchot as chief forester of a National Forest System. Pinchot believed in a decentralized agency, creating six regional management districts (presently 10 regions) with individual national forests under a regional forester. The division of administration strove to make decision making sensitive to local interests and needs. Pinchot also emphasized connections between the private sector and state and local governments. In these early years, the USFS maintained the national forests primarily for future timber needs and not immediate harvest. Lumber companies applauded the policy because it reduced timber supplies and boosted prices.

Pinchot sought to hire a professional workforce that included rangers, directors, and superintendents. He instituted civil service exams and fitness requirements with an underlying conviction that resources of the forests could be managed scientifically and by professionals. Pinchot developed the 1905 *Use Book* to provide guidelines for the "wise use" of forest resources. The *Use Book* directed forest employees to act in accordance with Forest Service policies that called for "preserving a perpetual supply of timber for home industries, preventing the destruction of the forest cover which regulates the flow of streams, and protecting local residents from unfair competition in the use of forest and range."

THE UTILITARIAN AGENDA

In the early years, grazing, rather than timber harvests, demanded the major attention of forest officials. The 1897 Forest Organic Act opened the forests to the possibility of grazing, especially if benefits could be derived and no harm occurred to forest resources. For example, it could be argued that sheep in some forests helped to prevent forest FIRE by preventing the buildup of combustible vegetation. In the forest reserves, the

Government Land Office offered a limited number of grazing permits to operators—despite sharp criticism from the preservationist-minded JOHN MUIR, who declared sheep "hoofed locusts." In 1901, Pinchot signaled his approval of grazing on government forest reserves. He noted the important role of stock grazing in the western states' economies, as well as the political strength of stock operators, whose endorsement was essential for the success of any future National Forest System. After the transfer of the forest reserves to his administration in 1905, Pinchot refined a grazing permit system (already in the preliminary stages of use by the Government Land Office). The permit system always asserted that grazing in the forest was a privilege granted to stock operators by forest officials and not a right. The U.S. Supreme Court in a series of cases endorsed this position by 1911.

Pinchot remained chief forester until his dismissal by President William Howard Taft (1857–1930) in 1910, when he came into conflict with Secretary of the Interior Richard Ballinger (1858–1922) over conservation policies. After Ballinger reopened some public lands protected during the Roosevelt administration for commercial use, Pinchot publicly protested. Despite Pinchot's argument that the act was illegal and in the interests of corporations, Taft and Congress sided with Ballinger and replaced Pinchot for his insubordination. Nonetheless, many of Pinchot's policies carried through to the next chief foresters, Henry Graves (1871–1951) and William Greeley (1879–1955), who served from 1910 to 1920 and 1920 to 1928, respectively. A major expansion of the National Forest System occurred under the Weeks Act of 1911, which allowed for acquisition of new national forestlands in the eastern portion of the United States for watershed protection. It also provided funding for cooperative efforts between the USFS and the states for fire protection. These provisions expanded under the Clarke-McNary Act in 1924 beyond fire protection to include measures for research into reforestation and issues of insects and disease.

WORLD WAR I (1914–18) saw large demands for both grazing and timber in the national forests. Forest administrators responded by permitting both large increases in forest grazing and timber cutting. The contracting market after the war never fully recovered throughout the 1920s. To protect national timber resources better for future use the agency also strove to support private forestry. Although Greeley was proindustry, he also responded to increased demands for OUTDOOR RECREATION and wildlife protection in the national forests. In 1924, he implemented the first designation of a "primitive area," in Gila National Forest in New Mexico—a precursor of wilderness protection measures that attempt to discourage resource uses and road building. During the 1920s, the USFS sought to increase grazing fees but generally faced fierce opposition from western stock interests. The collapse of the American economy after 1929 prompted the Forest Service to declare periodic moratoriums on the collection of grazing fees.

In 1933, when President FRANKLIN D. ROOSEVELT launched the NEW DEAL to fight the GREAT DEPRESSION, thousands of young men worked in the national forests under one of the New Deal's most popular programs, the Civilian Conservation Corps (CCC). The CCC fought fires, built EROSION control systems, and contributed to research and documentation of national forests. By 1935, projects diversified to include campground, trail, and road construction, as well as cabins, picnic areas, and other projects related to the nation's increasing interest in outdoor recreation. Many of these projects eventually served the demands of postwar tourism.

Despite significant activity in the forests during the 1930s, it was a period of bureaucratic hesitation and disappointment for the Forest Service. Although two decades removed from his position as chief forester, Pinchot continued to call for greater activism by the USFS to regulate private timber holdings. A 1932 internal report on forest influences envisioned extending Forest Service policies and conservation practices to private forest holdings. The failure to do so had a lasting impact in the following decade as private timber supplies dwindled rapidly and left large tracks of unproductive forestland. In addition, the Forest Service failed to expand its administration over the remainder of the public domain with the passage of the Taylor Grazing Act in 1934, the emergence of the Grazing Service to administer public grazing lands, and the formation of the BUREAU OF LAND MANAGEMENT in 1946. The publication by the USDA in 1936 of *The Western Range* lamented the deteriorated state of the range and noted pointedly that the USFS was the only agency that had dealt with matters of range administration and rehabilitation.

WORLD WAR II POLICY SHIFTS

Increased demands during WORLD WAR II (1941–45) for timber and the decline of productive private forests forced the Forest Service into greater emphasis upon timber use. These pressures continued in the postwar period. The Federal Housing Act (1949) and an expanding economy demanded an increased timber cut. The Forest Service complied and moved from a "custodial era" to a role as overseer of forest harvests. Instrumental in this shift was Chief Forester Richard McArdle (1899–1983), who served from 1952 to 1962. He encouraged increased cuts that called upon the Forest Service and its forestry scientists to employ technological and intensive management strategies to uphold goals of sustained yield over the long run in the national forests.

The result was an increased maximal allowance in the timber cut, which the USFS justified in myriad ways. The Forest Service constructed 65,000 miles of new roads in the two decades following World War II to facilitate LOGGING AND LUMBERING. New policies called for clear-cutting, particularly of old-growth trees that had maximized their growth potential. The process also involved continual upward revisions of sustained yield rates in the national forests. Not surprisingly, timber cut in national forests increased from 8 million board feet in 1950 to 167 million board feet cut in 1970. In response to harsh criticism of manipulated "sustained yield" figures to serve the demands of industry, the Forest Service defended its practices.

At the same time that the Forest Service increased timber harvest, it faced new use pressures from graziers, recreational groups, and ecological preservationists. Several regions saw a need to reduce stock on forest ranges and rehabilitate damaged areas. This development pleased recreation interests and conservation groups (soon to be more commonly called environmentalists). In 1957, the USFS initiated the first of its five-year plans to increase camping and recreational opportunities in national forests. The plan also called for an increase in wildlife protection, but logging proceeded apace in spite of mounting criticism.

In the face of competing users during the 1950s, it was clear that the Forest Service needed a wider mandate. In 1960, Congress passed the Sustained Yield Multiple-Use Act. Under the banner of "multiple use," the Forest Service hoped to serve all the users of the forests in a fair manner. While national forests had long been open to diverse users, the original language of the 1897 Forest Organic Act primarily identified the lands with the management of water and timber resources. Still, criticism persisted when the Forest Service designated some forests for the single use of timber production.

The demands of the consumer society in the postwar period prompted the Forest Service to be increasingly concerned with the destruction caused by forest fires. Fire destroyed valuable resources that could be turned into lumber. The Forest Service campaign against fire reached back to the first decade of the 20th century, when it adopted the extensive system of fire lookouts and demanded that all fires be attacked and stamped out in the same day (officially adopted as the "10 A.M." policy in 1935). Any arguments in favor of permitting fires to occur naturally in the forests were denigrated as "Paiute Forestry," a term born in the 1890s from observations of American Indian forest management that involved light burning to promote growth. The Forest Service after World War II took its antifire campaign to the public in well-planned publicity campaigns featuring SMOKEY BEAR.

ENVIRONMENTALISM AND BACKLASH

Much of the forest-related legislation after 1960 affected a burgeoning environmental movement. The WILDERNESS ACT OF 1964 mandated that federal land management agencies—including the Forest Service—designate wilderness areas for protection against development. Nine million acres of Forest Service lands immediately fell into this category. The ensuing controversies prompted the Forest Service to initiate several Roadless Area Review Evaluation (RARE) studies. The NATIONAL ENVIRONMENTAL POLICY ACT (NEPA) OF 1969 (which created the ENVIRONMENTAL

PROTECTION AGENCY in 1970) had a profound effect upon the USFS. It required environmental impact statements from all public land agencies addressing management policies. In addition, the ENDANGERED SPECIES ACT OF 1973 required the Forest Service to pay attention to habitat protection for threatened and ENDANGERED SPECIES. Environmental legislation, of course, posed a challenge to traditional forest resource users who held grazing permits and to lumber companies who demanded ever-larger timber harvests.

Besides the environmental laws that affected all federal agencies, Congress in the 1970s passed the Forest and Rangeland Renewable Resource Planning Act of 1974 and the National Forest Management Act of 1976. Both called for long-term SUSTAINABILITY management. The secretary of agriculture required officials at each national forest to draft and implement a resource management plan that conformed to the new environmental laws and protected future timber resources. The directives of the 1960s and 1970s helped create a basis for a shift in the USFS away from multiple use to a consideration of ecological management. This policy embraced many tenets of the multiple-use agenda but called for more intense management of ecological systems—meaning the protection of whole environments and not just marketable trees—while catering to the varied needs of national forest users.

As was the case with other land-management agencies, the Forest Service endured a backlash from user groups while it labored to apply what it judged as good ecological science. Many groups charged that the federal government had gone overboard in the application of environmental protection measures. By the late 1970s, western political interests backed by natural resource interests in timber, grazing, and mining launched a SAGEBRUSH REBELLION, demanding that federal lands should be controlled and even owned locally, preferably by the states.

After a decade and a half of a variety of new environmental laws, the election of President RONALD REAGAN in 1980 signaled an effort to thwart the intent and application of environmental protection on public lands. President Reagan's secretary of the interior, JAMES WATT, was an outspoken enemy of environmental restrictions. The administration drastically cut funding for the Environmental Protection Agency in the early 1980s and limited provisions of the CLEAR WATER ACT and CLEAN AIR ACT. Millions of protected acres in the national forests opened for logging—including the extremely controversial logging method of clear-cutting. But the administration faced a backlash of its own from nonprofit environmental organizations, notably the WILDERNESS SOCIETY and the SIERRA CLUB, whose membership increased significantly by the end of the 1980s. Even the Reagan administration, which once embraced the Sagebrush Rebellion, backed away from the idea of ceding public lands to the states.

Pressures from environmental organizations and dissent by employees within the Forest Service who disagreed with the agency's unrelenting commitment to forest harvests caused a serious review of policies in the 1990s. President BILL CLINTON's administration (1993–2001) facilitated a shift within the USFS toward the goals of ecosystem management, or ecological forestry. The Northwest Forest Plan (1994) represented a compromise among natural resource industries, ecologists, and recreationists in shaping federal land policy in the Pacific Northwest. Reversing the trend of increased logging, this plan called for endangered species habitat protection and wildlife and watershed protection and emphasized the need for monitoring and predicting sustainable timber harvesting in the region's national forests. For the Pacific Northwest, the measure occurred after most of the valuable forestlands had been logged and the region faced a timber shortage.

The efforts of the Clinton administration gave way to the presidency of GEORGE W. BUSH, from 2001 to 2009, which quickly returned to Reagan era policies. The salvage of timber from southern Oregon's 2002 Biscuit Fire contradicted many scientific recommendations and increased media scrutiny of USFS policy. By 2009, the goals of ecological forestry remained at a crossroads with the larger power of private timber interests and the U.S. Forest Service. At issue is the continued need for harvesting forest resources while integrating sound management of forest ECOSYSTEMS. It remains to be seen how President BARACK OBAMA's administration will approach these ongoing questions of multiple use and scientific integrity in the national forests.

See also CATTLE; CONSUMERISM; DEFORESTATION; ENVIRONMENTALISM, MAINSTREAM; FEDERAL LAW—ENVIRONMENTAL REGULATIONS; FEDERAL LAW—LAND POLICIES; GRASSES; HOUSING, PRIVATE; HOUSING, PUBLIC; SPOTTED OWL; TRAVEL AND TOURISM; UNITED STATES—PACIFIC NORTHWEST.

Peter Kopp

Further Reading

Hays, Samuel P. *Wars in the Woods: The Rise of Ecological Forestry in America.* Pittsburgh: University of Pittsburgh Press, 2007.

Hirt, Paul W. *Conspiracy of Optimism: Management of the National Forests since World War Two.* Lincoln: University of Nebraska Press, 1994.

Rowley, William D. *U.S. Forest Service Grazing and Rangelands: A History.* College Station: Texas A&M University Press, 1985.

Steen, Harold K. *The U.S. Forest Service: A History.* Seattle: University of Washington Press, 1976.

forty acres and a mule

The phrase "forty acres and a mule" refers to land and goods freedmen were promised upon their EMANCIPATION from slavery during and after the CIVIL WAR (1861–65). It specifically refers to an order Maj. Gen. William T. Sherman issued promising 40 acres of land to freedmen after his march through Georgia in 1864–65. Although no mules or horses were officially named in the order, many were dispensed to the freedmen to help them get started as freed farmers.

On January 16, 1865, Major General Sherman issued Special Field Orders, No. 15, promising land to former black slaves from the region. The property on the coastal lands and barrier islands promised to the freedmen went from CHARLESTON, SOUTH CAROLINA, southward to the St. Johns River in Florida. Many of these blacks had been freed during his march through Georgia to the coastal city of Savannah, and they had followed his army. In addition to promising up to 40 acres of land, or a quarter of a quarter-section (or square mile), Sherman and his army relinquished a large surplus of mules and horses to the freed slaves but did not mention it in Special Field Orders, No. 15. The former white residents were banished from these lands in the process. By June 1865, two months after the war ended, approximately 400,000 acres had been distributed to 40,000 freedmen along the banks of the Atlantic Ocean and on islands in these states. These lands become known as "Sherman's Reservation." Many of the former slaves spoke Gullah and were often called the Gullah Geechee people.

Historically, the potential for property ownership was an important pull for IMMIGRATION to the United States; however, race, gender, and property ownership were exclusionary conditions for suffrage rights from the inception of the nation. The redistribution of lands to freedmen would also provide the freedmen and their families private land for living and agricultural development. Thus, the prospects of freedmen's owning land would have elevated both the political and economic power of former slaves after the abolition of slavery.

Eager to reunite white northerners and white southerners and unable to envision a role for African Americans except as landless laborers, in fall 1865, President Andrew Johnson (1808–75) rescinded the order that gave lands to the freedmen. The federal government forced the freedmen off the lands, and former owners reclaimed the PLANTATIONS. Few, if any, former slaves kept their 40 acres. Deprived of any significant landholdings and facing an absence of other opportunities, many former slaves returned to work on these plantations as laborers. Eventually, many landowners divided their plantations into smaller parcels and opened their land to SHARECROPPING.

While the sharecropping system varied slightly from plantation to plantation, the owner agreed to allow the sharecropper or tenant to work the land in exchange for a share of the crop produced on the land. After the harvest and sale of the crop, the workers received a share of the money minus various fees, debts, and interest for living on the land. COT-TON and TOBACCO remained as the major crops in the region. Despite the obstacles posed by the sharecropping system, many African Americans gradually earned enough money to purchase the farmlands they worked. By 1910, blacks owned more than 16 million acres of farmland, and by 1920, an estimated 925,000 black farmers resided in the United States. By 1999, that number had dwindled to roughly 17,000 black farmers. The reduction in black-owned farms parallels the reduction in all family farms in the United States over the last century.

Today, the descendants of the Gullah Geechee people face some important environmental issues including, but not limited to, excessive development of coastal resorts, alleged nuclear leakage from the Savannah River Plant, coastline EROSION, and further breakdown of the unique cultural and linguistic history of the peoples. A Forty Acres and a Mule Bio Regional Office has been created in Charleston by the African American Environmentalist Association to help plan and ameliorate many of these growing environmental and cultural issues. "Forty acres and a mule" has also become a rallying cry for granting federal reparations to family members of former slaves, because some blacks believe the issue has represented the historical treatment of African Americans by the U.S. government.

See also ATLANTA, GEORGIA; CIVIL RIGHTS MOVEMENT; COASTLINE EROSION AND STABILIZATION; ENVIRONMENTAL JUSTICE; FEDERAL LAW—LAND POLICIES; RACISM AND DISCRIMINATION; UNITED STATES—DEEP SOUTH.

Marcus David Aldredge

Further Reading
Bullard, Robert D. *We Speak for Ourselves: Social Justice, Race and Environment.* Washington, D.C.: Panos Institute, 1990.
Oubre, Claude F. *Forty Acres and a Mule: The Freedman's Bureau and the Black Land Ownership.* Baton Rouge: Louisiana State University Press, 1978.
Reid, Joseph D., Jr. "Sharecropping and Agricultural Uncertainty." *Economic Development and Cultural Change* 24, 3 (1976): 549–576.
Royce, Edward Cary. *The Origins of Southern Sharecropping.* Philadelphia: Temple University Press, 1993.

Special Field Orders, No. 15
William T. Sherman (January 16, 1865)
In promising land to freed slaves near the end of the Civil War, Major General William T. Sherman hoped to do more than secure their loyalty to the Union. Although President Andrew Johnson subsequently rescinded it, Sherman's order, issued on January 16, 1865, reflected long-held American beliefs that private property and tilling the soil cultivated good citizens. It also reflected the belief of many Americans in the separation of the races.

Headquarters Military Division of the Mississippi, In the Field, Savannah, Georgia, January 16, 1865

1. The islands from Charleston south, the abandoned rice-field along the rivers for thirty miles back from the sea, and the country bordering the St. John's River, Florida, are reserved and set apart for the settlement of the negroes now made free by the acts of war and the proclamation of the President of the United States.

2. At Beaufort, Hilton Head, Savannah, Fernandina, St. Augustine, and Jacksonville, the blacks may remain in their chosen or accustomed vocations; but on the islands, and in the settlements hereafter to be established, no white person whatever, unless military officers and soldiers detailed for duty, will be permitted to reside; and the sole and exclusive management of affairs will be left to the freed people themselves, subject only to the United States military authority, and the acts of Congress. By the laws of war, and orders of the President of the United States, the negro is free, and must be dealt with as such. He cannot be subjected to conscription, or forced military service, save by the written orders of the highest military authority of the department, under such regulations as the President or Congress may prescribe. Domestic servants, blacksmiths, carpenters, and other mechanics, will be free to select their own work and residence, but the young and able-bodied negroes must be encouraged to enlist as soldiers in the service of the United States, to contribute their share toward maintaining their own freedom, and securing their rights as citizens of the United States. . . .

3. Whenever three respectable negroes, heads of families, shall desire to settle on land, and shall have selected for that purpose an island or a locality clearly defined within the limits above designated, the Inspector of Settlements and Plantations will himself, or by such subordinate officer as he may appoint, give them a license to settle such island or district and afford them such assistance as he can to enable them to establish a peaceable agricultural settlement. The three parties named will subdivide the land, under the supervision of the inspector, among themselves, and such others as may choose to settle near them, so that each family shall have a plot of not more than forty acres of tillable ground, and, when it borders on some water-channel, with

not more than eight hundred feet water-front, in the possession of which land the military authorities will afford them protection until such time as they can protect themselves, or until Congress shall regulate their title.

—◈—

Source: William Tecumseh Sherman. *Memoirs of General William T. Sherman.* Vol. 2. New York, 1875, 730–732.

fossil fuels   *See* ENERGY, FOSSIL FUEL; FUELS, FOSSIL.

4-H Clubs   *See* FUTURE FARMERS OF AMERICAN AND 4-H CLUBS.

Franklin, Benjamin (1706–1790) *writer, printer, diplomat, civic leader, business and political strategist, statesman, scientist, inventor*

Benjamin Franklin was an author, printer, political philosopher, and scientist, who helped shape the early American republic and imbue the nation with democratic values. Franklin's inherent curiosity also led him to look for explanations to the workings of the physical world around him, always reading or performing experiments to get answers.

Franklin's logical thinking processes aided his scientific studies and the development of many practical applications of his experiments. For example, his well-known experiments with electricity led to a proposal for the humane slaughter of animals for human consumption through a process of electric shock. This concern may have grown out of his interest in vegetarianism as a teenager. After reading a book extolling the virtues of a vegetarian diet, Franklin stopped eating meat, partly for moral reasons, partly for his health, but mostly for financial reasons, saving money to purchase books. Franklin eventually returned to an omnivorous diet, but his concerns stayed with him.

Franklin was born on January 17, 1706, in BOSTON, MASSACHUSETTS. The youngest son and 15th child born to his family, he attended the Boston Latin School for two years and continued his own education through his lifelong voracious reading. At age 12, Franklin became an apprentice to his brother James, a printer. Five years later, he ran away to PHILADELPHIA, PENNSYLVANIA, and worked in a number of print shops until he opened his own. In 1733, he began to publish *Poor Richard's Almanack,* which he continued for 25 years. Among other items, Franklin invented bifocal glasses, the Franklin stove, and a lightning rod.

Franklin was intrigued by the ENLIGHTENMENT writings that proposed religious truths were best discovered through the study of science and nature. He applied his own philosophy, logic, and theological ideas to his studies, writings, and experiments on aspects of the orderliness of the universe. Franklin wrote of natural phenomena in his newspaper the *Pennsylvania Gazette* and in *Poor Richard's Almanack.* He used the forums of the Junto, a club for artisans and tradesmen he had founded, and the American Philosophical Society, which he helped start, to discuss studies of nature.

Franklin's wide variety of interests, to name just a few, included music, psychology, perspiration and blood circulation, electricity, refrigeration, civic improvements, economics and population growth, comets, inertia, rotation of the Earth, density of air, absorption of light, the Earth's magnetic and geographic poles, the Earth's interior and its surface structure, the burning of wood, which led to his invention of a new Franklin stove that required less fuel, and—notably—weather patterns, movements of bodies of water, and wind that led to his mapping of the Gulf Stream and sparked later studies in meteorology and weather prediction. He also studied the usefulness of various parts of nature. For example, he extolled the virtues of various insects, including the bee and the silkworm, and the materials they provide for human life. Franklin's many experiments and inventions in many areas of study led to practical applications, many of which are still in use today.

Through his studies, Franklin helped shape our understanding of many aspects of nature, from the HUMAN BODY to weather patterns. His older brother John suffered from kidney stones, for example, prompting Franklin to develop the first flexible urinary catheter in America. His broad-ranging interests sparked many to follow in his footsteps and expand research in these areas. In particular, Franklin was among the first to put forth ideas of POPULATION growth, marriage age relative to number of children produced, and population density relative to available land.

Franklin took note of climatic and environmental changes during his lifetime. In the first two centuries of European exploration and settlement in North America, a period of cooling known as the Little Ice Age (although it did not actually constitute a true glacial age with the expansion of polar ice sheets and GLACIERS) exacerbated colder winters and extreme weather fluctuations. Franklin and other leading Americans such as THOMAS JEFFERSON concluded that the winters were increasingly warmer as the climate changed. They hoped to show that civilized human intervention could transform WILDERNESS and weather patterns, particularly by clearing FORESTS. Many colonial leaders believed that temperate climates offered the best chance for the emergence of a superior civilization. Franklin also examined Philadelphia, concluding that its founder WILLIAM PENN's plans for an orderly city had been overwhelmed by the dynamic commercial activities centered in its docks, warehouses, and artisan shops. The densely populated city, he complained, experienced AIR POLLUTION, excess noise, and congestion.

Many Americans best remember Franklin as one of the founding fathers of the United States. As a delegate to the Continental Congress, he served on the committee that drafted the DECLARATION OF INDEPENDENCE, although Thomas Jefferson was the primary author of the document. Franklin served as the U.S. ambassador to France from 1776 to 1785. Upon returning to the United States, he joined the convention that crafted the U.S. CONSTITUTION and debated, among other issues, the proper distribution of lands and resources west of the original thirteen states. Both the Declaration and the Constitution were imbued with theories of NATURAL LAW that influenced political philosophers in the 18th century. Franklin died on April 17, 1790, in Philadelphia.

See also ALMANACS; AMERICAN REVOLUTION; CLIMATE CHANGE; ENERGY, ELECTRICAL; FUEL, WOOD.

Caren Prommersberger

Further Reading
Brands, H. W. *The First American: The Life and Times of Benjamin Franklin.* New York: Doubleday, 2000.
Isaacson, Walter. *Benjamin Franklin: An American Life.* New York: Simon & Schuster, 2003.
Morgan, Edmund S. *Benjamin Franklin.* New Haven, Conn.: Yale University Press, 2002.
Opie, John. *Nature's Nation: An Environmental History of the United States.* Fort Worth, Tex.: Harcourt Brace, 1998.

Freedmen's Bureau

During the disorder at the end of the CIVIL WAR (1861–65), CONGRESS established the Bureau of Refugees, Freedmen, and Abandoned Lands, better known as the Freedmen's Bureau, to integrate newly freed slaves into the southern economy and society and to support former slaves and white refugees who had been loyal to the Union. Best remembered for its educational work, the Freedmen's Bureau, as it was commonly called, also provided more than 22 million rations to those who needed them and attempted to redistribute land throughout the South in ways, had it been successful, that would have largely destroyed the old system of PLANTATIONS and created a class of black small farmers. The Freedmen's Bureau was the federal government's first significant social welfare program.

The need for an agency to aid the transition of former slaves into freedom became apparent during the war. Escaped slaves had little ability to support themselves and were largely dependent on Union army handouts. Private freedmen's relief societies appeared during the war, but the four million African Americans freed by the northern victory overwhelmed their resources. Representative Thomas D. Eliot of Massachusetts first introduced a bill in December 1863 to create a bureau for freedmen, but it stalled in the Senate. Congress finally passed the bill on March 3, 1865, and President ABRAHAM LINCOLN signed it into law.

Entitled "An Act to establish a Bureau for the Relief of Freedmen and Refugees," the law established a bureau to administer relief for freedmen and loyal refugees, to supervise confiscated or abandoned lands, and to restore southern economic stability. Working within the War Department, the bureau was intended to operate for one year after the war. A commissioner appointed by the president was expected to name assistants who would control bureau operations in each former Confederate state.

Besides furnishing FOOD, clothing, and fuel, the bureau was expected to help freed slaves find work. Few had skills and experiences unrelated to agriculture. Recognizing this fact, the bill also allowed every "male citizen" to rent up to 40 acres of land for up to three years. The renter had the option to purchase the land. This clause apparently was the basis of the rumor among former slaves that each family would receive FORTY ACRES AND A MULE.

The implications of the program were enormous. By summer 1865, the Freedmen's Bureau controlled more than 800,000 acres of land and 5,000 pieces of urban property. Commissioner Oliver O. Howard and his assistants intended to make most of this land available to freedmen, thereby breaking up the large plantation holdings of wealthy Confederates and creating a class of black small farmers. Northern radicals favored the plan since it punished the South.

Howard's plan conflicted with President Andrew Johnson's hopes for a limited RECONSTRUCTION. Johnson hoped that most Confederate states would return to the Union within a few months and issued a Proclamation of Pardon and Amnesty on May 29, 1865, granting amnesty to all southern citizens who took an oath of allegiance, with the exceptions of Confederate military officers and government officials. Those who obtained amnesty received back their confiscated property, with the exception of slaves, as long as it was valued less than $20,000. At first, Howard and his assistants assumed the president's proclamation did not apply to the land they controlled and continued to make it available to freedmen. On August 16, 1865, Johnson specifically ordered Howard to cease distributing land and to restore it to the control of its former owners. Those blacks who already had rented land were forced to leave, although most were allowed to harvest crops they planted. Johnson believed, as did most Americans at the time, that permanent confiscation of someone's property by the federal government was unconstitutional.

Republicans in Congress responded in February 1866 with a new Freedmen's Bureau bill. President Johnson vetoed the bill. Congress passed a similar bill in June and overrode Johnson's veto. The new bill funded the bureau for two additional years and increased its power to intervene when African-American civil rights were threatened. Two-thirds of the bill dealt with providing land to former slaves. During the war, coastal territories in South Carolina and Georgia had been seized by Union forces. Much of this land was abandoned by Confederate sympathizers and taken by federal authorities for failure to pay taxes. In January 1865, Major General William T. Sherman had issued Special Field Orders, No. 15, granting freedmen the right to buy land held by federal authorities. The 1866 bill allowed freedmen who held valid titles to land that was returned to its original owners to rent 20-acre plots elsewhere from the federal government. Freedmen also received reimbursement for any improvements they made during their occupancy.

Outside the coastal territories, more land was made available to freedmen by the Southern Homestead Act, also passed in 1866. Modeled after the 1862 Homestead Act, it made 46 million acres of federal land in the South available to freedmen and white refugees. Each family could claim 80 acres, later expanded to 160. After making improvements and living on the land for five years, they would receive title for a five-dollar fee. Much of this land, however, was unsuitable for farming and was unclaimed.

The 1866 Freedmen's Bureau law also granted judicial powers to the bureau. Its agents were authorized to invoke military force to ensure freedmen received equal rights. While some agents used this power extensively, others did not. Public opinion in the North gradually turned against the cost of a hard reconstruction. In 1868, Congress enacted a law ordering the bureau to cease all activities on January 1, 1869, except for educational ones and the payment of veterans' pensions to black former soldiers. The bureau went out of existence in June 1872.

The Freedmen's Bureau failed to organize a massive land redistribution in the South, largely because of opposition from President Johnson. Most of the best agricultural land returned to white owners. Underfunded, the bureau was unable to assist many black farmers, reflecting the majority belief that the government should not undertake a large welfare program. Moreover, many freed slaves were encouraged to work as contract laborers for their original owners by local bureau representatives. As a result, an independent class of African-American farmers failed to materialize.

See also AGRARIANISM; AGRICULTURAL TECHNOLOGY; AGRICULTURE, COMMERCIAL; AGRICULTURE, SUBSISTENCE; CONFEDERACY; FEDERAL LAW—LAND POLICIES.

Tim J. Watts

Further Reading
Cimbala, Paul A. *Under the Guardianship of the Nation: The Freedmen's Bureau and the Reconstruction of Georgia, 1865–1870.* Athens: University of Georgia Press, 1997.
Crouch, Barry A. *The Freedmen's Bureau and Black Texans.* Austin: University of Texas Press, 1992.
Finley, Randy. *From Slavery to Uncertain Freedom: The Freedmen's Bureau in Arkansas, 1865–1869.* Fayetteville: University of Arkansas Press, 1996.
Oubre, Claude F. *Forty Acres and a Mule: The Freedmen's Bureau and Black Land Ownership.* Baton Rouge: Louisiana State University Press, 1978.

Free-Soil Party

The Free-Soil Party was a minor American political party that flourished in the presidential elections of 1848 and 1852. The party was more successful than most third parties because it was able to send two senators and 14 members of the House of Representatives to the 31st CONGRESS in 1849. The ideology of the Free-Soil Party gave voice to long-held American ideas about the links between tilling the land and DEMOCRACY.

Whigs and members of the failed Liberty Party formed the Free-Soil Party in 1848 at a meeting in Buffalo, New York. Many members were New York "Barnburners," who opposed slavery, rather than "Hunkers," who tended to be neutral on the subject. The Free-Soil Party drew its supporters from members of the DEMOCRATIC PARTY and the declining WHIG PARTY living in western New York, Massachusetts, Ohio, and other northern states. As a party, they supported the Wilmot Proviso, a congressional measure that never passed, which called for "free soil." They proposed that the lands obtained from Mexico in the MEXICAN-AMERICAN WAR (1846–48) should be "free soil," meaning they would be opened to settlement by free people only; slavery would be banned.

The party's ideology centered on its free-soil argument. In the mid-19th century, farming formed the basis of most of the American economy. Free-soilers believed that the use of slave labor in agriculture created a morally inferior society— inferior to a society in which free people worked their own land. The latter system, they argued, kept faith with the Jeffersonian ideal of an agrarian America of YEOMAN farmers who were independent and self-reliant, yet defenders of a democratic way of life. Slavery made labor undignified and created a class society that was undemocratic. The party's political theorists saw slavery as an inefficient form of labor, which, if contained, would eventually become so uneconomical that it would die off. Slavery created an ecologically exploitative system that neglected stewardship of the land. The free-soil philosophy encouraged small family farms, which nurtured stewardship; farmers cared for the land to leave a legacy for their children.

In the elections of 1848 and 1852, the Free-Soil platform called for no further extensions of slavery beyond its current boundaries. The party also campaigned for internal improvements and a homestead act to award farms to free people who would settle and work the untamed FRONTIER. The party also believed that the federal government needed

FREE SOIL — FREE LABOR — FREE SPEECH.

TEMPLE OF LIBERTY

MARTIN VAN BUREN.

CHARLES F. ADAMS.

This lithograph print created by the N. Currier firm shows a campaign banner for the Free-Soil Party candidates Martin Van Buren and Charles Francis Adams in the presidential race of 1848. Below their laurel-framed portraits is an oval vignette, between two overflowing cornucopias, of a farm scene showing a man working a field with a horse-drawn plow. Above, resting on a bed of clouds, is the "Temple of Liberty," a peripheral structure with a small dome and the figure of Liberty within. Perched atop the temple is a bald eagle with an olive branch and arrows. Inscribed above the eagle is the motto "Free Soil—Free Labor—Free Speech," an abridged rendering of the party's slogan, "Free Soil, Free Labor, Free Speech, and Free Men." *(Library of Congress)* the revenue provided by tariffs, but that tariffs, should not to be set so high as to result in protectionism.

At its 1848 convention at Buffalo, New York, the Free-Soil Party nominated the former president Martin Van Buren (1782–1862) and Charles Francis Adams (1807–86) for president and vice president. Van Buren, a Democrat, had served as president from 1837 to 1841. Adams was the son of the former president JOHN QUINCY ADAMS and grandson of the former president John Adams (1735–1826). Their slogan called for "Free Soil, Free Speech, Free Labor and Free Men." Other leaders of the Free-Soil Party included Salmon P. Chase (1808–73) of Ohio and John P. Hale (1806–73) of New Hampshire. Other important Americans identified with the party were the poet William Cullen Bryant (1794–1878), the poet WALT WHITMAN, the future vice president Henry Wilson (1812–75), and the educator Horace Mann (1796–1859). In addition to sending members to Congress, the party suggested a way for antislavery Democrats to join in opposition to slavery. Their influence was far greater than their numbers. However, the COMPROMISE OF 1850, which attempted to balance the expansion of slavery and antislavery interests, undercut the message of the Free-Soil Party as it entered the 1852 elections. Its candidates, John P. Hale as president and George W. Julian (1817–99) as vice president, received only 5 percent of the popular vote.

In 1854 antislavery members of the Whig and Free-Soil Parties knew that the failure to win any electoral votes and that the passage of the Kansas-Nebraska Act (1854) had ended their hopes. Meeting at Ottawa, Illinois, they joined in an alliance that was to become the REPUBLICAN PARTY.

See also AGRARIANISM; KANSAS-NEBRASKA CONTROVERSY.

Andrew J. Waskey

Further Reading

Blue, Frederick J. *The Free Soilers: Third Party Politics, 1848–54.* Urbana: University of Illinois Press, 1973.

Foner, Eric. *Free Soil, Free Labor, Free Men: The Ideology of the Republican Party before the Civil War, with a New Introductory Essay.* New York: Oxford University Press, 1995.

Smith, Theodore Clarke. *The Liberty and Free Soil Parties in the Northwest.* Whitefish, Mont.: Kessinger, 2007.

French and Indian War (1754–1763)

The French and Indian War (1754–63) was the last war fought between Britain and France in North America and was so named by British and American forces fighting against French and Canadian forces allied with the Algonkian nations. In Canada, the war is known as the Seven Years' War (1756–63), or la Guerre de la conquête. It was the fourth of a series of wars, sometimes known as the Intercolonial Wars, fought between the European powers from 1697 to 1763. The French and Indian War, however, was distinct in that it began in the colonies and spread to Europe when Britain declared war on France in 1756 to begin the Seven Years' War. The causes of the war were primarily economic, with both sides vying for access to the still-rich fur country of the Ohio Valley and the fertile fishing grounds off the coast of Newfoundland. American colonists disliked being encircled by French territory that curved from the Gulf of the St. Lawrence River to Louisiana and effectively blocked the British colonies at the APPALACHIAN MOUNTAINS. The Americans, however, who were largely Protestant, dramatically outnumbered the Catholic Canadiens and Acadiens, approximately two million to a thinly scattered 70,000. Both sides relied on their First Nations' allies. This was particularly important for the French, numerically weaker and claiming a vastly larger territory. From 1713, however, Britain considered the Iroquois Confederacy its subjects, and the Iroquois claimed the Ohio Valley as their own.

A series of FRONTIER skirmishes escalated tensions before the formal outbreak of war. As early as 1749, the French sent expeditions into the Ohio territory in an attempt to ensure the loyalties of Native Americans. In 1753, they began constructing a line of forts down the Ohio Valley. The next year, Major GEORGE WASHINGTON (the future general and president), on his second incursion into the Ohio, encountered a French and Canadian scouting party; the death of the French commander provoked an international incident, and the "Jumonville Affair," as it became known, demonstrated the gap between traditional European diplomacy and backwoods fighting. The next year the British took Fort Beauséjour on the Bay of Fundy and, doubting the allegiance of the French-speaking Acadians, expelled them from the area.

Most of the French and Indian War was fought in Upstate New York and Pennsylvania over such sites as Fort Duquesne (Fort Pitt), Fort William Henry, and Fort Carillon (Ticonderoga). It was a distinctly new-style American conflict in that it consisted largely of guerrilla-type fighting in the WILDERNESS and along colonial borders. The early years of the war generally favored French offensives, whose *canadien* militia were more accustomed to travel in the *pays d'en haut*, the French term for the forested interior of the continent. At the Battle of the Monongahela (or the Battle of the Wilderness) in 1755, for example, the British general Edward Braddock found himself enveloped by Canadians and Natives, while his officers unsuccessfully tried to reform units into conventional lines. In 1758, however, the tide turned in favor of the British for a variety of reasons, including William Pitt's leadership and France's weakening financial state and priority on its European theater. That year saw the fall of the fortress of Louisbourg on Cape Breton (Île Royale) to the largest naval invasion in North American history. In 1759, the marquis de Montcalm was defeated by General James Wolfe in the Battle of the Plains of Abraham at

Québec, and the next year, after the capitulation of Montréal, the governor of New France, the marquis de Vaudreuil, surrendered to General Jeffrey Amherst.

A final peace was signed between the European powers in 1763. In the Treaty of Paris, France surrendered all its North American possessions, except the fishing islands of Saint Pierre and Miquelon. As per Voltaire's derisive evaluation of Canada as *quelques arpents de neige* (or a few acres of snow), France preferred to regain the valuable sugar-producing islands of Guadeloupe and Martinique rather than its northern territory. But Britain's concessions to its new French and Catholic subjects in the 1774 Quebec Act would prove to be one of the Intolerable Acts that helped incite the AMERICAN REVOLUTION.

See also CANADA AND THE UNITED STATES; FUR TRADE; GREAT LAKES REGION.

Claire Campbell

Further Reading

Anderson, Fred. *Crucible of War: The Seven Years' War and the Fate of Empire in British North America, 1754–1766.* New York: Knopf, 2000.

Fowler, William M. *Empires at War: The Seven Years' War and the Struggle for North America, 1754–1763.* Vancouver: Douglas & McIntyre, 2005.

Steele, Ian K. *Warpaths: Invasions of North America.* New York: Oxford University Press, 1994.

French exploration and settlement—Acadia and Canada

At the beginning of the 16th century, fishermen from northern France and the Basque region of Spain learned of abundant cod populations on the Grand Banks, off the coast of Newfoundland. In 1534, on the first of three voyages to Canada, Jacques Cartier (1491–1557) claimed the territory for France, planting a cross on the shores of the Gaspé. He later sailed up the St. Lawrence River to Stadacona (the future site of Quebec) and Hochelaga (Montréal). The sieur de Roberval attempted to found a colony in 1541, but the principal concern of Cartier, his royal patrons, and those who followed was finding a NORTHWEST PASSAGE through the continent to Asia.

In 1604, Pierre du Gua de Monts (ca. 1558–1628) and Samuel de Champlain (ca. 1567–1635) established a small colony on Île Sainte-Croix, which relocated to Port Royal on the Annapolis River the next year. Here, the French made contact with the Mi'kmaq and the Maliseet. By 1607, the French (led by Champlain) had mapped the Atlantic coastline as far south as Cape Cod. But Champlain is known as "the father of New France" primarily because of his role in founding a settlement at Quebec in 1608. In pursuit of furs, the French tapped into a vast trading network by forming alliances with the Montagnais and other Eastern Algonkian nations and the Wendat (Huron) of southwest Ontario. In 1615–16, Champlain accompanied a Huron party traveling home along the Ottawa River to Lake Nipissing and thence down the French River, along what became the favored route of voyageurs for the next two centuries. This knowledge of the GREAT LAKES informed his last and most important map, *Les voyages de la Nouvelle France occidentale* (1632), which showed Lac St-Louis (Lake Ontario), *la mer douce* (Georgian Bay), and a *mer de l'ouest,* suggesting an interior water route. In the process, he involved New France in the traditional wars of the Montagnais, the Huron, and the Iroquois Confederacy. Upon the defeat of the Wendat—and the destruction of the most important Jesuit mission, Sainte-Marie, among the Hurons—in 1649, the Iroquois expanded north and threatened Canada until peace was made in 1667.

New France was also vulnerable to attacks from the British. Acadia was seized in 1613 and renamed Nova Scotia under royal charter in 1621; Quebec was taken by the Kirke brothers in 1628. France regained them in 1632, but Acadia changed hands again in 1654 and 1667. Subsequently, Canada and Acadia were caught up in a series of intercolonial wars lasting from 1689 to 1763. Despite quarrels in the 1640s between the colony's leaders, Charles de Menou D'Aulnay and Charles La Tour, the Acadian population grew along the shores of the Bay of Fundy, at such settlements as Beaubassin and Grand-Pré. *Grands prés* referred to the rich marshlands reclaimed from the tidal bay by use of a sophisticated system of dikes, levees, and sluiceways called *aboiteaux*. Their distinctive agricultural lifestyle engendered a prized sense of independence. When the Treaty of Utrecht gave Acadia (and Newfoundland) to England in 1713, Acadians insisted on a status of neutrality. France retained Île Saint-Jean (Prince Edward Island) and Île Royale (Cape Breton Island); here, they built a substantial stone fortress at Louisbourg, which quickly became a prominent seaport.

Given the importance of the FUR TRADE to the Canada colony, it is not surprising that it was largely entrusted to commercial companies, notably the Compagnie des Cent-Associés, until 1663. The Catholic Church became the most important social institution, responsible for hospitals and schools. In 1627, the quasi-feudal seigneurial system was established, wherein land was granted to a seigneur, or landholder, who in turn granted parcels to tenants commonly known as habitants. Seigneuries typically fronted on rivers (for transportation), with the land divided into thin strips of farmed land, creating ribbons of settlement along waterways. Coupled with the lure of the fur trade in the Pays d'en Haut, this kept the population thinly scattered, compared to the rapidly growing English colonies to the south. (In 1666, the first census revealed a colonial population of only 3,215.) In 1663, however, Louis XIV made New France

This lithograph print, created in the late 1800s, shows Samuel de Champlain and two companions exploring the Canadian wilderness.   *(Library of Congress)*

a royal colony, subject to the *Coutume de Paris,* a governor and *intendant* responsible to the Minister of the Marine, and a stronger military presence. The arrival of the first *filles du roi,* young women sent out with royal dowries to prompt family formation, likewise signaled this new administration.

But the fur trade continued to propel exploration westward. Pierre-Esprit Radisson (1636–1710) and Médard Chouart des Groseilliers (1618–96) reached Lake Superior in 1659; there they learned of a bay to the north. When France refused to sanction their explorations, Radisson and Groseilliers turned to London investors; the successful voyage to the bay of the *Nonsuch* in 1668–69 promptly resulted in the formation of the Hudson's Bay Company. Meanwhile, peace with the Iroquois allowed men such as Louis Jolliet (1645–1700) and Robert de La Salle (1643–87) to move west into the Great Lakes and the Mississippi. By the 1730s, Pierre Gaultier La Vérendrye (1685–1749) and his sons reached the PRAIRIES, founding Fort Rouge near present-day Winnipeg, Manitoba, in 1738.

On the eve of the Seven Years' War, or FRENCH AND INDIAN WAR (1754–63), France claimed a huge expanse of North America, reaching from the Gulf of the St. Lawrence to Lake Winnipeg, from north of Lake Superior to Louisiana. As tensions mounted, the British lost patience with the Acadians' reluctance to take an oath of allegiance, and in 1755 Governor Charles Lawrence (1709–60) ordered their deportation to the American colonies or to France. After early successes in the Ohio country, France suffered defeats at Louisbourg, the Plains of Abraham outside Quebec, and Montreal. With the Treaty of Paris (1763), France surrendered all its territorial possessions in North America except for the fishing islands of St. Pierre and Miquelon.

See also CANADA AND THE UNITED STATES; FRENCH EXPLORATION AND SETTLEMENT—NEW ORLEANS AND LOUISIANA; FRENCH EXPLORATION AND SETTLEMENT—ST. LOUIS AND THE MIDWEST.

Claire Campbell

Further Reading
Greer, Allan. *The People of New France.* Toronto: University of Toronto Press, 1997.
Marchand, Philip. *Ghost Empire: How the French Almost Conquered North America.* Toronto: McClelland and Stewart, 2005.
Moogk, Peter N. *La Nouvelle France: The Making of French Canada: A Cultural History.* East Lansing: Michigan State University Press, 2000.

A French Settler Discusses North American Abundance Nicolas Denys (1671)

In the 16th and 17th centuries, Europeans hoped to settle parts of North America that seemed to offer an abundance of natural resources for trade. A French aristocrat, Nicolas Denys (ca. 1598–

1688), engaged in the trade of timber, fur, and fish at New France's Cape Breton Island for more than 30 years. Upon returning to France in his old age, he completed his memoirs in 1671 and, still hoping to recruit settlers to New France, described "the goodness of the land."

The country there is very pleasing, and the land good. Along both shores of the river the trees are beautiful, and in great abundance, such as Oaks, Birches, Beeches, Ashes, Maples, and all other kinds that we have in France. There is also a great number of native Pines which have not the grain of the wood very coarse, but they are of forty to sixty feet in height without branches, [and] very suitable for making planks for building both for sea and land use. There are also many Firs *[sapins],* of three species, of which some have the leaf flat, of the length and breadth of a little needle, pointedly arranged along the branch, and this is the kind with the coarsest grain. The second species has really the leaves the same, but they come out all round the branches and they prick. The third has also the leaves all around, but thinner and separated and they do not prick; this is called Prusse [spruce] and has a grain much more compact than the others, and is much better fitted for making masts and is the best [of them all]. . . .

But to return to the River of Pentagoüet. Quantities of Bears occur, which subsist upon the acorns that are found there; their flesh is very delicate and white as that of veal. There are also a great many Moose or Elks, a few Beaver and Otter, but abundance of Hares, Partridges, Pigeons, and all kinds of land birds in the spring. In the winter there are still more of those of river and sea which occur there in very great quantity, such as Wild Geese, Ducks, Teal, Eiders, Cormorants, and several other species which in summer go towards the north, and return here in winter when the rivers freeze up, something which happens very rarely on the southern coast.

In front of the entrance of the river there are many islands a little way off, around which the English take a great number of Mackerel as well as at the mouth of the river, where lies the Isle des Monts Deserts. Going towards Baston there is still a number of islands where the English carry on in the spring their fishery for Mackerel, of which they make a great trade throughout their Islands of Barbadoes or Antilles, something which has greatly enriched them. As for Herring they have not much of that, but plenty of Gaspereau, which is one kind thereof, but is not so good by a great deal. During the winter only they fish round these islands for Cod, which they dry by freezing. Our French go there to buy [them] in the spring, and give the English salt, wine, brandy, and other goods in exchange. In the upper part of this river, there is a great deal of Salmon, Trout, and many other sea-fish.

⧫

Source: Nicolas Denys. *The Description and Natural History of the Coasts of North America.* Edited and translated by William F. Ganong. Toronto: Champlain Society, 1908, 107–111.

French exploration and settlement—New Orleans and Louisiana

France failed to colonize the Lower MISSISSIPPI RIVER valley until quite late, considering its possessions along the northern portion of the river. René-Robert Cavalier, sieur de LaSalle (1643–87), first traveled down the river in 1682 and named the lower Gulf Coast portion of the Mississippi River valley Louisiana for King Louis XIV. The lower valley is subtropical and has a humid climate that was conducive to agriculture on large PLANTATIONS.

French settlement of the Lower Mississippi Valley and Gulf Coast began with the establishment of a base on Mobile Bay in 1701. The French settlement began as an effort to secure the Mississippi at its southern outlet. A French port on the GULF OF MEXICO would also serve as a base to harass the Spanish while securing the area from further Spanish or English expansion. French colonization of the area was eased by the decimation of local Indians by epidemics, particularly SMALLPOX, introduced by Europeans. Nonetheless, the Natchez Indians opposed French colonization in the area. French power in Louisiana depended on alliances with local tribes, particularly the Choctaw, who were instrumental in the defeat of tribes such as the Natchez. A vigorous trade existed between the French and local tribes. The Indians gave the French pelts, food, INDIGO, and timber in return for European trade goods. Consequently, the trade led to the depopulation of many native species from overhunting and an increase in Native agricultural production, thereby creating intertribal conflicts.

In 1717, the French government granted the Scottish businessman and economist John Law's Company of the West the rights to colonize the region. In 1718, NEW ORLEANS, LOUISIANA, was founded near the mouth of the Mississippi River and four years later made the capital of Louisiana. With the establishment of New Orleans, France controlled the outlet of the Mississippi and its produce. Land grants were given, and settlers from the West Indies, Canada, and France began to immigrate. In addition, John Law (1671–1729) was able

to attract German and Swiss émigrés. Under the French, the colony never turned a profit, but a number of products were created for consumption in the West Indies and France.

The local landscape was fundamentally altered by agriculture as French settlers planted TOBACCO, indigo, RICE, and COTTON. Tobacco and cotton were produced in inland areas in small quantities over the course of the 18th century. Those two crops were labor intensive and robbed the land of nutrients quickly, giving them a comparative disadvantage over other forms of produce during the French tenure in Louisiana. Many colonists concentrated more on subsistence farming and individual trading practices with local tribes rather than giving their energies over to market agriculture and its instabilities. Nonetheless, the colony in its relationship with tribes was a colonial economy involved in the extraction of natural resources for use by the French metropole and its colonies.

Rice was the first major cash crop in the colony. In many cases, knowledge of the production of these crops was gained from African slaves, who were first imported to the colony in 1719. Rice production required a great deal of land and slave labor. Land was cleared of trees and brush, CANALS were dug, and then fields were flooded with freshwater. To grow rice, valves also had to be constructed to release water should water levels get too high. In addition, given that tidal lands were the best places for the crop, levees had to be built to bar salt water from entering the areas. Rice cultivation remained popular in Louisiana despite the labor cost, and it expanded throughout areas with tidal plains. Rice was consumed domestically and exported to the Caribbean. Rice cultivation declined as it depleted local soils of nitrogen, requiring more and more swamps to be cleared. The French also distributed land to settlers with river access, creating deep holdings with less river access, which also constricted rice cultivation. While rice cultivation cleared swampland, it also continued to rely on standing bodies of water, which did nothing to eradicate the MOSQUITOES in the area, so MALARIA and YELLOW FEVER continued to be prevalent in Louisiana.

Louisiana became a crown colony in 1731, and administrators under the direction of Jean-Baptiste Colbert (1619–83), Louis XIV's minister of the navy and trade, encouraged more agriculture production in order to make the colony turn a profit. Indigo was indigenous to Louisiana, but the French settlers only began to process the plant after the introduction of African slaves. In the 1750s, the crop took off. Indigo grew in drier areas and was, therefore, more suitable for growth in inland Louisiana. The crop, however, after a few years, robbed its land of nutrients, requiring that more land be cleared. DEFORESTATION increased as cypress trees were cut down to create the large tubs that were filled with water to collect the residue of the plant to create the dye.

The FRENCH AND INDIAN WAR (1754–63) began in 1754, but the fighting did not involve French colonists in Louisiana,

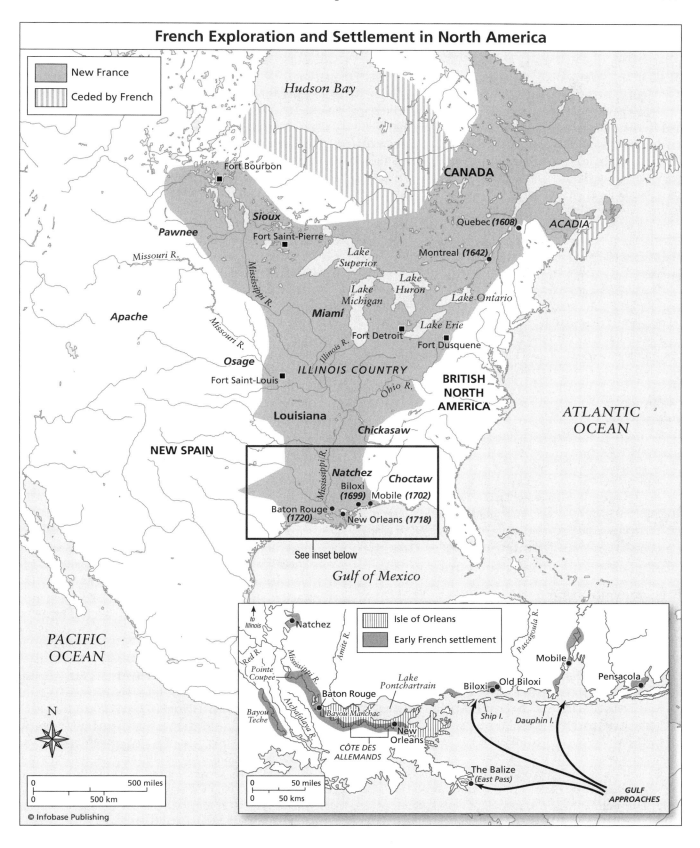

French Exploration and Settlement in North America

Legend:
- New France
- Ceded by French

Hudson Bay

Fort Bourbon

CANADA

Sioux

Fort Saint-Pierre

Quebec *(1608)*   *ACADIA*

Pawnee

Montreal *(1642)*

Missouri R.

Lake Superior

Lake Huron

Lake Michigan

Lake Ontario

Missouri R.

Apache

Miami

Lake Erie

Fort Detroit   Fort Dusquene

Illinois R.

Osage

ILLINOIS COUNTRY

Fort Saint-Louis

Ohio R.

BRITISH NORTH AMERICA

ATLANTIC OCEAN

Mississippi R.

Louisiana

Chickasaw

NEW SPAIN

Natchez   *Choctaw*

Biloxi *(1699)*   Mobile *(1702)*

Baton Rouge *(1720)*   New Orleans *(1718)*

Mississippi R.

See inset below

Gulf of Mexico

PACIFIC OCEAN

N

Inset legend:
- Isle of Orleans
- Early French settlement

to Illinois

Natchez

Pascagoula R.

Amite R.

Red R.

Mississippi R.

Mobile

Pointe Coupee

Lake Pontchartrain

Biloxi   Old Biloxi

Pensacola

Bayou Teche

Baton Rouge

Bayou Manchac

New Orleans

Ship I.   Dauphin I.

Atchafalaya R.

CÔTE DES ALLEMANDS

The Balize (East Pass)

GULF APPROACHES

0   500 miles
0   500 km

0   50 miles
0   50 kms

© Infobase Publishing

even though a large French troop presence was maintained in the colony. After losing the war to Britain, France turned over Louisiana to Spain. SUGAR planting arrived in Louisiana under the Spanish in the 1790s, and over the course of the 19th century, Louisiana led the country in its production.

The French exploration and settlement of New Orleans and Louisiana made significant changes to the environment. Louisiana's Native tribes were either displaced or subsumed into the greater colonial economy. The French Native allies then increased their extraction of timber, furs, and other natural resources for trade with the French. As the French presence in Louisiana grew, the colonists further transformed the environment as they turned to rice, indigo, and finally sugar production at the behest of colonial administrators in Louisiana and France searching for a crop that would make the colony profitable.

See also ENGLISH EXPLORATION AND SETTLEMENT—THE SOUTH; FRENCH EXPLORATION AND SETTLEMENT—ACADIA AND CANADA; FRENCH EXPLORATION AND SETTLEMENT—ST. LOUIS AND THE MIDWEST; FUR TRADE; INDIANS, DEEP SOUTH; INDIANS, GULF COAST; SPANISH EXPLORATION AND SETTLEMENT—FLORIDA AND THE SOUTH.

Michael Kelly Beauchamp

Further Reading

Eccles, W. J. *The French in North America, 1500–1783.* Markham, Canada: Fitzhenry & Whiteside, 1998.

Hall, Gwendolyn Midlo. *Africans in Colonial Louisiana: The Development of Afro-Creole Culture in the Eighteenth Century.* Baton Rouge: Louisiana State University Press, 1992.

Usner, Daniel H. *Indians, Settlers and Slaves in a Frontier Exchange Economy: The Lower Mississippi Valley before 1783.* Chapel Hill: University of North Carolina Press, 1992.

French exploration and settlement—St. Louis and the Midwest

Louis Joliet (1645–1700) and Jacques Marquette (1637–75) first explored the area of the Upper Mississippi River valley for France in the 1670s. René-Robert Cavalier, sieur de LaSalle (1643–87), traveled down the river in 1682 and named the lower Gulf Coast portion of the Mississippi Valley Louisiana for King Louis XIV. In 1699, the French established a trading post on the eastern bank of the Mississippi near current-day ST. LOUIS, MISSOURI, named Cahokia, site of a large ancient Indian settlement. This was a key site that would grow in importance, as it would eventually lie midway between the French positions to the north at DETROIT, MICHIGAN, founded 1701, and south at NEW ORLEANS, LOUISIANA, founded in 1718. Initially, however the site was well chosen, as it was near the confluence of the Mississippi and Missouri Rivers as well as the mouths of the Tennessee and Ohio Rivers. The French established Kaskaskia on the eastern side of the Mississippi in

the Illinois country and Ste. Genevieve on the western side of the river. A series of French settlers, for the most part missionaries and traders, spread west to the GREAT LAKES and then south into the Illinois country from Canada; other French settlers arrived from France or the West Indies by way of New Orleans.

In 1717, the French government officially made the Illinois country, Illinois, and portions of other midwestern states of the current-day United States a part of the colony of Louisiana. The Illinois country was a valuable source of furs and other animal products such as bear oil but also served to produce an agricultural surplus that made its way south to feed the population of French Louisiana. The French missionaries, traders, and soldiers cooperated with the local tribes in a symbiotic relationship to restrict the expansion of British power into the West in the latter half of the 18th century. The FUR TRADE was the basis for the relationship with the Indians, and the small French population posed little threat to Native American lands, thereby allowing the French to maintain far better relations with the Indians than their English rivals. Unlike in many other areas of settlement, the relatively smaller French population in the Illinois country had little effect on the environment in terms of agricultural production at first. It did, however, deplete BEAVER, DEER, and other species as the European demand rose along with the Indian dependence on European trade goods.

By the 18th century, the Illinois country was made up largely of Algonquian peoples who were refugees from Iroquoian aggression farther east. The Iroquois armed with British weapons gradually drove a number of Algonquian tribes from their traditional homelands and into the west, where they reconstituted themselves in new villages. Slaves from Louisiana were sold and used extensively in the region's agricultural production. The new dependence on agriculture changed the landscape as GRAINS depleted the soil of nutrients, even though CORN had long been planted in the same area by Indian civilizations. In essence, the Midwest was the link between the French colonies of New France to the north and Louisiana to the south that followed the Mississippi. The area depended on trade with local tribes but was also a center for expeditions that went farther into the West. In 1739, two French traders, Pierre (1704–51?) and Paul Mallet (1706?–53), made a journey to Santa Fe from Detroit. St. Louis served as a similar gateway to the West once it was integrated into the United States in the early 19th century. St. Louis would have served as an anchor linking the French possessions on the Gulf Coast with those in Canada, at the same time serving as an entryway into the American West for further trade and expansion.

After the FRENCH AND INDIAN WAR (1754–63), St. Louis was established in 1764. It was planted by Gilbert Antoine de St. Maxent (1724–94) and Pierre Laclede Liguest (1729–78) after Governor Louis Billouart de Kerlérec of Louisiana granted them a monopoly on trade in the area of the Upper Mississippi Valley. The Upper Mississippi region was rich in furs. French traders, through their relationships with local tribes, gained beaver pelts and deer and buffalo skins. From St. Louis, French and later Spanish merchants journeyed into Illinois and along the MISSOURI RIVER to trade with tribes while spreading French and Spanish influence throughout the West in competition with the British. The commodities gained were then transported to Canada or downriver to New Orleans, particularly after the British had full control of Canada, for use by the European metropole and the West Indian colonies. After losing the French and Indian War to Britain, France turned over Louisiana to the Spanish, who upheld the trade monopoly granted to the founders of St. Louis. St. Louis was on the west bank of the Mississippi and therefore in Spanish territory, and as a consequence French settlers throughout the Illinois country immigrated to the town once the British took control of the territory east of the Mississippi. In essence, even as French power had officially closed, a French population continued to dominate the Mississippi frontier. This influence lasted for generations even as the British and Spanish, and later the Americans, continued to expand into the region. French traders also retained good relations with the Natives, which further solidified their position as the preeminent traders in the area.

See also FRENCH EXPLORATION AND SETTLEMENT—ACADIA AND CANADA; FRENCH EXPLORATION AND SETTLEMENT—NEW ORLEANS AND LOUISIANA; RIVER TRANSPORTATION.

Michael Kelly Beauchamp

Further Reading

Eccles, W. J. *The French in North America, 1500–1783.* Markham, Canada: Fitzhenry & Whiteside, 1998.

Jaenen, Cornelius J. *Friend and Foe: Aspects of French-Amerindian Cultural Contact in the Sixteenth and Seventeenth Centuries.* New York: Columbia University Press, 1976.

McDermott, John F., ed. *The French in the Mississippi Valley.* Urbana: University of Illinois Press, 1965.

frontier

Few words in the American lexicon have been subjected to as much cultural revision as the idea of the *frontier*. In its earliest American usage, the frontier demarcated a clear line between civilization and the unknown wilderness. The frontier of post–Revolutionary War America was an open, empty space to be explored and settled. At the turn of the 20th century, historians such as Frederick Jackson Turner (1861–1932) pronounced the American frontier "closed." With the advent of American environmentalism, the frontier began to signify those places where nature, and especially wilderness, might still be found. More recently, revisionist historians, postcolonial critics, and Native American scholars have insisted that the idea of the frontier

has been a myth all along, a place where bourgeois Americans look nostalgically upon a preindustrial past. The frontier has even been absorbed into American popular culture, from dime novel westerns to the science fiction franchise *Star Trek*. Above all else, the frontier has always been a place of contention, both literal and academic, as few places so thoroughly embody the ideals, paradoxes, and contradictions of America's relationship to its land and environment.

ORIGINS

Etymologically, the term *frontier* has long been associated with some hypothetical "borderland" separating civilization from the WILDERNESS, a usage that dates as far back as the 15th century. This now-common meaning of the word, however, became especially prominent upon the settlement of the North American continent, beginning in the 17th century, where the stark contrast between the "civilized" and the "primitive" had never been more clear. Indeed, for the earliest European settlers of North America, the existence of the unknown beyond the frontier line of a village or town was an ever-present threat that clearly shaped daily life. Roderick Frazier Nash's seminal study *Wilderness and the American Mind* (1967) points to numerous examples of this attitude toward the frontier in the earliest writings of Americans, noting that "countless diaries, addresses, and memorials of the frontier period represented wilderness as an 'enemy' which had to be 'conquered,' 'subdued,' and 'vanquished' by a 'pioneer army.'" Most of the opening chapter of Nash's work is spent detailing the sizable rift that Euro-Americans created along the frontier in order to separate themselves from the "uncivilized" realities on the other side. As such, the indigenous plants, animals, and people found beyond the frontier were treated with hostility, a fact evidenced by the destructive land-use practices and treaty-breaking policies that soon developed there.

As America moved into its expansionist age after the AMERICAN REVOLUTION (1775–83), fear of the frontier morphed more into a disregard for it, commonly with the same catastrophic results for nature and Native Americans. The settlement of the frontier regions of the trans-Mississippi West symbolically began with the LOUISIANA PURCHASE in 1803 and the subsequent expedition of Meriwether Lewis (1774–1809) and William Clark (1770–1838). This began the age of the so-called frontiersman and resulted in the mythologizing of such figures as Daniel Boone (1734–1820), Davy Crockett (1786–1836), and ZEBULON PIKE, all of whom spent considerable time traversing America's frontier regions. On the heels of these explorers, wave after wave of Euro-American migrants and immigrants, along with events such as the MEXICAN-AMERICAN WAR (1846–48) and the passage of the Homestead Act (1862), pushed the boundaries of the frontier to farther and farther distances. As in colonial America, the frontier of this period was marked on maps with empty, open spaces and generalized terms like *Indian Territory*. But instead of posing a threat to small islands of civilization in vast stretches of wilderness, this vision of the frontier was viewed more as a challenge, as something to be overcome and an opportunity to expand the reach of MANIFEST DESTINY. This attitude toward the frontier can even be said to be part of the official policy of the American government during the 19th century, which rewarded those willing to push beyond the limits of civilization with legal and moral immunity, not to mention preference for gaining large tracts of land.

TURNER'S FRONTIER

This policy was so successful that the historian Frederick Jackson Turner was able to claim that the American frontier was officially "closed" in an article read to the American Historical Society in 1893, just in time for Chicago's World's Fair. As has the term *frontier* itself, Turner's place in American history has become one of contention among revisionist historians of the American West. Nonetheless, his "Frontier Thesis" and subsequent work *The Frontier in American History* (1920) undeniably shaped the way this concept has been discussed. The impetus for Turner's "Frontier Thesis" was a report by the superintendent of the Census in 1890 that the United States could no longer be considered to have a "frontier of settlement," as the nation had reached a saturation point of two people per square mile, a seemingly arbitrary number that nonetheless satisfied Turner and his contemporaries that the frontier in America had in fact come and gone.

Although Turner makes it clear throughout *The Frontier in American History* that his interest in the frontier is strictly academic, the work makes a number of overtly political statements as well. Take, for example, Turner's foremost definition of the term: "The most significant thing about the American frontier is, that it lies at the hither edge of free land." This notion of "free land" is problematic for a number of reasons, not least of which is the number of times it appears in Turner's writing. More than anything else, however, is the fact that the idea of "free land" completely discounts the claims of Native Americans that the frontier regions doled out by the U.S. government to settlers and homesteaders were not "free" for the taking. Turner, then, as did most of his academic and political contemporaries, accepted and promoted the notion that the frontier was ultimately an abstract or theoretical space, open for settlement once rightfully reappropriated through the political mechanisms of Manifest Destiny.

CRITIQUES

Intricately connected to Turner's ideas of the American frontier is the equally problematic concept of the American West. For many, including Turner, the settlement of the West goes hand in hand with the so-called closing of the frontier. In some cases, the ideas of the frontier and the West are indistinguishable, seemingly forgetting the century and a half of American settlement where the frontier did not reach beyond the APPALACHIAN MOUNTAINS. Nevertheless, it is Turner's ideas of the American West, and thus the frontier as well, that were critiqued by the "New West" revisionist historians of the latter half of the 20th century. These scholars tend to view earlier accounts of western American history like Turner's "Frontier Thesis" as turning a blind eye to many of the more negative components of frontier settlement, particularly the large-scale destruction of natural resources and the wholesale disenfranchisement, or slaughter, of Native peoples.

Writers such as Frieda Knobloch, whose work *The Culture of Wilderness* (1996) can be considered a touchstone piece of New West historicism, challenge earlier historians such as Turner, who she asserts was "preoccupied with an abstract, elusive process of the 'frontier' rather than a place called the West." In opposition to these overly general and abstract accounts of the western frontier, Knobloch and her colleagues instead express an interest in this region as a concrete, physical place where the policies of Manifest Destiny and the Homestead Act went a long way toward altering the real-world environments and ecosystems (the FORESTS of the GREAT LAKES, the PRAIRIES of the Midwest, the mountain rivers and streams of the ROCKY MOUNTAINS) found there. Instead of seeing in the frontier an endless tract of "free land," these historians of the New West find there complex webs of relationships among the land, its indigenous inhabitants, and those seeking to settle there. In this way, the frontier is not merely a dichotomy between wilderness and civilization; nor can it be reduced to just an abstract idea or physical space but also must be studied for its implications in the many political, ideological, and social forces of a given time and place. These forces in turn impose significant weight on those frontier environments, whether in the east or west, north or south.

Similar to such critiques of these New Western historians are those currently being leveled by Native American writers and scholars who are giving their own close look to the portrayal of the frontier in American history. As do their counterparts, the revisionist histories offered by postcolonial and Native writers seek to reconsider, reimagine, and sometimes literally retell the accepted stories of frontier settlement. Particularly troublesome for these writers are narratives of the frontier that depict Native communities as helpless victims who were easily subdued and glad to give up their land to the unstoppable progress of Euro-American advancement and Manifest Destiny. Far from the "free lands" of Turner's vision of the frontier, writers such as Gerald Vizenor, Gloria Anzaldúa, and Vine Deloria, Jr., have all offered their own visions of postcontact frontier life and none of them involves willingly acceding to the inevitable crush of "civilization." Furthermore, these Native critics are highly skeptical of the image of the frontier that has been cultivated over the years in American popular culture and looks back on this time and place nostalgically, lamenting the disappearance of the cowboy and the frontier town but ignoring the realities of human and ecological degradation. The Lakota scholar Deloria (1933–2005), for instance, writes of this very problem in his collection of essays *Spirit and Reason* (1999): "The great social experiment of the nineteenth century became a systematic exploitation of people during the twentieth century. For no sooner had the frontier been declared officially closed by Frederick Jackson Turner than people forgot about the thousands of Indians huddled on the desert reservations of the West. Nostalgia for the frontier overwhelmed public consciousness, and dime novels and the new motion pictures created a West that never was but which everyone *thought* existed."

POPULAR CULTURE

These "dime novels and new motion pictures" that attempt to tell their own version of the settlement of the frontier West have long been a mainstay of American popular culture: the novels of Louis L'Amour, the movies of John Wayne and Clint Eastwood, and television shows like *Gunsmoke* and *Deadwood*. Yet the mention of the word *frontier* in the phrase "Space: the final frontier," which serves as the opening line of narration for the *Star Trek* franchise, might be its most recognizable usage in American popular culture. The original *Star Trek* television series begin in 1966, placing it in the middle of the National Aeronautics and Space Administration's (NASA's) Apollo program and the effort to land a human being on the Moon. The idea of outer space is the "final frontier" is therefore not limited to this particular science fiction franchise but is a concept that has long permeated the national consciousness of Americans. Furthermore, this notion of space as frontier hearkens back to earlier usages of the term, particularly as the place of the unknown, but this frontier is also seen as a place to be explored and, perhaps eventually, settled. Many other analogies between the settlement of the American West and the exploration of space can be made, and the thematic similarities between dime novel Westerns and shows like *Star Trek* have been well documented.

Yet it is perhaps enough simply to ask whether this "final frontier," or even any of those few unexplored regions left on this planet, will suffer the same fate as the American frontier has in four centuries of Euro-American settlement and civilization. Or have enough lessons been learned that humans will tread more carefully on those grounds and in those regions where there is still a chance to preserve something of the unknown, the unsettled, and the uncivilized? This question has been asked with increasing frequency by the American environmental movement, which has seen its share of activists and writers searching for those places on the continent that remain untrammeled. EDWARD ABBEY went to the desert, BARRY LOPEZ to the Arctic, and Annie Dillard (1945–   ) to the remote islands of the PUGET SOUND, to name a few, all looking for the very same frontier that two centuries before was not just taken for granted by Americans but treated with open fear and hostility. How far, one must

wonder, will intrepid spirits have to go two centuries from now in order to find America's frontier?

See also FEDERAL LAW—LAND POLICIES; LEWIS AND CLARK EXPEDITION; NATIONAL IDENTITY, FORMATION OF.

Matthew Low

Further Reading

Anzaldúa, Gloria. *Borderlands/La Frontera*. San Francisco: Aunt Lute Books, 1999.

Deloria, Vine, Jr. *Spirit and Reason: The Vine Deloria, Jr. Reader*. Golden, Colo.: Fulcrum, 1999.

Knobloch, Frieda. *The Culture of Wilderness*. Chapel Hill: University of North Carolina Press, 1996.

Lewis, Meriwether, and William Clark. *The Lewis and Clark Journals*. Edited by Gary E. Moulton. Lincoln: University of Nebraska Press, 2004.

Nash, Roderick Frazier. *Wilderness and the American Mind*. New Haven, Conn.: Yale University Press, 1967.

O'Connor, John E., and Peter C. Rollins, eds. *Hollywood's West: The American Frontier in Film, Television, and History*. Lexington: University of Kentucky Press, 2005.

Slotkin, Richard. *Regeneration through Violence: The Mythology of the American Frontier, 1600–1860*. Norman: University of Oklahoma Press, 2000.

Turner, Frederick Jackson. *The Frontier in American History*. New York: Henry Holt, 1920.

Vizenor, Gerald. *Fugitive Poses: Native American Indian Scenes of Absence and Presence*. Lincoln: University of Nebraska Press, 1998.

White, Richard. *"It's Your Misfortune and None of My Own": A New History of the American West*. Norman: University of Oklahoma Press, 1993.

fruit and vegetable production

In spring 2009, Michelle Obama, the First Lady of the United States, started a kitchen garden on the South Lawn of the White House, the first since Eleanor Roosevelt dug a Victory Garden during WORLD WAR II (1941–45). Obama plans to use some produce from the garden to feed her family (her children love fresh vegetables) and to send the rest to soup kitchens in WASHINGTON, D.C. Obama hopes that this gesture, which is both practical and symbolic, will inspire other Americans to plant their own kitchen gardens. Kitchen gardens reduce monthly grocery bills, offer a ready source of fresh fruits and vegetables, provide an opportunity for physical labor, and allow participants to experience nature firsthand.

Nomadic humans initially foraged for fruits and vegetables that grew in the wild. Around 8000 B.C.E., humans around the Earth began to settle and cultivate indigenous crops, including varieties of fruits and vegetables. It took a long time for those plants to migrate around the world. Most migrations of fruits and vegetables have happened in only the last four

First Lady Michelle Obama plants the White House kitchen garden on the South Lawn of the White House on April 9, 2009.   *(Associated Pres/Charles Dharapak)*

centuries. The concept of growing fruits and vegetables in the backyard dates back to the beginning of settled civilizations and, in the 21st century, is still followed in developing countries with gusto. In the United States, however, fruit and vegetable production increasingly shifted to large agribusinesses at the end of the 19th century. Agriculture, including fruit and vegetable production, is America's largest industry, generating 20 percent of the country's gross domestic product. It employs, directly or indirectly, 22 million people in United States.

TYPES OF FRUITS AND VEGETABLES

A fruit is the ripened, seed-bearing part of plant that is fleshy and edible. Thousands of varieties of fruits and vegetables are available around the world and in North America. Promi-

nent among them are apples, avocados, berries (strawberry, blueberry, blackberry, etc.), cherries, citrus, grapes, melons, nectarines, peaches, apricots, pears, plums, prunes; specialty fruits like black sapote, bread fruit, cherimoya, kiwano, lychee, passion fruit, persimmons, pomegranate, prickly pear, quince, tamarillo, and others; and tropical fruits such as banana, carambola (star fruit), coconut, guava, jackfruit, kiwi, mango, mangosteen, papaya, pineapple, and sugarcane. Specialty fruits, which often are generally modified varieties created through precision breeding or gene therapy, are rare, unusual, and hard to find. Maximal varieties of specialty fruits are developed in the United States. For centuries, conventional plant breeders have produced new fruit varieties by crossbreeding existing tree fruit varieties to produce new varieties with certain desired traits. Examples of specialty fruits in the United States are ribes (currants, gooseberries, and jostaberries), aronia, elderberry, cranberry, beach plum, hardy kiwi, persimmons, pawpaws, mulberries, and medlars.

Sweet and nutritious tropical fruits are grown mostly in the Tropics or regions where tropical or semitropical weather conditions prevail. These fruits take on different characteristics when grown in different places because of variations in climate, soil, and precipitation. Citrus fruits, avocado, mango, papaya, banana are grown in Florida, Hawaii, and California with various levels of commercial success. Except citrus fruits, many of these are planted in the backyard for home use and as decorative plants. Pineapple, papaya, and various berries are grown in Hawaii along with many exotic fruits such as lychee, rambutan, starfruit, atemoya, purple sweet potato, and the candy apple banana. The California nurseryman Edward James Wickson (1848–1923) in his 1891 book *The California Fruits and How to Grow Them* describes tropical or semitropical fruits such as banana, custard apple, guava, jujube, loquat, persimmon, pineapple, pomegranate, melon, alligator pear, prickly pear, white sapota, natal plum, kai apple that were grown in California in the 19th century. Some fruits grew well, and some did not survive as expected. However, most of these fruits are still grown in California on a commercial or noncommercial basis. Other southern states also grow some tropical and subtropical fruits in people's backyards but not as part of a commercial venture.

The term *vegetable* refers to the part of a plant that is edible. Bulb vegetables include chives, garlic, leeks, onions, scallions, shallots, and water chestnuts. Fruit vegetables involve avocados, chayote, cucumbers, eggplant, okra, olives, peppers, squash, tomatoes, and tomatillos. Inflorescent or sprout vegetables are artichokes, broccoli, broccoli rabe, and cauliflower. The leaf vegetables are arugula, brussels sprouts, cabbage, chicory, Chinese cabbage, collards, cress, dandelion nettles, endive, lamb's lettuce, nasturtium, purslane, radicchio, Savoy, sea kale, sorrel, spinach, and others, of which the leaves are eaten. Root vegetables, which contain large amounts of iron and other nutrients, grow in the soil; examples include beets, burdock, carrots, celeriac, malanga, parsnips, radishes, rutabaga, salsify, and turnips. Stalk vegetables are asparagus, bamboo, cardoon, celery, chard, fiddlehead, fennel, and kohlrabi. Tuber vegetables, which also grow in the soil, include cassava, crosne, Jerusalem artichoke, jicama, potato, sweet potato, taro, yam, and others.

NUTRITIONAL EFFECTS OF FRUITS AND VEGETABLES

Fruits and vegetables are high in nutrients and provide many health benefits. Eating more vegetables and fruits of different varieties and color can reduce the risk of heart disease, stroke, some cancer, and blood pressure; decrease eye and digestive problems; and reduce blood sugar levels, lessening diabetes. Fruits and vegetables have low energy density (few calories relative to volume) and thus the regular consumption of them aids in appetite management, helping to control obesity. Vegetables and fruits are not sources of cholesterol. Many are a great source of fiber, which assists with digestion. The Centers for Disease Control and Prevention and National Institutes of Health provide important nutritional information on vegetables and fruits.

GROWING ENVIRONMENT OF FRUITS AND VEGETABLES

While Americans grow fruits and vegetables in their backyards, the vast majority of production within the United States is by commercial farms and orchards. Climatic conditions dictate which fruits and vegetables are grown in individual locations. Florida, for example, primarily specializes in citrus fruit farming. Blueberries, pecan, and peaches grow in large quantity in Georgia. Idaho has long ranked first among U.S. states in potato production. Grapes, apples, and a great variety of temperate climate fruits are grown in California's valleys. California possesses the largest agricultural economy of the 50 states and is the world's fifth-largest producer of food and agricultural commodities. Approximately $10.24 billion worth of fruits and nut crops grew in California alone in 2007. In that same year, income derived from vegetable production in California totaled nearly $7 billion. Therefore, California has been called the "fruit and vegetable capital of the United States."

ENVIRONMENTAL IMPACT OF FRUIT AND VEGETABLE PRODUCTION

Fruit trees and vegetable plants, as do other trees and plants, use atmospheric carbon dioxide (CO_2) for food preparation or photosynthesis and thus help reduce the amount of CO_2 in Earth's atmosphere. Most vegetables are annual or seasonal, but a few are perennial, recurring on a yearly or continual basis. As most parts of the vegetable plants are eaten, they do not release significant carbon to the atmosphere. Therefore, vegetables are carbon negative (meaning they help in CO_2 depletion). Generally temperate climates across much of the United States allow perennial vegetables such as asparagus, artichoke, and rhubarb to grow. The biomass produced from such forest plants or shrubs are carbon neutral, which means they do not contribute toward GLOBAL WARMING and do not reduce the CO_2 content in the atmosphere. Unlike the forest plants, which produce a lot of biomass, fruit trees are small and defined as carbon negative. However, when fruit trees die, they release some stored carbon into the atmosphere.

In many cases, farmers leave vegetable residues in their fields as green manure by tilling them into the soil.

Vegetable production helps produce fertile soil and results in nominal soil EROSION because of the intense soil and land-management processes used during production. The soil and land-management processes involved in vegetable production include row cropping, cover cropping, and soil fertility enhancement processes. The major negative environmental impacts associated with fruit and vegetable production in the United States involve the large-scale application of chemical FERTILIZER and PESTICIDES.

A growing, but still relatively small organic farming movement in the United States and across the world attempts to address this problem. Americans have increased their consumption of organic produce and of more varied fruits and vegetables beyond those produced close to their homes—from across the country and from other nations. This consumption depends on the transportation of these foods over great distances, transportation that relies primarily on the use of FOSSIL FUELS.

CONCLUSION

To feed the growing population of the world, many leaders are advocating an increase in personal fruit and vegetable production. Dr. Wangari Maathai of Kenya, who received the Nobel Prize in peace in 2004, developed the idea of holistic environmental restoration in the mid-1970s as a way to provide jobs for the unemployed in her home country. This Green Belt Movement has spread to most parts of Africa and other areas of the world. Fruit tree plantings have been a major feature of this movement because they provide FOOD and conserve the environment simultaneously. With the economic recession that began in 2008, many Americans, as many as 80 percent in one survey, expressed an interest in planting their own vegetable and fruit gardens, although Americans still rely on agribusiness production for the majority of the fruits and vegetables they consume. Another survey, in June 2009, found that nearly 43 million people in the United States grew vegetables in their backyard. Urban gardening has increased as community groups in poorer neighborhoods have utilized vacant urban spaces in the cities to grow vegetables and fruits for personal consumption and food kitchens.

See also AGRICULTURE, COMMERCIAL; AGRICULTURE, ORGANIC; COLUMBIAN EXCHANGE; ECOLOGICAL IMPERIALISM; HEALTH AND MEDICINE; MEXICO AND THE UNITED STATES; TRUCK FARMS; UNITED STATES—CALIFORNIA.

Sudhanshu Sekhar Panda

Further Reading
Centers for Disease Control and Prevention (CDC). "Nutrition for Everyone." Available online. URL: http://www.cdc.gov/nutrition/everyone/fruitsvegetables/index.html. Accessed April 21, 2009.

Food and Agricultural Organization. "Food and Agricultural Commodities Production Report, 2005." Available online. URL: http://www.fao.org/es/ess/top/commodity.html?lang=en&item=619&year=2005. Accessed April 21, 2009.
Naughton, P. "Big Agriculture Take Umbrage at Mrs. Obama's Organic Garden." Times Online. April 22, 2009. Available online. URL: http://www.timesonline.co.uk/tol/news/world/us_and_americas/article6146396.ece. Accessed April 22, 2009.
Panda, S. S. "Biomass." In *Encyclopedia of Global Warming and Climate Change,* edited by S. G. Philander, 126–127. Los Angeles: Sage, 2008.
Pew Research Center. "Luxury or Necessity? The Public Makes a U-Turn." Available online. URL: http://pewsocialtrends.org/. Accessed April 25, 2009.
United States Department of Agriculture (USDA). "Dietary Guidelines for Americans." Center for Nutrition Policy and Promotion, U.S. Department of Agriculture, 2005. Available online. URL: http://www.health.gov/DietaryGuidelines/dga2005/document/default.htm. Accessed April 22, 2009.
United States Department of Agriculture, National Agricultural Statistical Service. "California Fruit and Nut Review." Volume 20, no. 10. Available online. URL: http://www.nass.usda.gov/Statistics_by_State/California/Publications/Fruits_and_Nuts/200610f rtrv.pdf. Accessed April 21, 2009.

fuel, wood

Also called firewood or cordwood, fuel wood is any wood that is burned for biomass energy. It is usually measured in cords, or cubic units eight feet long, four feet wide, and four feet high. Fuel wood must contain less than 67 percent moisture to ignite, so it is usually air dried after harvesting. When partially combusted in kilns, it becomes charcoal—a pure carbon fuel containing almost no moisture. The energy transition from biofuel to FOSSIL FUELS was the critical step in the transformation of the United States and other nations from agrarian to industrial regimes. Although this is true for the energy demands of industry, most North American fuel wood was consumed by heating homes.

When North Americans wonder what happened to their FORESTS, they often imagine timber harvested for construction and shipbuilding, but historically the main agent of DEFORESTATION was the farmer who cut trees for agricultural clearing and for fuel. Depending on a community's needs, cleared land and cordwood were alternating by-products, but consumption of this biofuel continued long after clearing had ceased. It was still considered a major fuel source in the early 20th century, especially in rural areas where importing COAL was too costly. British deforestation was a result of iron and construction industries, but in North America it was more directly tied to comfort and the cold.

Native American communities used fuel wood intensively for heat, cooking, and swidden agriculture, and fuel supplies were a major factor in the rhythms of migration. Swidden involved clearing an area for temporary cultivation by cutting and burning vegetation. Both Natives and newcomers consumed an astonishing amount of fuel wood per capita because supplies were abundant and open fires and fireplaces were inefficient heaters. The average household consumed approximately 35 cords per year in northern parts of the thirteen colonies, and a large home with several hearths often burned up to 70 cords per year. Towns usually exhausted local fuel wood supplies within a few decades, and by the late 17th century, urban markets operated through fuel dealers and drew from farm woodlots up to 100 miles distant. The cost of hauling this bulky commodity over land for more than 25 miles was prohibitively expensive, but water routes and urban demand helped create elaborate supply chains. In the 18th century, severe fuel shortages plagued cities such as NEW YORK CITY and BOSTON, MASSACHUSETTS, and made fuel wood a luxury for the wealthy during the harshest winters.

By 1810, more than one billion cords of fuel wood had been processed and consumed in the United States—more than a quarter of it between 1800 and 1809—and consumption increased rapidly in the 19th century. Heating and cooking required weeks of chopping every year, and farmers knew their woodlots and energy supply chains intimately. A skilled chopper often cut and processed up to one and a half cords per day. This task was one of the most arduous and time-consuming jobs on a farm, and in turn it created its own energy demands. In mid-19th-century diaries, American farmers recorded cutting wood around 15 percent of their working days.

In 1850, biomass energy warmed more than 90 percent of U.S. and Canadian homes, but it also propelled most locomotives and steamboats and put extra pressure on riparian forests. Manufacturing industries, such as distilleries, brick kilns, and blast furnaces, consumed large quantities of wood and charcoal. Charcoal was produced by the destructive distillation of wood. The pig iron produced in the United States, in 1810, required the energy of about 1,000 square miles of forest that year, and even though efficiency increased, production quickly outpaced the capacity of U.S. biofuel supplies. Fossil fuels replaced most industrial biomass energy by the late 19th century. Eastern steam and railway companies switched to coal in the 1870s, although some transportation lines in the ROCKY MOUNTAINS and the farther north continued burning wood into the 1930s.

At some point, beginning in the Northeast, agricultural clearing ceased and fuel wood was harvested from dwindling woodlots. Some of the earliest energy crises involved wood shortages, and humans determined to live in northern climates responded with a variety of solutions: migration, lengthy supply chains, woodlot management and conservation, and increased fuel efficiency. The energy efficiency of biomass was often as low as 10 percent. The widespread adoption of high-efficiency wood stoves and fossil fuel heat occurred surprisingly late, and the average house still consumed 16 cords of firewood in the 19th century. Although fuel-efficient heating and insulation technology decreased the size of the average woodpile, it may also have encouraged larger and warmer houses. Clearing produced enough fuel wood to keep rural and urban houses warm without the extensive use of coal, and after clearing had ended, well-managed woodlots could still keep most rural and some urban houses warm.

The renewal of wood supplies was directly related to the concentration of population and industry. Native Americans often consumed wood resources until the point of exhaustion before moving to new areas, but their numbers rarely presented prolonged threats to forests. CAHOKIA Mounds was one settlement whose population density and stability ultimately depleted local fuel wood supplies. Other sedentary populations had greater difficulty finding adequate fuel wood, but the fact that they did for so long, even in the urbanized regions, suggests a relationship to woodlots that historians have not addressed.

The transition to fossil fuel was slow because biofuel systems were steady, and chopping fuel wood was flexible enough to fit around other time-sensitive farm activities. Fuel wood was sufficient for most of North America's energy needs before 1890, and it was valuable enough that farmers could sell it to urban consumers and steamboat companies using systems that were already in place for their own fuel.

See also ENERGY, RENEWABLE; FIRE; RIVER TRANSPORTATION.

Joshua D. MacFadyen

Further Reading
Cronon, William. *Changes in the Land: Indians, Colonists, and the Ecology of New England.* New York: Hill & Wang, 1983.
Hurley, Andrew, ed. *Common Fields: An Environmental History of St. Louis.* St. Louis: Missouri Historical Society Press, 1997.
Smil, Vaclav. *Energy in World History.* San Francisco: Westview Press, 1994.
Williams, Michael. *Americans and Their Forests: A Historical Geography.* Cambridge: Cambridge University Press, 1989.

fuels, fossil

Fossil fuels are nonrenewable forms of energy, which include petroleum, NATURAL GAS, and COAL. Other less common types of fossil fuels include tar sands, shale, peat, and methane clathrates. Accepted theory holds that fossil fuels form from the decay of plants and animals over millions of years. Over time, the high pressure and heat under the Earth's surface transform this decaying organic material into fossil fuels rich in hydrocarbons. Since this process takes millions of years and use depletes them much faster than they can be replenished naturally, fossil fuels are regarded as nonrenewable sources of energy. Humans have exploited fossil fuels since antiquity and continue to rely on them as the primary source of energy on Earth. Today, fossil fuels account for approximately 86 percent of the energy produced in the United States. Because of the nonrenewable nature of fossil fuels as well as the environmental costs associated with their consumption, efforts are under way to reduce the dependence on fossil fuels with renewable and cleaner alternatives.

COAL

Coal is a solid combustible fossil fuel composed mostly of carbon and hydrocarbons. There are four main types of coal with decreasing levels of potential energy per pound: anthracite, bitumous, subbitumous, and lignite (brown coal). Anthracite, or hard coal, has been traditionally used as a home and commercial heating fuel in the United States, since it burns cleanly and produces little soot. Anthracite is the rarest form of coal, accounting for 0.5 percent of coal production in the United States. Its high price and scarcity make it unattractive for power generation. Bitumous coal is the most common form of coal found in the United States, accounting for more than half the coal mined. Bitumous is used for power generation and as an important fuel and feedstock for the STEEL and iron industries. Subbitumous and lignite coal (brown coal) have the lowest energy content. These varieties are almost exclusively used for power generation, and subbitumous has become increasingly popular in recent years because of its low sulfur content (less than 1 percent), which translates into lower sulfur dioxide emissions, reducing AIR POLLUTION. Approximately 49 percent of the energy generated in the United States is from coal.

The environmental costs of using coal are substantial. Burning coal releases carbon dioxide, which may contribute to CLIMATE CHANGE through GLOBAL WARMING. Coal also contains heavy metals and toxins, such as uranium, thorium, and MERCURY, which are released into the environment during combustion. The burning of coal also causes ACID RAIN. Coal mining contributes to groundwater contamination and the release of coalbed methane, a potent greenhouse gas. Aesthetically, coal mining disrupts the landscape; strip-mining changes the contours and natural features of the land; leads to EROSION, air pollution, and WATER POLLUTION; and negatively affects wildlife. Underground mining can lead to subsidence and groundwater pollution. Despite its drawbacks, the ubiquitous nature of coal and its cheap price continue to make it an attractive fuel for electricity generation.

PETROLEUM

Petroleum is a liquid fossil fuel found in rock formations around the world. Commonly referred to as oil, petroleum is a complex mixture of hydrocarbons that is usually black or brown in color. Petroleum serves as a feedstock for refineries in the production of gasoline, diesel, jet fuel, and other important fuel oils. In the United States, about 84 percent of petroleum is converted to liquid fuels. Other uses of petroleum include electricity generation and the production of plastics, FERTILIZERS, cosmetics, and other petrochemicals.

Petroleum falls into two broad categories: conventional and unconventional oil. Conventional oil is normal liquid petroleum that may be extracted through drilling or pumping. Conventional oil is most easily processed by existing refineries and yields the most energy. Consequently, conventional oil has been most the heavily exploited. World reserves of conventional oil are estimated to be in excess of 1.2 trillion barrels, or approximately 40 years worth of consumption at present rates. In reality, however, much less of this total is economically recoverable.

Unconventional oil is an increasingly important source of fossil fuels. Unconventional oil generally includes tar sands, extra heavy crude, and shale; these solid or semisolid materials have large amounts of petroleum present but must be heavily processed to release the trapped oil. When compared with conventional oil, unconventional oil is much more common, with reserves in excess of 3.7 trillion barrels. However, unconventional oil is more expensive to extract and refine than conventional oil, reducing its overall value. As conventional sources of oil run out, unconventional oil will play a greater role in meeting energy demand.

Petroleum has overtaken coal as the most important source of energy on Earth. This is largely due to its versatility and high energy density. Like coal and natural gas, petroleum is a nonrenewable resource, which is rapidly being consumed; world consumption is nearly 85 million barrels of oil per day. Continued high levels of consumption are expected to lead to *peak oil,* when global production will reach a peak and subsequently drop off, leading to scarce supplies and high prices. Peak oil production was reached in the United States in 1971, and most other major oil producers have reached or are near peak oil.

The environmental effects of petroleum are similar to those of other fossil fuels. The burning of petroleum for energy releases greenhouse gases, which may contribute to global warming. Since crude oil is often transported long distances by pipeline and by tanker, OIL SPILLS are a persistent threat. Spills pollute the soil and water and are devastating to wildlife. The production of unconventional oil, particularly tar sands, is environmentally destructive. Tar sand production changes the landscape, since vast amounts of earth and water must be processed to remove the petroleum.

NATURAL GAS

Natural gas is a combustible gas composed primarily of METHANE, although heavier hydrocarbons such as ethane are also commonly found in natural gas deposits, along with other hydrocarbons and elements such as sulfur and helium. Natural gas is found in rock formations throughout the world and is often produced in conjunction with petroleum or coal. Unlike coal and petroleum, natural gas is also produced in quantity by microorganisms as a by-product of the decay of organic material. Common sources of this "biogas" include LANDFILLS, swamps, and even manure. Large deposits of solidified natural gas also exist under low temperatures and high pressures beneath the world's OCEANS. These methane clathrates may represent a substantial source of energy in the future, as well as a potential further source of greenhouse gases.

Natural gas is regarded as the "greenest" fossil fuel, since it burns cleanly and produces fewer pollutants than oil or coal. While some use of natural gas is recorded in ancient China, natural gas exploitation only became common in the 20th century. Prior to the development of long-distance natural gas pipelines in the 1920s, natural gas was commonly flared (burned) at the site of extraction or simply vented into the atmosphere, since it had little commercial value. As late as the 1940s, one billion cubic feet of natural gas was wasted annually in the United States. Natural gas is widely used for power generation, in homes for heating and cooking, as a feedstock for fertilizers, and as an industrial fuel in steel mills and other industries.

CONCLUSION

Despite efforts to find viable alternatives, it is likely that fossil fuels will continue to be an important source of energy for the foreseeable future. This stems from the reality that alternatives, such as biofuels, hydrogen, and nuclear, all have limitations when compared with fossil fuels. While nuclear fission plants produce no greenhouse gases, they are politically unpopular and extremely expensive to build and operate. The mining of uranium for nuclear plants also contributes to water and air pollution, and nuclear reactions produce extremely toxic and radioactive by-products. While attractive, renewable sources of energy such as wind, geothermal, and solar are not efficient enough or cost-effective enough at the present time to replace en masse the energy generated through the use of fossil fuels. More speculative sources of energy, such as nuclear fusion or hydrogen fuel cells, may be decades away from commercial viability.

See also ENERGY, ELECTRICAL; ENERGY, FOSSIL FUEL; ENERGY, HYDRAULIC; ENERGY, NUCLEAR; ENERGY, RENEWABLE; GREENHOUSE EFFECT; OIL, DOMESTIC; OIL REFINING; TRANS-ALASKA PIPELINE.

David Raley

Further Reading

Black, Brian. *Petrolia: The Landscape of America's First Oil Boom.* Baltimore: Johns Hopkins University Press, 2000.

Castañeda, Christopher. *Invisible Fuel: Manufactured and Natural Gas in America, 1800–2000.* New York: Twayne, 2000.

Smith, Duane A. *Mining America: The Industry and the Environment, 1800–1980.* Lawrence: University Press of Kansas, 1993.

Yergin, Daniel. *The Prize: The Epic Quest for Oil, Money, and Power.* New York: Free Press, 1993.

fuels, synthetic

Synthetic fuels, often referred to as synfuels, are liquid fuels obtained from sources other than petroleum, such as COAL, NATURAL GAS, oil shale, tar sands, or biomass. Early interest in synfuels dates to the 19th century, with the production of ethanol from CORN and coal oil from shale for cooking, heating, and lighting. With the rise of AUTOMOBILES during the early 20th century, farmers, politicians, and even HENRY FORD promoted the use of ethanol blended with gasoline or pure as a motor fuel. However, with the ready availability and relatively cheap price of oil, synfuel research has moved slowly. Moreover, while some synfuels burn more efficiently than FOSSIL FUELS, the use of fossil fuels in the production of synfuels causes its own environmental consequences.

An ethanol plant first opened in Kansas in 1936, producing more than two million gallons of ethanol over a two-year period. High costs, oil company pressure, and competition from cheap oil and gasoline doomed the operation. WORLD WAR II (1941–45) provided the conditions necessary for the development of a synfuels industry in the United States as well as abroad. Both Germany and Japan experimented with synfuels before and during the war, since neither nation possessed large petroleum reserves. Nazi Germany produced ethanol from POTATOES and other crops but also established a large synthetic petroleum industry utilizing coal-to-liquids technology through the Bergius process, one of several methods of coal liquefaction. By the beginning of World War II, Nazi Germany operated 14 synthetic petroleum plants, with six more under construction. These synthetic petroleum plants eventually supplied nearly half of the petroleum used by Germany, along with approximately 90 percent of its aviation gasoline, during the war.

The threat of petroleum shortages also encouraged the United States to experiment with coal liquefaction during and after World War II. In 1944, the U.S. CONGRESS passed the Synthetic Liquid Fuels Act, authorizing a five-year program to produce petroleum from coal. The Synthetic Liquid Fuels Program used captured German technology and scientists to jump-start American coal liquefaction efforts. By early 1949, a 200 barrel-per-day (bpd) facility was in operation at Louisiana, Missouri. This facility—the Missouri Hydrogenation

Plant—operated until 1953, producing synthetic gasoline and diesel from bituminous and lignite coal through the Bergius process. A second test plant, constructed nearby in 1951, converted coal to petroleum through the Fischer-Tropsch process, another method of coal liquefaction. This second plant only produced 40,000 gallons of fuel during its two-year operation. In 1953, Congress canceled funding for the synthetic fuels program, forcing the two plants to shut down.

After these closures in the United States, South Africa became a leading producer of synfuels. South Africa is rich in coal but lacks large petroleum reserves. Led by Sasol (Suid-Afrikaanse Steenkool en Olie), South Africa successfully built three large coal- and gas-liquefaction plants, the first in 1955 and two more in the early 1980s at Secunda, South Africa. However, while still entrenched in apartheid (a legal policy of racial segregation that limited the rights of the majority black population), South Africa found itself increasingly isolated from other nations. As international sanctions against the South African government tightened, Sasol's plants provided the fuel needed to keep the country functioning in the absence of petroleum imports until apartheid ended in the mid-1990s. Sasol subsequently licensed its technology to several international oil companies, and its three synfuels plants continued to produce synthetic petroleum from coal and natural gas profitably into the 21st century. The Sasol facilities at Secunda are also noteworthy in that they are the largest single source of carbon dioxide (a greenhouse gas) in the world.

Synfuels gained renewed interest in the United States in 1973 after the Arab oil embargo. The Organization of Petroleum Exporting Countries (OPEC), plus Egypt and Syria, imposed the embargo, coupled with production cuts, to punish the United States and other nations for their support for Israel during the Yom Kippur War. Americans felt the impact of the embargo almost immediately. Gasoline prices rose as the price of crude oil quadrupled between 1973 and 1974 to nearly $12 per barrel. Supply shortages resulted in long lines for gasoline, spurred inflation, and forced Americans to come to terms with their growing dependence upon foreign oil.

Among the many solutions offered to end this dependence on petroleum imports was the development of a domestic synfuels industry. Amid the threat of rationing, President Jimmy Carter signed the Energy Tax Act of 1978, which created tax incentives for the development and use of synfuels derived from biomass. The act made the gasoline-ethanol blend, known then as "gasohol," exempt from the four-cent federal excise tax on gasoline up to 1984. Additional tax incentives, credits, and exemptions encouraged refiners to blend ethanol and other synfuels in their fuels. Along with the federal government, many states adopted similar tax incentives designed to encourage the production of synfuels; corn-producing states such as Nebraska, Illinois, and Indiana led the way with subsidies for ethanol plants. Louisiana, a major producer of sugarcane, also promoted ethanol through tax

incentives. These efforts achieved some success, and by 1979, Amoco (now part of British Petroleum) marketed a gasoline-ethanol mixture in 13 states. Other companies followed suit, and by 1982, gasohol was widely available in the United States, with more than 234 million gallons sold.

In 1980, amid a new oil crisis brought on by the Iranian Revolution and the Iran-Iraq War, President Carter signed into law the Synthetic Fuels Corporation Act, establishing the Synthetic Fuels Corporation (SFC) with a budget of $19 billion over six years. The purpose of the SFC was to assist in the development of domestically produced alternatives to imported oil through a public-private partnership with private industry. An ambitious goal of the SFC was the production of two million barrels of synfuels per day by 1985 and 2.5 million barrels by 1990. Despite its early intentions, the SFC was plagued by mismanagement, charges of lavish spending by officials, and failure to invest in appropriate programs. By 1985, SFC had invested only $1.2 billion in three programs, although several new projects, including promising shale oil programs, were in the works. SFC investments yielded only about 10,000 barrels per day of synfuel production, a minuscule fraction of its initial goal and far too little to have any impact on supply or prices.

The SFC was a victim of its own mismanagement as well as of falling oil prices. After the Iranian Revolution and the start of the Iran-Iraq War in 1980, crude oil reached prices of more than $38 per barrel, a tenfold increase from the 1973 level. From its 1980 peak, crude gradually dropped in price as new production entered the market and demand weakened as the United States and other countries struggled with a prolonged recession in 1981–82. In 1986, oil prices crashed to just above $10 per barrel, ensuring that efforts to produce synfuels would not be competitive with cheap oil. Even before the price crash of 1986, President Ronald Reagan's administration had targeted the SFC for elimination, complaining that the SFC ran afoul of free-market principles by granting subsidies to private companies. In early 1986, the SFC was abolished, again ending public-private efforts to develop alternative fuels.

Interest in synfuels in the United States often seems to ebb and flow in response to oil prices. Low oil prices during much of the 1980s and 1990s further discouraged investment in synfuels research. By the early 21st century, this era of "cheap oil," which had fueled Western growth and prosperity for nearly 20 years, appeared to be over as the invasion of Iraq, Iran's nuclear saber rattling, unstable political climates in oil-producing regions around the globe, and rapid growth in India and China combined with continuing high U.S. demand to prompt record high oil prices. By mid-2008, oil prices briefly reached $147 per barrel, more in real dollars than the inflation-adjusted 1980 price of $38. As oil prices rose from 2003 to 2008, interest in synfuels grew in the United States. Several synfuels projects have moved forward, spurred initially by tax incentives and high oil prices, which make synfuels more competitive with petroleum. However, as oil prices fell below $50 in the final months of 2008, the profitability and interest in these projects became doubtful.

Synfuels, depending on their source, have a number of implications for the environment. Natural gas has been used as an alternative for petroleum-derived gasoline in fleet vehicles, among other uses. As such, it burns more efficiently and produces fewer emissions than gasoline or diesel. However, natural gas is widely used in homes, industries, and power generation, limiting available supplies for synfuel production. Other synfuel feedstocks, such as corn and sugarcane for ethyl alcohol (ethanol) and coal for synthetic petroleum, have heavy environmental and social costs. The use of corn for the production of ethanol has caused increases in food prices, putting pressure on the poor in the United States and abroad. The use of fossil fuels, such as coal, oil shale, and tar sands, in the production of synfuels also presents major obstacles. The conversion of coal to synthetic petroleum produces large quantities of carbon dioxide (a greenhouse gas), while the strip-mining typically used to extract oil shale and tar sands seriously degrades the environment, causing EROSION, loss of natural habitats, and contamination of surface water.

See also AGRICULTURE, COMMERCIAL; ENERGY, FOSSIL FUEL; OIL, DOMESTIC; OIL, IMPORTED.

David Raley

Further Reading

Cheremisinoff, Nicholas P. *Gasohol for Energy Production.* Ann Arbor: Ann Arbor Science, 1979.
Melosi, Martin V. *Coping with Abundance: Energy and Environment in Industrial America.* New York: Knopf, 1985.
Vietor, Richard H. K. *Energy Policy in America since 1945: A Study of Business-Government Relations.* Cambridge: Cambridge University Press, 1984.
Yergin, Daniel. *The Prize: The Epic Quest for Oil, Money, and Power.* New York: Touchstone, 1992.

Fuller, R. Buckminster (1895–1983) *architect, author, designer, engineer*

R. Buckminster Fuller was an engineer and designer who focused his life's work on the question of how humanity could survive and thrive on Earth. Among other projects, he crafted affordable, practical, and sturdy residential designs for the masses. Prescient about environmental matters, his designs incorporated such "green" technology as composting toilets, water catchment, and wind energy systems into his housing designs.

Fuller was born on July 12, 1895, in Milton, Massachusetts, to Richard Buckminster Fuller and Caroline Wolcott Andrews. He was educated at Milton Academy and later Har-

vard University, where he was expelled twice (once for misconduct and once for his "lack of interest") and never received a college degree. Fuller served in WORLD WAR I (1914–18) as a communications officer in the U.S. Navy, where he was struck by the efficiency of movement in naval vessels. Fuller married Anne Hewlett in 1917 and started the Stockade Building System with his new father-in-law by 1922.

Fuller's mechanical skills and creativity were combined in the Dymaxion House model first displayed at CHICAGO, ILLINOIS's, Marshall Field department store in 1929. The Dymaxion, or 4D House, was a rental home built from plastic and lightweight steel that would be suspended from a central beam similar to a ship's mast. The house would start with an interior room near the beam and expand outward in a hexagonal pattern.

Fuller and his design collaborator Isamu Noguchi (1904–88) introduced the Dymaxion Car in 1933 as part of the Chicago World's Fair. This three-wheel car featured a rear-steering assembly, a front-wheel drive built by Ford Motor Company, and a lightweight body designed by the yacht maker Starling Burgess. Fuller's car concept could carry 12 passengers, consumed half the fuel of a conventional car, and reached 120 miles per hour. Nonetheless, the car failed. The Dymaxion Car's fate was sealed when one of the prototype drivers was killed in an auto accident before the World's Fair started.

Fuller's focus returned to housing as WORLD WAR II (1941–45) descended upon Europe. The British War Relief Organization asked Fuller and the Butler Company to create temporary housing for military personnel after the Battle of Britain in 1940. Fuller developed temporary "silos" using the Butler Company's grain silo design that could be installed, filled, and removed in a matter of hours. The U.S. government utilized Fuller's design to house U.S. Army Air Forces pilots and ground personnel after 1941.

Fuller created the Dymaxion Dwelling Machine, often referred to as the Wichita House, in 1945. The Wichita House was Fuller's second-generation design for the Dymaxion House and used circular rather than hexagonal elements to create the structure. Fuller limited each sphere within the Wichita House to 10 pounds, added a rainwater storage system for household water needs, and priced the unit at $6,500. The Wichita House prototype was designed to withstand high winds, storms, and other elements without separating from its central beam. Fuller's Dymaxion Dwelling Machine was not mass-produced as accusations of project delays and profiteering plagued its development.

The world of academia helped Fuller find a home after the failings of the Wichita House project. While teaching, Fuller met his future collaborators Don Richter and Shoji Sadao at Black Mountain College in North Carolina (1948–49), James Fitzgibbon at Washington University at St. Louis (1955), and John McHale at Southern Illinois University

(1959–70). These collaborations yielded new ideas such as the Dymaxion Map, which answered distortions in the Mercator projection. Dating back to the 16th century, the Mercator projection became the standard map of the world because it facilitated navigation, but it also distorted the size of landmasses in the polar regions, presenting Greenland (836,109 square miles) as larger than Africa (11,668,598 square miles), for example. Fuller's alternative maps the globe onto an icosahedron, which unfolds into 14 triangular sections and diminishes the distortions Fuller found with the Mercator projection.

The focus of Fuller's work from 1948 to his death was the development of geodesic domes. These spherical, or partially spherical, shells formed from interlocking polygons embraced the designer's notions of using maximal space with minimal resources. Geodesic domes were built in Montreal in 1950 and the Museum of Modern Art in NEW YORK CITY in 1951. Fuller showed the flexibility of the geodesic dome design at the Milan Triennale in 1954 by using six folded pieces of cardboard carried in a suitcase from the United States. Fuller designed a geodesic dome in 1960 that could cover the entirety of Midtown Manhattan. The Manhattan dome would have been paid for within a decade, he claimed, solely from money saved in snow removal services. The geodesic dome design was a microcosm of Fuller's "Spaceship Earth" notion, which touted sustainable energy sources as the future of urban design. Americans and others have adopted domes for some specialized industrial uses and entertainment facilities, but less often for residential use. Fuller and Sadao designed a 20-story-high geodesic dome for the U.S. pavilion at Expo '67, the World's Fair in Montreal, Canada, which still stands today.

Fuller was a prolific writer and lecturer in the last four decades of his life. In addition to the 28 books written on technology and design, Fuller held 25 U.S. patents as well as a nomination for the 1969 Nobel Prize in peace based on his book *Operating Manual for Spaceship Earth* (1969). His views on ARCHITECTURE, resource conservation, and human nature were captured in a 42-hour film session called the "Everything I Know" sessions in 1975. Fuller died on July 1, 1983, of a heart attack at the age of 87 in LOS ANGELES, CALIFORNIA.

See also DEFENSE, DEPARTMENT OF; HOUSING, PUBLIC; HOUSING, PRIVATE; SUSTAINABILITY; URBANIZATION; WATER, DRINKING; WORLD'S FAIRS.

Nicholas Katers

Further Reading
Fuller, R. Buckminster. *Operating Manual for Spaceship Earth.* Carbondale: Southern Illinois University Press, 1969.
Gorman, Michael John. *Buckminster Fuller: Designing for Mobility.* Milan: Skira, 2007.
Pawley, Martin. *Buckminster Fuller.* London: Trefoil, 1990.

fur trade
The North American fur trade of the 16th, 17th, and 18th centuries was an intercultural web of human and animal relationships. Born of a European craving for fine animal skins and Native peoples' desire to obtain European manufactured items for purposes both practical and symbolic, the trade was made possible by the important, though radically different cultural and economic values that each party assigned to the process. The French and English colonizers sought to incorporate Indians and their animal goods into their home markets, where overhunting in western Europe made high-quality skins and pelts especially prized. The Native peoples of eastern North America valued the exchange, at least initially, as a means to maintain reciprocal alliances with the newcomers and to integrate certain European wares into their daily lives and cosmology. Yet, the cultural barriers that separated the two worlds yielded dramatic results for both the humans and the animals they hunted. The fur trade drew together disparate societies in a partnership that wrought complex changes on Indian culture and the ecology of the North American natural world.

DISPARATE CULTURES
Centuries of overhunting in western and southern Europe created the conditions that made possible the European thirst for North American furs. Between the 13th and 16th centuries, fashion trends among the wealthy varied from fur linings derived from animals such as squirrel, marten, and BEAVER to softer materials such as silk and velvet. These materials signaled an owner's affluence and sense of style. By the time of CHRISTOPHER COLUMBUS's arrival in the West Indies in 1492, however, hunters had nearly exterminated Europe's beaver population. Many other furbearing creatures had also become scarce in Europe as well as in the FORESTS of northern Russia. By the turn of the 16th century, the European fur market had bottomed out. Fur prices rose significantly as supplies fell and war and political instability across the continent disrupted international trade. Moscow, at the time considered the fur capital of western Europe, further compounded the problem when it turned its attention away from unstable markets in Europe to more profitable ventures in Asia. These factors made the European market ripe for new sources of animal pelts, supplies readily available across the Atlantic Ocean.

For Indian peoples living in eastern North America, the killing of animals for their skins and meat was deeply rooted within a spiritual and cultural context. These values governed the hunt, regulating the number of creatures taken as well as the important relationship between humans and their animal brethren. Prior to contact, Algonquin-speaking peoples of the GREAT LAKES region and Canada such as the Micmac and Ojibwa took only the animals needed to sustain the community. The meat was consumed for FOOD, the skins provided clothing and shelter, and the bones were fashioned into useful tools, weapons, or personal ornamentation. Beaver, BEARS, moose, caribou, and other game provided the elements of life for peoples who hunted and gathered in an environment that inhibited meaningful agriculture. They believed that spirits, called Manitou, inhabited the animals and protected them from wanton slaughter. Hunting was a negotiation between the Indian people and the animal spirits. The beasts gave their lives to sustain their human neighbors, and in exchange the latter agreed to honor and fully utilize animal bodies. Nothing was to be wasted. Unnecessary killing risked provoking the wrath of the Manitou, causing the game to be sent away and the specter of starvation to loom. Contact with Europeans would soon alter these cultural norms.

The fur trade began largely on the shores of the Newfoundland coast, in the late 16th century. By 1580, as many as 20,000 European fishermen spent the spring and summer months harvesting the cod-rich waters of the North Atlantic. While in port to dry their catch, the fishermen swapped metal items, glass beads, and other objects for Native-made beaver robes. The former believed they received a deal by trading seemingly simple items for pelts of superior quality. From the Indian perspective, however, the exchange was imbued with powerful symbolic meaning. Trade among Native groups was a form of gift giving rather than an economic transaction. Gifts between Indian nations established reciprocal relationships that cemented alliances, affirmed friendships, and brokered peace. Articles such as furs, wampum, and food sustained these ties and conveyed respect. Failure by either party to provide proper offerings could damage these connections. It was from this vantage point that the Algonquin speakers approached the European fishermen. What the latter conceived as lopsided transactions, the Native peoples saw as opportunities to forge ties with the new arrivals within their own cultural framework.

The realization that North America possessed significant quantities of excellent furbearers occurred as the European fashion pendulum swung back in favor of animal pelts. Participants in the fur trade exchanged the skins of a number of hairy beasts, but beaver hide was prized over all. Beavers living in the Great Lakes region and Canada grew thicker furs to guard against the northern climate's harsh winters. This protection became their undoing. Beaver pelts could be refined into a highly desired felt that by the turn of the 17th century was in demand by European tailors, particularly haberdashers. The increased popularity of beaver hats in Europe required an infusion of source material from the other side of Atlantic to meet the market's needs. As several scholars, most notably Richard White and Susan Sleeper-Smith, have observed, the demands of the fashion world led to the commodification of these animal resources.

ALLIANCES AND CONFLICTS

Competing imperial powers sought to control this lucrative trade by forming alliances with various Native groups. They utilized the network of waterways penetrating deep into the continental interior to build these relationships. While the English and Dutch settled on the Atlantic coast, the French began carving out their American empire farther north via the St. Lawrence River. In 1600, the French constructed the trading post of Tadoussac at river's mouth to load furs and other goods onto seafaring vessels for the return trip home. Eight years later Samuel de Champlain (1575–1635) founded the permanent settlement of Quebec as New France began an expansion west into the Great Lakes and surrounding territory, a region they termed the Pays d'en Haut, or "upper country." These movements were the first of many over the next 150 years that saw the French establish trading posts and settlements around the lakes, along the MISSISSIPPI RIVER into the Ohio country, eventually connecting with their colony in NEW ORLEANS, LOUISIANA.

The French cultivated ties with the Iroquoian-speaking Huron, who initially controlled the evolving fur trade by serving as intermediaries between the French and the Algonquian peoples of the interior. Champlain attempted to impose order on the trade by orchestrating the chartering of a series of monopolies as governor of New France, including the Company of One Hundred Associates. In exchange for domination, these cartels were expected to contribute to the imperial treasury, underwrite military expeditions, and encourage settlement of the colony. The latter proved especially difficult for all of New France's history. With these monopolies arrived many traders, some of whom lived among the people they bartered with, learning indigenous tongues and customs. In some instances, tribes arranged marriages between Indian women and French men, establishing kinship ties between the two that provided an insurance measure that traders would continue to visit Native villages. The fur trade also drew Jesuit missionaries, whose attempts to convert Indians to Christianity met with limited success.

By the middle of the 17th century, efforts to control the trade in beaver pelts erupted into war as part of a broader struggle for dominion over the continent. In 1649, the Five Nations Iroquois, a confederacy of allied tribes residing in what is now Upstate New York, launched a brutal assault upon the French-allied Huron to begin the Beaver Wars. Encouraged and armed by Dutch and later English traders who wanted to increase their market share, the Iroquois destroyed the Huron and assumed their role as the trade's intermediary. With the Huron out of the way, the Five Nations pushed into the Great Lakes, attacking villages in a campaign that reshaped the demography of the region. The Iroquois continued their raids over the next half-century. The conflict scattered the Potawatomi, Miami, Fox, Sauk, Erie, and others, forcing them to settle and resettle in refugee villages in the Pays d'en Haut. The Iroquoian presence made the eastern journey to Montreal especially dangerous for Indians desiring to trade pelts for European implements.

The French exploited the Iroquois-induced diaspora by forming new ties in a now more ethnically diverse Pays d'en Haut. They also invested more in their relationship with the Illiniwek Confederacy. In 1680, seeking to consolidate their power over the trade, the Iroquois attempted to annihilate the Illiniwek for their refusal to abandon the French and take their furs directly to the Five Nations. René-Robert Cavelier, sieur de La Salle (1643–87), however, offered assistance to the Illiniwek. A shrewd trader who understood the nuances of Indian diplomacy, La Salle developed alliances with the peoples affected by the Beaver Wars through gift exchanges. He built trading posts to collect and store furs in the Pays d'en Haut and among the Illiniwek near Lake Peoria that also enabled the Native peoples to acquire European goods. Later, his construction of forts and posts along the Mississippi River lent credence to France's claim of all lands from Hudson Bay to the GULF OF MEXICO. In response to La Salle's efforts, the Iroquois increased their attacks in the region, but by the 1690s, the fighting began to the taper off as French-armed Indians finally took the war to Iroquoia. In 1701, the Iroquois sued for peace.

SHIFTING FORTUNES

In many ways, the Beaver Wars cost the French their North American empire. Expansion into the Pays d'en Haut and the Mississippi Valley presented the French with territory simply too large to administer properly. Unlike the English, who settled their American colonies with successive emigration waves throughout the 17th century, the French had difficulty in attracting settlers from across the ocean. Great farms situated on the alluvial flood plains of the Mississippi Valley expected to feed a thriving colony never materialized. Compounding matters, illegal traders known as *coureurs de bois,* or "runners of the woods," defied the monopolies and took their furs to the likes of Hudson's Bay Company, chartered by the English Crown in 1670. The French also continued to spend more money providing the gifts needed to maintain friendships with their Native allies. Though they understood the subtle complexities of Indian diplomacy in ways the British and later the Americans never did, the financial weight of these obligations greatly strained the French colonial balance sheet.

New France's reliance on the fur trade made it susceptible to conquest. The exchange of pelts in the colony grew in importance relative to the British settlements because the former better understood the social and political importance of the trade to Indian peoples. Yet the French were not completely proficient in all of its degrees. Between the 17th and 18th centuries, the French sought to alter the nature of the trade by tying gift giving to services rendered or the promise of future assistance. It was not a successful endeavor. They also attempted to align the trade with market demand, but, as White noted, the Indians did not see price fluctuations from a Western economic perspective. The Native peoples' participation in the trade remained rooted within their own cultural context. The exchange of furs for goods might increase without issue, but a decrease in trade signaled a lack of affection that threatened to destabilize Franco-Indian alliances.

Sensing an opportunity, the English began to siphon off French trade and Native loyalty by undercutting their rivals' prices. They did so even as the overall trade in beaver pelts declined. By the 1720s, overhunting of the animal in the Pays d'en Haut, joined by a shift south by Algonquians fleeing renewed Iroquoian pressure, reduced the French take considerably. The combined trade value of Fort Frontenac and Niagara on opposite ends of Lake Ontario plummeted from 40,911 livres (France's currency until the late 18th century) in 1723 and 29,297 livres in 1724 to a remarkable 9,151 livres by 1725. By contrast, furs and hides amounted to 40 percent of the New York colony's total exports to London in this period. They accounted for roughly 50 percent of Pennsylvania's transatlantic shipments. Although the gradual diversification of the English colonial economy dropped these figures to 25 and 44 percent, respectively, by the 1740s, the damage to New France had been done. To stave off the English economic and political assault, French investment in the trade became more a means to preserve the boundary between the two colonial powers than to turn a profit. In the end, it mattered little. Despite early successes at the onset of the FRENCH AND INDIAN WAR (1754–63), Great Britain and its colonies conquered New France by 1763.

France's defeat in the Great War for Empire, or French and Indian War, marked the end of the fur trade's most important era. Although the French political entity was gone from North America and the tenuous middle ground between the competing imperial powers and the Indians dissolved, the French effect on the cultural landscape continued to frustrate the British. Alliances built carefully through marriage and gift giving created an important framework that the conquerors failed, or cared not, to appreciate. With the French threat now removed, the British had little patience for the finer points of Indian diplomacy. The fur trade became of less consequence as the colonial economies continued to diversify and an emerging political dispute between Britain and its American subjects grew into civil war. Victory by the United States in the AMERICAN REVOLUTION (1775–83) further reduced the trade's importance. The new republic's Indian policy focused more on assimilation and conquest than it did on commerce. The British, though, did enjoy some success in 19th-century Canada, primarily through the Hudson's Bay Company and the North West Company.

CONSEQUENCES OF THE FUR TRADE

The North American fur trade in this period produced a number of dramatic consequences. Scholars debate the extent to which Indian peoples grew to rely on European wares in their everyday lives, but it is clear that the desire to acquire these goods altered the cultural and spiritual relationship between animals and their Indian hunters. Prior to contact, Native peoples took animals for food and other practical purposes with the permission of the Manitou, the animal spirit guardians. European demand for beaver pelts and other skins changed this dynamic as Indians began taking animals for their coats rather than their meat. The ethnohistorian Calvin Martin has argued that the pressure placed on Indian societies by European diseases and Christian missionaries led to a secularization that enabled Native hunters to bypass their spiritual taboos. Without fear of the Manitou, they launched a war on the animals, taking the furs to obtain items such as metal tools and guns. Other researchers contend that European implements improved Indian quality of life, fostering a material dependency that drove the trade. Overhunting forced Natives to travel wider to find additional animal resources, putting them into contact with other peoples with often unfortunate results. Whatever the reason for Indian participation in the trade, the answer lay at the intersection of the cultural, economic, and cosmological spheres.

The craving for animal coats had a powerful ecological impact as well. While hunters took many creatures, the destruction of beaver populations was especially detrimental to North American ECOSYSTEMS. Overhunting nearly destroyed a species that by one estimate numbered 60 million prior to contact. Ecologists consider the beaver a KEYSTONE SPECIES, one that creates certain conditions other life-forms depend upon for survival. As the environmental historian Ted Steinberg has noted, beaver dams create ponds home to fish, turtles, frogs, and waterfowl. Other species take refuge in trees felled by beaver jaws. To kill them, participants in the fur trade ripped open beaver dams and took the old as well as the young. The indiscriminate slaughter forbade the possibility of a sustainable population. Advanced weaponry, often of European origin, made the killing faster and much more efficient. Ironically, the destruction of beaver dams benefited the colonists in an additional way. With the animals gone, their damaged dwellings went unrepaired. Structures that managed to survive annihilation collapsed from want of regular maintenance. As the dams gave way, they released rich organic material stored within the ponds. In some areas, such as New England, this natural FERTILIZER enhanced grasslands that fed the colonists' CATTLE.

The fur trade, then, was a transformative experience for humans and nature in the 16th, 17th, and 18th centuries. Devastated furbearing populations and evolving fashion trends in Europe created the demand for new resources. Contact with Europeans altered Natives' interaction with the natural world and with each other in unpredictable ways. Competition for control of the trade led to imperial war and shifting alliances. Unintended ecological consequences resulted from overhunting. The trade reordered the meaning of life for all involved parties. It also ushered in death on a grand scale.

See also ASTOR, JOHN JACOB; CANADA AND THE UNITED STATES; DISEASES, HUMAN; DUTCH COLONIAL SETTLEMENTS; ENGLISH EXPLORATION AND SETTLEMENT—THE MIDDLE COLONIES; ENGLISH EXPLORATION AND SETTLEMENT—NEW ENGLAND AND CANADA; FRENCH EXPLORATION AND SETTLEMENT—ACADIA AND CANADA; FRENCH EXPLORATION AND SETTLEMENT—NEW ORLEANS AND LOUISIANA; FRENCH EXPLORATION AND SETTLEMENT—ST. LOUIS AND THE MIDWEST; HUNTING, COMMERCIAL; HUNTING, SUBSISTENCE; RELIGION; WILD ANIMALS.

James P. Ambuske

Further Reading

Hinderaker, Eric. *Elusive Empires: Constructing Colonialism in the Ohio Valley, 1673–1800.* New York: Cambridge University Press, 1997.

Krech, Shepard, III, ed. *Indians, Animals, and the Fur Trade: A Critique of Keepers of the Game.* Athens: University of Georgia Press, 1981.

Martin, Calvin. *Keepers of the Game: Indian-Animal Relationships and the Fur Trade.* Berkeley: University of California Press, 1978.

Richter, Daniel K. *Facing East from Indian Country: A Native History of Early America.* Cambridge, Mass.: Harvard University Press, 2001.

Sleeper-Smith, Susan. *Indian Women and French Men: Rethinking Cultural Encounter in the Western Great Lakes.* Amherst: University of Massachusetts Press, 2001.

Steinberg, Ted. *Down to Earth: Nature's Role in American History.* New York: Oxford University Press, 2002.

White, Richard. *The Middle Ground: Indians, Empires, and Republics in the Great Lakes Region, 1650–1815.* New York: Cambridge University Press, 1991.

Future Farmers of America and 4-H Clubs

The National FFA Organization (FFA, or Future Farmers of America) and 4-H both have roots in agricultural education and focus on helping youth learn through experience. FFA is geared toward high school students enrolled in agriculture courses, with some opportunities for middle school and university students. Membership in 4-H is open to children of the ages of nine to 19, and the organization operates through LAND GRANT INSTITUTIONS' cooperative extension programs. Both FFA and 4-H function at the local, regional, state, national, and international levels and have programs focusing on environmental education.

FFA

With the Smith-Hughes National Vocational Education Act in 1917, CONGRESS established agriculture courses in the nation's schools. In 1926, the Future Farmers of Virginia (FFV) formed to assist young men in agriculture classes. At a livestock judging contest in Kansas City, Missouri, in 1928, students from 18 states used the FFV as a model to create the Future Farmers of America and encourage leadership development among agriculture students. By 1934, all states except Rhode Island and Alaska had associations affiliated with the national FFA; they joined in 1950 and 1976, respectively. Congress recognized the FFA in 1950 as officially part of the agricultural education program.

African-American farm boys began organizing their own associations in the 1920s, primarily in southern states, and formed the New Farmers of America for African-American males in 1935. The New Farmers of America merged with the FFA in 1965. The national FFA welcomed women in 1969. By 2006, the organization was more than one-third female, and women were nearly half of all state-level officers. In 1988, FFA voted to change its official name from Future Farmers of America to the National FFA Organization; this change reflected interest in providing career development activities for all agriculture-related fields. FFA currently has nearly a half-million members.

The FFA has long provided awards to its members, including two that address environmental concerns. Beginning in 1949, the FFA recognized proficiency in soil and water management at the national level; beginning in the mid-1990s, the organization recognized proficiency in environmental science.

4-H

Ancestral programs of 4-H began across the United States in the 1890s and early 1900s. They sought to provide youth with improved agricultural education. Notable among these were clubs for boys and girls established in 1902 in coop-eration with Ohio State University. The 1900s and 1910s introduced adoption of the four *H*s—Head, Heart, Hands, and Health—and the use of the clover symbol. In 1914, the Smith-Lever Act established the Cooperative Extension Service, with 4-H as a component; the act gave 4-H public financial support. The Cooperative Extension Service is a nationwide noncredit educational network. Each state has an office at its land grant university and local offices staffed with experts who provide research-based and practical information to agricultural producers, small businesses, youths, and others.

Early 4-H projects focused on FOOD preservation for girls and CORN and livestock production for boys. In the 1930s, girls' projects expanded to include home economics and nutrition, and boys' projects expanded to include SOIL CONSERVATION, ENGINEERING, and more diverse agricultural production. As 4-H grew, there was increasing emphasis on leadership, citizenship, and science in 4-H activities.

In 1965, 4-H overseers officially began encouraging 4-H in urban areas and minority participation in national 4-H events. In the 1970s and 1980s, more 4-H project options began to address environmental issues, including natural resource and energy conservation. In 1990, the 4-H curriculum changed to give equal focus to disciplines outside agriculture and home economics. At the beginning of the 21st century, 4-H has more than 7 million members.

See also AGRICULTURAL TECHNOLOGY; AGRICULTURE, COMMERCIAL; AGRICULTURE, FEDERAL POLICIES; CONSUMERISM; NATURE STUDY.

Lisa J. Powell

Further Reading

Miner, Paul. *Blue Jackets, Gold Standards: 75 Years of Living the FFA Legacy.* Evansville, Ind.: M.T., 2003.

Reck, Franklin. *The 4-H Story: A History of 4-H Club Work.* Chicago: National Committee on Boys and Girls Club Work, 1951.

Wessel, Thomas, and Marilyn Wessel. *4-H, an American Idea, 1900–1980: A History of 4-H.* Chevy Chase, Md.: National 4-H Council, 1982.

G

Gadsden Purchase

The Gadsden Purchase is a strip of land in southern Arizona and part of New Mexico purchased by the United States from Mexico in 1854. The Treaty of Guadalupe Hidalgo formally ended the MEXICAN-AMERICAN WAR (1846–48) in February 1848. Under the treaty, Mexico ceded nearly half of its territory—from Texas to the Pacific Ocean—to the United States. The treaty vaguely set the new U.S.-Mexico borderline according to an inaccurate map, and subsequently, a Joint Boundary Commission's survey of the Mexico Cession between the Gila River and the RIO GRANDE failed to settle the border dispute between the U.S. territory of New Mexico and the Mexican state of Chihuahua. The disputed region included the Mesilla Valley and the celebrated Stevenson silver mine.

When Franklin Pierce, a brigadier general in the Mexican-American War, became president in 1853, he repudiated the compromise achieved under President Millard Fillmore in which Mexico retained the Mesilla Valley. At the time, American political and business leaders, influenced by the idea of MANIFEST DESTINY and excited by the California GOLD discoveries, sought to link their nation from the Atlantic to the Pacific by a transcontinental railroad. The prosouthern Pierce and his secretary of war Jefferson Davis of Mississippi favored a route through the southern United States, which would strengthen the commercial and political influence of the South rather than that of the antislavery North.

Pierce appointed South Carolina's James Gadsden (1788–1858) as U.S. minister to Mexico. A former U.S. Army soldier who had fought against the British in the War of 1812 and against the Seminoles in Florida in the 1820s and 1830s, Gadsden became president of the South Carolina Railroad, the South's most extensive transportation system, in 1843. Secretary of State William Marcy (1786–1857) instructed Gadsden to resolve the boundary dispute with Mexico and to purchase a strip of Mexican territory south of the Gila River that was well suited for a railroad that could link California to Texas, and thus to NEW ORLEANS, LOUISIANA, and the East Coast.

Gadsden was authorized to purchase nearly one-third of Mexican territory, including Baja California. When Mex-

ico balked, Pierce moved 2,000 troops to the border, and Gadsden warned Mexican negotiators that the United States would begin seizing territory if Mexico refused to sell. This threat and Mexico's treasury deficit compelled the Mexican president, Antonio López de Santa Anna, to sign a treaty with the United States selling 55,000 square miles of land. The U.S. Senate subsequently reduced the Gadsden Purchase to 30,000 square miles for $15 million after northern abolitionists denounced it as a southern scheme to bolster slavery. They feared that a southern railroad would push California into the southern camp.

By ratifying the Gadsden Purchase, the United States acquired the fertile Mesilla Valley, rich copper mines at Santa Rita, and the Gila River valley, where the Mormon Battalion had first raised the American flag in Tucson during the Mexican-American War. The Gadsden Purchase prompted an influx of American settlers and ranchers as military outposts, mining boomtowns, and the development of the timber industry stimulated growth of livestock ranching in this arid region with limited water resources. When the new territory of Arizona was formed from the western portion of New Mexico territory in 1863, the portion of the Gadsden Purchase included constituted nearly 25 percent of it. Although the U.S. CIVIL WAR (1861–65) delayed construction, the Southern Pacific Railroad Company completed the United States's second transcontinental railroad through the Gadsden Purchase in the early 1880s.

Most of southern Arizona below the Gila River—a tributary of the COLORADO RIVER—falls within the Sonoran Desert, which contains a variety of unique plants and animals including the venomous lizards known as Gila monsters and the giant saguaro cactus. The Gila River valley was occupied by the ancestors of the Pima and Papago ethnic groups and contains the present-day San Xavier and Tohono O'odham Indian reservations. The population of Arizona has surged since the end of WORLD WAR II, making the Gadsden Purchase acquisitions of Tucson and Yuma the state's second- and third-largest metropolitan areas. Strewn with forests and mountains, southern Arizona contains national parks, wildlife refuges, and WILDERNESS areas, as well as the Barry M. Goldwater Air Force Range. While the Gila River and its tributaries have dams and

CANALS to provide hydroelectricity and water for vegetable and COTTON farming, exploding agricultural and residential growth threatens existing water supplies.

See also COPPER; MEXICO AND THE UNITED STATES; MINING TOWNS; RAILROADS; SOUTHERN NATIONALISM; UNITED STATES—SOUTHWEST; WORLD WAR II.

David M. Carletta

Further Reading
Faulk, Odie B. *Too Far North, Too Far South*. Los Angeles: Westernlore Press, 1967.
Gara, Larry. *The Presidency of Franklin Pierce*. Lawrence: University of Kansas Press, 1991.
Garber, Paul Neff. *The Gadsden Treaty*. Philadelphia: University of Pennsylvania Press, 1923.
Wagoner, Jay J. *Early Arizona: Prehistory to Civil War*. Tucson: University of Arizona Press, 1975.

game laws   *See* FISH AND GAME LAWS AND POACHING.

garbage

Garbage has changed more in the last 125 years than in its entire history. Greater consumption, increased packaging materials, and new standards of cleanliness have all contributed to this change. The quantity and composition of garbage have made its disposal a persistent and rarely resolved environmental issue.

Before industrialization, nearly all garbage was organic—waste material of animal or plant origin—and could be managed, although not always safely, by feeding it to PIGS AND HOGS, using it as FERTILIZER, or letting it decompose. When consumer goods became packaged and disposable, there was more consumption, leading to more trash; older methods increasingly were viewed as unsafe and impractical. Additionally, Progressive Era ideals of sanitation also made the old value of reuse fall out of favor in the early 20th century, as cleanliness began to be associated with newness.

While ordinary individuals became averse to handling their garbage at this time, businesses and "waste exploiters" saw it as a possible resource for profit. Some people called this interest the "romance of waste." Waste exploitation came into fashion at a time when people were interested in the "Gospel of Efficiency," a philosophy that promoted maximizing resources. Efforts to utilize waste generally proved unprofitable. During WORLD WAR II (1941–45), the need for scrap metal caused Americans to relive the old way of salvaging, but it was a brief revival.

The affluence the country experienced after World War II created more garbage than ever. In 1920, the estimated per capita waste production was 2.75 pounds a day. By 1969, concerned commentators speculated that Americans produced 5.3 pounds of garbage per day. In 2003, the ENVIRONMENTAL PROTECTION AGENCY (EPA) estimated the average Americans generated 4.5 pounds of garbage daily.

From the mid-1960s to the early 1970s, America faced its first "garbage crisis." Before the 1965 passage of the federal "Highway Beautification Act," litter remained unregulated. Large amounts of garbage were strewn about roads and within cities. The growth of and increased exposure to garbage made many people wonder what would happen if and when the United States ran out of space for LANDFILLS. Researchers and the MEDIA again speculated about the profitable recovery of resources from garbage and the minimization of waste. Innovators suggested various solutions, including mining garbage for minerals, converting it to fertilizer in a method similar to that used by the old reduction plants, and even using atomic energy to vaporize it down to its fundamental elements, which could then be reused. CONGRESS passed the Resource Recovery Act in 1970 to assist in these types of research, but it was the oil crisis of 1973 that prompted two federal energy agencies to join the EPA in funding demonstrations that promised to turn garbage into energy. When the price of oil declined in the early 1980s, the government abandoned these demonstrations.

While efforts to develop garbage as a resource faltered, other businesses and municipal governments viewed garbage as a possible commodity. In 1973, New Jersey landfill operators, concerned with losing revenue, joined some cities in Pennsylvania and New York in suing the state of New Jersey for imposing a new ban on the importation of out-of-state waste. The case of *Philadelphia v. New Jersey,* 437 U.S. 617 [1978]) went all the way to the U.S. Supreme Court, which ruled that the law banning out-of-state waste violated the interstate commerce clause and was unconstitutional. The court concluded that New Jersey garbage was no different from the garbage produced in other places. Therefore, the state could not invoke the exception to the commerce clause that allowed it to keep out hazardous materials. Additionally, states are not allowed to horde natural resources solely for the benefit of their residents, and the court equated landfill space with a natural resource. In *C & A Carbone v. The Town of Clarkstown* (511 U.S. 383 [1994]), the Supreme Court similarly affirmed that states could not enact laws that prevented garbage from leaving the state. These rulings treated garbage the same as any other commodity and shaped the current situation of waste management, where communities allow waste companies to handle and plan their waste disposal and to secure the companies' own waste streams and disposal sites.

While resource recovery was the emergent idea after the first garbage crisis, RECYCLING surfaced after the new crises of the 1960s and 1970s. In the 1980s, Waste to Energy (WTE) plants fought with recyclers for access to waste materials such as newspapers and cardboard that the plants needed to help

High-density development in urban areas creates huge amounts of waste. In the 1930s, New York was one of the first cities in the United States to establish sanitary landfills.   *(Library of Congress)*

garbage burn in INCINERATION processes. Both recycling and WTE proponents wanted to reduce the waste stream, keep materials out of landfills, and make use out of what people threw away. Despite these common objectives, the two groups represented opposing views of the environment, making garbage an important ideological symbol in environmental discussions. WTE advocates believe in technological solutions for environmental problems, while recycling embodies the older value of reuse and the newer value of sustainable consumption.

Garbage remains a resource, a commodity, and an ideological symbol in the 21st century. It is also both a messy headache and a sign of America's continued good fortune, making it, as one garbologist has suggested, the ultimate measure of the difference between the way we are and the way we think we are.

See also CARCINOGENS, POISONS, AND TOXINS; CONSUMERISM; PROGRESSIVISM; WASTE DISPOSAL AND MANAGEMENT.

Angie Gumm

Further Reading

Melosi, Martin V. *Garbage in the Cities: Refuse, Reform, and the Environment.* Rev. ed. Pittsburgh: University of Pittsburgh Press, 2005.
———. *The Sanitary City: Urban Infrastructure in America from Colonial Times to the Present.* Baltimore: Johns Hopkins University Press, 2000.
Rathje, William, and Cullen Murphy. *Rubbish! The Archaeology of Garbage.* New York: HarperCollins, 1992.
Strasser, Susan. *Waste and Want: A Social History of Trash.* New York: Henry Holt, 2000.
Zimring, Carl A. *Cash for Your Trash: Scrap Recycling in America.* New Brunswick, N.J.: Rutgers University Press, 2006.

gardens and gardening

The garden is a planned and demarcated space for the cultivation of plants that may have utilitarian or pleasurable functions. Throughout history, gardens were essential for the provision of FOOD and medicine. They also provided an aesthetically pleasing space for OUTDOOR RECREATION and contemplation and served as controlled spaces for scientific research.

As manifestations of both human effort and natural processes, gardens represent a unique human relationship to the environment. Created through human design, selection, and arrangement, the garden has been an expression of the culture from which it derives. Therefore, gardens are an example of social and cultural construction of space since they reveal values and behaviors, including the subsistence strategies and spiritual beliefs of the gardener and larger community. Gardens also express broader cultural patterns. Throughout U.S. history, for example, bonded and free laborers worked not only within the plantation system but also in the gardens of wealthy landowners. The American landscape garden thus also contains an invisible history of labor and class power.

The garden has been a significant concept around the world. It is not clear when humans first began to create gardens, but the cultivation of plants in small plots began 11,000 years ago. The idea of the pleasure garden originates from the ancient Near East, where archaeological and historical evidence shows that early Egyptian, Persian, and Mesopotamian cultures planted the first gardens designed for entertainment. The Babylonian city of Nippur, the Mesopotamian city of Eridu, and the Assyrian city of Nimrud all had pleasure gardens devoted to exotic flora. These cultures were the first to associate the garden with political power. The ability to collect and assemble botanical products from throughout the world illustrated elite power. A garden of exotic plants, akin to artwork, could display wealth and worldly knowledge. Inhabitants of the ancient world also established pleasure gardens. The Greek and Roman Empires built public and private gardens, and the garden has an extensive history in Asia. In China, the garden was a place to contemplate the human relationship to nature.

From its earliest inception, humans associated the garden with paradise. Indeed, Near Eastern gardens may have been influential to the biblical Garden of Eden story. In Judeo-Christian tradition, the story of Eden explains humanity's place as one of dominion over the natural world and affirms a connection between paradise and the garden. Thus, the first European settlers in the Americas did not only create gardens out of necessity; their gardens also represented godly order by defining and structuring the unbounded and hostile WILDERNESS.

Indigenous peoples throughout the Americas have cultivated food plants for approximately 10,000 years. The variety and sophistication of their gardens astounded European explorers, and early accounts indicate that, as elsewhere in the world, indigenous Americans cultivated plants for ornamental purposes. In colonial America, the utilitarian garden provided fruit, vegetables, and herbs for settlers. The kitchen garden was a staple feature of household production and distinct from the aesthetic flower garden or landscaped pleasure garden. Utilitarian gardens supplemented diets and income. Some African slaves in the American South, for example, tended gardens to improve their diets and produce for sale, but even affluent American households, such as George Washington's Mount Vernon in the late 18th century, had kitchen gardens that yielded plant foods for daily meals.

Regardless of time or culture, humans have frequently viewed gardens as pleasurable retreats. Ornamental gardening is an aesthetic, scientific, and cultural project that Americans have enjoyed since the colonial period. Many of the earliest settlements included designed gardens. Colonial Williamsburg and Jamestown both featured European-inspired gardens by the mid-17th century. Wealthy estates often featured pleasure gardens to showcase exotic or rare plants and to accommodate promenades and social gatherings. Many prominent American figures kept extensive pleasure gardens, including THOMAS JEFFERSON, who entertained and politicked in his gardens at Monticello. In such instances, prodigious gardens were not simply beautiful and enjoyable but visual displays of Enlightenment power and wealth. By the end of the 19th century, a uniquely American character had developed in landscape design and gardening. Led by Andrew Jackson Downing (1815–52) and FREDERICK LAW OLMSTED, SR., American landscape designers established cultivated gardens as public places. The result was the creation of a variety of public parks, ranging from the Smithsonian gardens to NEW YORK CITY's Central Park and the University of Washington in Seattle.

In Europe, the concept of a scientific garden emerged during the 16th century, when universities and hospitals established *hortus medicus,* or physic gardens, primarily to grow plant medicines and teach medical botany. During the 18th century, the aesthetically pleasing garden became a popular site for the botanical sciences. Imperial expansion facilitated a global exchange of plants and plant knowledge, stimulating the worldwide development of botanical gardens and BOTANY. Botanical classification and taxonomy often depended on colonial enterprises, since European naturalists relied on colonial networks to receive specimens and information from around the world.

Americans established their first botanical gardens during the 18th century. These sites included John Bartram's (1699–1777) garden in Philadelphia, the botanical garden in Cayenne in French Guiana, and the Royal Botanic Garden in Mexico. The colonial governments of Britain, France, and Spain, respectively, established and designed gardens to generate wealth and knowledge. In the early United States, universities and colleges usually supported botanical gardens, although the relatively affluent country had few compared to Europe. The Missouri Botanical Garden in Saint Louis, for example, is one of the oldest botanical intuitions in the United States. It has been a center for botanical research and education since the philanthropist Henry Shaw (1800–89) opened it to the public in 1859. Affluent Americans also created botanical gardens on the grounds of their estates.

Since it is both natural and managed, the garden illustrates the merger of nature and culture, often perceived as conceptual opposites. Gardens are multifarious spaces within the context of American history that evoke notions of paradise and the human struggle to establish order over chaos. Products of both human and natural efforts, they can supply basic provisions, create pleasure, and facilitate knowledge.

See also BUILT ENVIRONMENT.

Meridith Beck Sayre

Further Reading
Brown, Jane. *The Pursuit of Paradise: A Social History of Gardens and Gardening.* London: HarperCollins, 1999.

Delumeau, Jean. *History of Paradise: The Garden of Eden in Myth and Tradition.* New York: Continuum, 1995.

Drayton, Richard. *Nature's Government: Science, Imperial Britain, and the "Improvement" of the World.* New Haven, Conn.: Yale University Press, 2000.

Hedrick, U. P. *A History of Horticulture in America to 1860.* Portland, Oreg.: Timber Press, 1988.

McCracken, Donald P. *Gardens of Empire: Botanical Institutions of the Victorian British Empire.* London: Leicester University Press, 1997.

Sarudy, Barbara Wells. *Gardens and Gardening in the Chesapeake, 1700–1805.* Baltimore: Johns Hopkins University Press, 1998.

genetics

Genetics involves the scientific study of heredity, particularly the mechanisms of hereditary transmission and the variation of inherited characteristics among similar or related organisms. A distinctly modern science that emerged in the early 20th century, genetics has become increasingly important to developments in medicine, agriculture, and biology.

In the 1860s, the prescient monk Gregor Mendel (1822–84) laid the foundation for genetics, conducting meticulous experiments with varieties of garden peas in the abbey garden of the St. Thomas Monastery in the present-day Czech Republic. Mendel tracked the inheritance patterns of seven physical traits, such as yellow or green, wrinkled or round, of pea plants and discovered that the appearance of these traits conformed to a 3-to-1 ratio when first-generation plants were crossed and to a 9-to-3 to 3-to-1 ratio when second-generation plants were crossed. Rejecting Darwinian theories of blending that argue that offspring express an intermeshed combination of their parents' heredity, Mendel instead posited that each trait was the result of the independent assortment and segregation of discrete hereditary elements that could be divided into dominant and recessive. Furthermore, these hereditary elements, termed *genes* by the biologist Wilhelm Johannsen (1857–1927) in 1909, segregated randomly during reproductive cell division such that offspring had a 50 percent change of inheriting a dominant or recessive type. Because an individual needed a pair of recessives for a particular hereditary trait to be expressed, dominant traits, of which only one was needed, were three times more likely to determine what was eventually called *phenotype.* This principle helps to explain discrepancies between an individual's *genotype,* or genetic makeup, and its genetic expression, or *phenotype,* as is the case with humans who inherit one recessive sickle-cell anemia gene but do not suffer from the disease. However, they can transmit it to the next generation because they have the one gene.

During his lifetime, Mendel worked in relative obscurity; he received a lackluster response when he presented his findings to the local NATURAL HISTORY society. However, in

1900, two plant biologists, Carl Correns and Hugo de Vries, simultaneously discovered the same patterns of segregation and independent assortment that Mendel had hypothesized 35 years earlier. In due time, scientists recognized Mendel's extraordinary contributions and *genetics,* a term coined by William Bateson in 1905, began a meteoric assent, attracting scientists from fields as diverse as BOTANY, embryology, cytology, statistics, and psychology. Over the next 50 years, geneticists, often working in multidisciplinary teams, determined some basic principles about genes. Genes are located on chromosomes, and every organism has a specific number of chromosomes, including one pair of sex chromosomes. The closer the proximity of genes on a chromosome, the greater the likelihood they will segregate together. Genes mutate as a result of both random errors of cell division and environmental disruptions such as atomic radiation exposure. Genes are composed of nucleic acids, specifically deoxyribonucleic acid or DNA, and its four bases, adenine, guanine, cytosine, and thymine. The term *genome* refers to the entirety of an organism's genetic information, encoded in its DNA.

One of the crowning moments of genetics was the 1953 discovery of the structure of DNA, by James Watson (1928–   ) and Francis Crick (1916–2004). Working feverishly as they competed against other prominent geneticists to elucidate DNA's structure, Watson and Crick benefited from the sophisticated photographs taken by Rosalind Franklin, the foremost X-ray crystallographer of the era. Watson and Crick proposed that the shape of DNA was a double helix composed of twisting strands of interconnected nucleic acids held together by sugar phosphate bonds. This revelation propelled genetics into the molecular age. Geneticists became more and more interested in sequencing genes and understanding their role in cell function, especially the way genes code for the 20 amino acids that make up proteins. Geneticists soon realized the pace of their research depended on how quickly and to what extent they could copy or "clone" DNA. Thus, starting in the 1970s, geneticists figured out clever ways to induce DNA replication in the laboratory. The most notable was through the process of polymerase chain reaction (PCR), which geometrically reproduced DNA fragments. The 1990s saw the development of bioinformatics and computational techniques that could sequence DNA at rates so astounding that scientists affiliated with the National Human Genome Research Institute of the National Institutes of Health, founded in 1990 and initially headed by Watson, actually completed the sequencing of the entire human genome in 2000, three years ahead of schedule.

From its quiet beginnings in Mendel's garden, genetics has been entangled with nature. In the 20th century, many geneticists worked with plants to add precision, subtlety, and depth to Mendel's laws. For example, Barbara McClintock's pioneering research in the mid-20th century on gene expression and regulation in maize provided the conceptual framework to explain how DNA sequences, called transposons, can jump and sometimes mutate to different positions on a genome. Genetics has transformed agriculture as more crops have become transgenic, or genetically modified. In 2003, more than 105 million acres of genetically modified (GM) crops was planted in the United States, including 81 percent of soybeans, 40 percent of CORN, and 73 percent of COTTON. In addition, there are many types of transgenic FISH. For example, genetically altered SALMON can mature to market size twice as quickly as unmodified salmon. While some hail GM agriculture as a vehicle to equalize crop cultivation in poorer parts of the world and combat malnutrition, for example, by inserting a beta-carotene gene into the RICE genome to increase vitamin A content, others worry about the side effects of manipulating nature and potentially disrupting delicate ecologies. Over the past several decades, transgenic organisms have blurred the boundaries of nature and the definition of what is natural. How much of its original genome must a pig possess to retain its pigness? Moreover, questions about who should control heredity and to what extent they should modify DNA remain as relevant in today's world of routine genetic screening and stem cell controversies as they were a century ago when some geneticists became enamored of biased theories of eugenic breeding and biological selection.

See also AGRICULTURAL TECHNOLOGY; AGRICULTURE, COMMERCIAL; AGRICULTURE, DEPARTMENT OF; ANIMALS, DOMESTICATED; BIOTECHNOLOGY; DARWIN, CHARLES; EVOLUTION; GREEN REVOLUTION; HEALTH AND MEDICINE; PIGS AND HOGS.

Alexandra Minna Stern

Further Reading
Comfort, Nathaniel C. *The Tangled Field: Barbara McClintock's Search for the Patterns of Genetic Control.* Cambridge, Mass.: Harvard University Press, 2001.

DeSalle, Rob, and Michael Yudell. *Welcome to the Genome: A User's Guide to the Genetic Past, Present, and Future.* New York: Wiley-Liss, 2005.

Holdrege, Craig. *Genetics and the Manipulation of Life: The Forgotten Factor of Context.* Hudson, N.Y.: Lindisfarne Press, 1996.

Shiva, Vandana. *Biopiracy: The Plunder of Nature and Knowledge.* Cambridge, Mass.: South End Press, 1997.

geography

Although environmental history is closely identified with the larger discipline of history, scholars in other disciplines do research in the field. One such discipline is geography, a broad area of study that utilizes perspectives from the natural sciences, social sciences, and humanities to examine the human relationship with nature. Environmental questions have informed research in the discipline both in the past and in the present.

Some geographers argue that at one time almost all work in their discipline could have been called environmental history. From its founding as an academic discipline in the late 19th century, geography addressed relations between people and the environment over time. Early academic geographers argued that this focus made geography a unique field of study. In the early 20th century, geographers saw nature as strongly influencing the characteristics of entire cultures and civilizations. Pioneering American geographers such as Ellsworth Huntington (1876–1947) of Yale University and Ellen Semple (1863–1932) of the University of Chicago argued that the environment determined the characteristics of cultural groups and civilizations.

Environmental determinism fell into disrepute during the 1920s, in part, because of the critique of Carl Sauer (1889–1975), a cultural and historical geographer. Drawing on insights from the anthropologist Franz Boas (1858–1942), Sauer saw humans as active participants in the shaping of landscapes. "Culture is the agent, nature is the medium, and the cultural landscape is the result," Sauer wrote in 1925. In his research and the work of his graduate students at the University of California–Berkeley, Sauer examined how humans had modified the environment of the Americas since European contact. In many studies, Sauer revealed nostalgia for the lost landscapes created by Native Americans. Yet Sauer and his students also recognized the pervasive influence of Native peoples on the environment, a perspective that anticipated work by environmental historians decades later.

In 1955, Sauer co-organized a conference on the role of humans in environmental change. The conference and the volume it spawned, *Man's Role in Changing the Face of the Earth* (1956), served as an exhaustive overview of how people changed the environment over the preceding few millennia. The title was a deliberate reference to *Man and Nature,* the influential book written by the conservationist GEORGE PERKINS MARSH in 1864. Geographers were instrumental in organizing the conference and contributed many chapters to the volume. While many entries discussed the environmental history of the United States, they also made efforts to place environmental changes in a global perspective.

The volume had little influence outside the academy. Furthermore, in the 1960s, the discipline of geography moved away from environmental concerns at precisely the time that the public developed a keen interest in them. During these years, influential geographers sought to change geography into a quantitative and scientific enterprise modeled on the discipline of physics. There was relatively little room in the field for attention to the vagaries of past human and environmental change.

Despite these attempts to turn geography into a spatial science, some geographers continued to argue for historical research, often addressing environmental themes, albeit indi-

rectly. Historical geographers such as Andrew Clark (1911–75) and Donald W. Meinig (1924–) of Syracuse University examined the shaping of the North American landscape over the past five centuries. Although somewhat attentive to environmental matters, these geographers were primarily concerned with human patterns on the land. They frequently depicted nature as a passive stage over which people created settlements, cultivated crops, and built cities. The dynamic interplay between humans and nature that later became a hallmark of environmental history was largely absent from this work.

In the 1970s, developments in the discipline of geography took it further from environmental history as practitioners began to question the dominance of spatial science. Criticism arose in two quarters. Marxist geographers argued that the formation of landscapes, both in the recent past and in the present, must be understood in the context of prevailing power structures, particularly the capitalist economic system. Humanistic geographers argued that geographers needed to remain sensitive to human emotion and the way people experienced place, not just the physical location where they lived or the structures they built. Neither approach, however, carefully addressed environmental matters, even as environmentalism became an influential social movement outside the academy.

The failure of geography to capitalize on environmental concerns, coupled with the relative weakness of the field in the United States, left an opening for the development of environmental history. In other countries, such as Canada, Britain, and Australia, environmental history retains a strong presence in geography as well as history departments. In the United States, its institutional home is overwhelmingly in history departments.

Since the 1980s, the discipline of geography has played an important role in the study of environmental history research. First, historical geographers continue to produce environmental histories. In practice, the differences in work by historical geographers and historians on environmental topics are relatively modest. Both share a concern about changes in space, place, and nature over time and argue that the relationship between society and the environment is a dynamic one in which neither has a determining influence. Second, geographers influence environmental histories through the theories they produce. Given their home in the social sciences, geographers have more readily embraced social theory than most historians. Historians have drawn on these theories suggestively to examine topics ranging from the management of SALMON fisheries in the American Pacific Northwest to the development of urban environments over time.

Some environmental historians now employ tools from geography, such as Geographic Information Systems (GIS). GIS enables users to display large amounts of data spatially.

To date, the most prominent use of GIS in environmental history has been by historians, not geographers. The use of GIS by environmental historians seems likely to grow over time as they see the potential of this tool to help comprehend the significance of underutilized spatial data.

What makes geography unique is its explicit attention to space. Certainly, other fields, including environmental history, are sensitive to these concerns. Still, geography offers a broad set of perspectives and tools for the study of environmental history. Given their different disciplinary homes, geographers and historians have conducted environmental history research utilizing different, but complementary, perspectives on the changing relationship between society and nature over time.

See also MAPPING AND SURVEYING; URBANIZATION.

Robert Wilson

Further Reading

Kearns, Gerry. "Environmental History." In *A Companion to Cultural Geography,* edited by James S. Duncan, Nuala Christina Johnson, and Richard H. Schein, 194–208. Malden, Mass.: Blackwell, 2004.

Thomas, William Leroy, ed. *Man's Role in Changing the Face of the Earth.* Chicago: University of Chicago Press, 1956.

Williams, Michael. "The Relations of Environmental History and Historical Geography." *Journal of Historical Geography* 20 (1994): 3–21.

Wilson, Robert. "Retrospective Review: Man's Role in Changing the Face of the Earth." *Environmental History* 10 (2005): 564–566.

Geological Survey, U.S.   *See* U.S. GEOLOGICAL SURVEY.

George, Henry (1839–1897) *political economist, single tax advocate*

Henry George was a political economist best known for advocating a single tax on land. George believed that people should own what they produced, but that resources found in nature, including land, water, and minerals, belonged equally to all human beings.

Born in PHILADELPHIA, PENNSYLVANIA, on September 2, 1839, George left school by age 14. Among other jobs, he apprenticed as a printer. He moved to California in the 1860s. After failing in the mines, George settled in SAN FRANCISCO, CALIFORNIA, and held a number of odd jobs before working his way up the newspaper industry from printer to reporter to editor. As a newspaperman, George frequently criticized the mine owners, RAILROADS, and land speculators who dominated the economy in the western United States.

Concerned about the poverty he saw in U.S. cities, George sought to understand its causes and to identify the best way to mitigate it. George supported laissez-faire CAPITALISM but argued that monopolies did not act in the public interest. He believed that landowners, speculators, and monopolists captured a disproportionately large share of the wealth generated through industrialization and other economic activities. This concentration of unearned wealth, George concluded, caused the nation's staggering poverty.

George advocated a single tax that put value on the land as a common resource. He believed that this tax should replace all other taxes such as income tax or taxes on capital—thus the name *single tax.* Underlying the single tax movement and of most interest to environmentalists was George's belief that land was a resource that should belong to all. He believed this could be accomplished through a fee paid to the government for the use of the land. Since taxes on income and on production exacerbated poverty, his solution was to remove taxes on anything other than the use of land and natural resources.

The details of George's ideas were contained in *Our Land and Land Policy* (1870) and *Progress and Poverty* (1879). *Progress and Poverty,* one of the best-selling economics books of all time, earned him his greatest fame. He moved to NEW YORK CITY to promote the book and eventually entered the political arena. He ran for mayor as the candidate for the Labor Party in 1886, finishing second (although ahead of the future president THEODORE ROOSEVELT). George died during his second mayoral campaign on October 29, 1897.

More than 30 contemporary organizations exist to debate George's economic ideas. Those ideas also have appealed to many environmentalists. Some view his notion of a single tax as an early iteration of a tax on resource exploitation; government would secure, under this theory, royalties on oil, gas, and other minerals extracted from the land. Some environmentalists have used his writings to argue for ecological tax reform, believing that fees on pollution would act as a greater deterrent than the late 20th-century regulatory structure. Others embraced his philosophy, expanding it to suggest that the Earth is the property of all humanity.

See also ENVIRONMENTALISM, MAINSTREAM.

John-Henry Harter

Further Reading

George, Henry. *The Land Question: Property in Land, the Condition of Labor.* New York: Robert Schalkenbach Foundation, 1953.

———. *Progress and Poverty: An Inquiry into the Cause of Industrial Depressions and of Increase of Want with Increase of Wealth.* New York: Doubleday & McClure, 1898.

Laurent, John, ed. *Henry George's Legacy in Economic Thought.* Northampton, Mass.: Edward Elgar, 2005.

ghettos, slums, and barrios

Of all of the environmental problems posed by American cities, some of the most severe arise from the most neglected neighborhoods. Because of their marginal place in the socioeconomic and cultural landscape of any given city, ghettos, slums, and barrios have been beset by public health issues, a degraded and neglected infrastructure, increased pollution from nearby factories, and lack of city services. These environmental problems can be divided into two broad epochs: problems related to URBANIZATION and industrialization from the mid-19th century until WORLD WAR II (1941–45) and problems caused by deindustrialization, urban decentralization, and racial segmentation in the postwar era.

Although often used interchangeably, these terms, especially *ghetto* and *slum,* have specific historical meanings. *Ghetto,* originally used for Jewish neighborhoods in Europe, referred to places where different racial and ethnic groups in American cities were also forced to live because of de facto and de jure discrimination. A *slum* generally referred to an area of the city with severely degraded housing stock that attracted the poorest residents because of low rents. Historically, a slum was not necessarily a ghetto, and a ghetto was not necessarily a slum. However, the stratification of the American metropolis by class and race since World War II slowly erased this line, as the most decrepit and physically neglected parts of cities became the places where poor and working classes and racial and ethnic minorities lived. The English translation of *barrio* is simply "community" or "neighborhood." In the United States, however, barrios are often likened to ghettos or slums—neighborhoods that are populated mainly by poor Hispanics and have severely degraded physical infrastructures.

By the early 19th century, American cities were large enough to have significant environmental problems, but ghettoization did not begin in earnest until midcentury. As cities grew, immigrants and rural migrants populated older areas that the established and affluent abandoned. With the influx of eastern and southern European immigrants into American cities at the end of the 1800s, reformers and journalists began to notice the environmental problems posed by these cramped and unsanitary conditions in places such as NEW YORK CITY's Lower East Side and CHICAGO, ILLINOIS's West End. In *How the Other Half Lives* (1890), JACOB RIIS explained how landlords took advantage of a lack of housing to subdivide apartments and cram four families into a space designed for one with rudimentary sanitary facilities and little access to freshwater. His work sparked efforts by reform groups nationwide to expose how low wages and a lack of housing forced the poor to live in decrepit conditions. Earlier reformers blamed the slum dwellers for their unsanitary living conditions, attributing it to their lack of morals or ethnic and racial inferiority.

The study of slum and ghetto conditions became more systematic in the 1920s. At the University of Chicago, the sociologist Robert Park (1864–1944) developed the succession theory of slums and ghettos. Park and his associates argued that recent immigrants and racial and ethnic minorities moved to slums because these were the older areas with the cheapest rents, abandoned by more established groups. As these groups adjusted to urban life, they moved to newer areas with better housing and city services. The study of city housing conditions entered the political realm in the 1930s with the PUBLIC HOUSING movement. Reformers such as Catherine Bauer (1905–64) based their proposals for public housing on a negative assessment of the cramped, polluted environment of the modern city and called for clean and efficient modern housing for America's workers.

Although this prewar research examined the unique discrimination that African Americans faced, its relevance was bypassed by the hardening of racial segregation in the middle of the 20th century, especially when the second large great migration from the South (1940–70) caused a surge in urban black populations. In places as diverse as New York City, Oakland, California, and ST. LOUIS, MISSOURI, de jure and de facto segregation and economic decline brought about a profound shift in urban environmental problems. For the previous 100 years, the problems of breakneck growth plagued slums and ghettos: cramped, subdivided apartments; overburdened and insufficient city services; and a lack of access to parks and open space. Although the poor and working class felt these problems most acutely, environmental problems were spread more equitably among different racial and ethnic groups.

After World War II, those burdens fell predominantly on the poor, especially African Americans and Hispanics. The booming suburbs opened up single-family homeownership to a broad swath of America's expanding middle class. Discrimination in jobs and housing, however, meant that many Hispanics and African Americans could only find housing in older central cities. By the 1960s, these central cities suffered from severe economic problems, as individual factories and entire industries moved to newer plants in the suburbs or the rapidly growing SUNBELT. Urban leaders faced a number of difficulties and had a shrinking tax base with which to fund solutions. In response, they invested in projects such as stadiums and convention centers that privileged downtown business and property interests, or projects such as highways that actively destroyed central city neighborhoods.

Within this context, many Americans equated the slum with the ghetto. Places where racial and ethnic minorities were forced to live were also the cities' most degraded neighborhoods. Their apartments were not the overcrowded TENEMENTS of Riis's Lower East Side but buildings neglected and abandoned by their owners. Neglect exposed families to poor plumbing, insufficient heating, and LEAD poisoning

In the United States, lack of political influence makes ghettos, slums, and barrios especially vulnerable to environmental problems including waste sites and air pollution. This photograph, taken by Carl Mydans in July 1935, shows backyards in Washington, D.C. The Capitol can be seen in the background.   *(Library of Congress)*

from peeling paint and plaster. In the late 1960s, urban activists utilized the lead paint issue in places like New York and Chicago to argue that "slums kill." Childhood lead paint poisoning was only the most noticeable of problems. Tight budgets forced cities to curb trash pickup, and African-American and Hispanic residents felt that politicians unfairly targeted their neighborhoods. In the late 1960s, black and Puerto Rican New Yorkers dragged their GARBAGE into the streets in parts of Harlem and Brooklyn, an informal protest against the perceived neglect of their communities by the city government. Black Power advocates in cities across the country argued that the condition of inner-city neighborhoods was evidence of not just benign neglect but the colonial relationship between the ghetto and the rest of the metropolis.

Since the 1980s, activists described these environmental problems as examples of environmental RACISM and placed them under the broad purview of the ENVIRONMENTAL JUSTICE movement. Although the siting of toxic waste sites within minority and working-class communities was this

movement's original focus, activists expanded their critique to examine the increased AIR POLLUTION burdens and incidences of asthma in urban neighborhoods, lack of access to transportation and healthy FOOD supplies, and the density of BROWNFIELDS and SUPERFUND sites in minority communities. Environmental justice advocates are the most recent in a long line of activists, reformers, and commentators who highlighted the unique problems of the ghetto, slum, and barrio.

See also ALLERGIES AND ASTHMA; CARCINOGENS, POISONS, AND TOXINS; INTERSTATE HIGHWAY SYSTEM; PUBLIC WORKS; SUBURBANIZATION; URBANIZATION; URBAN RENEWAL; URBAN SPRAWL.

Robert Gioielli

Further Reading

Bullard, Robert D., Glenn S. Johnson, and Angel O. Torres. *Sprawl City: Race, Politics, and Planning in Atlanta.* Washington, D.C.: Island Press, 2000.

Gandy, Matthew. "Between Borinquen and the Barrio: Environmental Justice and New York City's Puerto Rican Community, 1969–1972." *Antipode* 34, no. 4 (2002): 730–761.

Hirsch, Arnold R. *Making the Second Ghetto: Race and Housing in Chicago, 1940–1960, Historical Studies of Urban America.* Chicago: University of Chicago Press, 1998.

Sussman, Carl. *Planning the Fourth Migration: The Neglected Vision of the Regional Planning Association of America.* Cambridge, Mass.: MIT Press, 1976.

Ghost Dance

The Ghost Dance of 1889–90, an American Indian religious movement, had significant environmental dimensions. For many tribes, it promised an environmental restoration in line with their spiritual conceptions of the natural world. Through their ritualistic dancing and singing, Ghost Dancers sought to bring forth a renewed earth where indigenous ecosystems would be restored, dead ancestors would be revived, disease would be eradicated, and traditional livelihoods would be revitalized. While there could be considerable variance among tribes on this point, many dancers believed that a series of massive natural events would usher in the new world and usher out Euro-Americans. According to the Southern Plains faithful, a conflagration would sweep over the existing world, which would then be plunged beneath the advancing new world. During the event, Ghost Dancers would take flight with their sacred feathers only to land after its completion. The Ghost Dance religion appealed to tribal peoples who had experienced land dispossession, resource depletion, the ravages of disease, and ongoing assaults on their cultures as a result of Euro-American colonization in the 19th century.

The Ghost Dance originated in the Mason Valley of western Nevada and spread rapidly across the Rockies onto the Great Plains. Its founding prophet was Wovoka, or Jack Wilson, a Paiute who had adjusted to Euro-American colonization by laboring in the local mining and ranching economy. While Wovoka (ca. 1856–1932) engaged in the market economy and even learned some Christian teachings from a white family with whom he had ties, he maintained his traditional Paiute beliefs and practices. Wovoka's life, however, took a dramatic turn after a solar eclipse on January 1, 1889. Perhaps induced by a bout with scarlet fever that had scorched through the Paiute population in the late 1880s, Wovoka fell into a deep sleep and was transported to the spiritual world. He met the creator, who gave him the message of the Ghost Dance. Upon Wovoka's recovery, the sun shone forth from the darkness that was about to engulf it, and Wovoka was widely credited among the Paiute with saving it. He proceeded to preach a message of moral living and ritualistic dancing in preparation for reuniting with deceased ancestors in the world to come, which would be teeming with traditional resources. Gaining adherents through such feats as ensuring rains in the midst of DROUGHTS, Wovoka's message took root among many Paiute. The promise of Wovoka's prophesied world attracted several western tribes, who sent representatives to learn more about the religion.

The Lakota were receptive to the message of the Ghost Dance. Discontent pervaded their reservations, where environmental conditions had deteriorated. Under an 1889 law, the United States shattered the Great Sioux Reservation into separate reservations and took an additional nine million acres from the Indians. On the reduced reservations, government agricultural policies were ill suited for the semiarid climate of the western plains, particularly during a late 19th-century drought, and thus undermined crop yields. With the great BISON herds decimated by Euro-American resettlement, the Lakota turned to government rations, which were always precarious. Suffering from malnutrition, some Lakota succumbed to measles, INFLUENZA, and whooping cough. Through emissaries who had visited Wovoka in 1889 and 1890, the Lakota learned of the prophet's spiritual message, which promised demographic, environmental, and cultural rejuvenation. Many joined the religious movement as a spiritual means for restoring the bison and their dead and expelling the Euro-Americans, who had distressed the Lakota environment and culture. Singing inspired songs, followers danced together in a circle in the hope of being transported to the spiritual realm for a glimpse of the world to come. Ultimately, the Lakota movement was cut short by the overreaction of Euro-American settlers and officials that led to the killing of Sitting Bull and the massacre of Bigfoot's band of Miniconjou Lakota at Wounded Knee in December 1890.

Wovoka's message had continuing relevance for many tribal communities beyond 1890. While some scholars end their treatments of the Ghost Dance movement with the Wounded Knee Massacre, others point out that the religion persisted among some western tribes in modified forms into the 20th century and has even been revived by some traditionalist leaders of the present day.

See also AGRICULTURE, FEDERAL POLICIES; BUREAU OF INDIAN AFFAIRS; FEDERAL LAW—INDIAN POLICIES; INDIANS, CENTRAL PLAINS; INDIANS, COLUMBIA PLATEAU AND GREAT BASIN; INDIANS, NORTHERN PLAINS; UNITED STATES—CENTRAL PLAINS; UNITED STATES—COLUMBIA PLATEAU AND GREAT BASIN; UNITED STATES—NORTHERN PLAINS.

John Husmann

Further Reading
Hittman, Michael. *Wovoka and the Ghost Dance.* Edited by Don Lynch. Lincoln: University of Nebraska Press, 1997.

Kehoe, Alice Beck. *The Ghost Dance: Ethnohistory and Revitalization.* Fort Worth, Tex.: Holt, Rinehart & Winston, 1989.

Mooney, James. *The Ghost-Dance Religion and the Sioux Out-break of 1890.* Introduction by Raymond J. DeMallie. Reprint, Lincoln: University of Nebraska Press, 1991.

Ostler, Jeffrey. *The Plains Sioux and U.S. Colonialism from Lewis and Clark to Wounded Knee.* Cambridge: Cambridge University Press, 2004.

Thornton, Russell. *We Shall Live Again: The 1870 and 1890 Ghost Dance Movements as Demographic Revitalization.* Cambridge: Cambridge University Press, 1986.

Utley, Robert M. *The Last Days of the Sioux Nation.* 2d ed. New Haven, Conn.: Yale University Press, 2004.

Gibbs, Lois Marie (1951–   ) *environmental activist*

Lois Gibbs first gained fame when she organized and led a group of homeowners in a campaign to force local, state, and federal governments to clean up the toxic waste dump in their neighborhood, LOVE CANAL, in NIAGARA FALLS, New York. She remains a leader in the ENVIRONMENTAL JUSTICE movement.

Lois Marie Gibbs was born on June 25, 1951, in Buffalo, New York, to Joseph and Patricia Conn. To support his working-class family, Joseph Conn worked as a brick-layer, providing a comfortable, if not extravagant, life for his homemaker wife and six children. Lois was a quiet, slim girl who often wore her hair in pigtails and tried to remain out of the spotlight in school. Her family lived on Grand Island, a small rural community in Upstate New York, located between Buffalo and Niagara Falls between the forks of the Niagara River.

In 1971, just out of high school, Lois married Harry Gibbs, a young man a year ahead of her at Grand Island High School. Harry Gibbs obtained a job at Goodyear Chemical Company in Niagara Falls, and the couple settled into married life. Lois Gibbs soon became pregnant and gave birth to the couple's first child, Michael, in 1972, and a daughter, Melissa (Missy), in 1975. Shortly before Missy's birth, the family moved from Grand Island to a modest home in a small neighborhood known as LaSalle on the outskirts of Niagara Falls.

Although LaSalle soon became famous as "Love Canal," the residents who filled the modest, inexpensive homes knew little to nothing about the neighborhood's history. To Gibbs, it seemed a perfect place to raise a family, with neat homes, clean streets, gardens and pools in backyards, lots of kids, and a school within walking distance. Unbeknownst to Gibbs, and most of the residents, their neighborhood had been constructed on top of a hazardous waste dump, whose history stretched back to before the turn of the century. In the early 1890s, the entrepreneur William Love began digging a canal to link the Niagara River to Lake Ontario, bypassing the dangerous falls. His plan fell victim to an eco-nomic depression in 1893, leaving the canal only partially completed. The city of Niagara Falls recovered from the depression and quickly developed into an industrial center powered by the water flowing to the falls. One of the companies situated in the area was Hooker Chemical, which soon began disposing of a variety of their waste products in the canal. After filling the canal, Hooker Chemical sold the area to the local school board for a dollar. Construction of a school for the rapidly growing population proceeded along-side the development of homes for working-class families in the area. After a series of heavy rains and snowfalls in the late 1970s, some of the buried waste bubbled to the surface and resulted in numerous complaints of strange odors, flooded basements and choked sump pumps, and illnesses, especially of children.

These illnesses also affected the Gibbs family. In 1977, shortly after he began school, Michael began to suffer from a variety of ailments, none of which doctors explained satisfactorily to Gibbs. He developed epilepsy, had mysterious low white blood cell counts, had surgery for urethral strictures, and had problems with ALLERGIES AND ASTHMA. Gibbs eventually connected Michael's illnesses with a series of articles written by Michael Brown, a reporter for the *Niagara Gazette,* about the variety of chemicals present at Love Canal.

An alarming announcement by the New York health commissioner, Robert Whalen, on August 2, 1978, further frightened the Love Canal residents. As a result of several studies, Whalen announced that Love Canal was a serious health threat to the people who lived near it. Whalen recommended the relocation of pregnant women and children below age two as a safety precaution.

Armed with knowledge about the area, and the health commissioner's warnings, Gibbs organized her neighbors into the Love Canal Homeowners Association (LCHA). Her working-class background consistently informed her leadership and activism. Thoroughly familiar with union tactics because of both her father's and her husband's ties, Gibbs frequently used marches, demonstrations, and pickets of the site to express her views. Area unions also supported Gibbs financially, as well as with people and resources. In addition, in her role as a working-class housewife, Gibbs found that appeals for help based on her status as a mother resonated loudly in the MEDIA. The LCHA consistently pressed for change to protect the health and safety of their children, a tactic known as maternalism.

Using maternalism, the LCHA worked for relocation of the neighborhood, along with compensation for homes, for the affected residents. Some of the residents escaped quickly, since the government decided to assist those closest to the canal not long after the Whalen announcement. The rest of the neighborhood, including a mostly African-American housing project, fought through three years of opposition and red tape before the government finally agreed to assist in 1981.

After the government agreed to purchase all the homes, Gibbs decided to leave Niagara Falls. Her marriage had disintegrated as a result of the crisis, as had many area marriages. Harry Gibbs wanted his family to return to "normal," with Lois Gibbs as homemaker. Lois, on the other hand, found her calling through her activism at Love Canal. She felt a need to continue her work and try to assist others with similar struggles. She moved to Falls Church, Virginia, where she established the Citizen's Clearinghouse for Hazardous Waste (CCHW) in 1981. The CCHW was later renamed the Center for Health, Environment, and Justice (CHEJ).

In her job as founder and executive director of the CHEJ, Gibbs works tirelessly to promote various environmental causes. The CHEJ currently extols the dangers of polyvinylchloride (PVC) plastics and has pressed for corporations as varied as Microsoft and Johnson & Johnson to stop using the material. In addition, the group provides organizing assistance and valuable know-how for hundreds of local resident groups across the country struggling with similar environmental problems. In addition to her duties at the CHEJ, Gibbs is the author of several books, including an autobiographical account of her activism at Love Canal. After her move to Virginia, Gibbs married Stephen Lester, who assisted with the scientific data at Love Canal and currently also works for the CHEJ. The couple have two children of their own, Ryan and Christopher.

Gibbs is still active in the fight over Love Canal. She struggled against the reintroduction of families into the Black Creek area directly north of the canal, arguing that even though the ENVIRONMENTAL PROTECTION AGENCY (EPA) had declared the area "habitable," no one ever declared it "safe." She also organizes rallies and events to commemorate and keep the memory of the Love Canal struggle alive.

See also CARCINOGENS, POISONS, AND TOXINS; CORPORATIONS, CHEMICAL; ENVIRONMENTALISM, MAINSTREAM; SUPERFUND.

Elizabeth D. Blum

Further Reading

Blum, Elizabeth D. *Enlarging the Picture at Love Canal: Race, Class, and Gender in Environmental Activism.* Lawrence: University Press of Kansas, 2008.

Center for Health, Environment, and Justice Web site. Available online. URL: http://chej.org. Accessed September 30, 2008.

Gibbs, Lois. *Love Canal: The Story Continues. . . .* Stony Creek, Canada: New Society, 1998.

Levine, Adeline Gordon. *Love Canal: Science, Politics, and People.* Lexington, Mass.: D. C. Heath, 1982.

Mazur, Allan. *A Hazardous Inquiry: The Rashomon Effect at Love Canal.* Cambridge, Mass.: Harvard University Press, 1998.

Lois Gibbs Testifies before Congress on Love Canal (1979)

Propelled to activism in 1978 when she discovered that her Love Canal neighborhood in Niagara Falls, New York, sat atop a toxic waste dump, Lois Gibbs led her neighbors in gathering data on diseases and birth defects, organizing protests, and forcing state and federal officials to relocate some 800 families and clean up Love Canal. On March 21, 1979, she testified before a congressional subcommittee and called for federal intervention. "We are the first," Gibbs told Congress, "but we are not likely to be the last."

March 21, 1979
Testimony Presented to the House Sub-committee on Oversight & Investigations
Lois M. Gibbs, President, Love Canal Homeowners Association

My name is Lois Gibbs and I am president of the Love Canal Home-owners Association (L.C.H.A.). The L.C.H.A. is a citizens group consisting of over 1,000 families representing more than 90% of the residents in the area. L.C.H.A. was formed to deal with the problem of living near the Love Canal chemical dumpsite. I became involved in this situation after discovering that toxic chemicals were buried two blocks from my home and that these chemicals could be aggravating my children's health problems, one of whom attended the 99th Street School located in the center of the dump. I started by canvassing the neighborhood to find if other residents had similar problems. I discovered that the majority of residents had what seemed to me an unusually high amount of illnesses. I then worked with residents to form an organization to identify their problems and to help them find solutions.

The L.C.H.A. was formed to voice the opinion of residents on the decisions made by State authorities which would affect our lives. . . .

The means and capabilities of the State and local resources were—and still are—simply not sufficient to protect the public health and welfare of the residents during such an emergency situation. . . .

Because of the fear of panic, the State did not know how far to involve the residents in the decisions and findings that were made. And officials often did not inspire confidence in the residents, which made matters worse. . . . Many of the chemicals in the canal were unknown as was the boundary of the canal. . . . These uncertainties frightened the residents and we demanded a safety plan and an on-site monitor to help provide protection for the residents in the event of an accident. What resulted was a meeting held by the Office of Disaster Preparedness during which a "total" safety plan was prepared and later presented to the residents at a public meeting. However, the confidence in this plan was greatly shaken by a statement made by a State spokesman who, when asked to comment on what he would do if toxic vapors were released through the neighborhood, replied: "I wouldn't wait for the bus, I'd run like hell". . . .

First of all it is apparent that a means for responding to environmental incidents such as Love Canal must be provided by the Federal government. A group analogous to the infectious disease response unit of the Center for Disease Control should be set up to respond to environmental emergencies that require immediate action and special expertise. Specialists in the effects of chemicals on skin disease, kidney disorders, urinary infections, and so on could be alerted and called in as needed. This did not happen at Love Canal. We are the first but we are not likely to be the last.

⸺◈⸺

Source: "Transcript of Testimony, Love Canal Collection, University Library, State University of New York at Buffalo." Available online. URL: http://library.buffalo.edu/libraries/specialcollections/lovecanal/documents/disaster_gif/records/gi bbs1.html. Accessed November 13, 2008.

Gilded Age

The Gilded Age, roughly the 1870s to around 1900, represented a paradox in terms of the environmental history of the United States. Rapid westward expansion and industrial and urban growth led to extraordinary damage to the environment. At the same time as the nation grew, so, too, did the middle class, and as time passed, it displayed an increasing concern about the cost of unbridled expansion and interest in protecting the environment.

MARK TWAIN coined the phrase "the Gilded Age," in his novel *The Gilded Age* (1873), cowritten by Charles Dudley Warner. He employed the term to satirize the extensive corruption and "all-pervading speculativeness" of the times. Historians have similarly used the term *Gilded Age* to describe the era following RECONSTRUCTION. As did Twain, they tend to portray the era as one of unbridled or unregulated industrial growth, extensive political corruption, and extreme aggregations of wealth and power. Chronologically, the Gilded Age also coincided with the rapid settlement of the trans-Mississippi West.

American BISON symbolized the harm done to the environment in the West during the Gilded Age. Prior to the CIVIL WAR (1861–65), bison had been so plentiful that observers used adjectives like *immense* and *countless* to describe the size of their herds. By the best estimate, about 30 to 60 million bison roamed free before HORSES arrived along with Europeans. In the middle of the 19th century, however, millions were killed each year, some for sport, many others for their hides. As a result, by the end of the 19th century, they were on the verge of EXTINCTION.

Western settlement by European Americans had a significant impact on other aspects of the Plains' ecology at the end of the 19th century. Miners dug up the earth in search of valuable metals, such as GOLD, silver, and COPPER; cowboys drove thousands of feral CATTLE overland to markets in Kansas and then (after the great era of the cattle drive had ended) grazed massive herds of livestock on the high plains. Farmers busted up the sod, replaced native GRASSES with MONOCULTURE crops, and turned a fragile but stable prairie ecosystem into a DUST BOWL in a few generations. Numerous other species of animals, such as WOLVES, which were seen as a threat to livestock, fared nearly as poorly as the bison in the face of unregulated growth.

The Gilded Age also witnessed the cutting down of massive FORESTS, especially in the Midwest, which in turn led to increased soil EROSION and more dangerous FLOODS. For instance, in the 25 years between the end of the Civil War and 1890, 95 percent of forests in Michigan were cut down. Likewise, thousands of acres of trees in Wisconsin were felled in the latter part of the 19th century to clear the land for farming and for building material and fuel. In 1889, the United States experienced one of its most deadly natural disasters in history when a flood, caused by a broken dam, leveled the city of Johnston, Pennsylvania, leaving more than 2,200 dead. While torrential rains and a poorly designed and maintained dam caused the flood, denuded or deforested hillsides contributed to its severity.

As rapidly as the West grew in the late 19th century, urban areas expanded even more dramatically. CHICAGO, ILLINOIS, with a population increase from 298,000 in 1870 to nearly 1.7 million in 1900, became the symbol of America's urban landscape. Chicago served as the transportation nexus and marketplace for the surrounding agricultural and mineral extraction regions. Its growth depended upon an ENGINEERING miracle, namely, the ability to change the flow of the Chicago River, so that it flowed into rather than away from Lake Michigan. This feat allowed the city to dump its waste into the GREAT LAKES, much to the detriment of the health of the lake itself.

Nearly every American city, including Chicago, became inundated with waste and air pollution. Dark sooty air was the rule, the by-product of factory smoke and COAL burning stoves and furnaces. Human and animal waste festered in city streets, and rivers died. The Passaic River in New Jersey, for instance, supported a substantial commercial fishing industry prior to the Civil War. By the latter part of the 19th century, however, factory and human waste not only killed most of the fish but left the river smelling so bad on hot summer days that factories had to close down. Overcrowded and unsanitary conditions also increased the risk of deadly diseases. CHOLERA, TYPHOID, and TUBERCULOSIS increased in frequency as cities grew.

Rapid westward and urban expansion generated a counterforce. Middle-class Americans sought respite from the dangers, environmental and social, of the cities where they worked and lived. Various forms of OUTDOOR REACTION, from camping and hunting to bird-watching, rose in popularity. Fearful that some of America's western treasures were in jeopardy, activists lobbied for federal protection. In 1872, Congress established YELLOWSTONE National Park—eight years earlier ABRAHAM LINCOLN had given California control of the area that became YOSEMITE NATIONAL PARK to protect. Ironically, some of the largest RAILROADS, the engines of industrial and westward expansion, promoted these parks so as to boost the tourist trade, which in turn would aid their bottom line. Several decades later, the federal government began to establish forest reserves. Similarly, cities witnessed the development of the CITY BEAUTIFUL AND CITY EFFICIENT movements. Most famously, NEW YORK CITY constructed Central Park. Many of these developments paved the way for the rise of a broader progressive movement in the early decades of the 20th century.

Finally, the Gilded Age served as the springboard for the modern environmental movement. From the writings and activities of GEORGE PERKINS MARSH, JOHN MUIR, and JOHN WESLEY POWELL grew a different sense of the WILDERNESS. Muir, in particular, even if he did not have the scientific understanding of modern ecologists, intuited the interrelationship of all parts of the natural world. Seeing the damage that overgrazing was doing to the subalpine regions surrounding Yosemite Valley, he lobbied successfully for the creation of a larger National Park. And when his fellow conservationists, such as GIFFORD PINCHOT, called for creating a reservoir in part of the park in order to meet the needs of the residents of SAN FRANCISCO, CALIFORNIA, Muir served as the champion of the rocks, trees, and animals whose innate beauty he judged as important as that of his fellow man. Others joined with Muir to fight the construction of the Hetch Hetchy Dam in HETCH HETCHY VALLEY, California, which would flood part of the original park, and to establish the

SIERRA CLUB, one of the cornerstones of the modern environmental movement.

In sum, the Gilded Age stood out as a period of environmental degradation. Rapid and unregulated growth depleted natural resources and created unprecedented damage to the nation's waterways. Yet, at the same time, as the economy expanded, so, too, did the middle and upper-middle classes. And, in time, these classes would provide the basis for a growing movement to protect the wilderness.

See also CONSERVATION; DISEASES, HUMAN; NATIONAL PARK SERVICE; PROGRESSIVISM; OLMSTED, FREDERICK LAW, SR.; POLLUTION, AIR; POLLUTION, WATER; URBANIZATION; WASTE DISPOSAL AND MANAGEMENT.

Peter B. Levy

Further Reading
Bilsky, Lester J., ed. *Historical Ecology: Essays on Environmental and Social Change.* Port Washington, N.Y.: Kennikat Press, 1980.
Melosi, Martin, ed. *Pollution and Reform in American Cities, 1879–1930.* Austin: University of Texas Press, 1980.
Worster, Donald. *Under Western Skies: Nature and History in the American West.* New York: Oxford University Press, 1992.

Gilpin, Laura (1891–1979) *landscape photographer, author*

Laura Gilpin was one of the nation's most prominent photographers. Best known for stunning portraits of Navajo and other southwestern Indians, Gilpin depicted the weathered, handsome, and dignified faces of people who built a rich, enduring culture in a harsh environment. Her photographs of the RIO GRANDE in the late 1940s revealed a river stressed by cultural demands on both sides of the U.S.-Mexico border.

Born in Austin Bluffs, Colorado, on April 22, 1891, Gilpin was a westerner by birth and outlook. Her parents, Frank and Emma Miller Gilpin, struggled to succeed at ranching, while their outdoorsy, unpretentious daughter explored the foothills of the ROCKY MOUNTAINS. At age 12, Gilpin received a Brownie camera. Using family members and surrounding scenery as her subjects, she showed an innate gift for PHOTOGRAPHY. Gilpin was educated at eastern boarding schools from 1905 to 1910, until dwindling family funds forced her to return to Colorado. Gilpin earned enough by 1916 to return to NEW YORK CITY and attend Clarence H. White School of Photography for two years. She improved her skills, met influential artists, and concluded that commercial photography was an acceptable career choice.

Returning to Colorado, Gilpin supported herself with advertising and portraiture work but explored the larger region in her free time. She photographed the Pueblo Indians and the ancestral remains of the Anasazi Indians in the gauzy, romantic style of her teacher, Clarence White. Her first book,

The Pueblos: A Camera Chronicle, appeared in 1941. In time, Gilpin exchanged White's approach for her own "hard-edged" style. Her friendships with many Native Americans, which began in the 1930s, gave her portraiture a sense of intimacy rarely captured by outsiders. She worked briefly as a photographer for the Boeing Company in Kansas during WORLD WAR II (1941–45) before relocating to Santa Fe, New Mexico. Her photographic studies revealed rugged country where human occupation, both past and present, was evident. She published two more books, *In Yucatan: A Camera Chronicle of Chichen Itza* (1948) and *The Rio Grande: River of Destiny: An Interpretation of the River, the Land, and the People* (1949).

Gilpin's book on the Rio Grande represented her strongest environmental statement. She wrote the words that accompanied her photographs. Gilpin tracked the 1,900-mile-long river from its source in Colorado's San Juan Mountains as it wends its way through New Mexico, Mexico, and Texas toward the Gulf of Mexico just beyond the twin cities of Brownsville, Texas, and Matamoros, Mexico. Historically, the Rio Grande served arid lands beyond the 100th meridian. Over centuries, as the Rio Grande descended from the mountains each spring, snowmelt swelled the river and slowly carved scenic gorges. During other seasons in desert country, the Rio Grande shrank to delicate, curvilinear traces on its way to the sea. Gilpin revealed the rich cultures that Indian, Mexican, and American people created along the river.

Her subjects, like the Navajo in her earlier work, are lean, dignified, hard-working people who live in a challenging environment. All took from the river in order to survive. Some, like the Native Americans, were more balanced than others in their withdrawals, Gilpin argued. Loggers, by contrast, cut away at adjoining forests that acted as natural water tanks during DROUGHTS, bastions of flood control, and nurturers of underground aquifers. Ranchers let CATTLE herds and flocks of sheep overgraze on soil-protecting grasslands and drove wild ungulates (hoofed animals) from long-established habitats. Farmers diverted the river for IRRIGATION, and industrialists harnessed its energy for hydroelectric power. URBANIZATION intensified river usage the farther south the river flowed.

Gilpin's photographs captured extreme drought conditions between 1945 and 1948. Presciently, she wrote, "The volume of the river has been diminished through misuse of vast drainage areas." She blamed indiscriminate DEFORESTATION and depletion of indigenous GRASSES. Gilpin's message about the increasingly compromised Rio Grande was unheeded even as the vivid beauty of her riverscapes and the solemn faces of their denizens drew recognition and accolades. In 1930, the Royal Photographic Society of Great Britain inducted Gilpin. She received a Guggenheim grant at age 84. She died on November 30, 1979. Gilpin's photographs, negatives, and personal papers are housed at the Amon Carter Museum in Fort Worth, Texas.

See also ART; DAMS, RESERVOIRS, AND ARTIFICIAL LAKES; INDIANS, SOUTHWEST; LANDSCAPE ART, AMERICAN; MEXICO AND THE UNITED STATES; UNITED STATES—GULF COAST; UNITED STATES—SOUTHWEST.

JoEllen Broome

Further Reading

Gilpin, Laura. *The Rio Grande: River of Destiny: An Interpretation of the River, the Land, and the People.* New York: Duell, Sloan and Pearce, 1949.
Sandweiss, Martha A. *American National Biography.* New York: Oxford University Press, 1999.
———. *Laura Gilpin: An Enduring Grace.* Fort Worth, Tex.: A. Carter Museum, 1986.

Girl Scouts   *See* BOY SCOUTS AND GIRL SCOUTS.

glaciers

Serene yet great, roaring yet silent, static at a glance but always changing—glaciers provide a substantial muse. Glaciers exist on every continent and in 47 countries, including the United States. Broadly defined, glaciers are massive rivers of ice, created by multiple layers of compacted snow, which form in the Earth's mountainous alpine regions and at the tremendously cold polar regions. Scientists classify glaciers as either alpine or continental. Although nearly 70 percent of the planet's freshwater can be found in the Antarctic ice sheet alone, the magnificence of glacial ice does not result solely from the fact that it is the largest reservoir of freshwater on planet Earth. Glacial ice has transformed Earth's surface and continues to do so, while playing a central role in the dynamic processes (hydrological, geological, and biological) of this planet.

As does other ice, glacial ice consists of just two hydrogen atoms attached to an oxygen atom, creating a molecule that is repetitively linked in a near-tetrahedral arrangement around a central molecule. Although deceptively straightforward, this fascinating chemical structure of ice, in response to repeated temperature changes and precipitation, allows for the formation of glaciers. This process is known as glaciation.

Since the 1820s, scientists have acknowledged the existence of numerous ice ages in the Earth's history, which were directly related to the cyclical fluctuations in the planet's orbit around the Sun. Since the discovery of these past ice ages, there have been correlating challenges about the origin and evolution of the Earth, especially from those who held to a literal interpretation of the revealed faith traditions. Nonetheless, this planet is immensely old and constantly changing. Humans have observed glacier changes for centuries.

Modern continental glaciers are invariably associated with the immense ice sheets of the Pliocene period. These glaciers once covered much of the planet's surface, including large portions of North America. Glacial deposits and large areas of striated bedrock evidence their existence throughout the northern United States and Canada. Continental glaciers do not currently exist in the United States and are found only in Greenland and Antarctica. However, numerous small alpine glaciers are located across the mountainous regions of the western United States. This sizable area encompasses California, Colorado, Idaho, Montana, Nevada, Oregon, Utah, Washington, and Wyoming. Larger alpine glaciers are found in Alaska and the ROCKY MOUNTAINS. Alpine glaciers are much smaller than continental glaciers. Alpine glaciers flow downward from high elevations as a result of internal pressure adjustments caused by external temperature and precipitation fluctuations.

Alpine glaciers in the U.S. and Canadian Rocky Mountains reached maximal size in the Holocene period during the time of significant cooling known as the Little Ice Age. This began around the 13th century C.E. and ended approximately in the mid-19th century. Most scientists agree that summer temperatures and winter snowpack control the net balance of glaciers in the western United States. Current research further indicates that U.S. glacier accumulation and ablation (the removal of ice or snow from a glacier) are strongly correlated with the Pacific Ocean's sea-surface temperature, atmospheric circulation, and regional snowpack patterns. Alpine glaciers have greatly affected the U.S. environment by carving and

Taking on various forms and sizes, glaciers and ice caps hold huge amounts of water—approximately 59 percent of the world's freshwater. Glaciers, however, are threatened by global warming and, if substantially melted, could dramatically raise the Earth's sea levels. Here, two kayakers watch ice calving from Muir Glacier Bay National Park. *(© Hulton-Deutsch Collection/CORBIS)*

accentuating large portions of topography. Glaciers are comparable to large conveyor belts and often transport materials far away from the zone of accumulation. Glacial erosion and deposition in the United States have created a variety of landforms: V-shaped valleys, U-shaped valleys, hanging valleys, cirques, tarns, arêtes, and horns. Glaciers, for example, helped form the GREAT LAKES. When the ice sheet receded at the end of the last ice age, it carved out large basins. These basins filled with melted water and became the Great Lakes.

At the end of the 20th century and beginning of the 21st century, scientific observation of glaciers significantly expanded. To a large extent, the heightened interest in glaciers is due to the link between glacier retreat and global CLIMATE CHANGE. As the priority of glacier monitoring increases, improved funding and new techniques have permitted more detailed and efficient data collection and analysis. Several organizations, such as the World Glacier Monitoring Service (WGMS), the UNITED NATIONS Educational, Scientific, and Cultural Organization (UNESCO), and the International Geosphere-Biosphere Program (IGBP), have consistently produced systematized data sets that demonstrate the relationship between climate change and glacier retreat. In 2007, these data sets composed a major part of the Fourth Assessment Report by the Intergovernmental Panel on Climate Change (IPCC). Glacial changes involve many variables. Variation in precipitation, also related to climate change, can affect glacial change. Furthermore, because of the gigantic size of many glaciers, the corresponding response to shifts in temperature can be somewhat delayed. However, scientists increasingly recognize glacial changes (length, area, or volume) as a phenomenon of global change in climate and living conditions on Earth.

The identification of the role that glaciers play has inspired geologists and hydrologists alike to understand the environmental processes that affect these slow-moving rivers of ice. Although individual glaciers present differing response and retreat times, depending on topography and orientation, by the simplest account, rising temperatures and the accelerated pace of glacial retreat are inextricably linked. This understanding bestows on the inhabitants of this planet the responsibility of allowing glaciation, and the dynamic processes it involves, to proceed on a natural and unchanged course.

See also CANADA AND THE UNITED STATES; GLOBAL WARMING; OCEANS; UNITED STATES—ALASKA.

Charles F. Goddard

Further Reading

Barry, G. Roger. "The Status of Research on Glaciers and Global Glacier Recession." *Progress in Physical Geography* 30 (2006): 288–306.

Bitz, M. Cecilia, and D. S. Battisti. "Interannual to Decadal Variability in Climate and the Glacier Mass Balance in Washington, Western Canada, and Alaska." *Journal of Climate* 14 (1999): 5–10.

Meier, F. Mark, and R. A. Walters. "Variability of Glacier Mass Balances in Western North America: Aspects of Climate Variability in the Pacific and Western Americas." *Geophysical Monographs* 55 (1989): 365–374.

Glen Canyon Dam

The Glen Canyon Dam on the COLORADO RIVER in northern Arizona is perhaps the most disputed dam in U.S. history, though the dispute largely postdates the damming. The late writer and environmental activist EDWARD ABBEY spoke for many when he said, "Surely no man-made structure in modern American history has been hated so much, by so many, for so long, with such good reason."

The rationale for the dam goes back to the Colorado River Compact of 1922. According to this interstate agreement, the Upper Basin (Utah, Wyoming, Colorado, New Mexico) could retain up to 7.5 million acre-feet of the river per year provided that it first supplied the Lower Basin (California, Nevada, Arizona) with the same amount. The Lower Basin—especially California—moved quickly to develop its share of the river. California found a willing partner in the BUREAU OF RECLAMATION. After WORLD WAR II (1941–45), the Upper Basin appealed to the bureau for its own comprehensive project. It believed it had to start using its allotment or effectively lose the water to the faster-growing Lower Basin.

As designed by the bureau, the Colorado River Storage Project (CRSP) called for a handful of large storage projects—notably Echo Park and Glen Canyon—and 11 participating projects that would actually deliver water. The role of the storage dam was crucial. By regulating the flow of the river, the proposed dams at Echo Park and Glen Canyon would permit the Upper Basin to draw water without fear of preventing its delivery to the Lower Basin. In other words, the Upper Basin had to build big dams so that it could build small dams. This was true both politically and fiscally. Using "river-basin accounting," the bureau offset the cost of the participating projects—most of which were blatantly uneconomical—against the projected revenue from hydroelectric generation from the storage dams.

Until the 1950s, everyone took the bureau at its word: Dams meant progress. But with the CRSP, the agency crossed a line. The proposed Echo Park Dam fell within Dinosaur National Monument. Conservationists organized in opposition; with unprecedented zeal and organization, they worked to prevent a latter-day HETCH HETCHY VALLEY fiasco (a controversy in the early 1990s that had led to the construction of a dam in California that many people had opposed). To their own surprise, they won the battle in CONGRESS. Minus the one offensive dam, the legislation for the CRSP passed easily in 1956. Construction soon began on Glen Canyon Dam. At the time, the preservation of a national monument (and, by implication, the sanctity of the entire national park system) overshadowed the loss of the Glen Canyon.

By the time that Lake Powell—the reservoir behind the dam and the second-largest human-made reservoir in the United States—starting filling in 1963, however, the perspective changed. Out of curiosity, then urgency, thousands of conservationists went to see the condemned canyon. They could not believe their eyes. The 170-mile-long Glen Canyon was a place of heartbreaking beauty, a place that deserved to be a national park. In 1963, the executive director of the SIERRA CLUB, DAVID R. BROWER, produced a famous book of regret and nostalgia about Glen Canyon, *The Place No One Knew*. To drain "Lake Foul" and restore the glen remains a quixotic dream of American environmentalists, who likewise hoped to return a wild river to the downstream GRAND CANYON. Edward Abbey fantasized about blowing up the dam in his 1975 comic novel about ecoterrorists, *The Monkey Wrench Gang,* and the radical environmental organization Earth First! chose the dam as the stage for its inaugural protest in 1981. But Lake Powell has also attracted vocal defenders, who, tellingly, tended to confound the obvious recreational and aesthetic merits of the reservoir with the abstruse political and fiscal purposes of the dam.

Located near the Utah-Arizona border, the structure itself rises 587 feet above the river and contains 4.9 million cubic yards of concrete. At full capacity, it holds back 27 million acre-feet of water, or about two years' flow of the Colorado. The Upper Colorado River Basin, however, experienced DROUGHT in seven of the first nine years in the 21st century, leaving the reservoir at approximately half-capacity and diminishing its OUTDOOR RECREATION facilities. Today, the Glen Canyon Dam remains a grand symbol of the conflict between progressive river development schemes and WILDERNESS preservation initiatives in the West.

See also CONSERVATION; DAMS, RESERVOIRS, AND ARTIFICIAL LAKES; ENVIRONMENTALISM, MAINSTREAM; ENVIRONMENTALISM, RADICAL; IRRIGATION; MEXICO AND THE UNITED STATES; NATIONAL PARK SERVICE; NONGOVERNMENTAL ORGANIZATIONS; PORTER, ELIOT; UNITED STATES—SOUTHWEST.

Jared Farmer

Further Reading
Abbey, Edward. *Desert Solitaire: A Season in the Wilderness.* New York: McGraw-Hill, 1968.
———. *The Monkey Wrench Gang.* Philadelphia: Lippincott, 1975.
Farmer, Jared. *Glen Canyon Dammed: Inventing Lake Powell and the Canyon Country.* Tucson: University of Arizona Press, 1999.
Harvey, Mark W. T., and William Cronon. *A Symbol of Wilderness: Echo Park and the American Conservation Movement.* Albuquerque: University of New Mexico Press, 1994.
Martin, Russell. *A Story That Stands like a Dam: Glen Canyon and the Struggle for the Soul of the West.* New York: Henry Holt, 1989.
Porter, Eliot. *The Place No One Knew: Glen Canyon on the Colorado.* San Francisco: Sierra Club, 1963.

global financial institutions

Global financial institutions are made up of a variety of different commerce and regulatory organizations that operate within the economic sphere of international trade, investment, and development. Unlike local, national, or regional financial institutions, global financial institutions work across borders, operating in most cases independently of governmental involvement. Critics of these institutions argue that they have worked to the benefit of more developed nations, such as the United States, while undermining the people and ECOSYSTEMS of less developed nations.

Modern global financial institutions are largely associated with the United Nations Monetary and Financial Conference of 1944, where representatives from 44 Allied nations met during WORLD WAR II (1941–45) to restructure international financial systems. Popularly known as the "Bretton Woods" conference in reference to Bretton Woods, New Hampshire, where the event took place, the meetings resulted in the formation of two multilateral organizations known as the International Monetary Fund (IMF) and the International Bank for Reconstruction and Development (IBRD)—now one of two organizations within the World Bank. Subsequent negotiations on the topic of trade regulation led to the creation of the 1947 General Agreement on Tariffs and Trade (GATT)—now known as the World Trade Organization. In general, these multilateral instruments were formed to oversee international finance, redevelopment, and trade in a post–World War II era.

INTERNATIONAL MONETARY FUND
The International Monetary Fund was established to remedy balance-of-payment discrepancies among nations that have a significant impact upon exchange rates. As a lending agent, the IMF also provides short-term loans to nations that seek assistance.

The IMF is made up of 185 nations that seek to cooperate within a broader international economy. These nations are represented by the Board of Governors, which convenes annually to steer IMF policy. In addition to the yearly duties of the Board of Governors, a 24-member Executive Board that represents the interests of all 185 member nations meets regularly to negotiate policies for IMF members. Legislative operations are based upon a system where nations receive voting rights in general proportion to their size within the international economy. Thus, nations with larger economies hold more voting power than nations with smaller economies.

INTERNATIONAL BANK FOR RECONSTRUCTION AND DEVELOPMENT/WORLD BANK

Unlike the IMF, the International Bank for Reconstruction and Development (IBRD) is rarely referred to by its original name. Instead, the IBRD and its sister institution, known as the International Development Association (IDA), are now more commonly referred to as the World Bank, an umbrella term designating the two organizations.

The World Bank was originally created to provide financial assistance in the rebuilding of nations that had been destroyed during World War II. However, since postwar reconstruction began after 1945, the World Bank's mission has been to combat poverty and the social ills associated with it in developing regions. The World Bank operations consist of lending monies to mainly developing nations through the use of public funds. These funds accumulate through bonds sold within international markets.

GENERAL AGREEMENT ON TARIFFS AND TRADE/ WORLD TRADE ORGANIZATION

During the United Nations Monetary and Financial Conference of 1944, gathering members discussed a need for an organization that would act as a mediating body to resolve trade disputes and establish accords for exchange among nations. Originally, one proposed body was named the International Trade Organization (ITO) and was intended to be a special unit housed within the United Nations. However, the ITO never received enough support and subsequently failed to materialize.

Despite the failure of the ITO, the international community had already negotiated a similar regulating body known as the General Agreement on Tariffs and Trade in Geneva, Switzerland. The mission of the GATT was to uphold commitments by nations in limiting tariffs on agreed-upon commodities.

Similarly to the World Bank, the GATT has undergone several changes. During the Uruguay Round of 1986, gathering nations proposed changes to the GATT in order to adjust to, and keep pace with, the emerging challenges of GLOBALIZATION. In 1995, the GATT also received a new title, World Trade Organization (WTO).

CRITICAL IMPACT OF GLOBAL FINANCIAL INSTITUTIONS ON THE ENVIRONMENT

In 2001, the World Bank stated that the maintenance of natural and human-made environments is essential to sustainable economic and social development and crafted an environmental strategy that emphasized protecting regional and global commons. The other institutions have expressed similar goals. Despite these objectives and the stated missions of such global financial institutions as the International Monetary Fund, World Bank, and World Trade Organization, critics of their operations have argued these organizations have confounded preexisting economic situations and contributed to major disparities between more industrialized nations and developing nations. Perhaps the three most destructive contributors to this disparity are mechanisms identified as (1) conditionality, (2) structural adjustment programs, and (3) debt. Conditionality refers to sets of provisions imposed upon recipients of multilateral finance. These conditions are packaged within larger undertakings known as Structural Adjustment Programs (SAPs), which may require a loan-receiving nation to meet specific criteria such as agreements upon interest rates, monetary policies, budgets, exchange rates, and privatization decisions. The conditionality and SAPs are often criticized for generating stringent agendas that ignore the interests of loan recipients. For example, IMF packages often require budgetary agreements that designate a specific amount of money for infrastructural expenses such as education and health care. Although such IMF packages would not explicitly state that finances should be diverted away from infrastructure, SAPs might imply that monies should not be spent on these other areas of development.

Critics of conditionality and SAPs argue that these stringent agendas are simply too difficult to comply with and therefore only serve to force nations into renegotiation where provisions become even more severe, creating greater debt for loan recipients. It is argued that debt then becomes a mechanism of control for more developed nations.

Thus, critics contend, such mechanisms have left developing nations with little room to protect their environments or address the public health needs of their citizenry. Many environmentalists have questioned the World Bank and IMF's support for multipurpose DAMS, RESERVOIRS, AND ARTIFICIAL LAKES that have displaced local populations and oil, gas, and mining activities that have contributed to GLOBAL WARMING and destroyed local ECOSYSTEMS while channeling profits to large corporations rather than indigenous people.

See also TREATIES AND INTERNATIONAL LAW; UNITED NATIONS ENVIRONMENTAL CONFERENCES.

Salvador Jimenez Murguia

Further Reading
Eichengreen, Barry. *Globalizing Capital: A History of the International Monetary System.* Princeton, N.J.: Princeton University Press, 2008.
McMichael, Philip. *Development and Social Change: A Global Perspective.* Thousand Oaks, Calif.: Pine Forge Press, 2000.
Speth, James Gustave, and Peter Haas. *Global Environmental Governance: Foundations of Contemporary Environmental Studies.* Washington, D.C.: Island Press, 2006.

globalization

Broadly defined, globalization means the international movement of commodities, people, capital, culture, and ideas, as well as the global dispersion of flora, fauna, and microbes. By this definition, globalization has been happening almost since the beginning of human history. All living beings and commodities have flowed across porous political borders for thousands of years.

ANTECEDENTS TO GLOBALIZATION
Global trade expanded rapidly during the early colonial period (1500–1800) as European powers absorbed raw materials from distant lands and new dominions: furs, timber, FISH, and TOBACCO from British North America; cocoa, GOLD, and slaves from Africa; SUGAR and rum from the Caribbean; sugar, gold, and silver from Latin America; tea, spices, silk, and porcelain from Asia. Ships crossed the OCEANS. Heading to the colonies, their holds were filled with settlers and manufactured goods; returning home, the galleons and clippers bulged with precious commodities. Plants, animals, and disease accompanied trade around the world, invading and altering local environments.

Still, international trade in most commodities during the colonial period constituted a small percentage of overall economic activity. It led to little economic integration regionally or globally. Trade mainly involved high-value-to-volume products. Merchants and investors grew immensely wealthy from trade, but its aggregate economic effect was small. In one of the most successful trading nations on earth, England, at least until the 19th century, domestic agriculture, not trade, was the most important economic activity, whether measured by share of national income, contribution to employment, or ability to generate large fortunes. Domestic transformations had a greater effect on local ecology and environment than global forces. The agricultural revolutions of the 17th and 18th centuries and the evolution of capitalist economic institutions, first in England and then in western Europe and North America, induced profound ecological and environmental changes, as the expansion of cultivated land wiped out marginal ECOSYSTEMS, indigenous human populations, and animal species.

A more precise definition of globalization—the one that finds common currency among economic historians today—describes the phenomenon as the integration of commodity, capital, and labor markets on a global scale. A benchmark sign of market integration, or globalization, is observed when commodity prices begin to converge: in other words, when prices for the same commodity in different regional or local markets around the world begin to approach each other. By this definition, there have been two eras of globalization, two global economies in world history: (1) 1850–1914 and (2) 1980–2008.

THE FIRST GLOBAL ECONOMY
Beginning in the late 18th century, the Industrial Revolution ushered in the first era of globalization. The invention of the

steam engine and the exploitation of COAL as a fuel source harnessed enough stored energy to power production and trade on a truly global scale. "Fossilized sunshine" liberated first England and then other societies from the "biological old regime," which depended on annual energy flows from the Sun, radically transforming manufacturing and accelerating the growth of international transportation. In the mid- to late 19th century, coal-burning steamships and RAILROADS lowered the costs of international transport and integrated new regions, new resources, and new workforces into the world economy. Mass trade in basic commodities—not just luxuries or high-value-to-volume products but lower-value-to-volume bulk products such as COTTON, WHEAT, jute, coffee, cocoa, lumber, tropical fruits, minerals, petroleum, nitrates, and guano—became profitable for the first time. Mass trade in basic commodities led to international price convergence in those commodities.

The spread of cheap steamship and railroad travel also spread people as well commodities. In the early years of the 19th century, growing exports of Canadian timber and American cotton to Europe gave rise to a considerable increase in unused space on return journeys, so that ship-owners increasingly looked to emigrants to provide part of the return freight. Adverse economic conditions, such as the Irish potato famine of the 1840s, or the disrupting effects of mechanization in agriculture and industrialization, forced many Europeans to seek better lives in the United States, other parts of the Western Hemisphere, and Australasia. Railroad developers in the United States encouraged IMMIGRATION, largely to create freight on their lines in the form of agricultural development by immigrant farmers. The abolition of the SLAVE TRADE in the early 19th century produced a labor shortage in economies based on PLANTATIONS (West Indies, East Indies, South Africa, and South America) and gave rise to indentured immigrants from India and China.

The first global economy displayed tremendous economic growth, social transformation, and environmental change around the world. With the symbolic repeal of the Corn Laws in 1846, Great Britain embraced free trade, and other countries eventually followed suit. By the late 19th century, many had done the same in linking their currencies to gold. However, globalization was also economically and environmentally destabilizing. The advent of new, highly productive heavy manufacturing industries and the ongoing cycles of boom and bust under the gold standard meant that the world economy, by the 1870s, was susceptible to chronic "overproduction" in both manufacturing and agriculture. National markets and increasingly international markets were not large enough to absorb the skyrocketing output of industrial and agricultural goods. Meanwhile, large parts of every continent did not experience rising prosperity whether because of colonialism, corrupt rulers, or unfair trading relationships. Even in regions that developed rapidly, gains from growth were distributed very unevenly. This produced growing opposition to globalization, radical challenges to political authority, and a bloody conflict—WORLD WAR I (1914–18)—that ultimately brought down the first global economy.

British and European domination of the world economy magnified the problems of local harvest failures and famines around the world. Widespread DEFORESTATION and depletion of soil fertility, both in societies that were escaping the biological old regime and in places that were still constrained by it, increased the widespread vulnerability of populations to climatic shock, especially in countries such as India, where the workings of the British colonial control and economic power had undermined the Indian textile industry and forced many Indians to turn to cash crops for export. When, in the late 19th century, the climatic phenomenon now known as El Niño grew to its greatest intensity in possibly 500 years, harvest yields boomed in the American Midwest (and remained largely unaffected in Europe), while DROUGHTS afflicted vast regions of Asia, northern and western Africa, and northeast Brazil, causing widespread subsistence crises. During the last 25 years of the century, perhaps 30–50 million people died of famine across Asia and in parts of Africa and Latin America. Famines weakened societies and governments, making them susceptible to a new wave of imperialist expansion and consolidation, thus widening the development gap between the industrialized world and what became the "third world."

DISINTEGRATION OF THE FIRST GLOBAL ECONOMY

The "new IMPERIALISM" intensified military competition between the great powers of Europe, culminating in the Great War, World War I, which sowed unprecedented death and disease. During the next two decades, the first global economy disintegrated. Global economic imbalances created by the postwar debt/reparations settlement and adherence to the gold standard by advanced economies magnified the financial crisis of 1929–31 and the ensuing GREAT DEPRESSION. Capital controls and protectionism broke apart global markets. Commodity price gaps returned to their 1870 levels. Mass immigration fell sharply. All advanced nations and many developing nations turned inward in the 1930s, experimenting with political and economic solutions to delink their domestic economies further from the world economy, marking a global swing toward economic nationalism at odds with globalization and leading to the cataclysmic WORLD WAR II (1941–45), resulting in an estimated 50–70 million deaths.

The United States emerged from World War II as the preeminent world power. In the late 1940s and early 1950s, under the political cover of fighting a COLD WAR against the communist Soviet Union and China, the U.S. president HARRY TRUMAN orchestrated the reconstruction of the world economy, anointing Germany as the industrial anchor in Western Europe, Japan the industrial engine in East Asia,

with both industrial regions supplied increasingly by American oil companies in the Middle East. However, restrictions on currency convertibility (profits earned in one currency could not be freely converted and repatriated) permitted under the Bretton Woods gold-dollar exchange monetary system established in 1945, along with the fact that trade was characteristically conducted on a bilateral basis, limited the process of market integration on a global scale.

During the 1950s and 1960s, nevertheless, a surge in production, trade, and population, all fueled by cheap and accessible hydrocarbons, brought about a 25-year period of robust global economic growth. By the late 1960s, however, decolonization and the extension of the cold war to the developing world in places such as Vietnam began to destabilize the international system. A global dollar glut and the assertion of control over the production and pricing of oil by the Organization of Petroleum Exporting Countries (OPEC) weakened the hegemonic leadership of the United States over the world economy.

THE SECOND GLOBAL ECONOMY

These developments ended the long boom in postwar capitalism and ushered in an extended period of stagnation in the world economy in the 1970s. They also set in motion events that launched a new era of globalization (as defined previously) around 1980. In 1971, unable to maintain the dollar's fixed value in terms of gold, President RICHARD NIXON terminated the gold-dollar monetary system, freeing international currencies from links to dollars or gold. The resulting deregulation of financial markets, combined with the spread of high-speed telecommunication links, spurred a dramatic expansion in global financial flows and networks. After the oil price shocks of the 1970s, the investment of petrodollars in international money markets increased liquidity for international banks and stimulated private lending to the developing world. Private loans dried up after the bursting of the developing world debt bubble in the 1980s, but they revived in the 1990s and 2000s after the collapse of communism and the liberalization of capital controls through debt restructuring.

For the first time since the interwar period of the 1920s and 1930s, many developing countries and East European economies were reincorporated into international capital markets as borrowers. But lending remained concentrated in the middle-income countries of East Asia and Latin America. Others, particularly the poorest developing countries, were largely excluded from private financial markets and dependent on official aid flows. Increased financial flows also made economies more vulnerable to destabilizing tendencies. The deregulation of financial markets in developing countries led to high levels of speculative activity in the 1990s, largely fueled by short-term capital inflows, and the financial collapse in the United States and Europe that began in 2008 may possibly have signaled the end of the second era of globalization.

ENVIRONMENTAL IMPLICATIONS

During the 1990s and 2000s, capital flows to emerging markets financed and stimulated substantial growth, with East Asia, Brazil, Russia, India, and China the chief beneficiaries. The tremendous expansion of international trade, the outsourcing of manufacturing to many parts of the world, and the massive increase in the consumption of energy and other resources in recent decades drew hundreds of millions of people out of absolute poverty. The environmental costs, however, were enormous. The growth of the second global economy was clearly associated with an alarming degradation of the Earth's air, water, soil, and biosphere.

As in earlier historical eras, much of the ecological damage was local. But even local damage that leads to species EXTINCTION had moral, aesthetic, and economic consequences for the planet. Increasingly, environmental degradation had international and global dimensions, including DEFORESTATION and desertification, the decimation of ocean FISHERIES, transboundary AIR POLLUTION AND WATER POLLUTION problems, lethal biological exchange and the transmission of disease, pressures on scarce natural resources, conflicts over resources and water, and global CLIMATE CHANGE resulting from the burning of fossil fuels, which is perhaps the greatest environmental challenge human society has ever faced.

See also AGRICULTURE, COMMERCIAL; CAPITALISM; DISEASES, ANIMAL; DISEASES, HUMAN; DISEASES, PLANT; LOGGING AND LUMBERING; MERCANTILISM; OIL, IMPORTED; SPECIES, EXOTIC AND INVASIVE.

Tyler Priest

Further Reading

Crosby, Alfred W. *Children of the Sun: A History of Humanity's Unappeasable Appetite for Energy.* New York: Norton, 2006.

Davis, Mike. *Late Victorian Holocausts: El Nino Famines and the Making of the Third World.* London: Verso, 2001.

Frieden, Jeffrey A. *Global Capitalism: Its Fall and Rise in the Twentieth Century.* New York: W. W. Norton, 2006.

Held, Davis, Anthony McGrew, David Goldblatt, and Jonathan Perraton. *Global Transformations: Politics, Economics, and Culture.* Stanford, Calif.: Stanford University Press, 1999.

Hornborg, Alf, J. R. McNeill, and Joan Martinez-Alier, eds. *Rethinking Environmental History: World-System History and Global Environmental Change.* New York: Altamira Press, 2007.

Marks, Robert B. *The Origins of the Modern World: A Global and Ecological Narrative from the Fifteenth to the Twenty-First Century.* New York: Rowman & Littlefield, 2007.

McNeill, J. R. *Something New under the Sun: An Environmental History of the Twentieth-Century World.* New York: W. W. Norton, 2000.

global warming

Global warming refers to the observed or projected increase in the Earth's global surface temperature. Human activities that decrease the fraction of solar radiation reflected directly back to space (albedo) by changes in cloud cover, alter levels of atmospheric particles or vegetation cover, and increase concentrations of atmospheric greenhouse gases alter heat radiation from Earth and drive global warming. The primary greenhouse gases include water vapor; carbon dioxide (CO_2) emitted from the burning of COAL, NATURAL GAS, and oil and DEFORESTATION; and methane (CH_4), arising from extraction of FOSSIL FUEL ENERGY sources as well as from ruminant livestock (such as CATTLE and sheep), LANDFILLS, and RICE cultivation. Other important greenhouse gases are nitrous oxide (N_2O), hydrofluorocarbons (HFCs), perfluorocarbons (PFCs), and sulfur hexafluoride (SF_6).

Greenhouse gases are critical for life on Earth as they prevent some of the Sun's heat from escaping back into space. Without a "natural greenhouse effect," the Earth's average surface temperature would be below the freezing point of water. Since the Industrial Revolution began in the late 18th century, however, the stock of atmospheric greenhouse gases measured as carbon dioxide equivalents has increased from 280 parts per million (ppm) to around 430 ppm. As a consequence, the average temperature of the Earth's surface has risen by 0.74 degree Celsius since the late 1800s. This rise has triggered various amplifying feedback mechanisms, such as melting polar ice and GLACIERS that reveal darker land and water surfaces. Darker surfaces absorb more heat, thus causing more warming and more melting in a self-reinforcing cycle. As a consequence, average surface temperatures might increase by another 1.8°C to 4°C by the year 2100. This change will probably cause EXTINCTION of numerous plant and animal species, more frequent extreme weather events, and rising sea levels. Despite uncertainties about carbon cycle feedbacks, one point is certain: Sustained or increased atmospheric emissions increase the probabilities and effects of various adverse consequences, including DROUGHTS, heat waves, and FLOODS. Greenland's ice sheet loss alone, for example, could eventually cause a several meter increase in sea levels.

The Swedish chemist Svante Arrhenius (1859–1927) is often mentioned as the first person to warn of global warming as a consequence of increased atmospheric concentration of CO_2. In an 1896 paper, he calculated that a doubling of CO_2 in the atmosphere would increase global surface temperature by an average of five to six Celsius degrees. He did not, however, consider warming a problem. On the contrary, he looked forward to better climates and abundant crops for the benefit of a rapidly propagating humankind. In 1938, the British steam engineer Guy Stewart Callendar (1898–1964) downscaled the estimated effect of a doubling of CO_2 to an increase in the mean temperature of two degrees Celsius. He, likewise, viewed warming as a beneficial change that

This polar bear managed to get on one of the last ice floes floating in the Arctic Sea.   *(Jan Martin Will/Shutterstock)*

would improve the conditions of agriculture at the northern margins of cultivation while delaying the return of glaciers indefinitely. In 1956, the Canadian physicist Gilbert Plass (1921–2004) estimated that doubling atmospheric carbon dioxide would prompt surface temperatures to rise by 3.6 Celsius degrees. Contrary to his predecessors, however, he regarded this as a problem. The following year, the scientists Roger Revelle (1909–91) and Hans E. Suess (1909–93) repeated the warning, calling the present rate of combustion of fossil fuels a large-scale geophysical experiment.

In 1979, the first World Climate Conference organized by the World Meteorological Organization (WMO) appealed to the nations of the world to prevent human-made changes in climate that might be adverse to the well-being of humanity. By 1988, the WMO and the United Nations Environment Programme jointly set up the Intergovernmental Panel on Climate Change (IPCC) to provide scientific advice on CLI-MATE CHANGE. Its First Assessment Report, released in 1990, stated that the threat of climate change was real and a global treaty was needed to deal with it. As a result of these findings, a number of nations committed support to the United Nations Framework Convention on Climate Change (UNFCCC), which established a framework for intergovernmental efforts to tackle challenges posed by climate change. The United States was one of the first among industrially developed nations to ratify this treaty with the aim of returning individually or jointly to their 1990 levels of anthropogenic emissions of carbon dioxide and other greenhouse gases.

As part of the UNFCCC, the 1997 Kyoto Protocol introduced legally binding targets to limit or reduce individual countries' greenhouse gas emissions. The United States signed the protocol on November 12, 1998, but failed to ratify it, arguing that curbing emissions would hurt the U.S. economy and that the agreement did not include legally binding commitments for developing countries. When Russia ratified the protocol in November 2004, the crucial threshold of being ratified by 55 nations accounting for at least 55 percent of total Annex I greenhouse gas emissions was nevertheless achieved, and the protocol entered into force on February 16, 2005. It required developed countries that ratified the protocol to reduce their aggregate emissions of the six main greenhouse gases by 5.2 percent below the 1990 levels between 2008 and 2012. With the inclusion of flexible mechanisms including emissions trading between countries, "joint implementation" that credited countries for "carbon sinks" such as FORESTS, and a "clean development mechanism" allowing developed countries to offset their emissions by investing in projects to reduce carbon output in developing countries, however, the actual emissions reduction required is substantially lower.

Negotiations for a climate treaty to succeed the Kyoto Protocol, which expires in 2012, continue. The United States remains involved as President BARACK OBAMA agreed with a target to keep global temperature rise below two degrees Celsius above preindustrial levels. As there is now a clear scientific consensus that global warming is human-caused and represents a grave economic, social, and environmental threat, many nations have pledged to lower their greenhouse emissions and to try to curb deforestation in an effort to slow the process of global warming.

See also AUTOMOBILES; ENERGY, ELECTRICAL; GREEN-HOUSE EFFECT; OIL REFINING; OZONE LAYER; POLLUTION,

AIR; TREATIES AND INTERNATIONAL LAW; UNITED NATIONS ENVIRONMENTAL CONFERENCES.

Jan Kunnas

Further Reading
Kunnas, Jan, and T. Myllyntaus. "Postponed Leap in Carbon Dioxide Emissions." *Global Environment* 3 (2009): 154–189.
Revelle, Roger, and H. Suess. "Carbon Dioxide Exchange between Atmosphere and Ocean." *Tellus* 9, no. 18 (1957): 18–27.
Stern, Nicholas. *Stern Review on the Economics of Climate Change.* London: HM Treasury, 2009.
United Nations. *Kyoto Protocol to the United Nations Framework Convention on Climate Change.* UNFCCC, 1998. Available online. URL: http://unfccc.int/resource/docs/convkp/kpeng-pdf. Accessed January 21, 2009.
United Nations Intergovernmental Panel on Climate Change. *Climate Change 2007: Synthesis Report.* Geneva: IPCC, 2007.

gold

Gold is the 79th element on the periodic table of the elements, in the same group of elements as COPPER and silver, and possessing very similar physical and chemical characteristics including high conductivity, a lustrous appearance, relative malleability, and resistance to corrosion. Gold is also an extremely rare element. These physical characteristics and its scarcity have contributed to its cultural value all over the globe and help to explain why gold is often used for coinage and jewelry.

Gold has long had an impact on the North American continent. Much of the Spanish exploration of North America was driven by the belief that the golden city El Dorado existed somewhere in the continent's interior. Then, in the middle of the 19th century, gold MINING in the SIERRA NEVADA of California launched the United States as a major gold producer, and gold prospecting and exploration from that point forward played a significant role in settling the intermountain regions between DENVER, COLORADO, and SAN FRANCISCO, CALIFORNIA.

Gold has been found in three major forms in the landscape of the western United States, and each of these forms of deposition is mirrored by a changing and increasingly more effective impact on the landscape where the mining takes place. Gold was also, it may be noted, almost always located in far-off places arrived at only after lengthy travel.

The original gold of the California gold rush was found as a dust in the bottom layers of creek beds in the foothills of the territory, which became a state in 1850. Placer mining excavated creeks and creek beds and sent soil and gravel and dirt downriver. But nothing compared to the practice of hydraulic mining, in which jets of water washed entire hillsides through sluices, generally decimating the landscape in the foothills of the Sierra Nevada and ruining the IRRIGATION potential of downriver farms. The creek bed gold dust had eroded from quartz depositions, as the miners quickly discovered. When they burrowed into the side of a ridge alongside a creek that had produced gold dust, they sometimes discovered gold-laden quartz deposits.

Tunneling replaced hydraulic excavation, and the stamp mill, usually run with a steam engine, replaced the long toms and rockers (tools that separated gold from dirt, mud, and muck). Stamp mills crushed quartz into a fine powder out of which the gold could be amalgamated with MERCURY. Piles of mine waste gathered behind stamp mills and at the mouths of mine tunnels, sometimes to be worked over once more by Chinese miners, whose collective methods allowed them to profit from lower-quality ores when they were denied access to more lucrative creeks beds and ore lodes. Timber was taken from the hillsides to support the interior of the mine tunnels and to fuel the steam engines.

Gold was also a component of the amalgam of metals found in the hard rock sulfur deposits discovered around the West in the 1860s and 1870s. The hard rock mining elevated the scale and scope of mining and mining impacts. Deeper mines required larger workforces, more energy for excavation, and exponentially more lumber for the mines. Smelters, a technology required to break down the sulfuric ores, belched orange clouds of sulfuric acid vapor out into the western air and washed heavy-metal-laden slimes out into enormous settling fields. Gold continued to be produced in impressive amounts in these industrial smelters, but the yellow metal represented only a fraction of 1 percent of the total amount of metal produced.

Today, most gold is recovered from large-scale open pit mines where soils containing trace amounts of gold are saturated with a cyanide solution, causing the gold to fall out. These operations attract enormous controversy in the United States, where WILDERNESS advocates oppose the required removal of entire mountains to make these operations profitable, but they continue to take place in the developing world, where some of the largest open-pit gold mines are to be found.

Today, the most common use of gold is in jewelry (about 78 percent of the gold in circulation), followed by electronics and microcomputing. An enormous amount of gold goes to waste each year as COMPUTERS and cell phones are thrown away instead of recycled.

See also EROSION; LOGGING AND LUMBERING; POLLUTION, AIR; POLLUTION, WATER; RECYCLING; ROCKY MOUNTAINS; SMOKE NUISANCE; UNITED STATES—CALIFORNIA; UNITED STATES—SOUTHWEST.

Kent Curtis

Further Reading
Morse, Kathryn. *The Nature of Gold: An Environmental History of the Klondike Gold Rush.* Seattle: University of Washington Press, 2003.
Safford, Jeffrey J. *The Mechanics of Optimism: Mining Companies, Technology, and the Hot Springs Gold Rush, Montana Territory, 1864–1868.* Boulder: University Press of Colorado, 2004.
Smith, Duane A. *Mining America: The Industry and the Environment, 1800–1980.* Boulder: University Press of Colorado, 1994.

Gompers, Samuel (1850–1924) *president of the American Federation of Labor*

Samuel Gompers was a formative figure in U.S. labor history, stamping American trade unionism with a conservative approach that emphasized the protection of members' rights and wages rather than the development of a broadly based, working-class political agenda. While not known for his work on environmental issues, Gompers joined others in the early 20th century who spoke out for the CONSERVATION of American resources.

Gompers was born in London, England, on January 27, 1850, and immigrated to the United States with his family in 1863. He joined the cigar-rollers union, eventually becoming the president of Cigarmakers International Union. In 1881, Gompers helped found the Federation of Organized Trades and Labor Unions, which re-formed as the American Federation of Labor (AFL) in 1886. Gompers served as the president of the AFL from 1886 to 1894, and from 1895 until his death on December 13, 1924.

Under Gompers's direction, the AFL pursued a moderate agenda that aimed to improve working conditions and increase wages of its members. For example, Gompers's AFL provided political support for a New York state law that banned cigar making in TENEMENTS. Although the law purported to protect residents of tenements from the environmental dangers of cigar making, the conservative New York Court of Appeals in *In re Jacobs* (98 N.Y. 98 [1885]) claimed that it was not a health law but instead was designed to interfere with the property rights of tenement owners who sanctioned cigar making. In an opinion that was subsequently criticized by later courts and legal commentators, the court overturned the law as a violation of substantive due process, arguing the state legislature had exceeded its police powers. On other fronts, the AFL also tried to block unrestricted immigration from Europe and all immigration from Asia. Gompers believed immigrants lowered wages and undermined his union members.

Gompers proselytized for a nonaffiliated AFL that supported legislative efforts designed to improve union members' wages and working conditions rather than alignments with a particular political party. He openly dismissed radical organizers who involved themselves in electoral politics. Gompers supported U.S. efforts in Europe before, during, and after WORLD WAR I (1914–18). He served on the wartime Council of National Defense and accompanied President WOODROW WILSON to the postwar peace conference in Paris, in 1919. His wartime efforts helped secure better pay and the eight-hour workday for many American workers.

As the conservation movement gained in popularity in the early 20th century, Gompers joined others in using its rhetoric to further his own goals. Gompers used the union's magazine to express his support for conservation efforts. He argued that in their eagerness to reap quick and large profits, capitalists abused the nation's resources. Ultimately, however, his larger concern was about the impact of such wastefulness on his members rather than the defense of nature. Gompers argued for greater regulation of the environment and of corporate management to ensure that reckless speculation did not create economic downturns that led to unemployment.

Gompers also developed a strong, hierarchical leadership structure within the AFL, which allowed his successors to push elected representatives and regulatory agencies to implement regulations that made workplace environments safer and healthier. In the last few decades of the 20th century, the AFL made the environmental protection of its workers a central part of its agenda. In 2007, the AFL, along with public interest and environmental groups, founded the Apollo Project, a $300 billion program to create three million new clean energy jobs.

See also LABOR, EXTRACTIVE INDUSTRIES; LABOR, MANUFACTURING; LABOR MOVEMENTS.

Stephen Kirby

Further Reading
Buhle, Paul. *Taking Care of Business: Samuel Gompers, George Meany, Lane Kirkland, and the Tragedy of American Labor.* New York: Monthly Review Press, 1999.
Greene, Julie. *Pure and Simple Politics: The American Federation of Labor and Political Activism, 1881–1917.* New York: Cambridge University Press, 1998.

"Conservation of Our Natural Resources" Samuel Gompers (1908)

During the Progressive Era, Americans in all walks of life spoke out in favor of conservation, linking its basic principles to their own objectives. Samuel Gompers was founder and president of the American Federation of Labor (AFL). In July 1908, he wrote an editorial for the AFL magazine American Federationist, *commenting on a convention of governors, foresters, and irrigation experts called by President Theodore Roosevelt. Gompers implicitly criticized corporate interests that exploited natural and human resources, emphasizing that the protection of both was essential to American success.*

These eminent citizens are gathered in obedience to a call, the inspiration of which strike the keynote of the nation's future policy in the field of civil betterment. It is the extension of the new school of political economy. It is in the nature of the great stewardship that underlies the brotherhood of man. No more noble incentive to that end can be imagined than is to be found in the impulse that prompts wise and far seeing statesmanship to build and preserve for the future. Happily, too, this convention will act as a check on the marauding instinct so flagrantly exercised in the exploitation of the nation's natural resources by men whose actions have hitherto been sanctioned by law. In respect of waste and extravagance in the economic sense, these marauders have placed the American Republic in a situation unparalleled in economic conservation among nations. In one item alone, that of fuel, it is figured out by one of the experts attendant upon this convention that 200,000,000 tons of coal are wasted every year in the mining processes of the nation, which is equal to $200,000,000, every ton of coal being worth a dollar at the mines. Add to this the colossal waste in the exploitation of timber lands, water power, and the like, and we have some faint conception of the load our economic energies are carrying. . . .

Perhaps the greatest form of waste from which we suffer at this time is the waste involved in the unemployment of immense numbers of our people, and this waste is due to no fault of the working people. Without affirming to whom is traceable the blame of the present condition of unemployment, no one can truthfully charge that the cause can be laid at the door of the working people of our country. It is perhaps the severest commentary upon the intelligence and understanding of economic and social conditions that there are at this time about two millions of our working people vainly seeking the opportunity of working and earning their bread by the sweat of their brows. . . .

For it must be borne in mind that labor energy is the foundation of all wealth. Nothing is accomplished without labor. . . .

When we are expanded and developed, our natural resources wrested from the hands of heedless marauders and conserved as the nation's patrimony; when our great natural waterways are connected with canals; when our denuded watersheds are rehabilitated and made verdant and fruitful; and when the nation through the people speaks, the working men and the working women, who in reality do everything that is done, will take their place of freedom.

Source: Samuel Gompers. "Conservation of Our Natural Resources." *American Federationist* 15 (July 1908): 532–536.

Gore, Albert, Jr. (Al) (1948–   ) *vice president of the United States (1993–2001), environmental activist*

Although Al Gore is best known as vice president of the United States during BILL CLINTON's administration from 1993 to 2001, his career as an environmental activist is equally noteworthy. Gore has been an activist on the issue of CLIMATE CHANGE for years and has done much to further climate change education through mass MEDIA. He also serves and has served as a board member on numerous environmental, governmental, and business boards in pursuit of revising climate change legislation and helping people, governments, and businesses understand how they affect the climate, positively and negatively. In recognition of his environmental activism, he received the Nobel Peace Prize in 2007.

Gore was born in Washington, D.C., on March 31, 1948. At the time, his father, Al Gore, Sr. (1907–98), was a member of the U.S. House of Representatives from Tennessee. He later served as U.S. senator from Tennessee until 1971. After graduating from Harvard University in 1969, Gore, Jr., enlisted in the U.S. Army and served in Vietnam, although in a noncombat position. Gore began his political career at the early age of 28, when he was elected as a representative for the state of Tennessee and served in that position from 1976 to 1984. He was then elected to the Senate and served from 1984 to 1993, until he became vice president. He ran unsuccessfully for president in 2000 but lost in a very close election to GEORGE W. BUSH.

Throughout his time in CONGRESS, Gore was attentive to environmental issues, such as climate change and toxic waste. He also served on the House Committee on Energy and Commerce and the House Committee on Science and Technology, where he used his interest in technology and COMPUTERS to push for their use to study how humans were affecting the world's climate.

Gore is widely known for using mass media to educate people about environmental problems. In 1992, just before he became vice president, Gore published his book *Earth in the Balance: Ecology and the Human Spirit*. In it, Gore emphasizes the numerous ways that people have hurt the environment. He also contemplates what the detrimental effects of continued environmental misuse may be, such as further GLOBAL WARMING and destruction of natural habitats. Finally, *Earth in the Balance* suggests some ways that people can help the environment, or at least stop hurting it. Many of these suggestions are related to the use of technology, such as inventing and developing cleaner energy sources. In 2006, five years after leaving the vice presidency, Gore took his activism one step further with the dual release of a book and a movie, both titled *An Inconvenient Truth*. They deal specifically with climate change: how human action has furthered climate change and how human intervention can stop it. While the scientific analyses of *An Inconvenient Truth* were questioned by conservative politicians in many countries, the film was praised by critics and performed well at the box office. It won the 2006 Academy Award for the Best Documentary Film.

Gore's activism has progressed beyond the political and educational realms. In 2004, he cofounded Generation Investment Management, a company that creates investment portfolios with environmental SUSTAINABILITY in mind. In this way, the company supports investment opportunities that are also proenvironment. He is also a board member for numerous companies, making sure that their business policies do not further climate change and are otherwise ecofriendly. Gore also has made certain that climate change has stayed in the international spotlight, helping to plan such benefit events as LiveEarth, a musical concert all of whose proceeds went to environmental causes.

The crowning moment of Gore's environmental career occurred in 2007, when he won the Nobel Peace Prize along with other members of the Intergovernmental Panel on Climate Change (IPCC). In particular, the Nobel Foundation celebrated the IPCC's "efforts to build up and disseminate greater knowledge about man-made climate change, and to lay the foundations for the measures that are needed to counteract such change." Gore continues to be a leading voice for climate change and other environmental issues.

See also DEMOCRATIC PARTY; ENVIRONMENTALISM, MAINSTREAM; GREENHOUSE EFFECT; NONGOVERNMENTAL ORGANIZATIONS; UNITED NATIONS ENVIRONMENTAL CONFERENCES.

Chelsea Griffis

Further Reading

Gore, Al. *Earth in the Balance: Ecology and the Human Spirit.* Boston: Houghton Mifflin, 1992.
——. *An Inconvenient Truth: The Crisis of Global Warming.* New York: Viking, 2007.
Turque, Bill. *Inventing Al Gore: A Biography.* Boston: Houghton Mifflin, 2000.

grains

The term *grains* is an anthropocentric term that encompasses the edible and highly caloric seeds of certain cereals and pseudocereals that humans have used as STAPLE CROPS. Most grains are annual GRASSES and cereal grains, which include CORN, RICE, WHEAT, sorghum, barley, rye, millet, and oats. Buckwheat, amaranth, lamb's quarters, and quinoa, which are pseudocereals and not true grasses, are also considered grains. Grains have been grown for human consumption, animal feed, and, increasingly, fuel in the form of biodiesel and ethanol. The relationship between grains and humans has often been one of codependency, and the effect on North American ECOSYSTEMS of large-scale grain agriculture in the United States has been far-reaching.

Certain grains, most notably maize (corn), are native to North America and have been cultivated for millennia by indigenous people. Maize has been cultivated in North America for at least 5,400 years and through careful seed selection has now forms significantly larger and more abundant cobs than its wild predecessor. The process of nixtamalization (soaking maize in lime or wood ash water to enhance its protein value) was developed around 1500 B.C.E., increasing maize's dietary role and spurring subsequent agricultural and POPULATION increases. Wild rice in the Upper Midwest, amaranth in the Southwest, and lamb's quarters throughout the continent have also long been cultivated and harvested as grains by Native Americans.

The arrival of European grains and agricultural methods in North America revolutionized the ecology of the continent. Unlike Native Americans, who most often used polyculture methods of growing maize, European-Americans grew grain as a MONOCULTURE, which involved clearing land to plant a field of one crop. Along with rice cultivation in the antebellum South and wheat and maize cultivation by Hispanic settlers in the Southwest, much of the grain grown by early European Americans occurred in New England, where maize, wheat, rye, buckwheat, and oats were predominant. For the first time in the history of the continent, grains were grown not only for the human diet but for the diet of their DOMESTICATED ANIMALS as well.

By the mid-19th century, monoculture grain production, which had necessitated massive DEFORESTATION in the eastern United States, had reached the Midwest and Great Plains. As a result of ancient glacial flows and subsequent millennia of the enriching life cycles of the perennial grasses, this land had particularly rich soils conducive to grain cultivation. This fact, along with the increased transportation abilities via the RAILROADS and technological innovations such as the steel plow and McCormick grain reaper, allowed farmers to grow vast amounts of grain throughout the region to sell at distant urban markets. The invention of the steam-powered grain elevator in 1842 particularly transformed grain production and marketing.

No longer sold in bushel sacks, grain was mixed with other farmers' grain, graded by a grain inspector, and sold as a commodity. The futures market, in which traders around the world bought and sold grain in much the same way company stock was traded, emerged in CHICAGO, ILLINOIS, by the late 1860s and illustrates the degree to which grain had become commodified. This commodification of grain led to a perceptual abstraction of the grain from the environment that bore it.

Around the same time, another form of perceptual abstraction of grain occurred through refining and processing. By 1880, mechanized rollers replaced stone grinding in the United States. These rollers removed the germ of the grain (and thus the oils contained within germ that turn rancid when exposed to air) and ground the remaining endosperm into a fine white powder with a longer shelf life. This transformation from whole to refined grains marked a revolution in many Americans' diets and cooking habits, a revolution that some studies suggest has led to lasting, deleterious health effects in the U.S. population.

A transformative era in agriculture known as the GREEN REVOLUTION began in the 1940s and marked the advent of widespread use of chemical PESTICIDES, fossil-fuel-based synthetic FERTILIZER, and high-yielding hybrid grain varieties. Although plant breeding is an ancient craft, breeders at this time developed dwarf varieties of grains that channeled a much higher ratio of their energy from the sun into seed formation. Growing lower to the ground, these varieties were also less likely to fall over from their own weight. As a result, grain production in the United States, as with the rest of the world, greatly increased in the mid-20th century. The average maize yields in the United States from 1930 to 1990, for example, increased fivefold. In the 1990s, genetically modified (GM) grains (using newly developed breeding sciences) began to be sold in the United States. Certain varieties of GM maize have deoxyribonucleic acid (DNA) recoded to produce their own "pesticide." These built-in defenses, however, can pose hazards to beneficial and benign INSECTS, and unintentional genetic drift through cross-pollination between GM and non-GM varieties can reduce the vigor and diversity of non-GM maize.

The effects of large-scale grain growing on U.S. ECOSYSTEMS have been drastic. The shift to large monocultures has generally contributed to depleted soil fertility, increased disease susceptibility, and EROSION. In the case of the Midwest and Great Plains, one effect of turning perennial grasslands into annually plowed monocultures is that the soil has nothing to hold it down and is thus susceptible to blowing away. This occurred in the years of droughts of the 1870s and 1880s, and again in the DUST BOWL of the 1930s.

With the scaled-up agriculture available through the Green Revolution, the magnitude of pollution and environmental impact from grain farming have increased dramatically. For instance, because the soil has been depleted or eroded away by unsustainable monocultures, farmers often need to add liberal amounts of synthetic nitrogenous fertilizer to ensure their crops will not fail. The ensuing erosion contains runoff with levels of nitrogen much higher than normally found in the environment. In this way, large grain-producing farms in the MISSISSIPPI RIVER watershed are largely responsible for a 7,700-square-mile (an area more than three times the state of Delaware) "Dead Zone" in the GULF OF MEXICO, where the extremely high nitrogen levels in the ocean from agricultural runoff have caused FISH and shrimp to disappear from the area. As this example illustrates, the environmental effects of grain production in the United States have often been broad, far-reaching, and severe.

See also AGRICULTURAL TECHNOLOGY; AGRICULTURE, COLONIAL; AGRICULTURE, COMMERCIAL; CHICAGO BOARD OF TRADE; ENERGY, RENEWABLE; GENETICS; POLLUTION, WATER; SOIL CONSERVATION; UNITED STATES—CENTRAL PLAINS; UNITED STATES—MIDWEST; UNITED STATES—NORTHERN PLAINS; WATERSHEDS.

William Randall Carleton

Further Reading

Cronon, William. *Nature's Metropolis: Chicago and the Great West*. New York: W. W. Norton, 1991.
Manning, Richard. *Against the Grain*. New York: North Point Press, 2004.
Pollan, Michael. *The Omnivore's Dilemma: A Natural History of Four Meals*. New York: Penguin, 2006.

Grand Canyon

A natural gorge 277 miles long, a mile deep, and up to 18 miles wide, the Grand Canyon cuts across the Colorado Plateaus in northeastern Arizona. Cut downward by the COLORADO RIVER as the plateaus were uplifted over the last 17 million years of Earth's history, its walls expose spectacular rock formations ranging in age from two billion to 230 million years old.

Native American hunter-gatherers settled in caverns along the canyon's inner gorge at least 3,000 years ago, leaving behind animal fetishes made of twigs. The Puebloans began to establish farming villages in areas surrounding the canyon from 500 to 1200 C.E., and the Navajo followed in the 1400s. García López de Cárdenas, a deputy of Francisco Vázquez de Coronado (1510–44), became the first European to encounter the canyon in 1540. Unable to cross the canyon or find natural resources nearby, he saw it as merely an obstacle. That view persisted among the Spanish for decades, and colonists avoided the canyon and overland trails skirting it.

Carved by the Colorado River over millions of years, the Grand Canyon was inhabited for at least 4,000 years before it became one of the first national parks.   *(Gary M. Stolz, U.S. Fish and Wildlife Service)*

GEOLOGY

The Grand Canyon was mapped by a succession of U.S. government–sponsored expeditions during the 1870s: efforts—led by the scientist-explorers JOHN WESLEY POWELL, George Wheeler (1842–1905), and Clarence King (1842–1901)—that were consolidated in 1879 into the U.S. GEOLOGICAL SURVEY. These expeditions of the late 19th century transformed scientists' understanding of the canyon. Previously seen as an isolated natural wonder, it was reinterpreted as part of a dynamic system of landforms that included the Colorado River, its tributaries and their valleys, and the surrounding plateaus. Expedition geologists such as Grove Karl Gilbert (1843–1918) and Charles Dutton (1841–1912) explained the canyon as the product of a complex geological history, shaped by wind and water EROSION, the uplift of the surrounding land surface, changes in rainfall, and the effects of volcanic eruptions. The Grand Canyon played a key role in establishing the geological doctrine of fluvialism: the idea that river valleys are formed by the erosive power of the streams moving through them. It was also one of the first environments whose landforms, topography, subsurface geology, rainfall, and other factors were studied and understood dynamically, as elements in an integrated whole.

The Grand Canyon remained isolated and largely wild until the early 20th century, when human attempts to manage it began. The canyon's size and cultural significance have made it, ever since, a focal point for debates about the proper stewardship of unique natural wonders.

NATIONAL GAME PRESERVE—NATIONAL MONUMENT—NATIONAL PARK

The first attempt to manage the canyon and surrounding areas occurred in 1906, when President THEODORE ROOSEVELT signed an act declaring one million acres on the north rim—the entire Kaibab Plateau—the Grand Canyon National Game Preserve. Designed to protect the local population of mule DEER, the preserve was biologically isolated by deep side canyons and surrounding deserts. Hunting of mule deer was banned, and (in keeping with then-current game management practices) the native species of predators were systematically killed off by U.S. FOREST SERVICE hunters. The mule deer population exploded, rising from 3,000 in 1906 to more than 100,000 by 1924. Henry Cantwell Wallace (1866–1924), then secretary of agriculture, ordered that the population be reduced to sustainable levels by hunting, but the order met with fierce opposition from conservationists. Time passed without action, the mule deer devoured the available forage, and starvation set in, causing the population to plummet. The case highlighted the limits of conventional thinking about wildlife management and inspired ALDO LEOPOLD and others to embrace a more holistic, integrative approach that took into account the balance of predator and prey, the significance of native plants, and the effects of seasonal (and larger) natural cycles.

The preserve, the canyon itself, and other surrounding lands were designated a national monument in 1908 and the nation's 17th national park in 1919. The age of mass tourism at the canyon was already well under way by then, ushered in by a railway line and, soon afterward, paved roads to and along the canyon's rim. The paved roads led to a boom in car tourism that the NATIONAL PARK SERVICE enthusiastically supported with parking lots, paved roadside overlooks, and motor-court-style lodgings. AUTOMOBILES, as did trains, concentrated visitors in a small area where the access route met the rim. Areas beyond the paved roads on the south rim, and all along the north rim, remained largely wild because they were inaccessible to all but the most intrepid tourists. The concentration of so many cars in so small a space—more than five million a year by the late 1990s— meant that the portion of the south rim that defined most visitors' experience of the canyon was increasingly affected by noise, exhaust fumes, and visual clutter. Air tours, which began in 1927 and accounted for 118,000 flights a year by the mid-1990s, raised similar concerns about the interior of the canyon. Under the administration of President BILL CLINTON in the mid-1990s, the Park Service moved to limit air tours and to phase out automobile access to the rim in favor of shuttle buses and a revived rail service. As with similar proposals for other parks—limits on snowmobiles at YELLOWSTONE, for example—the restrictions were decried as efforts by "environmental elitists" to limit the park access of "ordinary people."

DAMMING THE COLORADO RIVER

The damming of the Colorado River and its tributaries was designed to impound water for hydropower, IRRIGATION, and OUTDOOR RECREATION. Inevitably, however, there were side effects. The completion of HOOVER DAM, downstream, submerged the lower end of the canyon under Lake Mead in 1941. Upstream, the completion of GLEN CANYON DAM in 1963 regularized and sharply reduced the flow of water through the Grand Canyon. The water that *did* pass the Glen Canyon Dam was from the bottom of newly formed Lake Powell: cold and sediment free. The Colorado, once a warm, sediment-laden river whose flow varied with the seasons (3,000 to 90,000 cubic feet per second), became a cold, clear river that flowed at a steady but reduced volume (8,000–20,000 cubic feet per second). River otters, muskrats, and many of the species of FISH native to the Colorado have since disappeared from the canyon, along with numerous species of BIRDS, INSECTS, lizards, and frogs. The natural cycle of scouring and rebuilding that shaped sandbars in the river and beaches along its banks also has been interrupted. Invasive nonnative plants have taken hold alongside the river, and nonnative algae in the river itself, crowding out native species ill adapted to the new conditions.

The effects of the Glen Canyon Dam, both on the Grand Canyon and on Glen Canyon itself, raised sensitivity to the environmental effects of large DAMS, RESERVOIRS, AND ARTIFICIAL LAKES. This heightened awareness contributed to the defeat, in 1968, of the Marble Canyon and Bridge Canyon Dam projects, which would have further altered the Grand Canyon's ECOSYSTEMS. It also led to an effort to approximate the Colorado's spring flood by releasing a 45,000-cubic-feet-per-second flow of water from the Glen Canyon Dam for seven days in late March and early April 1996. A series of similar releases followed, but their ability to substitute adequately for natural processes remains in doubt. The Glen Canyon Dam has, accordingly, become a focal point of calls to decommission and remove dams whose environmental costs outweigh their human benefits.

See also BUREAU OF RECLAMATION; ENVIRONMENTAL-ISM, MAINSTREAM; ENVIRONMENTALISM, RADICAL; INDIANS, SOUTHWEST; REPTILES; SPECIES, EXOTIC AND INVASIVE; TRAVEL AND TOURISM; UNITED STATES—SOUTHWEST; VOLCANOES.

A. Bowdoin Van Riper

Further Reading

Farmer, Jared. *Glen Canyon Dammed: Inventing Lake Powell and the Canyon Country.* Tucson: University of Arizona Press, 2004.

Fradkin, Phillip. *A River No More: The Colorado River and the West.* 2d ed. Berkeley and Los Angeles: University of California Press, 1996.

Goetzmann, William H. *Exploration and Empire: The Explorer and the Scientist in the Winning of the American West.* New York: Knopf, 1966.

Martin, Russell. *A Story That Stands Like a Dam.* New York: Holt, 1989.

Pyne, Stephen J. *How the Canyon Became Grand: A Short History.* New York: Viking, 1998.

Young, Christian C. *In The Absence of Predators: Conservation and Controversy on the Kaibab Plateau.* Lincoln: University of Nebraska Press, 2002.

Grange (The Order of Patrons of Husbandry)

The Order of Patrons of Husbandry, or the Grange, is an agricultural organization and a fraternal order founded in 1867 to promote the interests of farmers through education, cooperation, and mutual protection. In its first decades, the Grange was at the forefront of efforts to preserve community-based family farms, encourage sound agricultural practices, and promote public accountability over the railroad industry. The contemporary Grange continues to emphasize the needs of the rural United States and its family farmers. Membership in the Grange has fluctuated considerably since its founding; the National Grange, located in WASHINGTON, D.C., currently claims 300,000 members in 3,600 local communities in 37 states.

Oliver H. Kelley (1826–1913) is generally credited with the idea of the Grange and its founding. Kelley conducted a survey of the American South for the U.S. DEPARTMENT OF AGRICULTURE in 1866. He detailed the plight of southern farm families, observations that contributed, in part, to the Grange's original emphasis on enhancing the status of farmers by drawing them into association with each other. In Kelley's book of the early days of the Grange published in 1875, he described his hope to elevate the occupation of farmer to make it an "honor to be a cultivator of the soil." Other accounts of the Grange's official beginning on December 4, 1867, in Washington, D.C., also emphasize the contributions of the cofounders William Saunders (1822–1900) (in whose office the meeting occurred), Aaron B. Grosh (1803–84), William M. Ireland (d. 1891), John R. Thompson (1834–94), Francis McDowell (1831–94), and John Trimble (1831–1902). Caroline Hall (1838–1918), Kelley's niece, suggested that women gain full membership in this fraternal organization when Kelley visited her in Boston after his southern tour. The inclusion of women in the Grange was an innovation at that time. The National Grange in 1892 recognized Hall as "equal to a founder."

The Grange Illustrated; or Patron's Hand-Book, published in 1874, provides insight into the names for the organization. *Patrons of Husbandry* highlights the unifying task of cultivating crops and raising livestock, while the term *Grange* refers to meetings of the order and to the membership in its collective capacity. The contemporary term *National Grange,* implies now as it did at the founding that the organization has multiple levels of organization: the Subordinate or local Grange, the Pomona or county Grange, the State Grange, and the National Grange.

The Grange movement emerged at the same time as unprecedented expansion in agricultural and industrial production in the United States. While the Grange explicitly disavowed engagement in religious or political discussions and activity at its founding, farmers still had to respond to the prevailing conditions of agricultural production and the sale of their products. This situation led to a modification of the Grange's original emphasis on fraternity and the elevation of the status of farmers to an organization oriented around mutual protection. In the last half of the 19th century, farmers who once produced for home and village consumption increasingly faced middlemen who extracted transaction costs for distant buyers. Uncertain and ever-increasing railroad transit expenses for agricultural goods compounded the financial difficulties. Overproduction of cash crops led to lower prices and soil degradation. Periodic insect infestations and ruinous weather contributed to farmers' growing inability to meet ever-increasing financial obligations. Debt on equipment purchases and the neglect of the production of needed food staples in certain regions added to the financial insecurities of farmers.

The Grange's direct attention to these pressing economic questions led to its phenomenal growth in the 1870s. Farmers flocked to the Grange once they realized the financial advantages that could be gained by becoming members. In 1872, some 1,105 granges were organized. Nearly eight times that number were organized in 1873 with a total membership of around 700,000. By 1875, membership reached 760,000 with Granges located across the United States, but concentrated in the Midwest and the South. After a period of membership losses after the initial flurry of growth, the Grange gained greater strength in the East and the West in the 1880s.

Interpretations of the ideological orientation of the Grange membership in the 19th century vary. Emphasis on its goals simply to preserve the family farm and traditional agrarian practices are met with claims that the Grange was also a radical agrarian organization dedicated to challenging CAPITALISM in favor of a cooperative vision of socialism. Multiple financial pressures on Grange farmers did promote the practice of cooperation in buying, selling, and producing farm and farm-related products. These cooperative practices, while not pursued vigorously by the Grange after the 19th century, suggested an alternative economic arrangement to large-scale industrial capitalism and the pressures of national and international markets.

The development of the national railroad grid in the United States at the same time as the Grange's initial founding and expansion posed a particular challenge. RAILROADS provided a new means to deliver an expanded range of goods to a greater number of markets from the site of production. Grange members were not unequivocally opposed to the building of railroads. The major concerns focused on the ultimate beneficiaries of the system and a fair rate structure. The Grange responded with the support of legislation (known then as the Granger Laws) in a number of states, particularly Illinois, Minnesota, Iowa, and Wisconsin, that ultimately led to state laws regulating the maximal rates that railroads could set for the transport of goods. While there was no immediate environmental benefit to these laws or the U.S. Supreme Court decisions (the "Granger Cases") in fall 1876 that decided in favor of these laws, the outcome did help establish the principle that private corporate interests are subject to public accountability. Of particular note is *Munn v. Illinois* 94 U.S. 113 [1876]), which reaffirmed the power of the state of Illinois to set maximal rates for storage in grain elevators. This case helped establish the principle that the state has the ability to limit corporate power.

The Grange's attention to the concerns of the family farm anticipated contemporary trends that emphasize locally produced products from small-scale nonindustrial farms. An example of the early emphasis on the small-scale farmer can be found in *The Grange Illustrated; or Patron's Hand-Book* (1874), published at the apex of Grange membership. John G. Wells edited this one-volume compendium of Grange history, rules and regulations, songs, recitations, and lore to meet "farmers' every-day wants." A key section entitled

"Agriculture and Horticulture" summarized optimal farming methods that are predecessors to contemporary notions about SUSTAINABILITY. The issue of small farms versus large farms, as well as advice on drainage, plowing, IRRIGATION, FERTILIZER, crop selection, optimal GRASSES for hay and pasture, and the best combination and number of livestock, were all devoted to practices that promote self-reliance and self-sufficiency. The point was to enable Grange members to avoid entanglement in systems of credit and indebtedness.

The National Grange continues to advocate farm policies that encourage CONSERVATION techniques and the maintenance of the best agricultural land. Similarly to the Grange of old described in the *Hand-Book,* the contemporary Grange seeks ways to protect farmers from the undue concentration of market power that makes it difficult for farmers to compete and impossible for new generations of farmers to enter this profession.

See also AGRICULTURE, COMMERCIAL; AGRICULTURE, FEDERAL POLICIES; CHICAGO BOARD OF TRADE; CORN; COTTON; GRAINS; POPULISM; UNITED STATES—DEEP SOUTH; UNITED STATES—MIDWEST; WHEAT.

Ken Estey

Further Reading

Buck, Solon Justus. *The Granger Movement: A Study of Agricultural Organization and Its Political, Economic and Social Manifestations: 1870–1880.* Lincoln: University of Nebraska Press, 1913.

Kelley, Oliver H. *Origin and Progress of the Order of the Patrons of Husbandry in the United States; A History from 1866 to 1873.* Philadelphia: J. A. Wagenseller Publisher, 1875.

Nordin, D. Sven. *Rich Harvest: A History of the Grange, 1867–1900.* Jackson: University Press of Mississippi, 1974.

Wells, John G. *The Grange Illustrated; or Patron's Hand-Book, in the Interests of the Order of Patrons of Husbandry.* New York: Grange Publishing Co., 1874.

Woods, Thomas A. *Knights of the Plow: Oliver H. Kelley and the Origins of the Grange in Republican Ideology.* Ames: Iowa State University Press, 1991.

grasses

Among the most versatile plants on Earth, grasses are so ubiquitous across the United States that Americans often fail to appreciate their significance. Yet over time, they have played varied and complex environmental roles from providing nutritional support for Native Americans and BISON before the arrival of Europeans in North America to acting as a source of aesthetic pride for suburban homeowners in the 21st century.

Grasses are plants from the Grameamean or Poaceae family. Most grasses are annual or perennial herbs that die and resurface from a root system at the start of the next growing season. Typically grasses have onionlike nodes at the base of the plants and have long narrow leaves with veins. Some grasses produce small monoecious or dioecious flowers called florets. Temperate zones throughout the United States dictate which grasses will thrive in a given climate area. Most grasses are successful in steppe or prairie locations, whose environments allow some plants to grow up to 11 feet tall. Between the MISSISSIPPI RIVER and the ROCKY MOUNTAINS there are two types of temperate zones. Near the river, taller grasses thrive as they receive more than 20 inches of rain a year, and closer to the Rocky Mountains shorter grasses succeed because of the colder winters and drier climate, with less than 12 inches of rain annually.

Today in North America, there are more than 900 native and 400 nonnative grasses from more than 600 genera. The most common genera are the panic grasses (*Panicum* spp.), the bluegrasses (*Poa* spp.), and the needle grasses (*Stipa* spp.). Most of the nonnative grasses were intentionally or unintentionally imported from different parts of Eurasia during the time of European colonization. From the 16th through the 19th centuries, European livestock, including HORSES, CATTLE, PIGS AND HOGS, and sheep, destroyed or overtaxed local and regional ECOSYSTEMS and native grasses across North America, compelling the colonizers to transplant nonnative plants. Some scholars have argued that similarities between European temperate zones and those in North America allowed European flora, mostly grasses, to thrive and often out-compete native plants, aiding in European dominance.

Humans living in the United States have used a variety of grasses for food, shelter, and OUTDOOR RECREATION and sports. Today these grasses fall into three categories: agricultural, pasture, and LAWN grasses.

WHEAT, an introduced plant originally from the Fertile Crescent region in the Middle East, has been an important agricultural crop throughout U.S. history. In the 19th century, American farmers adopted European agricultural practices, leading to MONOCULTURE farming, which departed from the Native American polyculture methods. With better production and transportation methods in the late 19th and early 20th centuries, wheat developed into one of the United States's cash crops. Today, wheat *(Triticum aestivum* or *Triticum vulgare)* is one of the important cereal GRAINS, used to make bread, pasta, noodles, alcohol, flour, and a variety of pastries. Wheat is a tall grass that produces flowering heads known as awns. However, some wheat have awnless heads. The central plains are one ideal temperate zone in the United States in which to grow wheat, although it has been grown elsewhere in the nation, because the mix-grass prairies are wet during the growing season and dry at the time of harvest. Wheat is produced year-round and is sown in the spring and winter.

CORN (*Zea mays*), a grass native to North America, flourishes in various temperate zones of the United States. The female plant produces a flower known as a cob with hundreds of flowers each producing a seed or kernel. Prior to European colonization, different Native Americans across

North America harvested corn to supplement their diets. Upon arrival, European migrants adopted corn as an agricultural crop and, as with wheat, developed it for commercial purposes. Today, corn can be steamed or boiled for food consumption or ground to produce a variety of products such as tortillas, cornflakes, corn chips, corn syrup, alcohol, cornstarch, and flour. In many parts of the United States, corn is used to feed large livestock herds after it goes through a fermentation process. Aside from nutritional value, corn was also used to manufacture ethanol in the latter part of the 20th century. When combined with liquid petroleum, ethanol is used as fuel for AUTOMOBILES. In addition to wheat and corn, Americans, today, use other grasses such as barley, sugarcane, and RICE for their nutritional and economic value.

Pasture grasses provide important forage for herbivorous domestic and wildlife animals. Before Europeans settled on the central Great Plains of the United States, DEER, elk, antelope, and BISON relied on the variety of grasses for food and shelter from natural predators. In turn, the Indians of the Plains relied on the bison for food, clothing, shelter, and tools. Today, only a small percentage of native grassland exists for domestic grazing; for this reason, humans grow, harvest, dry, and bale hay to feed livestock. Some of the more common types of pasture grasses, both native and nonnative, in the United States included timothy *(Phylum pratense),* rye grasses *(Lolium perenne* and *Lolium multiflorum),* meadow foxtail *(Alopecurus pratensis),* and cock's-foot *(Dactylic glomerata).*

Most lawn grasses, also known as turf, pitch, or green grasses, are imported species from Eurasia. Lawns, as we know them today, were a European introduction in the early 19th century, gaining popularity among the growing middle class shortly after the CIVIL WAR (1861–65). Some Americans use turf grasses to decorate their front and back lawns in urban neighborhoods, while others carefully manicure green grasses for recreational sports such as golf, football, baseball, and tennis. Most lawn grasses are adapted to different climates through selective breeding. In the United States, there are two types of turf grasses: cool grasses and warm grasses. Cool grasses grow well in climate zones that are extremely cold in the winter and warm/hot in the summer. During the summer months, these grasses receive regular intervals of rain. Cool grasses include bentgrass, bluegrass, fescue, and ryegrass. Dry grasses turn brown in the early winter months and require good soil to reseed in the spring. Dry grasses include bahia, Bermuda, buffalo, carpet, centipede, grama, St. Augustine, and zoysia. Humans have defined some aggressive lawn grasses, such as crabgrasses, as WEEDS. Humans eliminate them because they compete with desired turf grasses. Lawn grasses require significant maintenance, involving methods that are often extremely destructive to local and regional ecosystems. The use of PESTICIDE and herbicide to kill pests and unwanted plants causes damage to the environment, as these chemicals can reenter some water tables that supply humans with DRINKING WATER. Also, cutting grasses often requires the use of gasoline-operated lawn mowers, which contribute up to 5 percent of the AIR POLLUTION in larger cities across the country during the summer months. Finally, many Americans use excessive amounts of water to maintain their lawns during the planting season, depleting much-needed water resources in urban areas. In fact, many cities regulate the hours in which their residents may water their lawns. For some people, during the early summer months, many grasses affect the HUMAN BODY, as they pollinate, causing hay fever and ALLERGIES.

Finally, in the late 20th century, Americans also used grasses to prevent and correct some unintended environmental consequences of human activities in the United States. Grasses are especially useful in EROSION control. Through crop rotation, for example, grasses protect the top layer of soil from being blown away and regenerate much-needed nutrients for agricultural crops.

See also AGRICULTURE, COLONIAL; AGRICULTURE, COMMERCIAL; AGRICULTURE, SUBSISTENCE; COLUMBIAN EXCHANGE; HOUSING, PRIVATE; INDIANS, CENTRAL PLAINS; INDIANS, NORTHERN PLAINS; PASTORALISM; SPECIES, EXOTIC AND INVASIVE; SPECIES, INDIGENOUS; SUBURBANIZATION; UNITED STATES—CENTRAL PLAINS; UNITED STATES—NORTHERN PLAINS.

Jerry Wallace

Further Reading

Barkworth, Mary E., et al. *Manual of Grasses of North America.* Logan: Utah State University, 2007.
Crosby, Alfred. *The Columbian Exchange.* Santa Barbara, Calif.: Praeger, 2007.
Darke, Rick, and Mark Griffiths, eds. *Manual of Grasses.* Portland, Oreg.: Timber Press, 1994.
Malin, James. *The Grassland of North America: Prolegomena to Its History.* Lawrence: University of Kansas Press, 1947.
Smith, James. *A Key to the Genera of Grasses of the Conterminous United States.* 6th ed. Arcata, Calif.: Humboldt State University, 1981.
Sprague, Howard. *Grasslands of the United States: Their Economic and Ecological Importance.* Ames: Iowa State University Press, 1974.
United States Environmental Protection Agency. Office of Mobile Sources. *Small Engine Emission Standards.* Washington, D.C.: EPA, August 1998.

grassroots environmentalism   *See* ENVIRONMENTALISM, GRASSROOTS.

Great American Desert

In the 19th century, many Americans viewed the Great Plains as a desert. Although later discounted, this environ-

"Great American Desert"

mental misnomer influenced settlement patterns for much of the century, as Americans initially leapfrogged the Plains in search of supposedly more fertile soils. The Great American Desert, as it was called on many 19th-century maps, stretched over parts of the present-day states of Nebraska, Colorado, Kansas, Oklahoma, and Texas.

The Great Plains became a part of the United States when President THOMAS JEFFERSON made the LOUISIANA PURCHASE from France in 1803. Jefferson commissioned two official expeditions into the new territory. Although the more

celebrated LEWIS AND CLARK EXPEDITION from 1804 to 1806 noted the dryness and the absence of trees of the northern plains, its leaders refrained from characterizing the entire region as a desert.

ZEBULON PIKE led another expedition through the southwestern reaches of the Louisiana Purchase from 1806 to 1807. Pike denoted a region possessing attributes comparable to Africa's deserts. His descriptions, influenced by his experiences in a more humid and forested eastern United States, may have reflected an attempt to soothe government officials' anxieties regarding the Union's cohesiveness should its population rapidly spread westward. Pike assured his superiors that the "desert" conditions of the region would prevent overextension and a possible governmental fissure. Although more than a decade passed before the next official expedition into the region, it would leave an unequivocal impression of the region as a "Great American Desert."

In 1820, Major Stephen H. Long of the U.S. ARMY TOPOGRAPHICAL ENGINEERS followed the Platte River and its southerly fork westward across the Plains to the ROCKY MOUNTAINS. Long's expedition explored the Plains from the Platte to the Canadian River. The expedition's published report, compiled by the botanist Edwin James, portrayed the region as nonarable and regarded it as best left to a nomad population. Overwhelmed by vast treeless expanses of sandy soils covered by a veneer of grass, Long's expedition produced a map that referred to the area between the 98th meridian and the Rocky Mountains as the "Great Desert." The report's conclusions aligned with the climatic realities on the Plains at the time. The Long expedition occurred during regionwide extended DROUGHT. The nation soon set aside as Indian Territory the seemingly worthless area extending from present-day Nebraska to Oklahoma.

The idea of a "Great American Desert" dissipated after the 1850s as Euro-Americans settled the region in greater numbers. Reevaluations of the region's productive potential proliferated while federal legislation facilitated settlement of what was soon regarded as the Great Plains rather than the Great American Desert. Boosters used the "Great American Desert" in literature promoting agricultural settlement during the 1870s and 1880s. Advocating the myth that rain followed the plow, they claimed that the once-arid climate was transformed by the supposed rainmaking powers of agricultural settlement. Rainfall was plentiful on the Plains during much of this period, but it had nothing to do with increased cultivation. The Plains historically experienced cyclical wet and dry phases, and this era of agricultural settlement coincided with an extended wet phase. Settlers and boosters, buoyed by this cycle of rainfall, dismissed JOHN WESLEY POWELL's sobering calls in the 1870s for acceptance of and fundamental adaptations to the region's enduring aridity beyond the 100th meridian. The perceptions of a Great American Desert began to fade from American memory during the 1870s and 1880s.

An inevitable return of a dry phase undermined boosters' claims that aridity decreased with agricultural production. Rain and settlers evaporated from the Plains during an extended drought in the late 1880s and early 1890s. The drought, along with an economic depression, cleared the western plains of many small farmers and fostered a greater respect for the limits of traditional agriculture in the region. Yet, it proved a tenuous respect, as agriculturists adopted new methods, crops, and

technologies and pressed the region's environmental limits during the return of booming wet years, only to be repelled by the return of drought and extensive soil EROSION in the 20th century known as the DUST BOWL. Responsive federal programs and individual adaptations to this crisis slowed the tempo of this ongoing tango between the environment and human settlement on the Great Plains but did not end it entirely.

After WORLD WAR II (1941–45), new AGRICULTURAL TECHNOLOGY allowed farmers to reach the Ogallala aquifer, an underground water supply cut off from its ancient sources. By the 21st century, industrial farming made the Plains a consistently productive agricultural region, but the area faced soil and water depletion, and family farmers lost independence as government aid compensated them for low grain prices.

See also AQUIFERS; BISON; GRASSES; INDIANS, CENTRAL PLAINS; INDIANS, NORTHERN PLAINS; UNITED STATES—CENTRAL PLAINS; UNITED STATES—NORTHERN PLAINS.

John Husmann

Further Reading

Hollon, W. Eugene. *The Great American Desert Then and Now.* New York: Oxford University Press, 1966.

Opie, John. *Ogallala: Water for a Dry Land.* Lincoln: University of Nebraska Press, 2000.

Smith, Henry Nash. *Virgin Land: The American West as Symbol and Myth.* Cambridge, Mass.: Harvard University Press, 1971.

Great Awakening

The Great Awakening (often called the First Great Awakening) refers to a series of evangelical religious revivals in the British North American colonies, in the late 1730s and 1740s. These events stressed the importance of an immediate and personal experience with God and frequently occurred in rural outdoor locations. Many participants believed that a stronger connection with God was found in such natural environments.

The revivals, which began with Presbyterian communities in the Middle Colonies, soon encompassed other Protestant denominations. In the late 1730s, a dispute emerged in the Presbyterian Synod of Pennsylvania over the training of clergy and the nature of the relationship between the people and God. The older, more established members of the church hierarchy tended to be born in Europe and educated at British universities. The younger elements of the church, however, were largely colonial born and trained at Harvard University or Yale College.

By the 1730s, the latter group became disaffected by the structured nature of the church and boring sermons. The only way truly to know God, they believed, was through a passionate religious experience. Clergymen who had not undergone such an occurrence were not qualified to deliver the holy message. Led by men such as Gilbert Tennent, these preachers sought to awaken a "new light" in the people through a personal conversion experience. An itinerant preaching style distinguished these New Lights, as they came to be known, from the Old Lights. Traveling preachers moved from town to town, often to the annoyance of a village's resident minister, delivering emotional sermons designed to evoke powerful religious sentiments that emphasized an intimate relationship with God. In Northampton, Massachusetts, for example, the Reverend JONATHAN EDWARDS warned his congregates of the dangers of sin and eternal damnation. Although Edwards lacked an explosive speaking style, his methodical warnings induced fearful emotions in his flock.

Colonial newspapers helped to spread the word of the revivals among the colonies. Revivals had taken place in local communities before, but the rise of the colonial press in this period allowed faster communication between distant regions. The publication of personal conversion narratives and notices that highlighted impending visits by prominent itinerants contributed to a belief among colonists that God was at work in America. The colonists were further encouraged by reports, in 1738, that George Whitefield, a popular British evangelist, would soon visit the colonies. The transmission of information through the press, combined with Whitefield's arrival in late 1739, helped to transform a series of local revivals into a general, intercolonial Great Awakening.

George Whitefield arrived in PHILADELPHIA, PENNSYLVANIA, on November 8, 1739, to great fanfare. According to BENJAMIN FRANKLIN, an estimated 6,000 people heard Whitefield's sermon from the steps of the courthouse. A dynamic speaker, Whitefield was also an effective self-promoter. He generated enthusiasm for his appearances by placing ads in several newspapers. Large crowds appeared in other cities and towns, including a reported 20,000 people who heard Whitefield's farewell sermon at Boston Common on October 12, 1740.

Open-air revivals were a key component of Whitefield's strategy. Outdoor spaces conveniently enabled large crowds to gather, allowing Whitefield to utilize his powerful voice. More importantly, they allowed disparate groups of individuals to worship together in fields, woodland areas, and other nonurban places. This feature marked revivals led by other ministers as well. The natural world enabled thousands to strengthen their connection with God by communing in spaces displaying evidence of his power. Meeting houses were the artificial creations of human beings, and it was in the natural environment where God had first revealed himself to Adam and Eve. Some American colonists longed for the same experience, hoping that God might speak to them under an open sky.

The intercolonial nature of the Great Awakening had significant implications for American society. George Whitefield's tours and the burgeoning press contributed to a developing sense of a distinctive American identity. The newspapers enabled Americans to learn what was happening in other parts of the colonies while the revivals communicated a shared experience. By 1745, when the Great Awakening began to subside, the framework for an American community was ready to take its place. This foundation contributed to the colonies' ability to coordinate protests against British policies prior to the AMERICAN REVOLUTION (1775–83). The United States experienced subsequent awakenings, or periods of religious revivals, in the first three decades of the 19th century and at its end.

See also ENGLISH EXPLORATION AND SETTLEMENT—CANADA AND NEW ENGLAND; ENGLISH EXPLORATION AND SETTLEMENT—THE MIDDLE COLONIES; ENGLISH EXPLORATION AND SETTLEMENT—THE SOUTH; RELIGION.

James P. Ambuske

Further Reading

Bonomi, Patricia U. *Under the Cope of Heaven: Religion, Society, and Politics in Colonial America.* New York: Oxford University Press, 2003.

Edwards, Jonathan, and C. C. Goen, eds. *The Great-Awakening: A Faithful Narrative. The Distinguishing Marks: Some Thoughts Concerning the Revival, Letters Relating to the Revival.* New Haven, Conn.: Yale University Press, 1972.

Hall, David D. *Worlds of Wonder, Days of Judgment: Popular Religious Belief in Early New England.* Cambridge, Mass.: Harvard University Press, 1989.

Lambert, Frank. *Inventing the "Great Awakening."* Princeton, N.J.: Princeton University Press, 1999.

Lovejoy, David S. *Religious Enthusiasm in the New World: Heresy to Revolution.* Cambridge, Mass.: Harvard University Press, 1985.

Rutman, Darrett Bruce. *The Great Awakening: Event and Exegesis.* Problems in American History. New York: Wiley, 1970.

Great Basin   *See* UNITED STATES—COLUMBIA PLATEAU AND GREAT BASIN.

great chain of being, the

The concept of the great chain of being is a product of the tension between other-worldliness and this-worldliness that has animated the core of Western philosophy from classical to modern times. Stated simply, the great chain of being conceptualizes all existing things in nature as a vast hierarchy ranked from simple, inanimate materials to complex, spiritual forms.

This concept finds its genesis in Plato's cosmogony, or theory for the origin and evolution of the universe (articulated most fully in his fourth-century B.C.E. treatise Timaeus). Platonists and the subsequent Christian theologians, who for centuries sought to synthesize Platonism with scriptural sources, envisioned the world as derivative of "The Good," or, in other words, as merely a gross copy of the singularly perfect archetype. If the "eternal source" was indeed perfect, lacking in nothing, then it must be the ground for the actualization of all possibilities, containing the archetype of all things. This dimension of the great chain of being, generally referred to as the principle of plentitude, imagines an elaborately organized hierarchy of all possible beings emanating from the perfection of the One, placing each creature in its proper place: nonanimate objects at the base, superseded by plants, insects, animals, humans, and angels. It is worth noting that this cosmology offers a theodicy (a vindication of God's good in the face of evil) as well. Suffering is a necessary element of true plentitude; actualizing the full potentiality of the Supreme Being begets everything, even imperfections.

Through the Middle Ages, the great chain of being served to mediate between the perfection of the infinite and the imperfection of the temporal but also provided fertile ground for the birth and growth of the modern naturalistic sciences. The ubiquity of the notion of the great chain of being created the intellectual environment necessary for the scientific revolutions that the psychoanalysis founder Sigmund Freud (1856–1939) labeled as "blows to human narcissism." As the basis for orthodox speculation about nature, theoretical consistency with the great chain of being suggested an anthropology of humility: Human beings were but one link in a great chain, undeserving of any ontological privilege. Furthermore, if each link in the great chain were only infinitesimally different from the next, it followed that humans were in essence indistinguishable from animals. The development of the idea of the great chain of being had direct currency for the popularization of Darwinian EVOLUTION and the contemporary articulation of "biocentric" ethics.

In the 18th and 19th centuries, the great chain of being fomented two conceptual elements in the emerging biological sciences. The first was the idea of the niche: The central thrust of the "great chain" is that all living organisms inhabit a unique place in the scale of being; thus a key labor for natural scientists was to devise logically ordered systems that described the place appropriate to each creature. A number of environmental historians have argued that the very taxonomic enterprise formalized by the Swedish botanist and zoologist Carl Linnaeus (1707–78) is premised on the ontological presupposition of the great chain of being. The second conceptual element was the temporalization of the principle of plentitude. Intellectual giants of the 18th century argued that truly scientific NATURAL HISTORY lay in the observation of the unfolding of nature's possibilities, very much in accord with the ideas of the German philosopher Georg Hegel (1770–1831), who described world history as akin to the growth of an acorn into an oak. Given that nature was to be studied as a kind of ontological sequence, 18th-century biologists were fixated on the search for "missing links," and such an emphasis on the unfolding potentiality of nature certainly contributed to the later scientific cultures that would see the natural world in terms of complexity, speciation, and selection.

In the 19th and 20th centuries, especially in the United States, the great chain of being continued as a foundational concept for thinking about nature. For instance, the romantic transformation of nature in the writings of the American transcendentalists was accomplished with recourse to a language of organic interconnectedness that had its roots in the great chain of being. In fact, according to the historian Donald Worster, the great chain of being was more than a mere taxonomy; it was a "system of economic interdependence and mutual assistance . . . man and worm alike live to preserve each other's life."

While contemporary notions of ecological interdependence may have their origin in the great chain of being, the concept's emphasis on hierarchy persists as a problem for evolutionary theorists. Building on centuries of research on the *scala naturae*, modern scientists struggle to find ways to discuss evolution without reference to the hierarchy of biological forms, evolutionary teleology, or the progress of natural history, all traces of the lasting influence of the great chain of being.

See also BOTANY; ECOSYSTEMS; NATURE WRITING; ROMANTICISM; TRANSCENDENTALISM; ZOOLOGY.

Evan Berry

Further Reading
Glacken, Clarence. *Traces on the Rhodian Shore.* Berkeley: University of California Press, 1967.
Lovejoy, Arthur. *The Great Chain of Being.* Cambridge, Mass.: Harvard University Press, 1982.
Worster, Donald. *Nature's Economy.* Cambridge, Mass.: Cambridge University Press, 1994.

Great Depression

The Great Depression was the most wrenching economic crisis in American history. It began with the sudden crash of the stock market on "Black Tuesday," October 29, 1929, and quickly spread through the most critical sectors of the American industrial economy.

The automobile, STEEL, and other heavy industries suffered mightily; COAL mining, particularly in Appalachia, experienced a considerable downturn; and the housing and construction industries ground to a standstill. The percentage of unemployed Americans steadily increased until 1932, when a staggering 25 percent of the workforce was out of work. The Great Depression hit the agricultural sector with equal severity. Aggregate farm income plummeted from $6 billion in 1929 to just $2 billion in 1932, during which the value of the average family farm was cut in half. Behind these economic statistics lay anger, frustration, suffering, and resignation caused by hard times. Breadlines appeared in cities across America. Hundreds of thousands of unemployed and newly homeless Americans settled in ramshackle encampments derisively called "Hoovervilles," a contemptuous reference to HERBERT HOOVER, who, as president from 1929 to 1933, presided ineffectually over the catastrophe. In rural America, farmers threatened bank officials with violence as farm foreclosures became more frequent. When the Great Depression reached its lowest point during the winter of 1932–33, the American economy was as close to a state of total collapse as at any other point in history.

BACK TO THE LAND: THE SEARCH FOR ENVIRONMENTAL SECURITY

The severity of the economic collapse led many depression era Americans to embrace a sentimentalized view of a life on the land as immune from the vicissitudes of the modern industrial economy. BACK-TO-THE-LAND MOVEMENTS, expressing a sentiment always present in American culture, surged in popularity during the 1930s. "The farm is the safest place to live," the author and farmer Maurice G. Kains (1868–1946) wrote in *Five Acres and Independence* (1935), for, at the very least, the land guaranteed that a working man could provide "food for his family." Thousands of Americans took to heart the message found in works such as *Five Acres and Independence* or *Flight from the City: An Experiment in Creative Living on the Land* (1933) by another back-to-the-land proponent, Ralph Borsodi (1888–1977), and abandoned the city for a life in the country. This was particularly the case in the older industrial states hit hard by the Great Depression. Connecticut experienced an 87 percent increase in its rural population between 1930 and 1935, for example, and in Massachusetts, the rural population grew by more than one-third.

Nationwide, the net migration from the rural areas to the city declined to just two million during the 1930s, down from the six million Americans who left the countryside for the city during the 1920s. The nation's urban areas even recorded a net loss of population during the depths of the depression in 1932, a brief but telling reversal in the long-standing trend toward URBANIZATION in American history. But even for Americans who did not actually move back to the land, the glorification of the nation's agrarian past was a dominant feature of 1930s culture. The economic security and peace of mind that depression era Americans associated with an attachment to the land served as a common theme for some of the decade's most popular works of fiction, including Erskine Caldwell's *Tobacco Road* (1932) and JOHN STEINBECK's *The Grapes of Wrath* (1939). During the Great Depression, many Americans viewed the land as a refuge from the uncertainties of the modern economy. Theirs was a search for economic security through the environmental security commonly associated with life on the land.

AN ENVIRONMENT IN CRISIS

The physical state of the rural American environment left much to be desired during the 1930s. The Great Depression was as much an environmental crisis as an economic one. FLOODS, DROUGHTS, and soil EROSION compounded economic hardships. In 1936 and 1937, devastating floods in New England and on the OHIO RIVER and MISSISSIPPI RIVER, coupled with the memory of the catastrophic Mississippi River flood of 1927, underscored for many Americans the degree to which their environment remained dangerously beyond their control. Drought, soil erosion, and rural poverty, however, most clearly impressed upon Americans the capriciousness of nature. This lesson was most apparent during the cataclysmic DUST BOWL of the mid-1930s, the environmental disaster that led to the loss of millions of acres of soil to wind erosion on the drought-ridden southern plains and set off one of the largest internal migrations in American history as ruined farmers fled the land.

The dust bowl was the most glaring example of a larger environmental crisis endemic to rural America. Drought turned green fields brown from Virginia to Arkansas in 1930 and 1931 before moving on to the Great Plains, and only Maine and Vermont escaped the first half of the 1930s drought-free. Combined with poor land-use practices, the widespread drought conditions led to ruinous levels of soil erosion throughout rural America. U.S. DEPARTMENT OF AGRICULTURE reports produced during the 1930s repeatedly predicted environmental and economic catastrophe if the health of the land continued to deteriorate. Soil erosion "seriously threatens the welfare of large farming populations," one such report declared in 1934, and would soon condemn hundreds of thousands of Americans to "a condition of meager subsistence obtained through bankrupt farming on erosion-depleted land."

These depression era environmental problems took a psychological toll. Many Americans interpreted the disasters of the 1930s as nature's retribution for generations of misguided land-use practices, and the rehabilitation of the environment therefore became an urgent task. FRANKLIN D. ROOSEVELT, who served as president from 1933 to 1945, captured this national mood when he declared in 1937 that "the floods, droughts, and dust storms are . . . manifestations of nature's refusal to tolerate continual abuse of her bounties . . . we must act while there is still yet time if we would preserve for ourselves and our posterity the natural sources of a virile national life."

NEW DEAL FOR THE ENVIRONMENT

The environment was central to the NEW DEAL, the collection of legislative measures and programs crafted by the Roosevelt administration in response to the Great Depression. At the most basic level, the New Deal built upon earlier conservation policies. During the 1930s, for example, tens of millions of acres were added to the public domain managed by the U.S. Forest Service and the National Park Service, two conservation bureaucracies created during the Progressive Era. The New Deal, however, applied the Progressive Era principle of public ownership and management to entirely new environments. The Taylor Grazing Act of 1934 established permanent federal management of 80 million acres of grazing lands (expanded to 140 million acres in 1936), while the Flood Control Act of 1936 signaled a significant expansion in federal authority over the nation's rivers. The New Deal marked an evolution from earlier environmental resource policies in other ways. Roosevelt and the New Dealers believed that environmental conservation projects provided an ideal form of relief work for the unemployed. The popular Civilian Conservation Corps (CCC) put nearly three million American men to work planting trees, building trails, and fighting forest fire in the nation's forests and parks between 1933 and 1941. This was, in Roosevelt's words, "applied conservation" on a scale and scope unprecedented in American history.

The Great Depression and the New Deal also signaled a potentially revolutionary moment in the United States. The twin environmental and economic crises of the 1930s led many Americans to think in terms of environmental limits, of adjusting production to consumption, and of comprehensive planning for the wisest and most sustainable resource use. "The time has come when we must make concessions to nature," Hugh Hammond Bennett, the New Deal's leading soil conservationist, declared in 1935. At its most ambitious, the New Deal urged private landowners, particularly farmers, to make such "concessions to nature" by changing their environmentally destructive ways. The federal government created the Agricultural Adjustment Administration (AAA) in 1933 to help farmers curb surplus production of wheat, cotton, corn, and other key agricultural commodities that were having a ruinous effect on both the land and the agricultural economy by restricting the number of acres individual farmers could plant to these crops. The federal government established the Soil Conservation Service (SCS) in 1935 to encourage farmers to employ techniques such as fallowing, terracing, and contour plowing. Most controversial was the Resettlement Administration (RA), created in 1935, to remove farmers from agricultural lands deemed "submarginal" and beyond rehabilitation by New Deal agricultural experts.

Perhaps the Tennessee Valley Authority (TVA) best embodied the revolutionary potential of the Great Depression and the New Deal. Created in 1933, the TVA called for a series of federally constructed multiple-purpose dams, reservoirs, and artificial lakes on the Tennessee River to promote sustainable, long-term economic development through the coordinated planning of natural resource use on both public and private lands throughout the Tennessee Valley. Lasting economic recovery, it was thought, would be predicated upon profound changes in patterns of natural resource use. In short, the conjoined environmental and economic crises of the 1930s made many Americans receptive to calls for far-reaching reforms in natural resource use that would take into account nature's limits and would allow economic recovery to proceed upon a sustainable basis.

ROOTS OF THE ENERGY-INTENSIVE SOCIETY

In the end, the revolutionary possibilities of the Great Depression were unfulfilled, in part because other patterns established during the 1930s led to the emergence of an energy-intensive economy of mass consumption during the decades following World War II (1941–45). It is important to remember that not all industries were equally affected by the Great Depression. For the petroleum, chemical, electrical appliance, electric utility, and processed food industries—all industries that were instrumental in creating America's energy-intensive "affluent society" of the 1950s and beyond—the 1930s were years of innovation and growth. The petroleum industry, for example, buoyed by developments in the aviation, chemical, and automobile industries, had returned to precrash levels of growth by 1936. The domestic consumption of electricity doubled during the 1930s in spite of the depression. The processed food industry weathered the Great Depression relatively well thanks to technological and marketing innovations, as the number of supermarkets nationwide increased from 300 in 1935 to nearly 5,000 in 1939 and the number of retail outlets that had electric refrigeration increased 30-fold during the 1930s. These developments in the processed food industry dovetailed with the sales of electrical home appliances (the number of refrigerators in American homes tripled during the 1930s), one of the only markets in durable goods that did not collapse during the depression.

Moreover, it is clear that the New Deal was instrumental in establishing the political economic framework and, in some cases, the physical infrastructure necessary for the post–World War II energy-intensive society. The TVA and the Bonneville Power Administration on the Columbia River, for example, established a political economy in electrical energy that facilitated high rates of electricity consumption during the postwar decades. The New Deal's Electric Home and Farm Authority (1934) helped depression era consumers finance the purchase of electrical appliances. The petroleum industry certainly did not mind the fact that one-third of all New Deal public works projects were roads or highways. Originally designed to reduce agricultural surpluses by restricting cultivated acreage, the Agricultural Adjustment Administration ended up benefiting the chemical industry as farmers increased their use of artificial fertilizer, pesticides, and herbicides in order to boost yields on their remaining acres.

In these and other economic sectors, the New Deal established the framework for postwar economic growth. While the Great Depression and the New Deal had held out the prospect of a revolutionary reexamination of natural resource use during the 1930s, they just as surely laid the foundation for the post–World War II energy-intensive society. The roots of the affluent society that emerged during the second half of the 20th century can paradoxically be traced back to the depths of the Great Depression.

See also AGRARIANISM; AGRICULTURE, FEDERAL POLICIES; CORPORATIONS, CHEMICAL; ENERGY, HYDRAULIC; FEDERAL LAW—LAND POLICIES; GROCERY STORES AND SUPERMARKETS; OIL, DOMESTIC; SUSTAINABILITY; UNITED STATES—APPALACHIA.

Kevin Powers

Further Reading

Henderson, Henry L., and David B. Woolner, eds. *FDR and the Environment.* New York: Palgrave McMillan, 2005.

Kennedy, David M. *Freedom from Fear: The American People in Depression and War, 1929–1945.* New York: Oxford University Press, 1999.

Maher, Neil M. *Nature's New Deal: The Civilian Conservation Corps and the Roots of the American Environmental Movement.* New York: Oxford University Press, 2008.

Phillips, Sarah T. *This Land, This Nation: Conservation, Rural America, and the New Deal.* New York: Cambridge University Press, 2007.

Reisch-Owen, Anna Lou. *Conservation under F.D.R.* New York: Praeger, 1983.

Watkins, T. H. *The Hungry Years: A Narrative History of the Great Depression in America.* New York: Henry Holt, 1999.

Great Dismal Swamp

The Great Dismal Swamp is a massive marshy area straddling the border between southeastern Virginia and northeastern North Carolina. It once covered 2,200 square miles—an area almost the size of Delaware—but after more than three centuries of draining and clearing, it now consists of less than 600 square miles. The current Great Dismal Swamp National Wildlife Refuge makes up one-fourth of the swamp. Its most prominent and notable feature is the Dismal Swamp Canal, a 22-mile-long waterway connecting CHESAPEAKE BAY and Albemarle Sound by way of the Elizabeth and Pasquotank Rivers. The canal forms part of the Atlantic Intracoastal Waterway, which runs from Norfolk, Virginia, to MIAMI, FLORIDA. Of the many CANALS constructed throughout the United States in the late 18th and early 19th centuries, the Dismal Swamp Canal remains the only one from the early national period still in operation. It was listed on the National Register of Historic Places in 1988 and is designated as a National Civil Engineering Landmark.

Buried under an ancient sea, the Great Dismal Swamp emerged as a landform when the last shift of the continental shelf occurred. Many species thrived in the forested wetland. Cypress, black gum, maple, Atlantic white cedar, and pine trees provide habitats for black BEARS, bobcats, otters, weasels, and hundreds of species of REPTILES and amphibians. Archaeological evidence suggests that human occupation of the swamp began nearly 13,000 years ago, but by 1650, few Indians remained in the area. European colonizers initially showed little interest in the swamp as its environment appeared both alien and dangerous to them. Over time, European settlements grew up on the fringes of the swamp.

Colonel William Byrd (1674–1744) first proposed a canal in 1728. This British Crown surveyor also gave the region its notorious but undeserved moniker. Another young surveyor, GEORGE WASHINGTON, visited the area and also championed a canal to bisect the swamp. In 1763, Washington, Patrick Henry (1736–99), and several other wealthy investors facilitated the establishment of the Dismal Swamp Company. They planned to harvest the area's timber and establish arable farmland. For a price of 50 cents per acre, the company purchased 40,000 acres of the swamp. Soon after, the proprietors made plans to dig a five-mile-long canal to Lake Drummond—a lake at the center of the swamp and named for William Drummond (1637–77), North Carolina's first governor. Using slave labor, the company produced shingles and lumber and finished a waterway known as the Washington Ditch. The workers, including the black slaves, who dug the canals, cut the trees, and gathered turpentine and furs, often lived on the poquosins, or slightly elevated, drier patches of the coastal plain. In these regions, often away from their owners, slaves experienced a limited level of autonomy.

Lumbering and shingling did not prove economically viable because of the excess of water, but the very water that made the area a swamp proved a good seller throughout the new nation. In fact, it was "bottled" by the keg and highly prized by sailors, who early on realized that the tannic waters of the canal were resistant to bacteria and thus were a perfect, albeit bitter-tasting, hydrant for long voyages.

Between 1787 and 1790, state assemblies in Virginia and North Carolina chartered the Dismal Swamp Canal Company in order to complete a canal from the Chesapeake to the Albemarle. The Dismal Swamp Canal opened in 1805 after 12 years of construction. A feeder ditch was added in 1814, and during the 1820s, eight stone lift lock gates were emplaced. In addition to commercial traffic, the canal became a popular OUTDOOR RECREATION area. The 19th-century novelist HARRIET BEECHER STOWE and the poet HENRY WADSWORTH LONGFELLOW based characters on slaves they witnessed participating in the canal's construction. Edgar Allen Poe reportedly wrote parts of his famous poem "The Raven" while traversing its length.

Throughout the 19th century, the canal's drafts were deepened and the locks reduced in number to two. This canal also faced competition from the Albemarle and Chesapeake Canal, opened in 1859, for the lumber, COTTON, and TOBACCO that plied its route. In 1862, Union forces built and fortified earthworks around the canal to prevent its use by Confederates. After disrepair after the CIVIL WAR (1861–65), the canal company went through various iterations, to include being renamed both the Norfolk and North Carolina Canal Company and the Lake Drummond Canal and Water Company. A private concern revitalized the main canal, in the mid-1890s, by dredging it and cutting a new canal to Deep Creek.

By the 20th century, with more efficient modes of transport, operating the canal became uneconomical. In 1929, the federal government purchased the canal for $500,000 and designated the U.S. ARMY CORPS OF ENGINEERS to maintain and operate it for public benefit. Two decades earlier, the Camp Manufacturing Company had bought all of the defunct canal corporation's land property. It focused upon timbering and in fact was so efficient in that endeavor that it had removed the last original forestation by the 1950s. In 1973, the company's directors donated their holdings to the Nature Conservancy, and they were ultimately turned over to the DEPARTMENT OF THE INTERIOR.

The canal is still in operation but is now used solely for pleasure craft. While there have been rumors reporting termination of its operation, the corps actually has periodically engaged in significant efforts to save it. Approximately 1,700 boaters cruise the river on an annual basis. While it is used mostly by sailboats, the canal's centerline depth, maintained at more than six feet, does allow for motorboat access. Its length generally parallels U.S. Highway 17, and most boaters use it to travel between Norfolk and Elizabeth City. The canal has different depths at its starting and end points. Hence, water to the canal is fed from Lake Drummond in North Carolina and reachable by a feeder ditch or an electric railway. There are lockmasters at the operating locks and notably a portable bridge used for farming operations.

Travel on the canal has waxed and waned over the years, but the Great Dismal Swamp has been recognized for its rich environment. In 1974, CONGRESS established the Great Dismal Swamp National Wildlife Refuge after a donation of almost 50,000 acres from the last corporate owner of the land. Managed by the U.S. FISH AND WILDLIFE SERVICE, the swamp's brownish waters remain mostly unpolluted, while its woodlands have rejuvenated. Blue herons, DEER, and other wildlife abound along its course and are joined by a variety of other mammals, almost 100 species of reptiles, and 200 species of BIRDS. The Great Dismal Swamp remains a historic and environmental treasure.

See also FUR TRADE; LOGGING AND LUMBERING; MAPPING AND SURVEYING; NAVAL STORES; UNITED STATES—DEEP SOUTH; UNITED STATES—TIDEWATER; WILDERNESS.

Kent G. Sieg

Further Reading

Dennis, John V. *The Great Cypress Swamps*. Baton Rouge: Louisiana State University Press, 1988.

Kirby, Jack Temple. *Poquosin: A Study of Rural Landscape and Society*. Chapel Hill: University of North Carolina Press, 1995.

Royster, Charles. *The Fabulous History of the Dismal Swamp Company: A Story of George Washington's Times*. New York: Vintage Press, 2000.

Simpson, Bland. *The Great Dismal: A Carolinian's Swamp Memoir*. Chapel Hill: University of North Carolina Press, 1998.

Traylor, Waverley. *Haunts of the Great Dismal Swamp*. Chesapeake, Va.: Waverly Traylor Photography, 2002.

"The Slave in the Dismal Swamp" Henry Wadsworth Longfellow (1842)

Henry Wadsworth Longfellow (1807–82) was best known for lyric poems, such as "The Song of Hiawatha" and "Paul Revere's Ride," which presented stories of mythology and legend. In 1842, he published a volume, Poems on Slavery, *in support of abolitionism. In "The Slave in the Dismal Swamp," Longfellow writes of an escaped slave hiding in the Great Dismal Swamp. In doing so, he captures the sentiments of many 19th-century Americans, who viewed the swamp as a primeval and dangerous wilderness. It is only in such a seemingly uninhabitable environment, Longfellow suggests, that the slave can find refuge.*

In dark fens of the Dismal Swamp
The hunted Negro lay;
He saw the fire of the midnight camp,
And heard at times a horse's tramp
And a bloodhound's distant bay.

Where will-o'-the-wisps and glow-worms
  shine,
In bulrush and in brake;
Where waving mosses shroud the pine,
And the cedar grows, and the poisonous
  vine
Is spotted like the snake;

Where hardly a human foot could pass,
Or a human heart would dare,

On the quaking turf of the green morass
He crouched in the rank and tangled grass,
Like a wild beast in his lair.

A poor old slave, infirm and lame;
Great scars deformed his face;
On his forehead he bore the brand of
   shame,
And the rags, that hid his mangled frame,
Were the livery of disgrace.

All things above were bright and fair,
All things were glad and free;
Lithe squirrels darted here and there,
And wild birds filled the echoing air
With songs of Liberty!

On him alone was the doom of pain,
From the morning of his birth;
On him alone the curse of Cain
Fell, like a flail on the garnered grain,
And struck him to the earth!

Source: The Complete Poetical Works of Henry Wadsworth Longfellow. Boston: Houghton Mifflin, 1902, 26–27.

Great Lakes

No region in North America has characterized the possibilities of exploration, the engines of commerce, and the concerns for the environment as have the Great Lakes. The scale of the Great Lakes hydrological system rivals any geographical feature on the continent, with a surface area of 94,259 miles (244,160 km)—almost the size of Oregon—and 10,500 miles (17,000 km) of shoreline, holding nearly 20 percent of the planet's readily available supply of freshwater. The Great Lakes form a large part of the border between the United States and Canada. Their drainage basin includes 10 percent of the U.S. population as well as both peninsulas of Michigan; parts of Wisconsin, Minnesota, Illinois, Indiana, Ohio, and New York; as well as the panhandle of Ontario., Canada.

The geological forces that created the Great Lakes began approximately one billion years ago when the earliest portions of what would become the North American continent split apart, forming the Midcontinental Rift running under Lake Superior and Lake Michigan. Approximately 570 million years ago, during a period of supercontinental breakup, the St. Lawrence Rift formed under Lake Ontario, Lake Erie, and into the course of the St. Lawrence River. The lakes as

they are known today are primarily the result of glacial activity between 14,000 and 9,000 years ago. A sheet of ice approximately 1.5 miles (2.5 km) thick extended into the OHIO RIVER valley, covering the entire Great Lakes region. The already weakened rock was easily eroded by the ice sheet and formed a catch basin for much of the meltwater as the GLACIERS began to retreat. The weight of the ice sheet depressed the crust into the mantle. Recovery to its previous position continues to this day at a rate of approximately 21 inches (53 cm) per century in a process called isostatic rebound.

Some 120 Native peoples (referred to as Indians or Native Americans in the United States and First Nations in Canada) inhabited the Great Lakes region at various times in history. Most of these Native Peoples were part of Algonquin language family and lived in villages ranging from 500 to 900 inhabitants. The Iroquois lived in present-day New York State. Among the different groups were the Illinois, the Miami, Menominee, Ojibwe, Sauk, Fox, Ioway, and Potawatomi. These communities have subsequently been called Woodland Indians because they had adapted their cultures to the region's rich FORESTS. They utilized a variety of strategies to ensure their subsistence, including hunting, fishing, foraging, and agriculture.

In 1603, the French explorer Samuel de Champlain (ca. 1575–1635), in search of the NORTHWEST PASSAGE between Europe and the trading centers of Asia, became the first European to mention the Great Lakes, although there may have been undocumented contacts between Europeans and the region's Native Peoples in the late 16th century as well. Champlain wrote in his journal that there was a saltwater lake more than 250 miles long that he believed to be the Pacific Ocean. This illusion persisted for decades, as did grand schemes to use the lakes in commerce to the Pacific. In 1826, the Scottish engineer John MacTaggart (1791–1830) suggested using "the great inland seas" as part of a large canal system connecting Quebec with the Pacific.

Between 1650 and the end of the 17th century, a "middle ground" existed around the Great Lakes. Neither Indians who experienced population losses due to the introduction of European diseases to which they had no immunity nor Europeans who moved through the region in comparatively small numbers were able to dominate. Fluid relations and accommodations dictated interactions among the Indian communities and between Indians and Europeans. Indians increasingly participated in the FUR TRADE and adopted tools and weapons from Europe while Europeans needed to adapt to the kinship politics of the Native Peoples.

The long hoped-for Northwest Passage was not to be found in or created from the Great Lakes, but after Americans claimed the region at the end of the 18th century, they built a large network of CANALS in the first half of the 19th century, making the region a viable hub for industry and

Great Lakes Basin

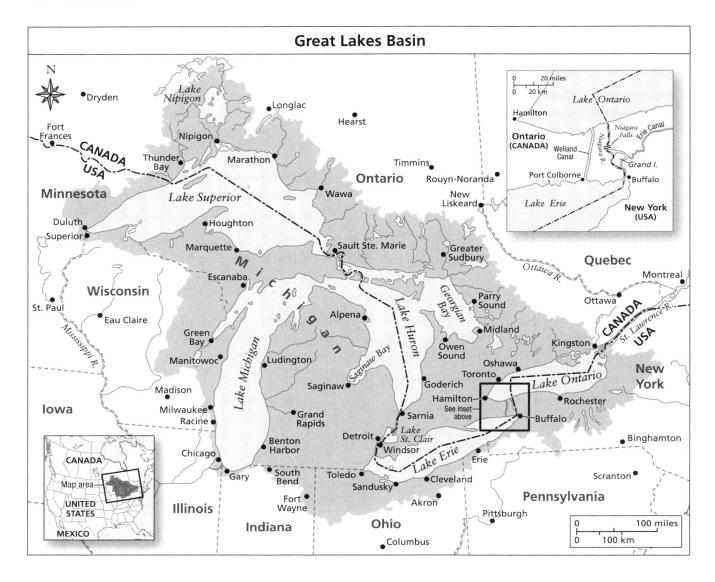

transportation. In 1825, the Erie Canal linked NEW YORK CITY to the lakes via the HUDSON RIVER, and in 1848, the Illinois and Michigan Canal connected CHICAGO, ILLINOIS, via the Illinois River, to the MISSISSIPPI RIVER. By 1850, goods could travel between New York and NEW ORLEANS, LOUISIANA, on inland waterways. The Great Lakes were a nexus for bulk cargo traffic in the 19th century, with GRAINS, iron ore, and COAL moving south to the steel industry, and food and supplies carried north. Despite their important role as a transportation corridor, for centuries, the Great Lakes have proven dangerous waters for ships. The first European vessel to sail the lakes, the brigantine *Griffon,* sank in 1677; most famously, in 1975, the SS *Edmund Fitzgerald* sank off Whitefish Point, Michigan, in Lake Superior.

Cities along the lakes emerged as manufacturing centers in the 19th century. Food processing plants handled the agricultural commodities of the wider Midwest. Furnaces at Duluth, Minnesota; Gary, Indiana; and Chicago produced STEEL. DETROIT, MICHIGAN, was long home to the U.S. AUTOMOBILE industry. The vast supplies of freshwater were also critical to the growth of industry along the lakeshores, both supplying water and providing a "sink" where regional residents dumped industrial, agricultural, and municipal waste. By the 1960s and 1970s, the impacts of dumping became too obvious to ignore. For example, Lake Erie experienced eutrophication, reduced oxygenation, and high nitrogen levels due to the introduction of nutrient phosphorus. Dead fish littered its shore. In 1972, the United States and Canada signed the Great Lakes Water Quality Agreement, which significantly limited the dumping of pollutants and runoff of phosphorus. Most of Lake Erie has become clean enough to allow sunlight to penetrate the water and promote algal and seaweed growth, but a dead zone persists in the central lake. And declines in American heavy manufacturing and steel production in the last decades of the 20th century have left the Great Lakes manufacturing sectors firmly entrenched within the United States's RUST BELT.

With its most prominent feature, NIAGARA FALLS, the Niagara Escarpment (a transitional zone between geological provinces usually characterized by a cliff or steep slope) formed a natural barrier between Lake Ontario and the other Great Lakes. The opening of the Welland Canal in Ontario, Canada, in the early 1800s allowed ships, but also many nonnative species to travel up the St. Lawrence River and the Erie Canal and into previously isolated ECOSYSTEMS, causing extensive ecological and economic damage. The Great Lakes are particularly vulnerable to EXOTIC AND INVASIVE SPECIES, not only because of their prior isolation but because their relatively young age means they have less BIODIVERSITY than might be expected in such a large water system. Before European settlement, there were roughly 150 native FISH species in the lakes. Now almost half of these are threatened or vanished, and at least 162 nonindigenous species have taken their habitat, reducing the opportunities for resurgence. In 2004, the Michigan Department of Natural Resources estimated that invasive species cost the state $5 billion per year.

The two classic examples of invasive species in the Great Lakes are the sea lamprey and the zebra mussel, and their introductions are emblematic of the introductions of many other invaders. The sea lamprey was first recorded in Lake Ontario in 1835, and while some believe it may be native to that lake, others think that it swam up the Erie Canal when it was opened in 1825. The deepening of the Welland Canal in 1921 to allow larger ships into the upper lakes allowed the lamprey to migrate as well, entering Michigan in 1936, Huron in 1937, and Superior in 1946. Feeding on large lake trout before they reach sexual maturity, the lampreys are responsible for a reduction in the value of the Lake Huron trout fishery from $1.5 million in 1937 to zero in 1947. Attempts to control the lampreys have been unsuccessful in part because improvements made to the lake system to help large, disabled native fish also help the lampreys.

The opening of the ST. LAWRENCE SEAWAY in 1959 caused a massive jump in the introduction of invasive species, principally in the ballast water of large saltwater ships. The zebra mussel, native to the brackish and highly polluted Caspian Sea, first appeared in the lakes in 1985, probably transported by way of the Baltic Sea. The highly efficient and prolific zebra mussel clogs intake pipes in municipal water facilities, has drastically altered the balance of algae, and has concentrated pollutants at the bottom of the water column. It is estimated that the zebra mussel does $500 million in damage per year. On the other hand, the zebra mussel, which can filter one liter of water per day, is credited with helping to reduce the eutrophication in Lake Erie.

As there is no effective way to remove an invasive species once introduced, both the U.S. and the Canadian governments have concentrated on preventing new introductions. Cooperation among national, state, and provincial governments on both sides of the U.S.-Canadian border on these and other environmental issues provides a model for balancing the interests of many stakeholders and weighing the obligations and limitations of a variety of treaties and laws.

See also CANADA AND THE UNITED STATES; CLEVELAND, OHIO; INDIANS, MIDWEST; INDIANS, NORTHEAST; SPECIES, INDIGENOUS; TREATIES AND INTERNATIONAL LAW; UNITED STATES—MIDWEST; UNITED STATES—NORTHEAST.

Katherine Keirns

Further Reading
Bogue, Margaret Beattie. *Fishing the Great Lakes: An Environmental History, 1783–1933.* New York: University of Wisconsin Press, 2000.
Dempsey, Dave. *On the Brink: The Great Lakes in the 21st Century.* East Lansing: Michigan State University Press, 2004.
Grady, Wayne. *The Great Lakes: The Natural History of a Changing Region.* New York: Greystone Books, 2007.
White, Richard. *The Middle Ground: Indians, Empires and Republics in the Great Lakes Region, 1650–1815.* Cambridge: Cambridge University Press, 1991.

Great Migration (1915–1970)

The Great Migration involved the mass exodus of southern blacks to northern, midwestern, and western urban industrial areas between 1915 and 1970. In a classic example of "push-pull" forces creating human migration, southern blacks fled the agricultural and urban South in two distinct waves of migration: 1.5 million from 1915 to 1930, and 4.5 million from 1940 to 1970. Migrants were motivated by the "push" factors of southern RACISM AND DISCRIMINATION, and crop failure due to EROSION, FLOODS, the COTTON BOLL WEEVIL infestation, and increasing agricultural mechanization. Black southerners sought the "pull" factors of burgeoning wartime and postwar industrial employment, coupled with access to greater individual freedom and the right to vote, denied them in the South.

The migration produced sweeping demographic changes that created a large black urban population outside the South for the first time in American history, engendering significant environmental change. After the CIVIL WAR (1861–65) overwhelming numbers of freed blacks became mired in the tenancy-SHARECROPPING system of agriculture, created to further southern agriculture using black laborers who did not have the benefit of landownership or capital. This usurious system trapped croppers in a cycle of debt to owners of PLANTATIONS and merchants, while the small tracts of land employed were farmed by archaic methods that fostered overproduction, soil erosion, and soil exhaustion. The invasion of the cotton boll weevil in the early 20th century, followed by severe flooding in the Deep South, left many southern blacks teetering on the economic brink just as racist segregation, disenfranchisement, and lynching became more firmly entrenched in the South. Moreover, black farmers were often the last to receive assistance, if they received any, from state and federal policies addressing the boll weevil infestation.

The growth of northern industrial jobs was spurred by WORLD WAR I (1914–18) armaments production, lessening European IMMIGRATION, and workforce loss to the wartime military. The small numbers of southern blacks already living in the North touted the availability of relatively high-paying employment to their southern peers, creating a migration fever among southern blacks that culminated in a diaspora to northern industrial cities starting around 1915. Many black tenant farmers with enough money for rail fare packed up and left with crops still in the field, while black land or house owners sold their lands for a pittance or even abandoned their property in order to move north. These developments began the demise of sharecropping in the South, signaling the rise of large-scale corporate agriculture and its attendant environmental concerns from runoff of FERTILIZER, PESTICIDES, and continued soil erosion.

While northern employment was indeed available, the jobs open to blacks generally were low-paying and involved menial labor. Local racism limited black residential areas to undesirable inner city GHETTOS that became prominent during the earlier mass immigration of Europeans. Inner city conditions were rife with HUMAN DISEASES and environmental contamination. Many white Americans fled from neighborhoods recently inhabited by blacks, contributing to greater SUBURBANIZATION and URBAN SPRAWL, which remain salient environmental concerns today. The influx of African Americans also taxed urban resources and infrastructure, while the additional labor fed an industrial complex that polluted lands, water, and air with little federal or state regulation before WORLD WAR II (1941–45).

The migration continued unabated during the economic expansion of the 1920s, and while it decreased during the GREAT DEPRESSION, southern agriculture was transformed by NEW DEAL farm subsidies and mechanization, reducing black sharecropping further. The explosion of wartime employment generated by World War II created a more expansive migration to urban areas, this time including western cities involved in shipbuilding, aircraft production, and other armament production sites. The introduction of blacks into western residential areas once again fueled the flight of many white Americans to the suburbs, adding to sprawl and urban industrial pollution. The migration continued throughout the economic boom of the 1950s and the racially charged era of the CIVIL RIGHTS MOVEMENT before ending in the early 1970s as southern migration reversed, as a result of an influx of population to the more economically viable SUNBELT of the southeastern and southwestern United States.

See also AGRICULTURAL TECHNOLOGY; AGRICULTURE, COMMERCIAL; AGRICULTURE, DEPARTMENT OF; ENVIRONMENTAL JUSTICE; RUST BELT; SPECIES, EXOTIC AND INVASIVE.

Aaron D. Anderson

Further Reading

Grossman, James R. *Land of Hope: Chicago, Black Southerners, and the Great Migration.* Chicago: University of Chicago Press, 1989.

Holley, Donald. *The Second Great Emancipation: The Mechanical Cotton Picker, Black Migration, and How They Shaped the South.* Fayetteville: University of Arkansas Press, 2000.

Trotter, Joe William, Jr. *The Great Migration in Historical Perspective: New Dimensions of Race, Class, and Gender.* Bloomington and Indianapolis: Indiana University Press, 1991.

Great Smoky Mountains National Park

A distinct family of high mountains in the southern APPALACHIAN MOUNTAINS, the Great Smoky Mountains today encompass a unit of the NATIONAL PARK SERVICE (NPS). Stretching into both North Carolina and Tennessee, the 520,976 acres of the Great Smoky Mountains National Park include the most challenging and scenic section of the famous APPALACHIAN TRAIL and some of the region's highest mountains (Clingmans Dome, 6,642 feet). The Smokies, as they are nicknamed, boast the greatest BIODIVERSITY in North America, and the national park's proximity to large cities makes it the most heavily visited park in the United States.

Unlike the western national parks, carved out of largely uninhabited land, the Great Smoky Mountains has a long history of human impact. As early as 8,000 years ago, Native Americans living in the Lower Little Tennessee and Pigeon Rivers gathered roots, seeds, nuts, leaves, and plants and hunted for DEER and elk in the mountains. Woodland Indians after 700 C.E. adopted the "three sisters"—CORN, beans, and squash. The Cherokee made considerable use of riv-

The first of the major eastern national parks, Great Smoky Mountains National Park was established via the removal of thousands of people from the area. By the 1960s, one of the highlights of the park were "automobile nature trails," where people could view the park from the comfort of their cars.   *(Library of Congress)*

ercane in the valley lands, and they utilized FIRE to keep down undergrowth in the forest. The 16th-century Spanish conquistador Hernando de Soto did not reach the Smokies but traded crops, including melons, pears, and cowpeas, with Native people who did. When the English developed a fur trading center during the 17th century in CHARLESTON, SOUTH CAROLINA, the Cherokee further shaped the environment by hunting white-tailed DEER, elk, and BEAVER. Because the Cherokee sided with their trading partners, the British, in the AMERICAN REVOLUTION (1775–83), they met with retribution from American soldiers, who destroyed their homes and fields. After the United States gained its independence, soldiers received land grants for their service. Some of the first white settlers in the Smokies were former soldiers; some purchased their land from those

who speculated in land grants; others squatted on Indian land until more land cessions were forced from the Cherokee. The earliest farmers, such as John and Lucretia Oliver, gained possession of the fertile bottomlands. Americans at this time looked on the WILDERNESS as a threatening place that needed to be tamed. Hence, the state governments paid bounties for wolf, mountain lion, and fox pelts, which nearly eliminated predators from the mountains. The farmers settled all the remaining valleys in the Smokies, clearing land for corn and letting their PIGS AND HOGS forage in the forest. They also retained the Cherokee practice of burning off undergrowth. On the tops of the mountains, farmers expanded any clear space to create the famous Appalachian "balds," meadowlands on the mountaintops where they grazed sheep and CATTLE.

At the end of the 19th century, an increasing number of commercial enterprises further shaped the Great Smoky Mountains. Farmers did some trapping as well as harvesting ginseng. Enterprising prospectors looked for GOLD and silver, and the Epsom Salts Manufacturing Company tried to process the minerals from Alum Cave. On Hazel Creek, competing mining companies tied up a sizable COPPER vein in legal battles. Before the Fontana mine closed in 1943, various owners extracted more than a half-million tons of ore. The most dramatic turn-of-the-century disturbance, however, was industrial LOGGING AND LUMBERING. With the help of narrow-gauge RAILROADS that could handle steep slopes and the steam-powered skidder, a cable system that carried trees to the railroad, lumbermen clear cut 60 percent, or 300,000 acres, of the Great Smoky Mountains, producing two billion board feet of lumber. With such large-scale DEFORESTATION was an increase in fire and FLOODS that devastated both mountain farming as well as the ecology of the region.

Concern about logging combined with an interest in promoting tourism created the impetus to establish a national park to the Smokies. Boosters in Knoxville, Tennessee, and Asheville, North Carolina, pushed the Southern Appalachian National Park Committee to choose the Smokies as the first national park in the eastern United States. Two organizations, the Great Smoky Mountains Conservation Association and Great Smoky Mountains, Inc., raised the funds necessary by publicizing the mountains and soliciting $1 million from private individuals, $4 million from the two state legislatures, and a matching gift of $5 million from the Laura Spelman Rockefeller Memorial Fund. Because more than 1,132 small farms and 18 large timber and mining companies owned the land, it took almost 12 years to acquire the terrain, and it would not have been possible without the states' power of eminent domain, which allowed North Carolina and Tennessee judges to condemn land and pay owners what government surveyors believed the land was worth. The Smokies became an official unit of the NATIONAL PARK SERVICE (NPS) in 1934.

Since its creation, the park has faced enormous challenges, including imported PLANT DISEASES, EXOTIC AND INVASIVE SPECIES, and AIR POLLUTION. In 1925, a fungus commonly referred to as the CHESTNUT BLIGHT arrived from China, eliminating the American chestnut, which once composed 31 percent of the FORESTS. In 1963, scientists discovered another Far East insect, the balsam wooly adelgid, which, over the next two decades, destroyed the Fraser fir species. Since then, the mountain forests have faced other menaces such as dogwood anthracnose, beech blight, Dutch elm disease, mountain ash sawfly, the gypsy moth, and hemlock wooly adelgid—all unintentional imports that have altered the composition of the forest.

Another impact, largely outside the control of the park, air pollution from COAL-burning power plants and heavy motor vehicle traffic, has given the Smokies the worst air of any national park. Poor air quality results in more than just a hazy view and warnings about ALLERGIES AND ASTHMA. During precipitation, the sulfur dioxide and nitrogen oxide particles reach the ground as ACID RAIN or acid snow. Lowering the pH or acidity of the streams diminishes fish life in streams and along with ozone pollution weakens vegetation, making it more susceptible to disease.

Despite these problems, the Great Smoky Mountains National Park also represents a remarkable story of restoration. After mammoth disturbance from farming, HUNTING, logging, and timber harvest, the forest has retaken the land. BEARS, deer, fox, and small mammal populations have recovered. Beginning with the Civilian Conservation Corps in the 1930s, the park worked to reintroduce trout into its streams. In 1983, scientists completely restored two extirpated species, the smoky madtom and the yellowfin madtom, to Abrams Creek. In 1986, wildlife specialists successfully released 11 river otters in the park, and they have repopulated the streams. In 1990, birders spotted the return of peregrine falcons. While less successful restoration efforts such as those of the red wolf and eastern elk command more publicity, NPS scientists have made considerable effort to restore native grasslands and rivercane as well as remove exotic plants that also affect BIODIVERSITY. Since 1991, the All Taxa Biodiversity Inventory (ATBI) has discovered 4,666 species new to the Smokies and an additional 651 species new to science and has confirmed that despite extreme environmental impact, these southern mountains are a remarkable treasure of biodiversity.

See also BIRDS; INDIANS, DEEP SOUTH; NEW DEAL; UNITED STATES—DEEP SOUTH; WILD ANIMALS; WOLVES.

Margaret Lynn Brown

Further Reading

Brown, Margaret Lynn. *The Wild East: A Biography of the Great Smoky Mountains.* Gainesville: University of Florida Press, 2000.

Hill, Sarah H. *Weaving New Worlds: Southeastern Cherokee Women and Their Basketry.* Chapel Hill: University of North Carolina Press, 1997.

Pierce, Daniel. A. *The Great Smokies: From Natural Habitat to National Park.* Knoxville: University of Tennessee, 2000.

Great Society

A rubric coined by President LYNDON B. JOHNSON in 1964, "The Great Society" described the far-reaching domestic programs that he initiated and CONGRESS approved during his administration (1963–69). Announced in a speech at

Ann Arbor, Michigan, on May 22, 1964, the Great Society's reforms focused on eliminating poverty and racial inequality; new federal spending programs addressed education, medical care, transportation, and the urban infrastructure, among other problems. Other new policies attempted to correct AIR POLLUTION and WATER POLLUTION, WASTE DISPOSAL AND MANAGEMENT, and ENVIRONMENTAL JUSTICE issues.

The agenda forwarded by the Johnson administration attempted to capture and restate in present time the ideals of past administrations, expanding the Bill of Rights to reflect a confident, affluent, and technologically sophisticated society deeply committed to democratic values. Of particular merit is the extent of research and legislation Johnson put into motion on behalf of environmental renewal.

Assuming the presidency in the wake of the assassination of JOHN F. KENNEDY on November 22, 1963, Lyndon Johnson put the weight of four decades of congressional experience to bear on his administration. Johnson understood in detail the changes in energy and technology that defined American culture in the 20th century. The presidency gave Johnson a novel opportunity to put into motion, at the national level, a comprehensive program to preserve and protect what was left of the American WILDERNESS, establish federal standards for clean air and water, and create urban parks where all people, regardless of race or economic status, could go to enjoy the outdoors, sports, and recreation.

Picking up the pieces of Kennedy's unfinished administration, Johnson worked with a talented and dedicated team of WASHINGTON, D.C., bureaucrats including Secretary of the Interior STEWART UDALL. In response to rising public concern for the alarming toxicity and degradation of the environment, Johnson, with the assistance of the First Lady, CLAUDIA ALTA TAYLOR "LADY BIRD" JOHNSON, made "America the Beautiful" a benchmark of the Great Society. Winning the 1964 election by a landslide, Johnson was the first president in history to model the emerging environmental values of the era, establishing task forces and signing trendsetting legislation on environmental pollution, natural resources, and natural beauty. A total of 12 task forces were initiated during his administration, focusing on pollution, resources, and "quality of the environment," setting the stage for federal action in the decades to come.

On February 8, 1965, President Johnson issued a special message on beautification to Congress, decrying the deterioration of the nation's cities and neighborhoods and calling into question the appropriate relationship of humans to the environment. In May 1965, the first White House Conference on Natural Beauty was held in Washington, D.C., under the direction of Laurance S. Rockefeller (1910–2004). Recalling President Kennedy's New Conservation, a term coined at the White House Conference on Conservation in 1961, Johnson addressed the daunting challenges ahead: the restoration and protection of natural beauty in the city and countryside, the development and enforcement of federal water quality standards, the need for new technologies to control waste products and for effective legislation to create and protect national parks, rivers, forests, and wilderness areas. He called upon the states and localities in the Union to hold similar conferences on natural beauty. The Environmental Pollution Panel published *Restoring the Quality of Our Environment* in October 1965, examining in detail the types and effects of known airborne and waterborne pollutants and sketching out in broad strokes a concerted federal program for environmental remediation.

The axis of President Johnson's program of environmental reform turned on classic tenets of CONSERVATION and PRESERVATION while raising the bar for the implementation of effective legislation, technologies, and standards to protect human health and control environmental pollution. Key environmental legislation included the WILDERNESS ACT OF 1964, the Land and Water Conservation Act (1965), the Water Quality Act (1965), the Solid Waste Disposal Act (1965), the Shoreline Erosion Protection Act (1965), the National Historic Preservation Act (1966), the Freedom of Information Act (1966), the Clean Water Restoration Act (1966), and the Air Quality Act (1967). Other precedents were established with the enactment of new consumer protection laws including the National Traffic and Motor Vehicle Act (1966), the Fair Packaging and Labeling Act (1967), the Federal Meat Inspection Act (1967), the Natural Gas Pipeline Safety Act (1968), and the Flammable Fabrics Act (1968).

Under the foresight and able administration of Secretary Udall, substantive changes occurred in the organization of the DEPARTMENT OF THE INTERIOR to meet the challenges of conserving resources while monitoring humankind's impact on the total environment. Working closely with the president, Udall coordinated an unprecedented expansion of the nation's parklands. During the Johnson administration, 46 new areas representing more than 15 million acres were added, including four national parks, 19 historical parks and sites, three national seashores, and two scenic riverways and trails. These additions, more than approved by any other administration, were chosen for their proximity to heavily populated urban areas and represented novel approaches to conservation. As a result of the President's Task Force on Natural Beauty and the National Historic Preservation Act of 1966, federal funds were made available to the states and localities to assist in the maintenance of the nation's historically significant properties and landmarks.

The President's Reorganization Plan No. 2, effective May 10, 1966, and Executive Order 11288 of July 2, 1966, transferred the Federal Water Pollution Control Administration to the Department of the Interior. Water resource development, including desalination research, was a subject that received Johnson's careful attention during his years in Congress. The Water Quality Act of 1965 enjoined the states to set water quality standards, monitored and subject to approval by the Department of the Interior, for major interstate and coastal waters. The Solid Waste Disposal Act of 1965 expanded the department's authority to monitor and control the disposal of mining wastes. The Clean Water Restoration Act, signed into law on November 3, 1966, expanded the scope of pollution control to include a three-year comprehensive study by the Department of the Interior on the effects of pollution on the ecology and wildlife of entire watersheds, estuaries, and river basins. A systematic analysis of air pollution was undertaken by the Bureau of Mines in 1963; the Clean Air Acts of 1963 and 1965 expanded the Clean Air Act of 1955, authorizing emissions standards, regulated by the Department of Health, Education, and Welfare, for stationary sources and AUTOMOBILES, respectively.

Johnson's Great Society established a pattern for greater federal intervention in environmental issues. This pattern continued with the passage of the NATIONAL ENVIRONMENTAL POLICY ACT (NEPA) OF 1970 and the creation of the ENVIRONMENTAL PROTECTION AGENCY under his successor, RICHARD NIXON in 1970.

See also CONSUMERISM; FEDERAL LAW—ENVIRONMENTAL REGULATIONS; FEDERAL LAW—INDUSTRIAL REGULATIONS; KEEP AMERICA BEAUTIFUL; NATIONAL PARK SERVICE.

Victoria M. Bretig-Garcia

Further Reading

Califano, Joseph A., Jr. "What Was Really Great about the Great Society: The Truth behind the Conservative Myths." *Washington Monthly On-Line,* October 1999.

Gould, Lewis L. *Lady Bird Johnson and the Environment.* Lawrence: University Press of Kansas, 1988.

Helsing, Jeffrey W. *Johnson's War/Johnson's Great Society: The Guns and Butter Trap.* Santa Barbara, Calif.: Praeger, 2000.

Melosi, Martin V. "Lyndon Johnson and Environmental Policy." *The Johnson Years.* Vol. 2, *Vietnam, the Environment, and Science,* edited by Robert A. Divine. Lawrence: University Press of Kansas, 1987.

Unger, Irwin. *The Best of Intentions: The Triumphs and Failures of the Great Society under Kennedy, Johnson, and Nixon.* New York: Doubleday, 1996.

greenbelts

Greenbelts are areas of undeveloped land that either surround or run adjacent to urban areas. They are created to control URBAN SPRAWL and provide green space for recreational and agricultural uses. The concept is not new, and examples existed before the 19th century, but it was the rapid growth of cities after the Industrial Revolution that led to the use of the modern greenbelt.

Social observers found the new industrial cities to be unhealthy places because of AIR POLLUTION and WATER POLLUTION created by factories and overcrowding of workers in substandard housing. The garden city movement in England at the end of the 19th century helped launch the modern greenbelt movement. Planners there called for cities to be encircled by parks and open spaces to constrain urban expansion. By the beginning of the 20th century, social reformers in other industrial nations similarly sought to mitigate the harmful effects of urban life by proposing the development of green spaces, such as parks and playgrounds, to promote fresh air and an improved standard of living through OUTDOOR RECREATION. As a result, municipal, state, and national governments created policies that responded to the social criticism.

While greenbelts exist in the United States, they have been employed more frequently in Europe and Asia. In the United States, the Regional Planning Association, founded in 1923, began advocating greenbelts almost from its inception. Under the NEW DEAL in the 1930s, federal funding for the construction of some 25 greenbelt towns was ultimately narrowed to the communities of Greenbelt, Maryland (near WASHINGTON, D.C.); Greenhills, Ohio (near CINCINNATI, OHIO); and Greendale, Wisconsin (near Milwaukee), settled in 1936 and 1937 as public cooperative communities. (The center of Greenbelt, Maryland, has been preserved as a National Historic District, but the other two communities have experienced significant changes.) The greenbelt idea was revitalized in 1958 when some 20 cities in the SAN FRANCISCO, CALIFORNIA, region formed the Greenbelt Alliance, a nonprofit land CONSERVATION and urban planning organization. New advocates emerged in the 1960s and thereafter as Americans developed a growing environmental consciousness and expanded their interest in outdoor recreation.

Municipalities have used different methods to create greenbelts. In Boulder, Colorado, beginning in the 1960s, and in Ann Arbor, Michigan, by referendum in 2003, public and nonprofit acquisition of open space and development rights provided the basis for its greenbelt. Other cities created greenbelts by regulating private land use. Greenbelts exist in Austin, Texas; Portland, Oregon; and Staten Island, New York, for example. For their proponents, greenbelts provided the most logical answer to the problems of industrialization and sprawl by both offering control of low-density construction at the urban-rural fringe and establishing green spaces. City planners began to utilize greenbelts in their plans of the cities of the future, some still in use today.

Whether through planning or policy, greenbelts are a fixture of the urban landscape and can be seen throughout the world. Today, proponents still claim that greenbelts are environmentally useful by controlling urban sprawl, providing needed green space, and offering improved air and water quality.

Critics contend that greenbelts do not necessarily offer such benefits and may do more harm than good. Instead of controlling urban sprawl, critics allege, greenbelts are simply bypassed and development continues unabated outside the belt. This continued development leads to new environmental problems as transportation lines are extended through the belt and commuters add to the urban pollution as they travel to work inside the belt. Critics also claim that greenbelts are economic barriers, keeping less affluent citizens trapped within urban centers while land prices outside the belt are only within the reach of the wealthy. Critics also charge that the claim that greenbelts provide clean air and water has never been proven, and that evidence showing a direct connection has never been offered.

Although most people would agree that greenbelts provide an aesthetically pleasing view in the urban setting, policy makers are left to debate their actual merits. Ultimately, the creation of greenbelts is a direct reflection of the social and cultural outlook of the communities that choose to develop and maintain them. More recently, some U.S. cities have selected an alternative to the rigidly controlled greenbelts and have opted for Urban Growth Boundaries (UGB). This alternative also seeks to control urban growth but allows for limited growth within planned time frames that are reevaluated at prescribed intervals. By 2009, the states of Oregon, Tennessee, and Washington required all cities within their limits to establish UGBs. Notable jurisdictions employing UGBs include the Twin Cities, Minnesota; Lexington, Kentucky; Virginia Beach, Virginia; Miami-Dade County, Florida; and Napa County, California.

See also CITY AND SUBURBAN PARKS; ENVIRONMENTALISM, MAINSTREAM; HOUSING, PRIVATE; MIAMI, FLORIDA; MINNEAPOLIS–ST. PAUL, MINNESOTA; PLANNING, URBAN AND REGIONAL; SUBURBANIZATION; URBANIZATION; ZONING.

Larry S. Powers

Further Reading

Hall, Peter. *Cities of Tomorrow: An Intellectual History of Urban Planning and Design in the Twentieth Century*. Oxford, England, and Malden, Mass.: Blackwell, 2002.

Knepper, Cathy D. *Greenbelt, Maryland: A Living Legacy of the New Deal*. Baltimore: Johns Hopkins University Press, 2001.

Pollack, P. "Controlling Sprawl in Boulder: Benefits and Pitfalls." *Land Lines: Newsletter of the Lincoln Institute of Land Policy* 10, no. 1 (1998): 1–3.

Reps, John W. *The Making of Urban America: A History of City Planning in the United States*. Princeton, N.J.: Princeton University Press, 1992.

green consumerism and marketing

After WORLD WAR II (1941–45), American environmental activism shifted from concerns with production to concerns with consumption. During the late 1960s, and through the mid-1970s, a series of environmental disasters changed public opinion and formed a consensus about the links among environmental health, consumption, and quality of life. Many of the ecological catastrophes during this period resulted from the production of consumer goods and clarified the link between consumption and the ecological well-being of the planet. This new awareness bolstered efforts to preserve resources but also sparked interest in more ecologically sensitive models of production. During this same period, technologically minded environmentalists helped reshape the American environmental movement, infusing it with a youthful energy and providing it with a new sense of purpose and direction. This new cadre heralded alternative technologies as solutions to contemporary concerns over production and consumption while embracing a new phase in the country's development. Environmentalists envisioned a "postscarcity" economy where advanced industrial societies theoretically possessed the means to provide abundance and freedom while reconciling nature and technology—if only they choose to do so. The alternative-technology movement led to calls for goods and services that used thoughtful techniques and technologies to produce more benign products.

Convincing American producers and consumers that a middle ground existed between CAPITALISM and environmentalism was no easy task. The authors Paul Hawken, Amory Lovins, and Hunter Lovins provided a captivatingly simple model for this reconciliation in their influential book, *Natural Capitalism: Creating the Next Industrial Revolution* (1999). They argued that an environmental ethic based on realistic use of existing appropriate technologies was the key to both the health of the planet and the future of corporate success and profitability. In some ways their model of "natural capitalism" harkened back to the "gospel of efficiency" of President THEODORE ROOSEVELT and PROGRESSIVE ERA conservationists. Unlike Roosevelt's cohorts, however, natural capitalists argued that environmentalism is best left to individuals and corporations using the free market to correct environmental waste and abuse.

Environmental consumerism and the desire for environmentally friendly alternatives drove national efforts to change American business practices without altering the fundamental economic system. One of the most successful of these attempts occurred in 1989. The grassroots "McToxics" campaign targeted McDonald's restaurants' use of Styrofoam packaging. This effort soon went national as consumers engaged in boycotts and "send-it-back" efforts against franchises that refused to switch to cardboard and paper packaging. Ultimately, the restaurant chain capitulated and replaced foam with paper wrappers. The "McToxics" effort illustrated the degree to which environmentalism had successfully infiltrated consumer culture and provided a model of an alternative type of consumer-based political action. It also juxtaposed Americans' commitment to using their economic power to advocate environmental issues and their unwillingness to challenge the basic economic system. In the 1990s, McDonald's worked with CONSERVATION groups such as Environmental Defense to improve their environmental image. By the early 2000s, even Wal-Mart got into the game when it hired the alternative technology visionary Amory Lovins to help the corporation's efforts to create a greener business model and building program to satisfy consumer demands for environmentally sensitive shopping. Although not a solution to centuries of environmental abuse, the greening of the American economy became the best expression of an everyday environmentalism that enabled individuals to integrate emerging concepts of ecological living into their homes and workplaces.

See also CAPITALISM; PROGRESSIVISM; ROOSEVELT, THEODORE.

Andrew Kirk

Further Reading

Gottlieb, Robert. *Forcing the Spring: The Transformation of the American Environmental Movement.* Washington, D.C.: Island Press, 1993.

Hawken, Paul, Amory Lovins, and L. Hunter Lovins. *Natural Capitalism: Creating the Next Industrial Revolution.* Boston: Little, Brown, 1999.

Hays, Samuel P. *Beauty, Health, and Permanence: Environmental Politics in the United States, 1955–1985.* Cambridge: Cambridge University Press, 1987.

McDonough, William, and Michael Braungart. *Cradle to Cradle: Remaking the Way We Make Things.* New York: North Point Press, 2002.

Steffen, Alex, ed. *World Changing: A User's Guide for the 21st Century.* New York: Abrams, 2006.

greenhouse effect

The greenhouse effect is the planetary rise in temperature that occurs when energy from the Sun is trapped by greenhouse gases in the Earth's atmosphere. This effect is essential for the survival of life on the planet; however, an increase in greenhouse gases can warm the Earth too much and cause problems such as CLIMATE CHANGE.

The greenhouse process begins with sunlight directed toward the Earth. Some of the solar rays bounce off the atmosphere and return to space. Those rays that reach the Earth—about half of those emitted by the Sun—warm the planet. The warmed planet then radiates infrared rays, some of which escape to space. The remaining infrared rays are absorbed by gases in the atmosphere and reflected back, raising the Earth's temperature to a level suitable for the existence of life. Were it not for this process, the Earth would be approximately 60 degrees Fahrenheit cooler.

The atmospheric gases that contribute to the greenhouse effect are known as greenhouse gases. There are numerous greenhouse gases, with some created by natural sources. These naturally occurring gases are the most plentiful and include water vapor, carbon dioxide, METHANE, nitrous oxide, and ozone. Other greenhouse gases are synthetic (human-made) and include chlorofluorocarbons, hydrofluorocarbons, perfluorocarbons, and sulfur hexafluoride. Clouds, although not gases, also contribute to the greenhouse effect by absorbing and emitting infrared rays radiated by the Earth.

Water vapor is the most abundant greenhouse gas and is created as liquid water evaporates. Temperature influences the amount of resulting water vapor in a positive feedback loop—as the temperature rises, more water evaporates, resulting in greater amounts of atmospheric water vapor; the more water vapor, the greater the ability to absorb and reflect infrared rays, increasing global temperature, which causes more water to evaporate, and so on. The water vapor eventually precipitates out of the atmosphere and back into liquid water and is subject once again to evaporation. Carbon dioxide occurs as a product of certain natural processes, such as animal and plant respiration, the exchange of carbon dioxide between the ocean and the atmosphere, and volcanic eruptions. Other natural sources of greenhouse gases include WETLANDS (methane), OCEANS (methane and nitrous oxide), and soils (nitrous oxide). Ozone is largely produced in the stratosphere in a reaction involving ultraviolet rays and oxygen.

Greenhouse gases that occur in nature can also be created by human activity. Carbon dioxide, for example, can be created by the combustion of fossil fuels, by the cutting and burning of trees, and by the use of certain industrial production processes and products. Methane emissions result from the use of LANDFILLS, livestock management, COAL mining, NATURAL GAS and oil production, and RICE cultivation. Human-related sources of nitrous oxide emissions include soil, sewage, and manure management and emissions from both stationary and mobile sources (e.g., factories and cars). Synthetic greenhouse gases are also produced through human activity, such as emissions that result from industrial processes.

Historical concentrations of greenhouse gases in the atmosphere have been determined by analyzing bubbles of ancient air trapped in polar ice cores. Partly on the basis of these levels, the UNITED NATIONS Intergovernmental Panel on Climate Change (IPCC) has reported that anthropogenic (human-influenced) emissions of carbon dioxide, methane, and nitrous oxide have increased significantly since the Industrial Revolution and far exceed the values established by ice core sampling. For example, according to the IPCC, annual emissions of carbon dioxide rose by 80 percent between 1970 and 2004.

Increases of greenhouse gases in the atmosphere are of concern because the greenhouse effect can raise the average temperature of the Earth. Worldwide elevations in air and ocean temperatures have been recorded over the past century, with the last decade the warmest on record. The IPCC attributes this warming trend to greenhouse gas emissions caused by human activity. Global temperature changes, even if small, can lead to significant climate change issues such as a rise in sea level and coastal flooding, DROUGHTS affecting FOOD and water supplies, harm to habitats and ECOSYSTEMS, and even species EXTINCTION if species cannot adapt to the change. Higher global temperatures can also lead to heat-related problems for humans as well as other health impacts related to AIR POLLUTION and WATER POLLUTION and changes in the human food supply.

Given these possibilities, many countries have made efforts to stabilize and reduce the production of greenhouse gases by enacting national laws aimed at reduction and ratifying international treaties such as the Kyoto Protocol. U.S. efforts to reduce greenhouse gas emissions include enactment and enforcement of air pollution and other environmental laws as well as efforts to create carbon sinks to help remove carbon dioxide from the atmosphere. However, the United States is one of only a few nations that, as of 2009, had not ratified the Kyoto Protocol, despite the fact that it produces approximately one-fourth of all global greenhouse gas emissions yet has only 5 percent of the world's population.

See also DEFORESTATION; ENERGY, FOSSIL FUEL; FLOODS; GLOBAL WARMING; OZONE LAYER; TREATIES AND INTERNATIONAL LAW; UNITED NATIONS ENVIRONMENTAL CONFERENCES.

Francesca Ortiz

Further Reading
Intergovernmental Panel on Climate Change. "IPCC Fourth Assessment Report: Climate Change 2007." IPCC Reports. Available online. URL: http://www.ipcc.ch/ipccreports/assessments-reports.htm. Accessed June 18, 2009.

Letcher, Trevor M., ed. *Climate Change: Observed Impacts on Planet Earth*. Oxford: Elsevier Science, 2009.

NOAA Satellite and Information Service. "Greenhouse Gases," National Oceanic and Atmospheric Administration. Available online. URL: http://lwf.ncdc.noaa.gov/oa/climate/gases.html. Accessed August 20, 2008.

Pew Center on Global Climate Change. *Climate Change: Science, Strategies & Solutions*. Leiden: Brill, 2001.

United States Environmental Protection Agency. "Greenhouse Gas Emissions." Climate Change. Available online. URL: http://epa.gov/climatechange/index.html. Accessed June 12, 2009.

Green Mountains

The Green Mountains dominate the physical and cultural landscape of the state of Vermont. These mountains, part of the Appalachian chain, were formed an estimated 380 million years ago, and they are composed primarily of metamorphic schist (or rocks) rounded out by EROSION during the last several glacial epochs. The range traverses the length of Vermont for 160 miles, and it extends to a width of between 21 and 36 miles.

Mount Mansfield, at a height of 4,395 feet, tops the Green Mountains, and it is the second-tallest peak in the APPALACHIAN MOUNTAINS range. The extreme conditions at the highest elevations mean that several peaks are crested with alpine microenvironments encompassing a number of arctic and tundra species. Soils throughout the range are thin, sandy, and acidic, and above 2,400–3,000 feet, they host boreal FORESTS of red spruce and balsam fir, while at lower elevations forest composition merges into a hemlock-northern hardwood mix.

Native bands ranged through the mountains until the 19th century, harvesting upcountry resources and hunting for game. They were joined by European settlers, who arrived in increasing numbers after the end of the FRENCH AND INDIAN WAR (1754–   ). Beginning in the early 19th century, farmers cleared much of the native forest to make way for agriculture. An early 19th-century sheep boom perpetuated DEFORESTATION, and by 1860, an estimated 75 percent of Vermont had been logged, including large swaths of the Green Mountains.

By the mid-19th century, the dairy industry and TRAVEL AND TOURISM began to replace sheep. Tourism first took root in the Green Mountains around scenic areas and natural springs. Mount Mansfield was the initial attraction: In 1858, a hotel was built on the mountain, and a scenic road was built to the top of the peak in 1870. The construction of mountaintop inns swept the state, and soon other mountains boasted their own tourist resorts. After the Green Mountains had been established as a pleasuring ground, the region developed a reputation as a destination for more strenuous recreation. In 1910, hiking enthusiasts established the Green Mountain Club, and this organization built the Long Trail, a "footpath in the wilderness," over the subsequent two decades. This trail, which meanders for 265 miles along the spine of the Green Mountains, claims the title of the first long-distance trail in the United States.

Reflecting the importance of OUTDOOR RECREATION and FOREST PRODUCTS to the state, Vermont's public officials were early participants in the CONSERVATION movement. In 1906, Vermont created a state forest system, which was followed by 1915 legislation to encourage the development of municipal forests and parks. In 1925, the state legislature voiced its support for the creation of a national forest, and seven years later, President HERBERT HOOVER dedicated the Green Mountain National Forest, which has grown to include more than 385,000 acres of mixed-use and WILDERNESS areas.

Numerous plans for the Green Mountain landscape emerged during the 1930s, and in 1934, the NATIONAL PARK SERVICE proposed the ill-fated Green Mountain Parkway, a road traveling along the crest of the mountains. Vermont voters rejected this project, but the state embraced other NEW DEAL initiatives, and the Civilian Construction Corps oversaw reforestation and PUBLIC WORKS projects, such as the construction of ski trails, throughout the Green Mountains.

Skiing emerged, in the early 20th century, as a wintertime diversion, and Vermont led in the development of winter sports, including the first U.S. ski tow, which was built in 1934. Since the 1930s, the Nordic and downhill ski industries have helped to drive the Vermont economy and minimized the reliance on forest products. Skiing and other outdoor recreation sites cover the Green Mountain landscape.

By the 21st century, afforestation left Vermont 78 percent forested. Today, boosters employ the mountain forests to evoke the attractions of this state. The Green Mountains are the backbone of the state's environmental awareness, and the mountains maintain a central influence on the culture and the economy of Vermont.

See also HUNTING, SUBSISTENCE; LOGGING AND LUMBERING; UNITED STATES—NORTHEAST.

Sara M. Gregg

Further Reading

Albers, Jan. *Hands on the Land: A History of the Vermont Landscape.* Cambridge, Mass.: MIT Press, 2000.

Johnson, Charles W. *The Nature of Vermont: Introduction and Guide to a New England Environment.* Hanover, N.H.: University Press of New England, 1998.

Klyza, Christopher McGrory, and Stephen C. Trombulak. *The Story of Vermont: A Natural and Cultural History.* Hanover, N.H.: Middlebury College Press, 1999.

Greenpeace

Greenpeace is an international NONGOVERNMENTAL ORGANIZATION known for its active campaigns to fight against environmental degradation and to conserve the Earth's BIODIVERSITY. It was founded by a small team of Canadian and American activists who set sail from Vancouver, Canada, in 1971 with the objective of stopping a second underground nuclear bomb test by the United States in Amchitka Island, Alaska. This island was the last refuge for many ENDANGERED SPECIES. Although they were intercepted before they reached the island, the group's journey aroused significant public interest. It was the birth of a huge organization that would attract compliments, and also criticism, for its actions to preserve the environment.

During the 1970s, Greenpeace built a more public presence and gained members. The decade's legacy of strong political youth movements fighting for ideals and the ideas of the GREEN REVOLUTION and ecologism as a form of living helped attract volunteers to fight for Greenpeace.

One of Greenpeace's most well-known successes happened in 1995, when Greenpeace activists occupied the Brent Spar oil storage facility in the North Sea. Their purpose was to stop plans to scuttle a 14,500-ton Shell installation that would contaminate the water. In the end, and with much public pressure, Greenpeace activists succeeded, and Shell Corporation agreed to dismantle and recycle the Spar on land. What was truly important is that Greenpeace's success led to a ban on the ocean disposal of such rigs by the international body that regulates ocean dumping. That victory helped to encourage nonviolent but active ways of achieving members' goals.

The organization is distinguished because of its use of direct action to attract attention to particular environmental causes. Today's numerous campaigns around the world include a strong commitment to stop and prevent GLOBAL WARMING; protect ancient FORESTS; prevent the irrational development of genetic engineering; stop commercial hunting of whales; implement sustainable management of the oceans, rivers, and lagoons; end reliance on nuclear power; reprocess waste dumping to eliminate toxic chemical threats to populations and ECOSYSTEMS; encourage sustainable and fair trade movements; and conserve the biodiversity of all life-forms.

Constant struggles have drawn Greenpeace criticism from many governments, private companies, and, on occasion, other environmental groups. Members are often arrested, most often for blocking ships, trying to stop the killing of animals, or protesting the disposal of dangerous wastes. Facing a determined opposition, Greenpeace crews grow larger and larger every day.

Greenpeace is a nonprofit global environmental organization, with its main office in Amsterdam. There are 27 national and regional offices around the world, providing a presence in 41 countries. Greenpeace has nearly three million supporters worldwide. Greenpeace's fleet is currently composed of four ships: the *Rainbow Warrior,* the *Arctic Sunrise,* the *Esperanza,* and the *Argus*—along with a balloon.

As a global organization, Greenpeace focuses on the most crucial worldwide threats to the planet's biodiversity, natural resources, and habitats. To maintain its independence, Greenpeace does not accept donations from governments or corporations. It relies on contributions from individual supporters, foundation grants, and a large number of volunteers.

See also ENVIRONMENTALISM, GRASSROOTS; ENVIRONMENTALISM, MAINSTREAM; ENVIRONMENTALISM, RADICAL; OCEANS.

Diego I. Murguía

Further Reading
Boettger, Conny, and Fouad Hamdan, eds. *Greenpeace: Changing the World.* Steinfurt, Germany: Rasch & Röhring, 2001.
Greenpeace International Web site. Available online. URL: http://www.greenpeace.org. Accessed August 22, 2006.
Hunter, Robert. *The Greenpeace to Amchitka: An Environmental Odyssey.* Vancouver, Canada: Arsenal Pulp Press, 2004.
———. *To Save a Whale: The Voyages of Greenpeace.* Vancouver, Canada: Douglas & McIntyre, 1978.
Jordan, A. Grant. *Shell, Greenpeace and the Brent Spar.* Houndmills, England, and New York: Palgrave, 2001.
Weyler, Rex. *Greenpeace: How a Group of Journalists, Ecologists and Visionaries Changed the World.* Emmaus, Pa.: Rodale, 2004.

Green Revolution

The Green Revolution dramatically increased agricultural productivity in developing nations, beginning in the early 1960s through the 1970s, with the introduction of hybrid high-yield varieties (HYVs) of grains and various PESTICIDES. The United States initially supported the Green Revolution, in part, as a socioeconomic COLD WAR strategy. The former United States Agency for International Development (USAID) director William Gaud coined the term *Green Revolution* in 1968 to describe the spread of new agricultural technologies: "These and other developments in the field of agriculture contain the makings of a new revolution. It is not a violent Red Revolution like that of the Soviets, nor is it a White Revolution like that of the Shah of Iran. I call it the Green Revolution."

The term *Green Revolution* has typically been used to describe advancements in developing nations, although crop yields increased worldwide during this period. The revolution enhanced agricultural management methods in less developed nations and employed other technological advances as agricultural production became further mechanized. International agencies such as the Ford and Rockefeller Foundations, many of which are based in the United States, led the agricultural advancements in developing countries.

The Green Revolution traces its roots to the 1940s, when U.S. researchers in Mexico created disease-resistant WHEAT with much higher yields. These SEEDS led to the Green Revolution first in Mexico and then in India. Both countries dramatically increased WHEAT production, helping to overcome financial- and famine-related crises. The U.S. agronomist Norman E. Borlaug (1914–2009) led the wheat research in Mexico and received the Nobel Peace Prize in 1970 for his efforts. During the 1970s, the Green Revolution spread throughout the world, although the movement has been plagued by criticism—many argue the negative environmental and social impacts far outweigh the positive aspects of the revolution.

Those lauding HYVs point to the impact they have had on food production in poor nations. High-yield varieties of grain—typically wheat and RICE, although some less successful experimentation has been done with CORN—boost harvests by up to four times and grow more rapidly, allowing for a greater number of harvests per year. Additionally, HYVs are better able to withstand DROUGHT, PLANT DISEASES, and climactic extremes than typical grains. The Green Revolution has most dramatically affected Mexico and developing nations in Asia and South America, although it has been attempted in parts of Africa with mixed results. Mexico, the Philippines, Pakistan, and India boast the greatest increases in crop yields. Almost all nations reported dramatic crop yield increases after employment of the new HYVs and accompanying techniques, yet the social and environmental costs have been high.

The results of the Green Revolution have not been all positive, and criticisms abound especially among environmentalists. They claim that although grain production increased in some regions, environmental disasters have accompanied that growth. Some environmentalists also argue that the new grains have replaced indigenous vegetation and reduced natural beauty and BIODIVERSITY. A number of scientists believe that the new grains require more energy to grow. New seeds need to be purchased with each new planting season as the HYVs do not regenerate fertility, a limitation that has increased cost of production for struggling farmers in several regions. Some growers believe that the new grains are actually less tolerant of disease and drought than their predecessors; the new grains, although resistant to many diseases, are not resistant to specific diseases in certain regions.

HYVs also require an abundance of pesticides and FERTILIZER, which can be damaging to the environment, animals, and humans and lead to other social problems. The fertilizers used increase growth of WEEDS in conjunction with grain growth, and growers therefore apply large amounts of herbicides to their crops. Many regions now rely on the United States and other Western nations to supply the herbicides, pesticides, and fertilizers, leaving developing nations even more dependent on them than in the past. Local waterways have been polluted as a result of the application of massive amounts of chemicals. The cost effectiveness has been challenged; many farmers cannot afford the large quantity of fertilizers and pesticides required for the new grains; often even lower yields than previously have resulted. The older GRAINS had adapted to the climactic and disease conditions in the region, opponents argue, and require lower amounts of the harmful chemicals. The larger yields and increase in numbers of harvests can quickly deplete soil, increasing the need for greater crop rotations. Moreover, a large amount of IRRIGATION is needed to support HYVs, and the greater number of harvests often diverts DRINKING WATER away from others in need.

Socially, many individuals and their families have been hurt through unintended consequences of the Green Revolution.

Many landowners now realize the profitability of their land and have refused to renew leases of it to smaller farmers. Affluent farmers have further prospered from the Green Revolution, yet the majority of farmers who need help have not gained from the revolution and in fact have been harmed by it. The results have been deepened class divisions and social problems in some societies as minority groups, women, and indigenous peoples have been displaced. Additionally, the Green Revolution has been counterproductive as exports of grains have increased dramatically in some areas, while the majority of those in need do not benefit from the greater grain production in their particular region.

The Rockefeller Foundation created the Consultative Group on International Agricultural Research (CGIAR), which opened research centers worldwide, primarily in developing countries, beginning in 1968. Despite the criticisms, 18 centers staffed with scientists from all over the world existed by 1992, primarily in developing nations. By 2009, CGIAR included both government and nongovernment members and some 15 centers remained open. The centers are supported by a variety of governments, foundations, and organizations, including the U.S. government and the U.S.-based Rockefeller Foundation. These centers generate substantial research, often aimed to dispel the criticisms.

See also AGRICULTURAL TECHNOLOGY; AGRICULTURE, COMMERCIAL; AGRICULTURE, DEPARTMENT OF; CORPORATIONS, CHEMICAL; DISEASES, PLANT; LAND GRANT INSTITUTIONS; MEXICO AND THE UNITED STATES; NONGOVERNMENTAL ORGANIZATIONS; STAPLE CROPS; STATE, DEPARTMENT OF.

Brian S. King

Further Reading
Brown, Lester Russell. *Seeds of Change: The Green Revolution and Development in the 1970s.* New York: Praeger, 1970.
Conway, Gordon. *The Doubly Green Revolution.* Ithaca, N.Y.: Cornell University Press, 1998.
Dahlberg, Kenneth A. *Beyond the Green Revolution: The Ecology and Politics of Global Agricultural Development.* New York: Plenum Press, 1979.
Osmani, Siddiqur Rahman. *Growth and Entitlements: The Analytics of the Green Revolution.* Helsinki, Finland: UNU World Institute for Development Economics Research, 1993.
Shiva, Vandana. *The Violence of the Green Revolution: Ecological Degradation and Political Conflict in Punjab.* New Delhi: Zed Press, 1992.

Grinnell, George Bird (1849–1938) *publisher, naturalist, ethnologist, outdoorsman, environmental activist*

George Bird Grinnell was publisher of *Forest and Stream* and *Audubon Magazine,* founder of the first AUDUBON SOCIETY, cofounder of the BOONE AND CROCKETT CLUB, and an environmental activist. A prolific writer, Grinnell is best remembered for his ethnographic studies of Great Plains Native Americans.

George Bird Grinnell, born on September 20, 1849, in Brooklyn, New York, was the eldest of George Blake Grinnell and Helen A. Lansing's five children. Grinnell's father made a fortune in TEXTILES and, after the CIVIL WAR (1861–65), became a stockbroker and banker. In 1857, the Grinnells moved to Manhattan's Audubon Park, the estate of the late artist and naturalist JOHN JAMES AUDUBON. In 1870, Grinnell graduated from Yale University with a bachelor's degree in paleontology. After his graduation, he went to work in his father's investment business. By 1873, Grinnell was writing for a new magazine, *Forest and Stream.* Grinnell also continued his studies in paleontology at Yale, finishing his Ph.D. in 1880.

In 1875, while a graduate student, Grinnell served as naturalist in a survey of YELLOWSTONE National Park. Grinnell declined an invitation to travel with George Armstrong Custer's ill-fated 1876 western expedition to the Big Horn Mountains. In 1883, he purchased a ranch in Montana. Grinnell traveled extensively in the West, exploring and hunting, throughout his adult live.

In 1880, Grinnell became editor of *Forest and Stream.* Through this publication, Grinnell advocated scientific CONSERVATION and responsible hunting. Along with his anger toward irresponsible sport hunters, who had no concern for the long-term viability of species, Grinnell was becoming increasingly frustrated with market hunting of BIRDS for millinery and other women's fashions. In an 1886 issue of *Forest and Stream,* Grinnell announced the foundation of the Audubon Society to protect birds from overhunting for fashion or sport. He also launched *Audubon Magazine* in 1887 to further the goals of the organization. Although the magazine was short lived, Grinnell would inspire the 20th-century Audubon movement. With his friend, the future U.S. president THEODORE ROOSEVELT, in 1887, Grinnell founded the Boone and Crockett Club an elite sportsmen's society dedicated to wilderness exploration, the protection of game animals and wilderness areas, and responsible hunting and fishing.

In 1902, Grinnell married Elizabeth Kirby Curtis. He sold his interest in *Forest and Stream* in 1911 but continued to be active in environmental causes. He became president of the National Parks Association in 1925. In his final years, he suffered from coronary disease, and he had a heart attack in 1929. He died on April 11, 1938, at the age of 88.

Grinnell is perhaps best remembered for his ethnologic studies of the Indians of the Great Plains, particularly the Cheyenne and the Blackfeet. Grinnell also authored numerous Boone and Crockett Club publications and the "Jack Danvers" series of youth-oriented outdoor adventure novels. He served as the director of the National Audubon Society for 26 years. Grinnell championed environmental protection of the Adirondack Mountains, better management and environmental protection for Yellowstone National Park, and the founding of Glacier National Park. In assessing Grinnell's achievements in his obituary, the *New York Times* hailed him as "the founding father of American conservation."

See also HUNTING, COMMERCIAL; HUNTING, RECREATIONAL; HUNTING, SUBSISTENCE; INDIANS, CENTRAL PLAINS; INDIANS, NORTHERN PLAINS; MEDIA; NATIONAL PARK SERVICE; PROGRESSIVISM.

Kathy S. Mason

Further Reading
Evans, Robley. *George Bird Grinnell.* Boise, Idaho: Boise State University Press, 1996.
Grinnell, George Bird, ed. *American Big Game in Its Haunts: The Book of the Boone and Crockett Club.* New York: Forest and Stream Publishing Company, 1904.
——. *The Cheyenne Indians: Their History and Ways of Life.* 2 vols. New York: Cooper Square, 1923.
——. *The Fighting Cheyennes.* Norman: University of Oklahoma Press, 1915.
——. Jack Danvers series. New York: Frederick A. Stokes, 1899–1913.
Reiger, John F. *The Passing of the Great West: Selected Papers of George Bird Grinnell.* Norman: University of Oklahoma Press, 1972.

grocery stores and supermarkets

Grocery stores and their larger counterparts, supermarkets, are retail outlets specializing in foodstuffs, beverages, and a range of household items. Depending on size, they can also feature nonfood items, such as pharmaceutical supplies, flowers, stationery, and seasonal gift items, in addition to FOOD. Smaller grocery stores, typically called convenience stores, generally sell only varieties of snacks and nonperishable items. Grocery stores and later supermarkets made food more convenient and affordable for most consumers. However, the rise of grocery stores and supermarkets also reflected and facilitated changing consumption habits and contributed to the evolution of foodstuffs into commodities. As a result, the United States witnessed the expansion of monocultural COMMERCIAL AGRICULTURE accompanied by the greater use of FERTILIZER and PESTICIDES and an increase of nonbiodegradable waste.

Originating in the late 19th century, grocery stores are an evolution of America's 19th-century trading posts—small local stores that contained not only nonperishable foodstuffs but also a range of other products such as furniture and household items. Groceries are nonperishable products, such as canned foods and bags of sugar and flour,

that originated in these new grocery stores. Sales assistants dealt with these products in a hands-on way, measuring out quantities and delivering personalized over-the-counter service. Perishable items such as meats, vegetables, and fruits were purchased at other locations, such as local farmers' markets and butchers' shops. Modern-day grocery stores now sell proportionally fewer household items and focus more on providing a wide range of groceries as well as fresh produce.

Representing the beginning of a new industrialized food industry, grocery stores were complemented by the creation of supermarkets in the early 20th century. The first supermarket to open in the United States was the Piggly Wiggly Store in Memphis, Tennessee, on September 11, 1916. A significant difference was that customers now walked down aisles with baskets in their hands, inspecting and selecting different goods for themselves. Today, the average supermarket contains more than 45,000 items within a large one-story building, where fluorescent lighting illuminates rows of stacked shelves in spacious aisles.

Supermarkets have been described as "landscapes"—albeit human-made ones—containing a wide variety of BIODIVERSITY. There is usually a fresh produce section as well as sections containing other kinds of food, including prepackaged and frozen "dinners." A separate meat counter containing a wide range of cuts of meat from different animals is common, emphasizing the freshness of the products and heightening their aesthetic appeal to shoppers. There is a similar idea behind the creation of seafood and cheese counters, with assistants in traditional uniform resembling those of a stereotypical historical fishmonger or butcher. This nostalgic approach is also employed in the package designs and advertising of foodstuffs, drawing on pastoral images emphasizing the "naturalness" of the products. Canned vegetables feature labels with images of freshly picked perfect produce, which is a far cry from the industrial environment in which they are processed. For much of the 20th century, this advertising directly targeted the American homemaker, long in charge of the shopping and feeding of her family, who wished to remain informed of what her family ate.

Prior to modern grocery stores and supermarkets, most foodstuffs were purchased in local communities. People were acutely aware of where their food originated. As a larger capitalist economy rose in the United States during the 19th century, the food industry was directly affected. RAILROADS allowed for transportation of goods over larger distances in shorter periods, meaning consumers could now enjoy products previously considered exotic, such as oranges, which found their way to northern cities. New inventions such as the "icebox on wheels"—refrigerated railway cars—solved the issue of transporting perishable goods a longer distance. Companies introduced additives into foodstuffs to maintain

Self-serve grocery stores and supermarkets in the United States emerged in the early 20th century. The vast majority of food now consumed in the country travels through these stores and requires transportation, packaging, and retailing.   *(Library of Congress)*

a longer shelf life once the product arrived in the store. These processes radically expanded the assortment in stores in large cities far from farms and feedlots, distancing consumers from the natural origins of their food.

Farmers responded to the new market's demands through specialization, rejecting a more traditional crop sequencing system. Similarly, livestock producers increasingly centralized the raising of CATTLE with large feedlots. With a new economic philosophy centered on increasing profit through mass production of goods, food, in many respects, transitioned in people's collective consciousness from a source of nourishment, directly from nature, into a commodity. Research has shown that humans today do not attach the same value to foodstuffs as to other consumer goods. Standardized pricing, as a result of the centralization of the food industry, means that many consumers neither question nor value quality enough to pay a higher price for it. Since the birth of supermarkets, consumers have been

confronted with a huge selection of competing products that are mostly prepackaged, making it impossible to make judgments on quality and taste without relying on brand reputations and increasingly more detailed labels.

The industrialization of the food industry has indirectly been linked to a range of health issues affecting the public. Popular foodstuffs sold in supermarkets tend to contain a high percentage of fats and sugars, such as corn syrup and transfats, known to contribute to diabetes and heart disease. Research has shown that these products are often significantly cheaper than healthier alternatives, thus promoting an unhealthy diet. As a result of this, a counterculture has emerged in America over the past 20 years, promoting healthy eating linked back to local environments. This local food movement promotes local farms and emphasizes consumers' knowing exactly where their food originates, providing an alternative to the anonymity of traditional supermarkets.

As the food industry has changed, so has the landscape supporting it. MONOCULTURE in farms and large feedlots along with the transportation routes supporting them have altered the landscape on an aesthetic level, and the increasing use of PESTICIDES has directly affected ECOSYSTEMS, creating new resistant strains of WEEDS and INSECTS. Local communities often found their economies depleted with the introduction of new supercenters, such as Wal-Mart, now dominating many parts of the United States. Containing entire supermarkets within their buildings, Wal-Mart stores also feature other services, such as tire and auto services, not traditionally associated with grocery stores and supermarkets. This development has led to smaller town's losing businesses and their individuality, as the recognized Wal-Mart signs and architecture take over the landscape.

Changes in the landscape have been paired with a new capitalist consumer-based idea of nature. Colorful packaging and food additives are now the norm from which human consciousness finds it difficult to divert. The supermarket experience is for many a natural part of daily life. Similarly, human dependence on the plastic bags used in many supermarkets shows no sign of receding, with some 100 billion plastic bags discarded every year by Americans alone. A large portion of these nondegradable plastic bags ends up in OCEANS and LANDFILLS, contributing to larger problems.

Grocery stores and supermarkets have had a profound, often double-edged impact on the human environment, health, and culture. They have facilitated the easy purchase of food and made available to consumers a wide range of products at reasonable prices. At the same time, they helped to distance humans from the environments in which these goods are procured.

See also HEALTH AND MEDICINE; STOCKYARDS AND MEATPACKING; TRUCK FARMS.

Anna Cecilia Rehn

Further Reading

Fishman, Charles. *The Wal-Mart Effect: How the World's Most Powerful Company Really Works and How It's Transforming the American Economy.* New York: Penguin Press, 2006.

Pollan, Michael. *The Omnivore's Dilemma: A Natural History of Four Meals.* New York: Penguin Press, 2007.

Vileisis, Ann. *Kitchen Literacy: How We Lost Knowledge of Where Food Comes From and Why We Need to Get It Back.* Washington, D.C.: Island Press, 2008.

Gulf Coast   *See* MEXICO, GULF OF; UNITED STATES—GULF COAST.

Gulf of Mexico   *See* MEXICO, GULF OF.

Gulf War

The Gulf War was a military engagement between Iraq and a coalition of 34 nations led by the United States from August 1990 to February 28, 1991. Sanctioned by the UNITED NATIONS (UN), coalition forces expelled Iraq from its small oil-rich neighbor Kuwait, which Iraq had annexed on August 2, 1990. The military technology employed in the conflict helped shorten the fighting, but it also had specific consequences for human health and the environment.

After Iraq's invasion, the United States launched "Operation Desert Shield," the mobilization of troops and materiel in Saudi Arabia. "Operation Desert Storm" commenced on January 16, 1991, when coalition forces began an aerial assault on Iraqi forces and installations in Kuwait and Iraq. The ground attack followed on February 24, Iraq withdrew from Kuwait on February 26, and a cease-fire took effect on February 28.

The Iraqi leader Saddam Hussein claimed a right to Kuwait dating back to the second millennium B.C.E. Under Ottoman rule, Kuwait was part of an Iraqi province. It became a British protectorate in 1899 and an independent nation in 1961. Kuwait occupied a strategic position adjacent to Iraq, Iran, Saudi Arabia, and the Persian Gulf. Furthermore, Kuwait was a country of immense wealth; its valuable oil fields produced nearly two million barrels a day. After a long war with Iran in the 1980s, Iraq owed Kuwait billions of dollars. Iraq also accused Kuwait of stealing its oil and of exceeding quotas set by the Organization of Petroleum Exporting Countries (OPEC).

Spearheaded by U.S. president GEORGE H. W. BUSH, the America-led coalition against Iraq sought to restore the balance of power in the Persian Gulf region. An Iraqi-controlled Kuwait threatened Saudi Arabian oil fields and the stability of world oil supplies. The UN and the United States also cited Iraq's poor human rights record, its production and use of BIOLOGICAL AND CHEMICAL WEAPONS, and its burgeoning nuclear weapons program.

Military combat during the Gulf War was brief: Iraq overwhelmed Kuwait in two days; coalition forces liberated Kuwait in six weeks with 240 casualties. Estimates for Iraqi deaths are controversial; they range from a few thousand to more than 200,000. According to most demographic experts, direct coalition fire accounted for approximately 3,500 Iraqi civilian deaths and 56,000 military deaths. Higher numbers cited by some commentators include indirect deaths due to postwar conditions. The coalition credited its overwhelming victory to superior technology and weaponry, particularly the so-called smart bombs utilized during the aerial assault.

The environmental impact of the war was more lasting. An estimated 11 million barrels of crude oil spilled into the Persian Gulf after Iraqi and coalition forces detonated tankers and offshore oil terminals. Iraq also pursued a scorched-earth policy by igniting Kuwaiti oil wells in their retreat; about 1.5 billion barrels of oil were lost and the 732 burning wells spewed soot and pollutants into the air and created toxic oil lakes. Western MEDIA images of dying cormorants stuck in oil slicks and the uncontrolled burning oil wells became symbols of Iraqi iniquity.

The war had a devastating effect on public health in the Gulf region. AIR POLLUTION caused respiratory illnesses. Land mines and unexploded ordnance were widespread. Destruction of civilian infrastructure led to water shortages. Lethal waterborne diseases, including TYPHOID and CHOLERA, ravaged Iraq, especially the Shiite-dominated south. Starvation and malnutrition were other problems; the air war destroyed IRRIGATION systems and disrupted the fragile desert ECOSYSTEMS of Kuwait and southern Iraq.

The war may have had broader, long-term public health and environmental impacts. Pollution from the burning oil wells was global and may have disrupted weather patterns in Southeast Asia. Exposure to Iraqi biological and chemical weapons may have contributed to Gulf War syndrome, a mysterious condition diagnosed in some coalition veterans. The U.S. use of depleted uranium in its ammunition also may have contributed to the syndrome and to enduring Iraqi health problems.

See also DEFENSE, DEPARTMENT OF; DISEASES, HUMAN; HEALTH AND MEDICINE; OIL, IMPORTED; OIL, SPILLS; POLLUTION, AIR; POLLUTION, WATER; STATE, DEPARTMENT OF.

Margaretta Brokaw

Further Reading

Atkinson, Rick. *Crusade: The Untold Story of the Persian Gulf War.* Boston: Houghton Mifflin, 1993.

Bloom, Saul, et al., eds. *Hidden Casualties: Environment, Health and Political Consequences of the Persian Gulf War.* Berkeley, Calif.: North Atlantic Books, 1994.

Hawley, T. M. *Against the Fires of Hell: The Environmental Disaster of the Gulf War.* New York: Harcourt, 1992.

Guthrie, Woody (Woodrow Wilson) (1912–1967)
folk singer

The singer Woody Guthrie provided a political voice for the working class of depression era America. Famous during his lifetime as a stage performer, radio personality, and writer, Guthrie wrote and sang songs, such as "This Land Is Your Land" and "Pastures of Plenty," that provided inspiration for social action in succeeding generations—particularly in regard to environmental issues. Guthrie's early music lamented the environmental and social degradation (the DUST BOWL) of the Great Plains, highlighted relationships between agricultural workers in California, and later captured the spirit of laborers

and nature in the dam building on the COLUMBIA RIVER. All the while, he also spoke to the beauty, spirit, and importance of diverse American landscapes.

Born on July 14, 1912, in Omeka, Oklahoma, Woodrow Wilson Guthrie was the son of Charles Guthrie, a businessman and politician, and Nora Belle, a homemaker and musician. Escaping a household broken apart by a series of ill-fated events including the death of his older sister and the institutionalization of his mother due to Huntington's chorea, the same disease that would later claim his life, Woody left Omeka by the time he was 17 to travel and work odd jobs in Oklahoma and Texas. In 1937, he migrated to California, as did thousands of other dust bowl refugees. Upon this backdrop of the GREAT DEPRESSION, Guthrie began writing songs based on the difficulties of poverty, the ills of CAPITALISM, and the intricate culture of the working class. As his radio popularity in California grew, so did his dedication to left-wing radical politics.

Guthrie moved to NEW YORK CITY, in 1939. There, he was recognized as an important musician by the folklorist Alan Lomax and made a series of recordings that captured his blended style of traditional folk songs and ballads, music inspired by his mother, as well as union hymns, political folk songs, and nationalistic anthems. Influenced by the early 20th-century union organizer and singer Joe Hill (1879–1915), yet capturing his own observations as a laborer and wanderer, Guthrie's words are poignant and demand lasting attention, although most of his melodies were borrowed from existing songs.

In 1941, the BONNEVILLE POWER ADMINISTRATION contracted Guthrie to write a series of songs centered on dam building along the Columbia River. Taking part in the building of the Grand Coulee Dam—destined to reshape further the second-longest river in the United States—Guthrie intoned the dramatic changes to the wild river and the spirit in which laborers changed its identity for use in hydroelectric power and IRRIGATION. The interval proved to be the most prolific songwriting period in his life, and many of these songs were captured in the album *Roll on Columbia*.

During WORLD WAR II (1941–45), the antifascist Guthrie first served as part of a civilian convoy in the Pacific in 1942 and later was drafted into the army, in which he served until December 1945. During this period, Guthrie continued to record and published his autobiography, *Bound for Glory*, in 1943. By the late 1940s, Guthrie was struck with Huntington's chorea—a debilitating genetic central nervous system disease. He continued performing and writing music, but in the early 1950s, his condition worsened and he was transferred in and out of hospitals until his death on October 3, 1967. Married three times, Guthrie had eight children, including Arlo, who became a prominent folk musician in his own right.

Woody Guthrie wrote more than 1,000 songs and influenced a wide range of folk, rock, blues, and country musicians, including Bob Dylan and Bruce Springsteen. In 1940, he put lyrics to a well-known folk melody to create the song "This Land Is Your Land," expressing his strong belief that the land existed for the well-being of all Americans. In 1966, the DEPARTMENT OF THE INTERIOR awarded Guthrie its prestigious Conservation Award, "in recognition of his life-long efforts to make the American people aware of their heritage and the land."

See also UNITED STATES—CENTRAL PLAINS; UNITED STATES—PACIFIC NORTHWEST.

Peter Kopp

Further Reading

Guthrie, Woody. *Bound For Glory.* New York: E. P. Dutton, 1968.

Klein, Joe. *Woody Guthrie, a Life.* New York: A. A. Knopf, 1980.

Santellit, Robert, and Emily Davidson, eds. *Hard Travelin': The Life and Legacy of Woody Guthrie.* Hanover, N.H.: Wesleyan University Press, 1999.

H

Hamilton, Alexander (1755–1804) *Constitutional Convention delegate, secretary of the treasury (1789–1795)*
Alexander Hamilton played many roles in the formation of the early United States as an officer in the Continental Army during the AMERICAN REVOLUTION (1775–83), as a delegate to the Constitutional Convention in 1787, and as the nation's first secretary of the treasury from 1789 to 1795. He became a vocal advocate of the idea that the United States must employ its vast natural resources in manufacturing to become self-sufficient and economically competitive with other nations.

Hamilton was born on January 11, 1755, on the British West Indian island of Nevis, the illegitimate son of Rachel Fawcett Lavien and James Hamilton, both from prominent trading families in the Caribbean Islands. He apprenticed as a clerk on the island of Saint Croix before his guardian, the merchant Nicholas Cruger, sent him to NEW YORK CITY in 1772. While studying at King's College (now Columbia University), Hamilton joined the political debates on NATURAL LAW and independence as the American Revolution drew near. He joined the New York militia in 1775 and, by 1777, had earned a commission as a lieutenant colonel and aide-de-camp to General GEORGE WASHINGTON, who took note of Hamilton's organizational abilities. In 1782, shortly after leaving the army, he was admitted to the New York bar and became an assistant to Robert Morris (1734–1806), the national superintendent of finance.

Hamilton also won election to the Continental Congress in 1782 and quickly campaigned for a stronger national government than the ARTICLES OF CONFEDERATION provided. He pursued this same goal as a delegate to the Constitutional Convention in 1787. A year later, Hamilton joined James Madison (1751–1836) and John Jay (1745–1829) in crafting a series of essays, now known as The Federalist Papers, that called for a stronger centralized government and executive and judicial branches that equaled the power of the legislature. The authors urged New Yorkers to ratify the proposed U.S. CONSTITUTION, and the voters did. After the ratification of the new constitution by the necessary nine states and with the formation of the new government, President Washington selected Hamilton as the first secretary of the treasury in 1789.

As a member of Washington's cabinet, Hamilton frequently clashed with Secretary of State THOMAS JEFFERSON over how the nation's resources should be distributed and to what end they should be utilized. Their arguments had begun in the 1780s over the terms of the Land Ordinance of 1785. Jefferson believed that hardworking Americans had a natural right to the land of the PUBLIC DOMAIN, and thus federally controlled lands should be sold at low prices. High prices, he contended, led to speculation by the wealthy that thwarted opportunities for the nation's YEOMAN farmers. Hamilton alternatively argued that western lands constituted the nation's greatest asset. He wanted to sell the lands for the highest possible price to help reduce the nation's debt and to fund other government operations. The land ordinance passed on May 20, 1785, set public sales at one dollar per acre, the standard price for the time but beyond the means of most average farmers. Subsequent amendments to the land ordinance supported Hamilton's position that land expansion should be the province of the big investors.

Hamilton and Jefferson also disagreed over whether the young United States should commit itself to significant industrial development. Jefferson worried that the poverty, noxious pollution, and human filth that defined English factory towns would undermine the republican virtues of the American citizenry. He believed that yeoman farmers strengthened local economies and prevented the concentration of wealth in the hands of a few. Cultivation of the soil supposedly taught people to be self-reliant and independent, although many historians suggest that Jefferson's idealized yeoman farmer was already a myth in Jefferson's time.

Hamilton argued for more extensive and more dynamic employment of the nation's natural resources. He wanted the federal government actively to promote manufacturing. Industrialization, he averred, allowed for substantially greater production of wealth than farming and would allow the United States to move away from its dependency on

England and Europe for manufactured goods. In his 1791 *Report on Manufacturers,* he promoted mechanization as the means to economic competitiveness. Hamilton urged the federal government to spark industrialization through protective tariffs, limits on the export of raw materials, public improvements such as ROADS AND TURNPIKES, and CANALS, and centralized planning. He wanted to control western expansion to ensure that essential natural resources, from FORESTS and minerals to hydraulic power sources, were placed in the hands of the most dynamic investors.

Hamilton helped the United States avoid bankruptcy as it worked to repay its debts, but he resigned as treasury secretary in January 1795 after a scandalous love affair and accusations that he had acted contrary to the directions of CONGRESS in the distribution of certain federal funds. Hamilton remained active in national politics, although he did not stand for office. In 1804, he helped organize the defeat of the then-vice president Aaron Burr (1756–1836) in the latter's bid for the governorship of New York State, including making supposedly insulting comments about Burr at a dinner party. Burr demanded an apology; Hamilton refused, claiming he did not recall the incident. Tensions escalated, and the two met for a duel in Weehawken, New Jersey, on July 11, 1804. Hamilton was mortally wounded and died the next day.

See also CAPITALISM; DECLARATION OF INDEPENDENCE; FEDERAL LAW—LAND POLICIES; SECTIONALISM.

Kathleen A. Brosnan

Further Reading

Andrews, Richard N. L. *Managing the Environment, Managing Ourselves: A History of American Environmental Policy.* 2d ed. New Haven, Conn.: Yale University Press, 2006.
New York Historical Society. *Alexander Hamilton: The Man Who Made Modern America.* Available online. URL: http://www.alexanderhamiltonexhibition.org/. Accessed August 29, 2009.
Opie, John. *Nature's Nation: An Environmental History of the United States.* Fort Worth, Tex.: Harcourt, Brace, 1998.

Hamilton, Alice (1869–1970) *leading physician of industrial medicine, progressive reformer*
Born on February 27, 1869, into a privileged family in Fort Wayne, Indiana, Alice Hamilton spent most of her long life exploring dangerous workplaces and the industrial toxins within them that threatened the health of workers. She was raised in Indiana and educated at home before attending boarding school in Connecticut. Eager to travel, Hamilton chose a career in medicine. "If I were a doctor," she wrote in her autobiography, "I could go anywhere I wanted—to foreign lands, to city slums." After graduating from medical school at the University of Michigan in 1893, Hamilton continued her studies abroad. Upon her return in 1897, she accepted a position as professor of pathology at the Women's Medical School of Northwestern University.

Hamilton had long been interested in the SETTLEMENT HOUSE MOVEMENT and had attended lectures by JANE ADDAMS and other Hull-House residents. In 1897, Hamilton moved into Hull-House in Chicago, Illinois, where she lived for more than 20 years. In the evenings at Hull-House, she taught classes on hygiene, first aid, and patent medicines. Hamilton used her medical expertise to study and explain the high rates of TYPHOID and TUBERCULOSIS in the community and recommended improvements in working conditions to strengthen the ability of workers to resist disease. She also established a well baby clinic at the settlement house.

Her experiences at Hull-House aroused her interest in industrial medicine and the toxic substances to which workers were exposed. By the turn of the 20th century, industrial medicine was well established in Europe. In the United States, however, very few physicians specialized in the field. Hamilton served on the Occupational Disease Commission, created by the governor of Illinois in 1910. Through this commission, she undertook a sweeping study of occupational poisons. She investigated phossy jaw, a disfiguring disease resulting from exposure to phosphorus in match factories, and concentrated especially on LEAD poisoning. Drawing on European studies, personal inspections of factories, and interviews with workers in their homes, Hamilton's report on the dangers of lead was comprehensive. She identified the ways in which workers were needlessly exposed to lead in rubber, paint, and other industries. Hamilton recommended specific changes in manufacturing practices and advocated workers' compensation laws.

Hamilton's report drew attention from advocates of labor reform across the country. From 1911 to 1921, Hamilton worked for the U.S. DEPARTMENT OF LABOR to reproduce her study on a national scale. Hamilton broadened her analysis of industrial toxicology to include a wide range of poisons and studied both acute and chronic exposure. Her study included the workplace as well as the homes of workers, where family members could be exposed to toxins carried on bodies and clothing. Hamilton researched the effect of radioactivity on workers who used radium to make luminous watch dials. Hamilton worked to call the plight of the largely female workforce, also known as the RADIUM GIRLS, to the attention of the government and the public. As the principal expert in industrial medicine, in 1919, she became the first female professor at Harvard. In addition to addressing the dangers of industrial pollution and poisons, Hamilton lobbied for protective legislation for women and children. Best known for her work in industrial medicine, Hamilton also worked broadly for social reform. She was an advocate for peace and authored *Women at The Hague: The International Congress of Women and Its Results* with Jane Addams and Emily G. Balch, in which they chronicled the women's efforts in international diplomacy.

Over her extraordinarily long life, Alice Hamilton made contributions in many areas of science and medicine and was an advocate of social reform. She coupled her pioneering research in industrial toxicology and occupational health with a commitment to improve living and working conditions for the urban poor and factory workers. As new substances flooded the marketplace, Hamilton strove to understand the consequences of these chemicals for human health. After her retirement, Hamilton continued to work for social justice and peace. Her decades of advocacy on behalf of women and workers and her efforts to call the workplace to the attention of science and medicine combined to make her one of the leading scientists and reformers of the 20th century. She died on September 22, 1970.

See also CARCINOGENS, POISONS, AND TOXINS; CORPORATIONS, CHEMICAL; HEALTH AND MEDICINE.

Kelly A. Roark

Further Reading

Addams, Jane, Emily G. Balch, and Alice Hamilton. *Women at The Hague: The International Congress of Women and Its Results*. New York: Humanity Books, 2003.

Gottlieb, Robert. *Forcing the Spring: The Transformation of the American Environmental Movement*. Washington, D.C.: Island Press, 1993.

Hamilton, Alice. *Exploring the Dangerous Trades: The Autobiography of Alice Hamilton, M.D.* Boston: Little, Brown, 1943.

Sicherman, Barbara. *Alice Hamilton: A Life in Letters*. Cambridge, Mass.: Harvard University Press, 1984.

The Obligations of the Industrial Physician Alice Hamilton (1925)

Dr. Alice Hamilton published widely about occupational health, toxicology, and the dangers an industrial environment presented to urban workers in the early 20th century. Worried about the health implications of new and untested industrial activities, particularly with chemicals and petrochemicals, she worked to make factories safer. In her 1925 book, Industrial Poisons in the United States, *Hamilton emphasized that an industrial physician's first loyalty was to the workers rather than the company, but in discussing immigrant workers, she also revealed some of the biases of American society.*

The task of education is not easy—it is exhaustive of time and temper alike, but it is a duty which cannot be shirked, especially in unorganized industries. Trade Unionists are to varying extent responsible for the conditions under which they work, but the great majority of the poisonous industries are unorganized. Much of the dangerous work is done by foreign-born men and women and toward these workers the responsibility of the management of the physician is far greater. Such people are like children in their readiness to accept the conditions of life, they will work long hours, in heat and filth and poisonous dust, they make no demands for security or comforts, they are quite free from the irritating interference of trade union officials. These are great advantages to the employer but if he accepts them he must accept the accompanying disadvantages. With child-like docility goes childish ignorance, recklessness and obstinacy. The management cannot throw upon such men and women the responsibility for their own health and safety. They are not capable of assuming it. For them the protection must be especially elaborate, it must be "fool-proof," the vigilance of the physician must be unrelaxed. . . .

In closing, let me beg the industrial physician not to let the atmosphere of the factory befog his view of his special problem. His duty is to the producer, not to the product. If measures which he knows to be necessary are declared impossible, because they interfere with production, he may have to yield, but let it be understood that such yielding is against his judgment. A sanitary engineer may be told by a city council that it cannot afford a pure water supply and he may have no choice but to accept the verdict. But he would be greatly at fault if he allowed the city fathers to believe that the halfway measures they plan will safeguard the community against typhoid fever. In the same way the industrial physician may be obliged to abandon his plans for protecting his charges against poisoning because the expense is greater than management will allow or because a change in the method might make the product less perfect. But in so yielding let him be careful never to sacrifice his won intellectual integrity nor adopt the standards of the non-medical man to whom the proper working of the plant is of first importance. His task is to safeguard the health of the patients who are entrusted to him, often without any volition of their own. The successful production of goods is outside his field. To the physician, always, life is more than meat and the body more than raiment.

⟢⟢⟢

Source: Alice Hamilton. *Industrial Poisons in the United States.* New York: Macmillan, 1925, 540–542.

Harlem Renaissance

The period between the mid-1910s and the late 1930s in the Harlem neighborhood of NEW YORK CITY was defined by a blossoming of black literary, theatrical, musical, and artistic talent and production. Harlem became a safer community for black southerners who began migrating to northern cities in the GREAT MIGRATION during the middle of the Jim Crow era of the South. The Harlem Renaissance was foundational for black Americans in terms of building greater cultural independence, challenging racist stereotypes, and eventually laying the foundations for the CIVIL RIGHTS movement of the 1950s and modern ENVIRONMENTAL JUSTICE movements such as West Harlem Environmental Action Committee (WEACT).

The Great Migration of rural blacks from the South to the North began in the mid-1910s and continued through the 1940s. Fueled by natural and social environmental issues in the South, more than 200,000 black residents relocated to Harlem by 1930. DROUGHTS, FLOODS, and a BOLL WEEVIL infestation in the 1910s decimated the agricultural fields black sharecroppers relied on for their already-tenuous livelihood. With a growth in industrial jobs due to WORLD WAR I (1914–18) and a decline of immigrants from Europe, the northern cities provided better unskilled and semiskilled job opportunities and a less oppressive and hostile cultural environment for day-to-day life. Although northern cities were far from free of RACISM AND DISCRIMINATION, many relocated blacks experienced greater economic, political, and social freedoms and opportunities than they had in the rural South. Black immigrants from the West Indies and the Caribbean also settled in Harlem and helped form this burgeoning community with a vibrant culture and a strong business and civic community. Inspired by writings such as W. E. B. DuBois's *The Souls of Black Folk* (1903) and James Weldon Johnson's *The Autobiography of an Ex-Colored Man* (published anonymously in 1912), black artists, writers, and musicians began to illustrate the black experience as a growing self-consciousness and prideful intellectual and creative community of "New Negroes." The term coined by Alain Locke signified a new confident spirit of racial consciousness and pride. BOOKER T. WASHINGTON's idea of black accommo-

dation waned with a new period of growing independence, pride, and conscious creativity and opinions of blacks in the United States. Marcus Garvey's arrival in Harlem in 1916 also encouraged black pride, expression, and self-empowerment.

Harlem became a blueprint for other black communities in America and a positive symbol for black culture in general, sometimes referred to as the "Negro capital," or the "promised land." A growing interest in black cultural products by wealthy whites was based on "primitivism," interest in African and Caribbean artistic products as representative of a simple, noble, yet uncultured rural life. These stereotypes of white audiences and publishers encouraged an oppositional consciousness among blacks that furthered black expressionism through creatively organic formats. This energy of creative expression flourished within this urban setting, which often appeared, paradoxically, distinctly separate from the rest of New York City. By developing exclusively black literary magazines, for example, Harlem writers and artists increasingly united to publish and produce their work in black formats. An abridged selection of major literary and philosophical figures of the Harlem Renaissance includes Alain Locke, Claude McKay, Jean Toomer, Langston Hughes, Zora Neale Hurston, and Countee Cullen. Prominent musicians included Duke Ellington, Louis Armstrong, and Fats Waller.

Besides the artistic and literary elements of the Harlem Renaissance, progressive black civic and politically oriented projects blossomed in this period—such as the Universal Negro Improvement Association (UNIA), founded by Marcus Garvey, and the NATIONAL ASSOCIATION FOR THE ADVANCEMENT OF COLORED PEOPLE (NAACP), led by W. E. B. DuBois and James W. Johnson during this period. More recently, in 1988, local residents formed WE ACT for Environmental Justice, a nonprofit, community-based organization to fight environmental racism and to improve environmental health and protection in Harlem.

See also ENVIRONMENTALISM, GRASSROOTS; FORTY ACRES AND A MULE; IMMIGRATION; NATIONAL URBAN LEAGUE; SHARECROPPING; UNITED STATES—NORTHEAST.

Marcus David Aldredge

Further Reading

Baker, Houston A., Jr. *Modernism and the Harlem Renaissance.* Chicago: University of Chicago Press, 1989.

De Jongh, James. *Vicious Modernism: Black Harlem and the Literary Imagination.* Cambridge: Cambridge University Press, 1990.

Harrison, Alferdteen, ed. *Black Exodus: The Great Migration from the American South.* Jackson: University Press of Mississippi, 1991.

Helbling, Mark Irving. *The Harlem Renaissance: The One and the Many.* Westport, Conn.: Greenwood Press, 1999.

Hill, Laban Carrick. *Harlem Stomp! A Cultural History of the Harlem Renaissance.* New York: Little, Brown, 2003.

Hawaii   See United States—Hawaii and the Pacific Islands.

Hawthorne, Nathaniel (1804–1864) *author*

A 19th-century writer in the romantic and transcendentalist traditions, Nathaniel Hawthorne wrote stories in which nature functions mainly as a peaceful place of solitude to escape society's temptations and distractions, although, as he reveals, humans can often conceive of the natural world as a threat to civilization and order.

Hawthorne was born on July 4, 1804, in Salem, Massachusetts, and educated at Bowdoin College, where he became friends with the poet Henry Wadsworth Longfellow. Although he took occasional extended trips to Europe, Hawthorne lived the majority of his life in New England and even spent a short time in the early 1840s at the Brook Farm commune organized by members of the transcendentalist movement. Hawthorne was the descendant of early Puritan settlers of Salem, Massachusetts; he added the *w* to the middle of his last name to distance himself from an ancestor who had been a judge in the Salem witch trials and had condemned innocent women to death. Hawthorne is known mainly for his novels and short stories, especially those that unfold as rich allegories, in which he explored topics such as the alienation of the modern individual, the legacy of Puritan New England, the conflict between fate and free will, and tensions between nature and society.

Hawthorne's stories set in big cities often condemn city dwellers as immoral. In the short story "My Kinsman, Major Molineux" (1832), for instance, the city acts as a corrupting force on Major Molineux, who devolves to such a state that he is barely recognizable to his young nephew, who travels from the country to find him. Hawthorne situates humanity's moral salvation in the preservation of the countryside and its agrarian values.

In other works, Hawthorne explores the legacy of Puritanism. His Puritan characters often view the woods and forests as a source of evil because it is in such uncivilized locations, they believe, that wild beasts, savage Natives, and the devil himself reside. In the short stories "Young Goodman Brown" (1835) and "The May-Pole of Merry Mount" (1837), the wilderness must be conquered by the Puritans because they see it as a place of disorder and temptation. The people of Merry Mount—who practice a form of nature worship— are innocent and live in harmony with the natural world, but they are quickly conquered by the Puritans and made to renounce their carefree ways and idyllic lives. Hawthorne's allegories often comment on American national identity,

in this case suggesting that its Puritan heritage informs the destruction of the environment. In his own time, Hawthorne observed the destructive power of the new railroads, the development of more factories in big cities, the loss of green spaces as cities expanded to accommodate new immigrants, and the ecological impact of the Civil War (1861–65).

Two of Hawthorne's short stories focus on the mistreatment of nature in the pursuit of science. In "The Birth-Mark" (1843), he discusses the loss of life that occurs when humans tamper with the natural world. Similarly, in "Rappacini's Daughter" (1844), he suggests that some secrets of nature should not be probed by science because the consequences could be devastating. In both of these stories, nature has a power that is lost on humans and their petty rationales.

In Hawthorne's longer works, such as *The Scarlet Letter* (1850), *The House of Seven Gables* (1851), *The Blithedale Romance* (1852), and *The Marble Faun* (1860), the beginnings of the forest on the outskirts of town can represent a safe haven for those at adds with the Puritan values of the town center. For the Puritans, the forest was the domain of the Natives and the place of pagan idol worship. To give God's message to the "new" world they had to civilize the wilderness. Hawthorne, as did other transcendentalists, wanted to rescue the concept of nature from its limited definition in terms of Puritan ideology or in terms of the scientific discoveries and capitalist profit motives that also justified the exploitation of natural resources. He imbues nature with a spiritual meaning, but one more sophisticated than that suggested by the symbolism of the pathetic fallacy, in which nature is a mirror for human emotion. The pathetic fallacy is invoked by Hawthorne—often in the play of light and dark imagery—when nature reacts positively to humans' achievement of a balance between human companionship in society and respect for the natural world. Also in his novels, he sometimes crafts nature's indifference to humankind and uses it as a tool to remind us of our insignificance and mortality. In doing so, Hawthorne borrows from the gothic tradition of nature as a location that unsettles or frightens humans. Ultimately, he sides with the transcendentalist movement in highlighting the wilderness as a place of temporary refuge where one recharges spiritually before returning to civilization.

Hawthorne died on May 19, 1864, in Plymouth, New Hampshire, while touring the White Mountains with another Bowdoin classmate, the former U.S. president Franklin Pierce. He remains a dominant American literary figure.

See also romanticism; transcendentalism; United States—Northeast, urbanization.

Kassi Hawkins and Lynn Houston

Further Reading

Halsey Foster, Edward. *The Civilized Wilderness: Backgrounds to American Romantic Literature, 1817–1860.* New York: Free Press, 1975.

Health and Human Services, Department of

The Department of Health and Human Services (HHS) is the U.S. government's principal agency for protecting the health of all Americans and thus is concerned about how environmental conditions affect human health. HHS also is tasked with providing essential human services to Americans but takes a particular interest in assisting those who are least able to help themselves. Thus, it protects specific citizens and their bodies. The history, a rather new subfield of environmental history, contemplates how diverse conceptions of the body influenced people, their actions, and their interactions with nature throughout history—conceptions that have influenced government health policies as well.

HHS functions include health and social science research, disease prevention, drug and food safety, and health service provision for those in need. Medicare and Medicaid are two of the most well-known agencies within HHS. In addition, the FOOD AND DRUG ADMINISTRATION (FDA) and the Public Health Service make up significant parts of HHS. Public health is that branch of medicine that addresses the health of the community as a whole.

The HHS came into existence in 1980, but there were many formal and informal precursors to this cabinet-level organization. In 1862, President ABRAHAM LINCOLN appointed to the DEPARTMENT OF AGRICULTURE (DOA) a chemist, Charles Wetherill (1825–71), who started the Division of Chemistry. Wetherill opened a laboratory, testing samples of FOOD, FERTILIZER, and other agricultural substances. Early research efforts focused on ways to preserve food, including the use of chemical preservatives. In 1874, the division reported on the adulteration of milk with water and chemicals. It also investigated the effects of arsenic and copper PESTICIDES on plant health and human health in the late 19th century. A precursor to the Food and Drug Administration, the division was renamed the Bureau of Chemistry in 1901 and continued to work to ensure that food—one of humans' most basic connections with nature—was pure for consumption both in its final form and in the processes and environments that produced it.

In other areas, the government's concern over disease and public health showcased which bodies and citizens concerned it most. In 1887, the federal government opened a laboratory on Staten Island, New York, to research disease. This facility, which became known as the Public Health Service's Hygienic Laboratory, laid the foundation for the National Institutes of Health (NIH), part of the modern HHS. Industrialization and the increasing concentration of population in crowded cities, as well as the influx of immigrants into the United States, had prompted new anxieties about the introduction of contagious diseases. In practice, this early health program focused on protecting white citizens, revealing a fear of foreigners grounded in racial prejudice and ethnic bias. At first, the government did not include immigrants or other racial minorities in its efforts to combat diseases.

By 1900, many states had passed food safety laws, but they proved inadequate in addressing nationwide problems. With industrialization and greater URBANIZATION, fewer and fewer Americans produced their own foods and thus needed to rely on others for their quality. Articles by muckraking journalists and UPTON SINCLAIR's novel *The Jungle* (1906) generated indignation about unsanitary production conditions among consumer groups and professional organizations, prompting CONGRESS to act. President THEODORE ROOSEVELT signed the Pure Food and Drug Act on June 30, 1906. The law authorized federal inspection of meat products and banned the manufacture, sale, and transportation of adulterated foods and dangerous patent medicines. It represented an expansion of federal authority as the government took control over the purity of foods and medications. The Bureau of Chemistry enforced the new law until 1927, when it was reorganized as the Food, Drug and Insecticide Administration and then again as the Food and Drug Administration in 1932. Because of the potential conflicts in the DOA's support of food producers and the FDA's mandated protection of consumers, Congress transferred the FDA to the Federal Security Agency in 1940. Created one year earlier, this agency addressed health, education, and social insurance and included the Public Health Service, which had previously been under the management of the Treasury Department.

Beginning in the 1920s, many government officials had discussed the need for a government agency to address issues of education and welfare. On April 11, 1953, President DWIGHT D. EISENHOWER replaced the Federal Security Agency with the Department of Health, Education and Welfare (HEW), the only cabinet-level department created through the president's governmental reorganization authority and the immediate predecessor to HHS. During those three decades, however, the federal government continued to act on issues of public health and the environment. The NIH, for example, emerged from the Public Health Service's Hygienic Laboratory in 1932. Formed in 1946, the Communicable Disease Center was the forerunner of the CENTERS FOR DISEASE CONTROL AND PREVENTION.

Although the FDA had been transferred from the DOA to the Federal Security Agency and then HEW, another connection to agriculture emerged in 1962 with the passage of the Migrant Health Act. This law provided support for health clinics for agricultural workers. Migrant workers are a high-risk group for occupational hazards, and the health centers offer information and services regarding environmental health. Thus, this act revealed a unique relationship between HEW (later HHS) and agriculture, while also illustrating changing ideas about workers' health and bodies.

Some of the most extensive government programs quickly came under HEW purview around this time. Created in 1965, Medicare and Medicaid extended Social Security services, making comprehensive health care available to millions of Americans. Medicare provided health insurance to people over the age of 65 or other people who meet special criteria. The former president HARRY TRUMAN was the first person to receive a Medicare card when President LYNDON B. JOHNSON signed the Medicare amendment in 1965. Medicaid is a health program for eligible individuals or families with low incomes and resources.

In 1966, led in large part by the U.S. Public Health Service, the World Health Organization began the International Smallpox Eradication Program. Introduced by Europeans to the Americas, SMALLPOX had devastated the indigenous human populations, who lacked immunities to the disease. As late as 1966, the disease still killed two million people a year worldwide. With vaccination campaigns, smallpox was eradicated around the globe 12 years later.

In 1979, Congress passed the Department of Education Organization Act; it relaunched HEW as the Department of Health and Human Services in 1980 and created a new cabinet-level organization, the Department of Education. HHS and its constituent parts quickly became involved with the worldwide acquired immunodeficiency syndrome (AIDS) crisis. In 1984, the NIH physician Robert Gallo (1937–   ) helped identify the human immunodeficiency virus (HIV). The NIH maintains an Office of AIDS Research.

In 1997, the Department of Health and Human Services added the State Children's Health Insurance Program (SCHIP). This program allows individual states to extend health coverage to more uninsured children. Along with Medicare and Medicaid, SCHIP provides coverage for more Americans who do not already have health insurance or those who do not have adequate coverage. By 2004, these three programs, Medicare, Medicaid, and SCHIP, made up approximately 80 percent of the HHS budget.

The new millennium presented new challenges to HHS. It dealt with its first bioterrorism attack in 2001, when a series of letters laced with anthrax were sent from New Jersey to influential members of the MEDIA and two prominent senators, Tom Daschle of South Dakota and Patrick Leahy of Vermont. The first wave of letters was sent on September 18, 2001, and the second dated October 9, 2001, within a few weeks of the attacks on the World Trade Center and the Pentagon. Five people died as a result of inhalation anthrax and 17 more were infected.

Finally, HHS also informs the nation of health trends and vital research. It publishes an established set of national health indicators every decade to ensure that people are aware of the country's health trends. In doing so, and in keeping with its legacy, the Department of Health and Human Services keeps a careful watch over environmental conditions and how they affect the health of the United States of America and the bodies of its citizens.

See also DISEASE, HUMAN; ECOTERRORISM; HEALTH AND MEDICINE; HUMAN BODY; IMMIGRATION; LABOR, AGRICULTURAL AND MIGRANT, PROGRESSIVISM.

Rebecca Vanucci

Further Reading
Butler, Judith. *Bodies That Matter: On the Discursive Limits of "Sex."* New York: Routledge, 1993.
Fausto-Sterling, Anne. *Myths of Gender: Biological Theories about Men and Women.* New York: Basic Books, 1985.
Frumkin, Howard, ed. *Environmental Health: From Global to Local.* Hoboken, N.J.: John Wiley & Sons, 2005.
Our Bodies, Ourselves for the New Century: A Book by and for Women. New York: Touchstone, 1998.

health and medicine

Diseases Americans face and the ways they have dealt with them in both the past and present have been very much a product of culture and environment. The history of health and medicine in the United States is more than a narrative of America's participation in the development of Western medicine. The history of health care in America is also part of the nation's overall development as a country. Historically, Americans' health and medical care have depended upon settlement patterns, economic development, educational infrastructure, and the environment, among other factors.

NATIVE AMERICAN MEDICINE

The history of health care in America begins with Native American medical practices and theories. While these systems of health management differed widely according to geographical, cultural, and chronological characteristics, traditional Native American health care was generally a combination of botanic, practical, and spiritual practices and concerns. For health care concerns in which the cause of the problem was external and obvious, such as injuries, or common and relatively innocuous, most Native American groups first relied on practical responses, which were frequently combined with botanic and herbal remedies.

For health problems in which the cause of disease was not obviously apparent, particularly serious or persistent health concerns, or in which the healing process seemed delayed or abnormal, many Native American medical theories looked not to environmental or natural causes but to supernatural explanations and responses such as spirit possession, witchcraft, and other religious concerns. Treatment for these health disorders was most often attended to by specifically trained community members and entailed medical theories and practices that incorporated that group's medical knowledge and religious beliefs.

THE INTRODUCTION OF WESTERN MEDICINE

During the colonial period and the early republic, European immigrants to America and their descendants introduced and cultivated a new system of health care management. While the medical traditions introduced by these groups often had religious connections or associations, these groups generally considered diseases to have natural rather than supernatural causes, which were often understood to have very close connections with the environment. One of the ways that environments affected American health care practices was through settlement patterns and economic life. From the early colonial era through the 19th century, the vast majority of Americans lived in rural environments, generally in small farming communities. Not large enough to support medical specialists, many of these areas supported general practitioners who worked out of their homes. Because most people made their living through farming, cash was scarce, and physicians were usually paid in trade. Few doctors supported themselves solely as health care providers; most physicians engaged in other occupations as well, such as farming or shopkeeping.

This rural, agricultural environment also meant that there were very few medical schools in America, and as a result, there were very few physicians with formal medical training. The first formal medical school in America, the Medical School of the College of Philadelphia, was not established until 1765, and while similar schools followed in its wake, most of their graduates practiced medicine in the more densely populated regions of America. Those few physicians who did receive traditional, formal training were known as "regular" physicians. Most health care providers received informal training through an apprenticeship system or self-education. With few doctors, most illnesses were addressed at home by the patient, or the patient's family and neighbors. They used newspapers, pamphlets, almanacs, oral tradition, and physician-published guides that provided everyday readers with guidance and instruction on how to maintain and restore health from within the home. In general, few people objected to this approach to medical training and practice. Most Americans saw the openness of the health care field as a positive characteristic and typically believed that practicing medicine required little esoteric knowledge.

BLENDING MEDICAL TRADITIONS

As a result of unsystematic approaches to medical training and practice, medical care varied widely throughout the colonial era through to the late 19th century, and formally trained physicians competed with a wide variety of practitioners and alternative therapies. While some practitioners relied on a singular, unified theory of medicine, most doctors practiced a blend of medical traditions, combining emerging theories about treatment with older remedies, passed down through families or local tradition.

In general, 18th- and 19th-century doctors believed blockages, excess matter, or disordered movement in the HUMAN BODY, which could be caused by a variety of factors including environment, caused disease. Many formally trained, or regular, physicians practiced heroic medicine, an aggressive approach to healing that used bloodletting, vomiting, blistering, and other such treatments in order to drain excesses, clear blockages, or restore the natural movements of a body's interior.

This approach to healing had detractors. Thomsonian healers, for example, criticized the techniques of regular physicians. Samuel Thomson (1769–1843), the founder of his namesake movement, was a root doctor from New Hampshire. As did many other healers, Thomsonian physicians relied heavily on botanic treatments in their techniques for medical care. Similarly, homeopaths opposed the medical practices of regular physicians. Imported to America from Germany in the 1820s, homeopaths held that sick bodies were best treated by very small doses of medicine, not by aggressive treatments with dramatic results.

THE CENTRALITY OF THE ENVIRONMENT

As suggested by the techniques of these physicians, environments not only affected the way that health care was organized and distributed in America, it also played a major role in healing practices. Prior to the widespread acceptance of germ theory in the early 20th century, most people, physicians included, believed that health and disease were largely a product of environment. In this conception of disease and health, bodies took on characteristics of environments in which they lived. As a result, the health of a person depended heavily upon whether one lived in a healthy or unhealthy environment. Environments that contained stagnant air or water, swamps, for example, were believed to contribute to stagnancy inside the body. This condition could supposedly cause bodily interiors to amass foul or rotten matter, thereby causing disease. Volatile or inclement environments that disordered natural flows of bodily matter could also cause disease. Healthy bodies, on the other hand, reflected healthy environments and allowed for regular, gentle flow of blood and other matter.

Given these beliefs, many sick people were treated by either changing their environment or removing them to healthier environments. The latter treatment became an especially popular option in the 19th century. URBANIZATION and rising incomes began to generate a population of wealthy Americans who could afford this type of health care and doubted the healthfulness of their home environments. Among patients who could afford it, resort spas became a very popular health care option. While some of these spas were primarily known for their health regimens, others were mainly celebrated for their healthy climates. Patients flocked to resorts offering seaside accommodations or those boasting hot springs, judging these environments particularly healthful.

Partially dissected cadavers lie on tables in the dissecting room of Jefferson Medical College, Philadelphia, ca. 1902. *(Library of Congress)*

GREATER PROFESSIONALIZATION

Approaches to health care and physician training changed dramatically over the course of the late 19th and early 20th centuries. As the United States became more urbanized and wealthy, most professions began to organize into coherent organizations with established educational institutions. Medicine was among the professions that underwent this change. As it became more organized, with a formal training process, licensing laws, and state and nationwide associations, medicine lost much of the pluralism that had once defined it.

A number of approaches to medicine, including osteopathy and homeopathy, established schools or received acknowledgment from licensing boards. By the early 20th century, however, regular physicians dominated American medicine. Their practices, likewise, also held sway over the way people thought about and approached medicine. Unlike holistic physicians, regular physicians typically thought of disease as being located in specific organs or bodily parts and not as an affliction of the larger bodily, social, or environmental system. This practice, along with a growing number of physicians, led to the development of medical specialists. Regular physicians of this era also invested a great deal of work in the construction of medical institutions, including medical laboratories, schools, and hospitals. As a result, these locations became increasingly important to the practice of medicine in the 20th century.

As this approach to medicine became the dominant model of disease and health care, medical approaches and theories such as those about germ theory and bacteriology, as well as chromosomes and GENETICS, encouraged

medical professionals, as well as everyday Americans, to rethink the environment's power to shape and affect the human body. Emerging cultural trends that attributed a growing significance to the role of the individual and that invested a great deal of importance in the concepts of self-improvement and self-development accompanied medical developments.

These changes significantly changed the way that people thought about the environment and health. Many popular ideas about health and disease that developed during this era weakened the connections between environments and health. Proponents of EUGENICS, for example, argued that many diseases and social problems were not caused by the environment but resulted from breeding and genetic inheritance.

Despite the popularity of technical medical advances, the importance of environments did not disappear from medical theory. Medical ideas about hygiene and sanitation remained particularly popular during the late 19th and early 20th centuries, and many medical works and organizations emerged that aimed to cleanse disease-causing agents from urban and rural environments. Unlike in earlier decades, however, proponents did not propose that environments caused disease. Rather, doctors viewed environments as benign mediums, inherently neither healthy nor unhealthy. Environments could, however, harbor disease-causing organisms if not properly maintained.

NEW VIEWS ON ENVIRONMENT AND HEALTH

The foundations laid by regular physicians in the early 20th century remain the dominant model of health care in the United States. The ways that Americans approach health care, and the ways that they think about disease, health, and the environment, however, have changed. One particularly important development in the history of health and the environment occurred in the early 1960s, in response to RACHEL CARSON's book *Silent Spring*. Her endeavor, along with similar works, revealed important ways in which environmental factors such as PESTICIDES, air quality, radiation, environmental toxins, and other environmental health factors affected human bodies. In the late 20th century, these studies were joined by investigations into the effect of CLIMATE CHANGE on human health worldwide.

Beginning in the late 1960s and early 1970s, Americans became increasingly interested in medicines and therapies derived from natural sources. Many Americans experienced a profound disillusionment with mainstream approaches to medical care. Some of these patients felt that orthodox medicine was too expensive, was too impersonal, and left too little room for the input or agency of the patient. Other people were frustrated that despite significant medical breakthroughs, physicians were unable or unwilling to treat chronic illnesses, especially those that did not manifest themselves in physically observable phenomena. Frequently, these Americans also identified with broader social changes that sought to improve society not through large-scale social reform, as had been the case with the hygienic and sanitation movement, but with a belief in the need for personal improvement and self-help.

As a result of these frustrations and beliefs, many people embraced approaches to health care that incorporated natural or holistic therapies. Drawn from diverse world cultures, featuring treatments that could be conducted at home, many of these approaches were adopted. Trained healers provided similar treatments but conducted them in a personal, rather than a clinical, setting. These practitioners advocated close patient-healer bonds that gave patients a greater role in their own healing processes.

By the late 20th century, orthodox medicine adapted to the popularity of these treatments, including homeopathy, acupuncture, and botanic medicine. In some cases, this development meant adapting doctor-patient relationships to allow patients to take on greater agency in their own treatment. In other cases, this meant learning to incorporate alternative therapies into a wider array of medical practices.

Modern experimental and laboratory medicine has also forged new relationships with the environment, however. These new relationships entail not only more sophisticated analysis of the environment's impact upon human health but also the manipulation of environmental factors to control health, as well as an increasing awareness and attention to the relationship between human and animal health. Made possible by technological advances in laboratory equipment, experimental medicine increasingly harnesses and manipulates biological traits of plant and animal sources in order to look for potential cures and treatments.

THE UNRESOLVED ISSUES

While many medical scientists have recently investigated the environment as a source of health care improvements, concerns such as human immunodeficiency virus (HIV) and acquired immune deficiency syndrome (AIDS) and other emerging zoonotic diseases have drawn new attention to the potential of the environment to introduce new diseases as well as to provide cures. Conversely, recent scientific and medical research, combined with modern environmental concerns, also has led to research and anxiety about health care's impact on the environment. One such example is the increasing awareness of residual medical compounds, particularly the hormones in some forms of birth control, which remain in wastewater even after treatment.

See also BOTANY; CARCINOGENS, POISONS, AND TOXINS; CENTERS FOR DISEASE CONTROL AND PREVENTION AND NATIONAL INSTITUTES OF HEALTH; DISEASES, HUMAN; DRUGS, PHARMACEUTICAL; HEALTH AND HUMAN SERVICES, DEPARTMENT OF; MIASMAS; PROGRESSIVISM.

Skylar Harris

Further Reading
Grob, Gerald N. *The Deadly Truth: A History of Disease in America.* Cambridge, Mass.: Harvard University Press, 2002.
Leavitt, Judith Walzer, and Ronald L. Numbers. *Sickness and Health in America: Readings in the History of Medicine and Public Health.* Madison: University of Wisconsin Press, 1997.
Stevens, Rosemary A., Charles E. Rosenberg, and Lawton R. Burns, eds. *History and Health Policy in the United States: Putting the Past Back In.* New Brunswick, N.J.: Rutgers University Press, 2006.
Toledo-Pereyra, Luis H. *A History of American Medicine from the Colonial Period to the Early Twentieth Century.* Lewiston, N.Y.: Edwin Mellen Press, 2006.
Whorton, James C. *Nature Cures: The History of Alternative Medicine in America.* New York: Oxford University Press, 2002.

heirloom animals

Heirloom animals, or heritage breeds, are livestock types that farmers customarily raised before the growth of large-scale livestock production or industrial agriculture. In many cases, heirloom animals were originally chosen for breeding because of characteristics that made them able to adapt to a specific environment, climate, or geography. As industrial agriculture became more common, however, farmers turned to certain breeds because of higher productivity levels and greater resistance to pests and disease. This preference resulted in genetic uniformity in those breeds. Over time, consumer preferences also changed in favor of these mass-produced breeds.

Heirloom animals have become less common, and some are now threatened or endangered. Smaller populations in a breed can result in the loss of that breed's genetic diversity. Genetic diversity is important because it makes a species more adaptable to environmental changes, parasites, and predators. If a species population becomes too small, important characteristics of a breed may not be passed on to future generations through a process called genetic drift. Small species populations can also result in inbreeding depression, which is a condition that occurs when small, related populations of species pass on harmful recessive genes. In either case, the species becomes more susceptible to loss or even EXTINCTION if a disaster occurs.

Of the 40 species recognized as domesticated worldwide, there are only 11 that are considered major domesticated species, although various cultures supplement this number with additional species indigenous to their locations. With only 11 major species, preservation of genetic diversity in individual breeds is important in the event that mass-produced breeds lose overall disease resistance and tolerance to varying environmental conditions.

Various organizations work to raise awareness among and provide education to SUSTAINABLE AGRICULTURE participants and others regarding heritage breeds. Although heirloom animals are not as commercially productive as their mass-produced counterparts, sustainable farmers try to conserve the breeds by raising them, without hormones or use of PESTICIDES, and cultivating a market for their products. In some instances, the farming is successful. The American Bronze turkey, for example, is a heritage breed that was farmed less after WORLD WAR II (1941–45) but had been a consumer favorite for almost 80 years. The breed was eventually abandoned in favor of other turkeys that could breed all year long, even though these industrialized turkeys could not reproduce naturally because of their oversized breasts and undersized legs. The traditional American Bronzes, although more expensive than mass-produced breeds because of their shorter breeding season and slower development rate, still found a consumer niche because they were more flavorful. The possibility exists, however, that even sustainable farmers could ignore other less profitable heritage breeds in preference for more profitable ones.

International agreements such as the United Nations (UN) Conference on Environment and Development, the Biodiversity Convention, and Agenda 21 each have recognized the importance of preserving the genetic diversity of livestock breeds. With that in mind, the UN Food and Agriculture Organization implemented the Global Strategy for the Management of Farm Animal Genetic Resources in 1992. This strategy provides for the creation of National Farm Animal Genetic Resources Management Plans to help preserve genetic diversity in domesticated animals and promote sustainable productivity.

See also AGRICULTURE, COMMERCIAL; ANIMALS, DOMESTICATED; BIODIVERSITY; ENDANGERED SPECIES; FOOD; GENETICS; POULTRY INDUSTRY, UNITED NATIONS.

Francesca Ortiz

Further Reading
American Livestock Breeds Conservancy. "Conservation Priority List," Livestock and Poultry Breeds. Available online. URL: http://www.albc-usa.org/cpl/wtchlist.html. Accessed December 28, 2008.
Dohner, Janet Vorwald. *The Encyclopedia of Historic and Endangered Livestock and Poultry Breeds.* New Haven, Conn.: Yale University Press, 2001.
Food and Agriculture Organization of the United Nations, Sustainable Development Department. "Farm Animal Genetic Resources." Available online. URL: http://www.fao.org/docrep/fao/009/x8750e/x8750e02.pdf. Accessed May 18, 2010.

heirloom fruits and vegetables
The University of New Hampshire professor William Hepler coined the term *heirloom plant* when using it to describe a package of beans he received in the 1940s. Today, the term refers colloquially to any precommercial variety of fruits, vegetables, and plants passed down through families and ethnic or religious communities. All officially designated and marketed heirlooms, however, have three defining characteristics. First, heirloom varieties must be open-pollinated and be able to reproduce from seed. This characteristic distinguishes heirlooms from conventional hybrid cultivars, whose SEEDS are infertile or do not grow "true to type," meaning that their offspring do not maintain parental phenotypes. Perennial plants that propagate vegetatively, such as through roots, bulbs, or cuttings, may also be considered heirloom, providing their stock fulfills the other requirements.

Second, true heirloom varieties must have been introduced to the United States more than 50 years ago. Although this date is largely arbitrary and highly debated, it corresponds to the general consensus that heirlooms predate the development of scientific plant breeding and hybridization, which occurred after WORLD WAR II (1941–45).

Third, heirloom fruits and vegetables must have a traceable history. Varieties are often linked to particular waves of IMMIGRATION or in some cases single families; Native Americans may have cultivated them as staple or ceremonial crops, or they may have been taken north by Mexican migrants. The recent popularity of such varieties has spurred a movement to retrieve these folk histories. Indeed, the tangible link to Americana documented in these stories draws many heirloom gardeners into the field.

Having been selected for taste and regional specificity, heirloom varieties are not suited to large-scale production, nor mechanized harvesting. Compared to hybrid crops, heirlooms have lower yields, have thinner skins, and are less uniform in color, shape, and ripening time. Yet, when carefully tended in the right locale, they can out-perform conventional varieties. Their longer harvest period has also made heirlooms a favorite among gardeners and small-scale producers who need a smaller and more extended yield.

Advocates of heirloom cultivation contend that they are not simply culinary novelties but critical reservoirs of genetic diversity. Since the emergence of commercial seed cultivation in the 1930s, thousands of fruit and vegetable varieties have been replaced by only a few hybrid varieties, leaving agricultural crops vulnerable to pest infestation and environmental change. Recognizing that these lost varieties may hold the genes for drought tolerance or pest resistance, yield an important medical or commercial compound in the future, or simply prevent inbreeding depression, the U.S. government maintains a National Center for Genetic Resources Preservation (NCGRP) in Fort Collins, Colorado.

Nevertheless, because seeds cannot be stored in perpetuity but must be regenerated annually, the majority of heirloom preservation is carried out by backyard gardeners and semiformal networks of seed savers such as the Seed Savers Exchange (SSE) and Native Seeds/SEARCH. In addition to collecting and propagating heirlooms, these grassroots organizations publish catalogs listing thousands of available varieties and help coordinate seed exchange among members.

Brandywine tomatoes are the most popular heirloom variety in the United States; other notables include Kentucky Wonder beans, Hubbard squash, and Golden Bantam CORN.

See also AGRICULTURAL TECHNOLOGY; AMERICAN INDIAN MOVEMENT; BIODIVERSITY; BIOTECHNOLOGY; FOOD; FRUIT AND VEGETABLE PRODUCTION; GARDENS AND GARDENING; HEIRLOOM ANIMALS; TRUCK FARMS.

Robin Jane Roff

Further Reading

Gillis, A. M. "Keeping Traditions on the Menu." *BioScience* 43, no. 7 (1993): 425–429.

Jason, Dan. *Greening the Garden: A Guide to Sustainable Growing.* Philadelphia: New Society, 1991.

Nazarea, Virginia D. *Heirloom Seeds and Their Keepers.* Tucson: University of Arizona Press, 2005.

Watson, Benjamin. *Taylor's Guide to Heirloom Vegetables.* New York: Houghton Mifflin, 1996.

hemp

Hemp has been cultivated for millennia. The plant's stalks and seeds provide an enormous range of products for both food and nonfood materials. Despite a long agricultural history in the United States, hemp is not currently legally grown anywhere in the country because of its connections to marijuana. Industrial hemp and marijuana are variants of the genus *Cannabis*. Since early 2007, however, 27 states have passed legislation to create pilot programs to reintroduce hemp farming.

Hemp was an important crop in colonial America; THOMAS JEFFERSON and GEORGE WASHINGTON touted the plant's benefits. American hemp composed a major source of agricultural production in the 19th century in several states, led by Kentucky. Despite its economic and military (especially naval) importance, hemp requires a labor-intensive process that makes it difficult to harvest. By the late 1890s, COTTON began to overtake hemp as a fabric source for clothing and sails since its production was increasingly mechanized and therefore more attractive to farmers. The subsequent development of petroleum-based synthetic fibers and wood-pulp paper contributed to the further demise of American hemp farming.

In 1937, CONGRESS passed the first law to discourage *Cannabis* production for marijuana, although the presumed intent of the law was to permit continued production of hemp for industrial uses. The government actively encouraged farmers to grow hemp during WORLD WAR II (1941–

45), when imports of substitute products slowed or stopped. After the war, hemp production in the United States once again declined, and it ceased entirely by 1958. Hemp production is currently controlled by the Drug Enforcement Agency (DEA) because of its familial relation to marijuana, *Cannabis sativa* or *C. indica*. Hemp may not be grown without a DEA permit. Modern industrial hemp, however, is bred to contain a minuscule percentage of tetrahydrocannabinol, or THC, the psychotropic element in marijuana.

Hemp advocates argue that hemp is valuable for its multiple uses and its role as a renewable resource. Mature hemp stalks reach heights of six to 16 feet in approximately 110 days. Positive elements of this rapid growth include the virtual elimination of herbicides since competing plants, including WEEDS, are unable to thrive without access to sunshine. Since hemp has few natural predators, PESTICIDES are rarely required.

Hemp's complex root structure also aids in the prevention of EROSION. Hemp depletes few nutrients in soil and aids the soil further through its absorption of heavy-metal contaminants. It can be grown in rotation with other crops and does not require FERTILIZER in the large amounts used on other fiber crops, especially cotton, the third most heavily fertilized fiber product. Hemp is considered a hardy plant resistant to DROUGHTS and requires considerably less water than cotton.

Fiber products made from hemp reduce DEFORESTATION, thus reducing topsoil erosion and destruction of natural habitats. Hemp paper, for example, does not require chlorine for bleaching, a typical process for wood-pulp papers. Hemp as a source of biofuel is currently eclipsed by the use of CORN for ethanol. Hemp also has an enormous array of other uses, ranging from plastics and animal bedding to fiberboard and insulation. Favored in commercial bird seed for decades, hemp seeds for human consumption are now touted for their healthful profile of high protein and excellent ratio of omega-3 to omega-6 fatty acids, essential for good nutrition.

Hemp experienced a resurgence of interest, first in Europe, and then in Canada, in the early 1990s. In the United States, interest has been particularly strong from MONOCULTURE farmers and from consumers interested in healthful FOOD and environmentally friendly clothing and cosmetics. Growing interest in environmental and health issues has spurred imports and hemp product sales; all hemp products sold in the United States are imported or manufactured from imported hemp materials. Increased "green" thinking coupled with the lure of agricultural profits may combine to raise pressures on federal and states legislators to allow American hemp production again.

See also AGRICULTURE, COLONIAL; AGRICULTURE, COMMERCIAL; GREEN CONSUMERISM AND MARKETING.

Ellen J. Fried

Further Reading
Rawson, J. *Hemp as an Agricultural Commodity.* Congressional Research Service. Washington, D.C., January 5, 2005.
Roulac, J. W. *Hemp Horizons: The Comeback of the World's Most Promising Plant.* White River Junction, Vt.: Chelsea Green, 1997.

Hetch Hetchy Valley

In the early 1900s, a major political debate erupted over the proper use of the Hetch Hetchy Valley, located adjacent to Yosemite Valley in the SIERRA NEVADA mountains in California. Specifically, Americans debated whether to dam the Tuolomne River, which ran from the High Sierras and into the valley, so as to create a reservoir that could help satisfy the water and, to a lesser extent, the electrical needs of SAN FRANCISCO, CALIFORNIA. This dispute revealed significant differences between individuals heretofore considered partners in the growing movement to protect the WILDERNESS. Noting that the Hetch Hetchy Valley had been designated as a protected area—it was part of YOSEMITE NATIONAL PARK—preservationists, such as JOHN MUIR, argued against building the dam. Contending that nature had to be used for the greatest good for the greatest number of people, conservationists, such as GIFFORD PINCHOT, advocated constructing the dam. The debate revealed much about America's views of nature during the early decades of the 20th century.

As San Francisco grew from just fewer than 150,000 people in 1870 to more than 350,000 in 1900, its demand for freshwater escalated. San Francisco's mayor, James Phelan (1861–1930), and others saw building a dam and reservoir in the Hetch Hetchy Valley as the answer to their needs. However, in the early 1900s, the secretary of the interior, Ethan Hitchcock (1835–1909), rejected applications to build a dam on the grounds that the dam violated the original mission underlying the creation of the National Park.

Several developments, however, bolstered the case of those who favored building the dam. The 1906 San Francisco earthquake and FIRE made the city's call for an expanded water supply appear more pressing. Gifford Pinchot's close friendship with President THEODORE ROOSEVELT and appointment as chief forester in 1905 gave the proponents of the dam an important ally in the nation's capital. Powerful business interests also favored constructing the dam.

At first, President Roosevelt, who also enjoyed a personal friendship with Muir, sought to straddle both sides of the debate. He asked engineers to look for a suitable alternative site for the dam. When they reported that there was none, he authorized a permit that appeared to open the way to building a reservoir.

Undeterred, Muir asserted that national parks served a fundamental need of the people, namely, their need for "beauty as well as bread," and he spearheaded a movement to make the case against constructing the dam. More so than at any time in the past, many prominent men and women rallied behind the cause of PRESERVATION. In the face of these lobbying efforts, in his final state of the union address, Roosevelt declared his support for maintaining YELLOWSTONE and Yosemite in their natural state. In turn, the proponents of the dam emphasized that the reservoir, which could serve as a place for hunting, fishing, and camping, would not spoil nature but rather make it more accessible to the multitudes.

To the chagrin of the dam's proponents, they could not convince President WOODROW WILSON's secretary of the interior, Frank Lane (1864–1921), a San Francisco native, to permit construction to proceed. Instead, he insisted that Congress make the choice. One crucial voice in the debate was that of William Kent (1864–1928), a congressman from California. Kent had displayed his strong belief in preservation, including purchasing land in Marin County, just north of San Francisco, and donating it to the government for protection. Named Muir Woods in honor of John Muir, it contained a large grove of redwoods. Yet, to the surprise of Muir and the SIERRA CLUB, Kent sided with the dam's advocates, partly on the grounds that the dam's construction would foster public ownership of hydroelectric power and partly because he agreed with Pinchot that conservationists should seek the most efficient use of resources for the greatest number of people over time, not prevent their use.

Ultimately, both houses of CONGRESS voted in favor of the dam, and President Wilson signed the bill on December 19, 1913. Nonetheless, the battle over the Hetch Hetchy Valley vastly increased pubic awareness of and support for the principle of preservation. Three years after Wilson authorized the construction of the dam, he signed into law the NATIONAL PARK SERVICE Act. It allowed for an expansion of the National Park system and a more systematic effort to preserve other wilderness areas. As Roderick Nash has forcefully argued in *Wilderness and the American Mind* (1967), "The most significant thing about the controversy over the valley was that it had occurred at all." Since its founding, the nation had chosen materialism or development "without any hesitation. By 1913 they were no longer so sure."

See also CONSERVATION; DAMS, RESERVOIRS, AND ARTIFICIAL LAKES; UNITED STATES—CALIFORNIA.

Peter B. Levy

Further Reading
Nash, Roderick. *Wilderness and the American Mind.* New Haven, Conn.: Yale University Press, 1967.

Righter, Robert W. *The Battle over Hetch Hetchy: America's Most Controversial Dam and the Birth of Modern Environmentalism.* New York: Oxford University Press, 2005.

hides *See* TALLOW AND HIDES.

Hill, Julia "Butterfly" (1974–) *environmental activist*

On December 10, 1997, a young woman named Julia "Butterfly" Hill climbed 180 feet into an old-growth redwood tree on land belonging to Pacific Lumber Company (PL) in northern California. Feeling a spiritual connection with the tree she identified as a being named Luna, Hill chose to live in Luna's branches without descending for two years to protest the cutting of Headwaters Forest, the last privately held stand of virgin REDWOODS. Hill's protest was the culmination of an environmental movement that began with

the women of the Save the Redwood League 100 years earlier—women with whom she felt historic kinship.

A native of Jonesboro, Arkansas, Hill was born on February 18, 1974. She acquired the nickname "Butterfly" as a child when a butterfly landed on her during a family picnic and remained with her for the remainder of the day.

Hill's tree-sitting action was not totally unique. She was not the first protester to tree-sit, although her protest was the longest in duration; nor was she the first woman to articulate her concerns about the environment through the rhetoric of spirituality. Indeed, throughout the 20th century, historians have detected an alternative language used by many female environmentalists, not because they were inherently different from men, but because their experiences with nature differed as a result of society's expectations about how men and women behave. Early in the century, for example, white female mountaineers tended to use the rhetoric of freedom to describe their WILDERNESS experience while men usually expressed their experiences through the language of

Julia "Butterfly" Hill, in the branches of the redwood tree Luna, in northern California. Hill lived 180 feet aboveground in Luna's branches in an effort to prevent the tree from being cut down in 1998. *(© Gustavo Gilabert/CORBIS SABA)*

conquest. Likewise, BOTANY (especially the knowledge of wildflowers) was perceived as an acceptably feminine form of studying nature, while geology was understood as more masculine.

Hill's ascent and the 738 consecutive days she spent in the tree touched off an extensive debate both within the immediate area and beyond it to a national and, eventually, a global audience. The image of a woman in a tree quickly moved into popular culture and was used in advertisements, television shows, and political cartoons. The debates that raged around Hill revealed the deep splits within American society over environmental issues and social values, especially the definition of productive citizenship (for example, whether working and paying taxes are essential components of citizenship). The local and regional papers expanded their letters to the editor section to deal with the massive outpouring of public opinion. Her action polarized the community in ways similar to the contemporary debates over the protection of the SPOTTED OWL in Oregon or the reintroduction of timber WOLVES in Montana.

Labor and productive property stood at the heart of all three of those debates. In the case of the redwoods, the dialogue revolved around the symbolic importance of work and accusations of exploitation. Local timber supporters described Hill as a nonworking parasite, in contrast with the hard-working loggers, and PL as an important source of local jobs and community benefits. Hill countered that globalized capital, in this case, the Texas-based Maxxam Corporation, which owned PL, was the real parasite. She accused Maxxam's subsidiary, PL, of holding the region in a colonial relationship in which it extracted the area's resources for the economic enhancement of outsiders through devastating clear-cutting practices instead of sustainable selective cutting. Hill argued that the repercussions of this relationship would ultimately be disastrous for both the labor force and the environment. Indeed, she was supported by the United Steelworkers Union after the Maxxam Corporation used PL workers as scabs at its Washington State Kaiser aluminum plants.

Hill left Luna's branches on December 18, 1999, after reaching a settlement with PL in which she and her supporters would pay $50,000 to keep Luna and a 2.9-acre perimeter safe from cutting. PL would then donate the money to the Humboldt State University's FORESTRY program. Weeks later, a vandal used a chain saw to cut halfway through Luna's trunk. After being treated with herbal remedies and stabilized with steel chains, the tree continued to experience new growth.

After her descent, Hill wrote *The Legacy of Luna* (2001), describing her personal journey and her arguments about environmental issues. She used the proceeds to found the Circle of Life Foundation, an organization that addresses issues of social and ENVIRONMENTAL JUSTICE.

See also CAPITALISM; ENVIRONMENTALISM, RADICAL; FEMINISM AND ECOFEMINISM; FORESTS; LABOR, EXTRACTIVE INDUSTRIES; LABOR, MANUFACTURING; LOGGING AND LUMBERING; MEDIA; SUSTAINABLE DEVELOPMENT.

Cathleen D. Cahill

Further Reading
Albanese, Catherine L. *Nature Religion in America: From the Algonkian Indians to the New Age.* Chicago: University of Chicago Press, 1990.
Hill, Julia. *The Legacy of Luna: The Story of a Tree, a Woman and the Struggle to Save the Redwoods.* San Francisco: Harper-Collins, 2001.
Schrepfer, Susan R. *Nature's Alters: Mountains, Gender and American Environmentalism.* Lawrence: University of Kansas Press, 2007.

hogs *See* PIGS AND HOGS.

Hollywood

Hollywood, a distinct district within LOS ANGELES, CALIFORNIA, is the center of the American film and television production industry. In addition to its physical location, however, Hollywood has become synonymous with the cinema of the United States. It has represented a kind of "dream factory," creating for people living in the United States and abroad fantastic and diversified imagery about the nation's landscapes, population, history, myths, values, and ways of life. This artificial vision might be just a series of constructed images, fables, or fiction. No matter how far these social representations are from reality, however, they are nonetheless used and often understood by viewers as reliable references to cities, deserts, and people in a given country or region. While American cinema has become a multibillion-dollar industry with its own ecological impacts, the movies produced by Hollywood have at times celebrated American prosperity but more frequently and perhaps more recently questioned the environmental and social costs of industrialization, militarization, and URBANIZATION.

Since their invention by the French filmmakers and brothers Auguste (1862–1954) and Louis (1864–1948) Lumière in 1895, moving pictures, or cinema, have always been understood as representations of different places and people, showing urban scenes to the most remote audiences, and vice versa, especially through newsreels and documentary films. The Lumière brothers, in fact, directed some of the earliest documentaries, in the late 19th century, as they traveled with their cameramen around the world, filming famous and exotic places so as to draw crowds to the cinema.

NEW YORK CITY was the first center of American filmmaking at the turn of the 20th century. Studios increasingly moved to California, however, because of the high number of days without clouds or rain. Some studios were in the open air; others had glass roofs to obtain more light. Powerful light was needed because of the film's limited sensitivity.

WHAT MOVIES CAN SHOW

All film genres have addressed nature and environment, from documentaries to fiction, science fiction, and even animation. Classic examples of animation include numerous cartoons produced by the Walt DISNEY Studios since the late 1920s, from the classic *Bambi* (1942) to *The Jungle Book* (1967)—which was freely adapted from the Rudyard Kipling collection of short stories—and later *Lion King* (1994). In these various Manichean (a natural world divided by the intrinsically good and evil) idealizations of the animal kingdom, humans often appeared as the bad characters, collectively guilty for endangering wildlife and polluting nature. While not as popular as some of the Disney films, perhaps the most disturbing animation film about environment was the American director Jimmy Murakami's *When the Wind Blows* (1987), a political and satirical fable about an old couple who face a probable nuclear explosion in their neighborhood but remain calm because they meticulously follow the instructions provided in a brochure distributed by the government. The most beautiful animation film about nature, life, and environment is probably Frederik Back's *L'Homme qui plantait des arbres* (*The Man Who Planted Trees,* 1987), which, instead of showing the dangers faced by natural life, shows the beauty of plants, the colors of nature, and the miracle of reproduction.

A frequent theme in science fiction, another significant genre, was the unknown danger that often emerged from the soil, as in many monster movies from the 1940s and 1950s (the Godzilla series from Japan in 1954 and after) or in the zombie genre (*I Walked with a Zombie,* directed by Jacques Tourneur in 1943 and set in the West Indies). Despite their limited technical qualities, these B-movies became milestones in the fantastic, gothic, horror, or gore genres that followed, such as Steven Spielberg's *Jurassic Park* (1993), in which with hubris, humans reverse the results of EVOLUTION and EXTINCTION by manipulating fossilized DNA to bring dinosaurs back to Earth.

During the COLD WAR, many movies predicted the end of the world in various scenarios; the most frequent plot was the invasion of the Earth from outer space, for example, in *The Day the Earth Stood Still* (1951) and *The War of the Worlds* (1952). In another variant, the film *The Day the Earth Caught Fire* (1962) presents our "out of control" planet as it unpredictably leaves its orbit as a result of too many nuclear explosions. In *Them!* (1954), nuclear tests in the New Mexican desert have caused the growth of gigantic mutant ants that threaten civilization. Although perhaps laughable when viewed more than half a century later, such stories captured common fears about a potential, global, nuclear World War III.

Other filmmakers succeeded in showing the supposed strangeness of animals. In Alfred Hitchcock's classic movie *The Birds* (1963), BIRDS of different species, seemingly working in unison and with intelligence, pose a threat to a remote village, with no apparent reason to explain their attacks on villagers and children. The film stands in sharp contrast with another movie about human-animal conflicts, *Wind across the Everglades* (1958) by Nicholas Ray, in which a group of exploiters kill countless birds in order to sell their feathers, or plumage.

Many of the first film classics claimed to present some images of the American people and historic landscapes, such as D. W. Griffith's *Birth of a Nation* (1915), which included episodes of the CIVIL WAR (1861–65), as did Buster Keaton's *Our Hospitality* (1923) and *The General* (1926). While celebrated for its technical achievements, Griffith's film became controversial because of its favorable treatment of the Ku Klux Klan. At a time when most people did not travel often from one country to another, these films often served as the only references and physical representations of the United States overseas. Charlie Chaplin's representation of Alaska in *Gold Rush* (1925) was linked with a historical event: the Klondike GOLD rush of the late 1890s. Filled with omnipresent cops and cars, Chaplin's chaotic vision of the urban American environment after the 1929 stock market crash remains salient in classics such as *City Lights* (1930) and *Modern Times* (1936). In a particularly funny scene from *Modern Times,* Chaplin, who plays a factory worker, opposes the inhuman urban world of monstrous machines with a brief dream of abundance, in a clear kitchen, in which grapes and their trees are easily reachable and a gentle cow generously gives some milk to a happy young couple. Here, escape from the unfair and imposing urban society seems to be possible only in the countryside. Indeed, the closing scene of *Modern Times* shows the same couple walking away on the desert road, turning their backs to the city that rejected them.

Some foreign films revealed similar criticisms of American cities. For example, the German filmmaker Fritz Lang's unforgettable representation of a gigantic city in *Metropolis* (1927) was inspired by his first trip to NEW YORK CITY in 1924. Many futuristic films, such as the American director Ridley Scott's *Blade Runner* (1982), were copied from this German masterpiece. *Blade Runner* presents a 2019 version of Los Angeles, whose corrupted society is matched by its polluted and degraded environment. In a similar way, the film *2001: A Space Odyssey* (1968) by the American director Stanley Kubrick paved the way for a new generation of science fiction films and influenced the way space and spaceships are represented (in movies and television as well) through a new set of animated images. The NATIONAL AERONAUTICS AND SPACE ADMINISTRATION (NASA) provided crucial technical help to the producers, aiding them to represent the Earth in a more realistic fashion; the animated demonstrations used for the Apollo expeditions were employed in the film as well.

FEATURE FILMS

In many movies, the representation of American history was an indirect way for Hollywood directors and screenwriters to define the United States as a nation, using landscapes and iconic ways of life to convey implicitly a basic social background. Above all cinematographic styles, the western as a genre contributing to create a common, almost mythical vision of the American past and its pioneers. As a genre, the western began as early as the 20th century, during the silent era, with *The Great Train Robbery* (1902), and culminated during the 1950s. The genre faded after the big-budget, star-studded *How the West Was Won* (1962) and John Ford's quieter classic *The Man Who Shot Liberty Valance* (1963), although there have been isolated resurgences, such as *Dances with Wolves* (1994), which retold the story of the western settlement from the perspective of "ecologically noble" Indians.

The western genre is often perceived as an almost exclusive, perhaps inimitable American contribution to the world's film history. Oddly, some of the masters of the western genre were actually born in Europe and emigrated in the United States as adults: Fritz Lang (*The Return of Frank James*, 1941; *Western Union*, 1942; *Rancho Notorious*, 1952), William Wyler (*The Westerner*, 1940; *The Big Country*, 1958), Michael Curtiz (*Dodge City*, 1939; *The Comancheros*, 1961), and Otto Preminger (*River of No Return*, 1954). Some nonwestern movies, however, also depicted the massive migrations to the western United States, such as John Ford's moving adaptation of JOHN STEINBECK's *Grapes of Wrath* (1940), in which California and its fertile farms are perceived as an oasis by the characters living on the plains of the DUST BOWL in the 1930s. Countless westerns magnified the monumental character of the landscapes of the American West. *Red Canyon* (1949), directed by George Sherman, for example, depicted the impressive landscapes of Utah. *Dances with Wolves*, while celebrating environmental sensibilities, also utilizes sprawling western scenery to convey its idealized story.

THE BORDER AS A LIMIT

In American and foreign movies, the representation of "the other" is an interesting test to demonstrate how nations can be different. Many U.S. dramas from the 1930s used other continents as geographical backgrounds to illustrate evil societies and environments: Josef Von Sternberg's *Shanghai Gesture* (1941) and *Macao* (1952), John Cromwell's *Algiers* (1938), Michael Curtiz's *Casablanca* (1942). A few decades later, Vietnam would represent the dangers of countless wars through Francis Ford Coppola's *Apocalypse Now*

(1979), Oliver Stone's *Platoon* (1986), and the Rambo series (from 1982).

For example, Canada, while similar to the United States, offers important environmental differences as a hostile environment or a haven, depending on the goals of the director. In William Wyler's *The Storm* (1930), two men and a woman are stuck in a blizzard in Canada. In Fritz Lang's *You Only Live Once* (1938), however, two runaways try to escape the United States and find refuge in Canada. Similarly, in Orson Welles's classic film noir *Touch of Evil* (1959), the drama is set on the U.S.-Mexican border. Mexico appears as a lawless zone, as stark and barren of morality as its deserts are seemingly barren of life.

THE ISLAND AS A DRAMATIC PLACE

The dangers of the OCEANS have appeared in the many films, including various versions of the *Titanic* tragedy: the first version was *Titanic* (1953) by Jean Negulesco, and, five years later, *A Night to Remember* (1958) was directed by Roy Ward Baker. James Cameron's blockbuster version *Titanic* was released in 1997. The *Titanic* tragedy also has allowed American filmmakers to comment on the arrogance of humans' wrongly presuming that technology allowed humans to control nature.

Through the years, maybe as much as the seas, the island has been set as a dramatic environment for countless stories in Hollywood movies, creating spaces where social rules, laws, and norms can be avoided. For example, Merian Cooper and Ernest Schoedsack's classic *King Kong* (1933) shows some American explorers going to a Malaysian jungle known as Skull Island where a savage, giant beast is captured and taken to New York City, as if such an enormous monster could not emerge from U.S. soil. Among other cases, John Huston's *Key Largo* (1948) is set in a hotel on one of the islands in the Florida Keys, where the stranded guests must grapple with what is the greater destructive force—a hurricane or the gangster who holds them captive. One of his only feature films shot in the United States, Luis Buñuel's *Robinson Crusoe* (1954, based on the Daniel DeFoe novel) shows a character living for years on a desert island, trying to recreate a society similar to the one he left behind. The recluse Crusoe makes a slave of the first man he meets in years.

ENVIRONMENTAL CRITIQUES OF AMERICAN LIFE

Environmental issues appeared more frequently in American popular movies after the 1960s, as filmmakers began to question some of the costs associated with American affluence and acquisitiveness. The U.S. nuclear industry, which has been the subject of significant criticism, suggested that the film *The China Syndrome* (1979) exaggerated the potential for a nuclear meltdown, but the accident at the THREE MILE

ISLAND reactor in Pennsylvania 12 days after the movie's opening seemed to give the film and the concerns it raised about dangers to human and ecological health greater credibility. *Silkwood* (1983, directed by Mike Nichols and starring Meryl Streep and Cher) is about the true case of KAREN SILKWOOD, a labor activist and technician who exposed the corruption and hazards of nuclear plants and died in a mysterious car accident in 1974.

Other Hollywood films have commented on pollution and hazardous dumping by U.S. corporations. *A Civil Action* (1998), starring John Travolta, tells the real-life story of the contamination of DRINKING WATER wells by two large corporations in a Massachusetts town and reveals the length and expenses involved in proving an environmental tort case. Two years later, in a film based on another true story, Julia Roberts portrayed the title character in *Erin Brockovich*. Working as a clerk in a California law firm, Brockovich uncovers evidence that the West Coast corporate energy giant Pacific Gas & Electric had discharged wastewater with hexavalent chromium that seeped into the groundwater and poisoned a small town's water supply. Despite unusually high incidences of cancer, birth defects, and miscarriages, the company systematically covered up its dumping activities for years. In real life, the $333 million settlement was the largest in U.S. history for this type of lawsuit.

DOCUMENTARIES

Since the earliest films were made, countless documentaries have shown nature, animals, and environmental issues at home and in remote nations. Perhaps the richest documentary on environmental issues is *The Journey* (1987) by Peter Watkins. The director's running commentary raises various issues such as the potential for complete environmental devastation but also attempts to integrate different political positions on these issues. For example, a train carrying nuclear weapons crosses many western states and faces the protest of environmental groups. The MEDIA, as Watkins demonstrates, often present the environmentalist as bizarre and irrational, but when U.S. and Canadian politicians unsuccessfully debate nuclear disarmament, the media rarely address the futility of their discussions.

Perhaps the most influential environmental documentary of the 21st century to date is Davis Guggenheim's highly praised *An Inconvenient Truth* (2006), which received a tremendous worldwide reception. In the film, the former U.S. vice president ALBERT GORE, JR., presents the standard lecture that he had delivered around the world for six years, alerting audiences about the issue of GLOBAL WARMING. The film won many prizes, including an Academy Award, and Gore received the Nobel Peace Prize. However, the film also created discomfort for some scientists and sociologists by cataloging the opponents (the "so-called skeptics") as unfairly biased. The film, however, in being overly critical of the skeptics, perhaps undermines scientific debate.

Another group of highly publicized documentaries such as *Planet in Peril* (2007) and Yann Arthus-Bertrand's *Home* (2009) present in a mixture of the spectacular and high drama the current issues of global warming and overpopulation. The common message of these films is for people to change their habits of overconsumption drastically. Some critics argue, however, that the productions of these films, which are shot by crews in distant locations from Greenland to Brazil with many aerial scenes, are in themselves damaging to natural resources. Nonetheless, these films about environmental hazards innovate at least in one way: They are often available free and legally on the INTERNET; therefore, large audiences have an unlimited access to their arguments.

See also CANADA AND THE UNITED STATES; CORPORATIONS, CHEMICAL; CORPORATIONS, UTILITIES; ENERGY, NUCLEAR; MEXICO AND THE UNITED STATES; UNITED STATES—CALIFORNIA.

Yves Laberge

Further Reading

Cavanaugh, Terence W., and Cathy Cavanaugh. *Teach Science with Science Fiction Films: A Guide for Teachers and Library Media Specialists.* Worthington, Ohio: Linworth, 2004.

Laberge, Yves. "Peter Watkins' *The Journey.*" In *Encyclopedia of Documentary Film.* Vol. 2, edited by Ian Aitken, 689–691. New York: Routledge, 2006.

Maltby, Richard. *Hollywood Cinema.* Oxford: Blackwell, 2003.

Homer, Winslow (1836–1910) *artist, painter*

Winslow Homer was a printmaker, illustrator, and painter, working in oil colors and watercolors. His subjects ranged from CIVIL WAR (1861–65) soldiers to scenes of rural life to the seascapes around Prout's Neck in Maine, where he spent his later years. Homer's style evolved from a naturalism that focused on contemporary themes to a more abstract and modern realism. This change is particularly evident in the seascapes of his last years, which have been thought to reflect Homer's more fatalistic attitude toward nature.

Born in BOSTON, MASSACHUSETTS, on February 24, 1836, and raised in Cambridge, Massachusetts, Homer began his career in Boston and NEW YORK CITY, where he studied at the School of the National Academy of Design between 1859 and 1864. In 1862, Homer spent five weeks with Union soldiers of the Army of the Potomac. Homer published his battlefield illustrations in *Harper's Weekly*, a New York–based magazine published from 1857 to 1916, which complemented the magazine's coverage of the war. Homer's painting of army life, *Prisoners from the Front* (1866), reflected these wartime experiences as well and earned him critical acclaim.

In 1866, Homer left for Paris, where he was introduced to Japanese prints and the Barbizon school, with its focus on rural landscapes and the people who lived in the country. He returned to the United States in 1867, and his time in New Hampshire's WHITE MOUNTAINS inspired *The Bridle Path, White Mountains* (1868). In this painting, the surrounding rugged slopes of Mount Washington, with their sense of depth and implied challenge, are as important as the fashionably dressed female tourist on horseback to whom one's eyes are first drawn.

Critics have argued that Homer, along with other GILDED AGE painters, helped to create an American national and artistic identity, but he also gained an international reputation. Whether he was painting events near the coastal village of Cullercoats in northeastern England (*Wreck of the Iron Crown,* 1881) or the vivid autumn colors of New York's Adirondack Mountains (*An October Day,* 1889), Homer's work demonstrated strong contrasts of color and textures, creating his own uniquely American style.

Children were important early subjects in his paintings (*Snap the Whip,* 1872 *Breezing Up; [A Fair Wind Home]* 1873–76), and their innocence is reflected in the landscapes that surround them. Homer's seascapes from the 1880s (*Eight Bells,* 1886; *The Gulf Stream,* 1899) reflect a far more serious and heroic interaction between people and nature, influenced by his firsthand observations of the sea and the lives of those whose existence depended upon its bounty and who lived with its dangers daily.

Although Homer did not leave behind any records that might explain his fascination with the sea, his seascapes are considered to be among his finest works. Fishermen in *The Fog Warning* (1885) and members of the American Life-Saving Service (a precursor of the Coast Guard) in *The Life Line* (1884) capture the perils of the sea. Fine critical reviews of *The Life Line* and the high purchase price paid by a well-known art collector draw Homer additional fame.

Homer's seascapes evolved into paintings within which the sea itself, rather than human figures, became the focus. For 27 years, from 1883 until his death there on September 29, 1910, Homer spent time at his studio in Prout's Neck. His work from this period focused on a range of seascapes: *Northeaster* (1895) is a seascape with dangerous waves crashing against the dark, rocky coast, and *West Point, Prout's Neck* (1900) depicts a somewhat less violent sea and a sunset-colored sky.

Both paintings reflect the isolated location in which Homer completed his work. In part to escape the harsh Maine winters that are reflected in the Prout's Neck seascapes, Homer traveled to the Bahamas and Bermuda. These visits inspired *A Wall, Nassau* (1898) with its bright orange foliage contrasting with the blue of the sea and the peaceful sailing ship. *Hurricane, Bahamas* (1898) offered dark gray storm clouds, a choppy sea, and palm trees bending in the wind.

Although he continued to be active and self-sufficient enough to travel, Homer's health suffered after 1900. During the last decade of his life, his paintings took on an abstract style, using a flatter perspective and allowing for a more immediate sensory experience. There is a sense of anxiety in *Kissing the Moon* (1904) and of desperation in *Shooting the Rapids* (1893), perhaps reflective of Homer's recognition of his own mortality. Winslow Homer's work gained increasing recognition after his death, and he is considered one of America's master painters.

See also ART; LANDSCAPE ART, AMERICAN; OCEANS; ROMANTICISM.

Kimberly A. Jarvis

Further Reading
Cikovsky, Nicolai, Jr. *Winslow Homer.* New York: Harry N. Abrams, 1990.
Levy, Sophie, ed. *Winslow Homer: Poet of the Sea.* Giverny, France: Terra Foundation for American Art, 2006.
Lucie-Smith, Edward. *American Realism.* New York: Thames & Hudson, 1994.

hookworm

Hookworm is one of the most troublesome parasites known to infect humans. By causing anemia and malnutrition, hookworm makes it difficult to learn and to work. Worldwide, it affects more than 600 million people (10 percent of the world's population) and kills about 550,000 annually. Once a major problem in the American South, through improved sanitation it became relatively rare in the United States by the mid-20th century.

Long before hookworm had been identified as a parasitic disease, its mostly white victims were a common sight in the South. Pale and listless, with vacant stares and winged shoulder blades, these "shiftless" southerners seemed to demonstrate the weakness of the southern way of life. In the early 1900s, the zoologist Charles W. Stiles showed that these negative traits had a biological basis when he identified *Necator americanis.* The hookworm had migrated to the South in the bodies of African slaves, moved into the larger predominantly white population, and thrived in its new environment. While Africans and African Americans also suffered from hookworm, there was little contemporary comment about their ailments, perhaps given the racial prejudices of the time, because many whites falsely assumed blacks were "shiftless" by nature.

A hookworm belt extends around the globe between 36° north latitude and 30° south latitude. The land in this region is sandy or loamy, while rainfall is more than 40 inches a year

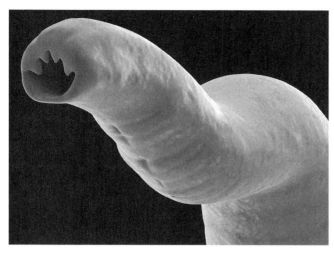

A hookworm, enlarged and shown here, is a parasite that lives in the small intestine of its host. These worms cause anemia, an iron deficiency due to a decrease of red blood cells. *(Sebastian Kaulitzki/Shutterstock)*

and the mean annual temperature is above 50°F. In these conditions, hookworm larvae thrive as long as they are not immersed in water or exposed for long to the sun. Hookworm spreads through fecal pollution of the ground. It is a disease caused by improper sanitation. Any contact of the skin with hookworm-infested soil is sufficient to allow hookworm infection. People typically become infected by walking through soil contaminated with the C-shaped worm.

The infestation cycle begins when the male and somewhat larger female hook themselves to the intestinal wall and suck blood over a life span that may last years. At some point, the male unhooks to find and mate with the female. Thereafter, the female may lay from 5,000 to 20,000 eggs a day, depending on her species. The host's daily bowel movement takes these eggs to earth, where under favorable conditions they hatch into rod-shaped larvae about 0.01 inch long. The larva feeds on bacteria, molts twice, almost doubles in size, and becomes a threadlike worm. It is aggressive when the ground is warm and moist. It can lash its way for a few inches upward along a plant, such as a blade of grass. The worm makes contact with bare skin and bores like a corkscrew through the tender skin between the toes. Once inside, if it enters a blood vessel, the worm will be carried alive through the circulatory system until it reaches the lungs, is pushed into the throat, and is swallowed to reach the gastrointestinal tract. Once in the small intestine, the worm bites into the mucus membrane lining. The worm drinks blood voraciously and quickly matures. Hookworms reach a length of 0.4 to 0.5 inch.

The burden on the victims of hookworms is often debilitating, and hookworms have historically been one of the greatest retarding influences in community development. The worms cause anemia, an iron deficiency due to a decrease of red blood cells. People who are infected with 25 to 100 worms may have pale, dry, yellowish skin and lack energy. Individuals with 100 to 500 worms will have yellow skin, depression, stomach pain, nausea, enlarged heart, chest pain, headaches, joint aches, frequent exhaustion, and dull reactions. In severe cases, victims have a pot belly, "angel's wings" or a protuberance of the shoulder blades, blurred vision, and a lack of reflexes. Hookworm itself is not a major cause of death, but it is frequently a contributory factor in fatalities from secondary infections. It is most dangerous in fetuses and children because it arrests both physical and mental development.

Hookworm disappeared in the United States largely because of the efforts of the Rockefeller Sanitary Commission. When Stiles reported his findings, many southern leaders rejected his conclusions and resisted calls for public health changes. In 1909, the commission sent experts to nine southern states to convince policy makers to take action against hookworm. In 1911, the commission shifted to treatment by offering thymol free of charge. The commission stopped work in 1915, when hookworm infections had dropped dramatically. The parasite was largely eradicated in the United States by 1940.

See also DISEASES, HUMAN; HEALTH AND MEDICINE; HUMAN BODY; SLAVE TRADE; SPECIES, EXOTIC AND INVASIVE; UNITED STATES—DEEP SOUTH.

Caryn E. Neumann

Further Reading

Ettling, John. *The Germ of Laziness: Rockefeller Philanthropy and Public Health in the New South.* Cambridge, Mass.: Harvard University Press, 1981.

Williams, Greer. *The Plague Killers.* New York: Charles Scribner's Sons, 1969.

Hoover, Herbert (1874–1964) *engineer, secretary of commerce (1921–1928), 31st president of the United States (1929–1933)*

President when the GREAT DEPRESSION began in 1929, Herbert Hoover promoted voluntary actions and limited government interventions in response to the crisis. Failing to end the nation's economic downturn, Hoover served as president for only one term (1929–33). As the secretary of commerce under presidents Warren Harding (1865–1923) and Calvin Coolidge (1872–1933) and president of the United States, however, Hoover attempted to protect the nation's natural resources by expanding the holdings of the NATIONAL PARK SERVICE and promoting ENGINEERING projects to control its waterways.

Herbert Clark Hoover was born in Cedar County, Iowa, on August 10, 1874, to Quaker parents. Hoover graduated with a degree in mining engineering from Stanford University at age 20. Upon graduating, he first found employment with the U.S. Geological Survey in California and then entered private engineering partnership. At the turn of the century, he traveled to Australia and China, where he oversaw the building of port facilities and the development of coal mines. Hoover later became an independent mining consultant, traveling worldwide before the outbreak of World War I (1914–18).

When the United States entered the war in 1917, Hoover abandoned his lucrative business and became head of the Food Administration in Europe under President Woodrow Wilson. By providing food to millions of people throughout war-torn Europe and Russia, Hoover became a prominent national and international figure.

After the war, Hoover became secretary of commerce under both Presidents Harding and Coolidge. In 1928, Hoover became the Republican presidential nominee and was later elected president. Eight months into his term, the stock market plummeted in October 1929, taking with it a great deal of Hoover's accumulated reputation and credibility. Hoover believed that government should lead by helping private industry be more efficient through guidance and assistance rather than mandatory regulations. He did not believe that the federal government should make major interventions to resolve the crisis. In spite of his more limited measures to mend the broken economy, many Americans blamed him for the collapse. By the 1932 election, Hoover's opponents portrayed him as a callous president, and he was defeated by the Democratic candidate, Franklin D. Roosevelt. Hoover returned to private business.

In 1947, President Harry Truman assigned the former president the task of organizing the federal government's structure and spending practices. The Hoover Commission, as it became known, was responsible for establishing new departments and policies to streamline government spending in order to maximize the value of the taxpayer's dollar. The Hoover Commission recommended formation of several key government departments, including the Department of Health, Education and Welfare Services and the General Services Administration—established to oversee buying, selling, and managing of government resources. The Hoover Commission, in place from 1947 to 1949, gained such high regard that President Dwight D. Eisenhower requested a second commission in 1953.

Throughout his life, Hoover revealed his appreciation of the outdoors and his concern for the preservation of the nation's natural resources. Nurtured in his youth in rural Iowa, these beliefs were often expressed by Hoover in what he called the democracy of fishing. "All men are created equal before fishes," he frequently asserted.

As secretary of commerce, Hoover encouraged waterways projects to control floods, increased the production of fisheries, and cleaned up rivers and harbors that quickly became the staple activities of the Bureau of Reclamation and the U.S. Army Corps of Engineers. The control of waterpower was of concern to both the public and private sectors during the 1920s. Ensconced in the conservation ethos of the Progressive Era, Hoover believed the nation's rivers should be harnessed for commercial activity and assumed any water that reached the ocean without experiencing such utility constituted a waste. In 1927, when the Mississippi River spilled over its banks, devastating thousands of acres of agricultural land, Hoover rushed to the scene to offer humanitarian and engineering assistance. He promoted a series of federal dam and lock projects along the Mississippi to provide electrification and manage flooding.

Some of Hoover's most important political engineering and environmental achievements involved the Colorado River. For many years, taming the Colorado River for irrigation, flood control, and electrical power had been an aspiration of residents of the American Southwest. As secretary of commerce in 1922, Hoover attempted to allocate the water resources of the Colorado River among the seven states through which it flowed—Arizona, California, Colorado, Nevada, New Mexico, Utah, and Wyoming. The ensuing Colorado River Compact, also known as the Hoover Compromise, attracted criticism over time, however. Negotiated at a time of abnormally high rainfall, the compact often results in shortfalls during droughts, which many scientists believe may be the more typical weather pattern for the region. Moreover, use of the river in the United States severely undermines its flow to Mexico.

The compact paved the way for later construction of Boulder Dam, which is also known as Hoover Dam. Begun during the Hoover presidency in 1931 and completed in 1935, the dam provided irrigation, electrical power, flood control, and outdoor recreation space for the people of the American Southwest. Boulder Dam ushered in a new era of expanded federal activity. Under President Franklin D. Roosevelt's New Deal and over the next six decades, the Bureau of Reclamation and the Army Corps of Engineers built more than 100 large multipurpose dams across the American West while the Tennessee Valley Authority constructed more than 40 such structures east of the Mississippi River.

Herbert Hoover died on October 20, 1964, in New York City at the age of 90.

See also Commerce, Department of; dams, reservoirs, and artificial lakes; fishing, recreational; food; Interior, Department of the; Mexico and the United States; preservationism; progressivism; Republican Party; United States—California; United States—Southwest.

Arthur Holst

Further Reading

Fausold, Martin L. *The Presidency of Herbert C. Hoover.* American Presidency Series. Lawrence: University Press of Kansas, 1988.

Nash, George H. *Life of Herbert Hoover: The Humanitarian, 1914–1917.* New York: W. W. Norton, 1988.

Smith, Gene. *The Shattered Dream: Herbert Hoover and the Great Depression.* New York: McGraw-Hill, 1984.

Hoover Dam (Boulder Dam)

Hoover Dam is a 726-foot-high concrete curved gravity DAM built to impound the floodwaters of the COLORADO RIVER. Located on the border of Arizona and Nevada about 30 miles southeast of LAS VEGAS, NEVADA, the dam was completed by the federal government in 1935; hydroelectric power generation began the next year. Hoover Dam dramatically altered the ecology of the Colorado River and sparked urban growth and agricultural expansion in the American Southwest.

As early as 1902, the federal U.S. Reclamation Service (renamed the BUREAU OF RECLAMATION in 1923) investigated the Colorado River for possible dam sites. Preceding this federal involvement in regional water projects, the privately financed California Development Company undertook an ambitious scheme to divert water out of the river near the U.S.-Mexico border and deliver it to the Imperial Valley in Southern California. Making use of an ancient river channel that extended through Mexico before crossing back into the United States, the company's IRRIGATION scheme worked well for a few years. However, in 1905, heavy FLOODS broke through the wooden gates protecting the canal and an uncontrolled surge of water poured into the Imperial Valley. More than two years passed before the flood was controlled, and, in the meantime, the lower sections of the valley were inundated and formed what is now known as the Salton Sea.

With the irrigation company's failure and replacement by the local Imperial Irrigation District in 1911, local interests began pushing for the construction of both a large flood control dam across the Colorado River and an "All-American" canal serving the valley that would not pass through Mexico. In the early 1920s, the Reclamation Service, in concert with Imperial Valley interests, backed a plan to build a large dam at Boulder Canyon to provide flood control and water storage. To help finance construction costs, the plan included generating hydroelectric power for transmittal and sale in the Southern California market. Soon, the city of LOS ANGELES, CALIFORNIA, and surrounding communities seeking electric power and municipal water supplies joined the bandwagon to promote the federal Boulder Canyon Project Act.

To boost political support, in 1922, California joined with other states in the Colorado River Basin to draft the "Colorado River Compact" and divide water rights between the Upper Basin States (Utah, Wyoming, Colorado, New Mexico) and the Lower Basin States (California, Arizona, Nevada). Although Arizona objected to the terms of the compact (it did not receive satisfaction until a favorable U.S. Supreme Court ruling in 1963), the compact mollified other states and proved vital to California's efforts to win congressional approval for the Boulder Canyon Project Act. By 1924, engineering studies by the BUREAU OF RECLAMATION (formerly the Reclamation Service) indicated that Black Canyon (located about 10 miles downstream from Boulder Canyon) offered a better dam and reservoir site, and Black Canyon subsequently became the focus of all work relating to dam design and construction. However, with the phrases "Boulder Dam" and "Boulder Canyon Project" already etched in the public consciousness, no change in project nomenclature was made.

Overcoming opposition from both Arizona legislators and proponents of the private electric power industry, Congress authorized Boulder Dam and the All-American Canal, and President Calvin Coolidge signed the law in December 1928. After completion of all preliminary planning, in 1930 Secretary of the Interior Ray Lyman Wilbur (1875–1949) named the structure Hoover Dam in honor of President HERBERT HOOVER. In 1933, President FRANKLIN D. ROOSEVELT's administration revived the name Boulder Dam, but in 1947, it was officially designated Hoover Dam again. Construction by Six Companies Inc. started in spring 1931. Concrete was first cast in 1933, and the final bucket was placed two years later; more than three million cubic yards of concrete went into the completed dam.

On September 30, 1935, President Roosevelt formally dedicated the structure, but the reservoir began to fill even earlier. When filled, Lake Mead, the dam's reservoir, has a capacity of more than 28 million acre-feet (an acre foot is equal to about 326,000 gallons). Relatively wet years in the late 1930s raised the reservoir to the spillway level for the first time in 1941. The only other time water passed over the spillway was in 1983. Usually, water releases to support the demands of agriculture, municipal supply, and power generation are of sufficient size to keep the reservoir below capacity. During times of low annual precipitation, ongoing water release demands are so great that reservoir levels can fall significantly on a year-to-year basis. In the first years of the 21st century, this problem became vividly evident as storage fell 50 percent below capacity and a prominent "bathtub ring" of salt residue marked the reservoir's boundaries

The environmental impact of Hoover Dam has been felt in four basic ways: inundation of the reservoir area, changes in salt content due to evaporation, changes to downstream ecologies, and agricultural and urban growth in Southern California, Arizona, and Nevada. Although settlement and development of the 247 square miles of the land inundated by a full Lake Mead were relatively sparse prior to dam construction, the reservoir flooded ancient

Indian ruins near Overton, the Pearce Ferry site; agricultural and mining communities, including the small towns of Callville and St. Thomas, Nevada; and two rapids at the extreme lower end of the Grand Canyon. In terms of salt concentrations, evaporation of water stored in the reservoir increases salinity levels because dissolved solids cannot evaporate into the atmosphere. Salt deposits are what form the white precipitate present along the edge of the reservoir.

Below the dam, the once-turbulent waters of the Colorado River (which ranged in flow from less than 10,000 cubic feet per second to more than 400,000 cubic feet per second in heavy floods) were tamed. Water diversions to the Imperial Valley, to greater Los Angeles via the Metropolitan Water District of Southern California's Colorado Aqueduct, and to central Arizona via the Granite Reef Aqueduct dramatically reduce the flow by the time the river reaches the Mexican border, drying up the once well-watered and ecologically diverse Colorado Delta that lay adjacent to the Pacific Ocean's Gulf of California. The vibrant character of the pre-dam Colorado Delta has been well described in a chapter of Aldo Leopold's classic book *Sand County Almanac* (1949).

Finally, perhaps the greatest environmental impact of Hoover Dam is evident in the ever-expanding urban growth of the American Southwest from the 1940s through the early 21st century. Whereas most of the water stored in Lake Mead once went to irrigated agriculture, over the past 30 years, more and more Colorado River flow has gone to foster suburban sprawl from San Diego County in California to greater Phoenix and Tucson, Arizona, and, last but hardly least, the burgeoning metropolis of Las Vegas, Nevada. Hoover Dam is no longer the only major dam across the Colorado (completed in 1964 near the Arizona/Utah border, the Glen Canyon Dam is of comparable scale), but it led the way in transforming the American Southwest from an arid desert landscape into an urbanized ecology supporting a human population of tens of millions.

See also Agriculture, commercial; Agriculture, federal policies; Indians, Southwest; Interior, Department of the; Mexico and the United States; oceans; Sunbelt; United States—California; United States—Southwest; urbanization.

Donald C. Jackson

Further Reading

Billington, David P., and Donald C. Jackson. *Big Dams of the New Deal Era: A Confluence of Water and Politics.* Norman: University of Oklahoma Press, 2006.

Hundley, Norris, Jr. *Water and the West.* Rev. 2d ed. Berkeley: University of California Press, 2009.

National Research Council. *Colorado River Basin Water Management: Evaluating and Adjusting to Hydroclimatic Variability.* Washington, D.C.: National Academies Press, 2007.

Ward, Evan R. *Border Oasis: Water and Political Ecology of the Colorado River Delta, 1940–1975.* Tucson: University of Arizona Press, 2003.

The Case for Boulder Dam
Edgar Lloyd Hampton (1922)

In his article "The Battle with the Colorado" in 1922, the author Edgar Lloyd Hampton made the case for federal construction of Boulder Dam (later Hoover Dam) to control flooding, manage irrigation, and generate power in the American Southwest. At the time, few people expressed concerns over the environmental implications of its construction, such as the disruption of fish migrations, changes in water temperature, and increased salinity.

Boulder Canyon Dam will stand, at its base, 665 feet above sea level. Its height will be 600 feet, its length at top 1000 feet, and it will impound an amount of water equivalent to almost two full years of the Colorado's annual run-off. By impounding the water during the flood period, and releasing it gradually for irrigation and hydroelectric purposes during the remainder of the year, the area now threatened with inundation will be permanently protected. The dam and its impounding reservoir, it may be interesting to note, will be many times larger than any similar project anywhere else on earth. The dam at Aswan, on the Nile, while much longer than the Boulder Dam, is less than ninety feet high and impounds a maximum of only 1,800,000 acre feet of water. The Boulder Dam will impound 31,400,000 acre feet, or seventeen times as much. The area of its reservoir is larger than the State of Delaware, and it will be navigable for more than one hundred miles.

Power Will Pay the Bill

While Boulder Dam is primarily a Government undertaking, and its original financing will be in Government hands, the entire construction and maintenance cost will later be repaid by the electrical energy which the project will develop. Always with the problem of Western reclamation runs the problem of electrical development—or, rather, electrical development is the solution; for it is to this source, and not to irrigation, that all such enterprises must look for their final reimbursement. The seven Western States involved, which to-day, with minor exceptions, burn $18 coal in competition with $4 coal at Pittsburgh, need and can use this electrical energy. They need it also in an effort to conserve the rapidly dwindling supply of fuel oil, and this condition the proposed development will bring about; for the Boulder Canyon Dam will develop 600,000 horse-power of electrical energy, which will displace annually 23,000,000 barrels of fuel oil now consumed in the development of power. Much more, indeed, could be said on the theme of hydro-electric energy, and the question is one that might well attract the attention of all thoughtful minds. The day of steam is all but past; our coal and oil are rapidly diminishing, and the world at large is swiftly approaching the golden age of hydro-electricity.

The cost of the dam will be $45,000,000, and repayment will extend over a period of twenty-five years. It is estimated that, in an effort to protect the various threatened districts, the Government has already expended of public funds more than enough to have paid the cost of the dam, with results that were only a partial success and with no hope of return. The Boulder Canyon Dam will permanently solve the problem, ultimately without cost to the Government.

Since the huge dam will also irrigate more than 2,000,000 additional acres of arid land, thus creating additional millions of wealth, Mr. Davis, of the Reclamation Service, at first reported that the cost of construction might be charged 15 per cent, against irrigation and 85 per cent, against electrical development. Later, and after further investigation, he reported that the entire cost must be charged against hydroelectric development. Thus will it be seen that the project, as reported and endorsed by the various Government heads, is the only one by means of which the cost of construction and maintenance may be met by the people in the territory involved. So the victims of the flood-infested lower Colorado basin are not without hope of ultimate salvation. The Government has taken definite steps; Congress at last is alive to the situation; one of the greatest constructive engineering minds of the present day, having endorsed the project, has been given definite orders to carry it to completion, and Mr. [Herbert] Hoover [then U.S. secretary of commerce] is not noted for delays.

Source: Edgar Lloyd Hampton. "The Battle with the Colorado: How the People Each Year Fight to Defend Their Homes against the Encroachments of a Flood-Mad River." *American Review of Reviews: An International Journal* 66 (July–December 1922): 530–531.

Hornaday, William (1854–1937) *author, wildlife conservationist, zoologist*

An advocate for wildlife, William Temple Hornaday is best known for his tireless CONSERVATION work in the 19th and early 20th centuries. He is often credited with transforming zoos by displaying animals in "natural settings" and working to ward off EXTINCTION of American BISON and Alaskan fur seals. Hornaday chronicled the decline of American wildlife populations and sought to reintroduce certain species to their native habitats.

Born in Plainfield, Indiana, on December 1, 1854, Hornaday grew up in Iowa. He attended Oskaloosa College and Iowa State College of Ames but left the latter in 1873 before taking his degree in order to work for Ward's Natural History Establishment in Rochester, New York. At Ward's, Hornaday learned the art of taxidermy and undertook a series of adventurous but grueling specimen collecting expeditions to Florida, Cuba, the Orinoco River valley, India, Sri Lanka, Malaysia, and Borneo. His memoir of the Asian trip, *Two Years in the Jungle* (1884), gave him a modest measure of fame. Hornaday made the jump from taxidermist to zoologist after a buffalo hunt in 1886. Both the hunt and his subsequent report, entitled *The Extermination of the American Bison*, convinced him of the need to preserve a core sample of each species as a safeguard against extinction. From 1888 to 1890, he served as the superintendent of the U.S. National Zoological Park in WASHINGTON, D.C.

In 1896, Hornaday accepted the position of director of the New York Zoological Park in the Bronx. He held this position until his retirement in 1926 and achieved his goal of making the New York Zoological Park, popularly known as the Bronx Zoo, one of the largest, most advanced zoos in the world.

Between 1905 and his death on March 6, 1937, Hornaday played instrumental roles in a number of successful wildlife protection measures, including the establishment of two bison preserves (1905, 1908) and a mountain sheep preserve in British Columbia (1908); the Bayne Bill in New York State, which banned the sale of game meat (1911) migratory bird protection (1913–37) the plumage ban in the tariff of 1913, ending the seal leasing system (1913); and the Migratory Bird Refuge System (1928). In addition, he worked to gain passage of many state HUNTING regulations. His book *Our Vanishing Wildlife* (1913) energized the wildlife protection movement with its graphic photographs and strong moral arguments.

Hornaday was essentially a force unto himself. His energy, lobbying skill, and prolific writing kept him in the forefront of all public debates concerning wildlife, even though he did not have an organization behind him. Instead, he cultivated a circle of wealthy philanthropists who financed his campaigns. By 1920, he had abandoned the sportsman constituency of the wildlife protection movement and became a spokesman for the nonhunting preservationists. While he achieved enormous results, he was a divisive figure who had alienated himself from most other wildlife conservationists largely through his self-righteous attitude and inability to trust the motives of others. His focus on hunting as the sole cause of wildlife decline led him to overlook various ecological factors.

See also BIRDS; PRESERVATIONISM; WILD ANIMALS; ZOOLOGY.

Gregory J. Dehler

Further Reading

Dehler, Gregory J. "An American Crusader: William Temple Hornaday and Wildlife Protection in America, 1850–1940." Ph.D. Diss., Lehigh University, 2002.

Dunlap, Thomas R. *Saving America's Wildlife: Ecology and the American Mind, 1850–1990*. Princeton, N.J.: Princeton University Press, 1991.

Hornaday, William T. *Thirty Years War for Wildlife: Gains and Losses in the Thankless Task*. New York: Charles Scribner's Sons, 1931.

——. *Two Years in the Jungle: The Experiences of a Hunter and Naturalist in India, Ceylon, the Malay Peninsula, and Borneo*. New York: Charles Scribner's Sons, 1886.

Isenberg, Andrew C. *The Destruction of the Bison: An Environmental History, 1750–1920*. New York: Cambridge University Press, 2000.

Trefethen, James. *An American Crusade for Wildlife*. New York: Winchester Press, 1975.

horses

Horses have long constituted an important part of the American environment. Prior to European arrival in 1492, the Americas had only one native horse species, which faded into EXTINCTION about 10,000 years ago, along with many other large four-legged species. The Spanish introduced the modern horse (*Equus caballus*) from Europe into North America and South America as a part of their colonization efforts beginning in the 1500s. Because of a similar climate and the lack of natural predators, horses thrived in the Americas, as did many other animals and plants introduced from Europe.

Before the modern horse first arrived in the Americas in the 1500s, Native Americans had very little experience with domesticated animals. Tribes in several areas quickly adopted horses as wild herds moved north from Spanish Mexico to the Great Plains. The Plains Indians, in particular, found horses to be a convenient addition to their culture over time. BISON hunting became more efficient for Indian tribes with horses. Bison grazed on readily available PRAIRIES and moved faster and farther than walking humans, but hunters on horseback could easily keep up with these migrations. Horses changed Indian cultures in other ways as well. Instead of using bison as only a part of their diet and supplementing it with agriculture and hunting-gathering, some tribes began specializing in bison hunting. Overhunting by Plains Indians played a small role in the decimation of the bison population that COMMERCIAL HUNTING accelerated in the late 19th century. The demise of bison prefaced the demise of Native American Plains populations.

The switch to horses also took a toll on land in the West. Both Native Americans and Europeans overgrazed grasslands with large herds of horses, causing the best grazing to be decimated quickly. In addition, the constant stream of wagons, horses, and other four-legged creatures used by Europeans crossing the continent over the course of the 1800s resulted in a loss of timber, damage to natural WATERSHEDS, and a general decline in health of ECOSYSTEMS.

Horses served as a powerful tool in the mechanization of agriculture that occurred over the course of the 19th century. Horses had long been used in dragging plows through the ground; by the 1870s, large teams of horses came into play when inventors developed large, heavy tools to thresh (cut) and reap (bundle) crops as they were harvested. Farmers also began using specialized draft horses, bred for size and strength. As steam and gasoline engines gained wide use in the early 20th century, horsepower became obsolete. By WORLD WAR II (1941–45), machines such as tractors operated more efficiently and allowed farmers to produce more, with less labor, on the same amount of land. Some organic farmers have recently reintroduced horses to farming as a way to reduce carbon emissions and dependence on foreign oil. In addition to uses in farming, horses have been (and continue to be) used on ranches to deal with moving, sorting, and caring for CATTLE and other livestock.

Throughout American history, horses also played multiple roles in warfare. Lighter breed horses carried individual soldiers in cavalry units in direct combat, while heavier breeds or mules pulled cannon, carts, and other equipment for soldiers. Great Plains Indians demonstrated considerable equestrian skills in warfare as well. Horses were especially significant during the CIVIL WAR (1861–65), with approximately 35,000 animals required for every 100,000 men. Confederate forces, because of experience, enjoyed an early advantage in horsemanship in the war. Southern terrain proved a liability to the North early on as well, with teams of mules or horses getting stuck in the mud and prohibiting movement. As the war dragged on, both southern men and horses suffered from widespread lack of FOOD and hunger. Northern soldiers, on the other hand, benefited from the greater amounts of food produced by newly mechanized farms. Again, though, as with agriculture, the horse's usefulness diminished with the growth of gasoline-powered engines. By World War II, mechanized vehicles had almost completely replaced any prior work-related uses for horses.

In addition to playing a role in the West in a variety of ways, horses played pivotal roles in history in the more populated areas of the United States. Horses and water transportation were the primary modes of travel and commerce well into the 19th century. Even with the advent of RAILROADS, horses still transported commodities within cities to their final destination and moved people around ever-growing urban areas. Horses also continued to provide sources of power for industry until the popularization of the steam engine.

Urban areas grew quickly at the end of the 19th century in the United States, with the horse population growing equally quickly. Although they provided useful city services, horses also produced tremendous amounts of waste—approximately 15–30 pounds of manure per animal per day. With about three million horses in urban areas at the time, the waste quickly piled up. Cities attempted to recycle horse waste back into the ecosystem by selling the manure to nearby farms as FERTILIZER. In turn, these farms produced vegetables and other food for the city.

Progressive Era reformers targeted horses as a source of vast amounts of pollution and disease. Reformers began to connect the issue of pollution, including the proliferation of manure, with the spread of flies and disease, particularly TYPHOID fever, which periodically swept through urban areas. Horse manure also produced AIR POLLUTION when it dried and swept along city streets. In death, horses produced problems as well. Horses were often overworked and abused in cities. Horse deaths on the streets were commonplace, often causing traffic jams and posing extreme difficulty for those responsible for removing the 1,000- to 1,300-pound bodies. In the 1880s, NEW YORK CITY removed as many as 15,000 dead horses from its streets in one year; CHICAGO, ILLINOIS, carted away nearly as many horse carcasses as late as 1912. Armed with this evidence, many reformers pushed for the use of AUTOMOBILES as a solution to horse pollution problems.

Although horses faded from city life for many Americans with the increased use of automobiles and electricity, they remained a vibrant element of American culture and imagination throughout the remainder of the 20th century. Horses became symbols of an idealized past, sports heroes on a grand scale, and tools to combat the spread of URBANIZATION. In movies, horses helped evoke a romanticized version

of European settlement of the West and visions of urbane city life during the 19th century. Periodically, exceptional thoroughbred racehorses have diverted national attention away from difficult social and economic problems, as the come-from-behind winner Seabiscuit did during the GREAT DEPRESSION. Recreational and competitive horseback riding continue to be popular in the United States today, while ranchers and farmers still use workhorses. There were an estimated 9.2 millions horses used for working, racing, competing, and OUTDOOR RECREATION in the United States in 2005.

Recent efforts focus on drawing the horse back into daily life among some people. "Equestrian communities" dot certain areas, particularly Virginia, North Carolina, and California. These "planned model communities" generally include a neighborhood centered around a riding stable, with arenas, show facilities, and extensive trails for riding, along with golf courses or other amenities. The Equestrian Land Conservation Resource leads the charge to develop these exclusive communities, citing fears of "losing" open space or the rural character of America as justifications. They have formed alliances with other CONSERVATION groups to develop their projects.

Horses have experienced varying tides of popularity within America. At first, an integral partner with humans in expansion, more extensive farming practices, and pollution of the urban environment, horses became obsolete for labor as gasoline-powered engines emerged. Recently, however, in addition to their use in recreation, some have begun to reintroduce horses in the living and working world of humans as a way to reduce pollution and human impact on the environment.

See also AGRICULTURAL TECHNOLOGY; AGRICULTURE, COMMERCIAL; AGRICULTURE, ORGANIC; ANIMALS, DOMESTICATED; GRASSES; HUNTING, SUBSISTENCE; INDIANS, CENTRAL PLAINS; INDIANS, NORTHERN PLAINS; PROGRESSIVISM; SPANISH EXPLORATION AND SETTLEMENT—FLORIDA AND THE SOUTH; SPANISH EXPLORATION AND SETTLEMENT—MEXICO AND TEXAS; SPANISH EXPLORATION AND SETTLEMENT—NEW MEXICO AND CALIFORNIA; SPECIES, EXOTIC; URBANIZATION; WASTE DISPOSAL AND MANAGEMENT.

Elizabeth D. Blum

Further Reading

McShane, Clay, and Joel Tarr. *The Horse in the City: Living Machines in the Nineteenth Century.* Baltimore: Johns Hopkins University Press, 2007.

Steinberg, Ted. *Down to Earth: Nature's Role in American History.* New York: Oxford University Press, 2002.

Tarr, Joel A. "The Horse—Polluter of the City." In *The Search for the Ultimate Sink: Urban Pollution in Historical Perspective.* Akron, Ohio: University of Akron Press, 1996.

White, Richard. "Animals and Enterprises." *Oxford History of the American West,* edited by Clyde A. Milner II, Carol A. Connor, and Martha A. Sandweiss. New York: Oxford University Press, 1994.

Letter from Mary Phelps Holley (December 1831)

In a series of subsequently published letters, Mary Phelps Austin Holley (1784–1846) described life in Texas during a visit to her cousin Stephen F. Austin's colony in 1831. The first book on Texas written in English, Holley's publication was credited with recruiting more American families to Texas, then a part of Mexico. Here she shared her observations of the Comanche, revealing how the Indians had adapted their society and economy to the horse.

❦

The Comanches are a noble race of Indians, inhabiting the country to the north and northwest of San Antonio de Bexar. They are a wandering race, do not cultivate the earth for corn, but depend altogether upon the chase for subsistence. They follow the immense herds of buffaloe which graze the vast plains of this region, often to the amount of thousands in one herd. These plains are also stocked with wild horses, which run together in droves of many hundreds. These wild horses are called, in the language of the country, *Mustangs,* and hence the figure of speech to denote any thing wild and uncultivated, as a mustang girl, applied to a rude hunter's daughter. These horses are not natives, but descended from the stock brought over by the first Spaniards. Domestic animals, and man himself, become rude, when removed from the associations of civilized life. The Comanches catch and tame these wild horses, and when unsuccessful in the chase, subsist upon them.

These Indians always move on horseback. Besides the bow and arrows, the usual arms of the Indian warrior, they are armed with a long spear, having a sword blade for the point. A war party of these mounted Indians is sufficiently formidable. They are headed by two squaws, who by their shrill voices, serve as trumpeters, and have, like them, various tones, to denote the different evolutions and movements. When they descry an object of attack, or pursuit, they dart forward in a column, like lightning, towards it. At a suitable distance from their prey, they divide into two squadrons, one half taking to the right, and the other to the left, and thus surround it.

Though fierce in war, they are civil in peace, and remarkable for their sense of justice. They call the people of the United States their friends, and give them protection, while they hate the Mexicans, and murder them without mercy.

❦

Source: Mary Phelps Holley. *Texas Observations, Historical, Geographical and Descriptive, in a Series of Letters Written during a Visit to Austin's Colony.* Baltimore: Armstrong & Plaskitt, 1833, 88–90.

household appliances

Households have always relied on tools to help complete tasks. The gourds of Native Americans or the one pot owned by many colonial families might not seem like an appliance, but they performed then what today's mechanical devices do in the home. The appliances of the 21st century are direct descendants of these more primitive tools, having changed significantly with technological advancements.

Prior to the Industrial Revolution, the majority of household helpers operated only with human energy. For example, the first aid for laundresses was the rather unimpressive washboard. Yet, this simple appliance, which required back-breaking work by its operator, was a welcome improvement over beating clothing on rocks in an open stream. From there, tub washers emerged—again these required someone to ensure that the agitator moved and dirt floated free of the fibers. It was not until greater access to nonhuman energy sources, electricity, oil, COAL, or other, that household equipment requiring little human power emerged.

As with most new technologies, early household appliances cost more than many budgets could afford. The first Singer sewing machine, for example, cost $100 at a time when the average annual family income was $500. In an effort to sell its products, Singer created a purchasing plan that permitted buying these coveted tools over time. This extension of credit significantly increased the consumption of these welcomed household helpers. Generally, the wealthy quickly adopted all types of technology, payment plan or not. Many upper-class households already employed domestics and realized that by purchasing a machine to do the work, they could not only be progressive in the adoption of technology but could save money in the long term. Slowly, ownership of appliances became a possibility for the middle class of populated portions of the United States, where there were significant disposable income and the utilities to operate the appliances.

During the early 20th century, there was great disparity between the use of appliances among rural and urban populations. In densely populated areas, electricity was available to operate both appliances and the equipment needed to get

Created at the turn of the century, this advertisement celebrates a century of sewing machine manufacturing. Today, the Singer Company is still in existence, based in La Vergne, Tennessee, near Nashville.   *(Library of Congress)*

water with the turn of a faucet. The reluctance of for-profit utility companies to pay for miles of high wires to reach isolated farms and small towns made modern living and household technologies impossible for rural people. Without electricity, women faced backbreaking work every day that included hauling water and sewing by the light of an oil lamp. The creation of the Rural Electrification Administration in 1935 made it possible for appliances such as irons and refrigerators to be parts of rural households. Although the extension of the high lines slowed because of WORLD WAR II (1941–45), by 1960, most rural homes had electric service, but in 1970, only 90 percent of rural homes had running water. This extension of utilities increased the overall consumption of household appliances and slowly brought consistency to the number of household chores completed with technical assistance. Even the environment in which families lived began to be altered because of these new appliances. Laundry rooms, for example, became a standard fixture in contemporary architecture and a purpose of remodeling many homes.

The growth and advocacy of government agencies and manufactures of the adoption of household appliances caused households to shift from a place of production to a place of consumption. Women slowly gave up their production and preservation of FOOD—purchasing goods found on the shelf of the local store replaced long-standing food preservation rituals. Women stopped sewing clothing in favor of buying ready-to-wear garments. These changes could also be found in the appliances available for purchases. The microwave, for example, permitted quick cooking and easily heated new convenience foods for the family on the go.

Historians and sociologists have demonstrated that, contrary to popular assumptions, increased access to appliances actually required that more time be devoted to housework. Certainly, the automatic washer has made doing laundry easier than the washboard or even the wringer washer run by electricity. However, the ease of operating the modern washer has resulted in the frequent changing of outfits and a higher expectation of cleanliness—causing increased use of water, electricity, and human time. Recently, hanging clothes on the line has become popular again as individuals attempt to reduce their use of clothes dryers. But this action has caused controversy in neighborhoods with restrictions against clotheslines and among neighbors who do not like the appearance of clothes drying on a line. In other efforts to lessen carbon footprints, utility companies have started bounty programs in which appliance owners receive a bounty to turn in their inefficient appliances and purchase energy star models.

Increased consumption of appliances from the basic to the mundane means more technological garbage. In the past, Americans gave little thought to disposing of broken electric can openers or a refrigerator. However, increased concern over how elements of discarded appliances such as hydrochlorofluorocarbon and chlorofluorocarbon affect the OZONE LAYER, MERCURY seeping into groundwater, and capacity of LANDFILLS has increased attention to what happens to appliances once they leave the home. Not only do governments at all levels have programs and guidelines for the disposal of waste appliances, but industry groups such as the Association of Home Appliance Manufacturers have implemented programs to encourage proper disposal. The success of these programs has resulted in "white goods" second only to old AUTOMOBILES as a source of scrap metals.

See also CARCINOGENS, TOXINS, AND POISONS; CONSUMERISM; ECOLOGICAL FOOTPRINTS; ENERGY, ELECTRICAL; HOUSING, PRIVATE; POLLUTION, WATER.

Sara E. Morris

Further Reading

Cowan, Ruth Schwartz. *More Work for Mother: The Ironies of Household Technology from the Open Hearth to the Microwave.* New York: Basic Books, 1983.

Hardyment, Christina. *From Mangle to Microwave: The Mechanization of Household Work.* Cambridge: Polity Press, 1988.

Strasser, Susan. *Never Done: A History of American Housework.* New York: Pantheon Books, 1982.

Vanek, Joann. "Household Technology and Social Status: Rising Living Standards and Status and Residence Differences in Housework." *Technology and Culture* 19, no. 3 (July 1978): 361–375.

housing, private

Private housing is physical dwelling spaces designed and constructed for habitation by individuals or family groups. In the United States, private housing has changed over time, reflecting differences in social class, race, ethnicity, and environment.

NATIVE AMERICA

In precontact North America, Native American concepts of communal property ownership and housing reflected the seasonal mobility that was a hallmark of many of the continent's indigenous peoples. Moving several times each year for purposes of planting, hunting, fishing, and gathering, Native Americans had dwellings, by necessity, that were easily taken apart, moved, and rebuilt. Women were largely responsible for constructing and moving these dwellings, which were made of natural materials, including tree bark, cut logs, and the skins of fur-bearing animals. Some groups, including the Iroquois Confederacy, lived in more fixed dwellings, including longhouses located in villages. Regardless, the mobility that was characteristic of most Native groups minimized their long-term impact on the natural environment because they left less of an ECOLOGICAL FOOTPRINT in any given area.

Archaeological evidence reveals that other Native Americans had at various times developed permanent settlements with extensive dwellings. The city of CAHOKIA began around 650 C.E. in the floodplain of the MISSISSIPPI RIVER in present-day Illinois and initially consisted of a number of small settlements. These followed a common pattern, with a central courtyard surrounded by houses and other structures. Excavations reveal that by 1000 C.E., with an increased population and a centralized government, these Indians built larger and more elaborate structures with the emergence of distinct, elite households. People lived in more centralized communities and constructed a defensive wall around the grand plaza in addition to Cahokia's distinctive mounds. Cahokia flourished for more than 650 years and was the largest city in the present-day United States until the 18th century. Residents abandoned Cahokia around 1400 C.E. as its large population overburdened local resources. For example, the population used copious amounts of wood to construct buildings and its defensive stockade and for fuel. This use of wood caused EROSION and increased flooding of the Indians' agricultural fields.

In the American Southwest, the Anasazi culture began building aboveground, multistoried mason structures in the eighth century C.E. After 500 years, erosion, DROUGHTS, soil salinity from prolonged IRRIGATION, and DEFORESTATION from pueblo construction contributed to the culture's decline. Most scholars believe the Anasazi became the ancestors of more recent southwestern Indians such as the Hopi, Zuni, and Pueblo.

COLONIAL AMERICA

The settlement of Europeans in North America, in the 17th century, introduced significant changes in ideas about property ownership and private housing. In the New England colonies, European notions of property, which stressed individual, private rights to land, prevailed and helped inform ideas about private housing as well. New Englanders designed and built their homes, intended for ownership and habitation by nuclear family groups, in permanent communities known as towns, which were often built on the sites of former Indian villages. The towns functioned as a means of social and political control for the Puritan elders. However, the ordered hierarchy that was a feature of Puritan society also found expression in their homes. Husbands and fathers were granted ownership of their homes and, by extension, of their families as well. Fathers and mothers often slept in the main room downstairs, while children slept in lofts, in garrets, and sometimes on the floor. Thus, the private home itself was a tool of patriarchal and social control. The environmental impact of the Puritan towns was much greater than that of their Indian neighbors. Countless acres of New England forest fell under the ax of Puritan home and town builders, for building materials, for fuel, and for fields to grow crops.

Private housing in the colonial Chesapeake was also designed and constructed for the purpose of habitation by nuclear family groups. However, in these more southern colonies, an important characteristic of southern private housing was the distinct lack of towns and communal living. Rather, fixed settlements known as PLANTATIONS became an important feature of European settlement in the CHESAPEAKE BAY area, in the 17th and 18th centuries. Plantations were settlements designed for the cultivation, production, and sale of TOBACCO and other agricultural commodities. At the center of these settlements, which often encompassed several hundred acres of cleared land, was a large multistory, multiroom home where the master and his family lived. These homes, though often constructed with local materials, especially lumber, were often filled with furniture and other fineries imported from Europe. In addition, parents and children often dwelled in separate rooms, and there were other rooms devoted to family dining, cooking, and entertaining. Many of the features of the European aristocracy, then, were transplanted and rebuilt in the Chesapeake plantations. The Chesapeake aristocracy's homes also served as symbols of the political and economic power they wielded in the region.

Much of the wealth that enabled southern planters to live in such luxury was derived from the labor of imported and native-born African slaves. Slave housing, though, was very different from that of their European masters. Many slaves lived in crude barracks constructed with wood boards and slept together on dirt floors. Some masters took away slave children and housed them all together in a single dwelling. On larger plantations, however, masters often allowed their slaves to live in nuclear family groups, where slave husbands, wives, and children were permitted to live together in crudely built cabins. There, living in one large room and sleeping on a dirt floor, slaves were allowed a small measure of autonomy. Slave parents used their cabins as a space to instill values and family history in their children and to develop marital and family bonds away from their masters. They often grew FOOD in adjoining gardens to supplement their meager diets. Older slaves often found themselves living inside the master's house and often sleeping inside closets or on kitchen floors, away from family and friends. Slave housing was never completely private, and ownership was circumscribed by the master's power and control.

Poor whites in the colonial South occupied a middle ground between the planter class and African slaves. Many poor whites squatted on lands in the mountainous and uninhabited parts of the South and, in many cases, rented or leased land from larger planters. Their private homes reflected their socioeconomic status. Many poor whites lived in conditions not much different from those of slaves, occupying rough-hewn shacks made of local materials and sleeping on dirt floors. Many poor whites were completely dependent on credit extended to them by the planters to move their goods to market, purchase seeds, and cultivate crops. Most poor whites therefore did not own slaves. Their impact on the environment was often quite destructive, as they scoured FORESTS and hillsides for food, fuel, and building materials. However, as did slaves, they lived in the shadow of the southern aristocracy.

THE NINETEENTH CENTURY: URBANIZATION, INDUSTRIALIZATION, AND IMMIGRATION

In the decades after the AMERICAN REVOLUTION (1775–83), the United States experienced three important social and economic shifts. The expansion of URBANIZATION, industrialization, and IMMIGRATION had important implications for further changes in the shapes, sizes, and textures of private housing. As rural populations exploded in the North after the Revolution, many farmers' children felt the tug of urban life and the region's cities boomed. At the same time, new technology that allowed the mass production of many goods once produced at home both provided unskilled men and women a new source of jobs and made life in the new industrial cities more livable. Finally, by the early to mid-19th century, waves of immigrants from northern and western Europe began arriving in the cities of the North, swelling their populations and providing a new source of labor for the region's burgeoning industries. All of these changes had a profound effect on private housing.

Urbanization, industrialization, and immigration helped to reshape the physical landscape of the Northeast's cities, in the first half of the 19th century. The rise of mass production factories helped engender a split between the workplace and the private home. Over time, workers, their employers, and their workplaces occupied separate neighborhoods within cities. The spatial layout of many cities was thus defined by social class differences. Managers and company officials often lived in nuclear family units in row houses or other private dwellings away from their workers' homes. Many urban upper-middle-class families construed the private home as a space where wives and mothers would raise children, perform domestic chores, and create a sanctuary for husbands and fathers to recharge after long days at the factory. Middle-class private housing, then, was designed to serve as an antidote to the ills and stresses of the urban industrial environment. With the development of MASS TRANSIT systems, a few middle-class suburbs began to emerge around the nation's major cities after the CIVIL WAR (1861–65).

Urban industrial workers, on the other hand, often lived in apartments or small houses located away from their employers. As lower-middle-class workers, often every family member, including wives, mothers, and children, was forced to work outside the home. Dwellings were often cramped apartments inhabited by nuclear families and extended kin. Crowded apartment buildings and TENEMENTS bred infectious disease, and quickly the urban environment in working-class neighborhoods became marked by the smell and sight of human waste, rotting food, deceased animal car-

casses, and piles of GARBAGE. With men, women, and children working dangerous jobs with long hours and low pay, and then returning to filthy, unsanitary, and cramped homes, many northern cities experienced public health crises in the mid- to late 19th century. A continual worsening of these conditions compelled public health reforms, which began in earnest in the decades after the Civil War, and these reforms transformed the nation's private housing.

The problems of the modern industrial city deepened in the late 19th century. The post–Civil War expansion of heavy industry was accompanied by a massive influx of "new immigrants" from southern and eastern Europe to the nation's cities. The growing population further exacerbated the already difficult problem of private housing and sanitation. With more men, women, and children cramped into an increasingly overcrowded housing stock, the public health crisis that had started earlier in the century intensified. Progressive reformers pushed city and state governments in the late 19th and early 20th centuries to build modern sewage and sanitation systems as part of an effort to clean up the urban environment. At first, only upper- and middle-class neighborhoods benefited from the construction of modern garbage and sewage removal systems. However, by the 1920s and 1930s, most American cities and states had sanitation and public health departments whose services were available to nearly all their residents. Repairing the public health crisis engendered by overcrowded private housing eased some of the burdens of living in modern industrial cities. However, neighborhoods segregated by race and social class, and cramped living conditions, persisted throughout the 20th century.

THE RISE OF PRIVATE HOMEOWNERSHIP AND SUBURBANIZATION

In 1920, the United States Census announced that for the first time, a majority of the American population lived in cities. Social, economic, and demographic shifts in the 1920s helped usher in important changes in private housing. As men and women moved into cities, they became more reliant on their jobs and paychecks for survival. The introduction of electricity into private homes, which accelerated during the 1920s, allowed city dwellers to enjoy the benefits of the new consumer economy and live a more comfortable life. Finally, more Americans moved out of apartments and into private homes, thanks to the expansion of mortgage financing and an increase in private home construction.

Many of these new homeowners owned AUTOMOBILES, which enabled many to move to the burgeoning suburbs and commute to work on the new parkways and highways. Suburban middle- and upper-class private housing was still centered on the nuclear family, though private homes in the early 20th century were much larger than their 19th-century counterparts. Parents and children often had separate bedrooms, with other rooms devoted to dining, cooking, bathing, and entertaining. The advent of the automobile made garages a new feature of many upper- and middle-class homes during this time. New suburbs replaced agricultural fields and FORESTS around the cities. Working-class and immigrant families, however, remained urban apartment dwellers, albeit with an improved standard of living.

The GREAT DEPRESSION that began in 1929 and stretched through much of the next decade caused one of the worst housing crises in U.S. history. Bank failures and rising unemployment caused hundreds of thousands of urban, suburban, and rural dwellers to lose their farms, land, and homes. New federal banking laws and financial regulations helped stabilize the financial system by the early 1930s, but through the decade, most of the nation's private housing stock fell into disrepair. Those who remained in their homes stopped making improvements, and dilapidated and abandoned homes often fell victim to vandalism and squatters. Many single-family homes suddenly had new occupants as homeless relatives, friends, and other kin moved in and "doubled up" with their more fortunate loved ones. For African Americans, most of whom lived in the South, the housing crisis during the depression only exacerbated long-standing problems. In the South, most African Americans were tenant farmers, sharecroppers, or domestic workers. Federal farm subsidy programs established under the Agricultural Adjustment Act of 1933 benefited only the largest planters and farmers, who often used their federal money to expand and mechanize, leaving tenants and sharecroppers homeless. While many African Americans moved north and west, the majority remained in the South, landless and homeless victims of the uncertainties of CAPITALISM.

The expansion of the industrial economy during and after WORLD WAR II (1941–45) generated another housing crisis. This time, however, there was not enough housing to meet demand. The problem began during the defense buildup, as 15,000,000 men and women went back to work, moving across the country for defense jobs. It became acute after the war, as millions of returning veterans began to look for jobs and new homes. The GI Bill of 1944 offered low-interest mortgages to returning veterans, and real estate developers and banks, eager to attract new clients, began a massive expansion of the mortgage market and the nation's suburbs.

The SUBURBANIZATION of the United States occurred at unprecedented rates in the 1950s and contributed to reshaping the nation's housing landscape. Postwar prosperity expanded the ranks of the middle class, and millions of middle- and upper-class urban dwellers left the cities to pursue the domestic ideal and American dream in the rapidly expanding suburbs. Discriminatory lending practices by banks and real estate developers prevented many nonwhite Americans from pursuing the suburban dream, and millions of African-American and Hispanic men and women became

trapped in rapidly decaying and crime-ridden urban centers. As the urban environment fell into decline, the natural environment on which the new suburban settlements sprouted also experienced significant changes. High demand led to rapid and sloppy construction practices, which had negative consequences in the years to come. Sanitation and sewage removal systems broke down very quickly, contaminating water supplies and sometimes flooding communities with human waste and garbage. The use of chemicals to remove insects and create perfect lawns sickened human beings and animal populations alike. And the increased use of automobiles contributed to snarled traffic and an explosion in carbon dioxide emissions. The suburban footprint on the natural environment, then, was a big one.

Private housing in the postwar American city also witnessed significant transformations as apartment dwellers in lower-middle-class neighborhoods often watched their homes fall victim to urban renewal projects. In NEW YORK CITY alone, the urban planner ROBERT MOSES's dream of a city laced with highways and bridges in the sky displaced hundreds of thousands of poor residents in the South Bronx, Brooklyn, and other areas. The ties of urban life, among private homes, small businesses, places of worship, and workplaces, were torn asunder by the high modernist visions and dreams of urban planners and real estate developers. By the late 20th century, many poor urban dwellers, especially nonwhite men and women, had been pushed out of the private housing market and into increasingly run-down and dangerous PUBLIC HOUSING projects across the country. For many, the urban environment conjured images of poverty, homelessness, filth, and decay.

CONCLUSION

In spite of differences based on social class, race, and ethnicity, private housing in North America, from the precontact period through the early 21st century, has largely been devoted to the survival and perpetuation of the nuclear family. However, designing and constructing these sanctuaries from the stresses and frustrations of the modern world have taken a significant toll on the nation's natural environment. The environmental movement of the past half-century has taken note of this impact, and the burgeoning green movement is attempting to reconcile Americans' demand for private housing with the need to protect the environment. It remains to be seen, however, whether the need to perpetuate the American dream of large nuclear family homes on ever-larger plots of land will be environmentally sustainable. Private housing itself may need to change significantly to make this accommodation.

See also CULT OF TRUE WOMANHOOD; DISEASES, HUMAN; ENGLISH EXPLORATION AND SETTLEMENT—CANADA AND NEW ENGLAND; ENGLISH EXPLORATION AND SETTLEMENT—THE SOUTH; HEALTH AND MEDICINE; INTERSTATE HIGHWAY

System; lawns; slave trade; squatting; sustainability; waste disposal and management

Clarence Jefferson Hall, Jr.

Further Reading

Beauregard, Robert. *Voices of Decline: The Postwar Fate of American Cities.* Cambridge, Mass.: Blackwell, 1993.

Caro, Robert. *The Power Broker: Robert Moses and the Fall of New York.* New York: Knopf, 1974.

Cronon, William. *Changes in the Land: Indians, Colonists, and the Ecology of New England.* New York: Hill & Wang, 1983.

Fischer, David Hackett. *Albion's Seed: Four British Folkways in America.* New York: Oxford University Press, 1989.

Hayden, Dolores. *Building Suburbia: Green Fields and Urban Growth, 1820–2000.* New York: Vintage, 2003.

Isaac, Rhys. *The Transformation of Virginia, 1740–1790.* New York: W. W. Norton, 1982.

Jackson, Kenneth. *Crabgrass Frontier: The Suburbanization of the United States.* New York: Oxford University Press, 1985.

Melosi, Martin. *The Sanitary City: Environmental Services in Urban America from Colonial Times to the Present.* Pittsburgh: University of Pittsburgh Press, 2008.

Rome, Adam. *The Bulldozer in the Countryside: Suburban Sprawl and the Rise of American Environmentalism.* Cambridge: Cambridge University Press, 2001.

Sugrue, Thomas. *The Origins of the Urban Crisis: Race and Inequality in Postwar Detroit.* Princeton, N.J.: Princeton University Press, 1996.

housing, public

Public housing is government-subsidized housing for low-income families. It was introduced in the 1930s, during Franklin D. Roosevelt's administration, to provide decent living conditions for the poor; to assuage conditions in decaying urban areas, particularly ghettos, slums, and barrios; and to provide jobs in depression era America. Since their inception, federal housing programs have undergone continual change. Although initially built to mitigate environmental concerns associated with urban blight and hailed as icons of architectural modernism, public housing projects soon became overwhelmed with their own problems and became symbols of "high-rise ghettos" that bred crime, poverty, and racism and discrimination. In the process, public housing altered the physical form of the cities and simultaneously changed the way Americans perceived the urban landscape.

Although federal housing projects commenced in the 1930s, they have roots in the Progressive Era Settlement House movement, which provided social and educational opportunities to the working class, many of whom were recent immigrants. Echoing Progressive Era social reformers, such as Jane Addams, who advocated raising living conditions of the poor, housing reformers during the Great Depression believed that the federal government ought to finance the elimination of slum conditions in the cities and construct new homes for the nation's impoverished. Housing reformers often denounced the physical unhealthiness of urban slums, citing their increased incidences of communicable diseases. In addition to housing reformers such as Edith Wood (1871–1945) and Catherine Bauer (1905–64), women's groups, minority organizations, and labor unions endorsed public housing.

The Public Works Administration (PWA), under Roosevelt's New Deal, pioneered government-funded housing. Its principal concern, however, was providing employment, rather than decent living accommodations. In 1937, Congress passed the Wagner-Steagall Act, which created the U.S. Housing Authority (USHA), replacing the PWA. The USHA financed slum clearance and the construction of low-cost housing. In addition, the Wagner-Steagall Act, named for its sponsors, Senator Robert F. Wagner (D-N.Y.) and Representative Henry B. Steagall (D-Ala.), declared public housing both a federal and a local government responsibility.

The physical form of early projects completed under the PWA and the USHA consisted of a monotonous cluster of minimalist low-rise apartment buildings or identical row houses. Instead of renovating existing dilapidated buildings, the public housing projects were new constructions built on former slum sites. These government-funded accommodations, however, were far superior to the slum dwellings they replaced. They boasted modern plumbing and household appliances. Private bathrooms for each family relieved the unsanitary conditions associated with the one toilet shared by several families in slum tenements. Most rooms in these new constructions contained windows that let in light and air, a luxury that many impoverished heretofore had not enjoyed. Public housing in these early years also offered low-income urban dwellers pleasantly landscaped surroundings, safer environments, a degree of open space, and play areas away from congested, blighted neighborhoods.

The advent of World War II (1941–45) temporarily shelved public housing programs. Government capital moved toward financing the war. The wartime economy based on military and defense spending attracted millions to urban centers looking for industrial job opportunities. After the war, Congress passed the Housing Act of 1949, which authorized the construction of 810,000 dwelling units until 1955. Although opponents managed to curtail annual funds over the next decade or so, by 1965, the public housing program had nearly 600,000 dwellings that housed more than two million persons.

After the war, residents of public housing also changed. Whereas prewar public housing tenants were largely working-class families, in the postwar years, dwellers were mostly welfare families. A majority of government-subsidized projects were all-black enclaves. Similarly to private

HOUSING, public accommodations became segregated. City housing authorities "reserved" certain projects for whites, such as Trumbull Park in CHICAGO, ILLINOIS. Plans for new public housing developments were limited to areas in which other public housing already existed. Locating all new developments in existing public housing and all-black areas caused many blacks to fear they would be "sealed" into their current ghettos. Most developments also were built near RAILROADS, factory and industrial districts, highways, traffic arteries, and other unfavorable locations. Many people lamented that the projects were designed to "contain" cities' undesirable, poor, and polyglot populations. Housing policies further polarized the wealthy and the poor, and whites and persons of color.

In addition to different tenants, the physical form of public housing transformed in the postwar era. To reduce costs, cities constructed rows of high-rise apartment buildings that housed more people for less money and occupied less space than clusters of low-rise structures. The dwellings quickly deteriorated, and crime and vandalism in the enclaves rose. The Robert Taylor Homes in Chicago, the largest public housing project undertaken, were disparaged by tenants as miserable and dangerous. The Pruitt-Igoe project in ST. LOUIS, MISSOURI, suffered a similar fate. Touted as the model for other cities, the Pruitt-Igoe buildings offered open galleries and communal spaces for their residents, described by project architects as "vertical neighborhoods." In addition, the areas between the rows of buildings were filled with trees and spaces for OUTDOOR RECREATION. A decade later, however, the vertical neighborhoods had changed to "vertical ghettos," and trash, drugs, and crime occupied the former pleasant outdoor spaces. Some residents argued that public housing cutbacks and inadequate maintenance by cities' housing authorities were the cause, while others claimed the sizes of the projects were too large to survive. At the same time, federal housing policies such as mortgage insurance, tax incentives, and highway building encouraged suburban sprawl but did little to alleviate the decaying central cities. As had the urban slums that they replaced, public housing became a symbol of physical unhealthiness, and the term *projects* became synonymous with crime, poverty, and overall negativity.

President LYNDON B. JOHNSON'S GREAT SOCIETY program created the DEPARTMENT OF HOUSING AND URBAN DEVELOPMENT (HUD) to address growing problems in urban areas. The Housing and Urban Development Act of 1965 allocated $2.9 billion for URBAN RENEWAL and public housing programs. Many of the programs, such as Model Cities, however, were overambitious and underfunded. Moreover, many later presidents' agendas had little sympathy for the urban programs of earlier years, leaving public housing to languish. In 1992, HUD introduced HOPE VI (Housing Opportunities for People Everywhere) to eliminate severely deteriorating public housing. Under this program, developments in decline have been renovated and also completely rebuilt.

Questions concerning public housing as an effective approach to eradicating poverty and environmental hazards, as in the past, resurfaced in the late 20th century. Opponents of public housing eschewed HOPE VI and other federal programs as simply entrenching a system that already forced the poor into decaying areas and into cycles of poverty. Whether espoused or opposed, public housing had, nonetheless, shaped the physical structure in and American perceptions of the urban landscape.

See also DISEASES, HUMAN; PROGRESSIVISM; SUBURBANIZATION; URBAN SPRAWL.

Jordan Bauer

Further Reading
Hirsch, Arnold R. *Making the Second Ghetto: Race and Housing in Chicago, 1940–1960*. Chicago: University of Chicago Press, 1998.
Hirsch, Arnold R., and Raymond A. Mohl, eds. *Urban Policy in Twentieth-Century America*. New Brunswick, N.J.: Rutgers University Press, 1993.
Teaford, Jon C. *The Twentieth-Century American City*. 2d ed. Baltimore: Johns Hopkins University Press, 1993.

Housing and Urban Development, Department of

Established on September 9, 1965, under President LYNDON B. JOHNSON, the United States Department of Housing and Urban Development (HUD) superseded the federal government's Housing and Home Finance Agency. HUD, the 11th executive department, gave federal housing and development programs cabinet-level priority for the first time. HUD has pursued a number of environmentally friendly programs yet hardly enough to offset the department's role in promoting residential sprawl.

Since its inception, HUD has overseen an extraordinary array of programs. It has worked with local governments in the construction of public and subsidized housing and has promoted homeownership through a variety of policies, including through its subsidiary, the Federal Housing Administration (FHA). It has had a hand in the wholesale creation of new communities in rural and suburban America, yet it has also helped raze large tracts of urban America, sometimes sparking the rejuvenation of previously struggling neighborhoods but often displacing thousands of local residents. In addition, HUD also runs the federal government's housing programs for Native Americans and has cooperated in financing many local public works projects, ranging from the expansion of suburban gas and sewer systems to the construction of local jails.

HUD has found itself drawn into some of the most heated political debates of recent decades, including disputes over the federal government's responsibility to the poor and the balance of power among federal, state, and local governments. Accusations of HUD's inefficiency, even corruption, have sparked further controversy—enough to fill a volume dedicated solely to the topic: Irving Welfeld's *HUD Scandals: Howling Headlines and Silent Fiascoes* (1992).

Perhaps the most famous and consequential scandals surrounding HUD occurred just years after its establishment, when exposure of corruption in the federal government's leading GREAT SOCIETY housing programs coincided with one of the most evocative and widely publicized images of the failure of U.S. housing policy up to that point: the 1972 demolition of St. Louis's Pruitt-Igoe housing project. Designed by the famous architect Minoru Yamasaki (1912–86), who also designed the World Trade Center in NEW YORK CITY, the housing project, completed in 1955, quickly fell into decay. Although a Missouri court decision in 1956 desegregated public housing, whites chose not to move into the 33 11-story towers located in a predominantly African-American neighborhood. At its highest, occupancy only reached 60 percent and soon began to dip. Poverty and crime were pervasive. By the end of the 1960s, only 600 residents remained in 17 buildings. The other 16 were boarded up. The failure at Pruitt-Igoe became an icon in debates about public housing.

These controversies sparked President RICHARD NIXON's announcement, in January 1973, that he would make the highly unusual move of placing a moratorium on all housing and community development programs to allow for the reassessment of federal government policy. The resulting Housing and Community Development Act of 1974 reordered HUD programs and remains the backbone of federal housing and redevelopment policy today. Rooted in Nixon's "New Federalism," with its belief in local control, and in a turn toward market-based ideology, two programs formed the new HUD's core. The Community Development Block Grant (CDBG) program bundled funding for a number of previously separate federal programs and gave local governments significantly more discretion in spending federal funds. The Section 8 program put a new emphasis on federal involvement in the demand side of low-income housing. Instead of primarily promoting the expansion of housing supply by encouraging the construction of new projects, as federal policy had previously, the federal government would now dramatically expand its subsidization of rental payments in already existing privately owned units. Although often forgotten, the original Section 8 made provisions for new construction, a policy gutted in the 1980s, when the federal government almost completely abandoned the construction and subsidization of new housing units.

The 1974 act marked the beginning of a period of retreat in federal involvement in housing and development issues. Although funding for programs such as Section 8 inched upward in the late 1970s under President JIMMY CARTER, these increases were quickly undone under his successor, RONALD REAGAN, who dramatically slashed funding in the 1980s for programs like Section 8 and, to a lesser extent, CDBG, along with federal funding to the poor in general. The administration of BILL CLINTON produced a brief renaissance of HUD in the 1990s, especially through HOPE VI, a program providing funds for the replacement of high-rise public housing with single-family, suburban-style developments. The Clinton administration also brought to fruition a new phase in public-private partnership in community development through the Enterprise Zone/Empowerment Community (EZ/EC) programs, which use tax incentives, among other mechanisms, to promote recovery in depressed rural and urban areas. While these programs continue, the administration of GEORGE W. BUSH in the early 2000s was characterized by Reagan era hostility toward HUD.

Throughout its history, HUD has made a handful of attempts to promote environmentally friendly policies. On the most basic level, all HUD programs must meet federally mandated environmental standards. In addition, HUD operated an open space and beautification program as early as 1965. It has also made attempts to promote regional planning and better land use and has sponsored educational forums to raise awareness of the environmental impact of rapid SUBURBANIZATION. Currently, HUD administers a program to reclaim industrial BROWNFIELDS. Yet despite these initiatives, HUD has also consistently promoted suburbanization and, along with many other federal agencies, has helped spawn one of the gravest environmental problems of our time: the overconsumption of land and energy rooted in an accelerating and dangerous rate of residential sprawl.

See also ENVIRONMENTAL JUSTICE; FEDERALISM; HOUSING, PUBLIC; NATIONAL ENVIRONMENTAL POLICY ACT (NEPA) OF 1969; PLANNING, URBAN AND REGIONAL; PUBLIC WORKS; ST. LOUIS, MISSOURI; URBAN RENEWAL; URBAN SPRAWL.

Daniel Amsterdam

Further Reading

Bauman, John F., et al., eds. *From Tenements to the Taylor Homes: In Search of an Urban Housing Policy in Twentieth Century America.* University Park: The Pennsylvania State University Press, 2000.

Hays, R. Allen. *The Federal Government and Urban Housing: Ideology and Change in Public Policy.* Albany: State University of New York Press, 1985.

Rome, Adam. *The Bulldozer in the Countryside: Suburban Sprawl and the Rise of American Environmentalism.* New York: Cambridge University Press, 2001.

Vale, Lawrence J. *Reclaiming Public Housing: A Half Century of Struggle in Three Public Neighborhoods.* Cambridge, Mass.: Harvard University Press, 2002.

Welfeld, Irving. *HUD Scandals: Howling Headlines and Silent Fiascoes.* New Brunswick, N.J.: Transaction, 1992.

Houston, Texas

Houston, Texas, also known as the Bayou City and the Energy Capital of the World, is located 60 miles north of the GULF OF MEXICO and about 100 miles west of the Texas-Louisiana border. With a population exceeding two million, it is the largest city in Texas and fourth largest in the United States. Bayous snake through the flat coastal terrain within the city's 619-square-mile boundaries. Surrounding the sprawling city, layers of suburbs and small towns further increase Houston's reach. In 1836, when the brothers Augustus (1806–64) and John Allen (1810–38) founded the city, it was nothing more than a few scattered homesteads. The brothers drew a grid for the future city off Buffalo Bayou and promoted it as an important trading nexus and future metropolis in the fledgling Republic of Texas. The city was named after Sam Houston (1793–1863), president of Texas. Since that time, city leaders have strategically used all of Houston's natural resources to promote the growth, economic reach, and national and international importance of the city, particularly in relation to the oil and NATURAL GAS industries.

HISTORICAL OVERVIEW

From its infancy, commerce formed the base of Houston's economy. Because of its proximity to the fertile Brazos River valley, COTTON quickly became the most important raw good traded through the city. COTTON's dominance lasted through the early 20th century. Unlike the island city of Galveston, the nearest metropolitan rival, some 50 miles to the southeast, Houston lacked a natural port. Early Houstonians, however, overcame this difficulty by utilizing Buffalo Bayou to transport goods and compete with Galveston. The city's proximity to the cotton fields enhanced its competitive advantage over Galveston, but significant developments loomed on the horizon.

The vast oil fields discovered in the early 20th century near Houston drastically altered the city's economic future. Petroleum quickly upstaged the cotton economy. People entered from across America to capture and capitalize on the newly found resource. Many moved to Houston to live and work away from the hectic, dirty, and sometimes violent boomtowns that surrounded the oil fields. These migrations encouraged the development of industries in Houston that supported oil production and OIL REFINING.

Buffalo Bayou finally met the dreams of Houston's commercial sector at the turn of the 20th century. After almost a decade of minor improvements, Houston received federal funding to create a proper interior route for oceangoing vessels to deliver freight to Houston. City boosters brought the Houston Ship Channel into being, funded by the U.S. government. It opened on November 10, 1914, and signaled the end of any urban competition with Galveston, which had not recovered from the devastation and loss of 8,000 to 12,000 lives in the 1900 hurricane. The discovery of oil in East Texas had made it an important shipping port, and it remains one of the largest ports in the United States in the 21st century. Under the influence of the Houston politician and entrepreneur Jesse Jones (1874–1956) and other oilmen, WORLD WAR II (1941–45) generated extensive expansion of Houston's petrochemical manufacturing complex, much of it along the Ship Channel.

For most of the 20th century, Houston's economy drew mainly on oil-related business, but through the influence of the city's boosters, the close of the century saw Houston with a diversified economy. Today, Houston remains the "Energy Capital of the World," but it is also home to the Texas Medical Center, one of the finest medical complexes in the world, and a wide variety of industrial and financial activities.

WATER AND WASTE ISSUES

As with most cities, water management played an important role in the city's environmental history. Prior to the 1880s, Houstonians depended on bayous generally and the Buffalo Bayou in particular for their water and sewerage needs. This mixed-use system proved disastrous. WATER POLLUTION and inadequate waterworks systems made the water undrinkable and unsatisfactory for firefighting. In the 1880s, Houstonians finally tapped into the aquifer beneath the city for municipal water service. However, the underground water solution did not last long. Houston's growing population and industrial demands drastically reduced the pressure of water from the aquifer. Additionally, overuse of AQUIFERS led to subsidences, up to 10 feet in some cases, in parts of the city. In 1944, the city began searching for funding to dam part of the San Jacinto River north of the city. This aboveground source of water has fed many industrial complexes along the Ship Channel in addition to serving municipal needs.

Houston's climate, low water table, and proximity to the Gulf of Mexico have made FLOODS a constant issue for the city's inhabitants. In the 19th century, poor construction and a lack of sewers turned the city streets into small waterways during thunderstorms and rainy seasons. At the turn of the century, street design improved. However, in the 20th century, the concrete-covered surface area of the city also helped to reduce the land's capacity to absorb rain. To address the problem, the city began building storm sewers, around the beginning of the 20th century, but construction repeatedly lagged behind needs. This trend prevailed into the 21st century. Tropical Storm Allison, in June 2001, flooded much of the city and caused extensive damage. The storm also killed 23 people in Texas.

Sewage disposal in and other pollution of the bayous have been other long-standing water problems in Houston. The first sewerage plan, developed in 1866, included three main lines that drained into Buffalo Bayou. Since Buffalo Bayou was the city's source for DRINKING WATER, the system required updating within a few decades. The city developed a second plan in the 1880s, but with budget restraints, implementation of a complete system was not possible. Increasing pollution in Buffalo Bayou and pressure from the federal government, which threatened to withhold funding for the Ship Channel, compelled city leaders to find a new system. The city created a plan to remove sewage to a modern filter beds system for treatment. In 1917, a state law went into effect preventing dumping of untreated sewage into waterways.

Houstonians disposed of solid wastes, or GARBAGE from residences and businesses, in the 19th century, through the services of a city scavenger, who in a time before organized garbage services removed from garbage those items that could be reused or sold, leaving the food scraps for animals or decomposition on the streets. Toward the end of the century, the city switched to private collection services that removed the waste to open dumps. However, because of the hot, humid climate, dumps proved to be an inadequate option as Houston grew. The city turned to INCINERATION to dispose of waste more quickly and inexpensively. The incinerators caused significant AIR POLLUTION, but given persistent RACISM AND DISCRIMINATION, the city did not immediately address this issue because most of the incinerators were located in nonwhite neighborhoods. By the mid-20th century, with Houston's growth, incinerator pollution became a problem for the larger population, and the incinerators themselves could no longer effectively handle the city's solid waste. The city gradually switched to sanitary LANDFILLS. The city abandoned most of the incinerators by the 1960s but did not demolish them.

TRANSPORTATION

Because Houston is a commercial city, the facilitation of transportation has been a long-term issue of importance for city government. The city tried to implement several different designs and materials for regional ROADS during the 19th century, but they were rarely successful because of the low-lying, boggy terrain. Transporting goods to and through Houston was a challenging process. Massive construction of RAILROADS improved this process, and by the end of the 19th century, Houston was the meeting place of 13 railroads.

At this time, Houstonians launched a streetcar network that helped create the city's first suburbs. In the early 20th century, however, Houstonians accepted AUTOMOBILES as their primary choice for transportation, and they quickly supplanted the streetcar. Highways built after World War II helped end the reign of the railroad in Houston. By 2009, Houston possessed an extensive highway system including two loops within the city limits and a third stretching around the edges of the metropolitan area. The solution to the resultant traffic congestion on the city's highways most commonly offered has been simply to widen highways reaching into the suburbs. The city's MASS TRANSIT system, the Metropolitan Transit Authority (METRO), created in 1979, primarily provides bus service within city limits. In 2004, METRO's first attempt at light rail opened for business. The current route is extremely limited in scope and service. It is merely a preview for the extensive mass transit systems METRO has planned to combat traffic and pollution, although its construction has been delayed for many years.

LAND USE

Augustus and John Allen, the city founders, had been real estate developers. They helped launch a tradition of unrestricted private development that has continued throughout the city's history. Houston is the largest unplanned city in the United States. Until 1905, the city limits were nine square miles. At that point, Houston began the process of annexation that took it to its current massive size. The city began small, first acquiring the Heights, a local streetcar suburb. Over time, the annexations became more ambitious. By 1948, the city quadrupled its size. Just eight years later, it again quadrupled in size. The city officials chose annexation as a strategy to acquire newly developing suburbs' property taxes and to prevent competition for local industry and housing developments. Houston became the dominant city in the region, but without any controls on growth or city planning, real estate developers had free reign to develop when, where, and what they wanted. Houston, a sprawling city with a scattered and sprawling suburban landscape, contained many acres of undeveloped land inside the city, a declining core, and a flourishing fringe. Houston today possesses multiple city centers accessible primarily by automobile.

CONCLUSION

Houston is one of the nation's most polluted cities. The expansive road system and almost complete reliance on the automobile combined with a large industrial sector (particular the petrochemical industry) to create air pollution that became very noticeable and distressing in the 1940s. With the city lacking strong antipollution regulations, the problem continued through the rest of the century, until initiatives to relieve it began in the 1990s. Water continued to be a challenge in the city. By the 1960s, the Texas Water Quality Administration labeled the Ship Channel one of the most polluted bodies of water in the United States and created the Gulf Coast Waste Disposal Authority to help clean up industrial waste in the channel. In addition, the city of Houston again reformed its sanitation practices to meet new water control standards.

From its infancy, Houston has been a probusiness city. City benefactors working outside and alongside city government have used their commercial, political, and personal influence to build and modernize the city. Their accomplishments in large part created today's Houston. They tied the city's fortunes to the nation's oil and gas industries and saw Houston emerge as a global energy metropolis. However, the influence of these industries throughout the city's history has blocked the passage of comprehensive city planning, pollution control, and improvement of city services in favor of commercial interests.

See also ENVIRONMENTAL JUSTICE; HURRICANES; INTERSTATE HIGHWAY SYSTEM; UNITED STATES—GULF COAST; WASTE DISPOSAL AND MANAGEMENT.

Stephanie Fuglaar

Further Reading

McComb, David G. *Houston: A History.* Austin: University of Texas Press, 1981.

Melosi, Martin. *Effluent America: Cities, Industry, Energy and the Environment.* Pittsburgh: University of Pittsburgh Press, 2001.

Melosi, Martin, and Joseph Pratt, eds. *Energy Metropolis: An Environmental History of Houston and the Gulf Coast.* Pittsburgh: University of Pittsburgh Press, 2007.

Platt, Harold L. *City Building in the New South: The Growth of Public Services in Houston, Texas 1830–1910.* Philadelphia: Temple University Press, 1983.

Thomas, Robert D., and Richard W. Murray. *Progrowth Politics: Change and Governance in Houston.* Berkeley, Calif.: IGS Press, 1991.

Hoyt, Minerva (1866–1945) *conservationist*

Minerva Hamilton Hoyt was one of America's greatest champions of desert conservation. She became a recognized GARDENS AND GARDENING enthusiast in the first decades of the 20th century and fought for the recognition and protection of desert environments and native vegetation in the American West during the 1920s and 1930s. In the NEW DEAL era, Hoyt gained the support of President FRANKLIN D. ROOSEVELT for her greatest accomplishment: the creation of Joshua Tree National Monument near San Bernardino, California.

In the first decades of her life, Minerva Hamilton seemed an unlikely proponent of desert conservation. She was born on a Mississippi plantation in 1866 to a wealthy southern family and attended finishing schools and music conservatories. Hamilton entered the American West only through her marriage to Dr. Sherman Hoyt, who moved his family first to New York and later to Southern California, in the late 19th century. In her new Pasadena area home, Minerva Hamilton Hoyt became deeply involved in local philanthropic causes and developed an enthusiasm for gardening. As a result of the knowledge of local plant life gained through gardening and frequent family trips to the desert, she developed a deep appreciation for the beauty of the desert environment and became an avid supporter of desert CONSERVATION. After the death of her husband and infant son in 1918, Hoyt's attachment to the desert became even more pronounced. She took frequent trips to the desert, which served as her place of comfort and quiet reflection.

Conservationists such as Hoyt were deeply troubled by new developments resulting from the spread of AUTOMOBILES and roads in the 1920s, which threatened to destroy the fragile desert ecosystem. The desert became a popular destination for motorists eager for the thrill of driving and sightseeing. Visitors to the desert frequently uprooted indigenous plants to take home as souvenirs to decorate their homes and gardens. Even more troubling was the popular trend to light Joshua trees ablaze as torches to guide drivers traveling through the desert at night. By 1930, many desert regions, once home to trees, yuccas, and cacti, were nearly picked bare of vegetation.

In the 1920s and 1930s, Minerva Hamilton Hoyt fought to raise the profile of American deserts and bring to light the wanton destruction of desert environments. She organized several successful exhibitions of desert plant life in cities such as NEW YORK CITY and BOSTON, MASSACHUSETTS. Hoyt and other concerned conservationists established the International Deserts Conservation League. As its first president, Hoyt guided the league in its support of national parks to protect desert environments. Additionally, the noted architect FREDERICK LAW OLMSTED, JR., recruited Hoyt to serve on a new California state commission to make proposals for new STATE PARKS. From 1928 to 1932, Hoyt and fellow conservationists petitioned the NATIONAL PARK SERVICE several times and insisted that the area south of Twenty-nine Palms in the vicinity of San Bernardino become a federal park. In the midst of THE GREAT DEPRESSION, President HERBERT HOOVER's administration showed little enthusiasm for Hoyt's desert conservation agenda.

Hoyt, however, found an enthusiastic ally in President Franklin D. Roosevelt upon his elevation to the White House in 1933. She gained additional support from Roosevelt's secretary of the interior, HAROLD ICKES. In an effort to create jobs and revive the American economy through his New Deal, Roosevelt lent a sympathetic ear to Hoyt's cause and agreed to establish Joshua Tree National Monument in the vicinity of San Bernardino, California. Although the initial recommendation called for a park encompassing more than a million acres of land, a conflict with preexisting RAILROADS and MINING claims forced the president to scale down the original plans to 825,000 acres of desert environment. President Roosevelt officially established Joshua Tree National Monument through a presidential proclamation signed on August 10, 1936.

Through her conservation efforts in the early 20th century, Minerva Hamilton Hoyt successfully raised the national profile of desert environments in the American West and drew attention to the environmental destruction of those fragile ECOSYSTEMS. Her agenda became an integral component of Franklin Roosevelt's New Deal program and job creation initiatives. Although Hoyt is best remembered for her role in the creation of Joshua Tree National Monument, she also labored on behalf of the broader desert ecosystem in the first decades of the 20th century. As a result of her tireless efforts in support of desert protection, Hoyt earned the nickname "Apostle of the Cactus." She died in 1945.

See also ANTIQUITIES ACT OF 1906; PRESERVATION; UNITED STATES—CALIFORNIA; UNITED STATES—SOUTHWEST; WILDERNESS.

Jason Hostutler

Further Reading

Sellars, Richard Wade. *Preserving Nature in Natural Parks: A History.* New Haven, Conn.: Yale University Press, 1999.

Thomas, Rick. *South Pasadena.* Charleston, S.C.: Arcadia, 2007.

Waite, Vickie, et al. *Twenty-Nine Palms.* Charleston, S.C.: Arcadia, 2007.

Zarki, Joe. "Joshua Tree National Park: A Park for Minerva." National Park Service. Available online. URL: http://www.nps.gov/jotr/historyculture/mhoyt.htm. Accessed July 23, 2006.

Hudson River

No river has made as large an impact on the history of the eastern United States as the majestic Hudson River. It is a river of paradoxes—both a free-flowing mountain stream and a lazy brackish estuary. It is a river of immense BIODIVERSITY, as well as an industrial engine.

The Hudson River system consists of several tributaries that combine to drain close to 5,000 square miles of the state of New York. Only 315 miles long, it is a relatively short river, but within this diminutive distance, it varies from a rushing mountain stream to a long tidal basin. The view from the river changes from the picturesque waterfalls of the Adirondack Mountains and the Upper Hudson River valley to the daunting cliffs of the Palisades and the skyscrapers of the island of Manhattan.

From the headwaters in the Adirondacks, the river descends rapidly. For most of the river's history, it was a free-flowing stream. However, since the 19th century, when the Hudson reached the town of Fort Edward some 200 miles north of NEW YORK CITY, it has been stifled with dams and locks. Nineteenth-century industrialists dammed the river to utilize the energy of its rapid waters to power their mills, control FLOODS, and foster transportation. The river remains bound by DAMS and locks from Fort Edward until the confluence of the Mohawk River and Hudson River at the city of Troy, New York. Thereafter, the river takes on a completely different character.

The Lower Hudson is a 154-mile portion that stretches from Troy to New York City. Here it resembles more of an estuary than a river because the current diminishes severely. An estuary is the lower, wider part of a river where its current is met by ocean tides. Estuaries are affected by marine influences such as tides, waves, and salinity, and riverine influences such as freshwater flows and sediment. On the Hudson River, the water moves so slowly that ebb tides sometimes flow all the way upriver to Albany, making the river highly saline. It is also through this stretch that the Hudson reaches its deepest points. As it passes through the rising mountains known as the Highlands, the river reaches depths of close to 200 feet. Residents and tourists have recognized this area for its staggering beauty, and the state of New York protects it through the Palisades park system. New York Harbor stands at the confluence of the Atlantic Ocean, Harlem River, and Hudson River. This natural port is the result of river and glacial EROSION, and it has been the hub of transportation and trade for centuries.

The Hudson River offers a biologically diverse landscape. Along most areas of the river today are mainly oak FORESTS, but at one time the landscape boasted stands of chestnut trees before DEFORESTATION and the CHESTNUT BLIGHT wiped them out. The aquatic life is still considerable despite industrial, agricultural, and municipal WATER POLLUTION. Sea sturgeons and striped bass are among the most important FISH in the river. However, the estuary has not served as a significant commercial fishery for more than 100 years.

Humans have lived alongside the Hudson River for thousands of years. Native American groups were present along the river in some capacity since at least 4000 B.C.E., and Europeans first sailed the Hudson in the 1500s. By that time, there were between 40,000 and 60,000 Native Americans living in the area. After the voyages of Henry Hudson, for whom the river is named, in 1609, Dutch settlers first settled in Manhattan in the early 1600s in order to exploit the FUR TRADE, and the British took control of the colony in 1664. Native Americans joined the Europeans in the fur trading economy, and together they severely damaged the animal populations along the Hudson. By the early 19th century, most of the indigenous animals that provided fur no longer resided in the area.

In the 17th and 18th centuries, colonists developed agricultural lands along the Hudson. In the next century, however, humans turned large portions of the estuary into a river of industry. The Hudson and its tributaries served as one of the nation's most important conduits for trade after engineers dammed and canalized the majority of the upper stream. Along the banks, industries and communities dotted the landscape, contributing sewage and industrial wastes in vast amounts. Some of the more damaging pollution was from paper mills, foundries, oil refineries, electrical service companies, and nuclear power plants. A particularly damaging agent, polychlorinated biphenyls (PCBs), entered the watershed and forced significant remediation activity. PCBs, once used by power companies as dielectric fluids in transformers and capacitors, are carcinogenic in humans and animals and are as persistent as DDT (dichlorodiphenyltrichloroethane) in the food chain.

In 1965, Storm King Mountain on the west bank of the Hudson River, just south of the town of Cornwall on Hudson, New York, and some miles 65 miles north of New York City, became the center of a heated environmental debate. The mountain, which had been a frequent subject for participants in the HUDSON RIVER SCHOOL of painting, was selected by the utility company Consolidated Edison to become the site of a pump storage power generator with transmission lines. The company proposed to cut away part of the mountain during construction. Local activists filed a lawsuit to halt construction, arguing that aesthetic considerations should be considered in such projects. In 1979, the company abandoned the project.

This litigation also highlighted a number of environmental problems. Until the 1960s, untreated sewage, including industrial wastes, flowed from Albany, New York City, and other major urban and industrial areas at alarming rates. Since that time, the river has made a comeback from a severely polluted condition. More communities began to treat their sewage. Additionally, many industries no longer operate along the Hudson, traffic has diminished significantly, and recreational boating has taken the place of trade along the canalized portions. The river remains picturesque in many places despite its industrial heritage, and the Hudson still evokes pastoral reminiscences.

See also BEAVER; CANALS; CARCINOGENS, POISONS, AND TOXINS; DUTCH COLONIAL SETTLEMENTS; ENERGY, HYDRAULIC; ENGLISH EXPLORATION AND SETTLEMENT—THE MIDDLE COLONIES; GLACIERS; INDIANS, NORTHEAST; OIL REFINING; RIVER TRANSPORTATION.

Joseph Stromberg

Further Reading

Boyle, Robert. *The Hudson River: A Natural and Unnatural History.* New York: W. W. Norton, 1979.

Tarr, Joel A. *The Search for the Ultimate Sink: Urban Pollution in Historical Perspective.* Akron, Ohio: University of Akron Press, 1996.

Hudson River school

The Hudson River school was the first group of distinctly American landscape painters; their works spanned the period between 1820 and 1880. These artists drew upon artistic techniques from Europe but used these styles in new ways through painting subjects inspired by natural scenery and the history of the United States. Many of the Hudson

River school painters lived and painted in the Hudson River valley, particularly in NEW YORK CITY.

ORIGINS AND INFLUENCES

The Hudson River school's artists focused on landscape art, which is the artist's interpretation of nature or natural scenery. These artists drew inspiration from European landscape painting. Early landscape painters who influenced the Hudson River school style included the 17th-century Italian painter Salvator Rosa (1615–73) and the French artist Claude Lorrain (ca 1600–82). In the 18th and 19th centuries, English landscape painters such as John Constable (1766–1837) and J. M. W. Turner (1775–1851) focused on the portrayal of light, sky, clouds, and atmosphere and their effects on natural landscapes.

European artists and their American counterparts found inspiration for their depictions of nature in romantic aesthetics. These ideas, from the British writers Edmund Burke (1729–97) and William Gilpin (1724–1804), offered the means through which to explain and examine an observer's relationship to nature. The first was the idea of the Sublime, where nature inspired awe, terror, and a sense of vastness and of magnificence. The second idea was of the Beautiful, which focused on a characteristic smallness and smoothness of form. The final idea, the Picturesque, suggested ruggedness and rustic landscapes. Landscape art was meant to convey the emotional reaction of the artist to nature and to inspire the same sort of reaction in the viewer.

THE HUDSON RIVER SCHOOL AND NATURE

While the first depictions of the American landscape were in the form of maps or William Bradford's 1620 dismal musings about Cape Cod's not very welcoming "howling wilderness," by the early decades of the 19th century, the image of the American WILDERNESS, now seen as more promising, became important for another reason. Since the United States was a new nation without a "past" familiar to Europeans, there was a desire to find, or create, a past, as well as to demonstrate how the United States was the equal of Great Britain and other European countries. Lacking European castles and cathedrals, Americans instead turned to scenic places such as NIAGARA FALLS, the northeastern mountains, and, later, the dramatic landscapes of the West and Southwest to provide a monumental and historic landscape that was uniquely American. In John Vanderlyn's (1775–1852) *Niagara Falls from Table Rock* (1801–02), for example, the grand and majestic falls dwarf the American Indian figures included in the painting.

Thomas Cole's (1801–48) ability to reflect these ideas offered a model for American landscape painting that influenced many of the members of the Hudson River school. Credited as the school's founder, the English-born Cole began his painting career along the Hudson River and in New England.

Cole's paintings were among the first landscapes to draw the viewer into the American wilderness, as it was depicted on his canvases. His *A View of the Mountain Pass Called the Notch in the Mountains* (1839) represents the intense and sublime beauties of nature through dramatic storm clouds and mountain peaks. Cole also includes a human figure on horseback as well as evidence of human habitation in the forbidding mountain valley. As he saw them, the dramatic natural settings he painted were God's work, and he reflected sadly in his writings upon encroaching human development in the almost sacred American wilderness.

Other writers and artists believed that the people of the United States had a special mission that helped to define them and their country's natural splendors and resources. This idea, MANIFEST DESTINY, was the belief that the United States's territorial expansion across the North American continent was inevitable and sanctioned by God. Artists such as Asher Durand (1796–1886), Frederick Church (1826–1900), and Albert Bierstadt (1830–1902), whose styles reflected and advanced that of Cole, painted their interpretations of the Hudson River valley but went much farther into the newly acquired interior territory of the United States as well. At a New York art gallery, exhibitions of these painters were well attended, and their paintings became popular with a new capitalist elite in eastern cities.

Durand was one of Cole's pupils, and he reinforced his teacher's ideas about the importance of reflecting God's glory when painting nature. As a result, many of Durand's paintings represent monumental aspects of nature. Yet, these paintings also draw the viewer even more completely into the wilderness landscape by excluding much of the artist's own emotional reaction to nature from the painting. Durand's *Kaaterskill Cove* (1866), which depicts a favorite Catskill Mountain location used by many Hudson River school painters, contains many of the same elements as Cole's paintings, but the effects of clouds, trees, boulders, and distant hills are treated more naturally, although not with photographic realism.

Church's *Niagara* (1857) demonstrated even more completely the ability of Hudson River school painters to draw observers into the landscape. Unlike Vanderlyn's earlier representation of Niagara Falls from afar, Church's viewpoint is from almost on top of the falls themselves. The detail of the water as it rushes over the falls offers a powerful and dramatic effect.

Equally dramatic representations of nature could be seen in the works of the German-born painter Albert Bierstadt. Bierstadt became famous for his monumental paintings of western landscapes. His *A Storm in the Rocky Mountains—Mount Rosalie* (1866) drew upon his trip through the western territories in 1863. Approaching dark storm clouds offer a dramatic background to equally

This oil-on-canvas painting, *Indian Pass,* was painted in 1847 by Thomas Cole (1801–48).   *(Thomas Cole, Courtesy of the Museum of Fine Arts, Houston)*

dramatic mountainsides that frame a lake, a forest, and an American Indian camp.

DECLINE AND SIGNIFICANCE OF THE HUDSON RIVER SCHOOL

The CIVIL WAR (1861–65), the increasingly widespread use of photography, and the influence of changing painting styles from France, including impressionism, led to increasing criticism and decline in popularity of the Hudson River school. The artistic developments of the school, however, remain an important reflection of the development of a cultural ideal that represented the growing sense of a new and distinct American identity closely intertwined with the natural beauty of the United States and with what was seen to be its ordained destiny of prosperity and success.

See also LANDSCAPE ART, AMERICAN; ROMANTICISM; TRANSCENDENTALISM.

Kimberly A. Jarvis

Further Reading

Barringer, Tim. "The Course of Empires: Landscape and Identity in America and Britain, 1820–1880." In Andrew Wilton and Tim Barringer, *American Sublime: Landscape Painting in the United States 1820–1880.* Princeton, N.J.: Princeton University Press, 2002.
Howat, John K., ed. *American Paradise: The World of the Hudson River School.* New York: Henry N. Abrams, 1988.
Milhouse, Barbara Babcock. *American Wilderness: The Story of the Hudson River School.* Hensonville, N.Y.: Black Dome Press, 2007.
Miller, Angela. "The Fate of Wilderness in American Landscape Art: The Dilemmas of 'Nature's Nation.'" In *American Wilderness,* edited by Michael Lewis. New York: Oxford University Press, 2007.

human body

Popular and scientific knowledge about human bodies underwent a number of significant changes from the colonization of the Americas to the present. While many of these changes resulted from developments in science and medicine, cultural shifts brought about other changes as professionals and laypeople alike sought to understand human bodies in ways that made sense within broader cultural and scientific frameworks. The study of this interchange of culture and science in relation to human bodies makes up a specific branch of historical study, generally referred to as the history of the body. The role of environments in shaping and affecting bodies remains particularly important to understanding the history of the body.

During the late 16th and early 17th centuries, as Europeans first arrived in and colonized the Americas, Westerners believed that human bodies developed differently, dependent upon environmental influence. Some Europeans believed a system of four humors maintained the structure and health of the body: black and yellow bile, blood, and phlegm. Each of these elements had particular associations with seasons, climates, elements, astrological bodies, foods, and various other external and internal influences. Every human body possessed a particular composition of these humors, which accounted for an individual's appearance and personality. Disruption of these elements caused disease, typically brought about by environmental change.

This understanding of bodies had important consequences for colonization and informed the ways in which Europeans thought about the original inhabitants of the Americas. European cultural biases held that Native Americans possessed physically, mentally, and culturally inferior traits, and the humeral theory placed the blame for these deficiencies on the American environment. This conclusion about the American landscape, made popular in the 18th century by GEORGE-LOUIS LECLERC, COMTE DE BUFFON, convinced many Europeans of the dangers of colonizing the Americas. The various health afflictions that plagued many early colonial outposts further reinforced this conviction.

Most Europeans, however, greatly desired the potential benefits that North America offered. Over time, they developed a new interpretation of the Western Hemisphere's effects on European bodies. As European colonies became more stable and healthy, and as Native Americans began succumbing to newly introduced diseases in greater numbers, Europeans increasingly concluded that the American environment was not as suited to Native American bodies as they had once believed. Rather, these colonists concluded, Europeans' ability to thrive in the Americas without undergoing significant bodily transformations naturalized and justified European appropriation of Native American lands. Likewise, some Europeans believed that supposed African inferiority stemmed from an unhealthy African environment. In the 18th century, however, Buffon developed theories that racial characteristics deemed inferior by Europeans remained constant regardless of environment, making slavery a supposedly appropriate destiny for non-Europeans.

By the 18th century, humoral theory in the Americas underwent important changes. Some particulars of humoral theory fell out of favor as a result of 17th-century anatomical studies, most notably the English physician William Harvey's (1578–1657) works on the structure and function of the circulatory system. Certain elements of humoral theory, however, retained credence. This development held particularly true in the emerging United States, where medical professionals and the general public alike continued to conceive of bodily structure and health as being the result of key bodily fluids.

Proponents of the balance of fluids theory believed that health relied heavily on the influence of external environments, and humors tended to mimic the movements of the surrounding environment. For example, bodies placed in an environment containing stagnant air or water risked developing similar internal stagnancies that could lead to putrefaction and disease. Bodies in healthy environments of gently moving air and water, conversely, supposedly developed similarly healthful internal movement. As a result, the search for and cultivation of healthy climates and environments, as well as avoidance of unhealthy ones, made up an important aspect of American settlement and expansion. In many cases, the earliest explorers and cartographers of newly accessible western territories were medical geographers sent to survey new lands and determine their healthfulness.

Starting in the very late 19th century, however, scientific and social changes began to take place that once again altered the way that Americans thought about human bodies' relationships with environments. Some of these changes resulted from new medical theories and technologies, such as germ theory and bacteriology. The discoveries of chromosomes and GENETICS also encouraged medical professionals, as well as everyday Americans, to rethink environments' effects on human bodies. Supplemented by emerging cultural trends, these medical advances attributed a growing significance to the role of heredity, as opposed to the community. New philosophies invested a great deal of importance in the concepts of self-improvement and self-development.

Combined, scientific and social trends helped produce a model in which human bodies were much less vulnerable to environments than earlier theorists had concluded. Human bodies, by the early 20th century, in comparison, existed as largely self-contained units. While microorganisms affected human bodies, environments had little effect on the health or composition of bodies.

This interpretation of human bodies contributed significantly to modern American conceptions of humanity. RACHEL CARSON's *Silent Spring* (1962), however, challenged this belief. Carson's book, along with other scientific developments, revealed important ways in which human bodies might be affected by environments. While *Silent Spring* focused on the health effects of PESTICIDES in the environment, subsequent studies investigated the relationships of environmental conditions such as air quality, radiation, environmental materials, and CARCINOGENS, POISONS, AND TOXINS to health problems and birth defects. These medical investigations, joined by environmental movements both cultural and scientific, encouraged a widespread focus on the care of natural environments.

See also BACTERIA; CHOLERA; DISEASES, HUMAN; ENVIRONMENTALISM, MAINSTREAM; EUGENICS; HEALTH AND MEDICINE; RACISM AND DISCRIMINATION; SLAVE TRADE; SMALLPOX.

Skylar Harris

Further Reading
Chaplin, Joyce E. *Subject Matter: Technology, the Body, and Science on the Anglo-American Frontier.* Cambridge, Mass.: Harvard University Press, 2001.
Lindman, Janet Moore, and Michele Lise Tarter. *A Centre of Wonders: The Body in Early America.* Ithaca, N.Y.: Cornell University Press, 2001.
Nash, Linda. *Inescapable Ecologies: A History of Environment, Disease, and Culture in the History of California.* Berkeley: University of California Press, 2006.
Valencius, Conevery Bolton. *Health of the Country: How American Settlers Understood Themselves and Their Land.* New York: Basic Books, 2002.

hunting, commercial

Commercial hunting is hunting that is carried out for profit, rather than for subsistence, sport, or ritual. However, these distinctions are far from clear. For example, the Makah Indians engaged in whale hunting for centuries and traded the products it generated for goods that made their subsistence more comfortable. Similarly, for many rural Americans who lived off the land in the 19th and early 20th centuries, the distinction between subsistence and commerce was less clear than it was for city dwellers who hunted occasionally.

In terms of the modern cash economy, commercial or "market" hunting began in North America in the 17th century and was restricted to the eastern and, later, central United States. Most settlers lacked the skills to hunt effectively, and it is likely that the first commercial hunters were Native Americans, as they are known to have traded furs for items such as metal pots and tools. Market hunting in the colonies and later in the United States increased as the human POPULATION increased, peaking in the second half of the 19th century. Populations of many species—white-tailed DEER, elk, moose, antelope, BISON, turkey, prairie chicken, waterbirds, and the passenger pigeon—were soon reduced, especially in areas heavily populated by humans

Hunting methods were often extremely destructive. In the 19th and early 20th centuries, for example, the punt gun, a giant form of shotgun designed for commercial hunting, delivered as much as 500 grams (one pound) of LEAD shot and killed up to 50 BIRDS at a time. These guns were so large and their recoils so strong that hunters mounted them on punts, or flat-bottomed boats. The hunters then maneuvered the boats so as to put large flocks of waterfowl within range. James Michener describes such a hunt in his novel *Chesapeake* (1978).

Other market hunting practices were equally and notoriously wasteful. Commonly, hunters in the West left most of the carcass to rot; only the best quality meat of antelope and deer (from the hindquarters and legs) and hides were shipped to eastern cities. Growing urban centers created the demand for meat. Commercial bison hunting after the CIVIL WAR (1861–65) was even more wasteful, since the extermination of the species was in part politically motivated (in order to destroy the Plains Indians' main FOOD resource). Hunters left huge numbers of carcasses strewn across the Plains and rotting with only the tongue and hide taken. Over the second half of the 19th century, the bison population fell from approximately 50 million to a few hundred.

The most spectacular casualty of commercial hunting, other than the bison, was the passenger pigeon. Before the 19th century, this was possibly the most abundant bird species in the world, and it is estimated that one quarter of all birds in North America were members of this species. Estimates of the total exports of bird carcasses for eastern markets from Michigan alone, for example, vary from 1.5 million to one billion. Over a few days in early April 1878, about 18,000 of the birds shipped from Petosky, Michigan; this was the last year that large flocks of the pigeon were seen in Michigan, and by 1889, it was extinct in the state. Although the bird had been used as food by Indians and others before, its slaughter increased after 1800. Passenger pigeons were communal in their habits and easy to bag in large numbers. Commercial hunters netted birds by using bait or decoys or shot birds at nesting sites or roosting trees. Because of its abundance and the ease with which it could be hunted, the bird was a relatively cheap food source for urban workers and for slaves on PLANTATIONS prior to the Civil War.

It is, therefore, tempting to believe that hunting, particularly market hunting, was the sole cause of this bird's extinction. Because the pigeons laid only one egg each year, whole colonies could be abandoned, along with nestlings, when hunters began firing, leading to the loss of the entire replacement generation. However, the loss of the passenger pigeon cannot be blamed wholly on commercial hunting. At its peak, the population consisted of several billion birds; at 100 birds per day, it would take 1,000 hunters 27.4 years shooting every day of each year to kill one billion birds. As with most species, extinction was a result of multiple human actions, including the destruction or modification of the birds' habitats. These birds nested in huge colonies covering hundreds of square kilometers, but in the late 19th century, American FORESTS disappeared rapidly as a result of URBANIZATION, COMMERCIAL AGRICULTURE, MINING, and other economic activities, and with this loss, the birds' food supply and nesting areas often vanished as well.

Other bird species suffered for fashion, in the last decades of the 19th century. The demand for "plumes"—feathers to decorate women's clothing, especially hats—devastated populations of waterbirds in North America, as well as tropical America and Europe. Herons and egrets in particular faced extinction. The easiest way to obtain the feath-

ers was to kill the birds, whose bodies were usually left to rot. Because the European trade, where most feathers were sold, was highly centralized in London, accurate figures of kills are available: For instance, in 1902, feathers from an estimated 192,960 North American egrets were sold. Thanks partly to the efforts of scientists, conservationists, and nature lovers, commercial hunting of most species was banned under the MIGRATORY BIRD TREATY of 1918, and populations have recovered to the extent that most species are no longer threatened.

The interests of market hunters and sport hunters inevitably clashed, and a group of the latter formed the BOONE AND CROCKETT CLUB to advocate what would today be called sustainable game management. Along with organizations such as the AUDUBON SOCIETY, the club lobbied for the establishment of national parks and wildlife refuges and for state regulation of hunting to protect wildlife. The Lacey Act, passed by the federal government in 1900, prohibited interstate commerce in illegally killed wildlife in an effort to end market hunting. However, the act did not provide adequate protection because there were few funds for its enforcement. As a result, from pre-European numbers of well over 20 million, the white-tailed deer population fell to less than half a million by the 1920s, while, in the mid-1930s, the population of wild turkeys fell to 30,000. The 1937 Federal Aid in Wildlife Restoration Act, which levied taxes on hunting equipment to fund CONSERVATION, helped reverse this trend: There are now seven million wild turkeys and 27 million deer. The Lacey Act also provided no protection for a number of nongame species including WOLVES (viewed as pests) and BEAVERS (trapped for their fur), both of which became almost extinct in the lower 48 states in the 20th century. Today, the U.S. populations of wolves and beavers are approximately 5,500 and 10–15 million, respectively.

Market hunting scarcely exists in the United States today. It is illegal to sell wild game, and the demand for venison and turkeys is met by game farms or intensive raising units; almost all of the genuinely wild meat served in American restaurants is imported from New Zealand (where the several species of deer are all introduced animals that have become pests) and Europe. Commercial hunting now takes the form of game ranches, where recreational and trophy hunters pay to hunt native and, increasingly, exotic species. Some of these operations offer genuine "fair chase" hunts with no guarantee of success; others offer what is disparagingly referred to as "canned hunting," in which animals that are essentially tame are confined to small areas. For instance, Oklahoma has 24 registered "big game" ranches: A typical example has 40 trophy standard white-tailed bucks on 250 acres, and the hunter is charged a sliding trophy fee from $2,000 to $11,000 (or even more), depending on the quality of the antlers. It is even possible to "hunt" on the Internet:

A tame animal such as a deer is lured to a feeding station that is in view of a rifle mounted on a stand, and the user remotely aims and fires a rifle.

See also DEFORESTATION; FISH AND GAME LAWS AND POACHING; FUR TRADE; HUNTING, RECREATIONAL; HUNTING, SUBSISTENCE; NATIONAL RIFLE ASSOCIATION; OUTDOOR RECREATION; WHALING.

Alastair Gunn

Further Reading

Dark, Alex. "The Makah Whaling Conflict." National Council for Science and the Environment, Native Americans and the Environment, 1999. Available online. URL: http://www.cnie.org/NAE/cases/makah/m5.html. Accessed March 23, 2009.

Dempsey, Dave. *Ruin and Recovery: Michigan's Rise as a Conservation Leader.* Ann Arbor: University of Michigan Press, 2001.

Glavin, Terry. *The Lost and Left Behind: Stories from the Age of Extinctions.* London: SAQI, 2007.

Kushlan, James Anthony, James Hancock, and David Thelwell. *Herons.* New York: Oxford University Press, 2005.

Notzke, Claudia. *Aboriginal Peoples and Natural Resources.* North York, Canada: Captus Press, 1994.

Schorger, A. W. *The Passenger Pigeon.* Madison: University of Wisconsin Press, 1955.

The Lacey Act (1900)

Passed by Congress and signed by President William McKinley in 1900, the Lacey Act attempted to preserve wild animals and birds by making it a federal crime to poach or kill game in one state with the purpose of selling it in another. The law also empowered the U.S. Department of Agriculture to block the introduction of exotic species of plants and animals into native ecosystems. Subsequent amendments expanded the categories of protected animals (1969) and changed the mental state required for a criminal violation from "willingly" to "knowingly," making it easier to prosecute poachers (1981).

Be it enacted by the Senate and House of Representatives of the United States of America in Congress assembled, That the duties and powers, of the Department of Agriculture are hereby enlarged so as to include the preservation, distribution, introduction, and restoration of, game birds and other wild birds. The Secretary of Agriculture is hereby authorized to adopt such measures as may be necessary to carry out the purposes of this Act and to purchase such game birds and other wild birds as may be

required therefor, subject, however, to the laws of the various States and Territories. The object and purpose of this Act is to aid in the restoration of such birds in those parts of the United States adapted thereto where the same have become scarce or extinct, and also to regulate the introduction of American or foreign birds or animals in localities where they have not heretofore existed. . . .

That it shall be unlawful for any person or persons to import into the United States any foreign wild animal or bird except under special permit from the United States Department of Agriculture. . . .

The importation of the mongoose, the so-called "flying foxes" or fruit bats, the English sparrow, the starling, or such other birds or animals as the Secretary of Agriculture may from time to time declare injurious to the interest of agriculture or horticulture is hereby prohibited, and such species upon arrival at any of the ports, of the United States shall be destroyed or returned at the expense of the owner. . . .

That it shall be unlawful for any person or persons to deliver to any common carrier, or for any common carrier to transport from one State or Territory to another State or Territory, or from the District of Columbia or Alaska to any State or Territory, or from any State or Territory to the District of Columbia or Alaska, any foreign animals or birds the importation of which is prohibited, or the dead bodies or parts thereof of any wild animals or birds, where such animals or birds have been killed in violation of the laws of the State, Territory, or District in which the same were killed.

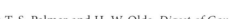

Source: T. S. Palmer and H. W. Olds. *Digest of Game Laws for 1901.* Washington, D.C.: Government Printing Office, 71–72.

hunting, recreational

Recreational hunting, as distinguished from COMMERCIAL HUNTING and SUBSISTENCE HUNTING, involves the stalking of wildlife for the challenge of the chase; the acquisition of trophies such as antlers, hides, or teeth; or the pleasure of interacting with nature in the intimate manner that the pursuit of prey provides. Animals hunted in the United States consist of big game such as DEER, elk, wild boar, pronghorn antelope, and cougars, as well as various species of grouse

Waterfowl hunting   *(U.S. Fish and Wildlife Service)*

and other upland game BIRDS; migratory birds including waterfowl; small game such as squirrels and rabbits; and so-called varmints such as COYOTES and gophers. Its popularity (evidenced in 2006, for example, by hunters' expenditure of $22.9 billion on licenses, services, equipment, transportation, and lodging) renders this practice highly consequential both economically and environmentally.

Recreational hunting has significant roots in the exploits of the famed outdoorsman Daniel Boone (1734–1820), whose prowess with a rifle earned him both fame and the admiration of an antebellum Euro-American society that otherwise frowned upon the practice of killing for sport. Celebrated in art and literature during the decades prior to the CIVIL WAR (1861–65), Boone and his adventuresome lifestyle presented a new, romantic model of autonomous masculinity and the conquest of nature that appealed to young men of the upper class and engendered a newfound esteem for recreational hunting. Subsequently taken up by wealthy men in the mold of THEODORE ROOSEVELT, the pastime spawned a sport-hunting culture that included field journals such as *Forest and Stream,* founded in 1873 and edited for 35 years by the Yale-educated naturalist GEORGE BIRD GRINNELL. In 1887, Grinnell collaborated with Roosevelt to form the BOONE AND CROCKETT CLUB, a sporting organization with a mission to promote manliness and advance the nascent philosophy of wildlife CONSERVATION through the establishment of wildlife preserves and the adoption of hunting regulations and a *fair chase* ethic. Indeed, as president in the early 1900s, Theodore Roosevelt designated 53 wildlife refuges, still regarded by many hunters as reservoirs to harbor animals they ultimately would hunt. A sport hunter himself, the 20th-century conservationist, wildlife biologist, and Boone and Crockett Club member ALDO LEOPOLD condoned the activity as a way to hone manual skill and foster self-reliance. While individual states established their own hunting laws and regulatory agencies from the late 19th century, the young U.S. FOREST SERVICE in 1915 adopted Leopold's *Game and Fish Handbook,* which described the scientific management of game animals as "forest products" and proposed the use of agency funds to enforce hunting laws on federal land.

Through the 20th century, recreational hunting grew less elitist as this pastime gained popularity across the socioeconomic spectrum, placing more pressure on public lands to sustain both game populations and increasingly heavy use by hunters. At the centennial of the Boone and Crockett Club's founding in 1987, 14.1 million Americans, more than 90 percent of them male, hunted. In the West, public lands play an important role in providing access to many of these sportsmen and sportswomen: State-owned properties supplement federal lands managed by the Forest Service or BUREAU OF LAND MANAGEMENT, all public holdings ultimately comprising substantial portions of the landmass in western states, Nevada with the highest concentration, at nearly 85 percent. But obvious differences in local environments and political geographies engender regionally distinct modes of hunting. In Texas, for example, where less than 2 percent of the land is publicly owned, hunters often pay private landowners for permission to stalk game on their property, while "canned hunts" demand premium fees for the privilege of shooting captive, often exotic prey in an enclosure.

Despite the prevalence of this type of artificial hunter-prey relationship, sportspersons in numerous instances have proved important in wildlife conservation, both directly and indirectly. Responding to the infamous mass slaughter of the BISON by market hunters who shipped millions of hides eastward in the service of late 19th-century industrialization, Roosevelt and the hunter-naturalist WILLIAM HORNADAY, in 1905, founded the American Bison Society, an organization that greatly aided in the recovery of this imperiled game animal. In a different way, falconers, who use trained raptors to facilitate the harvest of game birds, furthered the restoration of the once-endangered peregrine falcon, in the late 20th century, by funding research and reintroduction efforts and supplying wildlife biologists with scientific data on this species. Nevertheless, a segment of society remains opposed to the practice of sport hunting on moral grounds. In 1974, the author and humanitarian Cleveland Amory (1917–98) published *Man Kind? Our Incredible War on Wildlife,* a book that attacked both recreational hunting and wildlife management and ultimately inspired an antihunting movement in the United States.

To be sure, sport hunting has tremendous environmental impacts beyond its moral implications. The regulation of nature involved in achieving desired game population sizes at times proves counterproductive and highly disruptive ecologically. In one famous instance, on Arizona's Kaibab Plateau near the GRAND CANYON, government agents aggressively removed predators to produce higher numbers of game animals. As Aldo Leopold explained in his noted essay "Thinking Like a Mountain," "I thought that because fewer wolves meant more deer, no wolves would mean hunters' paradise." Leopold later concluded otherwise, after he witnessed, first, the rapid proliferation of Kaibab mule deer herds from 4,000 in 1906 to 100,000 in less than two decades, then their mass mortality by starvation, which resulted in a greatly decreased population of 10,000 by the onset of WORLD WAR II (1941–45).

The selective hunting many sportspersons practice involves less deliberate environmental manipulation.

Because individual prey selection by human hunters typically differs from that of nonhuman predators such as WOLVES and falcons, the impact of recreational hunting on prey populations is distinct from that of natural predation. Historically, sport hunters have favored the shooting of males because of an ethic that values the element of masculine competition in stalking large, virile males of a species and thereby condemns the killing of females as unfair and cowardly. However, wildlife populations that endure the harvesting of a disproportionately high number of males experience not only a preponderance of females and young but in some cases also decreased genetic diversity. Similarly, bighorn sheep herds, for instance, with which intensive selective harvest of large-horned males for their trophy mounts occurs, suffer declines in both genetic variation and the prevalence of trophy traits.

Some wildlife species undergo physical relocation to furnish hunters with sport, incidentally altering the ECOSYSTEMS they inhabit. In 1912, YELLOWSTONE National Park assumed leadership in a program to reestablish elk herds that had suffered extirpation resulting from Euro-American settlement or reckless market hunting, supplying 38 states and several nations with nearly 14,000 elk over the course of the next half-century. Of still greater consequence is the introduction of exotic species for the express purpose of hunting. While imported upland game birds such as the Eurasian chukar and gray partridge compete for habitat with related, native species, the widely distributed common pheasant, first imported to the United States from Asia in 1857, poses a threat to at least one high-risk bird, the Gunnison sage grouse, designated an ENDANGERED SPECIES by the International Union for Conservation of Nature and Natural Resources. Because pheasants are egg dumpers, laying their eggs in the nests of sage grouse, the host birds suffer reduced hatching rates among their own eggs, at times abandoning their nests altogether. The exotic game bird's parasitism, paired with its usurpation of habitat in wet meadows and riparian zones, areas critical to the grouse's survival, represents a menace to the native bird.

One of the most environmentally consequential conventions of sport hunting has been the use of LEAD ammunition. The lead shot overwhelmingly preferred by waterfowl hunters before the U.S. FISH AND WILDLIFE SERVICE banned its use in this type of hunting in 1991 often remained lodged in hit and abandoned birds that scavengers consumed; only three lead pellets ingested incidentally by an adult bald EAGLE can prove fatal. More importantly, the massive accumulation of these pellets in and around waterways continues to pose various environmental hazards, poisoning resident waterfowl and other riparian species that inadvertently ingest them and contaminating rivers, streams, and wetlands in some cases with several tons of lead shot that remains in place for years. Also susceptible to the toxicity of lead ammunition is the critically endangered CALIFORNIA CONDOR. Poisoning from lead is the leading cause of mortality in individual birds released as part of the reintroduction programs under way in California and Arizona, the highest toxicity levels occurring during hunting season due to the condors' ingestion of discarded entrails contaminated with lead bullet fragments. Since condor restoration efforts began in 1982, more than two dozen individuals have perished and hundreds became sick from lead poisoning associated with hunting ammunition. For this reason, the use of lead bullets and shot in much of the condor's range has been either discouraged or outlawed in the early 21st century.

Despite a slight decline in participation in recent years, recreational hunting remains an immensely popular mode of interacting with nature in the United States. In some states, such as Montana, where more than 25 percent of residents aged 16 and older hunt, a strong cultural tradition and a rich ecology together ensure the perpetuation of this activity. As a result, sport hunting continues to impact both game and nongame wildlife species and shape America's natural environment.

See also ANIMALS, WILD; ANTIQUITIES ACT OF 1906; BIODIVERSITY; DISEASES, ANIMAL; FEDERAL LAW—LAND POLICIES; FISH AND GAME LAWS AND POACHING; FISHING, RECREATIONAL; NATIONAL WILDLIFE REFUGE SYSTEM; POLLUTION, WATER; PUBLIC DOMAIN; SPECIES, EXOTIC AND INVASIVE; WILDERNESS.

Wendy M. Zirngibl

Further Reading

Herman, Daniel Justin. "The Hunter's Aim: The Cultural Politics of American Sport Hunters, 1880–1910." *Journal of Leisure Studies* 35, no. 4 (2003): 455–474.

———. *Hunting and the American Imagination.* Washington, D.C.: Smithsonian Institution Press, 2001.

Warren, Louis S. *The Hunter's Game: Poachers and Conservationists in Twentieth-Century America.* New Haven, Conn.: Yale University Press, 1999.

hunting, subsistence

Hunting for FOOD, shelter, and clothing is as old as humanity. For millennia after the advent of agriculture, which occurred approximately 11,000 years ago, hunting remained an important part of human survival. Since the 19th century, however, most Americans have placed less importance on subsistence hunting because commercial and transportation technologies allowed for acquisition of inexpensive commodities. By the mid-20th century, most hunting in the United States was recreational, creating tension between subsistence and recreational hunters over who would have access to wild game. Even so, subsistence hunting persists in isolated areas of the United States—typically near Indian reservations, in poor areas of Appalachia, and in other pockets of poverty. Subsistence hunting often runs into conflict with property laws, and hunters seeking mammals or birds for family consumption are often considered poachers. As a result of marginal agricultural conditions and a traditional subsistence hunting culture, Alaska is almost the only remaining area of significant subsistence hunting in the United States. More than 50 percent of households in Barrow, Alaska, for example, obtain half or more of their food through subsistence hunting.

In Alaska's more remote and rugged areas, farming is impractical and grocery stores are mostly nonexistent. There are no statistics on how many people of the 117,000–120,000 rural Alaskans, 20 percent of the state's population, subsistence hunt or how much game they take, but estimates are that combined take of fish and game reaches 43 million pounds, an average of 360 pounds per rural Alaskan. Some areas average 800 pounds, while others average little, and some areas depend mostly on SUBSISTENCE FISHING rather than hunting. In reality, however, some residents cannot hunt because of the scarcity of game, and subsistence hunters are generally restricted to areas near their homes and typically are not allowed to hunt in wildlife refuges and other protected lands. Federal jurisdiction over hunting includes 34 conservation system units in Alaska—parks, forests, refuges, and the like. Several of these sites ban subsistence hunting, including Glacier Bay, Kenai Fjords, and parts of Katmai and Denali National Parks. Subsistence hunters, however, often work in particular refuges and preserves set aside by the federal government.

The main difference between sport and trophy hunters and subsistence hunters is that unless subsistence hunters kill an animal, they may well go hungry. On the north coast of Alaska, for example, Inupiat Eskimos have traditionally endured eight months of winter without fresh game. To replenish food supplies, when spring begins, they take as much waterfowl as necessary. In 2009, however, they faced a threat from the U.S. FISH AND WILDLIFE SERVICE (FWS), which sought to protect Steller's eider, a threatened species of duck whose numbers in Alaska are perhaps down to as few as 500 birds. The Inupiat do not hunt Steller's eider, but the birds flock with the birds they do hunt and are often killed as a result. They contend that the birds have always been rare; that low populations result from predators, not hunters; and that natural increase will restore them eventually. The Inupiat also retain the right to hunt bowhead whales, preserving not only a food source but a basis for their cultural integrity.

In Alaska, similarly to many American Indian communities throughout the United States, community activities often center on the harvesting, butchering, eating, and sharing of food animals. State governments, however, often seek to restrict subsistence hunting in order to maintain healthy game populations. As human management of the natural world remains an integral part of modern societies, subsistence hunting offers a unique lens with which to view the history of not only CONSERVATION and PRESERVATION laws but also of the relationships between humans and environments.

See also FEDERAL LAW—INDIAN POLICIES; FISH AND GAME LAWS AND POACHING; INDIGENOUS PEOPLES, ALASKA; UNITED STATES—ALASKA; UNITED STATES—APPALACHIA.

John H. Barnhill

Further Reading

Bean, Michael J., and Melanie J. Rowland. *The Evolution of National Wildlife Law.* Westport, Conn.: Praeger, 1997.
Jacoby, Karl. *Crimes against Nature: Squatters, Poachers, Thieves, and the Hidden History of American Conservation.* Berkeley: University of California Press, 2001.
Warren, Louis S. *The Hunter's Game: Poachers and Conservationists in Twentieth-Century America.* New Haven, Conn.: Yale University Press, 1997.

hurricanes

Hurricanes are severe tropical storms that can produce powerful winds, huge waves, and flooding rains. These weather systems have inflicted catastrophic damage upon American communities along the Gulf Coast and the Atlantic coast. Inhabitants of the Gulf Coast from Texas to Florida, and of the Atlantic coast, particularly from Florida to North Carolina, are aware of the risk of tropical storms developing into hurricanes. These coastal communities have a long history of tropical storms, and approximately five hurricanes make landfall somewhere along the nation's coastline in a typical three-year period.

The dangers that hurricanes represent received greatly increased attention across the United States in August 2005, when Hurricane Katrina devastated coastal Louisiana and Mississippi. The long-term impacts of Hurricane Katrina are not fully understood at this time, but the extent of the flooding and damage in NEW ORLEANS, LOUISIANA, a major metropolitan area, made the storm the costliest of the natural DISASTERS in American history. Hurricane Katrina's economic costs, certainly in excess of $100 billion, were unprecedented, and the storm killed more than 1,800 people in Louisiana and Mississippi. As horrific as this 2005 storm was, it was not the deadliest hurricane in U.S. history, and it was far from the strongest of the hurricanes that have made landfall in the United States.

Hurricanes develop over warm ocean waters, and the storm systems that reach the United States typically originate off Africa's coast and travel across the Atlantic Ocean. Similar tropical storms also form over the Indian Ocean and Pacific Ocean, where they are usually called typhoons or tropical cyclones. All these terms refer to the same meteorological pattern, in which thunderstorms characterized by strong winds and heavy rains circle around a low-pressure center. In the Northern Hemisphere, hurricane winds circulate in a counterclockwise rotation, while cyclones in the Southern Hemisphere spin clockwise. The key to the remarkable power of these storms is the heat mechanism that fuels them. Hurricanes feed on the heat that is released when warm, moist air rises from the ocean's surface and the water vapor condenses. For this reason, the strength and size of these storms rapidly increase over warm bodies of water, and the storms weaken just as quickly over land.

Many of these ocean-generated storms never reach land, and hurricanes that reach coastlines usually do not cause major fatalities. But tropical cyclones that make landfall in densely populated, low-lying areas can be devastating. When these storms cause massive fatalities, it is typically because they create a rapidly flooding storm surge, which pushes seawater onshore, or because their torrential rains cause inland flooding. Hurricanes can combine with normal tides to raise water levels by 15 feet. The world's deadliest tropical cyclone flooded Bangladesh's Ganges River Delta region in 1970, killing more than 300,000 people, and the Atlantic's deadliest hurricane ravaged the Lesser Antilles in 1780, taking approximately 22,000 lives.

The deadliest hurricane in U.S. history struck Galveston, Texas, in 1900, and its floodwaters killed at least 8,000 and perhaps as many as 12,000 people. The city of Galveston is located on a low-lying barrier island, and the storm surge completely flooded the downtown area. The storm tides were 10–15 feet above normal water levels, and block after block of homes on the Gulf Coast side of Galveston were demolished by the seawater that swept across the island. The city's wealthier residents lived in homes on high ground in the center of the island, and many survivors found refuge in this section of the city. When the floodwaters receded, the residential area along the Gulf Coast had been scraped clean, and all that remained there was a wall of wreckage. Galveston had about 37,000 residents in 1900, and roughly 6,000 of the deaths were in the city, with the remainder of the casualties in the island's rural areas and on the mainland.

The survivors formed a new city government and undertook two huge ENGINEERING projects to protect the city from future storms. They erected a massive, 17-foot-high seawall made of concrete to defend the Gulf Coast beachfront, and they used sand dredged from Galveston Bay to raise the grade of 500 blocks of the city, some by inches, others by up to 11 feet. Galveston survived the disaster, and its recovery was celebrated as an example of American technological achievements over nature during the Progressive Era. Galvestonians resumed exporting COTTON and developed new facilities for tourism, but during the 20th century, other Texas cities grew much faster than the island seaport. More recently, in September 2008, Hurricane Ike made landfall at Galveston, destroying much of the city and other coastal areas near Houston, Texas, and leaving 195 people dead.

Florida has a long history of hurricanes, reaching back centuries before the 1900 Galveston storm and extending to Hurricane Katrina, which crossed the state before gaining strength in the Gulf of Mexico and striking New Orleans. The state of Florida was hit by three major hurricanes in a single decade between 1926 and 1935, and the 1935 storm was the most powerful hurricane ever to reach the United States.

The first of this trio of storms reached Florida in September 1926, and it was similar to the hurricane that followed in 1928. The 1926 storm passed directly over Miami, Florida, and Miami Beach, and every building in the young city's downtown was damaged or destroyed. If an equally powerful storm followed the same path today, the property damage would rival the costs of Hurricane Katrina. The storm caused Lake Okeechobee to flood, killing hundreds in Moore Haven, an inland community of poor agricultural workers.

The September 1928 hurricane was even more powerful, and it made landfall near Palm Beach, and again caused terrible flooding in and around Moore Haven. Lake Okeechobee's water level surged by six to nine feet, and more than 1,800 people died. These two deadly disasters played a significant role in bringing the 1920s Florida land boom to a halt, but economic boom times returned to coastal cities such as Miami and Palm Beach, while Moore Haven remained in poverty.

The third great Florida hurricane of this era roared through the Florida Keys in 1935, and it remains the most intense hurricane ever to reach the United States. The storm missed Key West, the main population center in the Keys during the Great Depression, but it killed more than 400 people. Most of the dead were World War I (1914–18) veterans sent by New Deal officials to work on the bridges linking the Keys, and the federal government's failure to protect or evacuate these men became a scandal. The veterans, like the African-American farmhands in Moore Haven, were economically disadvantaged Americans who were working in low-lying areas of South Florida during hurricane season with inadequate protection.

Hurricanes continued to reach U.S. coastlines in the decades between the 1935 Florida storm that set the record for intensity and the 2005 New Orleans storm that set the record for property damage, but few storms reached catastrophic levels between the 1940s and the 1980s. A second noteworthy 1930s storm hit Massachusetts, Rhode Island, Connecticut, and Long Island, New York, in 1938, demonstrating that hurricanes can reach the North Atlantic coast.

This "New England Hurricane" had a 10- to 12-foot storm surge, and it killed 600 people.

The ensuing decades saw a lull in major U.S. hurricanes, and in this era the United States developed better systems to track, predict, and measure hurricanes. The National Weather Service and National Hurricane Center developed aircraft, radar, satellite, and other monitoring methods to produce their official hurricane forecasts and advisories. Tropical storms are categorized by wind speed, ranging from category 1 to category 5. A storm becomes a category 1 hurricane when its winds reach 74 miles per hour, and winds of 96 mph, 111 mph, 131 mph, and 155 mph are required for designation as category 2, 3, 4, and 5 storms.

During the Cold War decades, hurricanes became better understood and their risks appeared to diminish. In the second half of the 20th century, many Americans left the Rust Belt for the Sunbelt, settling in coastal communities. More Americans could afford to travel to beach vacations. With these permanent and temporary increases in coastal populations, more people were in harm's way. During the middle decades of the 20th century, the nation experienced fewer destructive hurricanes, but there has been a notable increase in recent years. Hurricane Hugo in 1989 and Hurricane Andrew in 1992 each killed about 25 Americans, but the damage to real estate around Charleston, South Carolina, and Myrtle Beach, South Carolina, and in South Florida was estimated at $7 billion and $26 billion. These two hurricanes contributed to the popular view that tropical storms primarily pose a threat to property, not to American lives. Major rebuilding efforts followed these storms, and few citizens or public officials questioned the wisdom behind decisions to erect new buildings in coastal locations that had been devastated by a hurricane.

In August 2005, Hurricane Katrina made landfall on the Gulf Coast and the devastation it inflicted on the region forced Americans to reassess the dangers posed by hurricanes. Hurricane Katrina came ashore as a category 3 storm, weaker than both Hugo and Andrew, but its impact was much more like that of the deadly storms that ravaged Galveston in 1900 and South Florida in the 1920s and 1930s. Hurricane Katrina struck a densely populated, low-lying area, and as a result, the flooding caused extensive property damage and a shocking death toll of more than 1,800 Americans. The August 2005 storm, as had earlier hurricanes, proved particularly deadly to poor people, and many of the victims of the New Orleans disaster were African Americans living in poverty.

The systems of protection for the metropolitan region's inhabitants proved inadequate, as numerous experts had warned for decades. New Orleans sits in a bowl that is below sea level, and the levees and pumps designed to prevent a deluge of flood waters failed. The levees were both overtopped and breached, and much of the city and its eastern suburbs was underwater. Since these areas are below sea level, the toxic flood waters did not recede after the storm passed. Several years after the storm, the environmental cleanup, rebuilding, and recovery were still ongoing, and the future look and shape of New Orleans remained unclear.

The horrors of Hurricane Katrina received extensive television coverage, and many Americans became aware of the vulnerability of coastal areas to hurricanes and of the deep poverty and environmental inequality existing in today's United States. True recovery will require very costly investment in new systems to protect the city from future tropical storms. The vulnerability of the low-lying region and the high cost of infrastructure improvements have contributed to debates about the circumstances in which it would be appropriate to rebuild New Orleans. The fact that Hurricane Katrina was one of a series of major Atlantic hurricanes in 2005 has also increased debate about the possible impact of GLOBAL WARMING on hurricanes.

Since tropical storms are fueled by warm ocean waters, observed increases in sea surface temperatures are very troubling. Many scientists consider it likely that CLIMATE CHANGE caused by humans has been a contributing factor to recent increases in the intensity of tropical cyclones, and they predict that hurricane intensity will continue to increase during the 21st century. The legacy of Hurricane Katrina has yet to be determined, and it is entirely possible that no significant reforms or advances will result, but this tragedy also has the potential to be a watershed event in American citizens' views of natural disasters, climate change, and environmental inequality.

See also ENGINEERING; ENVIRONMENTAL JUSTICE; FLOODS; PROGRESSIVISM; PUBLIC WORKS; TRAVEL AND TOURISM; UNITED STATES—CARIBBEAN HOLDINGS; UNITED STATES—DEEP SOUTH; UNITED STATES—EASTERN SEABOARD; UNITED STATES—GULF COAST.

William C. Barnett

Further Reading

Brinkley, Douglas. *The Great Deluge: Hurricane Katrina, New Orleans, and the Mississippi Gulf Coast.* New York: William Morrow, 2006.

Colten, Craig E. *An Unnatural Metropolis: Wresting New Orleans from Nature.* Baton Rouge: Louisiana State University Press, 2006.

Dean, Cornelia. *Against the Tide: The Battle for America's Beaches.* New York: Columbia University Press, 1999.

Steinberg, Ted. *Acts of God: The Unnatural History of Natural Disaster in America.* New York: Oxford University Press, 2000.

hydraulic energy   *See* ENERGY, HYDRAULIC.

Index

Pages in **boldface** indicate main entries; *italic* page numbers indicate illustrations; page numbers followed by *t* indicate tables.

Alaska National Interest Lands
Conservation Act (ANILCA) **1:**240;
3:940; **4:**1302
Alaska Native Claims Settlement Act
(ANCSA) **3:**762; **4:**1302
Aldrin, Buzz **3:**944
Aleutian Islands **2:**425; **4:**1135, 1149
Aleut people **3:**761–762
Allen, J. A. **1:**179
allergies and asthma **1:108–109**
built environment **1:**206
grasses **2:**640
Great Smoky Mountains National
Park **2:**654
ragweed **4:**1100–1101
Allied Powers **4:**1408, 1410
alluvial mining **3:**915, 916
almanacs **1:***109*, **109–110**; **4:**1329
Alston, Dana **1:**23
Alta California **4:**1216, 1250
American Bison Society **1:**182; **2:**715
American chestnut **4:**1218, 1220
American Federation of Labor (AFL)
2:632; **3:**841
American Indian Movement (AIM)
1:110–111, *111*
American Indians. *See* Indian *entries*
American Recovery and Reinvestment
Act (ARRA) **3:**815, 956, 999
American Revolution **1:111–113**
ACE **1:**129
agriculture, commercial **1:**91
Articles of Confederation **1:**134
Boston, Massachusetts **1:**190
Charleston, South Carolina **1:**256–257
Civil War **1:**279
Cooper, James Fenimore **1:**330
Crèvecoeur, J. Hector St. John de
1:350–351
Declaration of Independence **2:**369
fur trade **2:**604
industrialization **1:**33
Ohio River **3:**1004
slavery **1:**29, 31
smallpox **4:**1198
Wheatley, Phillis **4:**1389
American Society for Environmental
History (ASEH) **1:**7, **113–114**
American West **3:**1046
Anasazi Indians
Colorado River **1:**299
drought **2:**409
housing, private **2:**697
Indians, Southwest **3:**760
irrigation **3:**785
ANCSA. *See* Alaska Native Claims
Settlement Act (ANCSA)
ANILCA. *See* Alaska National Interest
Lands Conservation Act

animal diseases. *See* diseases, animal
anthrax **1:**159, 249; **2:**674
antibiotics **1:114–115**, *115*
agricultural technology **1:**87
bacteria **1:**160
coral and coral reefs **1:**333
drugs, pharmaceutical **2:**411
poultry industry **3:**1075
tuberculosis **4:**1289, 1290
typhoid **4:**1293
Antiquities Act of 1906 **1:115–116**
Bush, George W. **1:**218
Clinton, Bill **1:**291
preservation **3:**1080
Roosevelt, Theodore **4:**1143
ANWR. *See* Arctic National Wildlife
Refuge
APA (Administrative Procedure Act)
2:494–495; **3:**799
Apache Indians **1:**183; **3:**760
APCD (Los Angeles County Air Pollution
Control District) **4:**1206, 1207
Apollo space missions **1:**22; **3:**886–887
Appalachia. *See* United States—
Appalachia
Appalachian Mountains **1:116–118**,
117*m*
Great Smoky Mountains National
Park **2:**652–654
Green Mountains **2:**659–660
Indians, Appalachia **3:**736–737
United States—Appalachia **4:**1303–
1304
White Mountains **4:**1391–1392
Appalachian Trail **1:118–119**; **2:**652;
4:1304, 1397
aquariums and marine parks **1:119–121**,
120
aqueducts
agricultural technology **1:**87
dams, reservoirs, and artificial lakes
2:359
engineering **2:**464
Mulholland, William **3:**937
aquifers **1:121–123**, 122*m*
acid mine drainage **1:**76–77
CVP **1:**255
Houston, Texas **2:**703
prairies **3:**1079
salt **4:**1161
San Antonio, Texas **4:**1164, 1165
United States—Southwest **4:**1336
Arab oil embargo **2:**600; **3:**1013
Arapaho Indians **2:**381, 382
arboretums **1:123–124**
Arches National Park **1:**75, 218
architecture **1:124–127**
automobiles **1:**153
built environment **1:**206

Charleston, South Carolina **1:**256
City Beautiful and City Efficient
movement **1:**277
Fuller, R. Buckminster **2:**601, 602
romanticism **4:**1137–1138
Wright, Frank Lloyd **4:**1412
Arctic National Wildlife Refuge (ANWR)
1:127–128, 291; **3:**940
Arizona
CAP **1:**250–251
Gadsden Purchase **2:**607
Hoover Dam **2:**689, 690
Phoenix **3:**1044–1045
Arkansas River **1:128–129**; **3:**1052
Army Corps of Engineers, U.S. (ACE)
1:129–132, *130*
agriculture, federal policies **1:**98
Great Dismal Swamp **2:**648
levees **3:**837, 839
mapping and surveying **3:**872
Mississippi River **3:**924–925
Missouri River **3:**929
nature and the state **1:**68
Ohio River **3:**1006
Tennessee-Tombigbee Waterway
4:1257, 1258
ARRA. *See* American Recovery and
Reinvestment Act (ARRA)
arsenic **1:**258, 337
art **1:132–133**. *See also* environmental
art; landscape art, American
Adams, Ansel **1:**81
Audubon, John James **1:**147–148
Catlin, George **1:**245
Comstock, Anna Botsford **1:**317
environmental art **2:**479–480
Homer, Winslow **2:**685–686
idea of nature **1:**17, 18
Remington, Frederic **4:**1115
Rocky Mountain school **4:**1133–
1134
romanticism **4:**1137–1139
Second Great Awakening **4:**1177
United States—Southwest **4:**1336
Articles of Confederation **1:**11, 67, **134–
135**, 327; **2:**525
artisan traditions **1:135–136**
ASEH (American Society for
Environmental History) **1:**7, **113–114**
Asian flu **3:**768
Aspinall, Wayne **1:136**; **4:**1399
assimilation **1:**207; **2:**518; **4:**1202–1203
asthma. *See* allergies and asthma
Astor, John Jacob **1:136–138**, *137*, 167
Atlanta, Georgia **1:**121, **138–139**;
4:1242
Atlanta Compromise **1:139–141**
Atlantic world, post-1500 **1:141–144**,
142*m*